Collected Works of Northrop Frye

VOLUME 9

The "Third Book" Notebooks of Northrop Frye, 1964–1972:

The Critical Comedy

The Collected Edition of the Works of Northrop Frye has been planned and is being directed by an editorial committee under the aegis of Victoria University, through its Northrop Frye Centre. The purpose of the edition is to make available authoritative texts of both published and unpublished works, based on an analysis and comparison of all available materials, and supported by scholarly apparatus, including annotation and introductions. The Northrop Frye Centre gratefully acknowledges financial support, through McMaster University, from the Michael G. DeGroote family.

The "Third Book" Notebooks of Northrop Frye, 1964–1972:

The Critical Comedy

VOLUME 9

Edited by Michael Dolzani

UNIVERSITY OF TORONTO PRESS
Toronto Buffalo London

Toronto Buffalo London

Printed in Canada

ISBN 0-8020-3542-6

Printed on acid-free paper

National Library of Canada Cataloguing in Publication Data

Frye, Northrop, 1912–1991
The "third book" notebooks of Northrop Frye, 1964–1972 : the critical comedy

(Collected works of Northrop Frye ; v. 9)
Includes bibliographical references and index.
ISBN 0-8020-3542-6

1. Frye Northrop, 1912–1991 – Notebooks, sketchbooks, etc. I. Dolzani, Michael, 1951– II. Title. III. Series.

PN75.F7A 2001b 801'.95'092 C2001-902089-9

University of Toronto Press acknowledges the financial assistance to its publishing program of the Canada Council for the Arts and the Ontario Arts Council.

University of Toronto Press acknowledges the financial support for its publishing activities of the Government of Canada through the Book Publishing Industry Development Program (BPIDP).

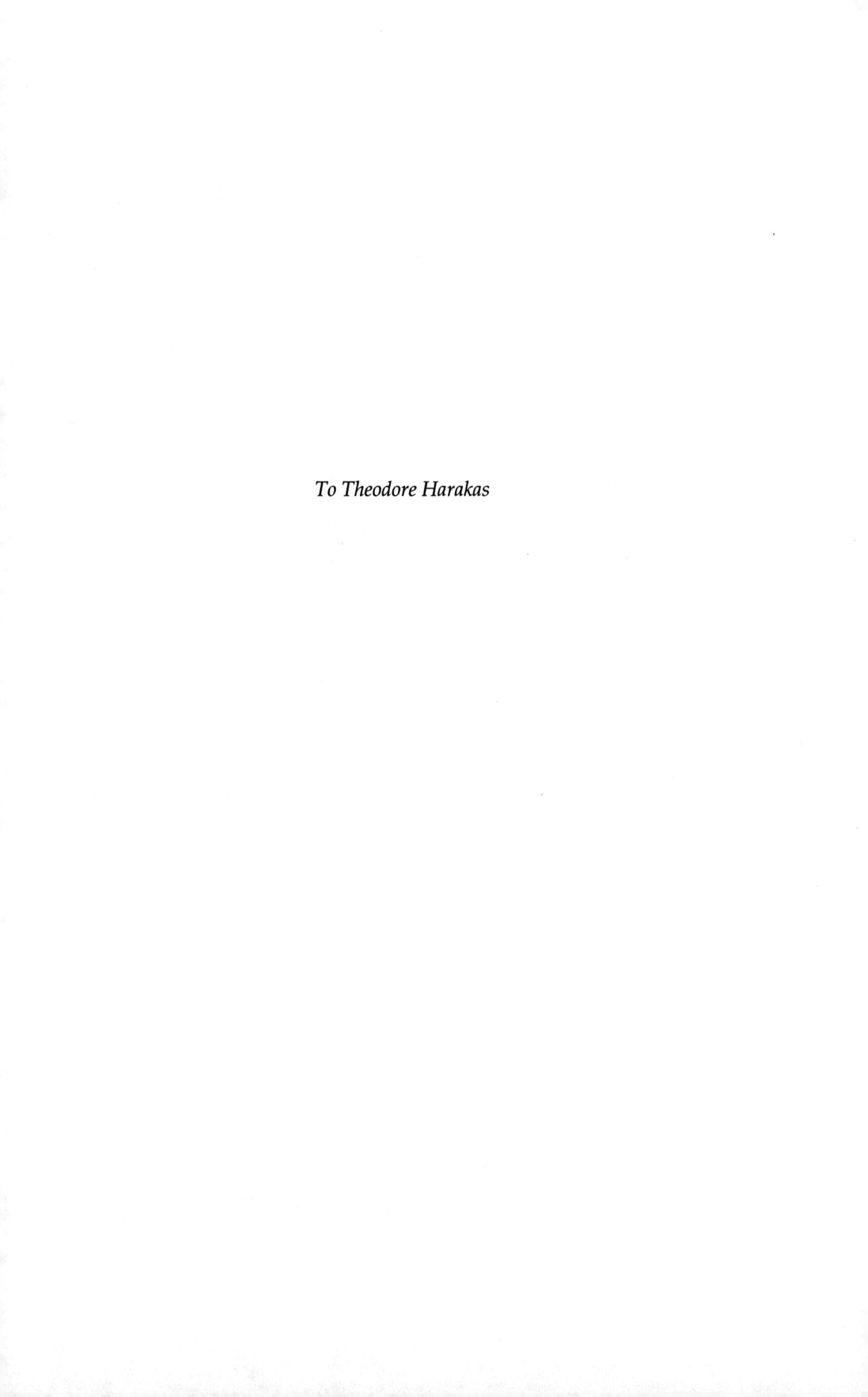

To Theodore Harakas

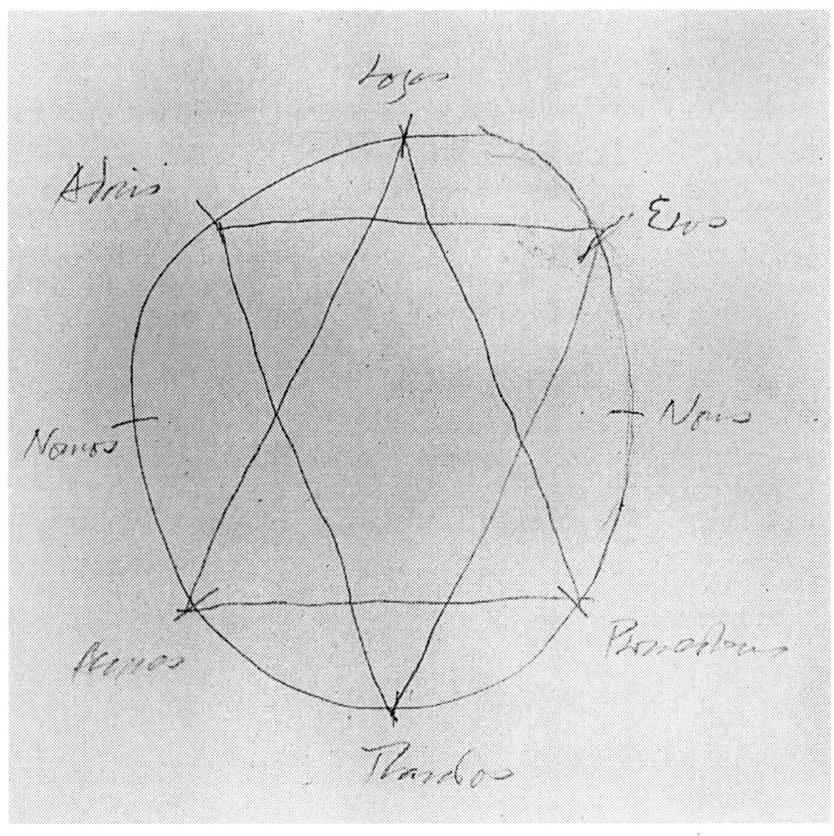

See p. xxix

From NFF, 1991, box 23, Notebook 11h
(courtesy of Victoria University Library).

Contents

Preface

The present volume consists of four of Northrop Frye's holograph notebooks—Notebooks 19, 6, 12, and 24—and one set of typed notes, which Frye titled *Work in Progress*. Despite the seemingly random numbering, they form a coherent body of material related to what Frye called the Third Book project, his third major book after *Fearful Symmetry* and *Anatomy of Criticism*, and were composed, for the most part consecutively, during the period 1964–72, a period of fresh beginnings initiated by Frye's sabbatical in 1964, his first since his Guggenheim fellowship year in 1950.

The numbering reflects neither chronology nor contents, and is a result of the vagaries of accession after Frye's death in 1991. Frye himself merely spoke (to the frustration of his editors) of "the red notebook" or "the brown notebook." Seventy-six holograph notebooks and hundreds of pages of typed notes survive among the Frye papers at the Victoria University Library in the University of Toronto. For further bibliographic information about them, I refer the reader to the Preface to *Northrop Frye's Late Notebooks, 1982–1990: Architecture of the Spiritual World* (*CW*, 5–6), edited by Robert D. Denham, and also to the same author's essay "The Frye Papers."[1] The final edition of the notebooks and notes, as coedited by Robert Denham and myself, will probably run to at least seven volumes.

Our ideal has been to reproduce what Frye actually wrote, without subjecting it to the kind of editorial standardization expected of published scholarly work. Hence, inconsistencies of spelling ("center" or "centre," "and" or "&," etc.), capitalization, and underlining have been preserved, although I have regularized Frye's placement of commas and periods in relation to quotation marks, and also silently corrected a few obvious misspellings and typographical errors. This edition italicizes anything that Frye underlined, and replaces his square brackets with braces: { }. Editorial additions have been placed in square brackets, including paragraph numbers and various interpolations intended to be useful. Among these are expansions of some of Frye's abbreviations ("Rcsm" for "Romanticism," "WT" for *The Winter's Tale*, and so on; those too frequent to expand at every repetition may be found in the list of Abbreviations); addition of first names if helpful; source information for Biblical, Classical, and modern texts where the edition is inessential; and question marks to indicate indecipherable (or at least undeciphered) words or phrases. The only omission has been three sentences in Notebook 19, a private reference to someone still living.

The annotations attempt to perform three functions, often more than one of them at a time. The first has to do with Frye's allusions and sources. In addition to identifying them and providing bibliographic information, the endnotes indicate whenever Frye's own library (now the Northrop Frye Library in the Victoria University Library) contains an annotated copy of the work in question, even though that is not necessarily the edition cited or quoted from in the endnote. To some extent, I have had to presuppose a general literary education of the sort that Frye himself assumed of his readers—whether or not such an education ever commonly existed or is in the process of vanishing. But at least readers who do not know that *News from Nowhere* was written by William Morris, or that the *Timaeus* is a dialogue of Plato—much less what those works are about—can easily look them up in very common reference books or anthologies. I have also had to assume the kind of knowledge about Blake's symbolic system that a student might pick up in an undergraduate Romantics course—who the four Zoas are, what an emanation is, and so forth. But, again, the answers are readily available in *Fearful Symmetry*.

The second function is that of cross-referencing. The Third Book project was never written, but its notebooks were the Gardens of Adonis from which the seeds to a number of Frye's shorter works were dispersed, and I have tried to indicate such relationships, along with connections to other material within the same notebook or within other notebooks in the present volume. The interpenetrating nature of Frye's ideas and references is so great, however, that limits have to be imposed upon the latter, and I have also tried to be conservative about references to notebooks or notes outside this volume. But not entirely so: one of the fascinations of the notebooks is the way ideas, or even minor source references, recur in notebooks separated by decades.

The third function of the annotations is interpretive, and here I have tried to be most conservative of all. Still, I have not hesitated to go beyond the mere identification of Frye's sources and references into brief explanation of what it is about, say, *Hamlet's Mill* or Plato's Circles of the Same and the Other in the *Timaeus* that Frye finds pertinent to the Third Book project. Sometimes the explanation takes the form of a more-than-usually-extensive quotation from the source itself. My rationale is that, unlike the notebooks for *Words with Power*, the Third Book notebooks have no final, published product to act as a potential key for the reader. Their pattern and purpose, without outside help, can emerge only from a lengthy period of co-habitation and close analysis, a process which I hope to foreshorten for future readers. The same is even more true of the Introduction, which lays out a blueprint of the Third Book project that is otherwise diffused through hundreds of pages of notebook entries. In fact, I have cross-referenced many endnotes to the Introduction; this may be inconvenient in one way, but ensures that the reader will eventually arrive at an explanation of, say, the "Seattle revelation" that is embedded in such a manner as to show its place within the total pattern of the Third Book and the even larger ogdoad.

For years now, the Frye notebooks have been a world in which I have lived as on a middle earth between two communities which have helped to make my work possible. Overarching the unpublished works project is the Collected Works of Northrop Frye to which it belongs. My thanks to the executors of the Northrop Frye estate for permission to be co-editor of the unpublished works; and to Alvin Lee, General Editor of the Collected Works, for his assistance and warm support both of this project and of *all* my work over the years. Thanks to Linda Oliver and her staff at the Victoria University Library at the University of Toronto for making repeatedly what the Third Book notebooks call the Hermes descent into the cave of memory in order to fetch me notebook volumes and books from Frye's personal library, housed in the underworld of the library basement. A very special thanks goes to Nicholas Halmi and Jean O'Grady, my in-house readers at the Collected Works project. They worked their way line by line through a very complex manuscript, making dozens of helpful suggestions and catching errors, improving the final project enormously. My gratitude also to Nicholas Halmi and Ward McBurney for preparing the index. To my copyeditor and friend

Margaret Burgess, an equal measure of gratitude for her extraordinarily painstaking job of copyediting an almost insanely complicated manuscript. No one has given more of herself, not only to this volume, but also to the entire Collected Works project, and beyond that to the real task to which we are all devoted: that of deepening the understanding of one of the greatest writers of our time. As time goes on, I grow more and more appreciative of the community of Frye scholars and readers throughout the world whose enthusiasm for the notebooks and faith in us has propped up my morale more times than I can say—especially at times when the transcribing and editing process has seemed in danger of lengthening, despite our best efforts, to Dead-Sea-Scroll proportions. Two people deserve deeper thanks than I have words to give. One is Jane Widdicombe, in part because it was she who made it possible for me to become Frye's research assistant for eleven years; but more largely because it is perhaps she, more than anyone, who has helped perpetuate not only Northrop Frye's work but also his spirit. The other is Bob Denham, who invited me to become his co-editor—admittedly before either of us realized what we were getting into. In Yeats's words, "And say my glory was I had such friends."

My other community, the one that has *grounded* me, the one that has lent me the firm foundation for all I have done, is the community of Baldwin-Wallace College in Berea, Ohio, to which I have belonged, as Frye belonged to Victoria College, since I was an undergraduate. I express my thanks to the college for two Faculty Development Summer Grants which helped fund my work on the notebooks and to the Reference and Circulation staff of Ritter Library, the former for help in research and the latter for its generous patience in the face of considerable demands placed upon its inter-library loan service. Also to Margie Martyn and her staff at Information Technology Services, who helped by converting files and by cheerfully performing the appropriate rites of exorcism whenever the poltergeist in my word processor became too much for me to handle alone. Similar thanks to my brother, Jeffrey Dolzani, who recreated virtually *ex nihilo* the machine on which I type these words after its software turned out to be hopelessly corrupted. But I also owe thanks to Baldwin-Wallace for less tangible benefits. Like Frye, I am primarily a teacher of undergraduates, and Baldwin-Wallace resembles, to some degree, Victoria College when Frye began his teaching career: a small, closely knit, Methodist-affiliated institution whose primary mission is liberal arts undergraduate teaching, which nevertheless desires to nurture scholarly endeavour without requiring it on a publish-or-perish basis. I do not think I could have completed this volume at any other kind of place. To those who know Blake's symbolism, the implicit comparison in my "middle earth" metaphor of Baldwin-Wallace to a type of underworld will not seem derogatory; for the caverns of Urthona, though hidden and largely unrecognized, are the location of the deep imaginative fires that can transform the world.

Once again, I owe a special thanks to two special people, from the generations before and after mine. One is Mary Aichlmayr, former student and friend forever, who spent countless hours helping me read the transcripts back against the original manuscripts for errors, and who also helped with the annotation. More than that, she understood and identified with Frye's kind of visionary mythmaking as deeply as any student I have taught, and in a very real way, the project became partly her own; I am glad to share it with her. My other debt is to the man to whom this volume is dedicated. *Fearful Symmetry* is dedicated to Pelham Edgar, the teacher who directed Frye towards William Blake. When I was nineteen years old and in his Romantics class, Ted Harakas, then my teacher and later my department chair, handed me a copy of *Fearful Symmetry* and said, "Here, given what you are, you should look at this." However melodramatic it may sound, that one act shaped not only my career but my entire identity. There are even deeper reasons for this volume's dedication, but, once again, I do not know how to put them into words.

Grateful acknowledgment to the following people who have contributed information incorporated into the annotations: Mary Aichlmayr, Laura Canis, Robert Denham, Scott Denham, Richard J. Finneran, Nicholas Halmi, Theodore Harakas, Kathleen Maresh Hemery, George Landow, Alvin Lee, Cynthia Lehman-Budd, Gerald McDermott, Jean O'Grady, Terry Martin, William Wright, Nancy Wurzel. To any I have forgotten, my sincere apologies.

All quotations from the Bible are from the Authorized Version (AV), and line numbers from Greek or Latin writers are given from the Loeb Classics editions. The following editions have been used for all citations from their respective poets: Dante, *The Divine Comedy*, ed. Charles S. Singleton, 3 vols. (Princeton: Princeton University Press, 1970, 1973, 1975); *Spenser: The Faerie Queene*, ed. A.C. Hamilton (London and New York: Longman, 1977); *The Riverside Shakespeare*, ed. G. Blakemore Evans (Boston: Houghton Mifflin, 1974); *The Riverside Milton*, ed. Roy Flannagan (Boston and New York: Houghton Mifflin, 1998); *The Complete Poetry and*

Prose of William Blake, rev. ed., ed. David Erdman (Princeton: Princeton University Press, 1982). Page numbers from the latter volume are identified by "Erdman" in the endnotes.

Notebook Citations

In the introduction and endnotes, a reference such as 12.345 means "Notebook 12, paragraph 345." When a specific notebook is being cited, but not a specific paragraph, the reference is simply to "NB 12." Citations to paragraphs within a given notebook are in the form "See par. 12, above," or "See par. 445, below." Citations to notes within the same notebook are in the form "See n. 74, above," or "See n. 303, below." References to paragraphs and notes in notebooks other than the one in which the reference occurs take the form "See 12.191," or "See 24.n. 131."

Abbreviations

AC	*Anatomy of Criticism: Four Essays*. Princeton: Princeton University Press, 1957.
Ayre	John Ayre. *Northrop Frye: A Biography*. Toronto: Random House, 1989.
CP	*The Critical Path: An Essay on the Social Context of Literary Criticism*. Bloomington: Indiana University Press, 1971.
CR	*Creation and Recreation*. Toronto: University of Toronto Press, 1980.
CW	Collected Works of Northrop Frye
D	*The Diaries of Northrop Frye, 1942–1955*. Ed. Robert D. Denham. CW, 8. Toronto: University of Toronto Press, 2001.
DV	*The Double Vision: Language and Meaning in Religion*. Toronto: University of Toronto Press, 1991.
EAC	*The Eternal Act of Creation: Essays, 1979–1990*. Ed. Robert D. Denham. Bloomington: Indiana University Press, 1993.
EI	*The Educated Imagination*. Toronto: CBC, 1963; Bloomington: Indiana University Press, 1964.
Erdman	*The Complete Poetry and Prose of William Blake*. Rev. ed. Ed. David Erdman. Berkeley: University of California Press, 1982.
FI	*Fables of Identity: Studies in Poetic Mythology*. New York: Harcourt, Brace and World, 1963.
FS	*Fearful Symmetry: A Study of William Blake*. Princeton: Princeton University Press, 1947.
FT	*Fools of Time: Studies in Shakespearean Tragedy*. Toronto: University of Toronto Press, 1967.

GC	*The Great Code: The Bible and Literature*. New York: Harcourt Brace Jovanovich, 1982.
LN	*The Late Notebooks of Northrop Frye, 1982–1990: Architecture of the Spiritual World*. Ed. Robert D. Denham. CW, 5–6. Toronto: University of Toronto Press, 2000.
MC	*The Modern Century*. Toronto: Oxford University Press, 1967.
MM	*Myth and Metaphor: Selected Essays, 1974–1988*. Ed. Robert D. Denham. Charlottesville: University Press of Virginia, 1990.
NB	Notebook
NF	Northrop Frye
NFCL	*Northrop Frye on Culture and Literature: A Collection of Review Essays*. Ed. Robert D. Denham. Chicago: University of Chicago Press, 1978.
NFF	Northrop Frye Fonds
NFL	Northrop Frye Library (the books in Frye's personal library, now in the Victoria University Library)
NFR	*Northrop Frye on Religion: Excluding "The Great Code" and "Words with Power."* Ed. Alvin A. Lee and Jean O'Grady. CW, 4. Toronto: University of Toronto Press, 1999.
NFS	*Northrop Frye on Shakespeare*. Ed. Robert Sandler. Markham, Ont.: Fitzhenry and Whiteside, 1986.
NP	*A Natural Perspective: The Development of Shakespearean Comedy and Romance*. New York: Columbia University Press, 1965.
OE	*On Education*. Markham, Ont.: Fitzhenry and Whiteside, 1988.
RE	*The Return of Eden: Five Essays on Milton's Epics*. Toronto: University of Toronto Press, 1965.
RW	*Reading the World: Selected Writings, 1935–1976*. Ed. Robert D. Denham. New York: Peter Lang, 1990.
SE	*Northrop Frye's Student Essays, 1932–1938*. Ed. Robert D. Denham. CW, 3. Toronto: University of Toronto Press, 1997.
SeS	*The Secular Scripture: A Study of the Structure of Romance*. Cambridge, Mass.: Harvard University Press, 1976.
SM	*Spiritus Mundi: Essays on Literature, Myth, and Society*. Bloomington: Indiana University Press, 1976.
SR	*A Study of English Romanticism*. Chicago: University of Chicago Press, 1968.
StS	*The Stubborn Structure: Essays on Criticism and Society*. Ithaca, N.Y.: Cornell University Press, 1970.

TSE	*T.S. Eliot*. Chicago: University of Chicago Press, 1963.
WE	*Northrop Frye's Writings on Education*. Ed. Jean O'Grady and Goldwin French. CW, 7. Toronto: University of Toronto Press, 2000.
WGS	*A World in a Grain of Sand: Twenty-Two Interviews with Northrop Frye*. Ed. Robert D. Denham. New York: Peter Lang, 1991.
WP	*Words with Power: Being a Second Study of "The Bible and Literature."* New York: Harcourt Brace Jovanovich, 1990.
WTC	*The Well-Tempered Critic*. Bloomington: Indiana University Press, 1963.
Xy	Christianity (Frye's abbreviation in the notebooks)
Xn	Christian (Frye's abbreviation in the notebooks)

Introduction

I The Retreating Nude

In "Literature as a Critique of Pure Reason," Northrop Frye notes that Bertrand Russell and Alfred North Whitehead speak independently of a "secret imaginative background" hidden behind the formal, public system of a philosopher's thought. Russell adds that if the philosopher is aware of it, "he probably realizes that it won't quite do; he therefore conceals it, and sets forth something more sophisticated, which he believes because it is like his crude system, but which he asks others to accept because he thinks he has made it such as cannot be disproved." Frye himself then goes on to say that "We get, then, from two highly reputable philosophers, a conception of philosophy as a verbal clothing worn over the indecent nakedness of something called its 'imaginative background,' so as to allow it to appear in public. It is this retreating nude that I have been trying to study all my life."[1] As we walked out in 1982 from hearing Frye deliver this paper as one of the Wiegand Lectures, a friend said to me, "I think he should title his next book *The Retreating Nude*." The phrase is still available, and it is tempting to apply it to the notebooks of Northrop Frye, for they are precisely the secret imaginative background of all his thought.

The metaphor of voyeurism latent in the preceding anecdote raises the question of how private Frye intended his notebooks to remain after his death. During his life they were used not to record the process of his thought but to give birth to it out of a matrix of preverbal intuitions. The fact that he thought by writing helps to account for the sheer quantity of notebook material, some four thousand pages of scribbling, beginning in the late 1930s and ending only with his death. The unpublished work is a vast sea on which his published work floats like Rimbaud's "drunken boat," an image he used to characterize the post-Romantic view of human culture and civilization floating atop a vast, mysterious otherness. To write a book was to build an ark, or, shifting the metaphor, to redeem an island of dry land out of the depths, like Prospero. Once his notebook writing had served his purpose, though, did he imagine any further use for it?

The fact that once or twice he explicitly says the notebooks are not intended for publication[2] is not necessarily definitive, for Frye was capable of contradicting himself, or at least of saying something quite different in a different context; after asserting repeatedly that no biographer could find the slightest interest in his life, he cooperated actively in the preparation of John Ayre's biography. Unapologetic about his refusal to give simple, direct answers to questions, he warned that such answers are traps; they imprison us within the limited horizon of the question's assumptions. So for him to say that the notebooks are not intended for publication or that he does not expect them to be published is not necessarily to say that he did not write them for an audience, and there is in fact compelling evidence that he did, the most extraordinary being perhaps the memo that concludes the present volume, a series of notes from 1972 that Frye titled "Work in Progress." In it, he not only explains the nature of the book he has been working towards through the four notebooks (Notebooks 19, 6, 12, 24) collected herein, but also how it fits into the enormous scheme of eight works that he has been contemplating all his creative life. "Work in Progress" explains the nature of each work in the "ogdoad," including its title and special designating symbol. Who is Frye talking to at such a moment? Certainly not to himself: he had been thinking in terms of the ogdoad's shorthand for over thirty years. He is clearly assuming an uninitiated audience who, without the "Work in Progress" and a few shorter but similar passages elsewhere in his unpublished work, would not have a key sufficient for comprehending a large part of the notebooks.

During the process of composing the thousands of paragraphs that comprise the notebooks Frye shifts back and forth between a subjective pole, where he is clearly writing for himself, and an objective pole, where he just as clearly is mindful of an audience. The most subjective notes are just that: notes, cryptic sentence fragments, occasionally even in second-person, reminding himself not to forget certain points. There are surprisingly few of these, however; most of the paragraphs are crafted in better prose than some critics publish. Moving towards the objective pole, this can evolve into what is clearly trial drafting, although this too is surprisingly rare. The majority of the paragraphs gravitate towards a centre that I would characterize as an implicit conversation with an intimate yet unknown other who is sometimes an alter ego and sometimes a kindred spirit. We may be reminded that the dialogue is a common form of Frye's favourite genre, the anatomy. In the most famous of all dialogues, the works of Plato, Socrates typically dominates the conversation. But Socrates also speaks at times of communing with a *daimon* or personal oracular spirit. Furthermore, he tells us in the *Symposium,* he received his own vision in conversation with a wise woman named Diotima (for the project he contemplated in the present volume, the so-called Third Book, Frye himself notes how often his *external* muses, the authors who have influenced him, turn out to be women. See NB 19.316–18). Perhaps *daimon* and Diotima are Socrates' versions of alter ego and kindred spirit. The point is that Frye's paragraphs can be conceived as himself speaking, yet also perhaps as something—or someone—speaking back to him.[3] Frye's notebook writing was a kind of divining, and it comes as no real surprise to find a sequence of paragraphs in Notebook 12 on the *I Ching*.

II The Maze in the Wood

Whatever use the notebooks were to Frye, what use are they to us? Fragmentary, written in a private code, and as endlessly self-erasing as a deconstructionist could desire, they can seem an impenetrable labyrinth to the reader who opens them for the first time, a version of the maze in the wood with which so many quest epics, from the *Divine Comedy* to *The Golden Bough,* typically begin. Frye himself mutters in frustration as a promising flicker of insight, pursued for many pages, turns into a will-o'-the-wisp, one of the misleading spirits in the dark wood of Milton's *Comus*. When we read in paragraph 20 of Notebook 19 that "The Utopia is a form of satire, & what it satirizes is anarchy," then discover that the very next paragraph begins "The combination of aristocratic . . . and revolutionary ideals makes the Utopia a romance, a vision of society with the irony omitted," we feel as if we are wandering in Blake's Beulah, an unborn world "in which contraries are equally true." Why not bypass the notebooks in favour of the published work, in which Frye has presumably discovered what he really thinks? There are a number of possible answers to this reasonable question.

The notebooks collected in the present volume were Frye's workshop for what he called the Third Book, that is, his third major book after *Fearful Symmetry* and *Anatomy of Criticism*. Many of their controlling ideas, images, and insights into specific texts did make it into print, almost thirty years later, as the second half of *Words with Power*, chapters 5–8. Yet it is arguable that discussions in the notebooks will not be replaced by their counterparts in the published texts but on the contrary will supplement them. If one limitation of the notebooks is their formlessness, their corresponding virtue is expansiveness, the relaxed freedom of an encyclopedic inclusiveness. His intermittent yearning to cast the Third Book in the form of one hundred sections or independent monads, a century of meditations, or inter-reflecting net of jewels like that in the *Avatamsaka Sutra*, points to Frye's own yearning for a freedom from the straitjacketing of discursive argument. By contrast, the incredibly condensed structure of *Words with Power*, part 2, forces Frye to boil down what began as interesting full-length discussions to a brief paragraph, sometimes even a single (and rather oracular) sentence.[4] It is both enjoyable and enlightening to tune in to ruminations about authors, from Proust to Lewis Carroll, whom Frye never found occasion to write upon at length; who would have known that Hawthorne and Melville bulked so large in his imagination without the repeated references in the notebooks? If we find ourselves wondering what he made of Anders Nygren's *Agape and Eros* or E.R. Eddison's *The Worm Ouroboros*, our most satisfying answer is in the notebooks. Moreover, by the time he completed *Words with Power* Frye had been trying to formulate some of its passages, in version after version, for several decades; much of the content of the present volume reappears (though at the service of a fascinatingly different structure) in *Northrop Frye's Late Notebooks, 1982–1990: Architecture of the Spiritual World*, edited by Robert Denham (CW, 5–6). While some readers may prefer the more aphoristic polish of the published volume, others may enjoy the fresher, more exploratory renditions in the notebooks.

The notebooks are also more uninhibited than Frye's published work, both intellectually and rhetorically. Frye's speculations are much more open, more daring, sometimes breathtakingly so, and he is more willing to risk venturing upon works which professional prudence restrained him from making extended public comments upon, even if they had greatly influenced him. These include, on the one hand, works whose language or culture was not native to him; on the other, books of ill-repute with whom respectable scholars feel they cannot afford to be caught in public, what he called the "kook books" of unreserved mythopoeic speculation, from Jacob Boehme to *Hamlet's Mill*, whose vision has affinities with his own project and which thus form part of its secret imaginative background even when their methods are flawed and their authors half-psychotic.

Frye's rhetorical orneriness in the notebooks is almost bound to get him in trouble in certain quarters. Biting comments on Catholics, feminists, Marxists, or anyone else he considered the oppressive agent of a closed ideology resemble the vituperations of Blake's marginalia; the deliberate, taboo-breaking use of four-letter words, some of them not politically correct even today, evokes Blake's *Island in the Moon*, or indeed the rhetoric of any satirist whose defiance of the superego-censor locates him or her within Frye's chosen tradition of the anatomy—Rabelais, for instance, whose influence looms so large throughout the Third Book notebooks, where he is discussed as a chief representative of the quadrant of Prometheus, revolutionary firebringer who cursed the gods and got nailed for it. Yet that is not to lose sight of the fact that, on their other side, notebook paragraphs verge upon, and occasionally even become, what Dylan Thomas called the conversation of prayer. On a more down-to-earth level, the natural spontaneity of the notebooks was probably a release for a man whose social interactions were constantly inhibited—if not outright frozen—by shyness on both sides: the shyness even of friends around the famous genius; the shyness of the introvert as public figure. What a relief to have an unselfconscious conversation, even if it has to be with a presence inside yourself.

But the most valuable feature of Frye's notebooks is that their form of organization—if that is the term for it—may, paradoxically enough, be more adequate to the kind of vision he was trying to convey than versions that dress for success by coming to terms with expectations of conventional logic, narrative continuity, and the conservative demands of peer-reviewed publishing. Despite thirty years of poststructuralist attack on the logocentric assumptions of the traditional book, it remains the form in which scholars are forced to write if they want acceptance in the academic power structure, if they do not want to be relegated to the margins as mystics, cranks, or creative writers. Yet Frye makes clear in the *Anatomy of Criticism* and elsewhere that, insofar as the anatomy is a type of satire, it is inherently distrustful of formal perfection, with its demands for "truth" (i.e., correspondence to the "facts" of an external reality) and "beauty" (i.e., ideal centripetal closure). Satirists make a hash of ideal form—the word "satire" in fact derives from a word for "hash"—and Frye claims that Marx identifies himself as belonging to the anatomy tradition by his inability to finish books: in such a context, to finish a book would mean to lock up its energies in an imprisoning structure like Ariel pent in the tree by Sycorax. I am not implying that Frye's published books are failures; unlike Coleridge, he was able to write in continuous prose without asphyxiating himself. But in his review of Kathleen Coburn's selection of passages from Coleridge's notebooks, he notes that her "method of anthologizing is much fairer to Coleridge than he was to himself because she preserves the aphoristic quality of his real thinking. . . . In his discontinuous notes, we get the bite and point of what he has to say because it is said in the rhythm of his thinking. Miss Coburn provides, up to a point, something that Coleridge badly needed as a discursive writer: an appropriate prose form." Now that we know the contents of his own notebooks, the paragraph that follows seems as much a meditation on his own struggles with prose form as it does a review of Coleridge:

> Like Bacon, Coleridge was much preoccupied with tables of contents, methodological axioms, schemes for others to work out, and intellectual projects and agendas of all kinds. But unlike Bacon, he could not be complacent about this or about the possibility that his vast opus maximum might never be finished. He seems to have felt it imperative to write a long piece of continuous prose in the conventional treatise form. Writing continuous prose is (as I think Kafka says somewhere) an art of causality, in which the ideas form a linear progression. But when Coleridge got an idea, it became a center to which other ideas simultaneously attached themselves.[5]

In the past decade or two, we have become increasingly familiar with a means of organizing language that is much less limited by the linear progressions of discursive prose: hypertext. As Jay David Bolter says in *Writing Space*, "The hierarchy (in the form of paragraphs, sections, and chapters) is an attempt to impose order on verbal ideas that are always prone to subvert that order. The associative relationships define alternative organizations that lie beneath the order of pages and chapters that a printed text presents to the world. These alternatives constitute subversive texts-behind-the-text."[6] By contrast, he continues, "A hypertext has no canonical order. Every path defines an equally convincing and appropriate reading, and in that simple fact the reader's relationship to the text changes radically. A text as a network has no univocal sense; it is a multiplicity without the imposition of a principle of domination."[7] Frye's word for such an ideal is interpenetration:

> And although Coleridge's thought remains fragmentary [he says], the fragments are priceless, not because they are imaginative, but because they are logia. Just as Blake urges us to see the world in a grain of sand, so in Coleridge we have to see the vast, ramifying body of the Logos in all the brilliant facets and prisms of these aphorisms, as they come tumbling over one another in a wonderful sweep of mental richness, like the drops in the Cumberland waterfalls that he loved so much to watch.[8]

Mention of Blake reminds us of the poet who began with the exuberantly discontinuous prose of *The Marriage of Heaven and Hell,* the irreverent marginalia, and various engraved plates of aphorisms. Blake wanted to write epic, but had to learn in *The Four Zoas* that the continuous cyclic form of the traditional epic was obsolete. To compose *Milton* and *Jerusalem,* he had to discover—or rediscover, in the form of "prophecy"—a new, non-narrative encyclopedic form, a discontinuous series of engraved plates; though he usually likens it to Dante, Frye's ambition to write a work in one hundred sections seems much closer in spirit to what Blake tried for in *Jerusalem.* Such a structure is, like the famous mystical definition of God, a circle whose centre is nowhere and circumference everywhere. That such a structure (and such a God) are paradoxical—that is to say, impossible—is, in Frye's definition of faith, no reason for not achieving them.

III The Search for the Centre

Hypertext by itself has no pattern other than the associative; enormously more efficient than conventional methods at nonlinear organization, it nevertheless remains a labyrinth without an Ariadne, a version of Borges's garden of forking paths or Library of Babel.[9] But the notes and aphorisms of Coleridge and Blake are more than ripples up and down an endless chain of signifiers; they are the potential epiphany of a larger pattern which is nevertheless not the framework of descriptive writing (with its linear sequence of causes and effects) or of conceptual writing (with its hierarchies of genus and species in outline form, based on similarity and uniformity). In *The Double Vision*, Frye adopts Blake's notion of two modes of consciousness, which disclose to us two levels of reality; there is only one world, but two ways of experiencing it, roughly corresponding to Mircea Eliade's profane and sacred. Ordinary or ego consciousness, being passive, lives in an external, given world, a subject surrounded by more or less alienated objects. This is the "factual" world of descriptive writing, the "logical" world of conceptual writing, the "real" world of Freud's reality-principle. But we learn in the opening chapters of *Words with Power* that behind the modes of descriptive and conceptual writing lies an "excluded initiative" (*WP*, 7–8). Even the most "objective" verbal structure has been rhetorically organized, though a good deal of trouble may have gone into concealing that organization; and rhetoric is the language of ideology, of what Frye calls the secondary concerns that bind any society together. The more we mature, the more we realize that an indefinite amount of what we had simply accepted as "the real world" is in fact a construct, a product of our cultural conditioning; even what we accept as a "fact" is selective. So far, Frye is in agreement with the main trends of contemporary critical thought.

But poststructuralist thinking typically stops at this point, passively accepting the ideological construct as a new limit: a given, external reality to be passively accepted. We can change our particular ideology; we can change the ideology of a whole society—what we cannot do is get beyond the horizon of the ideological itself. Ideology is an expression of human desire, more precisely human desire as culturally conditioned to live within a social contract; such conditioned, limited desire is what Frye calls secondary concern. Yet where did the whole, vast ideological construct of human culture, what Jacques Lacan calls the Symbolic Order, come from? Because we are born inside it, and the process by which it constructs our identity begins even before we are born, we are tempted to say that it is "always already" there, so that no creation myth is necessary.

But although nature is said by science to have come into being by the dynamic of its own inner processes, the symbolic order of culture is of human origin, even if we have to seek that origin in the depths of the human unconscious. When we do so, we find in the unconscious what Freud called primary process, and we have been calling the associative. And what we learn is that association is not free, that is, not arbitrary or random: it follows patterns. The basis of these patterns is sometimes called "resemblance," and it sometimes begins with resemblances, as when Wallace Stevens says that *Oak Leaves Are Hands*.[10] But "resemblance" can be misleading if it implies similarity or uniformity: as Freud said when he spoke of "the antithetical sense of primal words" in the unconscious,[11] a word or image is just as quickly associated with its opposite, as black with white. The real basis of association is not the outward patterns of descriptive reality but the inward patterns of desire. The verbal units out of which these patterns are constructed are myth and metaphor: these are the imagination's counterparts to the descriptive and the conceptual respectively, the linear or narrative and the structural or thematic aspects of humanly created reality. Both myth and metaphor build up larger patterns, as myths cohere into a mythology and metaphors cluster schematically, even diagrammatically. By the time this happens, it becomes clear that the imagination, the constructive power in the human mind, can and does indeed live and move and have its being beyond the horizon of the ideological, of the values and power structure of any particular society. For the slightest acquaintance with comparative mythology, despite the enormous resistance to this insight in both the social sciences and the humanities, shows that the patterns of myth and metaphor are overwhelmingly cross-cultural: whether by direct influence or spontaneous generation, the same patterns show up everywhere and in all periods of history, back to the first drawings in the Palaeolithic caves. That the history of institutional religion mostly shows ideology kidnapping mythology and using it for its own ideological purposes, making it in the process a mere instrument for its own will to power, does not obviate the fact that myth and metaphor are the excluded initiative of ideology. Like ideology, they are expressions of human desire, of what Frye already in the period of the Third Book notebooks was calling concern; unlike ideology, they do not express the narrow and provincial concerns of any particular social contract but what Frye was later to call primary concern, the desires which are universally human because they are for the bases of life: food and drink, sex, property, freedom of movement.

By this point we have gone far beyond the point at which Frye's thinking had arrived even by the 1972 "Work in Progress" notes that end the Third Book period. By the time of that document, he had just published *The Critical Path*, a spinoff of the Third Book project and his first full-length work to use the concept of mythology as the expression of concern. In fact, one of the most fascinating things about *Words with Power* is how little precedent its first four chapters have in the notebooks:

it is a very long jump from *The Critical Path* to the much more elaborate argument about primary and secondary concern, which was worked out mostly in a series of papers and public lectures during the 1980s, later collected in *Myth and Metaphor*. And the elegant scheme of excluded initiatives seems to have been worked out only very close in time to the drafting of *Words with Power*. In short, little in part 1 of that book has its origin in the Third Book notebooks, which are the source rather of part 2. What those notebooks are taken up with is the *telos* of the imagination, which begins with a labyrinth of associations and, out of that *prima materia*, creates the total pattern of a mythology.

IV The Finding of the Guide

So far, we have been speaking of what is worth examining in all of Frye's notebooks. But the notebooks for the Third Book project have a special value: they reveal a major mystery, perhaps *the* major mystery of the whole Frye corpus. We now know that, precisely because myth and metaphor build up out of the labyrinth of association a total form, all of Frye's works—written and unwritten—were variations upon a single pattern, whose emblem was a mandala. Frye did not call it that, but that is what it was: a circle with a cross inside it. He called it, delightfully, the Great Doodle. In the *Anatomy*, before clothing them with Aristotle's more dignified *melos* and *opsis*, Frye calls the rhythmic and visual initiatives of literature "babble" and "doodle." Out of the great babble of notebook associations arises the Great Doodle like Venus out of the sea, another retreating nude emerging from its secret imaginative background. Because we are in desperate need of some kind of guide in this labyrinth, some Ariadne with a functional map, it will be convenient to furnish an anatomy of the Great Doodle with its most frequently recurring features, cautioning ourselves that in one way the Doodle is more like Proteus than Venus: it is an unstable shapeshifter. As Frye plays with it over the years (in the *Words with Power* notebooks, play is for some time given as one of the primary concerns), it shifts names and identities like a foreign agent; even the diagram itself is metamorphic, as Frye adds and subtracts from it, turns it at right angles, and at one point even fissions it like an amoeba. So we must not mistake any variation of it for something definitive, but rather regard it as Joseph Campbell's "symbol without meaning":[12] the mandala not as containing and controlling form but as the bow that shoots an arrow, the latter image being a modulation of

Frye's ladder image in *Words with Power*. Both are images of *hodos*, the way. For all that, the following version will serve its purpose of initiating us into the mysteries:

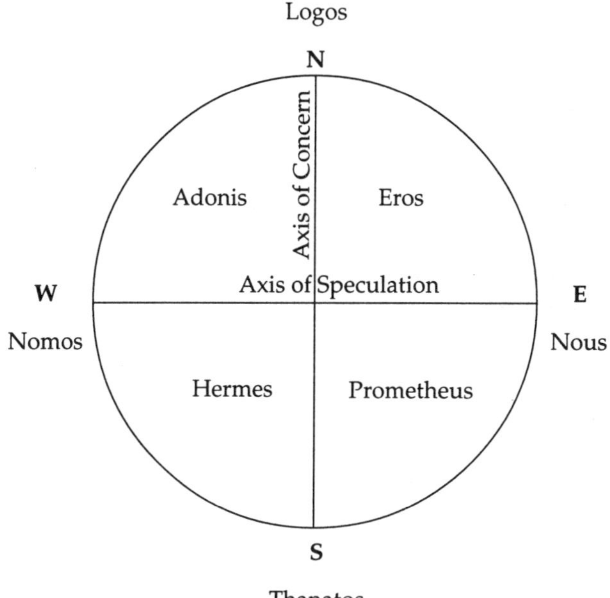

The Great Doodle

The Great Doodle is what Blake would have called his Vehicular Form, his visionary chariot, what Frye himself might have called the thematic stasis or epiphany of his entire creative process in a single form. The first four works of his ogdoad—four books whose names in eternity (that is, in the secret imaginative background of Frye's imagination) were Liberal, Tragicomedy, Anticlimax, and Rencontre—were the primary wheels of that vehicle (the other four books being their rather shadowy Blakean emanations or yin–yang counterparts); each would recreate it in a different aspect. By the cut-off point of the 1972 "Work in Progress" notes, Frye was expounding these as four volumes of a single project called *The Critical Comedy*. The "Dante and Balzac echoes will be frequent," he says, although adding, "I've always felt that Dante's trinitarian obsessions made him fail to see the real fourfold form of his poem, Purgatorio 27 to Paradiso 9 being the missing fourth world and scherzo movement" (par. 7).

Immediately afterward, the whole project, upon which he had been working since the late 1940s (the *Anatomy* was a spinoff and began as an attempt to write its introduction), underwent a metamorphosis. That is the positive way to put it, the way which emphasizes the continuity with what eventually emerged as *The Great Code* and *Words with Power*. But there is a radical discontinuity as well: the Third Book with the Great Doodle as its basis was never written; the present notebooks are all we have of it. The Doodle itself seems to have undergone a Jungian *enantiodromia* or transformation into its opposite, for beginning with *The Secular Scripture* in the mid-1970s Frye's diagram of choice was not a circle but a vertical axis. In *Words with Power*, the four quadrants of the Doodle become four ascending or descending movements upon the vertical axis; their names—Hermes, Eros, Adonis, Prometheus—repeated like incantations and meditated upon for hundreds of pages both in the Third Book and the *Words with Power* notebooks, receive a glancing mention on a single page. This is not choice of mnemonic but a crisis of vision. To some extent, Frye's perspective underwent the kind of reversal (Biblical *metanoia*, Eastern *paravritti*) or turning-inside-out, as in Blake's image of the vortex, that Blake's own vision underwent in its death-and-resurrection passage from the quarried-yet-abandoned *Four Zoas*, which retained the cyclical scheme of the traditional epic, to the later *Milton* and *Jerusalem*, whose organization is dialectical. Frye himself called this the switch from an Orc-structure to a Los-structure, undergone by Blake in the passage from the original to the revised versions of *Night the Seventh* in *The Four Zoas*, and the notebooks are invaluable insofar as they document Frye's own dark-night passage.

The Third Book notebooks at times anticipate the transformation; it is one of the things Frye means by "the book on its side." After a volume (often Liberal or Tragicomedy) which would lay out the Doodle in its cyclical form, Frye sometimes planned for a subsequent volume to expound it turned on its side; this apparently meant giving it a right-angled twist that would deconstruct it from a closed and static pattern withdrawn from external reality into an open-ended dialectical and teleological process which subsumes and transforms that reality. A frequent comparison is the difference of perspective between Yeats's two Byzantium poems: whereas *Sailing to Byzantium* is spoken by a dying old man caught in the natural cycle and longing to sail away from it towards the artifice of eternity, *Byzantium* sees the city from the inside, where it appears as an alchemical process transforming the natural life that breaks upon its shores. The two poems articulate the same vision, but from fallen and unfallen points of view respectively.

Thus, a fundamental ambivalence was inherent in the Great Doodle from the beginning: Frye always knew that it would have to have at least two different manifestations, related to each other in what he occasionally characterized as a Yeatsian double gyre. In its first form, the Great Doodle proper, designating a cyclical quest through the phases of human experience, signified by the quadrants of Eros, Adonis, Hermes, and Prometheus, in which the quester undergoes the conflict of opposites signified by the vertical and horizontal axes, lays out a fallen vision. Any diagram of human experience is inevitably a reduction, no matter how richly elaborated, and in this form the Doodle is only what Blake called the "Druid analogy"—not entirely false, because, as an analogy, it does capture something of the lineaments of the real; yet "Druid" because it is a kind of superstitious natural religion, an attempt to master life—and literature—by simplifying it into a drawing. At one point, Frye describes his "cycle of topoi, what I used to call the Druid analogy": "It has lyrical topoi & loci strung along as episodes on the Great Doodle which is the underlying form of all epics, or quest-epics at least." But he is careful to note that "It's Druidical & mother-centered because it's a cycle, a spatial & temporal cycle of then & there. So it's really a kind of Inferno, for all its ending in heaven, an Inferno close to FW [*Finnegans Wake*] & the Yeats vision. It's the cave of the dromena, the bound vision of shadows. It's full of literature, yet literature in it is circumferential & Tharmas dominated" (12.445).

In other words, Frye had always understood the kind of complaint so often made against the *Anatomy of Criticism*, that diagrams and schematic arrangements, so long as they remain mere abstractions, can be no more than a series of falsifying pigeonholes. The *Anatomy* begins with literature as a centripetal verbal structure withdrawn from an external reality, but it does not remain content with such a formalism or structuralism: the crucial Second Essay describes a dialectical process by the end of which that kind of internal/external duality is turned inside out. What it calls the "order of words," a Logos or total pattern of which any particular verbal pattern is a manifestation, is in itself what Blake would call a spectre, a ghostly illusion of the metaphysics of presence; it can thus never be described in itself, but only as it is always already undergoing a turned-on-its-side transmutation from static to dynamic, structure to energy, creation to recreation. Insofar as it is a sequel, the Third Book can be characterized as an attempt to clear up this primary misconception about the multiple schematic patterns of the *Anatomy*. As he himself put it, "AC dealt with the internal structure of literature & this deals with its external relations" (19.86).

V The World Between

A. The Horizontal Axis

That is why, after some remarkable introductory entries to which we will return later, the first of the Third Book notebooks begins with what will gradually take its place as the horizontal axis of the Great Doodle. Notebook 19, which Frye started in 1964, begins around paragraph 14 talking about contracts and Utopias. These ideas developed into the 1965 article "Varieties of Literary Utopias,"[13] but in their original context contract and Utopia are the western and eastern limits of what Frye was later to call the axis of speculation. In the west, sunset marks the end of the frontier, the limit of human freedom and the beginning of necessity with the establishment of the social contract and its manifestation as law. In Christian terms it is the fall, original sin, and the silhouette of the Crucifixion against the setting sun; in Classical terms it is Oedipus killing his father in twilight at a place where three roads meet; in individual terms it is, as the previous example suggests, the limiting, determining power of the past, the Family Romance we can never seem to stop playing out no matter how old we get and how much therapy we have paid for; historically, this location is the "evening land" or twilight of Western culture that Spengler's title speaks of in the original German. Life here is that of Spengler's megalopolis, the anthill collective, anxiously coercing its members into the only unity that law is capable of, that of uniformity and conformity.

Utopia, rising with the sun in the east, is the vision of social hopefulness, often located in the future. There are many varieties of literary Utopia, of course, and the more superficial are trapped in the ideological anxieties of law and contract: these reduce the axis from west to east to a myth of progress moving towards ever greater rational conformity made pleasant by ever greater technological innovations. But the greater works in the utopian tradition understand that the horizontal axis, the axis of the social, moves from the collective to the communal, and in doing so has to solve the problem of the Many and the One. If the Christian analogue of the western point is the fall, the eastern analogue is the apocalypse; and at the end of time the Book of Revelation, in a passage made much of by Milton, says that God will lay down the sceptre of the law and be "all in all." That is, the final form of human community transcends the isolation of individual egos in a kind of *homo Gestalt*: out of many, one. That is why the later name for the eastern point, starting with Notebook 12, paragraph 100, is Nous, universal (not just individual) mind, corresponding to Nomos, law, in the west.[14] Thus we have the first component of our diagram:

W ————————	E
Nomos	Nous
Law	Universal Mind
Fall	Apocalypse
Past	Future
Contract	Utopia

When following his plan to make the Third Book deal with the external relations of literature, discussion of the horizontal axis was often envisioned as taking up an entire volume, which would show how historical and political writings are displacements of this original mythical pattern: "The Third Book, then, is to be a book on literature & society, the reading for it to start at the end of 4k (Morris, Butler, Ruskin, Arnold, Mill) & work back. It's the Locke programme eventually, & includes the reading for the rcsm [romanticism] bk. DeTocqueville & things, of course. It's beginning to feel like that Spenglerian book of my dreams" (19.84). Here, 4k is the undergraduate course in "Nineteenth-Century Thought" which Frye taught in his earlier years under the old Honour course system at Victoria College, and which he mentions frequently in these notebooks. Although the course had a standard reading list and was also taught by other members of the faculty, the writers Frye mentions above, along with Carlyle, became central for him, something like a vast, intertextual conversation, an anatomy in dialogue form on the role of education and the arts in relation to power, ideology, and social class, a debate that took the subject forward from where Milton had left off. The

"Locke reading programme," referred to here and there throughout Frye's notebooks and left annoyingly unexplained every time, refers to some plan of reading one summer in the 1940s, presumably related to the issues in chapter one of *Fearful Symmetry*, "The Case Against Locke," in which the limitations of Locke's political ideals (horizontal axis) are seen as related to the limitations of his psychological, educational, and religious theories (vertical axis). At any rate, the essay "The Problem of Spiritual Authority in the Nineteenth Century,"[15] written during the Third Book period, is a kind of distillation of the projected volume. Notebook 19 shows how the Alexander Lectures, which became Frye's book on Shakespearean tragedy, *Fools of Time*, developed out of consideration of tragedy as revolving around Nomos, the epiphany of law. Other outgrowths of this phase include *The Modern Century* and, late in Frye's career, the essays on Samuel Butler and William Morris.[16]

However, there are conflicts in this diagram that creatively destabilize it and thus help to move it onward into the next phase of a total vision. Utopias are not really apocalyptic; usually they stop with a community of kindred spirits, often united through identification with one head, as in the apostles at the Last Supper, the Platonic symposium, or the knights of the Round Table. The reason is that it is hard to conceive of the universal without losing the individual; hence, the most interesting works in the Utopian tradition are, paradoxically, not Utopian: the Arcadia, whose controlling image is the garden, not the city, Eden and not the New Jerusalem, is individualized and anarchist in its tendencies rather than universalist. Those who know the Great Doodle in its entirety will realize the implication: the garden belongs to the imagery of Eros, the E–N quadrant; so the focus has begun to shift from horizontal to vertical. It is thus no surprise to find that the vertical axis, which Notebook 19 gradually shifts to discussing after the horizontal, is the axis between subjective and objective, in other words the axis of individual rather than social experience.

B. The Vertical Axis

The vertical axis in the first half of Notebook 19 has some kinship to the *axis mundi* of the second half of *Words with Power*, which is a distant development of it. But it is also a good deal different. As the basis for a separate volume or at least major component of the Third Book, it was to have provided the mythological backbone supporting a discussion of speculative, i.e., philosophical and theological, structures of thought. Yet the more it gets displaced into an ideological form, the more the vertical axis, soon to be characterized as the axis of concern, is cast as a hierarchy of authority. Two such hierarchies are central for Western culture: the *analogia entis*, or analogy of being, adapted by Thomas Aquinas out of Aristotle, and a more Platonic version utilized by Augustine, the pseudo-Dionysius, and others. The literary inheritance from these systems is the Chain of Being and related apparatus studied by students as part of "the Elizabethan world picture."

But even such ideologically contaminated structures leave visible the myth which is their secret imaginative background. The controlling myth of the horizontal axis is the fall, both into fallen nature (time and space) and into the social contract by which humanity tries to survive in the state of nature. The controlling myth of the vertical axis is Creation, kidnapped by the prevailing ideology to rationalize a top-dog structure of authority. But as such constructs are increasingly recognized as projections, the modern world has increasingly begun to consider what the vertical axis is a projection *of*, namely, the primary act of creation which is human perception. Thus, Frye arrives at a "Vertical axis of subject & object" (19.132), and his argument begins recalling aspects of the opening of *Fearful Symmetry*, especially the attack on the psychology of Locke, which turns the polarity of subject and object into what Blake called the "cloven fiction" of a passive ego-consciousness looking out helplessly upon a world of material objects from which it is alienated and yet which exist largely independent of it.

Blake agrees rather with Berkeley and the later phenomenological tradition that objects exist only to a perceiver; the assumption that any object exists outside of human perception may seem like the merest common sense but is really arbitrary and dogmatic, because it is asserted without evidence—the only evidence we can possibly have is the evidence of human perception. Nothing can exist except as perceived by a subject, says Berkeley. Thus, a dialectical progression begins to shape up as the real form of the vertical axis. We begin with ordinary ego-consciousness, the subject who, because passive, perceives a "given" external world, whether it is the world of material objects that Locke accepts from Newtonian science or the earlier world of the Chain of Being and its divinely-created Ptolemaic cosmos. This world is "the Creation" precisely because the subject did not create it himself; some external power and order-principle did, whether the "laws of nature" or an ordaining Logos.

Or so the subject believes: actually, it is the subject who is the true creator, and the world is not "given" at all but brought into the only kind of existence there is (except in the minds of dogmatists) by human creative power as it controls and orders human perception. The moment of enlightenment is that in which, realizing this, we begin to wake up; that is the moment signified by the centre of Frye's diagram, where the horizontal and vertical axes cross: *kairos*, the still point in the turning world. "In the centre is the education and initiatory-dialectic structure," Frye says (19.132), because such an enlightenment or awakening is the true purpose of education, initiating us into a dialectic whereby objective and subjective are progressively transformed. At this point Frye is continuing to develop the line of thinking set out in *The Educated Imagination*, which he had just published; related papers on this aspect of the Doodle include "Speculation and Concern"[17] and "Design as a Creative Principle in the Arts."[18] Art is at the centre of education because it can become a yoga or discipline for the transformation of perception. In a sequence meditating upon the notion of *telos*, Frye asserts that, while *telos* has been discredited as a concept in natural science, it is still perhaps the key to the humanities. For "The end of art is epiphany, perceiving the particular as universal, the grain of sand as the world" (19.159). Subject and object are transvalued by being gathered into the epiphany as its experiential and formal aspects. "Thus epiphany is (a) a subjective experience of a moment of identity (b) an objective telos or completed form clear of the wheel of process (c) the union of these two things represented by the experience of art (d) the identity of this union with the total person, Christ in Xy. This is the axis of concern . . ." (19.157).

VI The World Above

C. The Circle: Cycle and Quest

Surely this accomplishes enough for one book: Frye himself sometimes estimates a whole volume for the political and historical displacements of the horizontal axis, a second volume for the religious and conceptual displacements of the vertical axis, and a third volume articulating the dialectic of the centre. He calculates the years until retirement and wonders if he has enough time (19.231). Yet in the same breath he admits that the project is incomplete, and almost casually announces in paragraph 191, "At this point it will be convenient to transfer the great wheel from the drama notebook." And from somewhere about this point, the Third Book begins the modulation from a book of the axes to the book of the hemispheres or quadrants that it continues to be through notebooks 6, 12, 24, and the "Work in Progress" notes, which form a possibly overlapping but nevertheless fairly definite progression from somewhere around 1968 until 1972. After that, the four quadrants that had been four *loci*, journeyed through by a questing consciousness, each the environment for particular *topoi* or image clusters, became four ascents and descents on a vertical *axis mundi*. In both *The Secular Scripture* and *Words with Power*, the map of the journey was replaced by the journey itself: the "way" is defined more dynamically and experientially as action, not place. Thus, as we shall see, the later versions are less contemplative, more existential and involved.

But why was the containing circle introduced in the first place? Numerous passages make clear that Frye felt he could not discuss political and conceptual displacements without first summarizing the total mythical pattern that they are displacements of: when Frye uses the term "Great Doodle" in earlier notebooks, it does not yet refer to the four quadrants of Hermes, Eros, Adonis, and Prometheus, but merely to the cyclical journey of the ultimate quest-hero, the Logos, whose descent and return redeems the fallen world. The political and conceptual displacements are anchored to it at the four cardinal points where the axes meet the circle; in this context, those points N, W, S, and E represent junctures where the cyclical form of scripture, epic, and romance somehow modulates into the ideological, discursive, nonliterary prose forms of the axes. It was logical to think that the transition must be made through the intermediaries of the four forms of prose fiction (romance, novel, anatomy, and confession) as identified in the *Anatomy*, or else through what Frye off and on saw as four prose kernels, seeds from which the more continuous forms of prose presumably grew up. It is possible that these are parable, commandment, oracle, dialogue. Or parable, commandment, oracle, aphorism. Or commandment, oracle, aphorism, pericope.[19] The shell game Frye played for years shuffling prose forms and kernels, trying to get them to fall into place at the four cardinal points, began before the Third Book and continued after it, always collapsing into a series of unanswerable riddles: Does dialogue belong with the anatomy in the S, or with symposium forms in the E? The second table inside the front cover of Notebook 19 records a typically futile solution. No throw of the dice ever abolished chance in this area.

In *Anatomy of Criticism*, the interface of literature and mythology is the four *mythoi*, or generic plots, of comedy, tragedy, romance, and satire, which fit together as the four quadrants of a total cyclical quest-myth. There is no doubt that the four quadrants of the Third Book, Eros, Adonis, Hermes, and Prometheus, bear some resemblance (in that order) to the *mythoi*—so obvious a resemblance that Frye feared discovering that he was really just rewriting the *Anatomy*. But the *mythoi* belong to the literary, and thus to the fictional and hypothetical. The *topoi* of the Third Book belong on the other side of literature from its descriptive, conceptual, and ideological displacements: the side Frye was later to call the *kerygmatic*, or simply the spiritual. It is no accident that the two books that eventually derived from the Third Book project were books on the Bible. The four quadrants and their image-clusters can and do inform literature, but insofar as they do so literature itself approaches the metaliterary threshold of kerygma. What is merely the quest of the hero, any hero, in the *Anatomy* becomes the quest of the Logos in the Third Book.

Why do we need to take this step, especially since it is what Frye notes that Coleridge did and he himself refuses to do in the *Anatomy*, that is, identify the total form of the "order of words" with Christ as the Logos? To postulate a redeeming figure who descends, bringing a visionary model order whence the forms of all human culture derive—isn't that merely a form of projection? Why should humanity need a spiritual "other" to grant it its creative forms and powers from the outside? The traditional answer is that man is so fallen that he is utterly incapable of redeeming himself by his own efforts, and the twentieth century may be more in alignment with that traditional answer than it likes to admit. Socially, whenever the optimistic myth of progress that fuels both Marxism and capitalist democracy falters, we are again left face to face with the pessimism of Frye's first influence, Spengler. Even a booming stock market seems unable to allay the depressive anxiety that the Western world at the turn of the millennium is in irresistible cultural decline, as the natural youthful energies that Blake personifies as Orc age into the decadent frozen structures of Urizen. Psychologically, whenever the myth of healthy-mindedness fails that has fueled both humanistic or ego psychologies of various sorts and the millennarian revisionist Freudianism of the 1960s, we are left confronting the pessimism of Freud in *Civilization and Its Discontents*. As Frye likes to repeat, the natural man is a crazy Oedipus who wants to kill his father God and rape his mother nature, and much modern art and cultural theory is the recognition scene of Oedipus, the cry of agonized horror as he sees so clearly what he is that he has to put out his eyes.

The Great Doodle is the summation of the Third Book project; but, as already mentioned, the latter was an effort either to write one volume of the interminably postponed ogdoad project or perhaps to fold all of its four or eight parts into a single encyclopedic *magnum opus* as individual chapters. It might as well have been titled *Waiting for Ogdoad*; yet, though it never arrived, the Great Doodle is its prophet. The Doodle is a condensation (Frye would later say an enfolding) of the ogdoad scheme, which is the earliest form of Frye's spiritual architecture and goes back to the 1930s and early 1940s, not only before the *Anatomy* but before *Fearful Symmetry*. And that fact may provide some clue to the Third-Book crisis, for that means it is at least partially pre-Blake. That is important because Blake helped to radicalize Frye's religious imagination; the ogdoad pattern (at least in its first form as criticism rather than novels or symphonies) may have originated as an attempt to provide a Christian response more adequate than Arnold Toynbee's to Spengler's cyclical pessimism and the rise of Nazism and Fascism, but at that point it may have been still relying on a relatively conservative view of the Logos and its redemptive descent into the fallen world, in which it never entirely loses the appearance of being a *deus ex machina*. Such an external saving power will soon be contradicted by the Romantic notion that the only saving power is immanent in humanity, as in Blake's theory of the creative imagination sketched out earlier.

There is evidence for some ambivalence on Frye's part in the unified theoretical scheme that unites his student papers during this period into a single intellectual vision; historically, Romanticism is said in them to mark the beginning of cultural breakdown, a fragmentation of the vision embodied more coherently in the works of Spenser and Shakespeare, Bach and Mozart, and whose works for that reason are the great monuments and high point of Western culture. Even in *Fearful Symmetry* there is a rather puzzling attempt to assert that Blake was more akin to the Renaissance than to the Romantic revolution. The young Frye clearly identified with the Renaissance and did not think much of Romanticism—which he saw as ironic, "Kantian" in its epistemology, and all-too-German. It was only later that he moved towards a view more like that of M.H. Abrams's *Natural Supernaturalism*, in which Romanticism is associated with a hopeful political liberalism and a theory of the creative imagination, and which seems somehow English even when it is German or French.

The task of a critic who lives in a post-Romantic period of breakdown and fragmentation is to recreate the vision of unity when it has been forgotten, denied, or drowned out in the noise of the Tower of Babel. That is what the ogdoad scheme—and therefore still the Third Book scheme at its inception—originally was. As Frye himself says, he returns to it after each major book. The crucial Notebook 7 from the late 1940s shows Frye (until sidetracked by the conception, or what he called the "unwanted pregnancy," of the *Anatomy of Criticism* halfway through it) struggling to begin the ogdoad by writing a book on Christian epic (by which he really means Protestant epic). The Protestant epic marks the transformation of epic form from the Orc-cycle structure of traditional heroic epic to the Los-structure which identifies the quest hero as what Blake called "Christ in Luvah's robes of blood," the incarnate Logos who leaves the eternity of the Father and, out of *agape*, is sacrificed as the dying-god figure of the natural cycle. But in doing so he creates an identity between himself and the spiritual part of ourselves, an identity so total ("I am in Christ and Christ is in me," Paul says) that when he returns to his Father our spiritual self is taken up along with him and thereby redeemed.

Because the Bible is "the great code of art," in Blake's phrase, this myth as it unfolds through (usually) four distinct phases recreates the human order of words in its image, giving to literature its four major genres and four historical periods in a scheme roughly like the following:

1. *Liberal* (⅃), the first member of the ogdoad, is usually said to be an articulation of the Logos or total mythological vision in its full, unfallen encyclopedic form, as reflected in scripture, epic, and naive romance. Its symbol is thus the full mandala of circle plus axes, quadrants, cardinal points, and centre.
2. *Tragicomedy* (⌉), as its name suggests, moves from myth to ritual, from continuous cyclic forms to the episodic, though still cyclic, forms of drama. Its symbol is the circle, because the Logos-hero has descended from eternity into time; this is the form of his sacrifice (tragedy) and resurrection (comedy); the former is informed by Frazer's *The Golden Bough*, the latter by Colin Still's book on *The Tempest*, *Shakespeare's Mystery Play*, another very early influence. Insofar as Tragicomedy is concerned with all of literature, it views it as "dramatistic," that is, as episodes of a sacrificial *agon*.

3. *Anticlimax* (Λ) treats myth as *dianoia* or theme rather than as *mythos* (narrative) or *agon* (ritualized conflict). It includes both the political and conceptual displacements of myth, and so is associated with the horizontal and vertical axes, but also with the different kind of displacement towards plausibility we call realism. Its centre of gravity is prose.[20]
4. *Rencontre* (ʎ) treats literature in terms of irony and fragmentation; it begins in what Frye calls sentimental (i.e., self-conscious) romance, the form of some of Frye's favourite writers: Hawthorne, Melville, Poe, the Henry James of the occult stories, William Morris, some aspects of Proust. But it also includes the fragmented form *par excellence*, the lyric poem. Any fragment can be a random point; or it can be the Logos as microcosm, the world in the grain of sand.

Each of these four, which Frye identifies periodically with Blake's Four Zoas, is thus informed by and is an epiphany of one of the aspects under which the Logos as Great Doodle appears in the human order of words: as total mandala, episodic cycle, dialectic of crossed axes, and the isolated point. From the Logos-pattern derive the specific genres of literature: scripture, epic and romance, comedy and tragedy, realistic and thematic prose, sentimental prose romance and the lyric. It also gives us the diachronic pattern of literary history: scripture, epic, and romance are ascendent in earlier periods; then drama (Classical Athens, the Renaissance); realistic and thematic prose (Classical prose satire, the eighteenth–nineteenth-century period of the realistic novel); then lyric and postmodern prose. For want of any better guess, we may tentatively identify this pattern with what Frye called his St. Clair epiphany, a moment of crucial insight, often referred to in the notebooks, that he had in the 1950s while walking on St. Clair Avenue in Toronto, and which had something to do with a passage from epic to drama to prose. Further explanation is not forthcoming.

One cannot page far through the present volume without seeing these four names and symbols, and, more occasionally, their four emanations or counterparts in the full ogdoad: *Mirage* (V), a unified treatment of the whole circle of the arts; *Paradox* (⊢); *Ignoramus* (⊥); *Twilight* (variable: Γ, T, ⅃), aphorisms, a century of meditations in old age. Most often they will appear in tables of contents, parts of the Third Book (and so each corresponding to a piece of the Doodle, as above), whether expanded into entire volumes or contracted into single chapters. The whole scheme is breathtaking in its complexity and ambition, and Frye repeatedly doubts that he will ever manage to pull it off. Yet the final rupture had little to do with size and complexity; rather, it grew out of Frye's growing recognition that there was not one encyclopedic vision but two, one pre- and one post-Romantic, and that the one was the antithesis of the other.

VII The World Below

Frye had always known that the Great Doodle as the quest of the Logos demanded what he sometimes called a "second twist"—apparently this phrase means a kind of Hegelian *aufhebung*, a raising-up from simple to self-conscious, or from naive to sentimental, in Schiller's well-known terms. Frye's later term for the process was recreation, and it often implies a deliteralizing of the original narrative. If the Logos quest myth is to mean anything profounder than "Jesus saves," it is going to have to become a twice-told tale, with the second telling equivalent to the "secret" wisdom Jesus tells the disciples that he reserves for them, as opposed to the simpler and easier public message he gives to the crowd.

We have glanced at one version of such a twist, the idea of writing one volume, usually ㄱ (Tragicomedy), as a book on its side. There is perhaps a resemblance to Derrida's notion of deconstruction through "soliciting" a structure, setting it into motion and thus turning it from static to dynamic, synchronic to diachronic.[21] Even though it signifies a narrative, the circle of the Great Doodle is spatial and synchronic; given a twist, Tragicomedy, originally conceived as cyclical, would become a vortex, with the Doodle's centre becoming its apex, through which all reality might pass and be transformed. Three works with a special relation to this vortical recreation are *The Tempest, Paradise Regained,* and Blake's *Milton.* Through many years, in many notebooks, Frye thinks of them as a kind of consubstantial trinity, one theme in three manifestations: they are "my favorite 'centre' poems" (24.46). Only one is an actual stage drama, but the real subject of Tragicomedy is the dramatic structure of the *agon,* which *Paradise Regained* and *Milton* embody in the form of a dialectical debate; the Biblical type of such works (as *Paradise Regained* makes clear) is the Book of Job. Thus, *The Tempest, Paradise Regained,* and *Milton* are works about what Frye would later call the purgatorial process; not coincidentally, they are also works with a special autobiographical relation to their authors. What that points to is what is left out of the

Logos narrative of Christianity in its traditional form: namely, us. Considered in this light, Christianity is a divine comedy in a very literal sense: the only real actors are the members of the Trinity, and humanity is a passive creature, a princess bride waiting to be rescued from the dragon. Most human actions are pseudo- or parody-actions, as Milton shows in *Paradise Lost*; its real hero is Christ, who performs the only genuine acts. When a human being performs a genuine act, it is "not I, but Christ in me," or else the indwelling Holy Spirit which Christ sent down to relieve him after the Ascension. The problem that Romantics like Blake and Shelley had with *Paradise Lost* was that, despite Milton's revolutionary sympathies, it retained the orthodox doctrine of human passivity. During the cultural ascendency of Christianity during the Middle Ages and Renaissance, two phenomena appeared as attempts to supplement this lack in orthodoxy, mysticism and the cult of Eros known as Courtly Love; the erotic imagery of the former and the occasionally mystical rhetoric of the latter show that they are related, and Frye's interest in both of them is no doubt why he speaks of Eros as his great breakthrough into the four-quadrants version of the Great Doodle in Notebooks 6, 12, and 24. But, as the ending of Dante's *Divine Comedy* shows, the conservative or orthodox position is that both mysticism and romantic love have to become subordinated in the end to the patriarchal authority-structure of the Logos.

Yet Frye had never been satisfied with traditional Christianity. I suggested that the ogdoad scheme's limitations may have stemmed from the fact that it was conceived in part out of the usual modernist's distaste for the modern, as a way of conserving the great Logos-vision of the past in the face of the secularism, fragmentation, and confusion of the contemporary crisis. But Frye was no T.S. Eliot or C.S. Lewis; he valued institutional Christianity enough to become ordained, but hated it enough to write that "The effect of organized and institutional religion on society, for the most part, is evil. It isn't just reactionary or superstitious; it is evil, and stinks in the nose of God" (12.347). As a critic, Frye usually identified his affinities as being with the idealizing forms of comedy and romance, but his own form was the anatomy, and both his early reviews and *Fearful Symmetry* crackle with satiric energy and bite. As he became a more public figure, the satire was usually toned down to wit in his published works, but we now know that the residual subversiveness went underground into the notebooks. On the Great Doodle, Frye's spiritual mentor Blake is not located in the quadrant of Eros, moving like a Dante or an Eliot upwards towards identification with Logos at the north; he is a Promethean satirist busting out of an underworld in the south, whose fires are not the flames of torment but creative energies stolen defiantly from usurping gods.

Two developments influenced the evolution of the Third Book in its next phase. One was the spirit of the 1960s. It is instructive to remember that Frye's proposed work on criticism and society was not meditated in isolated tranquillity but within sight of the battlefields, so to speak, during a period of exceptional social upheaval. Like the French Revolution, which so influenced the vision of Blake and other Romantics, it was the best of times and worst of times. In his own country, the realization that Canada had come of age both culturally and politically gave rise to a nationalistic euphoria that reached its culmination in the celebration of the Centennial of Canadian Confederation in 1967, whose highlight was Expo '67, the World's Fair in Montreal that Frye has come back from visiting at the end of Notebook 19. Yet when Frye announces that he has reached the end of Notebook 12 on 30 August 1970, it is only two months from the October Crisis provoked by separatist terrorism in Quebec, the passage by the government of the War Measures Act suspending some civil liberties, and anxiety about whether Canada would survive as a unified society at all. The United States was caught up in its own version of the same manic-depressive rhythm. During his semester of teaching at Berkeley, Frye witnessed the People's Park crisis in May, 1968, and other aspects of what was, for a few brief years, another uprising of the revolutionary spirit of Blake's fire-haired Orc.

Frye himself made the connection with the Romantic revolution in a new preface to *Fearful Symmetry* in 1969. He had little sympathy for that part of the 1960s which, as a university professor, he got the closest look at. Still, he recognized that despite the unfocused and sometimes nihilistic anarchism of what he occasionally called "the children's crusade" (11f.184) it was a symptom of a much wider attempt at the liberation of human creative energies that Blake spoke of in *The Marriage of Heaven and Hell*. Not only had Frye chosen a revolutionary Romantic poet as his spiritual mentor, but he went on record during this period as saying that he had chosen him partly as a deliberate gesture of defiance against the cultural conservatism represented by Eliot's *After Strange Gods*. It must have been a strange experience, writing *Fearful Symmetry* at a time when the overwhelming majority of important writers and thinkers were reactionaries—almost as strange, perhaps, as finding himself twenty years later described by a Maoist pamphleteer as a "high priest of clerical obscurantism."[22] Yet, silly as that incident was, it reflected the fact that Frye was now a world-famous representative of an establishment about which he had deep reservations. If not a high priest, he was a clergyman and university administrator; yet he also accepted Blake's identification of creative vision with the revolutionary forms of Biblical prophecy and apocalyptic writing—so much so that the final form of the Great Doodle in *Words with Power* is the shaman's ecstatic ladder.

Frye was by this time well along in the second development affecting his critical project's shape, or lack thereof: a deeper understanding and insight into Romanticism. Articles such as "New Directions from Old"[23] and "The Drunken Boat: The Revolutionary Element in Romanticism"[24] had shown him that what Romanticism ushered in was not mere fragmentation but a momentous reversal of the whole structure of Western mythology. We now live in a different mythological universe from that of Dante or Spenser, one whose values are literally inverted. We have already seen how the Logos-structure of pre-Romantic Western culture projected Frye's vertical axis as a conservative hierarchy of top-down authority. This resulted in a descending four-level cosmos—heaven, paradise, earth, and hell—where good is up and bad is down. The primary social value is thus obedience to whomever and whatever outranks you.

As Frye shows in the chart on page 248 of *Words with Power*, the post-Romantic cosmos stands the traditional one on its head: at the top is a stupid and malicious sky-god who is really only a projection of the human death-wish; then a human civilization built (as Freud said) upon instinctual repression and maintained (as Marx and Nietzsche said) by a will to power; then a level to which everything sinks that has been repressed or "marginalized" (the unconscious, the underclass, the natural world pushed out by urbanization, etc.); and finally a deep source of creative power often imaged as submerged under the sea (Atlantis) or buried in some kind of underworld labyrinth or cave. The social values implied are radical, underdog ones; yet different Romantics had different attitudes toward and made various adaptations of this new cosmos and its imagery. During the composition of Notebook 19, Frye accepted the invitation to do a set of lectures at Western Reserve University in Cleveland which turned into his book *A Study of English Romanticism*. Notebook 19 discloses that book's secret imaginative background, which we could hardly have known otherwise, and it turns out to be that of the

Great Doodle in its quadrant form: South is demonic Romanticism (Beddoes); East revolutionary (Shelley); North oracular (Keats); West conservative and confessional (Wordsworth, Rousseau) (19.222)—later, Frye contemplates adding a chapter to cover this quadrant before the book is published (19.322).

The pre-Romantic cosmos has bequeathed us works whose imaginative power compels our emotional consent, despite our lack of sympathy with their ideology; even considered ideologically, their theme is more than a mere rationalization of authority. Their message, that there is a spiritual otherness greater than ourselves, whose ways are not our own, yet to whom somehow or other we belong, and with which we must struggle to keep faith, is not dead in our despairing century. Though he slay me, yet will I trust in him. Flawed and corrupted like all human productions, works written within the old cosmos of authority, including the Bible itself, possess, at least at times, rifts of an ore that glitters in our dark, even when it is surrounded by the ideological dross of dead white males. Self needs other, and if nothing else, texts from the old, conservative cosmos may counterbalance the tendency to an egotistical sublime that has been the chief temptation of the new, revolutionary cosmos since the late eighteenth century. At the same time, no one had put the case for the revolutionary, Promethean vision, in which the only redemptive power is the human capacity for imagination, intellect, courage, and love, better than Frye himself already had twenty years earlier in *Fearful Symmetry*. Antithetical values with antithetical maps, which can never be logically reconciled, yet Frye staked the entire second half of his career on the faith that they not only can but must be identified, however paradoxically, as double gyres of a total vision. This was the task that now began to emerge at the centre of the Third Book project, and whose final result was the dialectic of Word and Spirit in *Words with Power*.

If the second cosmos holds something of permanent value to the human race, its structure must be a missing piece of a total Logos-pattern, not just a parody-inversion of the older cosmos; also, that structure must not be a newfangled innovation but must have pre-Romantic antecedents stretching all the way back to the beginnings of mythology. Beginning in the last part of Notebook 19, Frye was much taken with the studies by G. Rachel Levy[25] of a mythological pattern that can be traced back to the Palaeolithic, whose central symbols included labyrinths, caves, and katabasis—the quest downward and inward rather than upward. Such symbols have age-old feminine associations, and although the present scholarship on "goddess cultures" did not yet exist for him to make use of, he was able to discern the outlines of an alternative mythology in which nature and the feminine were central—a mythology which has been repressed repeatedly by hierarchical power-structures. Writing "The Revelation to Eve" on *Paradise Lost*, first planned in Notebook 19, was his first tentative public exploration in this area.[26]

Frye's first solution to the problem of how to integrate pre- and post-Romantic mythologies is to regard what developed sequentially in history as in fact simultaneous possibilities to the imagination: the upper and lower hemispheres of the Great Doodle diagram. In this phase of his thinking, the two upper quadrants of the circle, Eros and Adonis, define the fundamental narrative of pre-Romantic mythology: a comic rising movement towards a revelation of the Logos-vision in the north, at what he had already called in the *Anatomy* the point of epiphany. The two lower quadrants, Hermes and Prometheus, though remaining permanent imaginative possibilities since the time of the cave cults, have only achieved cultural ascendancy in the post-Romantic period, the first thoroughgoingly revolutionary era in Western history. Frye was always uncertain what the best name for Hermes was; temporary candidates, including Oedipus and Theseus, add certain suggestive connotations to the quadrant, whose narrative is the katabasis into death and the underworld, where, at a point of demonic epiphany, the mysterious counterplayer to the Logos is manifest: Thanatos. Beyond that is Prometheus, the revolutionary rising movement.

The older, conservative era of culture was aware of the lower quadrants, but mostly just demonized them; there are few ideological perversions of mythology that provoke Frye's prophetic fury more than the Christian hell. Nevertheless, if the Bible is really the "great code" Frye thought it was, it must contain versions of both mythological frameworks, and, though to explore this would take us beyond the period of the Third Book, he eventually found them in the two creation myths conflated in the Book of Genesis: the P or Priestly version, not surprisingly, provides the basis for pre-Romantic mythology, with its sky-father; the J or Jahwist version retains vestiges of influence by the old earth-mother fertility cults. The J writer's story of the fall of man through woman, however, reinforces the ideology of authority; therefore tradition had added a second fall story, that of the revolt of the rebel angels, whose potential Prometheanism counters the authority of P's sky-father artificer.

This is the point at which Frye had arrived by the time of Notebook 6 in 1968. Notebook 6 is a curious production, not so much because it is organized by the clever trick of dividing the daybook in which it is written into four quadrants, with Eros and Hermes beginning on the pages for the equinoxes and Adonis and Prometheus beginning on the solstice pages; the real curiosity is that Frye, in filling out the sections, does not actually follow his own titles. The EROS section is actually about Eros; but ADONIS is actually about Logos; HERMES is about Adonis; and PROMETHEUS is about Thanatos. What this may suggest is that Frye was at this point still mostly preoccupied with the original contrast of two mythological structures rather than with four quadrants—the real focus of the notebook is perhaps the contrast of Logos and Thanatos.

Notebook 12 does fill in all four quadrants with a wealth of detail; it is one of the two or three longest and most complicated notebooks because Frye had come back from Expo 67 in Montreal with the plan of "writing the book in the fullest quest or labyrinth form" (19.354), which turns out to mean as a leisurely, meandering, encyclopedic meditation instead of a selective, driving, linear argument; this interlace style continues through Notebook 24. That does not mean that Frye is only exploring clusters of imagery, though; he is also attempting to construct a new quest narrative that will take into account the concerns of both conservative and revolutionary myths. He begins to pay greater attention to alternative interpretations of the Biblical creation myth such as that of Jacob Boehme, from whom Blake had drawn some of his notion that the original Creation was in fact a Creation-Fall, and that what fell was not only humanity and nature but also at least some part of God, as in various Gnostic cosmogonies. Why is the Great Doodle divided into polarized hemispheres? Because of a "sky-Father that splits the world in two between a Heavenly Creator and a demonic Mother Nature" (12.522). Then the Logos descends into the lower world by becoming the Promethean light-bringer; his gift of fire is the illumination that the division of reality is an illusion, and is abolished the minute we wake up and realize that it is such: "As long as the sky-Father is there the demonic world has to be there too: once the Logos emerges from the cycle, what Boehme calls the Father's empty shell of wrath & pain is abandoned" (12.523). The real Father with whom the Son is re-united is not the sky-father but more like

Heidegger's *Sein*, the Being that is the secret background of all manifest beings (6.31). The real Son is less the descending Word of the Creation in Genesis than the Promethean Christ of the Resurrection, who is also the God whose answer to Job amounts to a warning: don't focus on the star-maker God of Creation, for to look outward for an objective God is to fall into Blake's "cloven fiction," and all you will find is the sky-father God who is your own projection. The real God responds from the whirlwind vortex rising out of the underworld inside of us.

Because such a Christ is fully human, though, he is not just a superhero harrowing hell, but actually has to go through the misery, confusion, and despair of the human condition, whose mythological form is the Hermes katabasis. Orthodox Christianity pretends to insist on the complete humanity of Christ, but an attempt to explore the implications of that radical notion, such as Martin Scorsese's film *The Last Temptation of Christ*, is apt to provoke boycotts and demonstrations. Yet to identify the quest-ordeal of Christ with that of every human life means in return that the ordeal of every human life is identical to the quest of Christ: we are not mere sinful creatures redeemed by an all-powerful, perfect divinity, but rather "Thou art That," in the Hindu phrase. As Frye puts it, "We are in God; God is in us. . . . Perhaps this mutuality of awareness *is* identity."[27] The remote, inscrutable sky-father and his miserable worm of a human creature are objective and subjective illusions of the cloven fiction; the mutuality of awareness Blake called the human form divine is the only identity there is, and the quest of the Great Doodle is the journey from the objective northern pole to the subjective south in order to abolish their distance by uniting them in the common centre. The human yet divine identity that makes this journey is the creative power the Romantics called the imagination, the Promethean spark that bridges the subject–object gap, that jumps from north to south and realizes that A is B, Thou art That. This is the Word that shines like a light in the uncomprehending dark: Frye notes how the hymn that opens the Gospel of John reads like a recreation of the Creation myth in Genesis, and, imaginatively speaking, should have been put at the opening of the New Testament for that reason.

The Third Book was supposed to be a complete guide to the symbolic universe, however, and not another translation of myth and the Bible into Blakean terms. Some of the richest material introduced in Notebooks 12 and 24 shows Frye searching for versions of creative descent outside the English Romantic orbit. The next orbit outward in this solar system, so to speak, was sentimental romance, from Poe to Tolkien, which Frye was convinced fit somewhere into the ogdoad scheme, if he could only figure out where; whole notebooks are taken up with this material as far back as the 1940s, and the end result was *The Secular Scripture* just a few years after the "Work in Progress" coda to the Third-Book era.

The next orbit, perhaps via Poe, was that of French *symbolisme*, in particular Mallarmé, whose *Igitur* provided Frye with one of his major variations on the theme of the quest as a descent into nothing. The Hermes descent begins as the inherent alienation of ego-consciousness in an objective world, the state Heidegger calls "thrownness" and Thomas Pynchon calls paranoia. As the descent deepens and alienation intensifies, the subject is increasingly isolated; the connections are broken that made him feel that he was a part of his world and his world was part of him. In some myths this appears as the progressive stripping away of "property," beginning in the form of the possessions and appurtenances and relationships of life: the ritual stripping of Inanna (Ishtar) in Sumerian mythology, so that she arrives in the underworld naked, is an early form of it, repeated in the progressive losses of Job and King Lear. But one proof that the subject–object division is an illusion is that the stripping away of objects, of property, changes imperceptibly into the stripping away of subjectivity, of the "properties" that make us what we are and which we had considered inherent. The last property to lose is life itself: Inanna arrives in the underworld not only naked but dead. Subjects and objects are all such things as dreams are made on, and vanish leaving not a rack behind. Every human life ends in complete and utter loss, and is an epiphany of what the Renaissance called mutability, a fancy name for the common wisdom that you can't take it with you. At the bottom of the circle the Great Doodle is *nothing*, the key word in *King Lear*, whose protagonist says early in the play that nothing can come of nothing. So far, there is no quest, but only fate or destiny, a special Hermes theme. In Buddhism, which Frye at one point calls "the definitive night-vision" (12.436), enlightenment consists in seeing the phenomenal world as *maya*, illusion; reality, Nirvana, is "the void."

But Buddhism is not nihilistic; the void is not mere nonexistence but a state that can only reveal itself after both subject and object have been deconstructed. It can neither be said to exist or not exist, because it is beyond the antithesis of being and nonbeing, which belongs to the world of the cloven fiction. A Western analogue is Heidegger's *Sein*, the Being which is the ground of being, the secret background eclipsed by all the beings in the foreground of existence. In Christian terms, it is the Logos manifesting itself in the midst of the darkness of Thanatos, this time not as an objective order-structure perceived by a subjective consciousness but as recreated into a form beyond alienation. Thus the quester keeps looking for evidence of a hidden meaningful pattern in chance, chaos, vacancy; that is why Frye is so preoccupied with the symbolism of divination and games of chance in the Hermes quadrant, also why he is haunted by Mallarmé's *Un Coup de Dés*, with its throw of the dice which does not abolish chance. Oracles are another form of the search for the wisdom of the underworld at the south pole of the Great Doodle, and, like games of chance, are mostly sinister. Frye refers periodically in his notebooks, however (for example, 12.192), to an insight that occurred to him as a flash of revelation or peak experience in Seattle in 1950, in which the bottom of the quest is a *peripeteia* or turning-point at which the oracular turns into the wit of an answered riddle, accompanied by a regaining of the releasing power of laughter. Echoing a number of passages in the notebooks, *The Secular Scripture* says that "According to Plutarch, those who descended to the gloomy cave of the oracle of Trophonius might, after three days, recover the power of laughter."[28] To achieve enlightenment is to get the joke, as in the paradoxical humour of Zen. What's so funny? For one thing, the great, absurd comedy of life itself: when we tell the story of our earlier life, we often tell what was painful when we lived it with a humorous detachment that recognizes the element of illusion in all that angst. For another thing, perhaps the fact that we can never have any objective proof of the ultimate reality of the spiritual world—in this case, the joke's on us—which can only be a "supreme fiction," which is not to imply that it is a subjective hallucination either. What kind of reality a supreme fiction has, what evidence we can have of things unseen: these are the questions that increasingly became central in the final phase of Frye's life, as recorded in the *Words with Power* and *Double Vision* notebooks.

Where Notebooks 6 and 12 are largely concerned with working out the structural details and narrative scheme of a Great Doodle that could integrate both the pre- and post-Romantic cosmos, some of the most interesting sections of Notebook 24 work out a corresponding historical development. Revolutionary mythology must have a secret history; it cannot have entered the world for the first time with the Romantics. So Frye began tracing backward, beginning with the common knowledge that the roots of Romantic radicalism, especially in England, were in left-wing, inner-light Protestantism, along with the tradition of occult and esoteric writing, including alchemy, with which it has affinities. The invitation to deliver the Birks Lectures at the divinity school of the Université de Montréal in 1971 gave Frye the impetus to develop a scheme of the evolution of religious conscousness that he called the "three awarenesses." The first phase is conservative; it sets up a rational structure of authority with a visual focus. The second phase is revolutionary, prophetic, and iconoclastic. The third phase resolves the antithesis on the higher level of an "interpenetrating" vision. The cyclical conflict between the first and second phases, clearly analogous to Blake's Orc cycle, has played itself out in both the ancient and modern phases of Western history: in the ancient world when the Biblical religions opposed themselves to the rational monotheisms and monarchies of the great world empires; in the modern world when prophetic figures such as Luther revolted against the world order of Catholicism, the Romantic revolution being an aftershock of this great cataclysm. The third awareness is perhaps more a vision of potentiality than a historical occurrence, though Frye comes up with lists identifying various cultural and historical figures with each awareness.

One sign that the Third Book period was winding down was Frye's decision to spin off both this particular theory and more general thoughts about religion into separate notebooks, 11f and 21, a prelude to his commitment to write a complementary book on the Bible. Although they date from 1969–71, Notebooks 11f and 21 therefore belong with the notebooks for the book in which they resulted, *The Great Code*. More and more Frye is thinking of limiting the Third Book to literature, along the lines of his graduate course in "Principles of Literary Symbolism," which he continued teaching until a few years before his death. The graduate class dealt with the cycle of lyrics (excluding works not in English) that Frye had always hoped to arrange along the cycle of the Great Doodle, but the course never explicitly mentioned the diagram that was its secret imaginative background.

Meanwhile, plans for the Third Book were in increasing trouble. The Great Doodle diagram simply did not seem able to accommodate both the conservative and revolutionary mythological perspectives, which split in the latter part of Notebook 24 into two separate Doodles, one upside-down from the other. The scheme is so maddeningly confusing that most readers will be relieved when Frye quickly gives it up.[29] But, despite the confident assertion of a regrouping of forces in the "Work in Progress" text, progress for the Third Book had come to an end. When the notebooks for *Words with Power* resume the meditation again, after a gap of nearly a decade taken up with the composition of *The Secular Scripture* and *The Great Code*, what had been four quadrants quickly began rearranging themselves along an *axis mundi*: a new universe and a new vision.

VIII Quiet Consummation

Chapters 5–8 of *Words with Power* redistribute the quadrants of the Great Doodle. Chapter 5 actually does not correspond to a quadrant at all, but rather to the discussions of Logos imagery in Notebooks 6 and 12; the new Hermes which is its presiding deity, according to the list on page 277, is the informing presence of a higher wisdom and not a psychopomp to the land of the dead. Chapter 6 retains much of the Eros material of the notebooks intact, adding a rich level of discussion of such Biblical books as Ruth and Song of Songs. Chapter 7 is Adonis, still descending, but now below the horizontal level of our middle earth rather than above it and thereby incorporating some portion of the old Hermes descent, the rest of which is picked up by Prometheus in chapter 8, along with the original contents of that quadrant and what, early on, was Thanatos. The axes as they appeared in Notebook 19 are gone—and yet not forgotten, it seems, for a number of paragraphs at the end of the last *Words with Power* notebook sketch plans for taking up their subjects—contracts, Utopias, education—in a subsequent book, never written (*LN*, 225, 232–4, 235–6, 239–40). One brief note even speaks of reviving the circle somehow.[30] But the biggest change in *Words with Power* is the shift of focus to the up–down dialectic of Word and Spirit; the theme of the book is the dialogue (the last four chapters were originally called "dialogues" rather than "variations") between a divine humanity and a human divinity—human creative power and its spiritual other. This dialogue creates a dialectic whereby both Word and Spirit are redeemed by being recreated out of their fallen forms of false sky-father and egocentric creature, these being cast out into the only hell there is, the hell of illusion and nonexistence.

What does this add beyond the Third Book, indeed beyond all of Frye's other works? It adds an existential element, the necessity for a risk, a commitment, a personal stake. In doing so, it dares to face what

Richard Lanham in *The Electronic Word* calls the Q question[31]—Q for Quintilian, who asks uneasily at the end of his book on the orator whether all the orator's education and skill necessarily made him a virtuous man. Quintilian's answer is an anxious "They must," or the whole value of literature, culture, and education is called into question. But the Nazis wept at symphonies, and artists and academics hardly seem like better human beings than people with less education or creativity; Lanham charges that the humanities deserve their indifferent reputation in contemporary society because they avoid even honestly asking the Q question, much less trying to answer it. Does art really make us better people? Does intellect? Does religion?

While the Third Book notebooks are not as openly engaged with these ultimate questions, there are priceless moments in which Frye has intuitions of the questions he should be asking on his Grail quest. In fact, maybe it means something that on the first pages of Notebook 19, at the very outset of the pilgrimage, Frye lists four ideas for works of fiction or creative writing which read like Tarot-card emblems of the hundreds of pages to follow. We may add to those a fifth emblem, one of the most hauntingly enigmatic images in all the notebooks: the "chess-in-bardo problem." Frye refers to this over and over,[32] often accompanied by the hope of writing a book that solves it. Bardo is the other half of the cycle of existence in the Great-Doodle–style diagram implied by *The Tibetan Book of the Dead*. As we move from life to death, the dead move through this ghost-realm from death to rebirth again, unless they manage to gain the flash of wisdom that enables one to break free of the cycle into Nirvana. Chess in Bardo would be an *agon* in the underworld against a mysterious other: the reference in Notebook 24, paragraph 73, describes it as "opposed forces each with its own centre." If education, including the experience and interpretation of literature, is done for egocentric reasons, it can actually intensify egocentricity, acting as the mirror of Narcissus as we ask it who's the fairest of them all. We have all read interpretations in which the critic seems to have seen little in the work except the reflection of his own prejudices. For the act of reading to change us, it has to be chess in Bardo: the risk of a life-or-death engagement, Jacob wrestling with the angel in the dark, no guarantees. In that case, checkmate would not mean mastery, but recognition, a process that has two phases. Insofar as a work of literature shows us our own Jungian shadow, it helps us detach ourselves from its evil, both through insight and catharsis. In the final *Words with Power* notebooks, Frye prays to write at least one book free of ego before he dies. This is equivalent to the ordeals of self-transformation in Frye's "centre poems," *The Tempest* (which features a chess game in its fifth act), *Paradise Regained,* and *Milton.* Insofar as it requires a kind of self-sacrificial ritual, dying to everything we think we have and are, such a creative act would be the first of Frye's fictional ideas: a story with death the *cognitio,* or recognition scene.

On the positive side, the work of literature shows us a vision with which it urges us to identify ourselves; this act of metaphorical identification of reader with the text, A is B, is the moment when the text ceases to be merely fictional or "hypothetical" and becomes *kerygma,* a "myth to live by." This is the moment of Resurrection as a larger identity, and the Third Book notebooks never tire of making the identification of the Resurrection with the moment of illumination in which we expand into a greater identity that is beyond time and space. Another of Frye's fictional plots is the discovery of a fifth Gospel (19.11); if one were found, it would expound what he calls "a kind of Mahayana Christianity" (24.204) of this sort.

The third of his plots involves the invention of a machine that can see into the past (19.11); the theme of this story would doubtless have been that of several notebook paragraphs, that any true apocalypse would have to be retroactive, reaching back and resurrecting from the grave everything that has been lost, but also, I suspect, healing everything that never had a chance to live, or was forced to live crippled and amputated, physically or emotionally, and never had a chance to be whole. This is, of course, utterly impossible, "and is therefore one of the proper studies of faith" (*WP,* 141). The only excuse for its radical wish-fulfilment is love: the first thing Frye says about Eros is that it reverses the current of time back to the unfallen state. It is only important to keep in mind that Frye's Eros is not the traditional Eros of the creature returning to its Creator; it is Eros on the other side of Prometheus, no longer a projection but a supreme fiction. Yet a fiction to which Frye committed himself, making Eros his "myth to live by" after Helen Frye's death as recorded in the late notebooks, where she very literally becomes the Beatrice for whom he is attempting to finish *Words with Power* (*LN,* 145, 150).

Frye's final fictional idea is for a "century of meditations,"[33] a sequence of aphorisms of the type he often imagined as the form of *Twilight,* the last member of the ogdoad, and to be written in his twilight years. Its theme would be what is perhaps the central theme in all Frye's work, that of interpenetration, the ultimate reality being the vision of the world in the grain of sand, eternity in an hour, and the theme would be reflected in the form, each aphorism being a microcosm and a timeless moment. Considered thus, the Third Book notebooks are not the monument of Ozymandias but the ruins of time which build mansions in eternity.

Chronology

March 1961: Delivers the Page-Barbour Lectures at the University of Virginia. Published as *The Well-Tempered Critic* (1963).

1962: Delivers the Massey Lectures on CBC Radio. Published as *The Educated Imagination* (1963).

1962–63: Delivers "The Problem of Spiritual Authority in the Nineteenth Century" (the "Rice-Woodhouse paper") at Rice University during the year of its centennial celebration (*StS* , 241–56). Reprinted in a revised version in *Essays in English Literature from the Renaissance to the Victorian Age Presented to A.S.P. Woodhouse* (1964).

1963: Publishes *T.S. Eliot: An Introduction.*

March 1963: Delivers the Centennial Lectures at Huron College. Published, with an additional essay, as *The Return of Eden: Five Essays on Milton's Epics* (1965).

November 1963: Delivers the Bampton Lectures at Columbia University. Published as *A Natural Perspective: The Development of Shakespearean Comedy and Romance* (1965).

1964–65: Sabbatical, Frye's first since 1950.

1965: Writes "Varieties of Literary Utopias" (*StS,* 109–34).

October 1965: Delivers "Speculation and Concern" at the Conference on the Humanities at the University of Kentucky (*StS,* 38–55).

1966: Delivers an early version of "Design as a Creative Principle in the Arts" at a festival of the arts at the University of Rochester (*StS,* 56–65).

February 1966: Delivers "The Instruments of Mental Production" at the University of Chicago as part of the university's seventy-fifth anniversary liberal arts conference (*StS,* 3–21).

March 1966: Delivers the Alexander Lectures at the University of Toronto. Published as *Fools of Time: Studies in Shakespearean Tragedy* (1967).

April 1966: Death of Frye's sister Vera.

May 1966: Delivers lectures at Graduate School of Western Reserve University in Cleveland, Ohio. Published as *A Study of English Romanticism* (1968).

Fall 1966: Serves as Acting President of Victoria College for one semester, in addition to his duties as Principal of Victoria College (installed 1959).

January 1967: Appointed first University Professor at the University of Toronto. Acquires office in Massey College and (in 1968) his permanent secretary Jane Welch (later Jane Widdicombe).

January 1967: Delivers the Whidden Lectures at McMaster University in the centenary year of Canada's Confederation. Published as *The Modern Century* (1967).

1967: Visits Expo '67, the World's Fair held in Montreal as the highlight of the Canadian Centennial celebration.

1968: Writes "Dickens and the Comedy of Humours" (*StS*, 218–40).

Spring 1968: Becomes visiting professor for a semester at Cornell University. Delivers an address on "The Social Context of Literary Criticism," which is the germ of *The Critical Path*.

June 1968: Delivers "*Mythos* and *Logos*," which is very closely related to "The Social Context of Literary Criticism," at the summer session of the Indiana School of Letters in Bloomington, Indiana.

1968–72: Serves as part-time Commissioner for the Canadian Radio and Television Commission (CRTC).

1969: Writes "The Revelation to Eve" (*StS*, 135–59).

1969: Writes "The Top of the Tower: A Study of the Imagery of Yeats" (*StS* , 257–77).

1969: Writes "Old and New Comedy (*SM*, 148–56).

1969: Writes "Blake's Reading of the Book of Job" (*SM*, 228–44).

Spring 1969: Becomes visiting professor at Berkeley. Witnesses the People's Park crisis in May 1969.

1970: Publication of *The Stubborn Structure: Essays on Criticism and Society*.

1971: House of Anansi Press publishes *The Bush Garden: Essays on the Canadian Imagination*.

1971: Publication of *The Critical Path: An Essay on the Social Context of Literary Criticism*.

1971: Presents "*Agon* and *Logos*: Revolution and Revelation" at the University of Western Ontario to mark the tercentenary of the publication of *Samson Agonistes* and *Paradise Regained* (*SM*, 201–7).

April 1971: Signs contract with Harcourt Brace Jovanovich for a book on "The Bible and Literature."

October 1971: Delivers the Birks Lectures, on the subject of the Bible, at the Divinity School of McGill University.

1972: Produces *On Teaching Literature*, a manual to accompany *Literature: The Uses of the Imagination*, textbook series by Harcourt Brace Jovanovich, general editor W.T. Jewkes, 12 volumes. Volumes 1–6 edited by Alvin Lee and Hope Arnott Lee; volumes 7–12 edited by W.T. Jewkes.

1972: Writes 184-page introduction on the History of English Literature for a Harcourt Brace Jovanovich "Survey of British Literature" anthology, never completed. (Published in *Northrop Frye on Literature and Society, 1936–1989: Unpublished Papers*, 3–130)

Published and Forthcoming Notebooks

Published Notebooks

Notebook or "Notes" No.	*Volume Title*
6	*The "Third Book" Notebooks of Northrop Frye, 1964–1972* (CW, 9)
11h	*Northrop Frye's Late Notebooks, 1982–1990* (CW, 5–6)
12	*The "Third Book" Notebooks of Northrop Frye, 1964–1972* (CW, 9)
19	*The "Third Book" Notebooks of Northrop Frye, 1964–1972* (CW, 9)
24	*The "Third Book" Notebooks of Northrop Frye, 1964–1972* (CW, 9)
27	*Northrop Frye's Late Notebooks, 1982–1990* (CW, 5–6)
44	*Northrop Frye's Late Notebooks, 1982–1990* (CW, 5–6)
46	*Northrop Frye's Late Notebooks, 1982–1990* (CW, 5–6)
47	*Northrop Frye's Late Notebooks, 1982–1990* (CW, 5–6)
48	*Northrop Frye's Late Notebooks, 1982–1990* (CW, 5–6)
50	*Northrop Frye's Late Notebooks, 1982–1990* (CW, 5–6)
52	*Northrop Frye's Late Notebooks, 1982–1990* (CW, 5–6)
53	*Northrop Frye's Late Notebooks, 1982–1990* (CW, 5–6)
54:1	*Northrop Frye's Late Notebooks, 1982–1990* (CW, 5–6)
54:2	*Northrop Frye's Late Notebooks, 1982–1990* (CW, 5–6)
55	*Northrop Frye's Late Notebooks, 1982–1990* (CW, 5–6)

Forthcoming Notebooks

Notebook or "Notes" No.	*Volume Title*
1	*Northrop Frye's Notebooks on Fiction, Music, and Other Subjects*
2	*Northrop Frye's Notebooks on Fiction, Music, and Other Subjects*
3	*Northrop Frye's Notebooks and Lectures on the Bible and Other Religious Texts*
4	*Northrop Frye's Notebooks on Fiction, Music, and Other Subjects*
5	*Northrop Frye's Notebooks on Fiction, Music, and Other Subjects*
7	*Northrop Frye's Notebooks for "Anatomy of Criticism"*
8	*Northrop Frye's Notebooks on Drama*
9	*Northrop Frye's Notebooks on Drama*
10	*Northrop Frye's Notebooks on Romance*
11a	*Northrop Frye's Notebooks and Lectures on the Bible and Other Religious Texts*
11b	*Northrop Frye's Notebooks and Lectures on the Bible and Other Religious Texts*
11c	*Northrop Frye's Notebooks and Lectures on the Bible and Other Religious Texts*
11d	*Northrop Frye's Notebooks and Lectures on the Bible and Other Religious Texts*
11e	*Northrop Frye's Notebooks and Lectures on the Bible and Other Religious Texts*
11f	*Northrop Frye's Notebooks and Lectures on the Bible and Other Religious Texts*
13	*Northrop Frye's Notebooks on Drama*
14	*Northrop Frye's Notebooks on Romance*
15	*Northrop Frye's Notebooks and Lectures on the Bible and Other Religious Texts*
17	*Northrop Frye's Notebooks on Fiction, Music, and Other Subjects*
18	*Northrop Frye's Notebooks for "Anatomy of Criticism"*
20	*Northrop Frye's Notebooks on Fiction, Music, and Other Subjects*

Notebook or "Notes" No.	*Volume Title*
21	*Northrop Frye's Notebooks and Lectures on the Bible and Other Religious Texts*
23	*Northrop Frye's Notebooks and Lectures on the Bible and Other Religious Texts*
28	*Northrop Frye's Notebooks on Fiction, Music, and Other Subjects*
30a	*Northrop Frye's Notebooks on Fiction, Music, and Other Subjects*
30b	*Northrop Frye's Notebooks on Fiction, Music, and Other Subjects*
30c	*Northrop Frye's Notebooks on Fiction, Music, and Other Subjects*
30d	*Northrop Frye's Notebooks for "Anatomy of Criticism"*
30e	*Northrop Frye's Notebooks for "Anatomy of Criticism"*
30f	*Northrop Frye's Notebooks for "Anatomy of Criticism"*
30g	*Northrop Frye's Notebooks for "Anatomy of Criticism"*
30h	*Northrop Frye's Notebooks for "Anatomy of Criticism"*
30i	*Northrop Frye's Notebooks for "Anatomy of Criticism"*
30j	*Northrop Frye's Notebooks for "Anatomy of Criticism"*
30k	*Northrop Frye's Notebooks for "Anatomy of Criticism"*
30l	*Northrop Frye's Notebooks for "Anatomy of Criticism"*
30m	*Northrop Frye's Notebooks on Fiction, Music, and Other Subjects*
30n	*Northrop Frye's Notebooks on Fiction, Music, and Other Subjects*
30o	*Northrop Frye's Notebooks for "Anatomy of Criticism"*
30q	*Northrop Frye's Notebooks for "Anatomy of Criticism"*
31	*Northrop Frye's Notebooks on Romance*
32	*Northrop Frye's Notebooks on Romance*
33	*Northrop Frye's Notebooks on Romance*
34	*Northrop Frye's Notebooks on Romance*
35	*Northrop Frye's Notebooks for "Anatomy of Criticism"*
36	*Northrop Frye's Notebooks for "Anatomy of Criticism"*
37	*Northrop Frye's Notebooks for "Anatomy of Criticism"*
38	*Northrop Frye's Notebooks for "Anatomy of Criticism"*

Notebook or "Notes" No.	*Volume Title*
39	*Northrop Frye's Notebooks on Fiction, Music, and Other Subjects*
40	*Northrop Frye's Notebooks on Fiction, Music, and Other Subjects*
42	*Northrop Frye's Notebooks on Romance*
45	*Northrop Frye's Notebooks and Lectures on the Bible and Other Religious Texts*
54:5	*Northrop Frye's Notebooks and Lectures on the Bible and Other Religious Texts*
54:6	*Northrop Frye's Notebooks and Lectures on the Bible and Other Religious Texts*
54:7	*Northrop Frye's Notebooks and Lectures on the Bible and Other Religious Texts*
56	*Northrop Frye's Notebooks on Romance*

A selection of Frye's typed notes, not yet assigned a "Notes" number, will be included in *Northrop Frye's Notebooks on Fiction, Music, and Other Subjects*

The "Third Book" Notebooks of Northrop Frye, 1964–1972: The Critical Comedy

VOLUME 9

Notebook 19

By internal references, this notebook can with some confidence be dated 1964–67, with the latest entries possibly continuing into 1968. It follows pretty directly upon Notebook 18, the first post-AC notebook, which speaks of "what clearly ought to be my next job: a study of . . . the external relations of criticism" (paragraph 134), a phrase and an ambition repeated in paragraph 14, below. Various projects of 1963 are spoken of as if finished, including the Huron Lectures (RE) *and the Bampton Lectures* (NP), *both mentioned in paragraph 61. But the notebook begins before 1965 because some of its earliest paragraphs are notes towards the 1965 essay "Varieties of Literary Utopias." A substantial number of entries are taken up with the struggle to decide upon the final content of three upcoming lecture series that Frye has contracted to do: the Alexander Lectures, delivered at the University of Toronto in March 1966, which became* FT; *a series in May 1966 at Western Reserve University in Cleveland, Ohio ("the Clevelands"), which became* SR; *and the Whidden Lectures at McMaster University in Ontario ("the McMasters"), which became* MC. *These projects are regarded as satellites of the Third Book project. In paragraph 354, Frye says he has just come back from Expo '67, the 1967 World's Fair in Montreal, with a title for the Third Book:* The Critical Path. *He makes a similar statement in the Untitled Section at the end of Notebook 6, so these notebooks have a complex relation to each other, and may have been written to some extent concurrently, at least during the period 1967–68. One guess is that Notebook 19 was intended for notes related to the horizontal and vertical axes, while Notebook 6, soon to be followed by Notebook 12, was for material about the imagery of the hemispheres and quadrants, though this is clearly not a rigid distinction. The two tables (NF's term) reproduced on p. 4 were sketched on a preliminary page of the notebook, and are tangentially rather than precisely related to its contents. Notebook 19 is in the NFF, 1991, box 24.*

Axis of speculation
Urthona
Space–subject
Axis of concern
phil.
psych.
Tharmas
Space–object
Luvah
time–subject
rel.
hist.
Urizen time–object

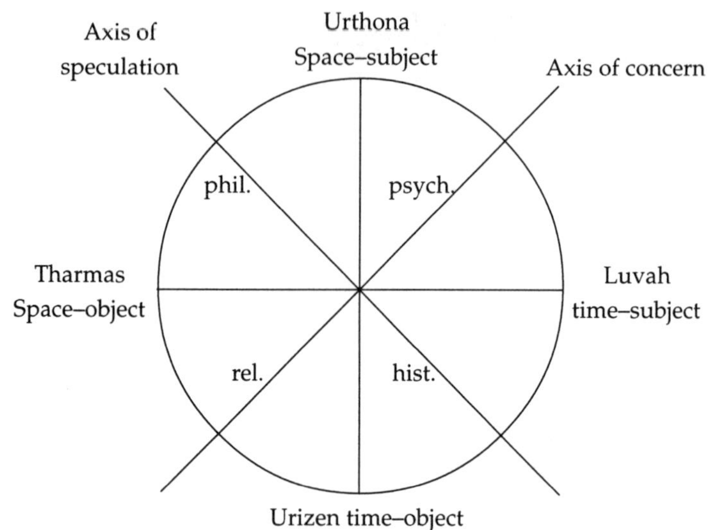

Table of Verbal Myths

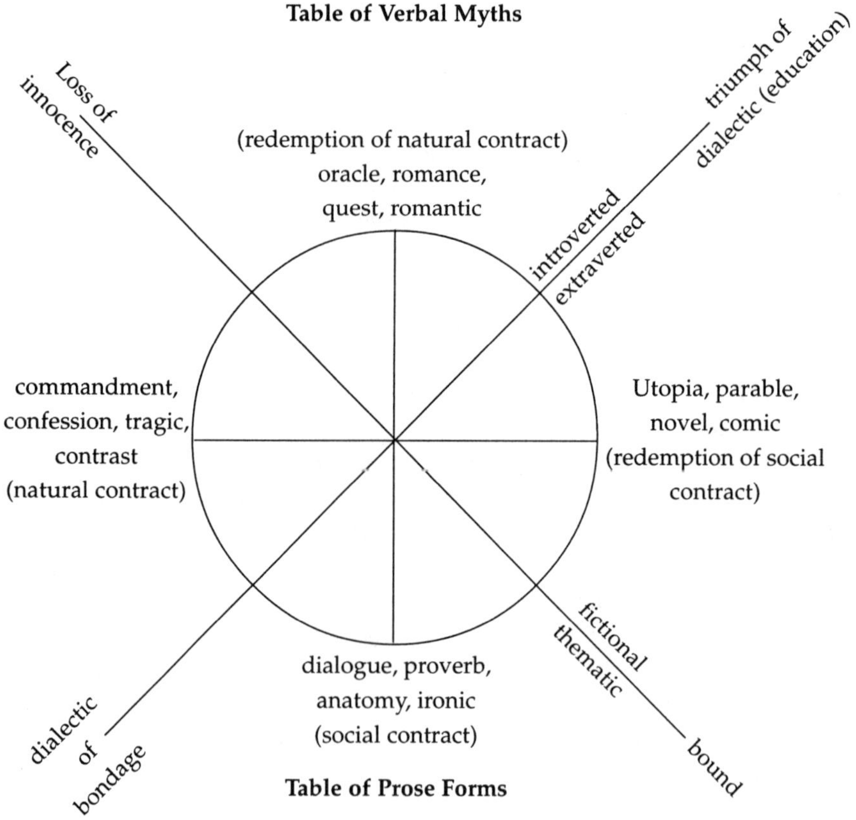

Loss of innocence
triumph of dialectic (education)
(redemption of natural contract)
oracle, romance,
quest, romantic
introverted
extraverted
commandment,
confession, tragic,
contrast
(natural contract)
Utopia, parable,
novel, comic
(redemption of social
contract)
fictional
thematic
dialogue, proverb,
anatomy, ironic
(social contract)
dialectic of bondage
bound

Table of Prose Forms

[1] I suppose the Third Book will really be an introduction to the study of literature, not so much along the lines of L-⅂-Λ [Liberal-Tragicomedy-Anticlimax] sequence, which is conceived generically, as an abstraction of the third Anatomy essay, expanded into a full-scale treatment.

[2] I don't know if I have any new ideas. The elements are the same as before: Biblical typology, the Druid analogy, dialectical & cyclical rhythms, tables of metaphors, history of imagery & the two frameworks. Also the humanizing of nature by analogy & identity and—what may be a new twist—the adjusting of the introduction to a possible curriculum sequence. These are the carry-overs.

[3] Keep in mind two other things: (nothing as yet).
In the red book: a work of fiction with death the cognito.
In the green book: centuries of meditation.[1]

[4] I've been saying that art drives a wedge between being & not-being. Wonder if it also drives a wedge between life & death. By death I mean not simple extinction, but shadow-life, Hades, the world we perhaps enter in dreams. I've always felt that the literary dream-world was different from the Freudian repressed erotic.

[5] I am aware that two things are overlapping here: the dichotomy of life & death & the dichotomy of sleeping & waking. But that's pretty standard in literature. All those primitive tales of a soul leaving a body in sleep make the connection, because frequently the man dies if the soul doesn't get back. In, e.g.[,] Tibetan belief that's what happens at every death. In Homer Hades is a place of shades or disembodied souls. In Celtic tales the other world is romantic, a world of youth & beautiful palaces. The ambivalence of the shadowy & the romantic evokes a similar one in the waking world, for life may be sweet or ironic. The Freudian identification of the waking world with reality won't work either, because reality is created as well as faced.

[6] Yeats says dreams are really dreamed by the dead, & create worlds we enter at sleep.[2] Has anyone explained why we need all that sleep? Hours & hours of it. It can't be to "rest the brain"—the brain doesn't work all that hard. And what, if any, is the biological function of dreams?

What use are they if nobody can understand them, least of all the dreamer? It's the same question that gets asked about the arts.

[7] However, I think I have ideas about dreams & art. The private Freudian wish-fulfilment dream is part of the egocentric subject, & partakes of the same unreality. There's an individual that isn't an ego, & there must be a dreaming individual that isn't just preoccupied with a wish to screw his mother. In waking life the storm clouds of the ego keep blinding us to reality, but every so often they clear & we see clearly & objectively. Something similar happens with dreams—everybody feels that some dreams are more oracular than others. But this doesn't tell me anything about the analogy between the dream world & death.

[8] In both dream & waking life the oracular *given* emerges as central: it *im*presses. In both too the created reality is at work.

Dream		Waking
subjective fantasy	Freud	objective reality
romance & comedy	Shakespeare	tragedy & irony
shadow	Homer	substance
resurrection-awakening	Blake	generation-sleep

[9] One must continually create reality, whether as artist or as saint, to produce or build up in oneself the kind of egoless objectivity which will enable one to recognize the oracular given when it comes. "The keys to. Given!"[3] The Tibetan Book of the Dead says the oracular given is presented at the moment of death,[4] which is the *Dry Salvages* point.[5]

[10] Our bodies are so conditioned that what we see (perceive with any sense) *can only be* the sub-human, or at most the merely human. What we see is inexorable law, Newtonian or Darwinian, struggles to survive & the like. What we create participates in our creation & comes as far alive as the limits of imagination permit.

[11] My fictional ideas include: a) a machine to see into the past b) a fifth

Gospel c) a story with death as the cognitio.[6] Can these be interconnected?

[12] Science tries to stay in the consciousness: art, being partly a skill, is a link with the unconscious. The phrase "liberal art" is really a tautology: all art is therapeutic.

[13] Should I do the Bible book after all?

[14] I think rather what I should do is a book on metacritics, on the external relations of criticism. First (perhaps), the structure of myth. Second, the informing of revelation by myth: the mythical basis of religion. Third, the informing of natural religion, or moral & natural law, by myth: the myths of contract & of Utopia.

[15] The form we call a Utopia is simply *a* social vision, society presented as a set of interlocking ritual patterns, as an intelligible conceptual structure. I could describe how I get to work in the morning in the idiom of a Utopia. However, the natural dialectic of literature creates the desirable & undesirable societies, the Utopia & the anti-Utopia. They are equally Utopian, but with the sense of the norm in different contexts.[7]

[16] There are two political ideas that can only be expressed mythologically, the Utopia & the social contract. One is the myth of *telos*, the secular apocalypse (millennium), the other the myth of origin, the secular creation-fall. Both are based on an analysis of the *present* facts of society. Plato's three-class Republic is based on the Aryan red, white & blue society studied by Dumezil.[8]

[17] Campanella's Trinitarian conception of the structure of knowledge,[9] parodied by Orwell.[10] The university ideal—lectures in Utopia, the informing symposium of Plato, Rabelais and the fay ce que vouldras community[11]—is close to the monastic ideal in More and Campanella. Both are parodied in Shakespeare's LLL [*Love's Labour's Lost*], & the monastic norm is still going strong in Carlyle's PP [*Past and Present*].

[18] The Utopia is a city ideal & the really important literary Utopia is the Arcadia, the pastoral, the vision of a world at play instead of at work. Natural society in Rousseau & Bolingbroke vs. Burke & Swift: today,

Western stories vs. *Lord of the Flies*. Thoreau reading the Bhagavadgita on the Merrimac is the ancestor of the Zen Buddhist & Dharma bum cults of today. Subversive society, destructive attitude to the social machine. Morris, NN [*News from Nowhere*]. Dissemination of aristocratic & revolutionary ideals inherent in the pastoral. Conspiratorial I-want-out group. Marvell's apotheosis of solitude as the condition of Paradise.[12]

[19] More's own Utopia is not an ideal state but an attempt to describe the form of society that results when the natural virtues are allowed to assume their natural forms. Hence, like Plato's Republic, it's not an external goal, a static ideal ending the historical process when you get there, but an informing vision of society that starts off social behavior, the latent vision underlying the axioms & assumptions of behavior, which it's the business of the Utopia to articulate.

[20] The Utopia is a form of satire, & what it satirizes is anarchy. It flourishes when we feel afraid of anarchy, as in 19th c. *laissez faire*. If we feel more afraid of order, the anti-Utopia results. Bellamy's *Looking Backward* would, or certainly could, be read today as a rather sinister book. Houston has no zoning laws: that indicates a strongly anti-Utopian sentiment in Houston; but no doubt Houston is building thruways & clover leafs & sewers and telephone exchanges on a vast Utopian scale.

[21] The combination of aristocratic (Wells' samurai)[13] and revolutionary ideals makes the Utopia a romance, a vision of society with the irony omitted. Hence the FQ [*The Faerie Queene*] is Utopian, & the university or educational ideal is linked with the relation of the Utopia to the Cyropaedia, as well as the Symposium-Cortegiano tradition.

[22] What I say of More goes with the Hythlodaye [Hythloday]-More contrast, & is equally true of Plato, where, as in More, the ideal is the dictatorship in the wise man's mind. The Book ix paradeigma[14] (check carefully) & the 7th Epistle.[15]

[23] There is a Utopianism of inertia—the *adjusted* vision. My Bali cartoon point: cf. the two views of Main Street in Sinclair Lewis, Carol's & the Swedish maid's.[16] This relativity shows how the Utopia simply describes the ritual structure, in itself. It's also society as a non-existential construct. Once you *live* in it, & the values become existential, the Uto-

pian feeling disappears. The only Paradises are those we have lost or are about to gain: no jam today.

[24] Perhaps the social contract is existential rather than conceptual: I don't know. Anyway, for revolutionary thinkers like Rousseau the anagnorisis of history would be the coincidence of contract & Utopia brought about by a revolution. That would be a "repetition" of the existential on another plane.

[25] This book is a book, I think, on the structure of myth, on myth as information, especially in social mythology (Massey 6),[17] religion, political theory, & of course lots & lots of literature itself. The Utopia is the one recognizable bit: I hope things will stick to it.

[26] Blooming, buzzing, blessed confusion.[18]

[27] Two American paintings: Erastus Salisbury Field's "Historical Monument of the American Republic" and "The Peaceable Kingdom" sum up the Utopian & Arcadian ideals.[19]

[28] What with *Lord of the Flies*, it seems to me the anti-Utopia is the central fictional form today. Note the social-science-study read as satire: *The Lonely Crowd, The Academic Marketplace, The Hidden Persuaders, The Insolent Chariots, The Status Seekers, The Organization Man.*[20]

[29] Poetry is the language of ritual, bound to time, an existential language of incantation & magic. Epic, & to some degree drama, are concerned with the arrival of the moment & the crucial act. Prose is a Cartesian language of myth & detached consciousness, dear to theology, which must always be commentary language. There's a third stage, the second twist on the four forms.

[30] Causality, a form of conceptual rhetoric, produces the literary rhythm of continuity or persistence in time, continuity being the literary equivalent of Hume's association.[21] There's more to the discontinuous aphoristic form than I've yet said. Is continuous prose intermediate between a ritual-poetic-fictional & myth-discontinuous-thematic antithesis? My own writing translates involuntary aphorisms into continuous prose. What I listen to crystallizes: what I aim at is a spread-out visual panorama.

[31] The life of the great man is an illusion of continuity, with the recognition in *act*: he's a ritualist bound to time, seizing the event. He (the Carlylean hero)[22] develops from the epic quest-hero. Drama is act-&-scene, tragedy, the hero-play, being closest to epic. There is no comic hero beyond the various eiron types, but when we reach the symposium-dialogue we get the Socratic hero, the incarnation of a dialectic, who swallows the act, or historical state. The Communist hero has affinities with this, as the Fascist hero has with the Carlyle act-man. But there's a third stage, the gospel or sequence of epiphanies, where the hero has acquired a transformation-body, & so has broken clear from the linear rhythm of act or continuity. The radio, addressed to the time-bound ear, produced the Fascist hero; the age of TV is the age of a Kennedy or Khrushchev, a dramatic act-&-scene hero. I don't know what the technical medium of the epiphanic hero is: supersonic planes, maybe.

[32] In a recent talk I got my symbolism-in-religion points a little clearer. Man creating gods talks in myth & metaphor: mythology in reverse, theology or revelation, uses the same language by accommodation. What Christians resist is conceptualizing myth, making it not an event, an *ἐγένετο*, & I'm not sure that I want to do that. But an event conceived as breaking into history cannot be presented as a historical event like the assassination of Caesar.

[33] The Utopian fallacy of making a personal life out of a community is perhaps after all the totalitarian one: the state must be in the long run a mere aggregate of persons, not itself a person. 7th Epistle clears this up in Plato.[23] Query: what is the vision at the end of a comedy? In my conception of the "idiotes"[24] I show how the balance between what Tillich calls essential centeredness & existential disruption is kept.[25] But there is in comedy a centeredness & disruption of a community coming the opposite way.

[34] Revelation is not actual knowledge: the immortality of the soul, or whatever the correct formulation is, is a part of revelation, but we don't *know* anything about it. It's mythical presentation only, with a Leibnitzian solution: the best possible one is the one that exists.[26]

[35] Maybe the kernel of truth in the leisure-class theory[27] is that society's finest flower is the parasite: the draft dodger, the religious person

who keeps clear of "organized religion," & the like. Or at least a very fine flower, that can't flourish in any other way.

[36] And is there a kernel of truth in the mythology of decline other than the ones I've been extracting? Perhaps since the Middle Ages there's been a steady decline in the power of cultural projection. The real creative power in society becomes steadily more internalized, democratized, hidden from view, as society becomes more highly organized & its cultural products become less distinctive & individual. A process analogous to the Freudian sublimination, or withdrawal of libido. Cf. my quotations from Coleridge & Keats in RR [*Romanticism Reconsidered*]:[28] Rcsm. [Romanticism] must be a crucial stage in this, if it exists.

[37] If this is so, then the art of our time has to be thought of as a direct reflection, not a projection, of inner structural principles. This accounts for its monotony: its functionalism, and its neo-neolithic geometrizing. What the hell difference there is between reflection & projection I haven't the slightest notion. Does it throw me back on the Ruskin ornament-imitation business?[29] Does projected art conquer nature & reflected art merely express the inner order?

[38] Blake's "Active Evil is better than Passive Good" is not sadism, as I've shown [*FS*, 198]: Blake simply has an ironic hell & a real one, & only the former can be active. Blake comes out for civilization. But the full sadistic content of the phrase needs to be explored. Blake rejected institutional Xy in order to recreate the New Jerusalem in the soul; a writer like Norman Mailer rejects fascism for a cult of individual violence which is really the same violence. It may be horseshit, & pernicious horseshit, but can evil itself be redemptive?

[39] Writers must follow convention in the same way that card players must follow suit, & they often get involved in cruel paradoxes. In order to express one's hatred of society & be as self-assertive as possible one must also follow that particular convention to the letter. The desire to be self-assertive is itself conventional.

[40] The fact that I consider

[41] Much has been said of the paradox of the Incarnation, but the para-

dox of Jehovism is much less conceivable. This is a matter of God's naming himself, of his deliberately limiting his essence to the God worshipped by the Jews. This is the fundamental paradox in the West. When we say the Moslems say "There is no God but Allah," we attribute the same paradox to them, but they're trying to repudiate that part of it: "There is no God but God" for them. So my "false god" idea only works when God has made himself "true" dialectically by naming himself: God is *this* god.

[42] In the acceptance of consistent evil one acquires the dignity that goes with consistency & with the identity of inner character & outward actions. The ditherer is undignified because he has spasmodic flashes of unredeemable behavior. Note this principle in Dante, down as far at least as Malebolge, after which the symbolism turns anal. In this connection I wonder about objective guilt. The writers of the Gospels say that crucifying Christ was wrong: it did not occur to them that crucifixion was wrong in itself (Luke 23:41).[30] Burning heretics is objectively wrong whatever the motivation, & this eventually draws out the discovery that the good subjective motivation was phony.

[43] One of the fundamental musical patterns is the Orpheus-in-Hades one, the contrast of diatonic Apollo & chromatic Dionysus, Haydn's representation of chaos & his cosmic chorus.[31] It's often the chorus however that's Dionysiac, & even more often the tempest figures, the basso buffo & the like, of Bach's Aeolus cantata & Purcell's Tempest.[32] In Bach's Phoebus & Pan I greatly prefer Pan's song to the pompous homosexual self-pityings of Phoebus, but we're not supposed to.[33] Incidentally, somebody says of Gluck's *Che Tano* aria[34] that it would have done just as well for a reunion: an example of my point about the audience-as-gods perspective of opera.

[44] I suppose the burning bush epiphany, God deliberately becoming *this* god & a partisan in history, accounts for there being no *re*incarnation in the Bible: everything is a single drama. Faust, disillusioned by good works, wants, like Yeats' Self, only to be reborn.

[45] I have occasionally played around with the idea that all determinisms are elements in a manifold criticism. Thus every literary work would have its sexual, "Freudian," erotic, or fetishistic aspect; also a cultural or class "Marxist" aspect; also a historical "Spengler" aspect, and perhaps a

primitive or Frazerian aspect. The first two, the green & the red, the conjunction of Venus & Mars, seem to me particularly obvious. They're both evolutionary; the other two are regressive.

[46] All myths of ascent, descent or quest are cyclical because we *go* only in a dream.[35] The goal of the quest is to integrate what we're getting with what we've got, & the only way to reach the goal is to wake up & find oneself in the same place. This is hinted at in Dante (because of its pre-apocalyptic or awakening of body symbolism); it's hinted at in Bunyan (Ignorance is the demonic opposed cycle); it's explicit only in Jacob's ladder.

[47] Ruskin's distinction of ornament & imitation[36] is fundamental to painting. Imitation is extroverted & phenomenal: ornament is abstract, introverted, & concerned with what is transcendental in the Kantian sense: the *categories* of form & design. In our day we go from extreme abstract expression around behind to an anti-painting based on the principle of the fetishistic (ornamental) aspect of the *objet trouvé*: this began in photography, & develops through types of futurism, surrealism, dadaism, like the pop art currently fashionable.

[48] The same, or at least an analogous, distinction holds in literature: prose is imitative, & when wholly descriptive it passes out of literature. Poetry is more ornamental & has a higher charge of introversion in it: it moves toward a more intense association of sound & sense. In Blake's pictures the pictorial conventions, haloes & the like, are abstract, as in all paintings: perhaps his huge & mighty forms are transcendental elements: they descend from the gods, which unites the two meanings of the words. Of course the link of myth & ornament is nothing new. One might define the god as a focus of ambiguities and associations.

[49] Anti-literature is, to begin with, the kinetic verbal world of advertising & propaganda, or the verbal experience which returns to the magical directing or releasing of emotion in which literature began. Pure "escape" literature is of this kind, because what escapes is mob emotion, as in thrillers. Again, the difference is in the use made, not in inherent quality. In pictorial advertisements the central element is the attention-getting emblem (i.e. fetishic or associative, usually erotically). In words it's the rhetorical stimulus.

[50] Ornamental literature is allusive, & allusion, as its etymology indicates,[37] has to do with playing. The extremely imitative or descriptive use of language is working with words: the ornamental tendency is toward play. Hence the central element of the fetishic anti-art is the *toy*, the thing made for pleasure, like the work of art. (I think of the o > i [ornamental to imitative] movement horizontally, but it's traditionally vertical, not from inside out but from the top to the bottom).

[51] I've spoken of the cyclical & dialectical rhythms, but there's a third, the creation rhythm of aligning along levels, the Shakespearean romance one. Creation & recreation are stratification movements, apocalypse dialectic, continuous life cyclical.

[52] This silly dictionary I've been reading says seven is a sacred number because there are seven directions of space: four compass points, up, down & the centre. There are seven directions of time in the Eliot Quartets: past, future, correspondence vision, rose-garden vision, present moment, subway vision, yew-tree vision. (Silly dictionary: Cirlot).[38]

[53] Further on the red-green, Marx-Freud symbols: both are revolutionary, both set up orthodoxies & define heresies. Why do only revolutionary structures do that?

[54] What's transcendental in Blake is not the statically geometrical, but the sense of arrested energy: the wriggling vines & snakes, flames & the like. This is what I meant earlier in talking of his Van Gogh classicism. It's an expression of the belief that every object is an event.

[55] If one thinks of a picture in this way, a painting becomes, obviously, a form of perception, not a subjective creation imposed on ordinary objective perception. Now, applying the same principle to literature: is there such a thing as a verbal perception? If so, what is the nature of it & what does it do?

[56] What is the literary importance of the monumental literary object: the leather-bound sets of the great classics, the plastic counterparts of these contributed by the book-of-the-month clubs, the monumental systematic theology or philosophy in a clergyman's study? Plainly it is in part an object of reassurance: contemporary philosophy, on the other

hand, distrusts the book as a literary genre. The *latter* feeling goes with specialization & with the existential: Austin's bits & pieces, or Wittgenstein's,[39] remind one of *Sartor Resartus*. Similarly with the distrust of the epic & narrative in poetry.

[57] The verbal perception, looking back to it, is a *Gestalt*, a vision of meaning in a previously meaningless area. Only "meaning" is too partial & specialized for poetry, where it's verbal pattern. Thinking has many analogies to perception: I can only think what is there, latent in what I've already thought.

[58] The opposite of the verbal perception is the presentation, the communicated message, what Marshall [McLuhan] talks about. Marshall says it's the form & not the content of the message that's important, which is why the nature of the medium is also important.[40] It seems to me that the form has this importance only as long as we're unconscious of it: to become aware of the form as a form is to separate the content. At that point the presentation goes into reverse & becomes a perception: the form comes from us then.

[59] Such reversal of movement (paravritti,[41] wider Kehr[42]) is of course a hinge of all my thinking. Marshall's "extensions of man" version of it comes from Samuel Butler.[43] A jet plane can move faster & a computer think faster than a man, but no machine yet invented has any *will* to do these things. The will is the reversal of movement from a receptive response to stimulus to a *Gestalt*. No machine can yet make this reversal: no camera, in Blake's phrase,[44] can look *through* its lens. I have a feeling that Marshall doesn't really get past the presentation at all, but I'm doubtless wrong.

[60] Other notebooks point out the Utopian relevance of Dante: the *Purgatorio* in particular shows the informing-vision aspect: life in this world, but in a symmetrical conceptual form. Note the affinity with science fiction.

[61] My Utopia paper is the germ of ∧ [Anticlimax], as the Huron Lectures were of ∟ [Liberal] & the Bamptons of ˥ [Tragicomedy], &, I suppose, the Random House book of ⅄ [Rencontre].[45] I don't know why I think of it as my third too.

[62] The Urizen-Utopia of adjustment I've mentioned: it's one step removed from the Tharmas-parody Utopia represented by Jefferies' *After London*. That in its turn is a step from the Inferno or We-1984 parody. The Orc Utopia of sexual fulfilment is The Land of Cockayne. The Los one is the informing vision, the Albion & Jesus one's the straight Paradiso. The Urizen one (Campanella, Bellamy) is conventionally the norm.[46] An Orc by-form is the kataplous[47] reversal of the normal world, the Saturnalia recall.

[63] The Utopia theme is closely connected with other themes I've noted elsewhere. One is the stylized conceptualizing of worlds in the epic tradition, where we have heaven, hell & the paradisal world of human nature presented & experience left out (Dante, Spenser, Milton). Another is the eiron basis of social relationships: it's the central act of courtesy to make oneself small & what is presented large. This hitches on to the conceptual-presented form of the Utopia vs. the minimized-process form of creation.

[64] The Langland-Carlyle vision of society at work is one kind of Utopia: its complement takes one into the theory of play, homo ludens, the creation of significant action by a mimesis of action. These are also intertwined with the informing vision, which is implicitly (Utopia, Republic) or explicitly (Cyropaedia, Rabelais) educational, with the university as its model (Rabelais, & to some extent Castiglione, where the court is interpreted as a university[)]. The monastic community is the model for Utopia itself, for Carlyle, &, in life, for Brook Farm[48] & the Shakers. Thoreau is the hermitage model. Also Campanella, of course. (monastic, I mean).

[65] Arguing from the individual to society produces the Platonic Republic as a projection of a wise man's mind: this is the paradox dealt with in my Milton lectures [*RE*, 99–103], where God the Father is so dismal a shit as a *social* model. The 7th Epistle makes it clear that for Plato the social projection is never existential, & that only the individual paradeigma is.[49]

[66] Arguing from society to individual produces the Castiglione courtier ideal: the individual as the microcosm of society. Cults of versatility & of (More to Brook Farm) alternating mental & physical work, as in Russia &

China now. This is the explicitly educational direction, & hence is the *myth* of education. If I can fish *this* up I'll be all set.

[67] What I got out of my last Milton lecture was the realization that, according to Milton, the really central myth of the human mind was Arcadian, one man alone in the world, because freedom is essentially individualization.[50] There is no *social* construct at the imaginative centre: the society that *should* have developed was patriarchal, an extension of the individual.

[68] Distinctions: the rational construct vs. the sense construct or land of Cockayne. The anxieties of society ensure that the latter is always satirical, directly or indirectly, the low-adjustment Utopia, or the Intourist guide. The high-adjustment one, the education of the Platonic guards & Wells' *samurai*.[51]

[69] Curious how slow the imaginations of Utopia-makers are: MacNie's *Diothas* have [has] some kind of car going at 20 miles an hour;* Poe has balloons crossing the Atlantic in 1000 years at 100 m.p.h.; Donnelly (I think) has aeroplanes taking 36 hours from Paris to N.Y.[52]

[70] Distinction of science fiction vs. technological fiction: it's the latter that becomes a bunch of Utopian fiction, starting with Bacon. Incidentally, the rationality imputed to Utopia-dwellers is simply the result of the literary convention used, which is that of a rational construct.

[71] There are few medieval Utopias, because the element of rational construct was so deeply involved in the life & thought of the time. Dante had only to extend the sacramental system into the very slightly more symmetrical world of Purgatory. There are no "common people" in his Paradiso, which confirms, rather than subverts, the hierarchies of this world.

[72] There are five modes of Utopia: the mythical Utopia (Dante); the romance Utopia (pastoral Arcadia); the high mimetic (the rational construct); the low mimetic (satiric mirror-world) & the ironic (hell or anti-Utopia).

---

* And even faster downhill!

[73] I've often said that the arts of *mousike* had a power of perpetuating themselves (print) that the arts of *techne* lack.[53] Travellers looking at the latter seem to do nothing but deplore ravages. They *age*, as the musical arts don't. Morris was caught by this. A lot of implications here I haven't got. One is that the conception of the unity of the imaginative life is the root of the Utopia, which is a projection of it. Medievalism, in fact any idealizing of any period in history, is another projection.

[74] Morris, by the way, has a wonderful phrase about "the eventfulness of form."[54] The function of the work of art is to epiphanize the centre, the centre being both oneself & what one is looking at: what I think of as the Avatamsaka centre, but could probably get out of Whitehead.[55] One primitive appeal is the charm or riddle that catches the epiphany in a trap: Morris's hair-entangling intricacies are linked to this.[56]

[75] In the study of history the arts consolidate one half of a moral dialectic, the other half being superstition, tyranny & cruelty. One survives in *mousike* and, crumblingly, in *techne*:[57] the other survives as rumor, as well as in presence. For presence always spoils the past.

[76] As man is essentially social, his social function is part of his individuality and his freedom. Hence work should be defined as creative art & as socially functional.

[77] In Morris pleasure is the increment of energy, decoration of design, value of work, art of life. His problem, as he saw it, was to transform the traditional art of unconscious intelligence into a conscious one, that being also a social revolution, from the past when art was the opiate of the people, to now when it should be their social function. The paradox is that art declines when the artist ceases to be exploited.

[78] The Christian form of Utopia, as it appears for instance in Milton, is that there is no divine archetype of the city, only of the garden. Hence Utopia turns on interim ethics. This Christian skepticism about the city ideal is reflected in Goldwater[58] American pastoralism. I'm really speaking of contract myths here, of course.

[79] The present American anti-Utopian mood is the result of thinking, quite correctly, that conscious design in society should be the result of a

process, the outward bound of energy. Otherwise it becomes a system in itself, hence a trap. The American feeling is linked to its social Freudianism, its belief in the setting free of energy.

[80] My ideas do hold together, God help me: the myths of contract & telos correspond not only to creation & apocalypse in religious myth, but to the first two essays of AC: the historical & the ethical contexts of a work of literature.

[81] The monastic community certainly isn't Utopian: it's highly ritualized because it's interim ethic again: the informing community. Hence its influence on More & Campanella. In More it's interim, in Campanella it's closer to being an end; in Rabelais the secular parody is Freudian: in fact Rabelais is the focus of that tradition.

[82] I think my general thesis is that American Utopianism today is mainly Arcadian & Freudian, in a tradition that runs through Thoreau to the anarchist people ([Henry] Miller, [Jack] Kerouac, the beats & Zens & I-want-out group). As that, it's a reaction to the Communist Utopian [word missing?] of the rational city.

[83] One important factor of course is the closing down of the spatial Utopia. 19th c. American experiments like Oneida[59] are out, except for religious groups that have adapted the monastic tradition. The end of Molière's *Misanthrope*: there are no such places anymore. Alceste & Timon vs. Thoreau getting his fine paid by Emerson [written above: Charon]. Mormons too.

[84] The Third Book, then, is to be a book on literature & society, the reading for it to start at the end of 4k (Morris, Butler, Ruskin, Arnold, Mill) & work back. It's the Locke programme eventually, & includes the reading for the rcsm [romanticism] bk.[60] DeTocqueville & things, of course. It's beginning to feel like that Spenglerian book of my dreams.

[85] I don't want to foul up this notebook with drafts. But this Third Book takes off from the Rice-Woodhouse 19th c. paper,[61] from the social mythology stuff in the last Massey, & perhaps from my curriculum-sequence lucubrations.[62] It would be nice just to toss in a curriculum-sequence aspect of the stew. Also the Rochester flop[63] & other things on the arts.

[86] I think of four main areas: one a summary of AC, turning on the allegory-archetypal framework distinction. AC dealt with the internal structure of literature & this deals with its external relations. Two, myth & religion; why historical fraud goes with revelation; the handicap. Maybe Dante. Three, the real balls of it, myth & social thought: contracts & Utopias; conservative & revolutionary myths; imaginative & social mythology. Four, the circle of the arts, Ruskin & Morris to read; mousike & techne;[64] my arts speeches. Something on media & messages, maybe, here or in Three. I want a wise book: my Book of Wisdom. Casual & relaxed in rhythm: not the drive of FS or the aphoristic crackle of AC. The dream book mentions St. Augustine,[65] who would come into Two under a discussion of city & garden myths. More systematic of course than the Jardin d'Epicure[66] type, but closer to that idiom.

[87] We could do with a revival of Utopian imagination now, in a less pastoral & anarchistic form, in order to study the logical design of the technological revolution now going on. In this process what will seem Utopian to one man will seem a Utopian satire to another (e.g. Skinner's *Walden Two*), but the dialectic will be useful. Skinner is no worse than Graves:[67] in other words the Utopia is one place where the two cultures can meet, instead of developing their infantilisms separately.

[88] The Utopia is a vision of the rational form of society, & it is best seen, not as an end, but as an informing principle. It's the objective aspect of what in subjective terms is ideal education. The Utopia & the educational treatise are closely linked in the 16th c.: in Rabelais, Castiglione, Spenser, where we have idealized courts and universities. Besides, education is the only way to develop the ritual habits needed, so Utopianism & the theory of education are inseparable, hence they must both be in my book. Educational theory hooks itself on somehow to the conception of the order of words.

[89] If we think of Utopian thought as informing, Milton's REW [*The Ready and Easy Way to Establish a Free Commonwealth*] is Utopian, as well as several Leninist & Marxist pamphlets.

[90] Present idea (I can't seem to resist drafting). One, the structure of literary mythology: summary of AC & satellite papers. Analogy & identity; absorption of nature by the imgve. [imaginative] universe; cyclical &

dialectical rhythms. Two, speculative myth. Religious, metaphysical, cosmological myths; the categories of time & space; of life & death & after-death & before-birth. Dante & St. Augustine. Three, social & political myth; contracts & Utopias; pastoral myths; myths of decline & advance (Ruskin & Gibbon parabolas); conservative & revolutionary myths; metahistorical myths. Forms of prose fiction. Four, the role of myth in education; the Renaissance educational treatise; media & messages (McLuhan); the circle of the arts & the place of literature in them & in society (Ruskin & Morris); curriculum & sequence; expansion of convention in 20th c. art.

[91] I see how the second twist is going to be applied all right: take St. Augustine, or, still better for my purposes, Rousseau. The book of Rousseau contains confessions, a contract theory, & an educational Utopia, revolving around a speculative myth of revolution.

[92] What is a speculative myth, the subject of Two? It's a myth designed to contain, and provide a vision for, experience. Therefore the further it gets away from actual evidence the purer it is. I've worked this out in some detail in my Bible lectures. For metaphysical cosmology, a much tougher job, I need Alexander, McTaggart & Whitehead.[68] It may become Three, but wherever it goes it's the chess-in-Bardo one.[69]

[93] This is the world of the Second Essay [of *AC*], the book of which Λ [Anticlimax] is the spiritual form. Its line of descent begins when at the age of ten, on 340 High St., I started trying to imitate the style of that idiot Cramb's book on Germany and England.[70] It runs through, God save the mark, my valedictory, my early Forum articles,[71] the 4k course, the two Ryerson essays,[72] my public speeches, the Bias article,[73] and, of course, that Rice-Woodhouse paper.[74] It's an aspect of my writing which has had very little critical comment or experimental teaching: the praise I've had has been for my rhetorical skill & not for the content. But it's a very deeply rooted aspect, yet I must remember to keep the literary tiller in my hands.

[94] Three is the Book of Luvah, Five the Book of Urizen, Four the Book of Tharmas, and Six the Book of Urthona. Subject to change.

[95] For most readers of Plato's *Republic* the argument ends with the 9th

book. The 10th is concerned with the final attainment of *nous*, the mythical existential which has no further need of the mythical imgve. [imaginative]. It's there to answer Adeimantus, as the rest of the book answers Glaucon: the opened vision over the two worlds.

[96] I don't of course simply want the Luvah chapter to rehash AC: it would incorporate some of my fictional-displacement themes (Uncle Silas-Egoist,[75] GE [*Great Expectations*], etc.), if I ever get to doing a Programme of fiction-reading. Perhaps some of my graduate poem-analyses,[76] but I have a notion that fictional displacement is what fits. It fits the second-twist idea & the general prose shape of the book. The Luvah chapter, then, is romance & novel, & the reading for that romanticism book[77] is included in it. The Tharmas chapter is confession & anatomy & their congeners (contracts, Utopias, metahistorical myths). The Urizen chapter is treatise & other second-twist forms, and the Urthona one is the teleological or dialectical skeletons common to the arts, especially music.

[97] In both Luvah & Urthona, I suppose, the poles are expression and communication, creation and revelation, subjective & objective. This is projected socially as the contract-Utopia polarity, and speculatively as the creation-apocalypse myth.

[98] Teleology: Socrates following a line (the inevitable metaphor) of thought in the Republic, with Glaucon supplying the punctuation. Mozart's symphonies, with the feeling that you could have written it yourself if you'd thought of the first two bars. My feeling that I had written FS in sonata form. Stretto in fugues & anagnorisis in drama.

[99] The AC tendency to think of the mythical as "undisplaced" is, I think, right & inevitable, but be careful not to think of it as necessarily the unprojected form. The creation-apocalypse myth might be projected from the psychological or even the political one. Otherwise you're in danger of religious determinism.

[100] The literary nexus of Luvah is romance & novel; of Tharmas, confession & anatomy; of Urthona the lyric & vehicular forms of Romanticism; of Urizen epic & encyclopaedic forms. Pity the Romantic forms are so unmusical: I may find more in the German area (Jean Paul & Novalis) or even base the whole chapter on musical form.

[101] Revision of table on p. 3 [par. 8]:

Area	Subjective	Objective
Process	Creation	Communication
Religion	Creation	Apocalypse
Society	Contract	Utopia
Psychology	Introverted	Extroverted
Prose Form	Romance-Confession	Novel-Anatomy
Romantic Form	Vehicular Epic	Epiphanic Fragment
Musical Tonality	Chromatic & Minor	Diatonic & Major

[102] The Romantic one is the basis of the Rcsm. [Romanticism] book,[78] I suppose: the long genetic process of Wordsworth's Prelude & other endless or unfinishable epics leading to Proust & FW [*Finnegans Wake*], with the epiphanic moment standing out as what's communicated, the *illumination*. Note that some of these—it may be important to understand whether it's some or all—are not antithetical but have a central connecting element. In religion it's the historical revelation in Christ; in society it's the educational system or cyropaedia.

[103] Say five to six thousand sentences, each one carefully written, & some prose good enough to be read on records.

[104] In working on Utopias the principle comes up again: the myth, being undisplaced, is not really the substratum of literary structure historically: the romance form is the substratum. That's why it's eternally revolutionary, & why its medieval incarnation is both a conservative (Carlyle-Ruskin) & a revolutionary (Morris) ideal. Besides, the romance (also legend & folktale) is less trapped in the religious & other allegories of canonization than the myth. Or maybe romance & myth are, respectively, the creative-revolutionary and the apocalyptic-conservative poles of culture, & belong across the page [i.e., in chart, par. 101]. That would make the Bible the supreme romance and Dante, at the height of the romance period, the supreme myth. But this is getting into a mythos = romance & dianoia or thematic stasis = myth pattern, which is confusing.

[105] My Utopia paper,[79] in its present form, leads logically to the spatial paradox: when ordinary society is global it is everywhere, & the question "where?" is always answered by "there." Utopia, which is in fact as in etymology nowhere, then becomes "here." What results from the temporal paradox? Part of it's the same thing: the answer to "When?" is "then," future shifting to past, & Uchronia is now. But there's outer time as well as outer space.

[106] Every so often I find myself, as now, at the bottom of the mountain, with everything I've done numbered zero. I'm in what Beckett calls the Belacqua fantasy,[80] in no damn hurry to climb. Prolonged, this state would be the paranoia I'm familiar with from Norma.[81] However, that's another story. I notice that in this state I tend to think about time, and more particularly the notion that time as we know it is a false or projected form of real time. This is one of the things I want to crack in the Urizen chapter. Simple location is a temporal as well as a spatial fallacy. Maybe that's why St. Augustine's name appears in the dream.[82]

[107] Certain structural principles: comedy with its three stages, the third a "repetition" of a recognized but unexperienced first (vs. subjective or sentimental, Blake's "memory"), comes into my Shakespeare lectures, my Utopia paper, & my Dante reflections. Beckett's *Murphy*, alluded to above [par. 106], is a chess-in-Bardo[83] book.

[108] Jay & Norma:[84] one is a poet & scholar, a Ph.D & a Professor; the other is a schizophrenic who passionately longs to be these things. Nothing at all can be done about it, yet how wrong it all is! I think of this here because the analogy is in Dante's salvation imagery too. It's as impossible for God to reach the proud as for me to reach a schizophrenic; as impossible for him to save Virgil as for me to treat Norma as authentically gifted. Now, of course, all things are possible with God, who is always *deus ex machina*. But the sense of *deus in machina*, God stuck in his own machinery, is part of what I call the intellectual handicap of religion, the assumptions of anxiety from which the archetypal framework is derived.

[109] I wonder how far I could get with the conception of faith as negative imagination—faith in the sense of asserting the existence of a construct and then making one's life a sacramental analogy of that. The

weak spot in imagination is that it has no subjective[85] counterpart, which is why people are always asserting that art is no substitute for religion.

[110] The aphorism is a verbal *perception*: that is, it's a verbal analogy of a *Gestalt* perception. We often speak of it as a perception. And the quality I so admire in Burton and struggle for myself is verbal *outline*, a verbal analogy of powerful sketching that contains a great mass of facts.

[111] The "existential" attitude rejects the tendency to think of reality as objective because this makes man an object, depersonalizes him and destroys his freedom. The total movement is: awakening from unconscious being into consciousness, & the *mirror* of awareness: from here to there, Sein to Dasein; and back. The awakening is exhilarating, a will to power turning around to look at itself: the emancipation of comic into discontinuous prose forms. But there comes a second awareness, in which this state is the tragic contract or epiphany of law, and the loss of identity. There follows the quest for the third awareness, back to here and Sein, where simple location is destroyed (Heidegger-Whitehead-Avatamsaka tie-up).[86] This last movement is repetition through time.

[112] This relates to the mythoi of AC thus: first awareness is the Romance discovery of quest, the imaginative key; second awareness is the tragic fall & contract; third is the ironic depersonalized vision; fourth the recovery. Luvah, Tharmas, Urthona (because the dialectic of identity that expands from verbal to total art begins there) and Urizen. Agon, pathos, sparagmos, anagnorisis—nothing really new, except in some of the referents.

[113] The second awareness doesn't have to be tragic—Hegel's doctrine of the Idea is second awareness philosophy—but it does have to be narcistic, as Hegel was: the tragedy can be of the H5 [*Henry V*] variety, with the abstract English pattern imposed on France. France is sick, but we see it from the exhilarated English point of view. Similarly, many ironists of the third awareness attempt to be tragic, like Heidegger. The first awareness is the romantic will on a quest, imposing itself in victory: the pure H5 kind. The Iliad shows this passing into a tragic sense of contract in Achilles' myth of the jars. And the rcsm. [romanticism] or ʎ [Rencontre] feature in romance is the sense of quest *as* an awareness, & so mental & allegorical.

[114] There are really seven steps: innocence, fall, contract, bondage, disintegration, redemption, recovery. Don't think of bondage (Israel in Egypt) as a mere duplication of fall (Adam in wilderness): for one thing, it's awareness of fall, which is quite different. Fall may be exhilarating & heroic: bondage is imprisonment, Angst, claustrophobia, froda & not forza.[87]

[115] The social argument contains my point, relating both to the categorical imperative and to the Marxist conception of a total social truth opposed to ideology, of a total or unconditional morality as the only moral standard for literature.

[116] I've done a series of lectures on Milton (L [Liberal]) and Shakespeare (˥ [Tragicomedy]). For 1966 I've accepted two series, the Alexanders in March and a series at Cleveland in May. The latter is to be on the Romantic poets (ʎ [Rencontre]) so the Alexanders clearly have to be the growing point of ∧ [Anticlimax]. That suggests a return to my old contexts of criticism idea: three of these are fairly clear now, on social, cultural & speculative mythology. I might anchor them, as I had originally planned to do, on the 19th c. authors. I could leave out the verbal key and deal with historical, conceptual, cultural and speculative myths. That way, the hell with the McMasters: they can wait.

[117] Another idea was to make the two series the two halves of the verbal key: one the Biblical topocosm & its thematic stasis in Dante, the other on the Rc. [Romantic] one and its stasis in the Proust-Joyce period. Or half that—the second half. Still another was to use the material & techniques of my graduate symbolism course. The thing is that lecture series have to come out of things already digested: I can't just sail into Dante, for example, even a year off. Yet the McMasters do worry me: if the Alexanders are the embryonic Book of Urthona, what in hell can they be?

[118] I've been impressed a good deal lately with something that came out of the end of my Utopia paper:[88] the difference in proportion between cultural products scaled to the human body, and those scaled to the mechanical extensions of the human body. Because it's scaled to the body, a great cathedral like York Minster represents the absolute maximum of vast soaring grandeur, and would even if a ninety-story sky-

scraper were erected beside it. The ragged streets of ancient cities are scaled to the body; Washington, laid out by L'Enfant[89] in 1800 in the great Versailles-Regency Euclidean period, is already in the age of the automobile.

[119] Something similar is involved in the greatness of the classic, the work that's definitive. Also in history: Greek history in the pre-Alexander period is body-scaled. It's an important element in the picturesque, when the sublime (i.e. things that *extend* the body, like mountains) marks a new sensibility. America was extended almost from the beginning (cf. Billings on his fuguing tunes).[90] So far extended man has been geometrical and nature-defying, not a larger body. Or rather he's astronomical and not earth-centered, as Blake said, a turnpike highway or jet trail, not a country lane.

[120] Late civilizations turn extended: the death of culture involved is symbolized in pyramids, the Tower of Babel, and above all by the crucifixion, which is linked to carfax, the crossroads where the vampire is staked down.[91] These are preliminary rehearsals for the vast neolithic change that begins around 1780 or so. Here there's an element that's death (Spengler) and something that isn't.[92] Culture perhaps must die to bring forth fruit.

[121] Nomadic tribes are always extended: culture has always been decentralized, having to take root in a very specific environment. Hence, e.g. the Mongols have been purely destructive forces, demonic Abels murdering Cain. But although the sense of culture as decentralized runs through Shelley & Morris to Eliot, it's an absolute idea. Our age is nomadic and omnicentral, if there is such a word, and it has the problem of bringing forth a new kind of creativity.[93] Much of this is the death of the old, hence the relevance of the pessimism in Spengler and Freud. And if the Nazis had won the war Spengler's fatalistic cyclical theory would have been unanswerable. (It isn't cyclical, but it works that way).

[122] Toynbee's correction of Spengler, the death-and-rebirth pattern brought about by a creative proletariat, adds another element. A preliminary rehearsal for rebirth occurs too, in Christianity as a nomadic crossroads religion, and earlier in the call to Abraham, Lot in Sodom, Daedalus in Crete: the "pilgrim's progress" quest archetype at five o'clock. (The

great wheel in one of the two brown notebooks,[94] either ∟ [Liberal] or ⌝ [Tragicomedy], belongs).

[123] Roman Catholic education has always been *summa*-centered, for obvious reasons.[95] In Newman all humanism & individual-centered education has to be sacrificed on the *summa* altar, or else. Hence Catholic intellectuals go in for great co-ordinating patterns, but are too timid & anxiety-ridden to try to get beyond this point. Or else, like Marshall [McLuhan], they work out their own line on the assumption that the *summa* is in the background ready to take care of it. Protestant thinkers are often worse off, because, not having a *summa*, they get stuck with what are really moral anxieties, and of course anti-religious people are anti-religiously anxious. I think the answer must be in some dialogue between *summa* and individualized humanism. I think this is a more genuine issue, *for me*, than the Word-Church dialogue, but I haven't much notion what individualization does to education yet. The question should be studied in the light of the principle that the theory of education is the connecting link between contract & *telos* myths. For initiatory education *is* a mythical corpus.

[124] Education is, or has something to do with, a process of transferring the continuum of identity from the ego and the memory to the individual and the imagination. In the process memory becomes practice memory or habit.

[125] The difference of ornament and imitation is connected, though not necessarily identical, with the difference between the continuous and the episodic. The geometrical ornament can be repeated indefinitely: Morris, influenced by his repetitive designs, is an intensely continuous writer, collecting epics and romances. The *symboliste* tradition, and Hopkins in England, is intensely episodic. Romanticism, by virtue of its "vehicular form," is continuous. The Gospels give us a discontinuous series of epiphanic revelations through the Son, with an inaccessible mysterious continuous Father in the background. After Christ's death, he becomes Jehovah, as Blake says,[96] a continuous Christ the same yesterday, today and forever.

[126] At present I feel that my Romanticism lectures could turn on four varieties of ambivalence in the Romantic movement. One is this continu-

ous & episodic business, applied to literary genres. One is the political ambivalence of revolution and reaction. One is the ambivalence of the creator's position, as being a prophet and medium of a message, or as being the place of a pure aesthetic experience, with authority deriving from that. One is the ambivalence of the world within, the goal of the quest, whether apocalyptic or demonic. That should hold the little bastards, as the man said.

[127] Of course I have never done a series of lectures on Shakespearean tragedy, nor done the kind of reading on tragedy that would bring it level with my command of comedy; yet that would be relatively easy to do.

[128] The difference between romance & comedy is that comedy attains, romance contains: one drives toward a telos, the other revolves around it in the circular quest shape. The *Purgatorio* is archetypal comedy; the *Paradiso* archetypal romance.

[129] There are fictional and thematic comic drives: one is the straight comedy pattern leading to new birth & a festive conclusion; the other is a conceptual or dialectic pattern leading to a separation of being & nonbeing. One is the As You Like It pattern, the other the Newman's Apologia pattern. I said in my British lecture[97] that one couldn't develop a serious belief in either a salvation or an enlightenment religion without accepting the validity of the comic structure. The Christian *commedia* is fictional; the Buddhist deliverance structure thematic, based on dialogues of an inverted Socratic type: in Zen the alazon questioner is the earnest disciple & the eiron the sage who makes some irrelevant remark or whacks him over the ear.

[130] Consequently any thematic stasis of the Christian *commedia* is likely to sound a trifle Buddhist, as the Eliot quartets do. So does the *Paradiso*, for that matter. The fictional emphasis is on escape from prison; the thematic on smashing the walls of a mental prison, the iron bar in Zen.[98] Romance, which presents this as contained, leads fictionally to Jerusalem & Eden; thematically to the Avatamsaka[99] conceptions of universal identity and interpenetration. Hegel is comic, and Marx: Whitehead is romantic. Ritual, including the sacramental analogy, is fictional; doctrine is thematic.

[131] It looks as though the informing of the applied verbal areas (roughly the historical, philosophical, psychological & religious) by the four mythoi were central; but I need to grapple more firmly with the conceptual forms of the mythoi. I mean the thematic ones. The only thing really new here is the pinning down of the Avatamsaka hunch to the dianoia of romance. This may be useful as a conception in the Cleveland lectures, which I think of as leading up at least to Morris, & so linking Romanticism & romance.

[132] Rearrangement: (I) The Instruments of Cultural Production, in two parts. The first the old Urthona chapter, the circle of arts & their hypothetical connexions. The second the verbal part of this, leading up to the informing of verbal structures by the mythoi. Or the other way round, as I'd originally thought. Then (II) the working out of this information on a Zoa-cross diagram. Horizontal axis of time and space: historical myths (contractual, Utopian, metahistorical) and philosophical myths (metaphysical constructs). Vertical axis of subject & object: psychological myths and religious myths. In the centre is the education and initiatory-dialectic structure.

[133] Dante speaks of Edward I of England as "better" than Henry III. Henry was peaceful & endowed churches & schools; Edward massacred Welsh bards & hanged Wallace & so on. I suppose the historical justification for such morality (which is also Shakespeare's) is ultimate: the warlike kings broke down the barriers of small civilizations & eventually what they did made for one world. At present we attach virtue to a defensive mentality, which hasn't that kind of goal.

[134] The epic is a stylizing of romance, and hence my L [Liberal] investigations lead toward the total content of the order of words that romance adumbrates. That means that L themes, extruded from AC, can reappear in Λ [Anticlimax] and ⅄ [Rencontre].

[135] Apparently stagnant history does not really exist, even if Spengler's thesis is essentially right. Cycles of Cathay & the notion of African history as simply "natives" aimlessly tormenting each other are ignorant history: greater knowledge brings the mythical shape inherent in knowledge. This principle is connected with other points: inconsistencies in a thinker removed by finding the verbal connexions. Of course one could

reverse the process, & see our own history as aimless torment from the point of view of someone on Mars. Something else I've suppressed for some reason.

[136] The vision of *techne*, of great works of the past crumbling as nothing comparable grows up in their place, is perhaps the one genuine *tragic* vision of our time—tragic because of the heroic element in its original greatness. The treatment, of course, as in *The Waste Land*, is usually ironic, or, as in Morris, elegiac.

[137] A great deal of the book may be concerned with the use of literary mythoi in actual life as well as in other bodies of knowledge. In many of the things I've done I see ironic patterns: if I weren't a literary critic I'd be forced to interpret them morally. Is all morality projected, a substitute for verbal insights? That is, is conscience, Milton's umpire,[100] simply humorous or ritualized criticism? The activities of compulsive critics, from Rymer to Leavis,[101] certainly suggest this, & so does the obsessive anxiety typical of the clergy.

[138] Only perhaps morality as such is not compulsive but simply deductive criticism. Conscience in the infantile please-mummy sense is what's compulsive, along with the empty anxieties of morality. But the sphere of ethical freedom *is* the genuinely aesthetic one, and literature is, exactly, a criticism of life. By conscience I mean the informing power of moral experience.

[139] If I could put all this together I'd have the Alexanders. I. The Instrument of Information (i.e. the total literary myth). II. The Social Analogy: first the Druid one out of Blake, then the contemporary pastoral-guilt one. III. The Moral Analogy, or law as a state of anxiety in the mind. IV. The Cultural or Creative Analogy: the redemptive nature of timing and the beginning of liberal awareness in the perception of irony. The interpenetration of moral & aesthetic standards. Simpler of course just to use the four Blake levels, which would make IV the speculative analogy: I have this somewhere else. But it's too big a theme, in that form, for four lectures. Four lectures on the social analogy, written in an easy WTC style, would be the ideal, it seems at present.

[140] It won't be easy to keep this clear of the larger pattern, which is still

the axis of speculation (time-space) and the axis of concern (subject-object). There are in the latter religious fallacies of objectifying & psychological fallacies of subjectifying, both reducing the central creative pattern. The traditional view of the creative pattern is that the subjective is formal & the objective material, but there must be something wrong with this. It's rather that the subjective incarnates & the objective is epiphanized: a principle of correspondence is involved which is the fundamental axiom of faith. This axiom is easier to see in pragmatic than in dogmatic situations: it's partly Crane's continuous recognition of a formal cause.[102] Death is not reduction of form to matter: it's deincarnation. All incarnation creates *a* centre which is *the* centre: in death the subjective centre disappears, which means also that it disappears *into the* centre.

[141] In this scheme the either-or business is the contrast between speculation and concern. Note that social & moral analogies are concerned (hence "ethical freedom"): an ad promising a cure of halitosis is more concerned than a metaphysical structure *as such*. Or perhaps the incorporation of knowledge into a structure is a process that could be called the impregnation of concern. It's not so much that communication overcomes entropy (Wiener)[103] as that structure defends against death-consciousness: Golgonooza.

[142] Of course what I can present of this I must present not as my own speculation but as what I find implied by the order of words, as what poets say when they're not saying anything.

[143] "Creation" is not only a metaphor: it expresses the fact that both life & art achieve an identity out of an analogy. Integritas is identity; consonantia is interpenetration; claritas is I+ (i.e. the recognition of identity, satori in the individual or the beatific vision in the analogical context, but usually erotic or sexual).[104] (What bothers me about all this is the turning of concern into speculation. But the previous note suggests that speculation is redemptive, being ultimately Eros, & that the Either/Or dilemma[105] is balls).

[144] Language is inherently Cartesian & split, & it's almost impossible to keep clearly in mind the unifying element on the axis of concern: the myths of religion are not there: we make them up; the myths of psychology are there: that is, both factors are always involved. St. Joan's answer

in Shaw: of course my visions are all my imagination: what else could they be? Religion is not just psychologismus; the Beulah mattress[106] isn't there either.

[145] Travelling on a train in Canada one looks out the window at a passing landscape. As it gets darker, more & more of the window reflects the inside of the carriage. Eventually there's nothing but reflection: one could assume that there was no world out there at all. A few lights appear that are difficult to reconcile with this thesis, but they could be ignored or explained away, like S.P.S. data[107] or flying saucers. But when the train stops, & you have to get out at a station, it's probably a help to believe it's there. That's a parable of the dilemma of trying to keep the subject-object split between a visible & an invisible world. Nothing really new here, of course: it's pure FS.

[146] What I'm after is different. Ruskin's ornament & imitation distinction:[108] traditionally, verbal structures have been thought of imitatively, as covering, explaining or arranging facts or reality. In the last half-century we've begun to be conscious of the element of construct in them, and this in turn should lead to a study of their relation to literature, which is pure & disinterested mythical construct. Oh, God.

[147] If you look through rose-colored spectacles, and then take them off, you naturally wonder how your naked eyes color what you see. That's the structural reaction: I suppose the "realist" thinks he's seeing "what's there." In fact you could divide the human race into two groups: those who say "Now I'm seeing things as they are," and those who say "I wonder how my eyes condition what I'm seeing." The latter are concerned with transcendental illusion, the illusion of structure. This is one of my main themes, & it's connected with what I call the verbal perception. And besides the verbal perception itself there's the verbal support of perception. "This pencil is green" expresses a conviction in my mind born of two parents, the mother a private and incommunicable sense perception, the father a verbal consensus: other people agree when I say it's green. I know that to a philosopher such problems are elementary in content & illiterate in formulation, but I am not writing philosophy: I am studying the social consequences of literary criticism.

[148] Just as the conventional is mad & the metaphor equally so, so the

archetypal is the illogical. When Yeats says [in *A Prayer for My Daughter*] his daughter oughtn't to have opinions because he once knew a beautiful woman who was silly & opinionated, one feels that logically he would have done better to have made a statistical survey. Yeats' argument, so-called, is a vision assimilated into the Venus-Vulcan archetype. It's valid as a vision of a bitch-goddess that Maud Gonne embodies, not as an inductive or collective observation on life. The latter is a displacement.

[149] I think my body-and-extensions of body point might be a central theme in the McMaster lectures, in view of the importance of abstract extension in Canadian landscape and (McLuhan) thought & culture. Perhaps the whole V [Mirage] aspect of my present complex, plus the initiatory summa education point, which seems to be getting shoved out of the 1966 Λ [Anticlimax]–ʎ [Rencontre] group.

[150] Nation means something socially born; nature means that which is born; principle means that which begins. The Aristotelian conception of nature is focussed on *telos*: I wonder if this is the real point in the Greek revolution? For without *telos* we're still in the Oriental world of maya, where things appear (get born) and therefore disappear (die), and where all reality has to be separated from appearance. The fact that birth implies death suggests an endlessly turning wheel. Telos is incarnation or embodiment in reverse, the wheel of chronos reaching a point of kairos. With Vico the maya wheel reappears in the West, & since then we have developed mayan process-philosophies, which tend to deprive the intellect of a focus. This focus or *telos*, the completed form, is the objective counterpart of individuality.

[151] This perhaps comes a little closer to defining the axis of concern. I wish I didn't have to think about it in such a private language: the communicable part of it isn't crystallizing. If I have to I may even specify a private-language final chapter, like Jeans' "Deep Waters" one.[109] In a sense that's always been inherent in the Λ [Anticlimax] conception.

[152] Epiphany is not a new experience: it is the knowledge that one has the experience: it's recognition or anagnorisis. The wise men did not need to journey to it: it was their own wisdom in the only form wisdom can take, the divine infancy or fresh beginning. Epiphany is the containing of change, or the other, by bringing it into line with identity: in short,

it's the awareness of growth, when the line pointing from the object to the subject reverses its direction. Death ⇆ Chih-Kai Bardo,[110] or Resurrection (ultimate anagnorisis).

[153] The object of knowledge is not, like the mere object, an It: it isn't Thou, unless a person; it isn't I. It's somewhere between I and It without quite being Thou. I don't know about a fourth dimension, but we sure as hell need a fourth-person pronoun. The Mad Hatter got as far as saying that time was Him and not It; Blake suggests that objects in their totality are space & that space is She (emanation). I suppose that there She has the same relation to Thou that He (in Blake the total perceiver, or Los) has to I: relation of identity, of course: but, hell, the object of knowledge, that's part of me because I know it yet forever itself, the phenomenon & not the Ding an Sich,[111] which is always It: what person is it?

[154] Now I must get down seriously to work on the Alexanders & the Cleveland set. They're Λ [Anticlimax] and ⅄ [Rencontre] cores, as the Hurons & Bamptons were L [Liberal] and ˥ [Tragicomedy] cores. The great advantage of the Cleveland set is that I know they're on Romanticism, so I can start reading there. The Alexanders thus would be introductory to Rcsm. [Romanticism], perhaps second-twist on prose forms, yet of course complete in themselves. For Rcsm. [Romanticism] see p. 47 [par. 126]; but the Rc. [Romantic] organism-machine Frankenstein myth fits my body and extensions of body, just as my Beethoven vehicular form points and the pastoral moral of my Utopia paper do. The McMasters are V [Mirage], & have to take their chance and turn: they'd be best thought of as a legacy-of-Rcsm. [Romanticism] series, attempting to define the "modern."

[155] My present Rcsm. [Romanticism] paper[112] turns on the point-of-epiphany construct of the *bateau ivre* on the sea. This is the pessimistic form of the telos-vs.-wheel point made above [par. 150]: in the telos-centered Cartesian tradition the mechanical is unconscious: with Vico the wheel of birth informs imagery, & the sea is another form of the wheel of birth, as various Buddhist constructs show. So the epiphanic moment, or transient glimpse, is an ironic parody of telos, the Cleopolis vision,[113] at least in part.

[156] The McMasters are to be called "The Modern Century," which fills the Confederation bill as well.[114]

[157] Thus epiphany is (a) a subjective experience of a moment of identity (b) an objective telos or completed form clear of the wheel of process (c) the union of these two things represented by the experience of art (d) the identity of this union with the total person, Christ in Xy. This is the axis of concern: the axis of time & space, of duration or being as existence and as essence, crosses it at right angles.

[158] On the speculative axis the vision is of an intelligible world of forms. On the axis of concern it's a vision of the source of compassion or charity or love. This is a luminous world of jewelled particulars, not a diagrammatic world. It's primarily not a world to see but to see by. It's the "other" world in the sense that death imposes a dialectic where we glimpse this world as an object (*because* we're dying), or don't, which is real death. The glimpse of it is the end of the quest, which of course has no end.

[159] The end of art is epiphany, perceiving the particular as universal, the grain of sand as the world. The end of non-literary verbal disciplines, and I think of mathematics, is the intuition of a network of relations or laws. Hence the difference I noted earlier with Yeats' archetype.

[160] Christmas note: the city-jewel world and the pastoral world are grouped around the infant Christ, the former with the wise men and their gold-shrouded gifts, the latter with the shepherds & the ox & ass in the manger. Gozzoli & Gentile da Fabriano[115] are particularly good on the jewelled-world setting of the wise men. In the calendar the pastoral reclamation comes on Christmas Eve, at the moment of birth: the renewed city at the very end, at epiphany, with the new year in between: millennium, end of the seventh cycle, & apocalypse. Note in Milton's NO [*Nativity Ode*] how the entry of the wise men is designed to follow the poem, the claritas succeeding the Incarnation itself (integritas) and the telos of time (consonantia).[116] Gold and green are the colors of new beginning.

[161] The anti-telos process bias of our time is particularly evident in the present linguistics fad for a "descriptive" attitude to language which is really anti-intellectual prejudice rationalized as scientific procedure. Spoken language is not the same thing at all as written language: O.K., for example, is one of the most useful & versatile expressions in the spoken language, and for that very reason is of limited usefulness in the written

language. The proportions of associative (process) and of prose (telos) rhythms are too different.

[162] Much of my writing, especially the Shakespeare-comedy lectures, is based on the traditional cross of becoming & being. A horizontal line, really a turning wheel, is process from origin to end. A vertical line from telos or being above to non-being below is the dialectical axis. Non-being is quite different from the *end* of the process, which is death, a mutation but not an annihilation, & not really an end but a new beginning, the horizontal line being a wheel in essence. This is the cross of the Eliot quartets, and in fact of the whole philosophical tradition from Heraclitus on.

[163] This is quite different from the cross I'm contemplating now, the intersection of the axis of speculation & the axis of concern. It may not be a cross at all, but I think it can be considered one. Religion is, almost by definition, on the axis of concern, but the principle of toleration means that every formulation of religious belief is speculative. I'm assuming, with Blake, that the basis of concern is the constructive imagination which identifies subject & object in the epiphany of art. Psychology & religion are respectively the subjective & objective analogues to art, and so turn out to be projections. But projection is speculative.

[164] Curious paradox in my own writing I should look into: I wrote the Masseys in a deliberately colloquial speaking style, to minimize the reading barrier. Yet this book sets up much more of a *personal* barrier than any of my essays that are written in normal prose. What I aimed at, & what I got, was the sense of a disembodied oracular voice speaking very clearly in the dark, not of me conversing with a reader. It had the same effect that I've noted in the discontinuous aphoristic form. In *epos* the personality disappears as it doesn't in the most objective fiction.

[165] The "up there" pre-Romantic structure of metaphors goes with the religious or objective projection of the creative life: that is, the perfecting of the persona. One lives or tries to live up to a critical watching God, to really be what others take one to be. Social conformity is the facile parody of this. The "in there" post-Romantic structure goes with the psychological or subjective projection, knowing oneself or trying to see through the ego. Egocentric self-awareness is the parody of this.

[166] I haven't yet read Marshall's "the medium is the message" book,[117] but (continuing the Masseys point) there is something magnifying in an address to the ear alone, something that reduces scale on a purely visual level. Hearing Hitler's 1939 speeches was a terrifying & hideous experience: Churchill, too, gave a sense of archaic greatness. True, all the visual effects of movies and photography helped build up Hitler; but I wonder if he could have survived television. For in television you can turn the sound off, & that would reduce Hitler to Charlie Chaplin in no time. I was circling around this in the first Bampton: Gower vs. Cleon & Dionyza in *Pericles*.

[167] I wasn't expecting this diary to turn personal, but it has. William James' dog in the library[118] raises the question of different levels of perception. I take in more of my surroundings than Aunt Lily does: she's deafer than I, but it isn't just perception: there's conceptual apprehension as well. Whenever I'm with Jay [Macpherson][119] I realize that her level of perception is higher than mine: I'm more short-sighted, but it's the mental patterns she creates out of her livelier mind that make the difference. Let's say that Aunt Lily takes in one per cent of what's there, I two per cent, & Jay three per cent. The maximum, limited by the structure of the human mind & by its biological need to select for coherence, maybe, let's say, ten per cent. Even above five per cent you'd have perceptions that we call psychic or extra-sensory: ability to read others' thoughts, awareness of the presence of the dead, & the like.

[168] So far I'm speaking of perception, of what's "there." Powers, I suppose, develop *pari passu* with perceptions, & powers are part of "creation." It's hard to think of creation except as the imposing of a subjective unreality on objective reality, but we should think of it as manifesting or bringing into being.

[169] The thing that ties *King Lear* together is the fact that Edgar is the emerging eiron young king, the mythical Prince Hal. Hence he has to go down the hell of nature with *Lear*, only he's born there, & Lear sees the process. The Fool is Lear's child, but of course not his heir: a fiercely loyal critic or unbroken Enobarbus.

[170] Locke & Rousseau have similar sleeping-beauty myths: the mind is a tabula rasa awakened by a messenger from the external world of

substance. To think of one's world as there, objective, preformed, is a Beulah withdrawal into a cocoon world. To think of creation as hallucinatory, forcing what's out there on what is, is spectral will. To increase perception is also to increase creative power, and vice versa, as we move from there to here. Hence education moves from the world man sees to the world man makes, & the latter is as much what's there as what's made. The goal of education would be this ten per cent awareness or whatever it is: the synthesis of perception & creation.

[171] In my Arts speech[120] I said that the annihilating of simple location underlay such things as abstract expressionism. I think too that the dissolving of location in our world has produced another Beulah cocoon, the fascination in the plastic arts & now music with chance. The powerful teleological will of Baroque music is Cartesian: Dada & Cage's music take us back by revolt to a body-centered response to sense experience as an end in itself.

[172] I have always distrusted what I call Reuben the Reconciler[121] in thought: the syncretism that "reconciles" Plato & Aristotle or St. Thomas & Marx. I think every great structure of thought or imagination is a universe in itself, identical with & interpenetrating every other, but not similar or harmonizable with any other. Syncretism is Coleridge's fancy playing with fixities & definites,[122] & it leads to the net of relations, not to the archetypal universal unique. My earlier notebooks, where I wanted to move all the big names in modern literature and thought around like chess pieces, were fanciful in this sense. What I now want to do is pick epiphanies out of them for my own purposes.

[173] Further on the Christmas note, p. 61 [par. 160]: one of the Magi is traditionally Negro, from the golden land of Ophir or Sheba. In the golden city of Venice the Negro suitor of Portia chooses the golden casket, & the Moor of Venice symbolizes what he has lost as a golden stone or chrysolite.[123] Gold & brown shit.

[174] One of my present master keys seems to be a recapturing of something that suddenly crystallized one Sunday morning & was written down in one of the brown notebooks.[124] It puzzled me at the time, because it seemed inconsistent with or peripheral to my main line of thought. It's turned up again as the three forms of awareness on p. 40 [par. 111].

[175] First awareness: a body-centered perception with the mind a *tabula rasa*. Reality is out there, to be perceived without manipulation. The selecting activity is unconscious, as it is in an animal. Those who try to push this perceptive attitude further than it will go, psychics & mediums & the like, get involved with hallucinations. Similarly with heaven or the "next world" regarded as a pre-fabricated place that we see around us in the same way that we see this world.

[176] The second awareness is mind-centered, & brings into being out of (apparently) nothingness an imaginative structure of religious faith, philosophical concept, or poetic imagery as a transformation of the world out there into a mental home. Such structures are always anxious, because they contain more of reality than is known about reality. That is, they are always partly hallucinatory, because of the underlying feeling of compulsive subjective imposing of intelligibility. Here one is, or becomes, concerned with the transcendental or mind-imposing categories. The least anxious of these structures is the scientific, because most closely related to the first awareness.

[177] When the mind takes over from the body it holds the body quiet, in study or concentration. Sense perception is directed & controlled. Some programmes of experience, such as yoga, assume a spirit-mind relationship parallel to the mind-body one. They say that the spirit is the real self, but can't emerge until the mind is kept quiet. The intellectual, with compulsive mental activity bucking and plunging around him, trying to achieve wisdom, is as baffled as a prizefighter trying to philosophize.

[178] So the third awareness often begins in ridicule of reason, as in Zen dialogues & in Browne's Tertullianism.[125] Or vice versa, as in Samuel Butler's Towneley.[126] But ultimately it has to be reasonable, just as the mental picture of the world as a ball spinning around the sun has to convince sense experience.

[179] It's difficult to describe the third awareness, because our language is Cartesian & dualistic, founded on the antithesis of the object out there & of the mental apprehension in here. When this antithesis disappears in realization, & not merely in conception (second level), we understand that the world man creates is the world that is really there. Education

leads to the threshold of this: the perception that the structure of the arts & sciences is the real world.

[180] This third awareness ought to be, ideally, a recapturing of the spontaneity of the first. There's a paradisal element in the first awareness that survives as a pastoral myth, & the anxieties of the second have to recognize it, if only by exclusion. In the first awareness there's no true individuality, except that the attachment to the group is unconscious. In the second there is a conscious effort to restrain the individual; in the third the sense of cleavage between social & individual aspects of the personality would disappear.

[181] These three awarenesses don't coincide completely with my educational ladder, but I suppose the same kind of progression is involved. The first awareness is the genuine child-nature. The second is on two levels: the social environment, which turns demonic very quickly, and the cultural environment, where a mimesis or mirror of the first state is established. The third is also on two levels: the axis of speculation, or Plato's *dianoia,* and the axis of concern or *nous.*

[182] For the Alexanders I might try the circle of mythoi, starting with tragedy, ending with romance, and concentrating on their dianoiai or thematic aspects: law & contract of tragedy; fall; establishing of time & space; the dialectic of separation; hybris & heroic decline. Of irony: theories of cyclical return; entropy; the all-too-human; the dystopia; naturalism in the sense of the assimilation of the merely human to mere nature. Of comedy: progress & evolution; metamorphosis; providential design; salvation & enlightenment; dialectic. Of romance: quest & pilgrimage; recognition of parentage; destruction of antitheses of subject & object, creator & creature, time & space; identity & interpenetration.

[183] At first I resisted so obvious a rehash of AC, but I can keep the Λ [Anticlimax] core if I throw the emphasis on the conceptual & thematic side, using the fictions for illustration. I'm really concerned with what Rousseau would call the moral effects of the arts & sciences. What do the mythoi mean? That is, what verbal patterns do they generate in non-literary verbal structures? My original titles were "The Information of" tragedy (and the others), but I'll probably modify that. I thought at first this scheme wasn't a good prelude to the ⅄ [Rencontre] set, but I can

make it one. Then the McMaster set can be educational, if I run out of time & energy.

[184] Tragedy, then, informs religion with the myth of fall and society with the myth of contract. It has much to do with *isolating* the hero or pharmakos figure: the isolation of the human race in the figure of Adam. It rationalizes ritual or prescribed action by setting it off dialectically from another world. Its epiphany of law includes a class struggle, law being the generating point of all social studies. I suppose my notions on the role of nature in King Lear will do as a starting point.

[185] I've just read Peacock's *Gryll Grange*, an extraordinarily rewarding book, & followed it with Virginia Woolf's *Between the Acts*. Both are secondary & derivative romances situated at or near the point of epiphany, & should come into the last section. Shakespeare could run through them all, of course: Peacock's book is WT and T-centered [*Winter's Tale* and *Tempest*-centred], VW's [Virginia Woolf's] Cy and T-centered [*Cymbeline* and *Tempest*-centred]. Maybe one of the things Morris' SF [*The Sundering Flood*] is is a P-centered [*Pericles*-centred] romance. All three are "last works." They cluster around Shakespeare's romances & the Purgatorio: the stuff in my myth paper,[127] only fiction & prose instead of Yeats & Eliot. The *cena* [banquet], as Plato suggests, is normally a point-of-epiphany setting: the *ultima cena* [Last Supper] is in an upper room. Yet the symposium as dialectic is comic, & the east cardinal point, not the north, which is rather the St. George & dragon one.

[186] This takes me back again to the great secret that I failed entirely to solve in AC, though I beat my head against it constantly; this is the relation of the four forms of prose fiction to the cardinal points of the wheel of drama, lyric, & rhetorical prose. The novel is in general a comic form, but its sense of history and its acceptance of a social contract put it solidly W. The anatomy fits E well enough, but the other two baffle me, & perhaps the anatomy is really S, being satire. What I hope for in this next phase is a new twist along the lines: confession; contract theory; educational theory; the city-garden ideal. S, W, E, N.

[187] Oh, God, do I have to beat my ears off over this again? Mythoi are tonalities, hence episodic forms are closely related to them, and continuous forms may resolve into any of them. The four forms of prose fiction

are comparable to, say, the epic. But what is the basis of classification of the four forms of fiction? The only thing I've got is introverted, extroverted, intellectual & social. The last two should have been fictional & thematic (other way round).

[188] Now: my idea was to work out the conceptual or thematic aspects of the four mythoi: this went on to the hypothesis that the cardinal points, the kernels of prose, are growing points of non-literary verbal structures. Will this work? And do I have to fall over the continuous-form problem in doing it if it does?

[189] Start again. The N point is apocalypse, St. George & the dragon, the pure dialectic & the cycle assimilated to it. The S point is irony, Jonah in the whale & Job in the leviathan, dialectic contained within the cycle. At E is the Leontes-Prospero figure who guides the dialectic out of the cycle, the comic dianoia;[128] at W is the Adam-Prometheus-Satan-Oedipus one who collapses the dialectic into the cycle. That much is clear, at least to me.

[190] Now: the W-E axis is what I've recently called the axis of speculation, time to space, music to painting, action to thought, will to intellect, history to philosophy, charm to riddle (the breaking of charm is the comic renunciation of magic). They're also my AC first two essays. If so, then the N-S axis ought to be the axis of concern. But I've been thinking of it as running from the psychological or introverted to the religious or projected, whereas it ought to run from an object-dominated dualism to a subject-dominated unity. At S, the ironic cardinal point, is the contrast of oracle & wit, the cave of Trophonius & the recovery of laughter.[129] Hence the confession is close to it, but so is the satiric diatribe. It's the area of my fourth essay, & although I call Freud a comic psychologist, he's really an ironic one, and that's why he's so powerful an influence.

[191] At this point it will be convenient to transfer the great wheel from the drama notebook:[130]

1. N. Birth of God: the Christmas concentration of golden city (wise men) & pastoral ["(green)" written above "pastoral"] (stable & shepherds; Matthew had never heard of either, & has Jesus born in a "house").

2. N-W. Birth of Hero: the coming of the dove & the strangling of the serpent: baptism or drawing out of the water.

3. W. Generation of the Presence of the Hero: Orpheus in the lower world: the Incarnation proper, as ministry, the temple-cleansing stage (Augean stables): arrival of unknown hero at court from forest.

4. S-W. Fixing of the pharmakos: hero dying as spectacle or crucified.

5. S. World of sparagmos & cannibalism: Jonah in whale; Christ in hell; vision of hell at point of demonic epiphany.

6. S-E. Escape of the dove (Leviticus); release of tricky slave or Barabbas; Ulysses escaping from Cyclops; birds flying from the frogs or serpents or Calibans.

7. E. Regeneration of the Presence of the Hero: Easter & resurrection (Harrowing of Hell is rather S.E.). Epiphany of Church as community, brave new world; release of bride: exhibition of birth-tokens ("secundum scripturas").[131]

8. N-E. Fixing of the Shadow: "conviction of sin" or kindling of candle of the Lord;[132] spiritual deliverance through dialectic. Comus stage.

9. N. Apocalypse or second coming of 1. (1 ["9" written above 1] & 5 are winter, 2 & 6 spring, 3 & 7 summer, 4 & 8 fall). Note that 3 is *not* a tragic phase but a contract one. Also I'm not sure but what the whole Easter business is really S-E & that E is the construction of a Utopia, the palace to house the victorious hero. No: the house may be N.E., but the escape of Ishmael from Moby Dick is not resurrection.

[192] 1 & 5 are water-worlds, 1 an Atlantis in the sea, represented conventionally by snow: in 9 there is no more sea. 2 & 6 have the ark-on-flood archetype, & the opposition of bird (dove) & serpent (leviathan). Then 3 & 7 could have the house: cleansed temple & rebuilt body-temple. Recognition of hero is physical & present in 3 & spiritual & past (flashback) in 7. 4 & 8 have pharmakoi: the illusory physical one in 4 & the real one in 8. At 2 & 6 there are massacres: of false gods as well as innocents in 2 (NO [*Nativity Ode*]): of suitors or shadows of the past in 6.

[193] Closing up another gap: the *cycle* of nature is a structure of analogies or similes; the *dialectic* emergent in comedy, achieved in romance & submerged in tragedy is a structure of metaphorical identity.

[194] And another one I've already closed: the first two essays of AC are W to E on the axis of speculation; the last two are N to S on the axis of concern. Whatever difficulties in analogy there may be, the novel, based on a sense of history and on acceptance of a social contract, is inescap-

ably W. The romance, the St. George & dragon completed dialectic, is clearly N, especially if there's anything in the conception on p. 37 [par. 104]. The anatomy, with its satiric affinities, is S, & the confession, the following of the dialectic of self-knowledge, must be E. But that sounds more concerned than S: still, irony is a deep pretense of un-concern: that's why it's ironic. This at least is. Oh, shut up, & start again with what you *can* see.

[195] The Tragic Contract | The Comic Community
The Ironic Cycle | The Romantic Pastoral
Confession (contract form) is *W*

[196] The Tragic Contract, or the Great Bond, will take some hard reading & thinking, but should bring my conception of tragedy up level with comedy: an obvious gap to plug. Examples from Shakespeare will run all through, and this one will feature a good deal of *King Lear* in particular.

[197] Tragedy is a mimesis of what in Christianity is the fall, the movement toward an epiphany of law. So much is in AC. Also what in Xy is the fall appears in political thought as the contract, the Greek dike & the Elizabethan nature. That's fine, but I shouldn't go all out for contract theories: I must keep the discussion within literature. Read Rousseau & Hobbes when you can, but it's more important to get Euripides clear & reread some Webster & Co., also a number of Restoration things like *Venice Preserv'd*.[133]

[198] Well, then: I've said that tragedy may happen to a good or a bad man. True, but the good man is typically one who has accepted a prominent place in the contract, like (Shakespeare's) Julius Caesar or the "meek" Duncan. His "hamartia" is, as in AC, simply being there. The primary tragic hero is the rebel against the contract, who normally starts a mechanical reaction by his rebellion.

[199] There are two steps in tragedy: Adam to the wilderness of contract; Israel to the Egypt of bondage. The second step ends in pure irony. I think there may be two stages of irony: a cycle, which is a higher consciousness, and an indefinite straight line, which is the ass-hole. There's a hint of this in Zamiatin's *We*.[134]

[200] The Alexanders are not the germ of the Third Book, but a transition to it from AC, and a unit in their own right. If I read tragedy & modern fiction I'll be all right: perhaps, as usual, I might start on the last two, which would be easier.

[201] I've been looking at three "science fiction" stories by John Taine. I read better stuff in The Boy's Own Paper at the age of nine, but it isn't their merits that interest me. They're all elementary displacements of golden age, fall & flood (earthquake in him) archetypes. Wonder if all science fiction is.

[202] Let's look at the existential projections of the modes in AC, which of course are different from those of the mythoi. If that of irony, which is also a mythos, is existentialism itself, then relativity, or rather relativism, the sense of any construct being potentially as good as any other, is part of it. Romance, at the point of epiphany, which is also the point of identity, sees the cycle from above, with its essential principle, interpenetration or the universal centre, as a reflection of that identity. Irony sees the cycle from below, with no fixed identity, & so sees it purely as a cycle, or as a straight-line void. This is the sparagmos vision, of course. I'd thought of Hawthorne, Melville & Morris as the romance-writers I was interested in, but I should see Samuel Butler's universal-family speculations[135] as a glimpse of interpenetration.

[203] Romance is irony inside out: Blake's Deism, or the *presented* design, becoming the created design. The "Deist" says, not all religions are one, but its opposite: all religions are equally true. Everything possible to be believed is an image of truth is the motto of my present job. I've said in my *1984* review[136] that lying weakens the will, because truth is not a virtue but the sign of a healthily functioning mind, & the weakening of will moves us nearer the mechanical or Robot existence. The sacrifice of truth to expediency (i.e. to some external will) is ironic: the sacrifice of presented to created truth is its genuine form. At the point of demonic epiphany we struggle for a network of causality and relationships (voids between the stars):[137] mathematic form.

[204] In the last two lectures, of course, the emphasis will fall on Utopianism (comic) & Arcadianism or the pastoral protest (romantic). The ironic is both the absorption of man into nature and the absorption

of individual into social will: tension resolved by exterminating the former. Tragedy sets up the antithesis of will; comedy overcomes it; romantic presents it as overcome.

[205] Symposium. The conspiratorial group reserving the upper room & dividing the body: embryo of the church emerging in E. Comedy is born in irony and moves toward romance. This do. What thou dost, do quickly.[138] Twelve form the embryonic community: the thirteenth joins the surrounding one. The dialectic is formed. Next night (winter) the wine is new and we eat the leviathan surround.

[206] There's a katabasis of irony, & I must work the stages out: symposium at the top & cannibalism at the bottom, for instance. At the bottom the single, dual & plural identity of comedy become solitude, pain, and stupefaction. The end of *1984* is also the end of the ironic religious vision: Nobodaddy, pure will & power with no motive behind him & no object in front of him, breaks & tortures & blindfolds & humiliates, & demands that we love him for it.

[207] I suppose one of the things that's bothering me is: are there epiphanic points at W & E, taking us into worlds of event & concept? Praxis. The great mystery of the heroic act that the poet can only watch and record. Theoria. The distant vision or Pisgah sight. The mystery of the act and of the scene. Perhaps those ∧ [Anticlimax] notes I collected that New Year's Day on St. Clair Avenue[139] were really about the E point of epiphany. Perhaps the W p. of e. [point of epiphany] is a sacramental world of imitative ritual: anyway, it has a lot to do with kairos, repeating the moment in time. From the Incarnation we go into the Pauline occasion-epistle. The note across the way [par. 205] about the *ultima cena*, on this theory, sounds W rather than S: the completing of the Presence. Yes: we could think of a W pt. of epiphany into a world of ritual based on analogy to myth. The E one is not strictly dream but the organizing or shaping power inherent in conscious thought. The W passage is Augenblick,[140] the moment of decision when art becomes significant or chosen act; the E is the moment of incarnate dialectic or recognition, when subjective idea & objective fact identify.

[208] Zamiatin's We:[141] demonic symbolism is anal, either full of shit like Dante, or unnaturally clean, as in this book. Incidentally, the

Nobodaddy point is made there too: the horrific state is descended from & the rebels are associated with the pastoral world & protest.

[209] Well, I think at least I have a cluster of things on the Western Gate to think about. I can't seem to read until I know what direction I'm reading in. That's not the same as knowing what to look for, which in itself is a closed deductive circle.

[210] What mainly emerged from my radio talk on *1984*[142] was: truth is less a virtue than a sign of a healthy functioning mind. Lying weakens the will & makes one like a machine, with no will of one's own, and instrumental to another's will. The link with the machine is of course modern, but the association of truth & liberty is of very long standing: links with the oratorical tradition. The Houyhnhnms abhor lying because they are free:[143] in the aristocratic code the lie direct is the deadliest of insults because the deadliest threat to social domination. The noble, unlike the base, can afford to tell the truth.

[211] In each mythos there seems to be a sequence of the integritas-consonantia-claritas kind,[144] which I suppose is simply the beginning, middle & end of any action at all. Irony, for instance, begins in the making of an individual pharmakos, proceeds to absorb him into a social or natural process, & ends by forcing him to surrender his identity. Comedy begins (this is quite important, I think) with the recognition of the ironic claritas as *absurd*. Thence it goes into the dialectic I've traced & ends with the recognition of identity. Romance starts here, with the hero recognized, and goes through interpenetration into existential identity. Tragedy begins here, with the fall of Satan or discovery of individuality, and works through the dialectic of the separating analogy to the epiphany of the marked individual, the point at which irony begins. The point of thematic concentration or dianoia is at the consonantia in the middle. I might call them the postulate, the education, and the discovery. In a sense all four begin with a contract: tragedy is the contract *par excellence*; irony begins with the second or Egyptian contract, the stage of bondage; comedy with the absurd contract or irrational law, & romance with the quest-contract & the destined saviour-hero.

[212] Everyman: a form that goes back to the stripping of Ishtar in the Sumerian underworld.[145] How much can be taken from one without

really taking anything from one? What is man's essence or identity? Not the sum of what he has done, as Everyman says. At least that doesn't feel right. Yet it isn't helpful to say that man is essentially what he is.

[213] I've been reading Rousseau's *Confessions* without much pleasure (that dreary paranoid whine is certainly an ancestor of Dostoievsky's *Notes from Underground*) and Diderot with considerably more. *Rameau's Nephew* is a dialogue in the Solomon-and-Saturn tradition,[146] one speaker Apollonian & the other, if not Dionysian, at least Lokian.[147] Damn it all, I wonder if I could do the Alexanders on prose forms and relevant reflections, starting with Milton and running through to the 19th c.

[214] Curious how in viciously authoritarian 18th c. France what we remember are radical writers, Voltaire, Rousseau, Diderot, & in liberal England the Tories, Swift, Johnson, Burke. Milton has no direct influence on France, more's the pity; it was the post-Miltonic England of Newton & Locke that influenced Voltaire, which leads to the paradox that Blake too is "Tory" in the sense of being violently opposed to the liberal ("Deist") tradition.

[215] Someone reading a foreign or unfamiliar technical language is grasping a grammatical structure without really knowing what it means. The centripetal verbal pattern does not have centrifugal resonance. Note that this resonance is a knowledge of essences or definitions as well as allusions. The latter is a secondary centripetal structure, the one the reviewer tries to pick up. This is a meditation on Diderot's "Encyclopaedia" article. French radicalism was encyclopaedic: Diderot begins with the dictionary as an abridged encyclopaedia: a dictionary is the most conspicuous product of 18th c. English Toryism.

[216] Another Diderot dialogue, *A Father & His Children*, is concerned with moral dilemmas: this is a prose form directly at the point of demonic epiphany, & the most powerful example of it in literature is Plato's *Euthyphro*. There's a difference between the primary social contract (excluding the paradisal or golden-age pre-contract) and the secondary moral contract, making bricks without straw. The second has no tragedy, only humiliation and absurdity, & its basis is the ritual-bound "humor."

[217] When I say in AC that animal imagery of the analogical cycle is

based on the choice of animal (deer in *Endymion*, rats in *The Waste Land*),[148] I imply a "humor" or character theory of nature (cypress melancholy, oak sanguine) which, like "poetic etymology," is superstition as fact and a structural principle in criticism.

[218] I wonder if things aren't beginning to take shape (again) around prose forms: I have the strongest drive to read in the anatomy tradition, I think. Unused bits from the old Manitoba article[149] like the Dryden passage. Also the Utopia, the educational vision (Castiglione), & the contract myth are all part of it. Perhaps the informing theme is the shape of the prose encyclopaedia. It includes the parody-romance themes of the marvellous journey & the kataplous,[150] as I've said, & the digression, which is an intellectual quest-parody. This is familiar: what's less so is the enormous importance of the sense of the influence of humors (Burton's melancholy), childhood experiences of an erotic or mythical kind (Rousseau, Proust) and of an odd "homunculus" image I haven't yet grasped in Diderot & Sterne. Something to do with the anti-hero theme: the microcosm seen as a bundle of responses to external influences.

[219] *Rameau's Nephew* is, as I said [par. 213], a Solomon & Saturn dialogue: one principle is the dialectic-building rational man, the Socrates; the other is the existential natural man. Both types are really act-dialogue people: one is a selective treatise-writer and the other is the fool, with a list toward the misanthrope (Lucian's Timon),[151] the emperor's-clothes child, & the Beckett ego-voice.

[220] The simplest scheme that occurs to me is: a) a paper on Utopia like the one I've done[152] b) a paper on contracts, including both the tragic & the ironic or Egyptian kind c) a paper on varieties of dialogue d) a paper on varieties of quest or parody-quest. Those seem to me to be E, W, S & N respectively, & to have points of contact with the four forms; but what points I don't know. Suppose they were: E novel, in its traditional comic form; W confession, because of the *initiation* & ritual (commandment) patterns in it; S anatomy & N romance? See the inside front cover, table 2: it fits the pp. 76–7 [par. 191] one all right.

[221] Plato: N Timaeus, NW Phaedrus, W Laws, SW Apology, S Euthyphro, S.E. Gorgias, E Symposium, NE Republic, N Phaedo. N is of course birth of god or definitive quest hero. NW is the second birth or

first epiphany: the drawing out of the water is an equivalent of losing or descending from paradise. W is the point that's been sticking me: the confession is the "all too human" form, the initiation that discovers contract & separating dialectic. SW is the second contract of bondage. S is the counsel of prudence, the sparagmos of ideas, the sense of moral dilemma. SE is escape by vision of the absurd, the Trophonius recovery of laughter.[153] E is the building of the physical house; NE the building of the spiritual one.

[222] Also I wonder if the Rcsm. [Romanticism] set[154] could box the same compass? W: conservative Rcsm. & the Rcsm. of confession, culminating for English with the Prelude; S: demonic Schopenhauerian & sadistic Rcsm; E revy. [revolutionary] Rcsm. (Byron, Shelley, Hugo); N oracular Rcsm, Keats, Blake, Novalis, maybe Nietzsche as a late form. That is, Confessional Rcsm; Demonic Rcsm; Revy. Rcsm; Oracular Rcsm. Again, you can't equate poets with these phases, only epiphanic points in their poetry, though Shelley's centre of gravity would be E & Beddoes' S. This scheme puts Wordsworth & Rousseau close together (Rousseau has a broader sweep NW & SW than the Prelude). The mother predominates in the W (Rousseau's C of L [Court of Love] set up & Wordsworth's Mother Nature); the sister in the S in the incest fantasies, the wife or mistress would logically be E & the daughter (or goddess) N. I think I'm on to something here, which is why I let myself blather.

[223] That clears up the Clevelands, & solves too the problem of the relation of the four forms of fiction to the four cardinal points of the episodic circle. The Whiddens are clear too, I think, but the Alexanders aren't, in the sense of knowing what to read & what to look for in it—I think they'll be prose from Milton to Morris all right. God, I'm a perverse bastard.

[224] Besides, I think they're going to be an expansion of the Daedalus paper,[155] concerned with contracts, Utopias, educational structures, pastoral myths, & cities of God. Maybe I shall look over Milton's prose & see what emerges. Where does Ruskin come in, if he does?

[225] Now that I have my eight books, or first four, associated with series of lectures, and therefore with *short* books & limited subjects, I could perhaps finish the lot of them. Something like the Mellons for V

[Mirage], the Weils for ⊥ [Ignoramus], the Giffords for ⊢ [Paradox], a series in my own honour, like the Couslands, at my retirement for ⌈ [Twilight].[156] Well, anyway, V reflections: in the kind of music I like there's endless repetition, without change, with very slight change, with only a key change. The "teleological," evolutionary, Darwinian affinities of this are obvious, & so is the subordinating of the actual musical "material" to the underlying rhythmical impetus. Again, what is implied by the conception "wrong note," which in modern music means only the note not corresponding to the one written down, but in Mozart or Schubert would be wrong in a musical context as well? Even in Hindemith or Shostakovitch there is a parody pattern of wrong notes. (The first part of this note, by the way, makes the Whiddens epicyclical, like the Page-Barbours[157] & the Masseys).

[226] I don't think my critical method is archetypal at all: I recognize the existence & importance of archetypes, but if I have a method, it would be better described as epiphanic. I look over a writer's work to see what shape its theme has, and then use the most revealing features of it to communicate that shape to the reader. As a method, it's a higher organization of commentary, because its basis is archetypal framework rather than allegory.

[227] Milton fits the circle thus, I think: W he has a conception of religious liberty based on a contract: the renunciation of temporal power to Caesar except when Caesar breaks the contract by claiming spiritual authority. E he has a conception of civil liberty that embraces revolutionary tradition. N he has a conception of Christian liberty based on the Biblical encyclopaedia. S he has a conception of domestic liberty based on (a) the humanist encyclopaedia (b) the Areopagitica sense of letting the Word circulate (though Areop. is really E).

[228] Simpler form of the circle: W is the primary or natural contract, S is the secondary Egyptian or social contract, the first tragic, the second ironic. E is the Utopian redemption from the social contract, the purging of the seven sins in Dante; N is the redemption from the natural contract, the Arcadian return to Eden. I've been trying to reverse W & S because the tragic hero is isolated from the community and the element of natural fate is so strong in irony, but I think this is right. It fits Lear better, & the natural gods of the Greeks. The fall of Adam into the wilderness is

tragic; the fall of Israel into Egypt ironic. The closing pages of my Utopia paper[158] do what all the Bamptons[159] don't quite do: elucidate the difference between comedy & romance. Speaking of Dante, the forza-froda distinction in the Inferno[160] (much clearer in Milton) establishes a similar difference (i.e. of the tragic & the ironic).

[229] W then is Blake's *Canaan*, the sacramental analogy (the interpreting of analogy as demonic analogy only was the one mistake I made in FS).[161] S is the latter; E the rebuilt city & N the promised land. (Note how the Megilloth[162] arrange themselves: Eccl. [Ecclesiastes] W (in spite of its anatomy form, it's the story of an old king living within the primary contract); Lam. [Lamentations] S; S of S [Song of Solomon] E, Ruth N. Esther is phony, so the symmetry is undisturbed). Why do I feel I must read *Emile* & not Euripides? I suppose superstition: the Alexanders should be prose & on the cycle, not a straight mythoi-circle which would make them epicyclical. I'm never quite sure of the difference between superstition, which deflects, and following my serendipitous nose, which usually points straight ahead, like the bird in Aristophanes.[163] At present it's pointing (or else my *a priori* superstitiousness is) to something prose, in the Milton > Swift > Rousseau > Burke > Arnold > Ruskin > Morris > Butler > Proust area. If the Great Eight[164] exist simultaneously, the Λ [Anticlimax] one doesn't *have* to precede the ʎ [Rencontre] one, if the Alexanders aren't Λ, & a straight mythoi job is logically prior to Cleveland, in fact it's ye nexte thynge.

[230] So let's decide: the big prose book this notebook started with is still a big book, the successor to FS & AC, and the Alexanders are something much shorter & simpler, in fact a mythoi chase. So let's get another notebook for them, & get them out of here. And I promised Kentucky to do something about the axis of speculation & the axis of concern.[165]

[231] By 1967 I shall have not finished the Third Book, in fact it's doubtful that I'll have begun it. If it's finished in 1977, when I'll be, if alive, 65, & anxious to have a fourth big job clear for my retirement, I'll be doing damn well. What I expect to have completed by 1967 are seven propaedeutic studies for it, for all my series are. I don't want it to be Coleridge's Logos-treatise, but it will be quite a book. I think its centre of gravity will be English prose from Milton to Ruskin & Morris, but a lot of

stuff I haven't considered—Plutarch's *Lives* & other works, Thucydides & Tacitus, the Bible as prose, besides all the contract > Utopia > educational treatise > dialogue clutter I've been talking about, will be there. The Rice & Utopia articles are still its only cores, but it takes off from the end of AC, just as AC took off from the end of FS.

[232] I've often said that criticism has to go beyond commentary, which is, if essential, also facile and doesn't build a structure. But I haven't said clearly that commentary is concerned primarily with what is displaced: vivid characterization & the like. Only structural poetics moves toward a *telos*.

[233] Milton's rule of charity is the only way of distinguishing belief from anxieties, the charter of freedom from the rationalization of bondage. It's also the only moral standard for literature, as well as the standard for education, or imgve. [imaginative] as distinct from social mythology.

[234] Part One: The Axis of Speculation.
Book One: (Luvah) The Circle of Mythoi.
Book Two: (Tharmas) The Information of the Mythoi.
Part Two: The Axis of Concern.
Book Three: (Urthona) The Structure of Verbal Education.
Book Four: (Urizen) The Limits of Verbal Expression.

[235] The principle of Book One is that the four great episodes of the encyclopaedic myth, creation, fall, redemption & apocalypse, *are also* the nodal points of the tragic, ironic, comic & romantic mythoi. I may not have tragedy & irony fully separated: perhaps the sacramental analogy is ironic, and illustrates the way that a pre-tension social contract makes a severe cadence to tragedy, as in the *Oresteia*. Analogy, after all, is the opposite of identity.

[236] Anyway, the scriptural encyclopaedia and its Druidic analogy[166] are the Book of Luvah; Tharmas is the philosophical study of the *dianoiai* of the four episodes: the *mythoi* as *dianoiai*. Causality, analogy, dialectic & interpenetration are the hunches.

[237] The *dianoiai* involve contracts & Utopias: the educational encyclo-

paedia is what emerges from them, based on *Cyropaedia, Republic, Courtier, Emile* & the like. It restates the circle of mythoi in terms of the concerned battle against the social analogical myth.

[238] What I don't want in II is the vulgar & facile equating of a whole philosophical structure with a mythos. Thus: Stoicism is tragic, Cynicism ironic, Epicureanism comic, Neo-Platonism romantic. What I do want is to locate the central conceptual analogies of the mythos. Thus Seneca shows real connections between Stoic philosophy & tragic form, but what I want to locate is some such conception as causality or natural law. I expect what I've been calling causality will turn out to be something more like *Dasein*, & that Heidegger will give me most of my clues to tragedy (some of it, such as the Sartre-Camus developments, will turn out to be ironic, just as tragedy itself does).

[239] For romance & irony I have, in AC, fictional *and thematic* forms as well as (mostly projected) conceptual analogies. Should I try to isolate distinctively thematic tragic & comic forms apart from the mimetic ones?

[240] With Don Quixote one distinguishes what he really believes in, which is apocalyptic, from what he thinks he believes in, which is quixotic. One is genuine & the other aggressive romance, one the genuine pastoral vision and the other the childish Walter-Mitty[167] fantasy. Much romance is aggressive, stories of invincible heroes; but the *dianoia* of romance in its genuine form is the higher identity in the mystical tradition.

[241] The Book of Luvah hasn't so far much to add to AC, but I think of it as comprising my old mythical encyclopaedia, which comes back into this notebook because the Alexanders have now become a straight series on Shakespearean tragedy. I want to do a lot of reading in Biblical & Classical myth for Luvah, and of course to reinforce my weak areas of tragic drama and fiction.

[242] The way it looks now, Urthona is the prose book properly speaking: educational because it shows literary experience deploying itself on the marches and boundaries, the detached prose consciousness following the old act > and > scene sequence, now Luvah & Tharmas. Strict literature, within the mythoi, and strict conceptual thinking, don't either

of them give the sense of *existential* profundity that you get in this Plato-Augustine (Dante)-Goethe-Rousseau-Nietzsche group. That's really where the inner secrets of the word-hoard are, and the Urizenic converse of Rabelais is the Bible.

[243] The theme of the whole book is a plan of the Tower of Babel, as it was before the confusion of tongues hit it. *Laborers of Babel.* Or even Milton's *Embers of Dead Tongues,*[168] the sense expanded to the general theme of the fertilizing of verbal process by verbal products.

[244] The deepest I have yet gone in this direction is the second WTC essay. If I bring it off, the Third Book will get completely away from the notion of commentary, or depending on the talents of greater men. It will also perhaps define a genuinely new verbal genre, the roots of which are in Spengler & Frazer. Frazer's roots go back to Macrobius & Varro, & so link with the anatomy tradition.

[245] I hope the Book of Luvah will solve such things as the chess-in-Bardo problem,[169] and that it will give some indication of what it feels like to live in a totally mythical universe, where a dragon is literally "the seeing one."[170] Note that I–IV is the progression from the mythical to the verbal universe, mythology to literature and what literature informs.

[246] The names of the Zoas don't really matter, but perhaps the axis of concern runs from Urizen to Urthona, not the other way. Thus Urizen, in the south, is the prose educational structure of the anatomy; IV then takes off from the mousike-techne distinction[171] and the circle of the arts. That would be the logical jumping-off point for a Fourth Book.

[247] I find immense difficulty in reading the *Iliad,* & have to get over it for personal as well as critical reasons. The age of childhood is the age of wrath, of aggressive rebelliousness that takes a conventional form. In my childhood I dreamed of the battles of red & blue toy soldiers, which I watched, directed, & determined victory for the red side. I also had dreams of a vast physical prowess I knew I didn't possess.

[248] So my resentment against the immorality of the Iliad is based partly on my own resentment at outgrowing my dreams of belligerence, which I didn't really outgrow but was forced to give up. I hate all those

gut-cut scenes; I'm a violent Trojan partisan; the apalling creatures they worship & their conceptions of an after-life horrify me; their social hierarchy outrages me; and so on. Give me the *Odyssey* every time, I say.

[249] But, of course, the *Iliad* is the world's definitive tragedy. Tragedy is pre-moral, as comedy & romance are post-moral; morality begins in and depends on the ironic vision. My natural attitude to literature is post-moral, comedy and romance-centered, starting with satire & ending with idyl. Hence I *need* tragedy, & must stop resenting the fact that everything interesting in the Iliad is a parenthesis, a hasty & abbreviated one because the poet wants to get back to his gut-cut.

[250] Tragedy shows man under natural law. The hero is not an individual: he's a species-man, the man nature has done her best work on. In Greek the gods exist to ratify this order of nature; hence the hero is sprung from the gods (it's simplest to read tragedy in post-Darwinian terms and translate).

[251] The social contract is ironic, or becomes so when tensions develop in it and the genuine individual appears. In itself the social contract, man helping to realize the one the gods & nature make, can be a serene full close to tragedy, as it is in the *Oresteia*.

[252] There's another tragic cadence connected with *doing* something, resisting the flux of nature & getting dissolved in it. If you kill somebody, that's something *done*, a magical dromenon, a deed of glory. If you get killed, you want to be buried, definitely planted somewhere in space with a grave as a marked achievement. (Of course you *can't* achieve anything: tragedy is a suspended illusion). You can't stand visible dissolution, or just being a wandering ghost like Hamlet's father, with no fixed abode in Hades (though he has one). The hero brings an identity down from romance he's terrified of losing: anything rather than not to be what he is. It's Job's "integrity."

[253] The gods are partisan in a way that seems wholly unjust: Hera & Athena hate the Trojans because they lost a beauty contest, & one judged by a mortal at that. Translating again: nature cares for the species, not the individual. To say, of course[,] that the gods are symbols of nature is not to say that they are personifications of natural forces or elements, though

they easily become so.* (Homer, by the way, probably did not know about the Judgement of Paris, but surely the Greeks read him in the light of it).

[254] We are reminded in the Iliad that although the gods seem to be cheering on the battle to the point of believing that the only good man is a dead man (which is sound Christian doctrine) they are, no less than the Christian god, losing their own sons in the struggle. The gods are absolutely essential to Greek tragedy: without the sense of an omnipotent divine aristocracy the vision would become purely ironic. It has even been suggested that tragedy can't survive in a religion like the Christian, where God's actions have to be explained away as somehow benevolent.

[255] Irony explores the tensions in the social contract: tragedy deals with heroes, that is, demigods in a social ether, with very limited social responsibilities and with nobody directly above them except the gods. "Prescribe us not our duties," says Goneril, and later: "the laws are mine, not thine," which is paranoid but within the tragic orbit.[172]

[256] In Euripides' *Heracles* the emphasis is thrown on Hera's activity as a perverse drive to madness within the soul. In Seneca's *Hercules Furens* the emphasis is on Hercules' return from the dead as a kind of portentous harrowing of hell that might bring with it the extermination of the gods. This emphasis is moving closer to irony, like Euripides' own *Alcestis*.

[257] Inexhaustible riches of wisdom in great philosophy & poetry, yet it is possible to be a great thinker or a great writer, an infinite source of wisdom, yet be not a wise man, even a positively foolish man. Wisdom in writing arises from the shaping of verbal patterns, the joy of realizing a shapeless potency of words. Wisdom in life arises from putting a shapeless potency of *experience* into proposed or hypothetical activity.

[258] Some are instinctively wise, but most have to depend, for what wisdom we have, on the sources of wisdom in the skill of writers, who

* Poseidon is a sea-god in Homer; Apollo is not yet a sun-god, but soon becomes one: Hera has no definite department of nature, but Juno became the air to later mythologists. The relation to nature is thus potential.

are often not wise. Wisdom is a quality in the consumer, not the producer: I'm a wiser man than Layton because I'm a critic.[173] Where shall wisdom be found? In the skills of the unwise.

[259] If I wanted to believe in reincarnation, I don't see why our ordinary perspective of time has to dominate it. Why couldn't one be reborn in the past, becoming in the future what he in another form has already been? That is, why should the past exist only as we know it? How do we know that it isn't existing in the present, & being reshaped? The past may be a purgatory & a foreshadowing paradise as well as an irremediably fixed hell.

[260] Following on a note in the blue book:[174] the eiron role, or making oneself small, is the foundation of all existence, not merely social courtesy.[175] I am a much better person to others than I am to myself: to myself I am a rather poor creature. What I am to myself tends in the direction of what in an omniscient mind would be the vision of justice. Ultimately I am nothing at all, which is what Buddhists mean by saying that things have no ego-substance. Immediately, I am a certain capacity for being remade, which is what I really want as distinct from what I think I want. As the latter, self-knowledge soaked in illusion, I would survive death only as a neurotic, whimpering, craving ghost, wanting to be "understood." The vision of others is also of course full of illusion, but it tends in the direction of what in an omniscient mind would be a vision of mercy. One remakes oneself, or tries to, for God's eyes alone: my social reputation is pure accident, like birth in the aristocracy. Still, here as elsewhere reality & illusion are turned inside out: the soul I am trying to save is more clearly revealed by what I seem to be to others than by what I wake up with in the morning. The instinct to make an obituary eulogistic is a sound one.

[261] Words are the only language of consciousness, and the art of words is the only art directly subject to the conflicts of consciousness. Anxieties can only express themselves verbally. They express themselves in two ways: formally, in clichés, and materially, in assaults on the structure. In paranoid writing, where the author is continually digressing to attack the Jews or his mother-in-law, we can see what we see in a different way in doggerel: that every structural achievement in writing is an ethical victory. The average sermon is full of digressions, because

parsons are occupationally anxious, anxieties being what the will substitutes for the grace of belief.

[262] Let's take a familiar example of the confronting of being with nothingness: I am standing in London on what the guidebook assures me was the very spot where something happened in 1150. The gap between my being & its nothingness is, essentially, time: the connection between them is essentially space. It's Newtonian space, which is why Newton called space the sensorium of deity,[176] following the Christian instinct to call Christ a real presence (space) rather than a real present (time).

[263] Beulah, or the Freudian unconscious, has two gates, the gates of birth & death. The gate of death is the dung-gate of nausea. Everything that nauseates us is a memento mori, an aspect of our own dead bodies. Death is not an enemy to be destroyed so much as the last crap: that is, the dead body is the last defecated stool. Just as the gate of death is the gate of nausea, the gate of birth is the gate of curiosity or exploration, the speleological imagination. Fiddling with the lock of this gate is a kind of fishing.

[264] The point of demonic epiphany turns up in every author who is religiously obsessed & complains that most men are not bad enough to be damned. Eliot on Baudelaire,[177] C.S. Lewis & Graham Greene, all are in Peer Gynt's position, preferring the dialectic of damnation to the button-molder & the returning cycle. *Jolly Corner* in James is pure p d e [point of demonic epiphany].

[265] I have never had the sort of experience the mystics talk about, never felt a revelation of reality through or beyond nature, never felt like Adam in Paradise, never felt, in direct experience, that the world is wholly other than it seems. I don't question the honesty, or even the factuality, of those who have recorded such experiences, but I have had to content myself with the blessing to those who have not seen & yet have believed—if one can attach the word "belief" to accepting statements as obviously true as the fact that I have seen New York. The nearest I have come to such experiences are glimpses of my own creative powers—Spengler in Edmonton and two nights with Blake—and these are moments or intervals of inspiration rather than vision. I'm not

sure that I want it unless I can have clarity about other things with it. What are all the miracles and divine visions of Bernard of Clairvaux to me when I know that he preached vehemently in favor of crusades? I had rather been inpercipient all my life than preach a crusade. And much as I admire the clarity of structure in the religious thought of Eliot or C.S. Lewis, I don't want it if it's inseparable from the controversial one-upsmanship of *After Strange Gods* or the 16th c. history. I feel I must have God on my own terms, because God on somebody else's terms is an idol.

[266] God of course would act on his own terms, but he would respect my own imaginative needs if he were a genuine Father, as I would my son's. The vision of nausea is very important, & the vision of moral nausea or conviction of sin or sickness unto death infinitely more so. But this kind of nausea is phony if it comes at second hand: something silly & masochistic & infinitely tedious, the very essence of tedium itself, which I want to kill in self-defence, because it wants to kill me.

[267] Every great work of art is profound, profundity being an essential part of the conception of greatness. Difficulty is the first stage of profundity: it represents the antithesis, the resistance, the otherness, in a work of art. Every work of art worth absorbing is difficult: the next step is the acceptance, the absorption, which is profundity. Difficulty is all that a teacher can deal with, & the job of a teacher of literature is the thankless one of showing that what looks easy really is difficult.

[268] The obviously difficult—Joyce, Blake's prophecies—is the more teachable: what seems easy—Blake's lyrics, Jane Austen, Dickens—is less teachable, & therefore (because it's another way of saying the same thing) the conviction of its difficulty is more strongly resisted.

[269] All men are distorted & crippled by their social function, by the hypertrophy that what they *do* forces on them. All women are too, whether their careers are those of nuns or housewives or tarts. The more socially acceptable the career, the less we notice this, but it's always there. Hence our dream of the complete or workless man, whom our aristocracies try to produce. The versatile man, who can do anything, and the entertainer or actor, who can pretend to be anything, are proximate dreams of the same kind.

[270] I've been asked to think about a university liberal-arts curriculum, & the central attaching idea at the moment seems to be the conception of the university as the *other half* of society. The 19th c. political thinkers, from Carlyle to Marx, were preoccupied with defining the society of producers ("workers"). In Huxley & Herbert Spencer this conception of primary society as producers led to an educational theory where subjects were either useful, geared to production, or ornamental & geared to leisure. Hence too the leisure or non-productive class as a dramatization of the other half. Martha & Mary; Cain & Abel. Adam tilling the ground & dreaming of Paradise. The monastic community with its division of labour & contemplation or study. And now a society where information is as important as production, & where the increase of information is so rapid that "retraining" is a constant necessity.

[271] So the old notion of four years of gentlemanly training in preparation for life during the mating season is on its way out. There's no longer that kind of race against time—the Spencer kind, I mean: how much can be squeezed into preparatory years? What's essential & what belongs to the fill-up-the-cracks stage. These questions are obsolescent. Herbert Spencer said: why learn the archaic superstitions of Greece & Rome when you could learn contemporary facts & ideas that would be useful? We say: why learn contemporary facts that will be archaic superstitions in ten years? Why try to "adjust" to a society that won't be there when you've adjusted to it? Educational Dagwoodism, trying to jump on a bus that's just vanished around the corner.[178]

[272] And now perhaps I can go back to Λ [Anticlimax], beginning with fiction reading, & gradually thinking of a big corpus of mythology, speculative *and* practical. Seems to me now that Luvah-Urthona, the context of literature and of the other arts, is a separate book, but it may fold in. λ [Rencontre] has always been a Luvah idea, & V [Mirage] an arts one. The tentative Λ title is "Criticism and Society." If Luvah were a separate book, the old epic dream that got squeezed out of AC & some of the blue-notebook[179] drafts could come into their own.

[273] At the moment what looms before me is a Λ [Anticlimax] book in which, first of all, I try to isolate what the whole subject is that literary criticism is part of. It's part of the conscious knowledge of what mythopoeia creates. As such, it's among other things the *theoria* of education.

[274] Part One of this book, the Book of Luvah, to some extent recapitulates AC by taking the *mythos* of *romance* as the key to all mythical structure. This incorporates the epic & the sentimental-romance speculations that got squeezed out of AC. From here one could go either into Urizen, speculative mythology in metaphysics and religion, by way of Dante & the church's thematic stasis of the Bible & the Druid analogy,[180] or (as I favor now) into the applied mythology of contracts & Utopias (Tharmas) by way of Rousseau, William Morris, & various second-twist prose forms, including those of St. Augustine.

[275] I like this scheme because the stone rejected from AC becomes the head of the next corner, just as the stuff I cut out of FS became the structure of AC. So far, the Book of Urthona is a chaos: perhaps a theory of education, perhaps a sketch of an aesthetic or unified field theory of all the arts, or that unregenerate part of my literary notions that goes under the general name of comminution, & which I've touched on only in some of the deepest passages in WTC.[181] In any case there ought to be something to be eventually squeezed out of it, to form the kernel of ʎ [Rencontre] & keep me alive.

[276] I start then, reading romance, especially naive romance, piling the epic on it, & gradually moving to sentimental romance. Rousseau & William Morris, especially the latter, are the points of transition I myself make from Luvah (myth informing literature through romance) to Tharmas (the quest theme as the political contract-Utopia myth), but Dante & St. Augustine will loom in the background as providing both that transition and the further one to Urizen. The Urizen part winds up in time and space speculations, such as Alexander's time-is-the-mind-of-space one,[182] and brings me to the essential informing myths of religion. Then, as I now think, Urthona is to this as Tharmas to Luvah, a practical application of the structure, this time to the learning process & a panorama of education (*not* a planned curriculum, of course). Or perhaps Urthona is simply the doctrine of interpenetration, the thematic aspect of romance, unless that's the conclusion of Urizen or the transition theme. Or maybe it's a three-fold structure, with no Urthona.

[277] Tharmas is not only contracts & Utopias; it's also the philosophy of history, & Hegel & Vico & the attempt to come to terms with Spengler, or at least with what Spengler did to me. I suppose I'll have to read

Collingwood[183] and add *those* chunks. It's in Tharmas where the 4k course & what I used to call the Locke pattern of reading[184] comes into its own.

[278] Luvah: the basis is probably Scott & Dickens, where the naive undisplaced romance pattern is fairly easy to extract from the sentimental one. There's a very suggestive one in [Sir Walter Scott's] *Peveril of the Peak*, if I could get hold of it; *GE* [*Great Expectations*] I think I have. And my Surtees[185] & Meredith stuff. Don't worry *too* much about the French & the Russians, though you'll need Flaubert's St. Anthony stuff. The thing is: can you start with medieval romance and work out something around the circle on page 76 [par. 191]? If not, the hell with it.

[279] The building designed to contain life, against the one designed to contain death. Browning's bishop; Blake's Pyramid; Yeats's soul & nun complex.[186] The city of peace is dead, the dead body of God. Mausoleums & most museums.

[280] Tr. [Transition] to phil. of history: I think the shape of tradition, like value, is always something that is just going to appear & never quite does. As for the cycle: the transition from "thus it appears to have been" to "thus it must be" is emotional, not logical, & if this is realized I imagine most of the Collingwood-Berlin stuff[187] falls to the ground.

[281] The Urthona chapter should include a good deal of what can only be called ethics: the interpenetrating of moral & aesthetic standards; my points about a mean between sincerity & hypocrisy where we are really talking *hypothetically*, and the *eiron* business of "making oneself small" & its significance. Some of this is in the blue book.[188]

[282] I musn't let my ∧ [Anticlimax] fantasies affect the actual shape of the book: possibly the Urizenic part of it, the speculative construct, is precisely what will get squeezed out. The Luvah part will be a gigantic romance construct.

[283] The total subject of which literary crsm. [criticism] forms part is not literature, there being no such subject apart from criticism. Its total subject expands from the theory of literature into the theory of myth, myth being the language of concern. As such it's really the theory of

verbal information. If the world is divided into secondary and primary qualities, the latter is mathematical in language: attempts of words to inform this world give us the imaginary, or spiritual-substance, world, the higher potentially visible world as distinct from the imgve. [imaginative] or created world. I wonder if "science" is really the criticism of mathematics?

[284] Rcsm. [Romanticism], I've said, brought in the conception of the *serious* writer, the writer committed to doing something more than finding his public & pleasing it. Not a new thing, but a new emphasis on it. This was another aspect of the revival of the mythopoeic, the story of peculiar seriousness in the centre of stories. Shelley was a serious writer; Byron serious by accident; Scott not serious.

[285] The autonomy of art & scholarship over the engrossing initiatory or anxious myth *is* spiritual authority, the engrossing governor. Obvious but essential link.

[286] Without the speculative myth, then, the book has three parts: The key, a romance literary construct; the lock, social mythology; the turning of the key, the theory of education. This last is what transforms the socially given, the contract, into the socially created, the Utopia. Science transforms the brutally given, the empirical fact, into the rationally understood, the marriage of nature & reason. Perhaps art is the marriage of gods and imagination. Perhaps faith is not only existential but is always & necessarily projected, hence it must die to be reborn as imagination. This took place for Xy with Blake. One starts as an eiron, making oneself small in front of the oracular given, and ends having swallowed the just state, which is the condition of wisdom.

[287] Marshall [McLuhan] says everything we do today is a potential item in a computer information file: cf. archaeology, & some history, which shows so obviously an apocalyptic perspective on the past. My old point about detective stories illuminating routine with knowledge, & the dystopia with its conception of a *demonic* last judgement, or life without privacy.

[288] Yes, it seems obvious at present that the Third Book is about praxis and the question of theoria or speculative myth has to be held over for a

fourth one. As I can hardly get to it much before I retire, it may be a foreshortened ⊥ [Ignoramus] project. One element in it is something squeezed out of FS that's haunted me ever since: the identification of the Neoplatonic-Dionysus-Erigena-Eckhart-Joachim-Cusa and later visionary traditions.

[289] Huizinga's book, *Homo Ludens*, doesn't distinguish contest play, like a game of tennis, from construct play: only the latter (except for some kinds of argumentative rhetoric) belongs in lit. csm. [literary criticism]. The opposite of play is (a) seriousness (b) work. This distinction has to do with the form-content one. Suppose I'm asked to give a Convocation address: I want to say something "serious" people will remember, & so I "work" at the speech. But the *form*, the whole symbolic set-up of a Convocation, is ceremonial play, a symbolic let's pretend. Chess is contest play, so chess in Bardo[189] is the repetition of agon, specifically the Oedipus agon or killing of the king.

[290] I sometimes think I am looking for the truth, in the sense of tremendous insights or intuitions that will illuminate the meaning of life—and of death. But of course I'm not: all I'm looking for is verbal formulations, to fit somewhere in some damn paper. Truisms are never true: the verbal expression of truth has to be sharply pointed to skewer an experience in the reader; but of course it doesn't directly communicate experience. Nor does it necessarily represent anything more than a potential one.

[291] The other day at the hymnal conference[190] I said that the basis of the impetus to produce hymns in Xy was the apocalyptic perspective. I think this is true: it isn't the sense of "another world," but of this world as open-ended, as opening up into the presence of God. Without that perspective, all hymns become either derivative or miserable.

[292] The Locke programme,[191] modified, and the ⅄ [Rencontre] set-up is the one involved in the Third Book. Victorian literature, apart from the prose of thought, including 19th c. fiction of all countries, is the primary thing.

[293] 19th c. too, at least for its roots, is the religious part of the argument: the nonconformist distinction between assent and conviction, and

Newman's parallel distinction between notional & real assent.[192] There is an ambiguity in the conception of faith that Newman dodges. The myth, down to Rcsm. [Romanticism], had two aspects, theoretical & practical. Theoretically, it was a structure of coherence, addressed to the reason or imagination; but accepted "on faith," because (a) it had no sense experience check (b) its major premises were simply given. This myth of coherence (theoria) was also a praxis, a programme of action. As such it's Pascal's wager, Vaihinger's conception of assumed fictions being the Kantian form of it.[193] Even *Grace Abounding* has a passage saying that Bunyan will wager on his structure of coherence even if it's horseshit.[194] Now, this program of action is the faith one is justified by: a man's real beliefs are what his actions show he believes. What he says he believes, or inwardly believes he believes, that is, his profession, is a symbol of belonging, a statement about the social institution he's attached to.

[294] In our day a myth may still be a programme of action, and is, but we demand a different quality from its theoria. We don't "believe in" myths any more: we don't accept authority beyond evidence with any real conviction (i.e. genuine connection with practical belief). It doesn't have to be "there" in time and space; the language of myth is now realized to be the language of presence, of the here and now.

[295] Regarding the literary status of such rhetorical works as those in the 4d course:[195] literature, being part (the central part) of the myth of concern, is profoundly impure. At the centre of literature is myth, which doesn't exist: around it are poetic, fictional, dramatic and rhetorical displacements of myth. Query: what relation has this essential but non-existent myth to the direct experience of literature?

[296] The religious displacement begins with the distinction of mechanism & organism. The oldest myths are organic: the world comes into existence through sexual activity and as a total seasonal cycle. This is really a female or mother-centered conception. Then along come Plato & the Hebrew Priest, father-centered, impressed by the "design" & "purpose" in nature, thinking of it as something made by a divine artificer. This creates God in the image of conscious, detached, subjective, aggressive man: it places him up in the sky, the abode of order; it makes the human soul female & submissive. What we do now is not, like Graves, to

go back to mamma, but to realize that the conception of incarnation has superseded the notion of creation, beginning as it did with kenosis.

[297] Politically, this distinction takes the form of the Burke inductive involvement followed by the deductive *a priori* contract conception of society as a thing made. Symbolically, it's swimming, first diving into a world of total involvement where the medium is the message, where communication is a total environment & consequently nothing is being communicated, nothing intelligible being said by A to B, but only an ambiance of noise & news. The next step is to get one's head, the place where one breathes & sees & hears & thinks, into its proper place. The world of total involvement is not our world: one has to be detached & withdrawn, not removed to another world, but using an alien element to keep you afloat in a higher one.

[298] Product, machine, creator, detached consciousness, being, are interrelated ideas; process, organism, participator, engaged consciousness, becoming, are also.

[299] The myth of the devil. Groups of people in an insurgent or revolutionary situation *must* create a myth of the enemy. This is the primary sense in which Sorel[196] uses the word myth. Communists must have some variant of a silk-hatted capitalist; Nazis a Jew; Protestant 17th c. England a skulking Jesuit; Elizabethan drama a Machiavellian. I notice how my students must have a "power structure" to buck, how faculty representation must have cigar-chewing businessmen on the board. This dialectical creation of a caricature is a tremendously important social force, and assertions that it doesn't exist have no effect on it.

[300] The devil is the father of lies, and the myth of the devil is what makes the big lie possible. The original devil was Eros-Dionysus, the erotic god with the exalted horn. The witch was the devil's dam. I suppose this myth is what Jung means by a shadow, something we have to embrace to outgrow.

[301] For the Third Book move (b) from Aristotle to Plato and (a) from the *Poetics* to the same conceptions recurring in the Ethics & Politics.

[302] The myth of the devil is ultimately the myth of the rejected projec-

tion. During the father-making-the-world phase the devil was Eros-Dionysus, & his dam the white goddess. I can't buy Margaret Murray's thesis[197] that the horned-god cult actually existed, but that obscene parodies of Christian rituals could be extracted by torture in an obscene parody of psychotherapy is obvious enough. The false devil is the buried Orc, the pharmakos victim of the social anxiety-structure; the genuine devil is the prince of this world, & is usually identified with God.

[303] I have been writing about the devil-myth ever since my undergraduate days: if I could establish its opposite, the myth of God, which is a myth of identity, I'd have cracked a tough nut.

[304] I wonder if I can really exclude metaphysical displacements from the Third Book. Surely I need some of this essential & primary displacement. I start, after all, with the symbolic or schematic universe. This schematic universe is not the objective world, but a mythical analogy of it. Still, attempts to fit it to the objective world have been constant & generally accepted before our own time. The most important conceptions seem to me to be:

a) Analogy, especially the Thomistic *analogia entis*.[198] I've been fascinated by this ever since my "general note" to FS.[199]

b) Coincidence of contraries, the doctrine of identity as manifested through the appearance of opposites: the Cusa-Bruno movement in the Renaissance and its Romantic revival.

c) The Augustinian doctrine of time as part of the fall: this develops the cyclical & dialectic (analogy of evolution) views of chronos & kairos.

d) A similar doctrine of space, which develops first the alienated space without direction, & second a presence or substantial space subsumed in the conception "universe." I don't of course know what the hell I'm talking about at this stage: I'm just working on a hunch. Luvah: The Vision of Plenitude. Urizen: The Language of Analogy. Tharmas: The Informing of Action. Urthona: Creation and Recreation.

[305] Luvah stresses the encyclopaedic, or universe-making, tendency in the arts. Not only literature: paleolithic caves, medieval cathedrals, & so on. Urizen deals specifically with the analogical encyclopaedia in discursive writing & thought: that way I don't get out of my depth going beyond the critical area. The Thomist doctrine of analogy[200] is central;

then the breakdown: Renaissance memory systems, Leibnitz, occult tendencies starting in Romanticism. Curious how women recur: Blavatsky, even reputable scholars like Yates and Levy: the old mother-womb cave keeps recurring.[201]

[306] What this leads to, whether it closes Urizen or opens Tharmas, is the stuff I have now on open & closed mythologies, and the separation of the existential from the objective vision. This leads directly to the Blakean finale of the unborn universe taking over the objective one, via the metamorphosis of time-space experience. On the way, of course, we get the contract-Utopia displacement of the containing time-myth, with the encyclopaedic vision of education appearing in the middle.

[307] The Bible says that the wisdom that dwells with prudence finds out the knowledge of witty inventions [Proverbs 8:12]. Depends on the translation of prudence: the wisdom that dwells with professional caution never finds out anything about anything.

[308] Dante is in II, Ruskin & St. Augustine in III, Jung in II, Bruno in II, Vico in III: I think I'm getting this clearer.

[309] In some way that I haven't begun to figure out yet, the book falls into two parts: the structure of myth & the function of myth. Each in turn has two parts: structure divides into the imgve [imaginative]-sensational & the conceptual aspects of myth. Function divides into the two manifesting aspects of the informing of social & of personal action.

[310] The Urizen chapter can be worked out if I stick to the relation between the discursive & poetic mythologies, to the writers who are literary philosophers (from Plato to Sartre), & to the philosophic influences in literary works (e.g. Bruno & Vico in Joyce). Seems to me that there's a dialectic & cyclical pattern in the discursive encyclopaedia too. The dialectic is formed by the antithesis of being (itself formed by *analogia entis*)[202] and not-being or the void. The cycle is formed by the coincidentia oppositorum, unity manifested as antithesis.

[311] The second half then deals with the informing of social action & the informing of personal action. Education is the transition, & the Urthona chapter deals with existential & religious paradoxes.

[312] The Luvah book outlines the symbolic universe, & the other three develop from this like the other three quartets from *Burnt Norton*. Urizen would, I should think, begin with the Summa form, the systematic (i.e. encyclopaedic) theological form that begins "Of God," runs through the Father, Son, Spirit, Creation & so on to Last Judgement—in short, the encyclopaedic Biblical myth in conceptual terms. From the Summa form the other conceptual mythical forms have descended: most contemporary ones start with the Fall, transposed to a butterslide or isn't-it-awful key.

[313] Cosmology is the process of assimilating science into a mythology. It's always temporary, because it's always wrong—that is, it's full of fictions. The use of mythical analogies to scientific principles (evolution, relativity, entropy, indeterminacy) is cosmological. See what comes out of Teilhard de Chardin.

[314] I think the Third Book will be an interesting & important book at the very least, because I have the material for such a book already in my mind. But if I can pull off the book I hope to write it'll be a colossal *tour de force*.

[315] What I want to do first is outline *the* structure of myth, in the form of a symbolic universe. Poetry assimilates nature through analogy & identity, & myth develops through assimilation. There's a dialectic principle derived from desire, but otherwise myths just keep eating other myths.

[316] I think I start with those two wonderful books of Gertrude Levy's: she's really one of the wise women. (And why so many women? Maud Bodkin, Jessie Weston, Gertrude Levy, Helen Flanders Dunbar, Madame Blavatsky, Frances Yates, Enid Welsford, Jane Harrison, Bertha Philpotts [Phillpotts], Ruth Benedict: whatever the level of scholarship, a woman's book seems to meet me wherever I turn).[203] Then the Jung things & Frobenius, & Frazer on Apollodorus & the Cambridge people on the Greeks.[204] Mircea Eliade's Comparative Religion & his Forgerons et Alchemistes.[205]

[317] I notice in *The Gate of Horn* a complex of underground cave with labyrinth: womb-tomb of birth, death, & rebirth, & what she calls "con-

ditional entry," symbolized by a meander (course of river also), a maze, or spiral.[206] The cave-tomb evolves into the pyramid & ziggurat pattern of a mountain-temple on top of a cave, where the risen god breaks through the top.[207] Ziggurats are seven-storey mountains. The things that keep recurring (apart from Dante, which she's aware of) are *The Tempest* ("forthrights & meanders")[208] & Blake's *Milton*, with its vortex in which the maze is formed by the spheres of the planets (as in Satan's journey in P.L. [*Paradise Lost*]).

[318] The fact that there is no dialectic or power of distinction in mythical thinking is something I have to face as a principle. It explains a great deal of fuzzy analogy-thinking, as in Bayley's *Lost Language of Symbolism*,[209] which degenerates into playing around with resemblances in words (the thing is that there probably isn't a universal language, whereas there could be a universal language of myth). There's no doubt a feminine link here: ideas indefinitely extending themselves by analogy. "Stubborn" facts & "hard & fast" distinctions are male metaphors.

[319] In *Milton* the vortex, the plow, & the red clay imagery all go back (according to Levy)[210] to Paleolithic patterns.

[320] Iconoclasm, whether Semitic or Protestant, goes with the total projecting of creative power away from man towards God. But there are advantages in setting up a dialectic structure in the mind & secularizing imagery: after all, all the things the butterslide people say started with Bacon or Ramus or Luther were there at least since Augustine.

[321] Well, anyway, as the chthonic cult rose into the air the seasonal cycle was assimilated to the solar one. But the solar one marks time more precisely, hence the rise of the prestige of measurement. As the king becomes the Sun King, the conceptual analogy of order & justice appears beside the image: what the king does must exemplify the time-order of the sun, & justice becomes the outward bound or circumference of the sun's energy (cf. the medieval fortiter et justus topos). Here's an example of the image-concept analogy. Levy refers to Hocart's book on kingship.[211]

[322] Incidentally, Levy speaks explicitly of the primitive identification of the road travelled with the body of both God and traveller.[212] I must

turn to the smaller jobs & see what comes out of them: I have greatest hopes of the Romanticism book, which I should like to expand with a chapter on Wordsworth's Prelude before the Beddoes & a rewritten commentary on Blake's *Milton* at the end.[213] This should make it possible to outline the whole cycle & not just the East side of it. Well, I could cut the Wordsworth, but the *Milton* idea does attract me.

[323] Strindberg calls his "Dream Play" a play where things happen arbitrarily as they do in dreams. That's balls: what has happened is a shift from projected to archetypal causation, as I say in a footnote about Poe's *Gold Bug* in AC [362]. This is a point I might use for Dickens.[214]

[324] Identity in the third book begins with the projected identity of the mythical figure (sun-god, etc.), and ends with the recovered identity through education to religion. Thus some element of the soul's quest gets into the narrative.

[325] The problem of *ethics* becomes more complicated with an open mythology. In a closed one it was assumed that conscience was equipped to tell one the right thing to do. Well, it soon became obvious that conscience itself was motivated by compulsions. So everybody jumped to the conclusion that ambiguity & relativism were the answers. But the thing is that one has to think of God, through the conscience or whatever it is, functioning as a literary artist, seeing a possible ironic pattern, a possible heroic pattern, a possible sentimental-romantic pattern (which he doesn't reject out of hand because he's a genuine critic), and so on. Jesus doesn't promise a Comforter to tell us the one right thing to do: his Spirit thinks the way he does, in parables.

[326] I know nothing about this, but it seems to me that contemplative mysticism is akin to mathematics, not to existential concern. Also that mathematics affords the only clue to what's left of the order & purpose that's out there. Pascal recognized the gulf, but his mathematical gift may have provided the bridge across it. Newton, of course, & Einstein.

[327] I probably have this in [par. 129]: the literary basis of Zen appears to be an eiron-alazon dialogue where the alazon is an earnest seeker after truth & the eiron tells him that there's no goal, no quest, no end. Keats, maybe. The serious "put-on."

[328] It's beginning to look as though the book on practical criticism I foresaw in the Preface to the Anatomy is shaping up after all, in a form indicated by the way my graduate course is taking shape. The two Western myth-constructs, expanded by the Greek one & by such studies as Miss Levy's,[215] & my speculations over the last few pages. I have a much more unified view of Shakespeare than before, as well as a better grasp of the Romantics. I think I could bring it off, & thereby crystallize the Luvah part of the Third (or Fourth, except that this is really the other half of AC) Book into something more manageable.

[329] Also I think my present impulse to add an essay on Blake's *Milton* to the Romantic book [see par. 322] is really connected with the above, because that poem, along with P.R. [*Paradise Regained*] & *The Tempest*, seem to be turning points in the whole structure.[216] The historical survey mentioned & ridiculed in the blue book[217] is now something I really have to do, in sketch form, for HBW [Harcourt, Brace and World].[218] Weak spots: Wordsworth, Tennyson, Browning, Lawrence, Conrad, Melville, Faulkner . . .

[330] If I'm going to work up a course in Theory of Drama[219] one of the by-products ought to be some reconsideration of music. The imminent collapse of the old chromatic-scale base, which has been the foundation of Western music since "early lowing" or plain chant days, raises tremendous theoretical questions that I'm not competent to solve as such, though I'd like to get at least a line on it that would connect with the rest of my world-picture.

[331] In traditional music I can see patterns all right: the way that the Romantic emphasis on organism and genetic metaphors, for example, appears in Beethoven's variation forms & germinal developments of themes.

[332] I wonder if I could revert to the original FS idea of 100 sections instead of chapters.

[333] Tactical directive: in beginning to plan a major work like the third book, *don't eliminate anything. Never* assume that some area of your speculations can't be included & has to be left over for another book. Things may get eliminated in the very last stage of preparing a book for publication, as an alleged "epic" chapter did from AC, but *never, never,*

exclude anything when thinking about the book. It was strenuous having to cut down from an encyclopaedia, but if the encyclopaedia hadn't been there FS would never have existed. That of course doesn't apply to single essays or short books made out of them, or public lectures on a definite theme; but major works are encyclopaedic & anatomic: everything I know must go into them—eye of bat & tongue of dog. It follows I suppose that all my major books are the same book with different centres of gravity: interpenetrating universes. Give me a place to stand, and I will include the world.[220] In FS I was standing in Blake's *Milton;* in AC I was standing in *The Tempest;* the only other place that I can stand that I know of is *P.R.* [*Paradise Regained*].

[334] All my life I have been resisting the demands of deductive verbal systems. First there was mother's Protestant Bibliolatry, demanding that I deduce everything from the Bible, as Canadian Methodism understood the Bible. Then there was Catholicism, demanding that everything should be deduced from that Wonderful Synthesis of everything the Church taught & was ever going to teach, even if it taught some damn fool thing like Papal Infallibility. Then there was Marxism, proving conclusively that nothing could be done about what was wrong with the world except what followed deductively from the principles of Marx. Freud was much less of a bother, but he did bother, and now there are close to a billion Chinese screaming their guts loose about the thoughts of Chairman Mao. In resisting these I don't feel that I'm necessarily defending or rationalizing bourgeois, capitalist or liberal-humanist values. I know the Marxists say that I can't have any ideas that don't ultimately rationalize my social context, but I know better. I want of course to be an important thinker in my own right, but that isn't all of it.

[335] Briefly, I do best by standing outside all these systems, including Protestantism, because by doing so I can chop a few holes in verbal systemization that I can see through & breathe through. I do want to try to understand the hold that such systems have on people, & the extent to which it's demanded of all thinkers that they keep their thoughts in verbal conformity with the Declaration of Independence or the Koran or whatever the hell it is. I have two leads. One is my structure of mythology point, and the distinction of closed-deductive & open-heuristic myth. The other is the point that came out of the end of the Keats paper: the community is based on (verbal) communication, which in turn is based

on communion, with God or the Ter-ewth[221] or, more frequently, the communion of saints.[222] (Notice how often the Master is the third of a line: Moses-Elijah-Jesus; Moses-Jesus-Mohammed; Marx-Lenin-Stalin or Mao, and, for me, I suppose, Shakespeare-Milton-Blake). What I want is the right to attempt a direct communion of my own, and the bourgeois liberal set-up I'm in, especially being in Canada & not in the U.S., is loose enough to let me do that.

[336] Graves says nothing prickles the hair in poetry except the white goddess. That's his mamma fixation. Everybody has a fixation. Mine has to do with meander-and-descent patterns. For years in my childhood I wanted to dig a cave & be the head of a society in it—this was before I read Tom Sawyer. All the things in literature that haunt me most have to do with katabasis. The movie that hit me hardest as a child was the Lon Chaney Phantom of the Opera. My main points of reference in literature are such things as The Tempest, P.R. [*Paradise Regained*], *Milton*, the Ancient Mariner, Alice in Wonderland, the Waste Land—every damn one a meander-&-katabasis work. I should have kept the only book Vera kept, *The Sleepy King*.[223]

[337] I know that the above note has a great deal to do with its predecessors. Similarly, ever since I understood the distinction between introvert & extrovert I realized that I was strongly introverted. Then I read a Pelican on mysticism by some vague soul who'd been talking to a doctor who said there was no such distinction, that introverts were just lazy & selfish people who didn't or couldn't live up to their obligations. This strikes me as a quite logical totalitarian view: it accounts for the pronounced dislike of introverts in books by educators, and for some of the frenzied energy of the closed-myth people. Also for the introvert's own self-distrust and feelings of inadequacy. Because, of course, he *is* lazy & selfish & unwilling to cope with his obligations. I am, anyway. On the other hand, there are all the look-within metaphors of religion. Now, I feel that extroversion is considerably more even than three-fourths of life, as Arnold said of conduct:[224] it's more like seven-eights. But there does have to be some residual or saving remnant of introversion, some sense of communion identity with something that isn't society. Call it nature or God, or, as I say in the Keats paper, it's important that different people should call it different things.[225] It's built on the introversion of the child, the retreat into the world made for his benefit.

[338] And I'm not so far from Graves after all, because of course the descent is always into mamma's cunt, which is what the Paleolithic caves represented, I suppose, with *their* meander-and-descent patterns. Extroversion has to do with striving onward & upward, trying to get through the wilderness & following the star, projecting everything on a father sky-God revealed through Papa Moses or Mohammed or Marx or Mao. So in the Middle Ages the introverted descent had to be blackened into an inferno. Such movements have a strongly anti-sexual bias (they're even anti-narcotic). At present there's a strong katabatic tendency in American civilization—the Freudian proletariat, the sexual obsessions of literature, the television vortex-tube, the weak, divided, self-distrusting intelligentsia. Hence it's produced me.

[339] I suppose Christianity belongs primarily to the onward and upward group. Its founder, apparently, was a homosexual with a beloved disciple and a mother fixation so intense that he even insisted that his mother was a virgin. Or somebody did. His point of introversion, the thing he kept dropping out of society to commune with, was his father, who of course couldn't possibly have had an earthly or incarnate form. Most of the points of retreat for pagan prophets were maternal—Diotima & Egeria[226] & the Athene & Venus of the epics.

[340] What I want to look into has a lot to do—it has a hell of a lot to do—with the issue raised in the third Alexander lecture. The "ecstatic" society holds loyalty tragically, by the two forms given in Carlyle: the extrinsic symbol, or the flag, & the intrinsic symbol, or the personality. The comic ecstatic society is a symposium, held by a verbal deductive pattern: the sacred book or the thoughts of Chairman Mao. In the tragic society the isolated figures are significant: the coward, the traitor, the hypocrite, the philosopher. In the comic society they are the same types in a different context: the parasite, the heretic, the comic hypocrite, the introvert. Cf. Jaques in AYL [*As You Like It*]. So I'm still revolving around the theory of comedy.

[341] Man, then, is born into a social contract, which in more highly developed societies always takes the form of a myth of concern. Adherence to the contract means deducing one's thought from that myth. Hence a verbal structure of concern develops an immense body of religious, philosophical, political thought which is really, in its form, com-

mentary, or criticism of the myth. Notice the enthusiasm with which, for instance, Coleridge insists that everything he thinks is deducible from the Christian myth. It is a fearful thing to be a genuine heretic, making a choice (*αἵρεσις*) of one's own road. Lonesome road with frightful fiend behind. One remark in AC which no one has noticed was the one about the intensity with which society demands the retention of verbal formulas—creeds, hymns, proverbs, manifestoes—and the prominence that this gives to what is essentially a critical activity. It was based partly on the first chapter of some book by Berdyaev that talks about the difficulty of the philosopher who just wants to philosophize, as against society's intense desire that he rationalize their myths.[227] There isn't perhaps anything very new here, except for the connecting of the verbalized myth of concern with the social contract, but I think some things are tying together.

[342] The next step takes me into a very dark & perilous cave indeed. One of the things that literature is all about is the relation of ordinary life, a current moving toward death, with whatever it is that begins with death. I know how violent the prejudices are on this subject, pro & con, but what the imagination, as distinct from rationalized commentary on traditional myth, says on the subject must be looked into. One lead is Yeats's remark that dreams are the current of the dead moving through us, the opposite way.[228] And my "point of ritual death" is really a point where the hero gets renewed strength from contact with the world of death. Well, it looks as though I hadn't yet thought enough about this to formulate anything new: I thought the context would help, but it doesn't. The point of introversion is perhaps always the world of the dead, disguised traditionally as gods, ghosts or what have you. Being is a life-death complex: I don't mean that the dead are still alive: I mean that to have been is a part of being. That which is to be is not part of being, but that which was is. It's the other half, like the world of anti-matter in physics, where entropy goes into reverse. God is dead; therefore God exists.

[343] I imagine that the third book will be heavily indebted to Vico, as heavily as an author can be who, like necessity, knows no law. I know of no other thinker who is as close to thinking of the entire structure of concern as a poetic myth. A much vaguer synthesis, also suggested by Vico, takes shape in the background, of an encyclopaedic spatializing of knowledge. The bases for this are Curtius' study of topoi, particularly

their literal sense as "places," the book of Frances Yates on the arts of memory and the idea of a cave-theatre holding all the ghosts of imagination like the one in PU [*Prometheus Unbound*], and the two books of Gertrude Levy on the early developments of meander & descent symbolism.[229] Compare Vico's "mental dictionary," apparently a table of the mythical constructs underlying language.[230]

[344] And so I get back to the type of speculation that begins this book. The dead is the unalterable: whatever reshapes the past performs an act of resurrection. There are two forms of reshaping: the tyrannical, selective or closed form, Orwell's controlling of the past by the present & hence the future by the past, and the free or open form. The first is argumentative & dialectic; the second is imaginative, & permits the dream to awaken. Maybe I should have put this into the Shelley essay,[231] where I more or less passed over the conception of a cave of myths, or encyclopaedic memory theatre. The point is—or one point is—that the world of the dead is also the world of the unborn. It's the cave-womb we emerge from, & knowledge in this world is an anamnesis of the cave of myths or memory theatre. Note too that there is no *time* in the memory theatre: it's a spatialization of knowledge. Or perhaps it's a world where time goes backward, toward its cause & not away from it.

[345] Correlation of noble birth & the freedom to be an original artist, in the sense anyway of being unconventional. Some very unusual writing in the music of Della Ciaja,[232] who I see is a Cavaliere, & one thinks of Gesualdo,[233] along with Byron in literature (not a good example technically, of course).

[346] The patent absurdity of a closed deductive myth doesn't injure its effectiveness: Marx's theory of surplus value, the pursuit of happiness, transubstantiation, etc. Query: does myth, in its role of imposing a convention and an intellectual handicap, *have* to be absurd?

[347] I have often asked myself what it is in Marxism that I find so irrelevant to my own interests. The core of the answer is in the total inability of Marxists to incorporate the tradition of literature, or to show any correlation whatever between literary centrality and political centrality. They talk about using drama for their purposes, but before Chekhov (and even he's a doubtful case) there is only one play, by Lope

de Vega[234]—a remarkable play, it's true, but still a fluke. Literature is all about something totally different.

[348] Marx himself was undoubtedly a great writer in the anatomic tradition: he had the satirist's truculence, excremental imagery, & inability to finish books. (This aspect of the ironic mythos is of course the counterpart of the endless form of romance). If Norman Brown's book[235] had been obsessed by Marx instead of Freud, & he had added Marx to his studies of Luther & Swift, he'd have written an even more remarkable book.

[349] The point is that literary criticism has to develop canons for—not judging, but—incorporating Marx, Freud, Luther, Paul, Jesus, instead of allowing determinists to make them a standard for critical categories.

[350] I've suggested several times that poets are instinctively reactionary, & revolutionary only as one form of reaction. The political perversity of our best writers—Yeats, Eliot, Lawrence—is not wholly explicable (a) on this basis (b) as bourgeois rationalizing—the Marxist answer (c) on my theory of the necessary absurdity of the containing form, though this is closest. I wonder how far back the regressive tendency of poets goes: Milton to the Renaissance Reformation of the early 16th c., Dante to the Dark Age wanderer, etc.?

[351] Marx evidently revolved around the Prometheus myth: images of incubus & vampires (= eagle) abound, & he is said to have reread Aeschylus every year.[236]

[352] The perversity of writers—Dante expounding hell with such relish, Shakespeare & the silly slaves of the sword, modern ferocious ironists, & the like—it's obvious that the "wounded surgeon" of that snarling part of *East Coker* [pt. 4] is the poet, not Christ. Hence we need a moral standard for relativizing poetry even though we can't accept any writer as a norm.

[353] Michelet, according to Wilson, said that history was the record of the struggle of man and nature, spirit and matter, liberty & fatality.[237] This implies that there is a passive principle represented by nature. I'd include the past in that: the past, the world of the dead, is also passive, &

culture includes the speaking of the open-sesame formulas that raise the dead, that make the valley of dry bones [Ezekiel 37] live. Marxism is a technique of controlling the future, but it can't really raise the past. At the same time the past can't be raised without its help: it does something—much—to bring the inarticulate & exploited to life. But that's not what I'm groping for: I don't know what I'm talking about.

[354] I've come back from the Montreal fair[238] with two ideas: one a possible title for the Third Book: "The Critical Path." The other is: instead of repeating a large section of the Anatomy argument for the Luvah section, couldn't I take care of some of that by writing the book in the fullest quest or labyrinth form? By "fullest" I mean the quality that Lord ascribes to Homer in *The Singer of Tales*,[239] and that I used to—in fact still do in some measure—ascribe to the symbolism of Xy compared to other religions.

[355] This concept of "fullest" takes me back to the old plenitude-vacancy aspect of my argument, where I distinguished the encyclopaedic from the mystical symbol—Giotto's O,[240] Aum, etc. The latter is the "undisplaced" one, really: all articulation, being growth, is a displacement. The undisplaced vision is the seed or unborn vision, from the circumference.

[356] There are two labyrinths. One is the maternal womb from which we escape by birth. It persists as the subjective or introverted labyrinth, where childhood experiences continually bring us to blank walls. It's the maze in the wood of *Comus* & the beginning of the *Inferno*, the chaotic sea of the *Tempest*, the heaven where Milton ponders the mazes of Providence,[241] Thel's world & the forest of the opening of *Endymion*. It's a paradise when directly associated with the pre-birth world—mazy error under pendant shades[242]—and becomes sinister only as this subterranean catacomb world of oubliettes and a hidden web of relationships that the unconscious establishes & that the reason is dimly aware of. Mother's tangling hair & all those symbols: Satan in chaos.[243]

[357] Then there is the objective labyrinth world to be explored in the quest. It's the same world, but looked at. If the reason alone tries to cope with it, we get Urizen exploring his dens; if the imgn. [imagination] does it, we have Los & his lantern.[244]

[358] In the agon the opponent is seen objectively; in the pathos he's seen in the identity of death; in the anagnorisis he's seen *as* death, the last enemy to be destroyed.

[359] I was thinking of a series of (somewhat melodramatic) titles for chapters. One, The Maze in the Wood; Two, The Finding of the Guide, who for this book is probably Vico. Only there's my 100-section idea too.

[360] Mythical thinking is what it is now fashionable to call both-and thinking. Thus, to use an example given before, Luke has the shepherds & Jesus born in a stable, Matthew has the wise men & has Jesus born in a house. On rational "reconciling" lines, where you're trying to reconstruct a historical event, you can pursue both-and thinking to the point of adding the wise men to the shepherds & having both, but you can't add the house to the stable: you simply ignore the house.

[361] I think I've always had in my mind *two* cyclical patterns. One is the ordinary progress from birth to death, which gets elaborated in literature as the ironic or white-goddess cycle of the Mental Traveller & the Gates of Paradise. Sometimes it extends past death to Bardo & a *ricorso*. The opposite cycle runs from the maze-of-Paradise creation-fall story to apocalypse by way of the katabasis, the stages of which are normally a) previous or preliminary trials b) the search for the beast c) agon d) pathos or mutual death, the third chamber of the labyrinth and the bowels of the monster e) sparagmos, loss of identity in the valley of dry bones f) anagnorisis, leading to the point of epiphany where one sees the cycle below g) apocalypse. This of course is stock: it seems to me that the heroic descent-quest is conceived in its totality as opposite in direction to the ironic one, like Yeats's double gyres, or more like his dream cycle moving against the waking one.[245] Only it's the ironic cycle of ordinary life that's the real dream: the heroic quest is the awakening to life, beginning in the middle like the epics (*nel mezzo* [in the middle] is the opening of Dante).[246] Roughly, the Friday-death, Saturday-disappearance, Sunday-resurrection pattern contrasts with birth, life & death; apocalypse to rebirth.

[362] A very small will, Paul's or Lenin's, can impose a quest-pattern on history & appear to reverse its direction. And I suppose the Hegelian dialectic is involved, as a conceptual displacement (Marx was right about

the personal or subjective (*not* material) force being primary. The Incarnation is conceived as the definite union of them[)].

[363] If I could flesh out this notion I'd have something pretty big. But of course the ironic cycle is also a double gyre, as the Mental Traveller shows: an Apollonian birth-death movement interpenetrating with a Dionysian death-rebirth one; and the two oppositions are easily confused. I've done a lot of the confusing myself.

[364] But there *must* be something here besides just my old stuff. When the descending hero is recovered from projection, we get man making (artificial creation myth), man exploring, fighting, surviving, and finally man confronting his own guiding vision.

[365] The finding of the guide might be concerned not simply with Vico but with the introduction to the descent quest that I give [get?] from Eliot, Yeats, & Joyce, hooking that onto the three great points, T [*The Tempest*], PR [*Paradise Regained*], & *Milton*.

[366] Tentative plan: One: An introductory, or maze-in-the-wood chapter, posing the problem of the total subject csm. [criticism] belongs to, why it isn't lit., & the place of myth as the centre of concern. Vico probably has to come here.

Two & Three (difficult to separate as yet): the Quest theme at the heart of narrative; the introduction to it that one can get from *The Waste Land*, Yeats & FW [*Finnegans Wake*]; the treatment of it in T [*The Tempest*], PR [*Paradise Regained*] & Blake's *Milton*; the pre-Rc. & Rc. [pre-Romantic and Romantic] constructs (i.e. the search for the father & the mother); the ironic cycle with its double gyre of Apollo & Dionysus; the double gyre (if it exists) between the apoc. [apocalyptic] quest theme beginning *nel nozzo* & moving towards rebirth, & the life cycle moving to death. This is my old Luvah idea, split in two, one part dealing with preliminaries & the other with the fundamental dialectic of concern & actuality, this latter corresponding to the agon of the quest.

Four & Five, then, dealing with the two political & conceptual displacements of the quest theme, would correspond to Tharmas & Urizen, pathos & sparagmos, respectively (Tharmas is more like sparagmos, but that doesn't matter). The political chapter deals with authoritarian & revy. [revolutionary] structures (A-D), along the lines of the Utopia paper, featuring Rousseau & the 19th c. thought people. The conceptual one deals mainly, I think, with St. Thomas & the analogia entis[247] (for 4 & 5 cf. my old *Ignoramus* ideas), along with the coincidence of opposites in Bruno & Hegel.

Six & Seven deal with two phases of anagnorisis. The first phase deals with the structure of humanistic education, & leads up to an apocalyptic, or rather encyclopaedic, vision of plenitude: the quest myth as education. Encyclopaedia Nuova. The second phase is the circumferential void; the possession of wisdom; the doctrine of interpenetration; the quest myth and religion. These two correspond to the restoring of imagination chapters in W's [Wordsworth's] *Prelude*.[248]

[367] This may take three volumes and ten years. The one where I most acutely feel my ignorance is 5; but I shouldn't get panicky & think I have to swallow the whole of philosophy & regurgitate. I should pick out one or two things with obvious literary relevance, like analogy & phenomenology (in Hegel's sense) and keep the anatomic tradition constantly in mind, as I do with Utopias. Only it's more the confessional tradition, the *personal achievement* of knowledge.

[368] All I'm really interested in, after all, in 5 are displacements of *myth*: the St. Thomas summa form, of the Bible myth; the Hegel stepladder, of the personal recovered myth. Perhaps *Summa Contra Gentiles* & *Phenomenologie des Geistes* are all I really need, along with briefer references. The City of God really belongs in 4.

[369] This gives me an oscillating movement, extroverted to introverted: after the Introduction, Chapter Two is anthropological, dealing with myth in society & history; Three is psychological, & deals with the conflict of the quest myth in the mind with ordinary life. Four returns to society & history; Five to the mind again; Six, dealing with education, is again socially oriented, & Seven returns to religion.

[370]

Introduction	Tuesday	Criticism	Maze & Guide	NW
Myth & Concern	Wednesday	Anthropology	Preliminary Tests	W
Myth & Anxiety	Thursday	Psychology	Agon	SW
Social Displacement	Friday	History	Pathos	S

Abstract Displacement	Saturday	Philosophy	Sparagmos	SE
Encyclopaedia	Sunday	Education	Anagnorisis I	E
Wisdom	Monday	Religion	Anagnorisis II	NE

[371] For the Introduction, Vico; Frazer in 2; Freud in 3; Rousseau, Marx, St. Augustine in 4; St. Thomas & Hegel, with Heidegger, in 5; Plato & Aristotle in 6; Kierkegaard in 7.

[372] One, Two & Three constitute the crystallization of all my encyclopaedia-of-myth ideas: the twenty-four preludes,[249] the zodiacal schemes, the Druid analogy[250] & the Biblical summa, the lot. Two deals mainly with the schematic structure of myth, its encyclopaedic organization, its pre-Romantic & Romantic structures. Also it incorporates the promised sequel to the Anatomy, as it sums up my graduate course.[251] It ends with a vision of the symbolic universe. Three is functional, as Two is structural: it deals with the conflict of father & mother myths, the quest theme & the white-goddess cycle. The uniting of the two is incarnation. I have yet to discover whether the crucial argument will come off or not, but what the hell, as Tennyson's Ulysses might say. The main line of argument, as I see it now, runs through the two double gyres: the Apollo-Dionysus one of rebirth and the quest-nature one of resurrection.

[373] I do think the seven parts are the boiled-down quintessence of the seven great books:[252] there are many signs that that haunting structure is taking over at last.

[374] Note that 3 leads logically into 4, and I should imagine that 5 will follow the same pattern, St. Thomas & Marx being its Apollo & Dionysus poles. 5 should work out if I know what to look for, as I will by that time: the summa displacement; the anabasis or ladder-of-perfection forms from Plato to Hegel; metamorphic or psychological forms of conversion & revolution; substance as a metaphor projected as object & recovered as subject.

[375] The Critical Path. Part One: Structure & Function of Myth. Part Two: Displacements of Myth. Part Three: The Reintegration of Myth.

[376] Incidentally, 5 will be perhaps more theological than philosophical or metaphysical, and the question of the extent of the informing power of

words comes into it. I suppose it's not impossible that the other arts could be taken as displacements, at least in their literary aspects. That would give me (I should think) three phases of anagnorisis. But it would probably get absorbed in 6.

[377] If I do what I'd like to do *Twilight* could be an aphoristic & discontinuous summary of the seven parts, and as such a sacred book for a new age.

[378] My mythology conception is of course the authentic form of the butterslide: a *religio*[253] is a myth of concern.

[379] It is almost impossible not to believe that Blake had read Vico, but of course he hadn't: that's our Newtonian notion of gravitation or attraction at a distance. We need a more Einsteinian approach, a crumpled continuum where a Zeitgeist does the thinking, becoming articulate in a certain focus, and, because articulate there, able to articulate itself again elsewhere without direct transmission. Yeats has hints of this, & suggests a subterranean communication in a sort of collective unconscious.

[380] Let's hope it will boil down to two volumes, the first extending to 4, which would be better in many ways.

[381] Vico, of whom I still have to make a long summary, says that the early wandering giants were frightened by the thunder into grabbing one woman & hauling her into a cave: monogamy began from the interruption of promiscuous coitus. This connects Vico with Tristram Shandy, as Joyce would at once have seen.

[382] The 1–4 sequence has for one of its main themes the recovery of projection. That's old, of course, but it's getting more concrete. The "religio" element in religion is, or first appears, as an external compulsory bond, acting first through the mysterious power of nature, later through the communal hypnosis of the state. Existentialism has worked out the theory of the recovery of *religio* for the subject. When Hegel, & Marx after him, places the absolute in the subject instead of in the (projected and objectified) conception of "substance," the history of philosophy takes a fateful turn. And of course myth itself moves from the projected story-of-God form to the revolutionary form (cf. Sorel)[254] of the

choice of a line of action. All this should be set out in the introduction. 2–4 is a gyre moving toward displacement; 5–7 the gyre running back the opposite way.

[383] The reservoir concept: the reality of the potential. Strictly, it's nonsense to say "I love you," apart from actions of love, or "I'm a genius, although I haven't written anything yet." Efforts to summon up a mirage of action ("I would die for you") only compound the absurdity. Yet the *feeling* of a love or a genius not yet expressed, perhaps not even expressible, is a genuine feeling. Power, wisdom, love, are often most impressive in their unborn or potential reserved forms. Is this acceptance of the reserved reality Platonic, or only pseudo-Platonic? Cf. Blake on conception & execution.[255]

[384] The Montreal fair:[256] what is the meaning of a billion-dollar fantasy world that is annihilated in six months? Civilization as a "happening." Part of it is descended from the aristocratic putting on of a show: cf. the 16th c. Field of the Cloth of Gold.[257] It's connected with the whole conception of drama, as the speech in T [*The Tempest*] indicates,[258] & it's in part a recovery of mirage, ghost, hallucination, & the epiphanic generally. This is the whole ritual or ˥ [Tragicomedy] side of myth, as distinct from the second-twist, verbalized, rational-escape Λ [Anticlimax] side.

[385] I've always said that the social judgements we make are an inseparable mixture of the moral & the aesthetic, & similarly our judgements on propositional writing are concerned not only with truth but with such categories as "pretentious," "flippant," "dull," & "obscure." Nothing new, but this has to do with the informing power of words.

[386] Two, by the way, could take the title of Structural Poetics. Three, whatever it's called, is really Rhetoric or Functional Poetics. Six & Seven reverse the procedure: Six is Mythology *for* itself, Seven Mythology *in* itself.[259]

[387] Meditation on Hegel: some terms, like God or mind or soul, have practically no meaning as point-terms (denotative meaning). They are circumferential terms. Zoology is the study of animals, but it's of no value to zoology just to think of "all animals." One spends one's life filling in a tiny part of the area covered by this circumferential term. But

then *all* conceptions are circumferential: when we point at them we see at most only their shells or seeds. Again, I just record this: I don't know what I'm talking about, but am revolving [around] the notion of interpenetration again.

[388] I suppose the Introduction will swell into a whole book, that the other six parts will remain unwritten because the introduction has swallowed them, & that then the introduction, now the third book, will be a third zero. That's all right, but I had hoped that the idea on page 1 [par. 3], the work of fiction with death as the cognitio, would be the form of this book.

[389] Berdyaev, in a chapter I've probably mentioned before [par. 341], complains that people don't want philosophers just to philosophize: they want him [them] to rationalize their myths. But of course the philosopher is conditioned by these myths too. When he wants just to philosophize, what he really wants to do is attack those myths.

[390] Curious how systematic philosophers back away from their work: they envisage a total system & then produce a two-thousand-page outline of a preface to the introduction to the beginning of the prolegomenon to the exordium. Starting out with a structure like the labyrinth pattern I'm thinking of now does have some advantages.

[391] I must go back to my point about Plato: that comedy and the triumph of *dialectic* are closely akin. When one form of life is superseded by another, we get the positive advance through a greater comprehension; but the negative aspect produces the dilemma-tragedy. Plato celebrates the triumph of dialectic, but revolves around the dilemma of the death of Socrates: similarly with Hegel & *Antigone*. Plato, Hegel, Shelley, perhaps even Dante, are preoccupied with an intellectual & dialectic comedy which they see as a more mature form of *bodily* resurrection. I must go back to my original hunch about the sun in the *Paradiso*.[260] It's closely connected of course with my T [*Tempest*]-P.R. [*Paradise Regained*]-*Milton* notions. The fact that Xy depends on the bodily resurrection, not the expansion of *Geist*, suggests that art comes nearer than philosophy to expressing the real dialectic: philosophers can't get beyond expansion & progress, at most rebirth. Their perspective is, oddly, not ultimately philosophical but historical. Hence the anti-dialectic direction of Job.

[392] If I see a sign advertising a four-square gospel church, I don't go in, because I know what I'll find: infantilism sustained by hysteria. Infantilism, which is part of what I mean by an intellectual handicap, is, I suppose, the negative side of the preserving of the eternal child that Christ talks about.

[393] The Plato-Dante business & the ramifications are the central theme of 6, not little farting educational noises like Rousseau's *Emile*. This was where I came in in this notebook, & I'm still there. 6 after all recaptures *Paradox*, and the anagnorisis *has* to be literary, not with an eye swivelling out to education & religion. The two stages could logically be the thematic *commedia* outside the Bible (6) *and* the Bible (7).

[394] Introduction: Maze in the Wood (∟ [Liberal]). Vico, Frazer, Freud.
The Wandering (ᒣ [Tragicomedy]). The katabasis quest in T, P.R. & M [*The Tempest*, *Paradise Regained*, and *Milton*];[261] the WL [*The Waste Land*] & Yeats introduction: the epic shape.
The Agon (Λ [Anticlimax]). The dialectic of myth & reality: the separation of vision.
The Pathos (ʎ [Rencontre]). Social & historical displacements; contracts & Utopias; second twist on confession or identity quest-forms (Augustine & Rousseau).
The Sparagmos (V [Mirage]). Conceptual displacements of analogy, coincidentia oppositorum, telos, paradeigma, & similar alienation > < recognition forms. Second twist on Anatomy forms. St. Thomas, Bruno, & perhaps Kant; Kierkegaard's repetition.
The Anagnorisis, Phase One (Γ [Twilight]). The commedia of Eros in Plato & Dante; Shelley & Hegel; the symposium & the triumph of dialectic. A lot of *re*-summarizing of ᒣ.
The Anagnorisis, Phase Two (⊥ [Ignoramus]). The Bible & the final commedia: the double gyre with the dead; rephrasing of Λ in terms of total identity.

[395] Hegel, more particularly *The Phenomenology of the Spirit* [*Phenomenology of Spirit*], appears to be the great philosopher of *anabasis*: one goes upward through morality, art & revealed religion to pure reason. Perhaps he's the recovered St. Thomas, in the way that Goethe attempted to be, at least, a recovered Dante. His scheme however appears to be based on the assumption that there is no difficulty about, and no limits to, the

informing power of words. He wrote before the sciences became so informed by mathematics that no one could really tackle such a Pisgah vision without wondering how far words are a reliable ladder, or at least whether concepts aren't displaced images. I suppose the vision of an *upward* metamorphosis away from alienation is what caught the Marxists, the existential rather than the poetic Hegelians.

[396] If, then, 6 is primarily a recognition of the anabasis ladder, its focus is purgatorial, and 7 is the paradisal vision, with its demonic reflection, the "democratic" effort to go beyond the anabasis vision of Marxism.

[397] This vision reverts to the original Hegelian programme of recovering the past, *harrowing* hell & not turning one's back on it as Dante does. Perhaps the anabasis vision is the recovery of conceptual space & the paradisal one the recovery of time, the demonic being of course clock time. The double gyre is centrally involved in the last part, the world of time & space, life *to* death, that neither is nor isn't but disappears moving against the created world that neither is nor isn't but appears. In this latter world of teleological time the effect precedes the cause.

[398] Two, then, on the katabasis or epic descent-quest, corresponds to its recovery in 6. It's concerned with continuous fictional forms, epic & romance. Three is on the dialectic separation at the bottom of the quest, and is concerned with dramatic or episodic fictional forms. Four starts off with the great St. Clair intuition,[262] & deals with thematic continuous forms, confessions & quests for identity, in the course of which social & historical displacements are established. It's the Augustine-Rousseau book, as aforesaid. Five deals with all my comminution ideas,[263] and is the second twist on the anatomy.

[399] Tactics: I think of the total scheme as in three volumes. The first volume, in itself, does the two things I've been promising to do for the third book. The introduction, which outlines the whole scheme, also does the job of externalizing criticism, establishing its context & the kind of importance it could have if critics knew what they were talking about. This is the maze in the wood, the finding of the guide (Vico, mainly) and the breaking of the branch. (*The Golden Bough*, of course, also begins with a maze in the wood). Next comes the practical-criticism survey, based on

my course as it's developing, and outlining the topocosmoi. Except that it's more intensively related to long narrative forms.

[400] The book then concludes with a cycle of epiphanies based on what comes out of my embryonic drama course.[264] This part occupies the place of ∧ [Anticlimax], but ∧ has now considerably expanded: the old Second Essay idea is now mainly Volume Two, & this section of course is more related to ⅂ [Tragicomedy]. The hell with that. This volume shouldn't take more than about three years, the introduction being the most difficult part. It's emphatically a first essay, & a rewriting of AC only in the sense that AC was a rewriting of FS.

[401] I'm still very ambivalent about my labyrinth pattern: experience indicates that one should let such things disappear in the course of writing, but this particular schema may possibly be of some help. For instance, the essential agon is the vision of the enemy, hence the dialectic pattern of 3 fits. But I should think it more logical to expound the narrative creation-apocalypse pattern in 2 & use 3 for the topocosms (my own & the two historical ones). That fits too, except for the displacing of the Introduction, which may be ∧ [Anticlimax]. Note the similarity of agon & Rencontre, pathos-sparagmos & Mirage.

[402] In this scheme there is as yet no place for any discussion of the other arts; 6 perhaps instead of education, which is 4 (*my* education, of course, in the HBW sense,[265] is a theme of 1–3).

[403] A revolutionary attitude is a deductive one, and tends to accept a sacred book as the basis of deduction. The most profoundly disturbing aspect of the contemporary world is the Red Guard millions waving the little red book of Chairman Mao's thought. The Koran or the sword; the word of God as a two-edged sword: Protestant bibliolatry. It has something to do with the voluntary limiting of the number of possible premises or principles of thought. Old & tired cultures like ours fall into an anarchy of ideas, a democracy which is mob rule, where envy as well as a disseminated equality of vision prevents a leader of thought from emerging. Democracy levels up in education and levels down in stock response. The sacred book of revolution unites the two things.

[404] I want the Introduction to be something colossal, something to

rank with the Preface to Hegel's *Phenomenology*. I want it of course to set up the conception of the verbal structure of concern, with its two great branches, the imaginative and the conceptual. Then I want it to summarize the argument of the entire labyrinth, anticipating Parts Four to Seven, so that the book will be complete in itself if I never live to finish it completely.

[405] The summary of Four will involve me in Marx & Sorel,[266] in contracts & Utopias, in the inductive-conservative & revolutionary-deductive contrast, in historical myths, in the 4k orbit. This part of Vico's argument is devoted to law, on which I'm not competent to enter, but even Vico's view of law is subordinated to a revolutionary theory of history.

[406] I suppose it would be logical to leave the Introduction to the end, doing the introductory summaries of 2 & 3 after I've finished those chapters. Three, I imagine, is reasonably complete in my mind now.

[407] The concept of alienation is the core of the myth of the fall. I call alienation a conceptual displacement of the fall myth. But why shouldn't the fall myth be called a displacement of the concept of alienation? I seem to use the word "projection" when I take this stance. Displacement is, first, a historical term, because the story precedes the concept, and, second, a topical term, because I assume that literature is in a "centre" and informs the disciplines on either "side" of it.

[408] I know this sounds like an obsession, but for anyone living in 1967, the thought of millions of Chinese yelling their guts loose & waving the little red books of Chairman Mao's thoughts in the air ought to be pretty central. Anything can happen, but one thing that certainly can happen is that China will unify itself around the "thought" of Mao, & become strong enough to wipe us out with the back of its hand in a very few years. An old & sophisticated bourgeois civilization like ours thinks in terms of the variety of its ideas, of the intensity of criticism, and above all, of the fact that to be intellectually weak & open to criticism is to be ineffectual. Great is truth & will prevail. For any bourgeois intellectual it would be a miserable impoverishment to confine oneself to the thoughts of Chairman Mao. Nobody's thoughts can be all that good: words can only do so much. But China is very probably enjoying a more intensive &

widespread intellectual activity than we are. It doesn't matter whether the thoughts are vulnerable to criticism or not if you suppress the criticism, including the criticism in your own mind. It doesn't matter how true they are if a powerful social will is determined to make them principles. Eventually, of course, the Chinese myth of concern will complicate itself & become critical too, but that's much later.

[409] There isn't anything in the internal consistency of the Koran, the New Testament or the thoughts of Mao that accounts for their power. There is an imaginative kernel, as I've said in FS, & some stylistic or rhetorical features: what there isn't is any necessary or inherent truth. Note, incidentally, how such a narrowing of the myth of concern limits the field. The Christian Church didn't struggle with atheists & infidels: it struggled with Arian & Monophysite Christians, whom it called atheists & infidels. Mao isn't fighting bourgeois revisionism: he's fighting Liu Shao-Chi's version of Communism,[267] which he calls bourgeois revisionism. It was Lenin who revived in modern times this trick of replacing the theoretical opposite with the heretical one: Mensheviks *or* capitalists.

[410] Browning's Cleon,[268] a pagan intellectual, said that Christianity was insane: the moral Browning himself intended was that Xy was better intellectually than Cleon thought. But Cleon was dead right. The Xns had a colossal will (or faith) to hold to certain principles through persecution & martyrdom. It was the "existential" power of the faith that mattered. The sources of that power are pre-predicative: they can only be located in some point where the structure of myth and the dialectic of history join.

[411] Perhaps I could do a Milton-based paper called "The Revelation to Eve,"[269] which would deal with the fact that Milton's imagination is broad enough to take in both the conservative pre-Romantic construct (Adam, the supremacy of reason, the vision of the Bible) and the revolutionary Romantic one that arises through the subconscious. Both have regenerate & demonic aspects. The original temptation of Eve was by dream, and her expression of it was mythopoeic. This is connected, somehow, with the aesthetic or mood-controlled religion of Il Penseroso; and I suppose too the pastoral retreat of L'Allegro is Eden as we reconstruct it as sons of Eve. The Bachofen white-goddess cult descends from Eve by way of Eurynome, I suppose.[270]

[412] This tedious business of value-judgements: I have nothing new to say about them, and I wish to hell people wouldn't dream up ways of making me repeat what I've already said. Value-judgements are part of the muttering & mumbling of criticism on its way to the understanding of literature. I'm not contradicting myself when I say "this is a good poem," but my feeling, or hunch, that it is good is pre-predicative: it leads to the study of the poem, & its whole value is propaedeutic. Some critics have the whole subject backside to: they think the study of literature leads to a set of criteria that will make further study unnecessary. No critic that I know of imagines that such criteria exist ([I.A.] Richards made a gallant attempt to formulate a set in *PC* [*Practical Criticism*], but it didn't take [)], but there are still a lot of people with pious hopes, demanding why I don't help to establish such criteria instead of saying they don't & can't exist. (They can with a closed mythology, of course, which is what most Americans want). It's a difference in the conception of the context of the work of literature. To me it's obvious that the context *is* literature, & criticism *is* literature studied. To them the context is removed, so it reappears in a set of social & moral & religious values the critic himself holds, these values being symbolized by an imposing set of noble brows labelled Homer & Shakespeare & Dante & others of "the great tradition." Wellek's argument that even on my premises v-js [value-judgments] have to collide to increase the understanding of literature won't work either, because the only thing that can resolve a conflict in v-js is greater knowledge.[271] The noble brows of the great tradition can never express anything except the critic's own values, hence all value based criticism is solipsistic. The more solidly a value is established in practice, the more the value of discussing it diminishes. We don't accept theses on the greatness of Shakespeare: we might accept one on the Birthday Odes of Colley Cibber, simply because relatively little has been done on them. We should go by our practice, which is intelligible, & not by our theories, which are not. The practice may be right or wrong, the theories cannot be either.

[413] The solipsism is partly concealed by the fact that the critic's social, religious, etc. values are attached to other communities. Hence he represents, not himself, but a "point of view," and csm. [criticism] breaks up into schools & isms & other consequences of nobody's knowing very clearly what they're talking about. The schools are not legitimate divisions of labor, like linguistics or the history of ideas. They are seldom

genuine schools: I have been lumped with Miss Bodkin, whose book I have read with interest, but whom as a critic I resemble about as closely as I resemble the late Sarah Bernhardt.[272] And so on: I have to spew all this out, but it's dreary filling up this important book with it. Intelligent people wandering in their wits.

[414] Two other things to get rid of. It's no use saying I like resemblances more than discriminations: literature is an art of analogy & identity, and resemblances are positive. Again, it's no use saying my genres are a false analogy to biology just because it's impossible to work out an *a priori* theory that things must be so. Even if you start with a completely chaotic view of art, like McLuhan's view that art is anything that A can put over on B, the next step will tell you that putting over involves the conventionalizing of what you say, & so genres arise.

[415] I do wish I could follow my nose & make 2 narrative of meander-descent & 3 thematic stasis, as I want to. But clarity of exposition will probably demand the reversal of this, along with the sacrifice of the whole maze-in-wood scheme. But that's what looks like following on from the Introduction, which involves some comparative religion points.

[416] It might be easier to take Victorian England a century ago as an example of what I mean by myth. The double meaning of religion as *religio*[273] and as the belief in some dimension of life other than the life-death progression. The Darwin rumpus & the evidence of something that is not myth separating from mythology, the fact that myth on the defensive is anxious. Robertson Smith,[274] Colenso,[275] the higher criticism movement,[276] & the anxious movements of both Catholics & evangelicals. I start with religion because it's more closely connected with mythology in the literal sense.

[417] Of course one can have a positivistic scientism which is really anti-mythical mythology: that is, it's directed primarily against the extra dimension, the aspect of religion that isn't *religio*. Butler saw this coming in Darwin & Huxley, & being a conservative he rationalized superstition, to the extent of feeling that one's attitude toward the "Musical Banks" shouldn't be too rigorously consistent.[277] His feeling that this scientism could be the worst of tyrannies if it became the established mythology is pretty central. The other-dimensional aspect of religion is based on ana-

logical language: the sharp teeth in religious persecution are always social & institutional. Not much new here: but hell, the third book isn't all new: it's a summary of my life.

[418] I should distinguish the purpose & meaning (dianoia) of myth, which is concern, from its co-ordinating & synthesizing *mythos*. The latter is derived from the tendency in myths to form a mythology. It isn't just concern that makes a myth effective, but its Pisgah vision or enlargement of perspective. Its "truth" is in its theoretical breadth & its practical effectiveness, not in its correlation with any body of phenomena. The distinguishing of myth from what is not myth is of course a pretty tricky subject. Progress is mythical analogy of evolution; but while I know it's only an analogy, I don't know how clearly I can explain why. "Demythologizing" is necessary for clarity, but the silly Bultmann line of course has to be avoided.[278]

[419] I think of comedy as allied to the philosophical search for the same (identity), and as linked with anabatic & dialectic forms. Hence 6. The theme of 7 is the quest (not of tragedy but) of romance, the search for the other, that which *continues* identity. At the same time there is a most important shift in comedy itself between the closed community & the open-ended community of individuals (Dante's sun).[279]

[420] I suppose my "mythology" follows the line of Dilthey & others who have talked about the typology of Weltanschauungen & Geisteswissenschaften.[280] Also Husserl's *Philosophie als Strenge Wissenschaft* [*Philosophy as Strict Knowledge* (1911)] is an attempt to say what is not myth. Now, while literature is central to mythology, what about criticism? Seems to me we need a distinction between the unconsciously & the consciously mythical. The unconsciously mythical doesn't know what the hell it's talking about, & so preserves the element "imaginary" in the concept of the mythical. Medieval science in many aspects was unconsciously mythical in this sense.

[421] And fallacious or evaluative criticism is unconsciously mythical too, because it replaces the mythical structure of literature with a private & hence largely incommunicable mythology. The latter produces the "interpretation" that Susan Sontag attacks.[281] Narcism: what X essentially means is what Y thinks he ought to mean. The willing suspension

of *belief*, not disbelief, is what matters. I don't, as I say, understand Husserl, but I gather his "reduction" is a suspension of this kind. He compares it with the *epoche* of Greek skepticism, & says that fully carried out it would lead to a metamorphosis (*Wandlung*) of the personality. It's evidently an intuitive *Gestalt* that *doesn't* reduce, in the usual sense, or over-simplify. The myth doesn't *exist*: it's an intentional object, something there to be thought about: so are genres & conventions. Every valid form of csm. [criticism] is applicable to all literature (myth csm., rhetorical csm., historical csm., *are* legitimate divisions of labor, despite what I said above [par. 413], or would be if the theory of csm. were more coherent). Pickled butterfly notion that every serious effort at csm. "kills" literature (notice how the metaphor gives direction to the meaning). There is only one thing that "kills" literature, and that is the stock response, including the stock response to csm. Real csm. annihilates the stock response by bringing it to life with a new understanding. A value-judgement is not understanding: it is only a rhetorical stimulus to understanding. It represents the passive or achieved side of the critic's competence, hence the more one trusts to it the more one is pulled down to stock response, which is *always* founded on prejudiced, ignorant & unacknowledged value-judgements. When it comes to the production of junk, lit. critics have no reason for feeling superior to educators.

[422] Further on phenomenology: I wonder if the metaphor is that which annuls reduction, and leads us back to existence, not directly, but within the genres & conventions formed by the myth, which has the metaphor at its core. The point of reduction is not so much to cut off existence as to cut off *objective* existence: one then returns to it with the language, which *has* to be a metaphorical language, of the world behind subjects & objects. Obviously one can think about myth in both ways: there are no myths apart from verbal formulations of them, yet the stories of Ulysses & Jason are equally great stories even though the latter never found a poet the size of Homer to tell it. Hell, I've *said* all this.

[423] George MacDonald's *Lilith*:[282] gives me the impression of having started his imgn. [imagination] off into the labyrinth, got scared, & then went through it again in a state of infantilism, trusting only to the traditional signposts. As a result the story is reshaped as an allegory, an allegory being a way of avoiding experience and substituting a way of talking about it. A fatuous introduction by C.S. Lewis indicates how

scared he is too when he can't make a stock response to the Christianized *content*. But of course MacDonald is a genuinely imgve. [imaginative] writer. He has a diva triformis, who is Eve, a regenerate Enitharmon, "Mara" (i.e. Rachel or the church in the wilderness) and Lilith, queen of hell (i.e. this world, a city of selfish merchants obsessed by the purity of their race), and much of it reads like a commentary on the second half of *The Mental Traveller*.

[424] The church in the wilderness of Rev. xii is an archetype I haven't used much, although it's central to Blake's *Jerusalem*. The *real* Jerusalem, like the real Jesus, is not established in the centre: it's reversed its role and has become a Hagar or Mary in Egypt. Hence she's in the romantic role of a) the Esau-Ishmael line b) the Andromeda prospective victim. Seems to me that only Protestantism (and Jahwism, of course) can make this figure central. MacDonald's Mara is the opposite of C.S. Lewis's Mother Kirke. I think this image is central to Milton, & it's only in connexion with Milton that I've mentioned it.

[425] In myth the question is not whether a given conception is true or false, but whether it is alive or dead. A connection here with the presumptuousness of critics "evaluating" a literature they have hardly begun to understand: all value-judgements on literature are really value-judgements on our own comprehension of literature, and similarly our professed belief in a mythology is our "position," a statement of our own social context.

[426] I'd like to write an anatomy some time in the form of a dialogue with a computer, which replies in various idioms, as the oracular, light verse, Zen koans, & the like, gradually changing the character of the inquirer from a bumptious and arrogant know-it-all to a penitent confessing before what he finally has projected as God. All kinds of things one could do, once I'd figured out the point.

[427] When the Korean war began, I wrote in my diary that just as the first half of the 20th c. saw the end of fascism, so 2000 would see the end of Communism.[283] I was whistling in the dark then, because the Communists had just taken over China. But now I really begin to feel that I'm living in a post-Marxist age. I think we're moving into something like an age of anarchism: the kind of violence and unrest going on now in China,

in the city riots (which are not really race riots: race hatred is an effect but not a cause of them) in America, in Nigeria, in Canadian separatism—none of all this can satisfactorily be explained in Marxist terms. Something else is happening.

[428] The age of Rousseau ended around 1850, although the things it started—Bonapartism in France, Prussian imperialism and Romantic culture—kept going for over a century later. After 1830 came the age of Marx, which lasted up to the Russian Revolution, starting things which are still going on, and will for a long time yet. After 1920 came the age of Freud, which is now beginning to produce what I call the Freudian proletariat.

[429] There were always two sides to anarchism: one a pastoral quietism, communal (Anabaptist, Brook Farm) or individual (Chaplinism). Its perfect expression, in an individual form, is *Walden*, in a communal form, *News from Nowhere*. The beats & hippies with their be-ins and love-ins, the "Dharma bums,"[284] are the first faint beginnings of a new pastoralism. The hysterical panic about organization, full employment, keeping the machines running, & the like, is now waning as it becomes possible to do other things besides work. The hippies seem to be only parasitic, but the fact of voluntary unemployment, of a cult of bums, is new. In the depression the statement "these people just don't want to work" was the incantation of the frivolous, trying not to think seriously. But now there are such people, and the values they challenge are equally bourgeois and Marxist values.

[430] The other side was violence & terror, without aim & without direction, like the rioting sweeping the world from Canton to Detroit, Lagos to Amsterdam. These riots are local & separatist: they have no intelligible point or aim; they simply show the big units of society breaking down. They aren't poor against rich, young against old, or black against white; they're just the anxiety of destruction against the anxiety of conservation.

[431] Where are the "Freudian" countries of the future? In Western Europe, I suppose, and perhaps Africa. The United States is still a Rousseauist country, and Russian Marxism will tend to approximate it, just as Asiatic Communism, especially the Viet Cong, seems to be drift-

ing toward anarchism. The latter has some affinities with Trotsky's version of Marxism, I suppose, and perhaps the hippies and other anti-anxiety people indicate the only way that "permanent revolution" can go.

[432] Rousseau is the cornerstone of 4; Kant of 5. The whole summa is based on the last two centuries, though of course Augustine haunts 4 & Thomas 5. The Kantian distinction of pure reason, which is limited to phenomena, and the practical reason, which participates in the noumenal by engagement, is the basis of a vast *metaphor of opposition* which runs all through the modern world. Hegel formulated the theory of this; Marx applied it to society; Kierkegaard drew from it the "either-or" aesthetic-ethical opposition which the conception of mythology, and that alone, transcends. The two-party system is democracy's adaptation of it.

[433] This opposition also extends to the two philosophical attitudes. One is existential, & is all commitment & engagement and resolute decision: it's a rationalizing of an uncritical attitude. It's roots are in Burke, the Kantian practical reason, and the various Catholic & Communist grammars of assent. The other is phenomenological & is concerned with an *epoche* or withdrawal to contemplate the vision of essence. Marx made a colossal effort of *epoche*, but Marxists insist on uncritical commitment & the indissolubility of theory (reading Marx & Lenin) and practice (doing what you're told). The Anatomy begins with an *epoche*, seeing the thing taken for granted, literature, as a new problem. This is my informing vision, as the other is my possession of literature. I also have the two attitudes in my *Fools of Time*, where the *epoche* is represented by Enobarbus & Mercutio.

[434] Here too I bring out what I suppose is Sartre's view of "nothingness": the withdrawal from being present in all consciousness. The traditional Christian view was existential: "I believe in order to know." The *epoche* here could only be made by Christ. Somewhere in here is the solution of a central comedy problem: the Platonic connection with the triumph of dialectic, where the withdrawing Enobarbus-Mercutio spirit wins out. And how to fit that to the unformulated pragmatism of comedy.

[435] In Milton work out the Word as male and the Church as female, and the Word in the heart as the unborn Christ in the hortus conclusus.

Sons of Adam see & reason; sons of Eve dream & rebel. In both passion naturally dominates over reason, but the male rebellion is prophetic (Rintrah) & the female one social (Palamabron).

[436] One of the most important passages in the McMaster lectures is the one about the incorporating of the ballad idiom into Romantic poetry.[285] Note the history of this: how totalitarian movements have tried to exploit it & turn it into a slogan song. The poets themselves have tried this too: vide Yeats's fascist songs.

[437] Reverting to Milton: the period of his life after 1660 was a prophetic male divorce from an unfaithful Israel who had gone over to the Philistines. The hatred for Milton felt by mother-fixated people like Graves, Belloc (Mother *Church*) and probably Eliot has a real basis. On the other side, note how inevitable the final line of PR [*Paradise Regained*] is. The mother dreaming of her mighty son.[286] A lot of the suggestions, such as the appeal to (Mother) earth at the end of REW [*The Ready and Easy Way*], are of course too tenuous to use; but some kind of pattern is there, as Blake saw clearly enough.

[438] If I'd written my Romantics book on German instead of English Rcsm. [Romanticism], my three poets would probably have been Kleist, Heine, & Hölderlin.[287] Substituting Heine for Shelley would make some things a lot clearer, such as the Trinity business, where Heine (the second Mountain Idyl in the Harz journey book)[288] openly adopts the Joachim of Floris historical third-age scheme.[289]

[439] Ordinary perception of a poem is seeing in it what one expects to see, which is the conventional expectation, which is really a Narcissus-mirror of oneself. The expression of this is the value-judgement, the articulating of what one thinks one knows. Perception with *epoche*, or recognition, is the genuine or original critical response. My Tom Sawyer point[290] is a test case: people simply beg me to see that the cave structure isn't there, or oughtn't to be noticed if it is.

[440] The split between pure & practical reason, which makes the former essential & phenomenological and the latter existential, means that there is a real connexion between the Hegelian & the Husserlian senses of the word phenomenology. One is informed by a comic & the other by a

tragic myth, & they're combined in irony. Hegel is the point at which the anabasis vision, or purgatorial climb upward, is reshaped into the quest vision, or pilgrimage onward.

[441] The principle emerging at the end of my Dickens paper [*StS*, 240] is something like this: the traditional belief in Providence, or a designing force in life, is a projected literary conception. The Word of God tells human life as his story, and if we knew the whole story we could see the design. This existential & immanent design is to be distinguished from the objective or teleological design in nature. When we stop projecting the latter, we get science; when we stop projecting the former, we get a philosophy of history.

[442] Thus the proverb "pride goeth before a fall" recognizes a tragic or ironic pattern in experience. "Seems sort of meant, like," recognizes a romance or quest pattern. We speak of the irony of fate, as though fate were a poet, and the happy endings of comedies are often explicitly associated with a benevolent Santa Claus providence. The belief that one's life is designed by a superior power for good or evil, that one is intended to be a man of destiny like Napoleon or a castaway like Cowper,[291] is, when taken literally, paranoid, hence morbid. Social projections of it appear generally in morbid forms: manifest destiny, the Marxist historical process, progress, are all efforts by a society to recognize or assume a quest-design. The original martyrs were witnesses or actors in a divine play (of which in another context they were also spectators): Paul uses this dramatic metaphor somewhere. If I were to ridicule blind people & then become blind myself, I and others would think of Providence as having brought off a symmetrical ironic design in my life. We like poetic justice because we think, faced with the hanging of Cordelia: "I should not have done that if I were God."

[443] The only genuine feature of evaluation is registering the history of taste. Dickens, for instance, presents us with a great deal of melodrama, sentimentality, & humour. The 20th c. accepts the humour, but finds the melodrama & sentiment embarrassing, so tries to ignore it, or deprecates it, or says Dickens is great in spite of it. Meanwhile, this age is an ironic one, so we find all the ironies & ambiguities we can in Dickens, & make his comedies as "dark" and full of social criticism as possible. In doing this we produce a hideous caricature of Dickens which gradually be-

comes an accurate & revealing caricature of ourselves. The evaluation reflects not Dickens but our own anxieties, & is parallel to that of the Victorians who asserted that a truly great writer, like Shakespeare, is always distinguished by the purity & chastity of his language, especially in the Bowdler edition. If we're obsessed with evaluation, we collapse at this point into a helpless relativism: but there are genuine questions of right & wrong involved, and a genuine distinction between critic & evaluator.

[444] Of course evaluation has to go on: there are far more people engaged in teaching literature than can possibly have anything to say about it, and for them, evaluation is the only possible form of occupational therapy, giving them in the eyes of the dean's office the status of a "productive scholar." Again, few teachers will preserve the ambition of being a transparent medium for their subject. Many will find it easier & more fun to become an opaque substitute for literary experience: to develop charisma, in short, which is Greek for ham. They will insist that values come from them instead of through them.

[445] There are three stages of education in literature. First is the stage of literacy, the immediately practical learning to read and write, as fundamental a need as food & shelter, yet in itself only the ability to follow instructions. Next is the stage of liberality, participation in a *free* society, then participation in the myth of concern. And this, by God, is the first notebook I've ever filled completely in thirty years of keeping notebooks.

Notebook 6

Unique among the notebooks, Notebook 6 is written in a diary with Year Book 1968 *printed on the cover. Frye's entries begin at five different places in the diary:* EROS *on 21 March (spring equinox),* ADONIS *on 21 June (summer solstice),* HERMES *on 21 September (autumnal equinox),* PROMETHEUS *on 21 December (winter solstice), plus an additional untitled section in the diary section titled "Memorandum" after the end of the year. This final section speaks of plans to call the Third Book* The Critical Path, *thus echoing the end of Notebook 19. The notebook, then, is probably to be assigned either to the later part of 1967 or the earlier part of 1968, and perhaps to both. Notebook 12 is fairly obviously the sequel to Notebook 6, greatly expanding its elaboration of the imagery of the four quadrants of the Great Doodle, and its earlier entries definitely come from 1968. Notebook 6 is located in the NFF, 1991, box 22. Throughout Notebook 6, NF uses braces { } to mark off certain portions of his own text for unknown reasons, possibly to indicate material that corresponds to or overlaps with similar material in the closely related Notebook 12.*

EROS

[1] The fundamental idea of Eros is the reversal of the movement of time. It is based on the sense that, as Norbert Wiener doesn't quite say, the creative act (he says communication) overcomes the habitual inertia in life that leads towards death (he says entropy, if that means anything {except a myth, of course} outside its thermodynamic context).[1]

[2] {Hence Eros goes back in time, towards childhood, towards the mother or father, towards earlier stages of history & culture, towards a

lost Paradise. The propelling movement is of course sexual, but it drives through the sexual act to a rebirth, into a world really unborn, where total possession and totally being possessed are the same thing.} Buddha promises an unborn world; Jesus a paradise or unfallen world.

[3] {The simplest & most direct object of Eros is the mother,} whose body is a garden or *hortus conclusus*, the traditional form of paradise. The Song of Songs is an Eros poem, or begins there. {The Courtly Love tradition is based on the maternalizing of the mistress, who in the pure convention is the unscrewed-inscrutable, often symbolized by the moon at which a phallic mountain points.}

[4] Dante, the greatest of Eros poets, except Plato—no, I shouldn't talk that way: every great poet has an Eros side to him—gives us one typical form of Eros progression, the purgatorial upward movement around a spiralling cone of a mountain. What he seeks is his own childhood, not his individual childhood but generic childhood as Adam yet unfallen in Eden. When he enters Eden, he meets Matilda, a sister-figure representing a pre-sexual idyllic pastoral state. Then comes Beatrice, who nags & scolds away like a typical Italian mother: that is, the first we see of her is in a scolding-mamma role. She quiets down after a while in the Paradiso, but as compared to Virgil she's a lousy teacher: when Dante asks a question she tells him it's a stupid question.

[5] The Eros or Beulah phase in Dante starts with the entry into Eden and ends at Par. ix., when we pass the shadow of the earth's cone in going from Venus to the Sun. From then on it's as pure Logos as a medieval poet can get. The world is polarized by the figure of Beatrice the Virgin Mother at one end and by Rahab the foreign harlot at the other, corresponding to the Virgin & the Magdalen at the crucifixion, the woman in blue & the woman in red, & the Virgin of the Epiphany with a fallen nature hiding her guilty front in Milton.[2] As a grotesque {contrast of lofty rationalizations and "low" physical impulses is a feature of Eros, we have in Dante the device of demonic parody to separate the two: Dante has a dream of a siren's cunt and a vision of Beatrice unveiling her mouth.[3] Compare Faunus' glimpse of Diana's cunt in the Mutability Cantoes [canto 7, stanza 6, ll. 45–6].}

[6] Freud is the great Eros thinker of our time, of course, and he takes us

on a journey backward in time to the birth trauma. The search for the spontaneous or immediate moment, one of the main Eros themes, naturally produces the kind of orgasm mystique that we find in so many writers from D.H. Lawrence on. But, as Norman Brown in particular has urged, {the erotic community, as an ideal, is polymorphous, not sexual.}[4] The Eros theme is normally comic, and the erotic drive in New Comedy, though it crystallizes around marriage, takes in a great number of "incestuous" sub-themes on the way.

[7] {One Eros theme is the attempt to get rid of the shadow} (cf. the earth's shadow in Dante). A great deal is made of Dante's shadow, and the shadow archetype—the twins, the doppelganger, the shadow as burden in Bunyan's PP [*Pilgrim's Progress*], Narcissus, & the doubled characters of comedy & romance (animated portraits like the picture of Dorian Gray are frequent in sentimental romance) usually refer to the mythical kernel of the word "reflection," shadow as used in Eliot's *Hollow Men*. {In ordinary experience (Adonis) action & thought, being separated by an instant in time, mirror each other: Eros seeks the pure immediacy that the orgasm symbolizes.}

[8] The woman as inspiration, the C of L [Court of Love] mistress, the Diotima of Plato's Eros Symposium, Egeria,[5] the *ewig-weibliche* [eternal feminine] of Goethe,[6] is of course a part of Eros: the Isis or Solveig[7] figure belongs to Adonis. In the Eros myth poetry, in all creative effort, is what ethologists (see Lorenz) call a *displaced* activity of the lover.[8] I suppose it's the displacement that leads him away from explicit sex towards the mother: even {Buber, whose *I & Thou* is mostly in Logos, says there's something motherly about his Thou.}[9] Hence a series of sexual sublimations. After the Mother, the glorification of male friendship, the higher Aphrodite—but surely this is Eros going *down* the cycle again into Adonis (Plato, N.T. [New Testament], Spenser Q4 [*Faerie Queene*, bk. 4], Shak. [Shakespeare] sonnets).

[9] I know about the tremendous difference between the mother-dominated mythology, with its subordinated dying-god figure (Bachofen & Graves),[10] where the creation myth is sexual, and the father-dominated one where the world is made as an artefact. Both are projected myths: the mother-myth, when recovered, becomes the Eros myth: the recovered father-myth is the Prometheus one. In Plato the Prometheus myth enters

Protagoras, where the subject said that man was the measure of all things. Today the U.S.A. is Eros-dominated & the U.S.S.R. is Prometheus-dominated. The relation between them is not clear to me, but Prometheus, as {his name suggests, is closer to Logos, leaving behind his erotic brother & Pandora, who is a baggage, i.e. Pandora is herself her box.}[11]

[10] Eros poetry, especially, is based on a sexual symbolism of nature in which the male is above & the female below. The sky, rain, clouds, the sun, and most birds are male: flowers, rivers, caves, streams issuing from underground, and the earth itself are female. Trees & mountains are often son-symbols: mother's son if thought of as arising out of the earth, father's if struck by lightning or a link in a descending movement, like Mt. Sinai. I worked this out in Milton's poetry:[12] of course in Milton we shift over from the mother-sexual "pagan" myth to the father-artefact Christian one, and hence Eros shifts to Agape, as we'd say now. Nature is no longer a mother or bride but a schematic piece of design, a part of Logos.

[11] The central Eros ascent is the purgatorial one, as in Dante: the mountain climb remains very frequent in Eros structures, & often turns out to be the mother's body, as in [W.H. Auden and Christopher Isherwood's] *The Ascent of F6*.[13] The arrow is of course a central Eros image: in Dante's Paradiso there's an arrow image in practically every canto. All ladders of love or perfection, Platonic or mystical, are erotic.

[12] The earthly paradise, then, is on top of the mountain, and it has the two Beulah gates, the gods' entrance from above and the cyclical one below. Either way goes through a vortex, the lower one being usually the Bardo vortex of reincarnation.

[13] I've thought that all conceptual ladders or mountains leading to Logos were erotic, like Hegel's *Phänomenologie des Geistes*, and they may be. (Kierkegaard was an Adonis figure, & I suppose the book called *Stages on Life's Way* is the existential & tragic answer to Hegel, though it begins with some brilliant remarks about Eros & the comic). Incidentally, Kierkegaard speaks of the thorn in his flesh:[14] Eros shoots arrows; figures stuck full of arrows, St. Sebastian & Actaeon, are Adonis figures.

[14] So we have an undisplaced mother-goddess who renews her vir-

ginity each spring, displaced in various ways. Christian has the permanent virgin mother & the redeemed harlot; Classical has Diana, who's also the moon pointed at by the tower, & Venus, who's both the mother of Eros & the restored mother of the Adonis *pieta*. Dante has the Biblical pattern, also the siren who displays her *ventre*, contrasted to the Beatrice who unveils her mouth[15]—as clear a case of displacement as one could ask for. Diana is related to women in childbirth. The Lady in Comus revolves around the undisplaced feeling that chastity & redeemed sexuality are the same thing. What unites them doctrinally is marriage, but marriage to Milton is consummated only by death. In C of L [Court of Love] there's an uneasy tension of frustration & possession, but you enter the Promised Land through Rahab.[16] The fall of the walls of {Jericho is the breaking down of the barrier to Paradise, & is the anagogy of Babel & Finnegan.} [Written beneath the previous sentence: Jericho & the moon]. Of course the obvious image uniting virginity & sexuality is the bride, & in *The Tempest* a great to-do is made about not anticipating the consummation. The symbol here of the p of e [point of epiphany] is the wedding masque of {the earthly Paradise & the world saved from the flood. Venus is excluded from it. The point is N, opposite the S point of the flooded world} where there's an older man & a preserved female infant. There is something to the *Mental Traveller* version of the cycle: if we adopt it, the male is born N, escapes from the mother in an Adonis descent, takes possession of his bride in the Henry V role, which is W, deserts her and wanders in a lower world approaching the S point of the infant Miranda & Perdita. The pull up the east side is an ewig-weibliche [eternal feminine][17] attraction: that's why Shakespeare so often makes the comic resolution depend on the activity of the female. Cf. also Diotima in Plato.

[15] Jung seems to focus around the p.d.e. [point of demonic epiphany] & the Prometheus quadrant. His main archetypes are Prospero and Miranda, the old wise man and the infant female who grows into an anima. The shadow, again, is accepted here, just as it's shuffled off somewhere near the end of Eros. I suspect the Valéry poem about the Jeune Parque[18] is mostly about this area too.

[16] My enemies would call this just mere accordion playing, but I wonder if Old or Aristophanic Comedy, however highly stylized in its present form, isn't a type of comedy that's the only viable comic alter-

native to New Comedy with its new-birth gimmick, & hence the form that contemporary dark comedy has returned to: I never did follow up my original hunch about Prospero & the Aristophanic *genre*. Nor have I seriously considered the question whether Old Comedy can be generalized in the way that New Comedy can be.[19] It's even possible that Plato's links are with Old Comedy, as the *Symposium* suggests, & that here's the answer to my E problem about the comic triumph of dialectic. I'm thinking mainly of the procession of characters in the last part of the play, but there may be more: this would be a major breakthrough if there is.

[17] Speaking of this last, I suppose there are E & W points of epiphany as well as N & S ones: if so, this would completely survey the critical path. The E one is the conceptual displacement of Nous, more or less: the top of the Hegelian ladder & such: the Marxist one too, in spite of its generally essential bias. The identification of opposites, fitting the stasis of E, seems central. It looks as though I'm heading for an explicitly religious book.

[18] I suppose Hermes would be the best name for the E epicycle, in his Trismegistus aspect at any rate.[20] He's a psychopomp going W to S, but his "mercurial" associations are comic. I've never been sure about prose fiction (since I established the confession as W), whether the anatomy was S (because of its sparagmos affinities) or E. If S, the novel's E, & I should note its recurring tendency to the dead centre of society: Tom Jones, Middlemarch, Main Street & Babbitt, Bouvard et Pecuchet.

[19] I think Orpheus symbolism, and still more David symbolism, belongs to Eros but not to Prometheus: magic seems to hang around the NE quarter, & to be preparatory to the music of the spheres culmination. Shakespearean comedy is E to N, mostly. I know the Tempest journey is S to E, but as I say there are two levels to that play. The absence of the lower level in MND [*A Midsummer Night's Dream*] accounts for the autonomy of Oberon. It would be funny if the four quadrants all disappeared in the writing & the whole damn book became a discussion of the two axes. It could, you know. For one thing, the same archetypes recur all over the circle: the labyrinth or maze turns up in every quadrant, & while the contexts are often distinguishable, they may not be theoretically divisible.

ADONIS

[20] Eros develops to the point at which it can either go "up" into Logos or around the cycle into Adonis. This point is what I called in AC the point of epiphany. In Milton, Dante & most Christian poets Eros gets as far as Eden or the terrestrial Paradise, and Logos begins when the Eros mother or bride figure becomes Wisdom the daughter of the sky-father. {Nature then changes to an artefact to be looked at rationally and schematically. L'Allegro & Il Penseroso lead respectively to an earthly Paradise & an "aesthetic" hermitage or old man in the tower: these are the twin peaks of the Eros-Parnassus, the beautiful and the sublime.} Above this is the rational order symbolized by the music of the spheres, the force that keeps unsteady Nature to her law.[21]

[21] Central to the Christian view of Logos is the downward, God-initiated redemptive movement that follows the track of the Adonis passion but completes it: the Agape descent & return, opposite the Eros-Adonis cycle. In the Gospels Jesus descends to earth in the Incarnation, redeems it, & returns in the Ascension; he descends to hell after his death, harrows it, & returns in the Resurrection; in [Blake's] Milton he descends to Beulah, creates the unfallen world, & returns: a fourth movement of second coming & total apocalypse is prophesied. The four stages of the total myth.

[22] The progress from the top of Eros into Logos is often regarded as a progress through a "cloud of unknowing" or "dark night of the soul" which is often mystical, leading to a sense of undifferentiated unity. Truth changes from truth of correspondence to truth as direct revelation of being. In Christianity truth is the revelation of the person of Christ, where the understanding of a book enables the Spirit to perform again the resurrection of the Word. The only literary form possible for this kind of revelation is that of a discontinuous sequence of epiphanies.

[23] The feeling that this "sequence" ought to suggest the cycle of totality produces the conception of the Logos as an alphabet of forms. The I Ching, the Tarot pack, & the like, are the Alpha-Omega aspect of the Word. These schemes are used for divination, as is natural, because they're conceived as above time, but they are expressions of the schematic

("all imagination")[22] shape of mythical apprehension of reality. Yeats' circle of the moon and Poe's Eureka cloud of unknowing.[23]

[24] Note that *music* has always had a close association with this area, and that music as we have known it in the West has been a schematic alphabet of forms. Of course mathematics & geometry hover around the fringes of these mythical compasses with their 32 points, but the element of *concern* disrupts them.

[25] Logos means structure and rational order; it also means discourse or dialogue, & I think Buber's great intuition, which for the first time formulates my own dissatisfaction with mysticism, is pretty central to it.[24] There is also the point at which the medium really does become the message, where the ordinary A-B-C progression becomes a straight A-C one. Some discontinuity certainly does enter here: I suppose the alphabet of forms is really the crux of the argument, because it's a point at which the logical turns into the mythical.

[26] I don't know whether my AC tables of metaphors have to be repeated here, but it seems to me that somewhere the great doodle of the hero's progress needs to be looked at as a whole. This would be just before returning to the cycle, perhaps.

[27] The question arises: is the Utopia a Logos theme? It seems to me that the element of logical ordering as an expression of an integrated (educated) mind means that it is, even though all Arcadian & pastoral ideals are quite clearly Eros. That makes me much less confident about things like Hegel's Phenomenology as an Eros mountain. It's bound up with my uncertainty about Marx & the Prometheus myth. Certainly there's a lower & higher Logos, & the former could in practice easily become a Thanatos parody.

[28] Christianity says you got born but you don't die; Buddhism says you die but you never got born. One is a will-religion thrown forward to the future, Kierkegaard's "repetition," the other, which is closer to Plato, is an enlightenment-religion thrown back to a "recollection" of reality before the fall. The latter is the Eros theme that enters Christianity very early, as Nygren says,[25] and produces purgatory and mystical ladder-climbing. The former is the Agape theme in which the hero makes the

Adonis descent into Thanatos & comes back. Note that the Adonis theme is also the Prometheus theme, the crucified human martyr. One is the Genesis myth, referring back to an original breach of harmony; the other is the Job myth, referring forward to deliverance out of death. The question is: can you have a Logos myth that doesn't use either the backward myth of Eros or the downward myth of Adonis to get there?

[29] There's some connexion between chess or cards and the alphabet of forms. Chess in *The Tempest* is an Eros mingling[;] Miranda, like Alice, becomes a queen & the king dies (shah mat).[26] In Thanatos visions they're emblems of fatality & enmity: the chess & Tarot pack of *The Waste Land*. Wonder if it has something to do with the triumph of the female will that goes all through Eros, & is parodied by the femme fatale.

[30] In a sense (see Thanatos notes) there really isn't any Logos symbolism, because the Logos is what symbols point to, and everything expressed in imagery is the word in the world, incarnate. One can have visions based on total identity or correspondence, as in Burnt Norton IIa, Revelation & Paradiso 10–33, but they're still structures of imagery, & to that extent they're still part of the masque. The dark night of the soul is at the same point. But even the vision of correspondence in BN [*Burnt Norton*] is looking down from the p of e [point of epiphany], not really up. Whatever you do you're involved in another structure of imagery, and never get clear of it.

[31] However, you start with the p of e [point of epiphany], and see the tragic cycle below. As Yeats saw in *The Dialogue of Self & Soul*, & as Nietzsche thought he saw, the deliverance from the wheel consists not in escaping but in accepting recurrence. Hence the Christian symbolism of the sacrament: the active seizure of the repetition of sacrifice. The action reintegrates the Logos body, just as passively watching it leads to the Gerontion vision of sparagmos & disappearance.

[32] The real Logos is, I suppose, the being or *Sein* that hides itself behind all formulated Daseins, and it manifests itself as time, of which the incarnate or spatialized form is the Word. Poetically speaking, it's the Father of man. At first it is thought of as man's Creator in nature, & hence as manifest in the order & design of nature, the harmony of the

spheres and such. As the belief in that declines, mother comes back in Rcsm [Romanticism], but by the end of the 19th c. the imgn. [imagination] has broken through to hell again and the rediscovery of the Father becomes a matter of some urgency. At present the Logos is apprehended mythically (and verbally) as the *concerned analogy of science*. That is, it's what seems to make human sense in the world, but isn't allowed to be miraculous, or violate our sense of external reality. It's what can respond when it's externalized, in a dialogue, as the scientific world can't.

[33] When Paul Tillich was asked whether he supported the Protestant theory of two sacraments or the Catholic view that there are seven, he answered that he didn't think there was any future in counting the sacraments.[27] I wonder if there's any future in counting the Persons of the Godhead. There may be three; there may be four and a half; there may be three hundred and sixty-five billion. If it's bad luck to number Israel, it may be even worse luck to number the names of God. Nowadays we have a stronger feeling about the reality of polytheism, or what Emily Dickinson calls refunding our confiscated gods.[28]

[34] In a sense established religion, which thinks of its God as triumphant, reverts to the Creator God of the O.T. [Old Testament]. For centuries the essential reality of the *suffering* Logos was hardly understood, and now that it is understood, the atonement or reconciling with the Father is what's hard to understand. It's the conservative block in our revolutionary myth, the thing Shakespeare keeps. I suppose what's really projected about God is this Creator. The Word projected as Deed, as Faust claims,[29] & the Deed or Act apprehended as number. There's also the projection of Word as *logical* or reasonable order—the Nous projection.

[35] The point of epiphany is first a locus amoenus—or rather first a maternal hortus conclusus, then a locus amoenus—and then a sexual element regresses to the polymorphous & finally vanishes. At the vanishing point it turns into harmony, the unchanging response of the creature to the Creator. In the next stage it becomes the discontinuous epiphanic sequence of the Logos proper, but I don't know how as yet. The breakdown of unitary mysticism into personal dialogue is involved somehow in it.

HERMES

[36] The poetry of experience converges on the figure of Adonis, the youthful hero who forsakes a maternalized Venus for (war and) hunting. It's the world of tragedy & epic, of mimetic displacements, and it seeks the moment of *fated* time, which is neither the unborn moment that Satan can't find[30] (Eros) nor the natural moment of death, but the *sacrificial* moment.

[37] The Adonis theme in the Gospels starts with Jesus leaving his mother (and father) to be about his father's business: the inheritance of a destiny is part of the complex. The reason why Christianity is so much more primitive a religion than Judaism or philosophical Hellenism is that the story of Jesus is given the Adonis or passion form: Jesus is clothed in Luvah's robes of blood, as Blake says.[31]

[38] As such, the story of the tragic hero follows the familiar outline. The hero's paternity is more mysterious than his maternity, and he grows up in obscurity. Two themes appear here of some significance. One is the dismissal of the old man, in the Gospels the *nunc dimittis*[32] theme extended to the doctors & the wise men. The rejection of Falstaff is demonic parody. The other is the maze in the wood, the beginning of the labyrinth theme, with which Dante (and Frazer's *Golden Bough*, of course) begins. Sometimes there's an older man as guide (Virgil, FQ2 [*The Faerie Queene*, bk. 2]). The maze in the wood, where the hero meets beasts who may be friendly or menacing, is in the temptation scene in the Gospels. I have a good deal of this in AC, of course.

[39] After that, the whole labyrinth sequence unfolds itself: agon, pathos, sparagmos and anagnorisis as rebirth. The white goddess forms part of this, but in the role of persistence through time, the potential energy of earth renewing its "virginity" each year. Note the contrast of eternal recurrence that got Nietzsche all giggly with the Logos redemption movement.

[40] For some reason I've thought that sentimental romance, Scott to Morris, was a key to Adonis mythology. I don't know if it is, but there's the double or shadow theme (Grave's "tanist")[33] that runs all through. In the Gospels this is the "Barabbas" theme: it appears in all the 19th c.

mirror, twin, doppelganger, portrait, Narcissus and puppet (i.e. Frankenstein's *mechanical* double) themes. Eros moves away from the shadow; Adonis towards it.

[41] Closely linked with this is the theme of friendship or male love: Plato's pupil-teacher love is perhaps—in fact certainly—Eros, but the beautiful youth of Shakespeare's sonnets, the theme in FQ4 [*The Faerie Queene*, bk. 4], the beloved disciple of Jesus, are all Adonis figures.

[42] Everybody who knows, including Blake, agrees that Eros and Adonis are the same person, the continuous identity of an Orc-Luvah who is born as one and dies as the other. And yet there is an opposition of directions between innocence & experience, the comic journey to birth & the tragic journey to death, Eros & Anteros,[34] love & war. Dante meets three beasts, turns away from them and explores the worlds of Thanatos, Eros & Logos. His whole effort, like Plato's, is to get to Logos through Eros. The great Protestants, notably Milton and Kierkegaard, recapitulate that Logos-Adonis incarnation of the Gospels. (I'm not saying that this is characteristically Protestant or Dante characteristically Catholic, though Nygren strongly hints this).[35] Both focus on a rejection of Eros, Milton on divorce, opposition to the C of L [Court of Love] code, and everything else inductive to the sin of Eve, Kierkegaard on the refusal to marry a woman who was in the "aesthetic" sphere—Dido's abandonment again. Under Eros I've got the St. Sebastian-Actaeon figure of Adonis stuck full of arrows & S.K.'s [Søren Kierkegaard's] thorn in the flesh.[36]

[43] To be born is to acquire a shadow: this may be the mortal part of oneself, the Narcissus reflection of what one really is. Or it may be projected as the enemy, a personal fate, with whom one is identified because he's my death or I'm his. Enemy or opponent within: crude in Jekyll & Hyde; subtler in [Henry James's] *The Jolly Corner*. At death one enters a ship: either one is saved by, and as, the ship (ark), or one sinks into the sea & identifies with the watery reflection.

[44] I've spoken in the AC of the contrast between knowledge of the present gained from the gods above, in the Classical epics, and the dark, mysterious, often forbidden knowledge of the future gained from the gods below. Knowledge of the certain future, of the future as present, is

possible only in hell (Thanatos): at the p.d.e. [point of demonic epiphany] is the prophetic oracle of the kind of thing that will happen, usually hopeful about the future, as in Aeneid VI, P.L. XII [*Paradise Lost*, bk. 12], and the oracular caves of Shelley. Maybe Nietzsche's (and Yeats') visions of recurrence really belong here, though I've got them at the p.e. [point of epiphany]—and maybe the confusion is theirs & not mine. Certainly this is the kind of thing that most worries me about them both.

[45] Paradiso 10: the Father beholding the Son as a manifestation of himself:[37] assimilates the Adonis myth to the Agape myth by a version of the Narcissus theme with which the Adonis progression begins.

[46] I've been confusing areas with directions. Eros & Adonis are opposed directions in the upper world that I've been calling Eros, & which is really Beulah or the romance world. The Adonis movement, which is N to W, ends in the "solemn sympathy"[38] of the dead lover & the purple flower, which continues into the W to S quadrant. This takes place in Generation, & hence is normally ironic & displaced; but *this*, surely, is the world that sentimental romance is the key to. It's the Oedipus world, the world of the discovery of the guilt underlying tragedy. Its symbols include: metamorphosis, or the locking up of subjects and objects (note that this is described by Keats as the *second* war).[39] Nympholepsy, the teasing & elusive daughter-figure. The impotent king or senex iratus, as elsewhere. The ironic tragedy of survival, which takes the form of isolation, solitude, misunderstanding, accusation, wandering in deserts & forests. The oracular cave into which Oedipus is finally received. The ship crossing water at death. The cave of myths—Morris's *Earthly Paradise* is actually a p.d.e. [point of demonic epiphany]. The labyrinth of Leviathan's bowels, this being the sparagmos completion of the Adonis death. One difficulty: this lower world seems still to be Beulah, though Beulah in the submerged revolutionary position. Maybe there's a complete displaced Generation cycle as well. How else can SE be *ironic* comedy? *Old* comedy, partly.

[47] Nietzsche & Yeats both think they can release from guilt by accepting the cycle. I have a hunch that Yeats buggered up his vision by getting hold of a lunar cycle moving clockwise, with the "primary" or Christian movements going down towards death & the heroic ones up to life.

Mine, which fits the facts of both literature & religion, very much better, is a solar cycle going anti-clockwise. In this one comedy rises & tragedy falls, as it should, or as they should.

[48] In the life of Christ there is an Oedipus descent following his death, the descent to hell of which Gethsemane & the Temptation (cf. P.R. [*Paradise Regained*]) are proleptic anticipations. Similarly the Transfiguration & Palm Sunday, in the general upper Eros level, are proleptic anticipations of the Promethean Resurrection. The Resurrection is the basis or assumption of comedy, just as the Crucifixion is the basis or assumption of Oedipus or guilt-tragic irony. But the E epiphany is ironic when it's rebirth, as in the MT [Blake's *The Mental Traveller*].

[49] There are two Eros ascents, an allegro one to the Earthly Paradise and a penseroso one to the lonely tower of mathematical vision. One is youth & the other age—problem here. Similarly, there are two forms of guilt, the Don Juan love-guilt and the Faust wisdom-guilt. Both betray women. Note the W to S associations of Byron, vs. the N to W associations of Sidney. You can have youthful figures at the p.d.e. [point of demonic epiphany], just as you can have lonely old men in the p of e [point of epiphany] tower. Of course the Virgin Mary & the SS [*Song of Songs*] little sister are youthful, & they're certainly N. But daughter-figures hang around the S: the baby Miranda accompanying Prospero on the W to S tragic journey before the comic action (which significantly begins with a shipwreck) begins.

[50] The S to E quadrant is the progress toward the new built city. Aeneas leaves the burning Troy (W), then wanders W to S until he reaches Carthage (S) and Dido. The sixth bk. recapitulates this journey, as he meets Dido again. *The Tempest* is founded on the same journey, & its action has two levels: the Prometheus S to E one for Prospero & the court party, and the Eros E to N one for Ferdinand & Miranda. *The Waste Land* combines the two, adding Augustine. The first section is W to S descent, substituting desert for forest, then the Dido chess world & death by water (Carthage & Phoenicia), then the final exit from the world of falling towers & the fisher king & Teiresias with the risen Christ. It also absorbs the Dante escape from hell through the centre of the earth (upside down in air were towers).[40] Thus this Carthage-to-Italy progress

is a Classical parallel to the Egypt-to-Jerusalem Hebrew one, the escape from Africa, vs. the Rasselas descent into it. Thus once again the Exodus prefigures the Resurrection. The content of all this is old,[41] but the overall shape is getting clearer. I see more clearly why "Sicily" haunts Shakespearean romance: it's the land of the two levels of Proserpine, and of Arethusa. For the action of WT [*The Winter's Tale*] exists on an old Leontes-Hermione level & a young Florizel-Perdita one even more obviously than that of *The Tempest* does. Perhaps this is the reason, not only for Shakespeare's anxiety to have the parental figures taken care of, but for the change that the romances make in the green world symbolism.

[51] I think Conrad & Melville are among the best places to look for Adonis symbolism simply because they wrote about the sea, and the sea is a Narcissus or mirror-image. What it mirrors, especially in a calm, is at once nature and the complementary half of human nature: the becalmed Ancient Mariner finding his release in accepting his own shadow in the deep. Note the tying of the shadow theme to the sea theme in Conrad's nigger,[42] significantly called "Wait," the pun on the name being established at the beginning, and of course in *The Secret Sharer*.

[52] Man is a divine child, & therefore his maternity is obvious; his paternity has to be taken on faith. In the age of faith he was a lost son of God; when the conventional & conservative symbols of heaven began to give out, the descent from Mother Nature was what was obvious. So physical nature becomes the complement of human nature, sublime & unspoiled at first, then "wild," then increasingly primitive & savage (in the French sense of *sauvage*). D.H. Lawrence is the culmination of this: the next stage is the breakthrough to the rediscovery of hell, for which Conrad's *Heart of Darkness* seems to me a profoundly significant work, wrapping up as it does *1984*, the *Penal Colony*, & all the rest of the nightmares.

[53] The thing I originally started on as an Adonis pattern, the meander-and-descent theme, now seems to me to start W at the Oedipus quadrant. The Elizabethan etymologists were right: Adonis is Adam, and the W point is the limit of contraction as well as the point of tragic fall. Of course it's also the moment of triumph, the Psalm 45 moment,[43] for the conquering Messiah *is Time*, like Shakespeare's Henry V. Hence it's also the Palm Sunday point of Christ's taking on Luvah's robes of blood.[44]

PROMETHEUS

[54] I know very little about Thanatos symbolism as yet: I do know that parody of the other three patterns is central to it. Ironic parody, of the kind that ranges from *The Rape of the Lock* to *Don Quixote*, is a very different thing from demonic parody, which is much further down. I have to do a good deal of reading in fiction from Celine onward to get the progression from the demonic circle, the frozen form of the great doodle, into an absurd world which parodies the elusive discontinuous epiphanies of the Logos. After absurdity comes, I think, anti-teleological *chosisme*,[45] which is the parody of sense of absorption or mutuality or identity in the Logos.

[55] I have a hunch that at a certain point we re-enter a world where the stars are again visible. The greatest Thanatos works of literature are the Iliad (ultimately that, I think, rather than Adonis tragedy) and the Inferno. In the latter the undisplaced journey begins with Dante entering Satan's mouth & being shot out of his arse at the bottom of everything, so that Dante is literally a Diogenes Teufelsdröckh,[46] a God-born devil's dung. The interval being the point of mysterious return frequent in epics, corresponding to the cave of the nymphs in the Odyssey.[47] (I wonder if I really can work it out on this kind of map: I've been assuming that the cave of the nymphs was the two-gated Beulah or Garden of Adonis, which I think is right, but in what sense, other than the fact that it's a romance, is the Odyssey an Eros poem? I've got a hell of a lot more thinking to do).

[56] Anyway, the mountain Satan piles up behind him as a result of his fall, an ironic Babel mountain, turns out to be the genuine Eros mountain. Similarly, I wonder if I don't get to some point, probably Genet, at which demonic parody becomes the perversion of perversion[48] & so turns into a reflection of the genuine thing. I've had a feeling—there may be nothing in it—that I have to go through a period of Pococurantism[49]—Jesus was a homosexual with a mother-fixation so strong he even insisted his mother was a virgin; Plato saying that everybody's stuck with ten thousand years except homosexual school teachers who get away with three thousand; Augustine, asked whether virgins sinned who got raped, saying no if they're quite sure they got no fun out of it. At some point there's a blind world of whispering voices like a radio play.

[57] Thanatos begins with the point of demonic epiphany, the John Barleycorn[50]–Mental Traveller-Juan at Winter Solstice[51]–Finnegans Wake vision of life as a closed cycle. Note the discontinuous aspects of the Mental Traveller cycle as compared with the Crystal Cabinet & Gates of Paradise: the continuity in MT [Blake's *The Mental Traveller*] is really the illusion of identity that continuity imposes.

[58] Ultimately there is a moral conflict between the art that shocks & outrages us & the mass media that try to accustom us & desensitize us. I've often spoken of Gertrude Stein as a practitioner of an associative style, but there's every difference between that & the Dick & Jane readers with their phony pumped-up excitement ("Run, Jim, run!") which educate primarily for the reading of advertising, with its exclamatory exhortations. The slogan is the demonic opposite of the koan or text, or formulaic pattern.

[59] Pococurantism[52] would extend to the Iliad & Inferno themselves. The Iliad itself is a poem I loathe, and the Inferno was an act of treachery to the human race far lower than Judas, who could not possibly have acted from motives so debased as Dante's "practical" ones were. This demonic shadow appears in the hell sermon in Joyce's *Portrait* [chap. 3], in its prototype the evangelist's talk in *The Way of All Flesh*,[53] & in the demonic priest at Ophelia's grave in *Hamlet* [5.1.226–34].

[60] Adonis or the tragic area deals not with death but with the cutting off of life: the sacrificial moment. The old man or impotent king figure is a Thanatos archetype, probably: Eliot's fisher king, Yeats' mad old man, the senile giants in Dante's hell, Priam at the end of the Iliad, Blake's Albion at the bottom of the sea, and Lear. He puts out to sea in the ship of death, as in Eliot's *Marina*. The arrow of Eros falls short of the virgin, describes a trajectory which is an upper semicircle and falls on the red Adonis flower. I've got that, more or less: what I want now is the other semicircle. This goes down in the West through all the David & Absalom complexes to the oracular cave, whence it returns in an image usually linked to a ship or floating ark, because it just misses hell, as the arrow misses the moon. (What corresponds to the arrow, the golden bough?) Strictly speaking, this speculation doesn't belong here, because this cycle doesn't really get into Thanatos. But it's related to Thanatos imagery as L'Allegro's is to Il Penseroso. You can go into a Cyclopean cave, even

drown in the sea like Phlebas, and still emerge through the S.E. birds & frogs gate. If I could crack this one I think I'd have reconciled pre-Romantic and Romantic myth. The thing is that if I have comedy & tragedy describing only quadrants, I need two other categories; or perhaps my old notion of romantic vs. ironic comic & tragic patterns would fit. I might have known I'd get the damn thing the wrong way round: it should go clockwise. But ironic hardly fits the damn Romantics, & they're all snuggling down there in the cave of winds. (No: counter-clockwise is right: it's my current Eros-Adonis semicircle that's wrong). This way there isn't a way out of hell, strictly: hell is a progressive series of parodies all along. My early satire paper[54] went through the point of demonic epiphany: it didn't go into hell at all.

[61] There are two kinds of old men at the point of epiphany: the Pisgah one (Moses-Virgil-Simeon-Magi) who can't get in but depart in peace, and the hermetic hermit in the tower—though of course they could be identified. At the point of demonic epiphany is the impotent king: the Priam-old Adam figure that forms part of Lear. Now, the old man in the tower is a Prospero who can realize the masque of the earthly Paradise: that is, he brings it about & sees it but can't finish it, like Moses. The old man at the p.d.e. [point of demonic epiphany] is, besides the impotent king, the *senex iratus*, who, as Yeats saw, includes Lear and Timon, the bitter impotent rage of experience which, as Sartre says, is nothing brought into being.[55] It's really the masque of hell. A softer form is the vision of Gerontion in Eliot, the underside vision of Christ in terms of sparagmos-disappearance. Teiresias the bisexual is close to the archetype; Prufrock more displaced.

[62] I'm beginning to suspect that there is no Logos or Thanatos in art at all, only a series of hints of what's beyond it or below it. As I've said, Celine & Genet are morally significant because they shock & horrify: they help to prevent us from becoming what we behold. Hell is not knowing the difference: it's the world of sub-art and anti-art. But everything that *is* art goes through the p.d.e. [point of demonic epiphany] and contemplates it. Similarly at the top, where everything that's literature is an analogy or masque of heaven.

[63] So what I have to think about right now is the tragedy beyond tragedy, that mysterious Lear-world that the Mental Traveller goes into

after the birth of Rahab, and the comedy antecedent to comedy, the comedy of which Cupid's first arrow is an anamnesis or recognition. This antecedent comedy comes out of a buried green world or cave of myths, the world of Queen Mab's dreams. Female figures include a sterile witch & whore ambivalence corresponding to the Venus-Diana one on top.

[64] I don't think I'm just boxing the third essay [of *AC*] compass again, certainly not if I succeed in tying up the Ro-pre-Ro. [Romanticism–pre-Romanticism] antithesis. And wouldn't it be extraordinary if what is partly a historical sequence, & has always been assumed to be exclusively so, turned out to be a completing of a total pattern? I do suggest this in my Harvard myth essay—no, my Yale one—on a substance-and-reflection basis, but the way I've modified it in my Romantic book does suggest this total circle theory.[56] But then what happens to displaced & realistic forms?

[65] I seem to be saying now that the real unborn world, that is, the more literal one, is the cave of myths in the p.d.e. [point of demonic epiphany], the shadow world of Thel; but *that* makes no bloody sense at all. Falling out of the p of e [point of epiphany] masque is surely birth. Or is it?—Jesus, it's hard to know. Limbo, the place of unbaptized (symb. [symbolic] of ungenerated) infants, is p.d.e., but where the hell's Alice? I think I'm onto something: I never did know what the second half of the M.T. [Blake's *The Mental Traveller*], the *female* life, was all about, & it must be underneath, being female. *Lear* is an Adonis tragedy, of life cut off, only in relation to Cordelia. Are *Iphigenia* & *Antigone*, then, also in the W to S area? S is physical birth & spiritual death, N the reverse.

[66] One thing, I'm pretty sure the S to E area is where Prometheus goes, the antecedent comedy of liberation on which all Eros comedy is founded, and the typical comedy of both Reason and realism (modern). Earlier, the postulate of comedy, so to speak, was the Promethean resurrection of Christ. The W to S area is the Lear one of second tragedy, as I say, only it's the Rc. [Romantic] world of [Shelley's] Alastor. The isolated or nympholeptic wanderer. (If he isn't nympholeptic he's deserted or betrayed the female, as with Aeneas & Theseus). I need a name for this quadrant: it's really the Oedipus one, opposite to the Promethean Christ as Yeats

says. It's the world where guilt, as the source of tragedy, is discovered.

[67] The definition of the S point frequently involves the theme we have in the middle of WT [*The Winter's Tale*] and the beginning of the total action of T [*The Tempest*]: the older man and the infant girl, corresponding to the birth of the Female Babe in MT [*The Mental Traveller*] and opposite the calumniated mother & infant boy theme of Perseus & [Chaucer's] The Man of Law's Tale. At the S point we have often both the sea and a devouring monster: Antigonus' bear.[57] This is the Scylla-Charybdis duality, revealed by Satan in Milton at the p.d.e. [point of demonic epiphany] of his universe, the gate between chaos & hell. The devouring monster recurs in the three beasts of Dante, reduplicated in Cerberus, & the leopards of *Ash Wednesday*, where the desert is symbolically a sea as well. Light-hearted parody of p.d.e. in *The Miller's Tale*: female arse & the man expecting Noah's flood.

[68] Is Thanatos ultimately a person like Logos? The one who comes nearest to suggesting this is Beddoes, and then there's Yeats. Because Yeats is interested in heroism rather than tragedy, he's got his literary categories all bass-ackward. All natural literary metaphors have tragedy falling (hence "catastrophe") and comedy rising. But he's got comedy all buggered up with a "primary" & objective culture, & tragedy with an "antithetical" one that *rises* out of it. He should have followed the direction of the mouths on the masks. But as it is he's got, as I said, God in the place of death. Hence his remark that wisdom (Logos) is the property of the dead, and a consequent identification of the Logos & Thanatos. But Yeats *is* a great poet, and there may be more in it than just buggered-up symbolism.

[Untitled section]

[69] The book I want to write, to be called *The Critical Path*, with an epigraph from Kant,[58] is to be a kind of critical Divine Comedy, surveying the entire symbolic universe of myth. It sounds like an impossible project, & may prove to be; but of course I'm not concerned with all subjects, only with the total subject of which criticism forms a part.

[70] The notes in this book are in one of the possible arrangements; but I

think the most practicable one is Eros-Adonis-Thanatos-Logos. It's very difficult to stop going up when you get to the upper limit of Beulah, but I think it's equally practicable to finish the cycle, then close it, and then open it up by whatever the opposite of parody is.

[71] The four "levels" of imaginative existence are as a rule arranged dialectically, two being "good" & two "bad." Thus:

	a. "good"	b. "bad"
1. Logos (order)	music of spheres	automatism & fatality
2. Eros (energy)	green & gold world	nature as world of will
3. Adonis	ordered city	fallen cycle of time
4. Thanatos	inner identity	life imprisoned in death

The combination 1a, 2a, 3b & 4b is the Classical or pre-Romantic one; 1b, 2a, 3b & 4a is the revolutionary Romantic, 1a, 2b, 3a & 4b the conservative Romantic; 1b, 2b, 3a & 4a a reversed post-Rc. [post-Romantic] tonality.

[72] Now that there appear to be four quadrants rather than two semi-circles, six parts are shaping up. And there may be eight, if I could establish E & W epiphanic points, one in conceptual & the other in social displacement. The E point is the resolution of my comedy paradox, how what is pragmatic in comedy becomes a revolutionary triumph of dialectic when it goes into conceptual reverse. This displacement is most of my St. Clair ˥ [Tragicomedy]-Λ [Anticlimax] illumination:[59] not all of it, because the discontinuous epiphanic sequence belongs to Logos. I suppose I could call this E point Hermes. On the other side is an existential social displacement, related to law but not easily held in a conceptual synthesis. This is where the stuff goes I got into the Alexanders about the conditioning ecstatic society and the "thrown-ness" of the subject.[60] It could be called Ares, who takes over at this point as the lover of Venus.

[73] That gives me Blake's diagram of a mundane egg with four chaotic universes around it,[61] so that my Zoa pattern has shifted to the epicycles. Mine is upside down compared to Blake, with the North at the top. Hence the E is a Tharmas area, & Orc has his specifically dying-god role

in the West. Blake's Milton, then, I have coming in from the NW, a meander-and-descent pattern heading for the p.d.e. [point of demonic epiphany]. I take the latter to be, among other things, the limit of opacity: the Adamic limit of contraction would be, for me, W rather than the p of e [point of epiphany]. The line across the circle is the line of fall, the dying god's death, & descent into hell, crossed N to S: the line of resurrection and physical rebirth, the birth often of a comic society, crossed S to N.

[74] Now: I know that my Logos & Thanatos sections are likely to turn out to be a series of parallel parodies: I wonder if Hermes & Ares represent a similar set of parallels, the tragic & comic antitheses. I wonder too if Apollo isn't closer to what I mean by the praxis-displacement than Ares is: Nietzsche's Dionysus, the complement, is less of a dying god for him than the Prometheus-Eros figure I've got at E. Plato's myths certainly converge around Eros & Prometheus: Orphism, an outgrowth of Dionysus, is in the E to N area. Perhaps Apollo-W & Orpheus-E is right: the Eurydice fiasco corresponds to the C of L [Court of Love] starting point. But it seems funny not to have a conceptual term at the point of Theoria-displacement when I have Logos & Thanatos N & S. But of course Logos turns out to be a personality, & perhaps the central question humanity can ask is: Is Thanatos a person too?

[75] So what I've got now is my old symbolic universe idea, seen as an inner circle of four quadrants, and then the two axes, of speculation E-W, of concern N-S. The only thing missing from a *total* scheme is the V [Mirage] theme of the context of literature in the arts. But all the other things are back, & now, of course, the old scheme underlying this book is buggered, not that that matters. Perhaps two volumes: first, the way in, the cycle of imagery; second, the way out, the dialectic of the axes. I have a notion that there's a speculation : spatial :: concern : temporal pattern involved. I'm not sure that Apollo & Hermes are quite right, though they're close: what I'm after is the "pagan" spatialized sky-father versus god of the shades below, as distinct from the "real" Logos-Death one.

[76] The top half of the circle is female-dominated, with the youthful Orc in his two aspects. At the W point we have the Oresteia, passing into a male dominated cycle—so that's where *that* goes. What I call Apollo is this creative male sky-linked artefact god. The lower half is male-

dominated, with father-daughter groups around S & the reborn male making his Promethean comeback E. The real Logos is clear of the sexual cycle: as clear as Thanatos is. And he *doesn't* make the world: that's the Genesis fallacy and not the Job revelation. That is, he doesn't make the mirror or speculative world out there: all he makes is the real world.

[77] One thing that bugs me is the fallacy suggested by this circle arrangement. I doubt if there are any significant patterns except at the quadrants. Or rather, there's an Eros imagery, but I shouldn't be fooled by the Dante aspect of it to think that that's a pattern characteristically ENE, another NE, & so on. The whole damn world is Eros to an erotic, & shouldn't be thought of as approaching anything else.

Notebook 12

Notebook 12 can be dated confidently 1968–70. Paragraph 68 speaks of an early version of CP *that Frye delivered as a lecture at Cornell University in March 1968, and paragraph 193 says it has been eighteen years since the Seattle revelation (see Introduction) of 1950. On the other end, in paragraph 573, Frye writes, "I arrive at the last page of this notebook on August 30, 1970." The longest notebook until the final* WP *notebooks at the end of Frye's life, Notebook 12 takes up from the end of Notebook 6 the plan to write the Third Book as* The Critical Path, *and develops much further its meditation on the quadrants and cardinal points of the Great Doodle. In the course of this evolution, the book eventually published as* CP *split off from the main project, taking the title with it, and is spoken of as finished in paragraph 560. Notebook 12 is located in the NFF, 1991, box 24.*

[1] I wish to make my third large book a study of the symbolic universe, a kind of Divine Comedy in criticism. Its tentative title; based on the coincidence of a common business term publicized by Expo and the last paragraph of Kant's *Critique of Pure Reason*, is "The Critical Path."[1] Its theme, like Dante's, is that of the passage through and out of the labyrinth (another Expo echo).

[2] I have been thinking about this book for years, but my first real lead into it came from a paper I did on Milton's imagery.[2] There I discovered the principle of the anabasis of Eros, the ascent of the soul towards its Creator, and the imagery that goes with that. In Milton, as in much Christian poetry, the anabasis of Eros has to be complemented by the katabasis of Agape, divine grace taking the initiative, but that's only one

of several possible patterns. Spenser's Four Hymns follow the Miltonic pattern, or rather anticipate it.

[3] Well: the symbolism of Eros starts with the conception, based on Ovid, of the writing of poetry as being what ethologists call a displaced activity of a frustrated lover.[3] Its basis is a sexual imagery in which the male (sun, sky, wind, rain, bird) is above the female (moon, earth, flowers, caves & rivers, especially rivers springing from underground). The female principle acts normally as a retreating eiron, an *ewig-weibliche* [eternal feminine] inspiration which grows more maternal as the lover becomes more dependent on it. That is, the Eros journey is really a journey *toward birth*, and its archetype is the purgatorial journey in Dante.

[4] The purgatorial journey is towards the original place of birth, or earthly Paradise. It goes up a mountain or upstream to the source of a river.* It's the Israelite wilderness wandering toward the Promised Land: note the paralleling of Virgil & Moses. Similar journeys to rebirth occur in [T.S. Eliot's] Ash Wednesday & several poems of Yeats. Often the earthly Paradise is a place of sexual fulfilment, but more often the journey is towards the pre-sexual world of "innocence." Dante's ring of fire is like a recognition of a birth trauma. The drive of Menandrine New Comedy is toward a sexual fulfilment which is also a *social* birth. The pastoral world is often innocent (*and* poetic) in the same sense. Freud's Eros-journey is also a recapitulation of childhood, a continuous recognition of blocks with the birth trauma at the end.

[5] The paradox of a vision of Eros involving *chastity* is completed by the higher Eros vision that descends from Plato and is the theme of Dante's *Paradiso*. Here the vision is often mathematical, symbolized by the harmony of the spheres. In Christianity this higher vision is a participating in the divine love or *agape*, but I'd prefer the term Logos for the vision of the top world: it has the Christian overtones of the union of divine & human, as well as overtones of reason, more particularly dialectic, of the supremacy of the Word (symbolized as music), and a number of other things.

---

* Hence the "happy valley" in a mountainous landscape.

[6] In Milton, L'Allegro is an Eros vision of "unreproved pleasures free" [l. 41], leading to the Earthly Paradise; Il Penseroso is an aesthetic or mirror vision of Logos, the old man in the Tower, the Platonist, the hermit or sage devoted to the vestal virgin. *Comus* is the natural virtue of chastity going as far as it can, hearing the music of the spheres, and establishing the mysterious magic rapport with the natural spirits symbolized by Orpheus (& Prospero). Ariel & the Attendant Spirit return to their own elements.

[7] The place of rebirth is a point of epiphany, symbolized by a Tower, lighthouse, mountain-top, tree in forest, directly under the moon. This place is a hortus conclusus, or body of the mother as earth, with two gates, one above & one below. It's a vision of the whole cycle, & hence may be the Gardens of Adonis: it's also a place of seed.

[8] I start with my old four-levels diagram, then with the cycle, divided into innocence & experience, in the middle, & symbolized by Eros & Thanatos. Now why the hell did I write that? I mean Eros & Adonis. Thanatos is the lower consolidation of tragedy, the world of the Iliad & Dante's Inferno, just as Logos is the higher consolidation of comedy. Logos & Thanatos are the dialectical opposition.

[9] It would be more traditional to start, as Dante does, with the world of Adonis, the world of the maze in the wood. The images of this world are those of war & hunting. Adonis deserted Venus for hunting, & it's the world, I think, of the animal chorus, the beast-headed rout. Anyway, it's the world of epic action, and has three main divisions. Socially, it's the world of the epic & tragic leader; erotically it's a phallic world symbolized by the satyrs in Spenser, by Aristophanic Old Comedy; by Cleopatra's Egyptian world in Shakespeare. This is the primary world of agon, and is the John Barleycorn[4] world of Frazer, who also begins with a maze in a wood.

[10] There follows the meander-and-descent pattern of the penetration into the labyrinth, which closes round one until we reach the beast in view. The world of Thanatos is a world of repetition, of the same dull round, of life assimilated to ritual. I don't know much about it yet: I've always hated this world, and the Iliad & Inferno are my bugbears. We escape from it out the back door: Dante in his undisplaced vision enters

Satan's mouth, prowls his bowels, & gets shat out of his arse. Two things are involved in the back door escape: the bird-and-serpent symbolism, the SSE point of my diagram, and the theme of mysterious return to the world that turns up in the Classical epic.

[11] On the other hand, I know considerably more about the Eros vision, with its purgatorial, pastoral & comic patterns. The journey of the wise man to the infant ties up a lot of it. Then we go through the mother's body (this extends in Dante from Purg. [*Purgatorio*] 28 to Par. [*Paradiso*] 9, from Matilda to Rahab)[5] into the full Logos vision. This is in part the analogical vision of plenitude, the apocalyptic table of identified metaphors & their demonic shadows,[6] where correspondence, figure & the dance of the elements are the organizing elements, and in part a dark night or vision of vacancy, not demonic but simply wordless, the musicless harmony of the tonic chord.

[12] I have always wanted to write a book that will be schematic in form as well as in content. The original version of FS had a hundred sections. Eros: twenty-eight sections, the lunar number of the cycle. Logos: twenty-two sections, the last one, corresponding to the Fool in the Tarot pack, dealing with the theme of redemptive descent. Adonis: twenty-eight sections again, and then Thanatos, twenty-two sections, with the escape theme the last one. Only, of course, assimilated to the two patterns in the Gospel: the Incarnation descent and Ascension return to & from Generation; the Harrowing of Hell descent & Resurrection return to & from Ulro.

[13] One difficulty with this scheme is that, aside from being over-restrictive, it may not fit the rhythm of criticism. It may require, as in Dante, the tremendous concentration of poetry to have so many stages. Critical treatment of *The Tempest* (top of Eros), *Paradise Regained* (opening of Logos), & Blake's *Milton* (redemptive descent) has to be extended, whereas if there's more than about three or four pages to a stage the critical path will get discouragingly long, & its readers will start thumbing rides on the Anatomy again.

[14] And if this book shows the least sign of becoming just a rewritten AC out it goes into the ash-can.

[15] I have to keep an eye open on the philosophical analogues, aside

from the fact that Plato, along with Dante, is the chief guide to the Eros & Logos visions. It seems to me that Hegelian dialectic, & the kind of reversal-through-exhaustion progression that one gets in the *Phenomenology of the Spirit* [*Phenomenology of Spirit*], is the intellectualized counterpart to the Eros climb. I suppose Thomas is the angel of the Logos vision: Kant & the riddle of the thing in itself as unknowable is the presiding genius of Adonis: I don't know who the devil of the lower stairs is. Very probably Augustine and the metaphysic of the absurd which descends from him through Pascal, Kierkegaard, Nietzsche. Also the political ones: Eros is revolution, Logos utopia, Adonis education & Thanatos contract. Note that the hell of narrowing circles, being leviathan's guts, eventually becomes the absurd, which includes my old comminution[7]–communication-fragmentation hunch, the sparagmos *digesting* of vision & divine personality. Man eats the red & white body & blood of God on the sacramental ascent: similarly love unites the red phoenix & the white turtle. At the other end the gods eat man & tread the winepress with his blood. This is red, white & black, the colors of the stairs in the Purgatorio [canto 9, ll. 94–102]: red, white & green (or sometimes red, gold & green) are the colors of the amorous bodies united with nature.

[16] Of course Dante had only one universe to deal with: I have at least two. The sexual imagery I start out with splits into a pre-Romantic father-god who makes the world & a pre-Christian and post-Romantic mother-god who remakes it, or rather gives birth to it. Hence I have to deal with both the traditional projected myth & the modern psychological or recovered one. That gives me a lot of descending Eros patterns: the Rasselas-Thel-Endymion-Erewhon (etc.) theme of guilt in the unborn world (or does this logically go at the beginning of Adonis?). The Shelley-Yeats-Lawrence type of *autonomous* Eros vision is quite different from the sacramental kind. In the Logos vision there's the projected God who really creates by the Word, & the revolutionary Prometheus who makes things. Blake's blacksmith god & Marx's chief symbol (also of course Morris's). The *mousike* projected & the *techne* recovered maker.[8]

[17] In Logos time & space are a real present & a real presence, the eternity of now & the infinity of here. In Eros time is an expression of the rhythmical exuberance of energy & space is a possessed home. In Adonis time & space are as we experience them; in Thanatos time is pure duration, one

clock-tick after another, & space pure alienated recession. (Experience time is a *mixture* of straight line & cycle, space a mixture of recession & home). Hence the function of art (Burnt Norton, section 5) is to express the combination of time & space ("pattern" of music & "rhythm" of painting) that the innocent world expresses by the images of heavenly spheres spinning around in circles & creating harmony by doing so.

[18] At the top of Eros one either goes on into Logos or returns to experience. *The Tempest* does the latter, as the brave new world is adult experience for Miranda and a repetition for Prospero. Here again there's the emphasis on chastity. Note that even Norman Brown drives away from the sex act towards the infantile polymorphous.[9] I suppose in a sense even Blake's *Milton* does the same, as Milton is still, like Enoch & Elijah in Paradise, the old man seeing the infant—or rather, in Blake he's without his emanation, & is hence in a pre-sexual state.[10] In Dante, after Satan shits him out of the Inferno, he shits Satan, in the form of the accusing memory, after Lethe & Eunoe at the top of purgatory.[11] Similarly in Blake's *Milton* the casting out of the devil (as in P.R. [*Paradise Regained*]) is the climactic action. In 19th c. fiction there's a lot of emphasis on the return to experience as a kind of voluntary or conscious fall. [Nathaniel Hawthorne's] Maypole of Merry Mount—that sort of thing. I suppose there are a lot of Adonis & Thanatos symbols in Hawthorne & Melville. Hawthorne even has a big red capital A. Adonis could well begin (after the redemptive descent) with the entry from Eros, & Hawthorne would be useful there (likewise Melville & Conrad with their poisoned-paradise imagery).

[19] On the schematizing of this book: a certain number of loci or topoi, whether 100 or not, would be useful in classifying notes, but apart from that I should let the book grow as my other books do & then see if a schematic division fits. There has to be a good deal of introduction, for one thing, and an immense number of things cluster around the points of epiphany & demonic epiphany. I only think of schematization because all my ideas about this book seem to turn that way. Preludes in all the keys, e.g. The schematizing of Dante is solemn, but the over-designing of a detective story is amusing, & Yeats's *Vision* comes somewhere between.

[20] Incidentally, I speak of *loci & topoi*. Wonder if there's a distinction—the distinction of fictional & thematic or conceptual myths?

[21] Adonis depends on the romance stream in 19th c. fiction, because romance is the skeleton key to displaced or realistic literature. In the AC the passage from irony to myth, through the exhaustion of naturalism, is a typically Hegelian progression through antithesis. Wonder if this is an organizing principle, connected with the mirror-reversal theme that runs all through from Ovid's Narcissus & Dante's specchio & spero symbolism[12] to Alice. Upside down in air were towers[13]—the demonic consolidation of the apocalypse by reversal.

[22] One reference to the total scheme & then I leave it. In AC I tried to give the world some notion of what's in L [Liberal], and similarly this book will do the same for ˥ [Tragicomedy]. There should follow two studies of displaced myth, one on metaphysical & the other on social & political displacements, Λ [Anticlimax] & ⅄ [Rencontre], both based on critiques of prose forms. Then a reintegrating study, V [Mirage], of the languages of all the major arts & their roles in education. Then two gigantic anagnorisis summaries, Γ & ⅃, of dialectic comic & existential tragic recognition respectively, and finally, Y, an axiomatic summary of the lot.[14] As I expect to die or go senile early in the progression, I have to shoot the works with every book I write.

[23] Certainly what seems the easiest is to start with the ascent of Eros. The post-Romantic form of the myth perhaps isn't an insuperable difficulty, once the reader has grasped the expendability of spatializing metaphor. In any case (a) there is some underlying connexion between the two myths, as my use of Yeats & Eliot to expound the earlier construct indicates, which I haven't grasped yet (b) I have to avoid the temptation to spread out my 100 loci in a single mental landscape.

[24] Still, the Eros pattern is fairly clear, & it's mostly ascent-to-youth metaphors. Dante puts the analogical vision at the top of Purgatory, but I think it has to open the Logos vision. That leaves room for the existential & fragmented things on the other side of the great revelation, and I suppose the whole Logos scheme is a parabola, with descent patterns like the Nativity Ode & the Book of Rev [Revelation] coinciding with immanent ones. Blake's bounding outline & Hopkins' inscape go here,[15] and I think there's a point of silence at the top of Logos & the bottom of Thanatos. Thanatos itself starts with the point of demonic epiphany & goes through the demonic analogy to Rimbaud's *Saison* [*en Enfer*] & from

there to Genet's evocation of the conventional images as the perversion of a perversion.[16] This scheme is infinitely more flexible than the old birth-of-hero Joseph Campbell way of getting at it, but I have a wheel of that too, of course, & have to keep it in mind.[17] Perhaps it's the vision of the cycle that's at the point of epiphany, to be immediately followed by the dialectic of analogical vision.

[25] Probably I've got the proportions wrong: the Eros climb to youth may be about equal in length to the Agape descent *into* the cycle. The Logos parabola at the top begins with the analogical vision, goes on to implicit or fragmented archetypes, reaches a point of silence, and then begins to consolidate another unified vision as it descends. God in Dante contemplates himself in his works, as Rachel looks in a mirror; hence the descent is a voluntary fall of Narcissus.[18] So the Eros climb (which is both Christian and autonomous) is repeated in a descent to experience, & so forth. Similarly the escape from Thanatos may be a repetition of the descent into, but a road that takes one through tragedy. At this point I'm assuming, really, an E-N-W-S-E progression, and if I started at N I'd start with the birth of the hero & end with the analogical vision. That would be difficult, because of keeping the expository key to the end.

[26] I originally thought of a summarized symbolic universe as an introduction to a study of the external relations of mythology.[19] Now that it seems to be becoming a separate book, I'm worried about its withdrawing too far from those relations and becoming a second Anatomy. My previous worry was the opposite extreme: that I'd stray off too far from what I really know to become an amateur writer on metaphysics or political theory. As this present book seems to be in part an adaptation of the book on practical criticism suggested in the Preface to AC, I have two extremes to avoid there too. One is the danger of losing an integrating pattern in a series of illustrations; the other is avoiding the impression of what Geoffrey calls a cheap tour of mythland.[20] (I think he was wrong, and that the Eliot book for all its faults is something of a *tour de force*, but still I want the sense of immense technical skill to show through, & it isn't just vanity that makes me want to).

[27] In any case I want to establish the essential links of ∧ [Anticlimax] & ⋌ [Rencontre], while making this book still essentially a study of the symbolic universe. Thus the Eros ladder has links with Plato & Freud,

not impossibly with Hegel; the Logos vision is one of analogy. Note the link between the projected: I think God, therefore God is, and the recovered Cartesian cogito ergo sum. The epiphanic vision of God is the primitive root of religious reality, because it attaches the reality to the experience, as Paul identifies the resurrection with his conversion.[21] That doesn't make it "subjective," of course.

[28] Subject to change without notice, the goal of the Eros vision seems to me to be identity-as, the goal of the Logos vision identity-with. The Eros vision begins in the Ovid-Petrarch displaced-lover theme, and develops toward the one-pointed concentration on the released creative power, which is human liberty. Liberty is the result of discipline, hence the Eros vision develops through purgatorial and yoga progressions. It begins in sexually inspired dreams, and ends in created visions which are not subjective. The fact that it moves simultaneously toward adult free will & reconstructed childhood leads to the y-choice at the point of epiphany: rebirth *or* progression to the Logos, though either choice, if honestly made, turns out to include the other—this is what's at the top of Yeats' tower.[22] In the East it's the Bodhisattva.

[29] Eros runs against the current of entropy in ordinary life, as communication does according to Norbert Wiener.[23] It's the uniting of the sexual instinct with the intelligence. Hence it's the creative world proper, where the poet studies himself. In Adonis sex & intellect split apart: Mark Antony is either in Egypt or in Rome. Logos, on the other hand, begins in the analogy of God & ends in the modern semi-recovered analogy of science. The latter part has to deal with the mystery of the *genuine* analogy to what's there—the kind of thing I've so far dodged in separating the myth of concern from the science. *Complete* separation of course makes the myth of concern solipsistic or paranoid. The sense of intuitive or recovered spontaneity of thought in Logos visions, as in the monologue of Lilith at the end of Shaw's BM [*Back to Methuselah*], is very strong.[24]

[30] It would be nice if I could bring off a recognition scene of the impasse of the culture of the sixties, after wearily plodding down through Rimbaud & Beckett & Celine & Mailer & Genet to a point at which—possibly in Genet's perversion of a perversion[25]—some upturn begins to look possible.

[31] So far, all I've really got is just my old AC book over again, Eros, Logos, Adonis & Thanatos being just my old four mythoi in a new setting. Of course the new setting is important, but my resolve holds.

[32] Anyway, there's the green or Eros vision, leading up to the white vision, the earthly paradise or vision of chastity under the moon. Once attained, this lunar or white vision turns into the full Logos or golden vision. Dante enters the full Logos vision at Canto X of the Paradiso, the sun beyond Rahab the forgiven harlot and the earth's shadow.[26]

[33] I have a hunch that romance, being the least displaced form of mimetic fiction, is the main thoroughfare for the red or Adonis vision. Naive romance, including the folktale quest patterns of the Two Brothers,[27] then the Greek romances, Apuleius, & the others down to Sidney; also the medieval romances, the Tristan & Parzival & other Arthurian & Grail legends, the Sagas, the Romaunt of the Rose (though of course the de Lorris part of that at least is an Eros vision), & the later Italians, Ariosto & such. Sentimental romance is my old notion of a pattern of imagery *and* quest structure (Hopkins' under-thought & over-thought)[28] running through Scott, Poe, Hawthorne, George Macdonald, William Morris & Tolkien, with ghost stories & German parallels & miscellaneous Gothic (LeFanu & Brockden Brown). Then the displaced forms. First, epic, more particularly the Aeneid, which, besides being the definitive point-of-demonic-epiphany vision, sets the model for the epic pattern of war & hunting succeeding the pastoral Eros vision. Hunting was what Adonis preferred to Venus. Second, low mimetic fiction, where I distinguish, heuristically, the primary displacements still close to romance (Melville, Conrad, Lawrence, Virginia Woolf) from the secondary ones (Balzac, Tolstoy, etc.).

[34] My colors are Dantean: red & white are those of the cycle of experience & innocence: red, white & black, the colors of the stairway to purgatory,[29] of the cycle closed off, the sublunary world. Red, white & green are the Eros vision moving up to the pastoral earthly-paradise green & gold. Above, there's a blue and white sky & cloud vision, centering on the Virgin & the Dove. Of course there's both Melville's demonic white and St. John of the Cross's dark night. Above the blue and white lower-Logos vision there's the higher red-gold one of the Seraphim, the "mutual flame" in which the red (female) phoenix & the white (male) turtle are united,

where in Little Gidding the ineffectual efforts to achieve a vision of immortality by burning a rose have given place to a world where the fire & the rose are one. This is Donne's "canonization," the fiery apotheosis of Eros, which in Yeats's *Byzantium* is seen as a total Heraclitean process from mire to "fury" and includes the journey across the sea of *Sailing to Byzantium* and *News for the Delphic Oracle.*

[35] The Adonis vision starts—at least I think it starts—with the folktale of the Two Brothers. This is the tanist theme of Romulus & Remus, the identical twins of *Amis & Amiloun*[30] & of various New Comedy plots, Poe's William Wilson & other doppelganger stories (Dupin and "O" in The Purloined Letter). The Biblical archetype is the brother accepted in the Promised Land & the brother wandering in the wilderness: Isaac & Ishmael, Jacob & Esau: the Romantic shift of sympathy to the desert wanderer marks the intensification of the Adonis vision. (Query: if the order is Eros, Logos, Adonis & Thanatos, could I postpone introducing the Romantic cosmos to the beginning of the Adonis vision, in spite of Virgil & the medieval romances? Anyway.). First, there's the Leviticus pattern of the chosen victim and the released scapegoat [Leviticus 16], Jesus & Barabbas. This intensifies into the demons chased out into the wilderness or the deep (Azazel and Lilith, who brings a female element into the complex).[31] Blake's spectre of Ololon [in *Milton*]. I don't know if the hero: victim :: tanist: demonic scapegoat always works, but there are many other forms.

[36] The commonest of these is the exile as rightful heir, who returns & chases out the pretender. Jesus is of the line of Jacob, but the Messiah of Isaiah 63 returning from Eden is an Esau, as Blake says. The hero : recognized ruler :: tanist : pretender pattern is in Shakespeare's Falstaff, Spenser's Braggadocchio, & all the eiron-alazon confrontations. Again, the exile in the desert may be a witness, Moses or Elijah, incarnate in John the Baptist the solstitial twin. All these shifting & varying shapes—Shelley's Zoroaster,[32] Eliot's shadow meeting himself as substance in *Marina*—recur in the author-persona relation: Swift-Gulliver, Proust-Marcel, Joyce-Stephen (cf. the Primas-Caddy business in FW [*Finnegans Wake*]).[33] I think the flounderings of critics over this question can be cut through.

[37] The order-figure of my Alexander lectures[34] is a lower Logos figure

who typifies the essentially split world of Adonis: split, as the world of Eros is not, between the social & the sexual, authority and love, loyalty & sympathy. The total alienation of sympathy from this figure is a frequent dramatic paradox: Henry V at the rejection of Falstaff, Caesar at the fall of Antony, and—centrally—Jesus in P.R. [*Paradise Regained*]. Also, of course, the great Adonis hero Aeneas, who also deserts his Venus (Dido) for war & hunting, rationalized as duty: sum pius Aeneas.[35] This is where my point goes about an interpretation valid for *The Tempest* being nonsense for A & C [*Antony and Cleopatra*].

[38] The difficulty, as well as the pleasure, of writing such a book is the elaborateness of the counterpoint: an endless fugue in forty parts. Thus when I spoke of demonic white & benevolent black I forgot the white goddess and the black bride. According to the Epithalamion, "Majesty" is the child begotten by Jove on Night.[36] Of course the dark night of the soul takes off from the black bride's search for her bridegroom in S.S. [Song of Songs] 3. Moby Dick on the other hand is male, even if he does have a remote female ancestor in Tiamat.[37]

[39] Chess: I think in its normal context it's an Eros symbol, a love game rather than a Kriegspiel [war game]. As it clearly is in *The Tempest*, in some naive romance (including the Mabinogion, where it's replaced by an unspellable & probably unpronounceable Welsh equivalent) and perhaps in the Egyptian Book of the Dead, where whatever game it is is translated "draughts" by Wallis Budge.[38] The Eliot one is ironic, of course, and there the 32 pieces of chess have some connexion with the poor creature's teeth that have to come out in her 32nd year.[39] Poe was interested in chess (*and* in checkers) as well as in teeth—Berenice's, that is: all 32 of them.[40] Going back to the Book of the Dead, I should remember that most Eros settings are, like Dante's, on the other side of this world, which means often the underworld, a quite different world from the world of Thanatos, which is Hades or hell, a world of life *in* death. In short, I have to remember that spatial projections are variable.

[40] Remembering that Lewis Carroll is a very knowledgeable guide through certain parts of the labyrinth, it's significant that the story about cards ends in a lawsuit and the story about chess (where the pieces are the Eros colors red and white) in a catechism (and banquet). Chess is Platonic Eros, linked to the victory of dialectic (the Russians are the best

chess-players) and the symposium. Cards have overtones of divination & fate (Pushkin's Queen of Spades; the Methodist horror of them, etc.): it marks the victim or it's the *deus ex machina* trump.

[41] One possible progression is: start with Eros, & go as far as the point of epiphany, but follow Yeats & descend into the Adonis world: agon & pathos. Then down to Thanatos & sparagmos, where the Hegelian progression from naturalism to demonic myth could then go through another reversal into the vision of Logos or anagnorisis, ending the book with a series of tremendous recognition scenes, including not only the table of metaphors but the great wheel of episodic forms & the hero's life & quest that holds them together.[41] That's really the form I want, though it's terrifically hard to bring off. It would give the quality of continuous story to the book and might even sublimate the death-recognition story I've always wanted to write.[42] It might however put too heavy a weight on contemporary literature, especially Genet, who's surely not all that important except as a personal symbol: le Byron de nos jours.

[42] Adonis is a mixture of Eros & Thanatos. The war & hunting theme is a social one in which the essential drive or impetus is ironic. Hence the lower-Logos order figure: the split from Eros is symbolized in Greek tragedy by the satyr-play following the trilogy; in Shakespeare by the opposition of Falstaff & H5 [Henry V], Antony & Octavius; in Spenser by historical allegory *and* by satyrs, etc. Speaking of the poet as personal legend, note the Adonis figure of Sidney (Spenser's *Astrophel*), Byron "killed" in Greece, & the like. Sidney & Byron are also lovers & love-poets. In low mimetic fiction the social-sexual split is represented by such things as the light & dark heroine, one associated with bourgeois domestic virtues, the other sexier and spicier, but often killed or rejected.

[43] In medieval society we have the nobility & the priesthood, red men & white men, as Eros symbols, both to some extent making themselves eunuchs, not for Christ's sake as Paul says, but for respectively the phoenix & the turtle, the Courtly Love mistress & the virgin mother of God. The Adonis split appears in the contrast between the crusade, the holy war which (ideally) united warrior & priest and abandoned the woman and the rejected sexual & Dionysian devil, which separated Rahab (Paradiso ix also refers to the crusades) from the witch or devil's dam, the degraded earth-goddess.[43]

[44] In mimetic times there's a social establishment in the middle of society, with an upper & a lower class both dependent on it, parasitic to that extent, and hence, qua classes, essentially animal classes. The aristocracy acquires a powerful sexual smell from Romanticism once Lord Byron & the Marquis de Sade inherit the devil, along with the Gothic heroes. They get this partly from the fact that Eros has shifted from pastoral & garden metaphors to the numinous nature of forest and wilderness. The sexual symbolism of a lower class is less easily established, but there are traces of it in [Wyndham] Lewis's *Paleface*[44] images: Nazi sadism & the whipping of Jewesses ([Robert] Briffault's *Europa*);[45] the black man as a sexual symbol; the virile worker & the effete bourgeois (Lawrence's gamekeeper; even Heathcliff). The beat & hippie people revive the childlike radical of aristocracy which makes it an Eros symbol, including the cavalier symbol of long hair. The "artist" too, of course, is an intermediate figure between aristocrat & beat, with the same satyrical display of balls.

[45] Dante is dead right about Virgil: he's all Eros & Adonis, with a glimpse of Thanatos in Aeneid VI, but with his centre at the p.d.e. [point of demonic epiphany], no real Logos vision, & a glimpse of the top of Eros in the 4th Eclogue, the vision of the divine child. Much the same limits are true of Eliot, which may be why Eliot had an affection for Virgil that I doubt he had even for Dante. What about Homer & Shakespeare, who don't seem to have had Logos visions either? Shakespeare is more difficult: I think that after going all the way down Thanatos & establishing, first the p.d.e., then the cyclical analogy, then Druidism, then perversion (i.e. absurd violence as an end in itself), then the perversion of perversion,[46] one would find it all contained in the blind skull that dreamed the Iliad, as Keats said.[47] As for Shakespeare, he clearly understood everything, even if he doesn't say everything. Hopkins' overthought & underthought[48] is the way to approach him: the progression of metaphors & images takes in all four worlds: what's actually said is only what satisfies Elizabethan anxieties. Eliot's burglar.[49]

[46] At the centre of the Adonis world is the beleaguered Troy, which attracts our sympathies because it's beleaguered & because it falls. At its heart is the Adonis figure of Paris, the archer beloved of Venus. The beleaguered and captive Israel is a cy [contemporary]-form. Both socie-

ties move westward, in Morris' words, until they reach the east again.[50] Morris links the "good land" of his romances with Iceland, with More's Utopia and, in general, the spatial myth of Utopia (the myth of the spatial Utopia is what I mean, dammit) and with Rousseau's buried society. The trouble is that even the most realistically minded l9th c. writer can hardly avoid giving this "good land" notion the overtones of Bardo, reincarnation, fairies, and the whole wonderland bit.

[47] One very important link in this argument is to take some 19th c. writer who begins and/or ends archetypally but goes into a naturalistic phase in the middle. There don't seem to be many English examples, but Ibsen, Strindberg, Hauptmann are Continental ones. A writer with an archetypal framework and a naturalistic "phase" puts the question of displacement beyond doubt. Morris has no naturalistic phase, but his lectures on socialism & the like represent something analogous.

[48] I don't see how I can avoid the Eros-Logos-Adonis-Thanatos sequence: I can't really introduce the great Logos visions negatively: there has to be a recognition scene at the end which is a recollection (Plato) or a repetition (Kierkegaard) of what has preceded. I think after the thematic apocalypses I go on to the fact that at a certain point in the Logos vision we pass beyond the possibility of conceptual displacement, or intellectual system. The latter is always founded on the conception of analogy or correspondence as the form of truth. At this point truth becomes, not truth as correspondence, but truth as revelation of being through personality. At this point the Bible as definitive myth becomes the Bible as a sequence of discontinuous epiphanies, as the point where the archetypal passes into the anagogic, where the medium really does become the message. Even so there's a correspondence between Son & Father, word & being: when that disappears we're back on the cycle again, ready to begin Adonis.

[49] I have a feeling—probably it's just one of those would-be profound feelings that it's comfortable to have—that I cannot really get at the centre of a problem unless something in it goes back to childhood impressions. Thus my New Comedy ideas, the core of everything I did after Blake, probably go back to my [Horatio] Alger reading, and now I think the clue to this labyrinth is the sentimental romance of the 19th century, the roots of which are in Scott. While I lived on Bathurst St.[51] I was

constantly reading ghost stories with similar patterns in mind, & Poe & Hawthorne have always been favorites. Underground caves; the Phantom of the Opera, & the like, are all part of the Urthona penseroso pattern.

[50] Well, anyway, the main problem is embarrassment of riches. When a writer lets his imagination go his writing starts to bristle with archetypes. [Charles Maturin's] *Melmoth the Wanderer* has more demonic symbols than I've ever encountered in a single work of literature.[52] On the first 25 pages of [Sheridan LeFanu's] *Uncle Silas* I get about the same number of major archetypes. Among them are: daughter with mysterious (Swedenborgian) father; daughter with gullible father (cf. *Egoist*); face at the window (cf. *Wuthering Heights*); captive Psyche & formidable female jailer (cf. *Pamela*); narcist image of the portrait with a life of its own (cf. *Melmoth*, Poe's story,[53] *Dorian Gray* & *The Sense of the Past*); secretary or old cupboard with mysterious letters or such (cf. [George MacDonald's] *Phantastes* & for the key the Bluebeard arch. [archetype]); haunted old country house & sense of past accumulated to point of independent or autonomous life; psychopomp walk to temple in woods where mother is buried, etc., etc. I must of course guard against assuming that certain genres belong wholly within one of my four areas, and no doubt a good deal of sentimental romance is in Eros, as so much naive romance is. But it's mostly Adonis, and I can get into Thanatos by way of the strong Gothic element in Henry James (cf. the reference to *The Sense of the Past* above). Note that ironic parody, which sets experience against innocence & has its focus in *Don Quixote* (a major archetype to the Romantics for that reason, who took him very seriously)[,] is different from demonic parody. The former is really part of Adonis.

[51] I've certainly got my Zoa structure back again with a vengeance. The Eros-Adonis axis is Luvah-Tharmas, though I'm not certain which is which. The Logos-Thanatos one is Urizen-Urthona, but again I'm not sure which is which. It might be simpler to think of Tharmas as Eros, looking at him in the 29 perspective,[54] and of Urthona as the underworld descent that turns out to be the Los recognition. As Stevens says, an age believes (green, Eros) or denies (Adonis, red).[55]

[52] Spatially, the aim of literary symbolism is the macrocosm, the universe as human counterpart. Only, the individual or one-God conception

is not the only one. It may be a Holy Family, a society, or even a crowd. The skeleton of comedy is symposium, the reborn *society*.

[53] I think the book is more likely to take shape around (recapturing an old hunch of mine) an equinoctial or cyclical axis of imagination and speculation (Eros-Adonis; Tharmas-Luvah) and a solstitial axis of dialectic concern (Logos-Thanatos; Urizen-Urthona). This is the core of truth in Kierkegaard's either-or dilemma, which is otherwise nonsense. Eros is the birth of the hero and the search for the secret garden which is both the lost paradise and the mother's body. Adonis is the passion of the hero. Eros is usually the poet's own quest; it goes up ladders & other ascents. Adonis is usually the projected hero. Eros leads to the mother & one of its presiding deities is Socrates the midwife. Adonis begins with a quest in relation to a father & often ends in a youthful sacrifice to prolong the father's life. So what else is new?

[54] Thanatos raises the old question of demonic analogy: here's where my point about Jesus as a homosexual with a mother fixation goes.

[55] In the 19th c. the Eros people are optimistic, progressive & systematic: Hegel's Phenomenology uses one of the old Eros love-ladders, whose every opposite is identical with itself. Kierkegaard is an Adonis-figure, fascinated by the idea of a sequence or chain of pharmakoi (martyr-rulers), wanting to be a hero (in that sense) & not just a poet & genius. I suppose *Stages on Life's Way* would be his answer to Hegel. His life was father-dominated & he renounced his girl-friend. He actually begins the demonic, not only as a conception but because of his notion that the hero is an individual eiron who provokes the fury of the crowd by being one, & who discovers that God *points*: to create is to designate.

[56] It's always been a feeling of mine that my conception of myth was the resolution of all "either-or" dilemmas, not only Kierkegaard's, where it's fairly obvious that "either" is just as mythical as "or," but the far more impressive Marxist one, where it's either revolutionary action on the right line or some evading ideology. Different versions of either-or dilemmas are constantly turning up: the martyr for a cause we sympathize with always raises guilt feelings. Kierkegaard was obsessed by this notion, contrasting the poet-genius whose human essence is imaginative, hence unreal, with the saint-martyr, like Socrates & Jesus. He says,

quite truly, that the poet's life is a satire on his work. The business of one man's loins, the reversal turning on one man's opposition to the world, is genuine enough: in Milton[,] Enoch & Noah represent a reversal of the Adamic fall.[56] But the leap is from conventional acceptance to personal appropriation, whose truth ceases to correspond with objective facts and begins to reveal the person: the same leap that makes for originality in the arts. Where was I? Oh, yes: the situation in which martyrdom is appropriate is a historical incarnation of a myth, which in itself is timeless & ought not to have any martyrs (because they'd be only ritual sacrifices). Kierkegaard didn't see the historical situation of his time very clearly, hence the cruel ironies in his life (a) the *effective* martyrs in his day were liberals & atheists (b) his influence survives as a "contribution to culture." Of course I say myth is projected on gods & recovered for man: Kierkegaard thought of the poet as projecting his life aesthetically and urged its ethical recovery. One does this through ironic kenosis, emptying oneself of the knowledge that puffs up: is recognition after Thanatos, Eros reached through the gate of Anteros.[57] (Note the demonic parody of kenosis, as well as atonement, at the end of *1984*: China is now kenoting itself on a vast scale).

[57] In simple repetition (e.g. ritual) the ideas of indefinite number & randomness of selection are involved: definitive repetition is final. Agape, or the taking on by Christ of the Adonis role, is a definitive repetition of the Adamic fall simply repeated in us.

[58] Suppose I started with Adonis: the opening chapter, the maze in the wood, would set up the fall-and-rise rhythm that underlies both (in fact all three, counting the Hellenistic) the mythical frameworks. The next chapter, the finding of the guide, would distinguish mythical or parabolic language from (a) factual language (historical or propositional) (b) ethical or existential language. And I seem to be straying away from my social displacements. I suppose the Utopia, as Plato indicates, is a central Eros motif, so that the contract is part of the war-and-hunting world. Why the hell did I ever think that sentimental romance was the key to the Adonis world?

[59] I've been reading Nygren's *Eros & Agape*[58] and find I already know most of what it says: nobody reading my Milton essay or my Romanticism book would believe I hadn't read it then. I should think a lot of the

argument is wrong or oversimplified. The story of the prodigal son, for instance, is in his terms a pure Eros-myth. He says Plato has a rising Eros but no fall, like Plotinus: he must be overlooking the *Timaeus*. He also ignores (though it isn't really his business) the way that the Agape theme of definitive descent fastens on the *Adonis* myth, with its Perseus & Jonah extensions. It's the incorporation of this myth that makes Xy so *primitive* compared with Judaism & Hellenism.

[60] I must be careful not to fall into a simple Eros = Comedy Adonis = Tragedy pattern, though these equations are involved. One Eros theme is the triumph of dialectic, the perception that Logos in the sense of discourse, rather than myth in the poetic sense, succeeds and crowns it. Thus Plato's reaction to tragedy & Hegel's optimistic system are Eros-Logos progressions. But there is, of course, a point at which the system or set of relations (Blake's voids between the stars)[59] gives place to the aphoristic revelation of personality, Logos as incarnation, and that again to the interpenetrating epiphany.

[61] [Marshall] McLuhan[60] has of course enormously expanded my thesis about the return of irony to myth. His formulation is hailed as revolutionary by those who like to think that the mythical-configuration-involved comprehension is (a) with it (b) can be attained by easier methods than by the use of intelligence. Hence everyone who disagrees (as in all revolutionary arguments) can be dismissed as linear or continuous. But there are two kinds of continuity involved: one is the older detached individuality, the other the cultural and historical continuity of preserving one's identity and memory in moving from one to the other. The issue here is a *moral* issue between freedom of consciousness and obsessive totalitarianism, plunging into a Lawrentian Dionysian war-dance.

[62] Plato's attack on poetry is an attempt to recover myth, substituting the reason in the human mind as authority, for the *received* myth or legend. The present (religious) crisis is connected with a shift from logos back to mythos, except that mythos this time has to be fully recovered.

[63] Kierkegaard's Either/Or is something I won't buy, & with my conception of myth I can't. There's no such thing as an "aesthetic" category as long as aesthetics is identified with the arts. Still, the category

does mean something. Jay [Macpherson][61] was remarking recently about the difference in two treatments of the same theme—a mother murdering her illegitimate child—in Bunyan's Badman & in Monk Lewis's House on the Heath, & certainly something like the ethical-aesthetic difference is involved. (Very important to note that the ethical is more realistic, hence more displaced).

[64] The aesthetic is thus the erotic-romantic: as soon as one seizes the ethical (nomos) one doesn't go upward into Logos but round the bend into Adonis. That's why the ethical almost disappears into the religious in the later book called *Stages on Life's Way*. In Logos one realizes instead of contemplating the myth: in Adonis one tries to imitate it sacramentally.

[65] The systematic thinker is a conqueror who solves his problems, as Nietzsche says, *en passant*, as incidental to his conquest.[62] In that sense Hegel is as erotic as Alexander the Great. The conqueror, however, does not *inhabit*. To inhabit is to live specifically and partially, not generally.

[66] I had the usual childish fantasies, when very young, of wanting to be a "great man"—fantasies that in our day only Churchill has realized. But Churchill's greatness was archaic: his funeral really buried that whole conception of greatness as a goal of ambition. Then I had fantasies of wanting to be a great composer & a great novelist—both obsolete conceptions today. The novel is breaking up into other forms & is no longer central as it was in the 19th c.: the great composers ended with Bartok, and Boulez & Varese & Cage are not "great composers," they're something else. When I settled into my real line I naturally wanted to be "great" there too: but maybe the great mind is obsolete. In the 19th c. one wants to read Hegel & Marx & Kierkegaard & Nietzsche; are there really any 20th c. equivalents of that kind of "great thinker"? Sartre, perhaps. But something about greatness *ended* around 1940. We're doing different things now. Marshall McLuhan is a typical example: a reputation as a great thinker based on the fact that he doesn't think at all.

[67] Out of the mouths of babes . . . The silliest remark ever made about me was made by a fool of a woman in Manitoba who said, apropos of *Fools of Time*, that I was back with 19th c. thinkers like Blake & Nietzsche instead of with contemporaries like Bill Wimsatt. And yet: my parents were born in 1870, my grandparents around the 1830s, my great grand-

parents close to, if not actually in, the 18th c. I must be careful not to get trapped in an archaic labyrinth.

[68] I did a public lecture for Cornell that came off fairly well, but (it's really a because, not a but) it restated a lot of things I've already thought about.[63] It turned on the two defences by Sidney & Shelley. Both tell us that it isn't what poetry says but what it illustrates or shows forth that's its real meaning. Sidney's conception of this real meaning is based on allegory (i.e. it's representational) and Shelley's is based on archetypal framework. In the latter mythical & logical confront, but myth doesn't reflect logic, as in Sidney: it swallows or absorbs it.

[69] The next step is to try to explain just how myth is a mode of knowledge: how to get rid, in short, of the "objective correlative" fallacy that the myth is an emotional counterpart to something intellectual. Concealed love is the answer to why Plato attacks poetry & yet uses myth. Religion is of course involved: also the *temenos* [sacred closed circle], the circumferential indication of the sacred. Also the point of analogy after the external reference collapses.

[70] The book should be an introduction to mythology (recognizing that 99% of mythology is literature), and a guide to an age that's moving from the Christian & creaturely fish-*in*-the-water to the water-*container*, the circumferential mythical configuration pattern. As for the peripheral patterns, they should take account of the pattern of such interests in poetry: in philosophy, speculative & cosmological metaphysics; in history, patterns like Spengler's that are assimilable to symbolic patterns, like that talk I gave the Historical Club once on the four mythoi in history.[64]

[71] The logical procedure is surely to work out the symbolic cycle first in the form that I think I have: the Eros E to N quadrant (New Comedy & Courtly Love, leading to the twin peaks of L'Allegro & Il Penseroso, the sexual & asexual erotic). Then the Adonis quadrant, N to W, dying god elegies & naive romance, along with certain types of tragedy. Then the Oedipus quadrant, W to S, meander & descent patterns to the death-mother: the second tragic area, explored in *Lear*, *Heart of Darkness*, etc. Then the Prometheus quadrant, S to E, the preliminary comic one, the revolutionary pattern. I associate these quadrants respectively with

Venus, Mars, Pluto & Neptune. Then comes the axis of speculation, W to E, Apollo & Hermes. The former is the historical-existential patterns associated with tragedy; the latter the symposium-dialectic ones associated with comedy. Finally, the great analogical patterns of the axis of concern, Logos & Thanatos, N to S. I associate the four cardinal points thus: Apollo Jupiter (replacing the sun); Hermes Mercury; Logos Venus (replacing the moon); Thanatos Saturn.

[72] It looks at present like three volumes. First, the circle of images, Eros-Summer, Adonis-Autumn, Oedipus-Winter, Prometheus-Spring. (Though they're actually transitions: Eros is spring-to-summer, etc.). This is the real ⅂ [Tragicomedy] scheme. Second, the axis of speculation, taking in the cores of ∧ [Anticlimax] (the E or Hermes point, with most of my St. Clair stuff in it,[65] though some is N) and of ⋌ [Rencontre] (the W or Apollo & Phaeton point). Third, the climax of my life & not to be attempted before retirement, the axis of concern, the cores of ⊢ [Paradox] (N, though Blake would say S) and ⊥ [Ignoramus] (S) & the analogies of plenitude & vacancy, faith & doubt.

[73] This scheme doesn't explicitly include ∨ [Mirage], which I imagine gets swallowed up somehow in the axis of speculation. The immediate intuitions are, first, that ∧ [Anticlimax] and ⋌ [Rencontre] probably and ⊢ [Paradox] and ⊥ [Ignoramus] certainly, are so closely related to each other that they have to be done together: they're theses or half-themes now, not full themes independent of each other & a book apiece. Second, & more important in the foreground, the ⅂ [Tragicomedy] scheme, the inner circle of images, is *all* the images there are. There aren't any Logos & Thanatos images except as a series of reflections from the two points of epiphany. And of course the W-E axis is history & philosophy, not literature.

[74] Perhaps two volumes of *The Critical Path*, to be subtitled *The Way In* and *The Way Out*. The first is the Eros-Adonis-Oedipus-Prometheus circle of images, involving certainly the two points of epiphany, and perhaps even the four epicycles if there really are specific images for them. If so, the second volume would be a quite different book, dealing with first the axis of speculation (Apollo-Hermes, W-E) & then with the axis of concern (Logos-Thanatos, N-S). The former is spatial, the latter temporal; the former is logical & the latter mythical. Speculation con-

cerns the existential-essential antithesis, and perhaps "Apollo-Hermes" includes the Son-Father conflict so far as that is a pattern of renewal & rebirth rather than dialectical separation. (Spatial : temporal :: temporal : timeless). The last projected or spatialized metaphor is time: as soon as one passes within it into being, one is on the N-S axis, & in the country of concern.

[75] I've got some sense now of the Eros ladder & its two summits of *allegro locus amoenus* & *penseroso* old man in the tower. As my next paper is to be on Yeats,[66] I have to think of the Eros-Adonis pattern as not only an ascent E-N followed by a descent N-W, but as a double gyre: Jacob's ladder on which angels both ascended and descended. The apex of the descending cone, Venus looking at the dead body of the Adonis who has left her for hunting, coincides with the base of the ascending cone, the lover turning to seek his lady.

[76] The Eros pattern seems to begin thematically with a state of mind: it picks up some narrative patterns of an anabasis kind, mostly comic, but its main narrative pattern is that of *return*, the second half of a movement. The Adonis one is more naturally fictional. The most frequent theme is the son leaving the father, or the younger brother the elder brother.

[77] When Yeats says he wants Oedipus descending into the earth [in *Oedipus at Colonus*] to "balance" Christ crucified standing up & ascending into the abstract sky,[67] he may be indicating a double S resolution corresponding to the *hortus* & the Tower in the N. And what, really, is the relation of the upper & the lower semicircles of imagery, when so many of the patterns repeat? Are they connected somewhat as the two axes are?

[78] Anyway: the double top of Eros has a lot of modulations. The *topos* of the assembly of gods disturbed by a complaint or revolt has, as its Biblical archetype, the Prologue to Job, &, as its Classical one, the apple of Eris.[68] Normally this assembly is presided over by Nature & Jove, the mother & father figures at the point of epiphany. Mutability Cantoes, of course. The same topos is repeated in the Arthurian stories, where the Round Table holds court and a figure representing either the marvellous (green knight) or the oppressed breaks the harmony. The invasion is

ultimately of *illusion*, & is an alternative to the fall. Or rather it's a *reported* fall, the invader being a messenger of dismay. (In P.L. [*Paradise Lost*] iii the Father does his own invading, though Satan at the lower point of epiphany is what prompts his harangue).

[79] There must be a series of epiphanic points, as in *Burnt Norton*. Arthur's court is lower down, nearer the W-E diameter (law & order). Below it is the point of *ironic* epiphany, or subjective withdrawal. In BN [*Burnt Norton*] this is the point of the yew-tree, which is explicitly said to be lower than the ironic detachment of the subway. Similarly the vision of correspondence (penseroso design theme) seems to be higher than the rose-garden point (allegro h-c [hortus conclusus] theme).

[80] The demons of the four quarters are Jung (N), Spengler (W), Heidegger (S) and Husserl (E): four clunk-headed Teutons.

[81] I suppose I should be thinking rather of the different aspects of a point of epiphany rather than trying to stretch them through space. The bardo reconciliation world is one such aspect, prominently assoc. w. Arthur in *Parzival*.

[82] Apparently *mab* is Welsh for youth, and eventually got to mean "story"—in other words a quest-romance or Orc story.[69] *Queen* Mab would then be from the country of the young, the Irish Tirnanog, and as such she makes an appropriate appearance in *Romeo & Juliet*. My Adonis quadrant is really a Percival quadrant: if I could crack the code of *that* legend I'd have it. And how the Alice books do keep creeping back! It may have been wrong to have once made a WT [*The Winter's Tale*] : cards :: T [*The Tempest*] : chess association, but something in there is central. The mock-battles of the red & white knight & of Tweedledum & Tweedledee have something to do with the chess symbolism. So chess has a war-*and*-love aspect, and the red & white (or black & white) opposition is part of it. And of course there's the Grail & cards business—note that in Alice no suits except hearts are mentioned, & of course the heart *is* the Grail suit. I wonder if this damn book is going to turn out to be a gigantic preface to Shakespeare?

[83] Anyway, Perceval is it: he'll clear up the Adonis quadrant, I hope, & lead me to *The Waste Land* again via Wagner and Jessie Weston's 1894 tr.

[translation] of the *Parzival*,[70] which should help with Oedipus. Eliot says Malory is a favorite writer of his.[71] I bet the Fisher King business just comes straight out of *Parzival* & doesn't need the *Ritual to Romance*[72] book at all. Then I can go on to Sidney, the Elizabethan Adonis figure, & the "Phoenix nest" & *Love's Marytr*[73] symbolism.

[84] Chess is on the Eros side: the will co-operates with fate, and because everything's displayed it can be a love game. The medieval symbolism of chess, I understand, associated the Queen with the Virgin Mary & the King with her Son. The castled king then is Amalthea hiding her florid son,[74] & checkmate is not, or not only, the dead fisher king, but the disclosure of the infant divine child by the surrounding Titans. Cards, on the other hand, are concealed from the opponent & so suggest fatality. In Yeats's terms, cards are antithetical and chess primary. (The contrast Yeats draws, by the way, between Oedipus going underground & Christ ascending from the standing position of crucifixion (ignoring the burial, but let that go) shows how he's got his symbolism arsy-versy—antithetical falls, primary rises). The disclosure of the child of love by the Titans, or birth in a world which is hostile to it but temporarily awed & silenced because it doesn't dare touch the frowning form,[75] is certainly one form of the point of epiphany. Only fully-developed chess could symbolize this, but any board game would be emblematical of love & war.

[85] Cards, on the other hand, are the *parental* figures, polarized by the movement of the seasons. Lance & grail are the male & female sexual symbols of the solar centre or winter solstice: sword & dish, with the severed head, of the John the Baptist summer solstice & the lunar night.[76] The first two are red, the second two black. In chess white plays against black or red. When black wins the babe is born a boy & the cycle turns: when white wins the female babe springs from the hearth.[77] I think I'm inheriting something here from the Nova Scotian lady.[78] Of course there's demonic chess, associated with rape & 32 teeth by Eliot,[79] and erotic cards, as in Alice in Wonderland, with gardeners painting white roses red.

[86] Birds: Eros shoots arrows & they hit himself as Adonis or St. Sebastian. The lecherous sparrow, the bird of Eros, kills the Adonis bird cock robin with the red breast, & the (female) nightingale pierces her breast with a thorn to sing. Red is the fundamental identity of passion & death.

Then there's all the wren-hunting business: the tiny wren is described in terms of a kind of Leviathan.[80] It's the female babe again, not the dialectic uprooting of all mystery but only the genesis of another cycle. Like the nightingale, the wren is female—Jenny Wren. Our Mutual Friend has a Jenny Wren and a Wrayburn (Robin). Speaking of Dickens, the mother shelters her son N & the daughter her father S. If not a preface to Shakespeare, maybe a commentary on the PT [*The Phoenix and the Turtle*]. I don't know if I've said anywhere that the bird of loudest lay[81] could be the *male* phoenix in a Joseph position, with the C of L [Court of Love] unity going on outside him. There's a male and female phoenix in Robert Chester.[82]

[87] The colors of romance are green (Eros going up, hope, vegetable life in growth), red (Adonis going down, love, animal life in death), white (the purity which is part of love) and black (the secret origins of nature).

[88] In Wolfram, white is heaven, constancy & loyalty, black evil, mutability, inconstancy.[83] After the consummation the black lead Saturnian casket of nature is broken and gold leaps out of it, the hidden fire within nature, the sun at night. Then gold goes into the sky to become the other color of regenerate nature (with green) and similarly blue breaks out of the cloud of white.[84]

[89] I've been having a lot of difficulty distinguishing the end of comedy from that of successful romance. The Odyssey should have given me the clue: in comedy there's a new birth; in romance the sense is of return home. The theme of reconciliation is typical of romantic comedy, as it's halfway between comedy & romance. The ironic cadence, when on the comic side, is a parody of *nostos* [return], a sort of "as you were" feeling. And, of course, as I said in the Milton book, the return home is a renewal caused by finding what you were looking for, or doing what you set out to do.[85]

[90] Eros goes back in time: Prometheus looks forward to the future. Oedipus seeks the fulfilment of time (death): Adonis is the quadrant of dislocated Time. Tennyson is an Adonis poet: his obsession with Arthurian themes, his carpet-knight treatment of the Duke of Wellington & the Crimean War, his laureateship in the service of a Queen, his elegiac masterpiece on the early death of a close friend [*In Memoriam*], his romanticized and anti-intellectual view of females, his heavily romanti-

cized treatment of Classical themes (Ulysses in him is closer to Dante than to Homer), and, above, the sense of a present moment *torn in two* between a subjective nostalgic past and an objective future. Ever since I fell over this in the Alexanders [*FT*, 89–90] as one of the essential aspects of tragedy I've been fascinated by it. I mean by the theme of the dislocation of time.

[91] The father & older brother stay home for the Adonis descent: hence Joseph & John the Baptist (often painted as an infant older brother of Christ, & certainly an Esau-figure). The reverse of this, where the older brother or rightful heir is exiled, has quite different overtones. Thus the bird of loudest lay might be announcing an Adonis theme.[86] That's balls: I mustn't just scribble.

[92] But I do have to think clearly about what I mean by calling Tennyson an Arthurian poet. I think, as I've said, that the Round Table is dead centre, essential "historical" order & existential moral pact. Being on the W-E axis, it's where the order-figure is in Shakespeare. It's a convention that nobody eats until they've seen a marvel—i.e., something coming out of the world of illusion. This will lead the knight to either, or both, of the points of epiphany. Giants & tyrants & ogres & marauders are demonic; above is the world of the lady, Spenser's Queene, the Grail that's really the virgin's womb, Beatrice's unveiled mouth.[87] Eventually W sinks to S, the Arthurian court breaks up in tragedy & adultery, & E rises into the abstract sky of N, as a vanished chivalric ideal. Yuh. I wish I could get a real lead.

[93] I have to know a great deal more about the axes before the first part will clear, and that means going on scribbling convocation addresses & keynote speeches on education until something busts loose. Meanwhile, my Cornell paper[88] was useful in consolidating some of the AC position. The question of what is the meaning of a poem has been traditionally solved by rephrasing a poem in prose, and the meaning of literature, similarly, is referred to its ethical & historical (including biographical) significance. The revolt against this drove us into centripetal meaning & ambiguity: a poem means itself. The reaction was right, but limited. The traditional way of arriving at meaning was *allegorical*. The reaction to explication has left a misbegotten superstition behind: that there is some virtue in depriving a poem of its context. This notion seems to be based

on some hazy analogy between the "unique values" of the poem & the respect for an individual in society.

[94] Well, anyway, the meaning of a poem can only be understood from its context in literature. The fact that what a poem means *is* its literary context (cf. Heidegger for this conception of meaning)[89] that its context is essential to what it *is*, that resonance is essential to value: nobody who ignores these basic principles is a serious critic anymore. The principle is more obvious in music, where there is no allegorical meaning whatever: all the meaning is derived from structure in relation to context.

[95] It may be thought that the very question "What does a poem mean?" is illegitimate, like asking what a flower means. But, first, this contradicts our experience, for we do try to grasp (allegorical) meaning when we read. Second, a flower in a crannied wall also has meaning, though a meaning derivable only from the whole horizon of reality it's in. So Tennyson's statement is a quite simple & literal one.[90] Third, there's the related question, "What is a poem (flower)?" which can only be answered by seeing it as an individual of a class.

[96] Time, space, and matter are *stupid* categories. The residual theism that's in all of us instantly says "Well, we're stuck with them," and gets an orgy of masochistic satisfaction out of feeling realistic. The impulse to chuckle approvingly over Carlyle's answer to Margaret Fuller[91] is an example of how fat-headed and brainwashed we are on such points. They're stupid. Any God who created them was an ass; no God did: we did, and we damn well should have done better. No point in that: I don't even feel better.

[97] Writing is lineal & successive: it answers to our need for a temporal continuum. The function of an image in a poem is to crumple up the continuum, to force us to group our impressions around a configurative centre.

[98] Eros images: the May morning vision of medieval poetry means (a) Eros is spring (b) the poet is a lover escaping alienation by reversing the ordinary current of reality & going up with the dream instead of down against it (d) May is also Beltane, a year's hinge & a gathering of ghosts[92] (e) the dream is often related to the *future*, which (as in Dante) introduces

the theme of *repetition*. Note the Mayday setting of MND [*A Midsummer Night's Dream*]. Then there's the walled garden, often with repulsive statues or carvings on the outside: the defended castle, the little wicket-gate & similar displaced-cunt symbols. Why does the image of the beloved statue turn up so often? Tristram, Pygmalion in RR [*Le Roman de la Rose*], WT [*The Winter's Tale*].

[99] Logically the first chapter of the book should be on allegorical and archetypal meaning. The latter has to come clear before the former takes its real shape as the axes of speculation and concern. That gives my London subway diagram: inner circle, the central line going E-W, & the black-brown & blue lines going N-S.[93] And though I recurrently feel that the axes are involved with the circle, this way of beginning makes the 3-volume-probably-unfinished scheme possible.

[100] Establishing archetypal meaning leads to the structure of mythology, in its projected & recovered forms. I'm pretty sure that my present diagram of the eight phases has something: if it hasn't it'll dry up as I work on it. I think I should call the W-E axis the Nomos-Nous one, the speculative vision of law in nature & in reason. Of the four mythical names, I seem to want to keep them all Greek, but Oedipus might be confusing in view of its strong Freudian, hence Eros, overtones for the modern reader.

[101] Naturally, if I could work out the second chapter I could work out the whole book, so the sooner I get down to it the better. The first chapter has much to do with the difference between the originality demanded in a writing culture and the sense of "the tale" that the oral poet has. There's a strong sense of "the tale," of what's complete & what fragmentary, of what belongs & what's unauthentic, of some definitive form that often a modern scholar (like Bédier with Tristram) is in a better shape to see than a medieval poet.[94] D.H. Lawrence says trust "the tale":[95] the archaic word points to an earlier notion of form.

[102] An example of the allegory-archetype distinction is the passage in *King Lear* about Lear having a daughter

> Which redeems nature from the general curse
> That twain have brought her to.[96]

Hence the prose-sense meaning of "twain" is Goneril & Regan, but the passage is a hyperbole unless we think of them as contained within, so to speak, Adam & Eve.

[103] There's a wonderful remark in Conrad's *Nigger of the Narcissus* about the silent work of anonymous people redeeming the clamor of sages for an empty heaven that seems to me the clue to the whole lower semicircle, especially the Promethean side.[97]

[104] From Blake on, it is impossible to be inspired by the conception of Jesus as a pattern of *moral* perfection. That is, we can no longer feel that it's the absence of *sin* that makes him divine, but rather the presence of suffering & rejection. The old notion, accepted by the Gospel writers themselves, was that it was only wrong to crucify him because he was innocent & hadn't done anything. In these days of objective guilt & of deliberately victimizing innocent people in order to terrorize the rest, this won't do. And there is a point I've mentioned elsewhere, that in these days of irresistible torture we can no longer feel that Jesus endured the limit.

[105] Thus the traditional Christ, down to P.R. [*Paradise Regained*], was a morally pure Eros romance Christ; the modern one is a Promethean Christ. The Agape descent is Adonis in the Passion: the lamentation is a peculiar form of Eros descent represented by Marvell's drop of dew[98] & various unsullied maiden themes in Dickens, Lewis Carroll & Shakespearean romance (Marina). Milton has his descent-of-harmony patterns. I did have a note on upper & lower katabasis somewhere that didn't get into the *Anatomy*, & I need it now.[99]

[106] What I've been calling the Logos vision at the top of Eros is a mathematical vision, a set of numerical inter-relationships. Many mystical visions are of this kind—Ouspensky, I remember, and some geometrical fantasies like Huxley's LSD ones.[100] Such visions are really of an *unborn* world: the speaking of the word is always an incarnation.

[107] The note wasn't really so useful: high k. [katabasis] is the drop of dew, low k. [katabasis] sparagmos & descent into hell; middle k. [katabasis] metamorphosis or identity with nature through death. Then there are anabasis patterns: low as escape from Polyphemos; high as

sacred marriage & such; middle as purgatorial ascent. I've got sound intuitions, but I wish I could get away from the tyranny of the circle: it won't all go on it, & I badly need another lead.

[108] Song of Songs bride turned black by the sun working in the vineyard—Blake's VDA [*Visions of the Daughters of Albion*].[101]

[109] Instead of projected & recovered, I should talk about projected *toward* & projected *from*. We start our experience of time by assuming that everything is lost—everything essential or precious, that is—hence all achievement is discovery. The quest is for hidden treasure or a lost city; eventually this becomes an allegory of the creative process which fishes unknown things out of an unknown depth.

[110] I think this is important, because I'm beginning to feel that the real contrast between Rc. [Romantic] & pre-Rc. [pre-Romantic] symbolic patterns is one of direction of energy: i.e. whether it's a return (pre-Rc. [pre-Romantic]) or an original movement. The original four levels are still there in Yeats, yet he thinks of the "antithetical" as original & his "primary" goes with the return pattern. Kierkegaard's contrast of recollection & repetition may be useful too. The chain of being, and the special-pleading term "creation," are downward or Agape movements: transformation & alchemical myths go up.

[111] Still, that doesn't really help with my efforts to distinguish Eros from Prometheus comedy (which I've been assuming is also the distinction of Old (P) & New (E) comedy). Everything in Prometheus has to do with escape from a womb-tomb cave: Vico's extraordinary beginning myth of giants frightened into caves by thunder & starting private property by dragging their wives after them is typical, & still survives in folklore about "cavemen." Old Comedy starts from a death-point; New works toward the phoenix burning which is both sexual intercourse and "death" (new birth).

[112] I'm coming around to the point at which I should once more realize that I always get into trouble when I start planning a series of books. Try to think of one book. An introduction of, as I now see it, two chapters, one on the difference between allegorical & archetypal meaning, the other on the structure of the literary or symbolic universe.

(Possibly there's a third form of meaning, created or concerned meaning). Then one or two sections on the four archetypal areas of symbolism, if there are four & if I've got them right, then a section on Nomos and Nous, then a section on Logos & Thanatos. The second one contains my informing-by-words thesis, the third my Utopia article[102] & what I know about religion.

[113] The two big things I'm fishing for I may not get. One is a key image or idea for the literary universe itself, something so overpoweringly obvious & convincing that nobody will be able to argue with it. The other is the formula for what kind of genuine knowledge, as distinct from mere desire, mythical or concerned thinking is based on.

[114] The Catholic tendency is to expand from the cycle to the encyclopedia, and take in the whole nomos-nous world that may be imaginative or imaginary. The tendency beginning with Luther & Calvin is to sharpen the dialectic of concern and mark it off from the external perspective, which after Protestantism becomes increasingly a detached and unconcerned science. God becomes increasingly, with Protestantism's emphasis on the Bible, a projected author of a plot—Puritan sermons on salvation and Poe's Eureka.

[115] And there's a third thing I'm fishing for, more important than either of the others: the way in which informing ideas in history, philosophy & religion are derived from poetic myths. This I've been avoiding because I've been over some of the ground before & because, partly for that reason, it seems only a facile extension of AC. But I do have to sort out my ideas on these matters, hackneyed as some of them are. I've aligned historical myths with the four mythoi, but that may need some expansion.[103]

[116] What's in front of that is to get these quadrants either cleared up or abolished. I want to think about Old & New Comedy as, possibly, Promethean & Erotic, and about Lear along with Oedipus & Job.[104] Oedipus is the man who has learned the secret of Nomos, that he has killed his father & lain with his mother, and so his tragedy has the sense of what I call in another context the second awareness.[105] This second awareness is the answer to the question that Percival ought to ask: why this continued pain & sterility? Nomos has two sides: the side of fairness

or justice, represented by the Oresteia, and the side of irrational wrath, represented by the first Oedipus play & by Antigone.

[117] My hunch about Aristophanes is what's hinted at in the Beddoes essay and in my early comedy paper.[106] A good deal of poetry & drama tries to articulate the chain of being: Old Comedy is a drama of unchained being, where life can be mixed up with Hades (*Frogs*), Olympus (*Birds*), ideas (*Clouds*), or allegories (*Peace*). The teleological plot of New Comedy works toward a conclusion which is exoterically marriage & esoterically a new birth or rebirth. Old Comedy is a theatre of the absurd, out of which dialectical conflict seems to emerge. If Aristophanes approves of one side, it wins & we have a kind of comic melodrama: usually there's a tremendous upsurge of some kind of power but we don't know whether it's less absurd. It's a dialectical action leading upward to an assumed *nous* which the audience is supposed to have.

[118] Old Comedy characteristics: episodic structure, continual encounters of two people (agon): series of visitors driven off or otherwise chased off; fantasy (the chorus suggests the direction of the fantasy; and here's my old SSE birds & frogs hunch coming back again). Fantasy is represented in Aristophanes by masques & a chorus: when New Comedy plots become operatic they turn into parody. The parabasis (which appears in only a few of the eleven plays) is a species of the harangue or monologue, which is an O.C. [Old Comedy] feature & again (as in Jaques' speech in AY [*As You Like It*]) lends a touch of parody (Shaw) in N.C. [New Comedy]. The use of actual or personal targets like Euripides or Socrates may have been a historical accident: its root is rather the character of archetypal significance, who may have an allegorical name (Disceopolis, Lysistrata).[107]

[119] In my original comedy paper[108] I said that *New* Comedy was Aristotelian and Old Comedy Platonic, seeking the Form of the Good or the escape from the cave to the sunlight. I imagine Rabelais is a great genius of the SE; and in the contrast of quadrants & cardinal points there may be a clue to my earlier puzzle about fiction (romance N-W, confession W-S, anatomy S-E, novel E-N). Don't forget the "Aristophanic" play in Peacock's *Gryll Grange*.[109]

[120] Hell, when I was reading Rousseau, that time I was sick, I was

really geared to something: why did I drop it? My Utopia paper, my Chicago liberal-education paper, and something I've never done but have often felt I could do on religion belong to Part 3.[110] My educational writings gravitate on that too. My spiritual authority paper, the Kentucky & Cornell papers, & the Indiana paper probably belong to Part Two.[111] I have the feeling that nothing in this book is really crystallizing as pieces of the AC did, but that may be only because of a growing dislike of putting my pieces together. I'd like to collect these essays in a book, and I hesitate to dismantle & reassemble whole books. The alternative is to construct the CP [*The Critical Path*] out of either new or completely rephrased material; and I shrink from that.

[121] Eros moves from alienated to spontaneous knowledge, the latter being incorporation into a mother & the casting off of the old man shadow. Over the W sunset the hero learns the knowledge of this the other way, in terms of original guilt. The hermit tells Parzival that Cain violated his grandmother Earth.[112] Each quadrant has a parallel complement (Eros-Prometheus), and a contrast complement (Eros-Adonis) and a parody-complement (Eros-Oedipus).

[122] Remark found in an old diary: *Paradise Regained* deals with the withdrawn vision of wrath, the rejection of all act, within which the universe of myth is reborn.[113] This puts Christ into the S.E. upheaval which carries him all the way to the N. That's his position in Dante, too, where the Eros climb is an imitation of Christ.

[123] Part Two begins with the old Renaissance diagram of poetry as between praxis & theoria.[114] First I show how metahistory & metaphysics get informed by myth, then how the informing gradually pulls away from the detached & disinterested vision of Truth, which eventually breaks off into a scientific vision which is intellectually detached and emotionally alienated. At this point the mythical information consolidates into a structure of concern. My terms speculation & concern are confusing me because speculation is the negative of concern: mythical structures of history & philosophy aren't just speculative. As I say, the Reformation is stage one; Rcsm. [Romanticism] stage two; our own time is three.

[124] If I'm right, this arrangement has 3 flowing logically out of 2, and 2

will flow logically out of 1 if my diagram is roughly right. Of the three things I'm fishing for,[115] the key image is in 1, the mythical informing of praxis & theoria 2, & the genuine knowledge in myth 3. If I can bring it off, or even indicate how it can be brought off, it'll have everything, even my fictional death-cognitio scene.[116] And it certainly makes the allegory-archetype business the inevitable opening chapter.

[125] So my Utopia stuff really belongs in 2, on the Nomos-Nous axis. The vision of the just state is polarized by, at W, the scene at the end of the Oresteia where revenge is absorbed into law, & the maternal cycle into the paternal creation, and, at E, by the trio Socrates, Agathon & Aristophanes talking about tragedy & comedy at the end of the *Symposium*. (If it had only been Euripides, or if only Agathon's plays had survived!).[117] Arthur's court, the assembly of gods, & the complaint of illusion probably all belong here. The Logos point is indicated at the opening of Paradiso X, the mirror image,[118] and the Thanatos point at the paradise-lost theme in Proust. (Sartre & Genet as commentary).

[126] I've been thinking so far about three parts, but probably I should settle for my usual four. Eros & Adonis are both forms of Orc, the eniautos-daimon,[119] and the Orc cycle underlies the Nomos-Nous encyclopedia. Oedipus & Prometheus run the other way, from death to birth, and are both, I think, forms of Urthona. Anyway, this part of the mythical universe, polarized by the meander-descent pattern of Oedipus & the volcanic explosion or deliverance from the sea pattern of Prometheus, is dialectic, & underlies the separation of Logos from its mirror of Thanatos.

[127] One thing that's bad about the diagram is the semi-circle. The Orc cycle can exist in its truncated Adonis form or its full Urizenic form: in either case there's a dead youth in the middle of it, but it's a complete cycle. As Yeats saw, & said in Byzantium & elsewhere, the other is the redeeming one. It's a complete cycle too, an Urthona-Tharmas cycle, but in either case there's liberation in the middle of it. The Eros ascent is a genuine ascent only when seen in its context as a Promethean *repetition*. The redeeming cycle gets its start by voluntary descent, by repeating the tragic act.

[128] The eniautos-cycle is the cycle of reality, & it's a normative cycle.[120] The kairos-cycle[121] is the cycle of dream & wish-fulfilment, & it moves

away from time (as in Blake & Shelley) towards identity: the rebirth of the same, not the other. And just as the Urizen-shadow or mystery of the Orc cycle is the mystery of the end, so the Tharmas-shadow mystery of the Urthona cycle is the beginning, the original Oedipal awareness of tragic guilt. The door of death has oracle on one side & wit on the other: when one goes through it one recovers the power of laughter.[122]

[129] This contrast of Orc-rebirth-cycle & Los-resurrection-dialectic has always been with me, but certain aspects of it weren't very clear. In FZ [*The Four Zoas*] & elsewhere the Orc cycle (Books V–VIIa) is followed by the Los dialectic (VIII–IX), but the point of *Milton* is that it annexes the Tharmas beginning or context of the Los revolution. Milton's descent repeats that of Christ, which in turn repeats that of Milton's Satan. And the MT [*The Mental Traveller*] is an Orc-Urizen cycle only. There isn't any complete cycle, because Los goes the other way. You *sympathize* with Orc only when you realize that Los is his restraining father: when you see the Eros quest as a repetition of the Promethean.

[130] The movement from Utopia to Jerusalem, the Nomos-Nous axis to Logos, is the Job movement from Beulah to Eden. That is, Job for Blake is entirely on the Los cycle: his fall is a Tharmas fall, & he's the opposite of MT [*The Mental Traveller*] & GP [*The Gates of Paradise*]. The S to E upthrust separates, or begins to separate, the world made from time, Los's halls, from what simply *has happened*, the slag-dump of echoes & rumors and sighs from hell explored by spiritualists & such like.

[131] The Quartets, too, begin with the kind of activity that cuts off all possibilities, & moves toward the recapturing of possibilities as a part of one's original identity. (That's a pretty optimistic view of those great but dismal poems).

[132] When have I had sudden runs like this (if this is one) and is there a pattern in them? There's the oracle-wit stuff in Seattle, the mind-soul-body stuff, undated, but a Sunday morning, and the stuff at the beginning of the "mystical" notebook in 1946.*[123]

---

* Also the St. Clair Λ [Anticlimax] stuff,[124] which seems slightly out of key with this, but may define the whole relation of 1 to 2 & 3. 2 anyway. I wonder if the right order is Eros-Adonis, Nous-Nomos, Oedipus-Prometheus, Thanatos-Logos? I doubt that,

[133] The Orc cycle leads to the projected God, to Jesus as a pattern of moral perfection who articulates the chain of being by his descent, & to the doctrine of analogy. The Los cycle projects from the God-Man, Jesus being divine through suffering & endurance, who explodes out of unchained being to identity. I don't know if I shall actually return to the point in FS where the external world is the fallen body turned inside out, but the final recognition scene of the book will be, I think, of Thanatos as the mirror-reflection of Logos.

[134] 2 is a visual-conceptual world dominated by the canons of writing & prose sense; in 3 the ear-world of the Word begins to take over. At one end is the articulating Word that creates; at the other is the chaos or unchained being of Vico's stupid giants frightened by thunder, who appear in the Inferno, GT [*Gulliver's Travels*] & FW [*Finnegans Wake*], always in connexion with inarticulate language. The so-called gift of tongues is the babble of chaos with the cerebral cortex turned off.

[135] If the contrast of Orc & Los cycles is not only the basis of 1 but the basis for distinguishing 2 & 3, there'll be some danger of rewriting FS instead of AC. Particularly if Orc = objective reality & Los = created reality, Orc = pre-Rc. [pre-Romantic] projected cycle & Los = post-Rc. [post-Romantic] recovered one. Orc is a martyr because killed by Urizen, projected as his father but actually his older self who gets taken over by the female will, hence the end of the Orc cycle is the Druid analogy[125] & Yeats' *Vision*, as opposed to the Los cycle which is the Byzantium one & starts from the world of the dead. Oh, well, there are doubtless worse things to do than rewrite FS. Nor should I overlook the possibility of a tertium quid incorporating both earlier books.

[136] Milton points: creation *de Deo*[126] corresponds to the Virgin Birth, because creation by God out of something else, as the prepositions show, would involve a co-eternal female consort. And if Christ in heaven, in

because the Eros-Adonis cycle is a mere abstraction without the rest of it. Think of the way Wolfram's Adonis poem on Parzival dives straight for Amfortas' balls—still, that doesn't really reverse the movement. Something about the L'Allegro-Il Penseroso double-climax of Eros reappearing as Nomos & Nous: one the maternal cycle & the other the paternal (projected) creator. But the Orc cycle is a *complete* cycle, not a semicircle.

history & in the Church are identical, so are the City of God, the human body, & the Church.

[137] The Tower is a *clock* tower, dammit, and time as the enemy of the locus amoenus, as in Spenser, needs more thinking about. Alice books: the rabbit taking out his watch; the March Hare doing the same later: the discussion of Time as "him" with the Hatter; lessons "lessoning" for eleven days: the grinning old man in LG [*Looking-Glass*]. Poe: that article on his clocks.[127] The article is a good one, but leaves out (I think) two things. One is The Bells, with its evocation of the four levels of time: time as exuberance, as ritual, as the significant moment of crisis, as mere duration. The other is the close connexion of the clock & the Narcissus reflexion or doppelganger, both obsessive themes in Poe. Existence is invisible until projected: you can't see your face except in some kind of mirror: you can't see time except in some kind of dial or clock face.

[138] Stewart's book on the *Hortus Conclusus* & Rostvig's on the Happy Man (also the edition of Hils's tr. [translation] of Casimire) should be kept in my bibliographical register.[128]

[139] The sexual & sublimated goals of the Eros ascent represent an antithesis that recurs in Adonis in the Lotus-land theme. Retirement is a regular episode in the heroic quest, but of course the quest itself always prefers the boar to Venus. I suppose that the p.d.e. [point of demonic epiphany], like the p.e. [point of epiphany], has two culminations: one on the W. side is tyranny & anarchy, the collapse of Nomos, the other absurdity, the collapse of Nous. Nomos & Nous themselves seem to be the Oedipus C. [*Oedipus at Colonus*] & Resurrection points Yeats speaks of in *A Vision*.[129] That almost suggests that the *penseroso* peak of Eros is on the W. or Nomos side, so that Eros does go up the sexual side after all. The Adonis hero is torn between hunt & cunt.

[140] The Nomos-Nous axis is the Libra inserted, according to Milton, between the Virgo of the p. of e. [point of epiphany] & the Scorpio below.[130]

[141] In each quadrant I have to be aware of the underlying mythical patterns. The king as woodwose:[131] the Nebuchadnezzar theme which survives in the stories of Lancelot & Orlando Furioso and enters here.

[142] I want to try to work out the difference between Old & New Comedy as a difference between Prometheus comedy and Eros comedy.[132] The chief feature of the latter is the teleological plot, which was exoterically a marriage & esoterically a new birth. My only hunch about Old Comedy is the phrase "unchained being." That is, gods, mystes,[133] allegorical figures & so on are all mixed up. Parabasis or harangue speech. Non-teleological conflict in which some force emerges of a highly ambivalent kind. Series of visitors or strangers, often driven off. Agon or sense of being very close to the satyr play & the escape from the Cyclops. I think there may be (or, as my hostile critics would prefer to have me say, I want there to be) a parallel distinction between Old & New Tragedy. One is Aeschylean & probably Sophoclean, the other Euripidean & Senecan. New Tragedy is, I suspect, fundamentally dilemma-tragedy, or at least all the Neigung-Pflicht [inclination-duty] stuff is in it, & gives a teleological twist to the plot. King Lear works its way back to Old Tragedy but keeps a New Tragedy structure in the Gloucester subplot. To keep the general scheme intact, its duty-impulse plot should reflect the hunt vs. cunt Adonis one. Not much of this is clear yet, & there may of course be nothing there, but if there is it'll clear up the quadrants.

[143] I keep vacillating between the feeling that there are four areas & the feeling that there's just one area with variations. Thus Oedipus seems to be the labyrinth one, but there are labyrinths in Eros too. Prometheus is the emergence from the labyrinth or cave: it features follow-the-leader games, where (see a passage in Yeats) an ordinary man gains immortality through attaching himself to his shepherd king.[134] Harrowing of Hell. Egypt: Book of the Dead. (Hero as the dead king moving toward identity). Blake's picture of Earth in GP [*The Gates of Paradise*]; Caliban; Borges' story "The Immortals."[135] Parodied by Satan's journey through chaos in P.L. [*Paradise Lost*], with its Ulysses echoes. Old Comedy: the Odyssey as a *narrative* Old Comedy, labyrinth followed by dialectic emergence of identity of Odysseus at Ithaca.

[144] The archetypal man faces us: Nomos is his right (droit, Recht): Nous is his revolutionary & dialectic left. His subordinates are a comitatus on the right & a symposium on the left. In Plato we fear & dislike the guards: the shadow of the comitatus on the other side of the symposium.

[145] I mention Borges, who seems to me one of the guides, along with

the Alice books & Poe. He says in connection with Quixote that literature not only begins but ends in mythology, & he tells the story of the man who rewrote Quixote—a parable of the way every great work is polarized between meaning then & meaning now.[136]

[146] Heraclitus' double gyre seems to be a diagram of something pretty central. In waking life things go upward from earth to the dry light of fire, which brings one into contact with the universal Logos.[137] An implied comparison between fire & gold links this to the alchemical process. The reverse process is that of death, dreams, & retreat into private worlds. But it seems that after death one becomes a guardian angel or daimon, like Lycidas, so perhaps the reverse process takes place not after death but before birth: the Oedipean unconscious fall vs. the Bodhisattva descent, which is Adonis area. I think my main hunches are right, because they do genuinely illuminate things, but some very central principle is still missing.

[147] The conventional colors are: Eros green, Adonis red, Oedipus blue, Prometheus orange, Logos white, Thanatos black, Nomos purple, Nous yellow (gold). Cf. Hopkins, "Spelt from Sibyl's Leaves."[138]

[148] I was wandering the streets of Moncton,[139] thinking how, in the course of time, memory tends to distribute itself between waking life & dream life. Some of my most vivid dream settings have been on Moncton streets. Streets are, of course, a labyrinth symbol, full of Eros: they recapture not past reality but *my* reality, reality for me. I wish I knew what I meant: something eludes me. Cf. Joyce's hallucinatory Dublin, the name Dedalus, the Count of Monte Cristo.

[149] Certainly the Heraclitean double gyre informs Hopkins, Eliot & Yeats. In the first two it's attached to the Incarnation-Resurrection movement: Hopkins' Windhover vs. the Heraclitean Fire one. The imagery of Hopkins, when E, seems to me to be Promethean rather than Erotic. One great Promethean writer, as I've realized ever since FS, is Rabelais: the last chapter seems almost definitive: it even mentions Prometheus. The whole Λ [Anticlimax] association with the kataplous[140] theme in prose fiction has to be thought about. Also the oracular priestess of Rabelais[141] recurs in Shakespeare's CE [*Comedy of Errors*]-Pericles conclusion and in Plato's Diotima, to say nothing of Apuleius' Isis.

[150] The Adonis hero has the mysterious quasi-divine birth: the Oedipus hero has the crime before birth: one descends from a higher world; the other is already imprisoned in a lower one: Adonis wilderness vs. Israel's Egypt. I hope this isn't *all* just a lot of shit.

[151] The reason is limited by the reasonable: by the impersonality of truth. Beyond that limit we get rationalizing, or providing a rational covering for something irrational. We may resist this distinction, which in theory is extremely vulnerable, but in practice we all know it's there. The imagination is limited by the imaginable: beyond this limit is the kind of fantasy that provides an imaginative varnish over something unimaginative. The rationalized irrational has something to do with ideology, depending on established system or procedure (not that I think only conservatives have ideologies); the imagined unimaginative has something to do with the egocentric side of the creator.

[152] The most obvious things come last: the Exodus pattern of the Eros ascent in Dante reappears in Blake in a revolutionary form, but it's the same pattern.

[153] I noticed in Jordaens[142] a familiar iconographic pattern: the Holy Family with the Dove & the Father over them. The sexual Trinity & the genuine one interlocked. The Dove is not the Virgin's lover but the genuine form of the Virgin—virginity means a transcending of sex. Similarly the Father who begets his Son is the genuine form of Joseph the old man who can't beget one. (Orc isn't Urizen's son).

[154] We enter the Thanatos vision through the mouth of a hermaphroditic monster, who includes the terrible mother (Earth & Death, the worm-sister) & leave it through the arse-hole of Satan, the false father. The p.d.e. [point of demonic epiphany], like the p.e. [point of epiphany], has two gates. We enter the p.e. through mama's cunt, only mamma has to be a virgin when approached from this direction, and we leave it through the door of Agape, the mouth of the articulate Logos-Spirit. The former, the Theseus-Prometheus cycle, is the ingesting & excreting of food which is in particular the natural cycle. You slither down the labyrinthine guts in quest of an oracle of drink, as in Rabelais. The upper quest is the one that turns on the inevitable sex-and-creativity associa-

tion. Their closed-in forms are Milton's greed & lust, miserly suicides in the shit & aggressive swimming in blood.[143]

[155] The lower cycle is the Bachofen mother one,[144] the female using the male, the male descending for the oracular lance-grail food & drink cycle-turning talismans. In the upper cycle the male uses the female.

[156] Then there's the cycle of Nomos & Nous, which is really the Orc-Urizen cycle. Society is held together by commitment: this generates a revolutionary body which begins in Utopian vision but soon demands a tighter & more intolerant commitment than the conservative nomos-society calls for. Hence an intolerant streak in Xy vis-à-vis paganism, reinforced in Protestantism vis-à-vis Catholicism, to say nothing of the totalitarian groups of our time. Plato's Republic shows the whole cycle, ending with the turning spindle of Necessity in Book X.

[157] Certain themes may be important: one is the doctrine of imaginative arrest. The moment of consciousness is a withdrawal from being, but as that it tends, when persisted in, to project a dead world. The imaginative arrest is rather a revolt against the habit of being, which includes a habit of perception. Shelley is the first to stress the imagination's revolt as what Wordsworth had called a recollection but which Kierkegaard saw, more accurately, to be a repetition.[145] The effect of it is that the familiar world bursts into strangeness, a brave new world which is a picture, hence *ut pictura poesis*, & needs brave new words to describe it.

[158] I don't know if I have anything new to say about the pattern of myth. There are two grand movements, down & up, the tragic & the comic, the Genesis Eden-to-Egypt one and the Exodus Egypt-to-Promised-Land (also apocalyptic) one. There are two forms of each, thus:

upper	lower
paternal sky-god	maternal earth-goddess
creation as artifact	creation as sexual
sex as creativity	sex as fertility

conservative-romantic	revolutionary-ironic
hero as son of Father	hero as son-lover-victim
Eros-Adonis	Theseus-Prometheus
food > sex-freedom	cycle > sex-food

(By this I mean that food, & the interested greed-quality it suggests, seems to dominate the lower cycle: Rabelais' descent to a drink oracle, Prometheus & the cheating of the gods, Persephone confirming the cycle by eating, etc.). In the story of Jesus we get

Incarnation	Descent to hell
Ministry	Harrowing of hell
Ascension	Resurrection

Note how the left *contains* the right one. The infant in the cave or manger surrounded (threatened or protected) by giants & animals. In conservative versions the sky-gods defeat the earth-giants, who congregate around the p.d.e. [point of demonic epiphany]. Gulliver in Lilliput, Finnegan, Keats' Hyperion. The S.E. quarter is that of the escape of Prometheus, of Ulysses from Polyphemus, David from Goliath, of "blind Orion hungry for the morn,"[146] with his child on his shoulder (Xn equivalent is St. Christopher, who has Atlas & Albion overtones). The giants win in the revolutionary version.

[159] I also see four historical stages going up the circle: first the early maternal, food-gathering, worship of animals, sacred place caves, male god an infant threatened or protected by giants. Second the later maternal, food-planting & agricultural (the first is nomadic), male god the son-lover-victim dying-god figure. Then we cross the Nomos-Nous axis and enter the early paternal, city-centered & aristocratic, gods as a departmentalized autocracy enforcing a cult of the dying *hero*. World-empire brings the later paternal monotheism, the Father with the world-ruler his adopted son. The first stage is certainly lunar & the fourth certainly solar, but I'm not so sure of the middle two. The colors, I think, are maternal red, white & black; paternal red, white & blue. Gold & green are the revolutionary or growing colors.

[160] Why are nearly all myths of the origin of fire myths of *stealing* it? Why is Prometheus, always the benefactor & in some versions the creator of mankind, never worshipped?

[161] The poet in world one is the Teiresias or blind prophet of the lower world; in world two he's the poète maudit or Actaeon figure; in world three he's the displaced lover; in world four he's the unacknowledged legislator. The sowing of ground with dragon's teeth to produce fighting warriors, & the belief that the earth goes barren with the shedding of blood, are myths of the transition from 2 to 3.

[162] The Eros journey gets rid of the shadow: the Adonis one acquires it. Jesus is first in relation with the older brother-figure John the Baptist, an Esau desert-figure, then with Barabbas. In between comes the beloved disciple, the incarnation of the Spirit, who waits his second coming.

[163] There are two fundamental mythical sequences: the Genesis one and the Exodus one. The Genesis one is the archetype of the tragic & ironic: it starts with a creation myth, with man in a paradisal setting, with the fall, & ends with Israel in Egypt—not as yet unhappy there, but in an alien country. The Exodus one is the archetype of the comic & romantic: it starts with alienation, and goes on to the themes of voluntary exile, wandering in the wilderness, & entry into the Promised Land. The Christian redemption-apocalypse myth is a double of the Exodus, & is built on its model. Note that it's potentially a revolutionary myth: it begins with rebellion against the alien kingdom.

[164] The Greek myth is fundamentally a Genesis myth: it begins with creation myths in Hesiod, goes on to the four ages of man, its equivalent of the Hebrew fall from a paradisal state, & goes down to the Trojan war and the mostly disastrous *nostoi*.[147] It has often been remarked that the Greeks write about the Trojan war as though it were a defeat. The Iliad, ending with the terrible myth of Achilles in Book 24, takes us into the Thanatos vision.[148] The Argonaut quest ends in the death of Jason's children and the escape of Medea. It's a shadow-world, where the shadow of Heracles & Achilles in hell is all that's left of them. (Heracles has both a shadow in Thanatos & a real form in Olympus: similarly Theseus is harrowed from hell but his Tanist Perithous is left there).[149]

[165] The Roman myth is an Exodus myth, worked out in the Aeneid. Its basis is the resolved *nostos* of the Odyssey, the pure cycle, where Ulysses prefers Penelope to Calypso & so emerges from the cave of the nymphs at the mortal end.[150] The Aeneid is also a return, because Dardanus came from Italy in the first place.[151] Virgil *had* to stick this in, because he couldn't take in the notion of renewal apart from a turning cycle. The Fourth Eclogue is a vision of rebirth *opposed* to resurrection, Virgil's only god, as Blake said, being Caesar: it's *anti*-Christian, a Yeatsian full-moon-in-March vision. Dante was perfectly right in his indicating of the circumference of Virgil's orbit. However, the Hebrew Exodus is also a return home, & so is the Xn vision founded on it: back to Eden where we started, the East Coker *larger* circle (not the ironic one in the poem), the creature returning to its Creator.

[166] Point in passing: *East Coker* has an ironic cycle which is seen sacramentally as an image of the bigger cycle of returning to the beginning. Similarly Yeats has an ironic cycle of man as creator, expressed in his lion-&-honeycomb & bone-shop of the heart imagery.[152] But in what sense is the absorption into the artifice of eternity in SB [*Sailing to Byzantium*] a return home? I don't know; I'm not sure that Yeats does.

[167] Anyway, the Genesis myth is down from the past. It implies a creator sky-god Father, who in Hesiod is really a Jacobean usurper of Mother Earth. The more the maternal & sexual basis of creation is stressed, the more strongly we are possessed by the feeling of up from the monsters. Similarly, the down to the future antithesis of apocalypse is the descent into hell, involuntary in damnation, voluntary in quests for future wisdom. So the Prometheus & Theseus quadrants appear as complements of Adonis & Eros. Prometheus & the return of Esau in MHH [*The Marriage of Heaven and Hell*].[153]

[168] The revolutionary basis of the Exodus myth, so carefully minimized by Virgil, is brought out by Blake, whose Eros pattern is the same as Dante's, but with a more explicitly social basis. The centre of the difference is his view of Jesus. The traditional mystical or, more simply, the *pious* view is of Jesus as the morally sinless man, hence the model of conduct. For Blake this is a sterile view: the fruitful view is of Jesus as society's definitive sinner or outcast.

[169] Then there's the principle that both kinds of past & future myths are projected from the present. This connects with my notion that the political conceptual displacement, contracts & Utopias (to which one should add, I suppose, theories of progress & decline), are projected from a theory of education. It also connects with my sense of myth as the language of the present, and the conception of awareness as an imaginative arrest.

[170] Present visions tend to be passive (fatalism, astrology, the cycle, & all views in which the future, because it must happen, has already happened) or active. One tried & reliable version of the active present is the alchemical one, as we have it in Yeats' *Byzantium*. Yeats sees this as half of the Heraclitean process: he doesn't define the sinking half, but obviously it's the relapse into mob passivity, & sacrifice & scapegoat ritual. I've got this in the *Anatomy*, though, along with the incorporating of the projections of ritual and dream.

[171] I suppose I shall have to work out a sequel to my Mythos and Logos paper.[154] There I dealt with the contrast between centrifugal (Sidney) and centripetal (Shelley) criticism. The former is allegorical context criticism, to which Marxism returned; the latter is archetypal myth criticism. Ed Honig[155] asked me why I didn't use more "abrasive" personalities like Whitman & Rimbaud. I don't know much about Whitman, but for years I've pondered the possibility of contrasting Rimbaud and Rilke (or perhaps Mallarmé). And of course I've thought a lot about Poe, & his development through Wilde's *Decay of Lying*.

[172] I may of course change my views on this, but it seems to me that there's always something of the *temenos* [sacred closed circle], the place marked off from experience, in the work of art, & that the cult of "happenings," which tries to dissolve art back into experience, is mob art, the dérèglement which Rimbaud fled from & later condemned as "bad," the kind of thing going on in [D.H. Lawrence's] *The Plumed Serpent*. It has something, I don't know yet what, to do with reversing the dream in the direction of medium & séance. The question "can you tell the truth without lying?" has two answers: one at the top connected with myth, one at the bottom connected with "tactics" and propaganda. At the top the "lie" may be partly the nothingness concealed in being. Perhaps truth cannot render being, & only myth can render the mixture

of being & nothingness. In any case this paper belongs to the general problem of discontinuity.

[173] The introduction to the third book, in any case, would have to begin with the centrifugal-centripetal distinction, which is also the allegory-archetype distinction. Centrifugal *criticism* treats the poem (or whatever) as a document. There are two orbits of this: the lesser orbit takes it as a biographical document, & hence develops toward psychological criticism, which at present has a strongly Freudian slant. The greater orbit takes it as a sociological & historical document: this is where the conventional philological, "history of ideas" and Marxist techniques go. The centripetal direction has the lesser orbit of explication and the greater orbit of the context of literature.

[174] The Marxists don't like me, and I can see why, but of course Marxism has never understood that the humanities are subjects, like the sciences. You can't have just any criticism you like that squares with your prejudices: you must accept the criticism that explains the facts of literature.

[175] That is, criticism has instinctively started with the centrifugal aspect of meaning. So it becomes documentary. The next step is the allegorical, the "history of ideas" & other treatments by manifest content. Then we go on to the latent-content Freudian & Marxist techniques, as above. If we stop there, we stop with determinism: if we go on to the "formalist" explicatory, linguistic (whatever they are) and archetypal techniques, we recognize the autonomy of literature. Of course literature eventually turns out to be a social product, but only through recognizing its autonomy & breaking with determinism can we see what its real relation to society is. The Marxists are right from their own point of view: to begin by recognizing the autonomy of literature is to end by recognizing the plurality of social mythologies.

[176] I suppose it would be simplest to start with the Logos vision as total metaphor or apocalypse, repeating the table from the anatomy, & going on through Revelation & Paradiso 9–33[156] to *Sailing to Byzantium*. The complications involved in the Romantic disruption of the creature-returning-to-creator pattern would soon raise the Exodus & Eros themes, however. So far, I've been insisting that there are really only two pat-

terns, the pre-Rc. [pre-Romantic] & the post-Rc. [post-Romantic], but the more accepted view that *symbolisme* added something to Rcsm. [Romanticism] needs to be looked at. The Logos vision gets involved with that interrelation of being & nothing that I have to learn something about from Hegel & Heidegger (& Sartre), & which makes Mallarmé's *Coup de Dés* a Logos vision.[157]

[177] This inter-related being & nothingness is already in the Logos concept, not as apocalypse but as the epiphanic & discontinuous life of Christ. Christ's life can only be told mythically, but as the myth is so obviously a human invention the myth cannot be the *real form* of the revelation.

[178] What actually happens when we cross the axis of nomos & nous is as mysterious as ever. But the Theseus quadrant has something to do with Heidegger's thrown-forwardness, the death-consciousness which in its pure form is the sense of total future in Dante's hell.[158] Again, Eros poetry, from medieval May-morning visions to Mallarmé's Faune,[159] hitches the imaginative life on to the (erotic) dream & moves against the current of human life. But the Prometheus vision has something to do with hitching *death* on to the imgve. [imaginative] vision & moving against life *that* way. But of course there's the whole phoenix business at the top of Eros, & the general scheme of reduplication.

[179] In the ironic vision death *informs* life, a cause preceded by its effects; in the romantic vision it's the concluding incident of life. All forms of murder, including war & judicial executions, are romantic. Ziba in Beddoes refuses to let Athulf poison himself: he has no death-consciousness.[160]

[180] I think my general analysis of Old & New Comedy, & of all Shakespeare as essentially New apart from TC [*Troilus and Cressida*], is sound.[161] But the feeling about the problem comedies AW [*All's Well That Ends Well*] & MM [*Measure for Measure*] still needs to be accounted for. MM [*Measure for Measure*] analyzes the interpenetrating of life & death that makes life essentially discontinuous. AW [*All's Well That Ends Well*] analyzes the irony inherent in the title: the lack of correspondence between a convention of literary form & the facts of experience.

[181] Primitive religions seem to accept a conception of vicarious immortality, through a king or hero. In some of the 19th c. artist-religionists, like Mallarmé on Gautier's tomb, the idea of immortality in the form of an artist's art reappears.[162] Is this supposed also, by implication, to harrow his readers' hell?

[182] The Logos vision exists as apocalypse or total metaphor; it exists as cosmic coherence (music & mathematics) & it exists finally as a coup de dés[163] or epiphany of coherence. In between comes the discontinuous epiphanic Logos of the Gospels. I suppose the cosmic coherence one reflects in part the intense schematism of the arts: music as arbitrarily conventional as a chess game, painting as the permutations of Euclid, etc. In Mallarmé [*Un Coup de Dés*] the birth of a god from a virgin is transformed to the birth of a poem from an undifferentiated purity broken into, even defiled, by the creative act. Azure & the white page are the most common images. Also how epiphanic fragment breaks free of the encyclopedic synthesis. In Mallarmé Victor Hugo is a kind of demonic leviathan who has swallowed all the themes of poetry in his rhetoric.[164]

[183] The symbolic universe will probably take a complete volume: I don't see how I can do both it & the displacements at once. But it's possible that the displacements will fall together. Thus Eros is the mystical, idealistic, ladder-climbing quadrant of Plato & Hegel; Adonis is the Aristotelian-Thomist being-as-substance imperium, explicitly linked to the tragic fall by the Xn Passion. Theseus is the existential quadrant of the thrown-forward-in-time concern of Augustine, Heidegger, Nietzsche; Prometheus is the revolutionary-technological Marx-Freud quadrant. All four are primary displacements of *experience*, the metaphysical, religious, political or psychological areas being, from my point of view, secondary. This will make it less essential for me to plunge into the subjects & thereby lose perspective. In other words, the real theme of Part Two is the relation of theory to practice, myth to experience. Naturally it would be just as good, perhaps better, to think of One as the projection of Two & not the other way round. The thing is that Two can only be dealt with in some continuous verbal form.

[184] My much suppressed & censored hunch that the symbolic universe

must have the form of a conventionalized human body is still there. The Logos vision of order is the spherical head. The romance section is the trunk, with the point of epiphany at the brain stem. I've always thought of this as square, but it may be more naturally an upward-pointing triangle. The ironic section is certainly a down-pointing triangle, with the point of demonic epiphany at the prick, the "instrument of production" from which all revolution starts. Below this is the cloven fiction of feet & legs, or the advance through contraries, depending on how they're used (often with a cyclical vision attached, like Molloy's bicycle in Beckett).[165] The end of the Theseus quest is of course the arsehole, which is why there's so much anal demonic symbolism. In the centre[,] the axis of nomos & nous, is the systole-diastole movement of heart & more especially the lungs, with its alternation of inspiration & expiration.

[185] If I can keep a hazy set of referents to Part Two in mind, I should be able to concentrate on Part One all right. The general Eros-Adonis pattern is a familiar one: Plato & Aristotle, Eckhart, & the great 12th c. Platonists & St. Thomas, Leibnitz & Kant, the individual journey vs. the philosophy of the imperium. Kierkegaard then filters down into Theseus, Hegel, probably, into Prometheus, where, however, the presiding genius is neither Freud (who is now also there) nor Marx, but Luther. It's possible that the book, or its sequel, may absorb my sonata-form ideas.

[186] I think I have to start with the four peripheral points, & relate the quadrants to them. I start with the Logos vision. It's the traditional one, & at its heart is that tremendous ambiguity between the speculative (mystical) and the systematic (Aristotelian being-as-substance) that I discovered in Dante's sun.[166] But I have to get over thinking that north is always the top of the map. There's also the Nomos vision, which I develop out of my Fools of Time, Old & New Tragedy, the systematic Oresteian contract & the designated absurdity of Job & Adam excluded from Paradise. (The social contract is not a derivation of original sin: rather the other way round: the contract settles down & excretes its victim, like Satan & God betting on Job). Here again is the contrast between the systematic being-as-substance & the existential-absurd. In the Thanatos vision the key ideas are Nothing, death, chance, & absurdity; but absurdity is polarized between the metaphysical absurd and the absurdity of *design*, the coup de dés in the middle of hasard.[167] Nous relates Old & New Comedy, Rabelais & Plato.

[187] It would be immensely convenient & simplifying if I regarded the peripheries as forming a historical progression. Logos the traditional tonality, the Hebrew-Classical tradition; Nomos the institutional counter-tradition; Thanatos the reversal of the father's usurpation & the reestablishing of the mother, the place we're in now; Nous as the immediate future. Anyway, each periphery has an encyclopedic & an epiphanic form. I'm beginning to wonder if what I used to call the Druid analogy[168] isn't really W, the tragic cyclical calendar. Then the encyclopedia as sacred book, the deductive synthesis, is E. The W epiphany is the heroic pharmakos; the E one is the dialectic-incarnate leader, the Marxists, Mohammed, Christ risen *secundum scripturas*.[169] The Protestant Bible is a book of revolution, vs. the Catholic Bible as a guarantee of the sacramental cycle. What's Thanatos, then? The bottom of the sea, the womb as an epiphany of the tomb.

[188] Hence the Thanatos vision could be the recovered Rc. [Romantic] one, with the inverted Jerusalem at Atlantis. But whether I try attaching Eliot & Yeats & the rest to it instead of the regular Logos tonality I don't know. According to Onians the head & the balls are closely associated in primitive thought.[170] Anyway, everything mirrors its opposite: Eros is mirrored by the Theseus descent; Prometheus is also Dionysus, the reborn Adonis. I don't at the moment know, for example, whether Eckhardt "belongs" in Eros with the mystics or in Theseus with the existentialists. All counterpoising is speculation, i.e., mirror-divination. All concern is drawing into the centre.

[189] I suspect too that the Nomos-Nous axis is that of mathematics & the spatial arts (including the technologies). The "idea" & visual area is E. The Logos-Thanatos axis is partly that of words & music: the mystery of S. is partly music's lack of informing power. The *fear* of music, especially Wagner & his nihilistic cycle, is intelligible on this basis.

[190] Contiguous quadrants are complementary: therefore antithetical; therefore opposed quadrants mirror each other. I doubt if there is any contiguity in the peripheries: they simply hold adjoining quadrants together. Also, thinkers tend to stay in a quadrant; poets don't. Mallarmé can write orthodox Eros poetry, just as Dante can write an Inferno.

[191] What's in the centre of concern? The simultaneous epiphany of

Logos, or real presence, & Thanatos, or nothing: around it, the encyclopedia of the educational contract, drawn from the axis. The axis is visual: the N-S longitude aural. I mean oral. For even E is the written or visual word.

[192] I've known since Seattle that the S. gate was oracular & witty.[171] I associated it then with the lyric. But perhaps wit is the epiphany of oracular mystery—hence the recovery of the power of laughter in the cave of Trophonius.[172] The fragmented or comminuted[173] vision out of the dark, the coup de dés. I suppose ultimately there's only one encyclopedia, the educational contract, of which all the "disciplines" are quadrants & all works of art epiphanies. I suppose the association of the S-gate with music is not new—it's in Blake's Urthona—but it's useful all the same.

[193] And after eighteen years[174] I come around to exactly the same confusion again—the superimposing of hell, the city of future-directed life in pain, on the rather benignant vision of the oracular mother. Cf. Shelley's Prometheus & Mother-Earth: it's partly the Enion lament.[175] It can't be just a question of tonality, i.e., the descent theme blackened into hell during the domination of the Logos set-up. Though that's part of it: the "Apollo-Dionysus" opposition in which the latter becomes the devil or goat-god.

[194] If I'm on the right track, then, the simplest order would be: the Logos, in its apocalyptic & epiphanic form: the imagery of Eros & Adonis, with the point of epiphany; then the upside-down world of Thanatos, simply hell in Dante, recovering more oracular qualities with the Romantic revival of the mother. Then the Nomos-Nous axis; the contract-and-fall duality of tragedy; the symposium-and-sexual union of comedy. And finally the centre. That may still be two volumes, breaking off just before the axis. Volume One, in that case, is mainly centred on Narcissus, the imagery of birth in the past (point of epiphany) being reflected in the pool of death in the future. In that event the conceptual displacements will be almost entirely the concern of Volume Two.

[195] Or, perhaps, the Mercator-projection laid down out of what I know & teach, which is mainly lyrical poetry;[176] a second volume based on fiction and the *sequences* of imagery; a final volume making the St. Clair

vortex illumination from drama to concept.[177] That's my old scheme again with L [Liberal] & ʎ [Recontre] identified. Which is perhaps the answer I've been groping for for so long. ʎ was always a demonic, Romantic, fragmented book; L always an epic & encyclopedic one. Now I seem to be working toward the idea of encyclopedia manifesting itself in epiphanic fragmentation. The real ʎ might be concerned with the informing languages of experience, and/or the book of the centre.

[196] I need to know something about the language of astrology (including numerology) for the Logos half & something more—considerably more, in view of Yeats & Rimbaud—of the language of alchemy. Alchemy seems to run up the whole E side, from Rimbaud's "season" in hell to Marvell's "annihilation."[178] Also games: chess, like alchemy, runs up the E. side, or at least all board games do: card games go down the W. side, & dice, from mummers plays to Mallarmé, hovers around the south. Some kind of labyrinth game-of-Troy dance[179] belongs somewhere, I think.

[197] The different versions of the cycle are subject to the rule that a cycle is really a p.d.e. [point of demonic epiphany] perspective, at best an axis one. The Mental Traveller can *only* have the boy born N., going through Tirzah at N.W., Vala at W., completing his quest at S.W. The Female Babe is born at S.: then he goes through the Promethean Bardo, & reaches E. where the Exodus imagery begins, after which he rolls up to the N. again. Whether my hunch that Yeats' Vision will work out as a reversed or S.-pointed vision in which the tragic runs up & the comic falls away I don't know.

[198] Something in the centre: traditionally a centre of authority, Arthur's court & the like, to be reversed into the inner authority of the educational contract. Why are there no pictures or statues of Christ in meditation, as there are of the Buddha? And what has that, if anything, to do with Xy's avoidance of a spiritual centre? The pure presence of the Logos wedded to Nothing?

[199] The book has to be, of course, a *tour* de force, like all my books. Its success will depend on its convincingness as a total structure explaining a vast amount of difficult poetry, & showing how many poems speak the language of poetry & inhabit its landscape. The second volume, a literal

ᒣ [Tragicomedy], will start from the N-N axis, incorporate my ideas of "old" ironic & "new" romantic tragedy & comedy, & then go on to take in all my hunches, present & future, about (drama and more particularly) fiction. Volume Three (Λ [Anticlimax]) will be on conceptual displacements—the lot, metaphysical, political, psychological, and religious, as a bunch. Then there should be a wind-up volume taking off from religion & dealing with the metamorphoses of the images of authority in the centre.

[200] All books are double, thus: I, L & R; II, T. & P; III, A & I; IV, M & Tw. [I, Liberal and Rencontre; II, Tragicomedy and Paradox; III, Anticlimax and Ignoramus; IV, Mirage and Twilight]. The book in the second series (apart from—no, not apart from anything) is the shadow or other half of the first. Now, for God's sake, rest, perturbed spirit.

[201] I always thought that the distinction between fictional & thematic modes was a particularly useful one in the *Anatomy*, & I'm not sorry to see it organizing the first two volumes. Volume I is encyclopedic & epiphanic: it deals with the whole circle, illustrated by *episodic* forms, lyric mainly, at most drama; but based on the traditional ∟ [Liberal] epic sequence (which always was simply Homer, Virgil, Ovid, Dante, & Milton). I start with centrifugal & centripetal criticism, outlining my own approach; go on to the place of mythology; outline the mother & father creation myths, the Genesis & Exodus narrative myths, & then start on the Logos as apocalypse. Why is the apocalypse a world of total metaphor as well as a world of desire?

[202] Then the Eros climb to the point of epiphany, emphasizing the Biblical parallels, Dante, Milton, Spenser (including Q1 [*The Faerie Queene*, bk.1] and its counterpart in Ariosto), Ash Wednesday, Mallarmé (the Faun & Prose pour des Esseintes[180] particularly), and so on. The Agape movement as Adonis (Spenser's HHL [*An Hymne of Heavenly Love*]).[181] Parzival & the Grail search. The King of the Great *Clock* Tower in Poe[182] & the Twin, doppelganger & Narcissus themes. How I can keep all this separate from ᒣ [Tragicomedy] I don't know.

[203] Then the meander-and-descent patterns: Waste Land & Pound Cantoes; journey through Leviathan's bowels to his arse; anal symbolism & the future-thrown search for the oracle. That difficult ambiguity be-

tween papa's arse & momma's cunt. Maybe this is the corresponding ironic Logos: wind blowing where it listeth might be, as in the Limbo of Vanities, father's fart. Anyway, Rimbaud can help me into the world of the giants: FW [*Finnegans Wake*] , Rabelais, Vico's myth, Blake's MHH [*The Marriage of Heaven and Hell*].

[204] I still have to get several hunches clear before anything emerges that will make ⅂ [Tragicomedy] a separate book up to standard. The old puzzle about the place of the four continuous fictional forms on the doodle (confession finally went west) is a minor one, I suppose. Others will have to emerge from some extensive reading in Scott & Balzac & that Gothic stuff that Jay [Macpherson][183] knows all about.

[205] Fictional Logos	Thematic Apocalypse
Bible as narrative (history)	Bible as visionary stasis
Mathematic order of stars	Sevens & Twelves
Logical Discourse (philosophy)	Total Body of Metaphor
Passion of Christ in Time	Second Coming & End of Time

[206] The ironic side of the Logos vision is, of course, the chaos of the last days: the harvest & the vintage; the repetition of the plagues of Egypt; Armageddon; the hosts of Gog; Dr. Strangelove. There's a father, a spirit who's really & originally a sexless mother, the unified form of the body of angels, and a demonic dies irae, treading the winepress & the like, as part of his epiphany as the repeating Logos.

[207] At the other end there's an oracular life-giving earth-mother, a shadowy father-figure I haven't yet defined, a dying god-son, and, of course, the demonic or Titanic world. In Jewish tradition giants & devils are sprung of the Gen. vi 1–4 business.[184]

[208] Ecclesiastes: deals squarely with the three A's: anxiety, alienation, absurdity.[185] *Not* pessimistic or weary but a shrewd tough-minded attack on the bromides of popular proverbs, which he collects, but tests with his touchstone of *hebel*, mist or vapors. "Vanity of vanities" really means something like "nuts" or "bullshit." The basis, as with all wisdom literature, is the contrast of wisdom, the tried & tested way, & folly, the

new idea which is the old fallacy. The fool is the "one-dimensional man" in a sense opposite to Marcuse's:[186] the man chasing the donkey's carrot of a definable future ideal, not realizing what's established by the cyclical vision at the beginning: that all future goals really come out of the past, a mixture of historical & childhood myth.

[209] Well: anxiety is death-consciousness, & has to be accepted (in time of youth remember your grave). But this often develops a belief in continuity and accumulation as you get older, & therefore wiser. Eventually you discover that there isn't any accumulation of wisdom through continuity, & that's where *real* wisdom starts. It starts in *dis*continuity, the accepting of experience without *a priori* moral judgements (a time for all things). This is the counter-anxiety of living in the moment, the opposite of a stylized *carpe diem* philosophy. Absurdity is the metaphysical absurd. The fact that all logic leads to suicide is not just Schopenhauer: it's a universal principle: Yeats' "wisdom is the property of the dead."[187] To go on living (as a "live dog") in spite of logic sets up counter-absurdity. Out of this the counter-absurdity of design in creativity comes, though this goes a step farther than Koheleth does.[188] Alienation is based on the sense of futility: the race is not to the swift, & there isn't any providence of the kind Job's friends invoked. This reverses itself as soon as we drop the "what for?" search for motivation, & accept the experience as an end in itself. Out of the dropping of motive comes the sense of acceptance, the context in which Koheleth invokes God, & I think the only one.

[210] If I'm right, & I'm pretty sure I am, that the real L [Liberal] is the old encyclopedic L combined with the fragmentation theme of ʎ [Rencontre], then perhaps I can go back to sentimental romance & get a few clues for ˥ [Tragicomedy]. For I must have some central principle for ˥ before L will clear up. My inhibitions about reading fiction are connected with the absence of real guiding conceptions. Dickens didn't do much for me: I wonder if Scott will.[189] What I need is some sort of stations-of-the-cross sequence for the four fictional forms. L is the Symbolic Universe; Λ [Anticlimax] Conceptual Displacements of Myth, & ʎ (really V [Mirage]-Γ [Twilight]) The Source of Authority. I haven't a working title for ˥ yet. I notice my old device of setting up a long sequence of things & then starting at the last one: from the Davidson to the Woodhouse Festschrift,[190] it's been pretty well the same thing shot at. The Locke programme summer & 4k.[191]

[211] What have I got for ˥ [Tragicomedy]? Damn little: mostly notes on a few scattered things: Meredith's *Egoist*, Surtees' *Handley Cross*,[192] Huxley's *Antic Hay*, & some quite full marginalia on a lot of others. Wonder if I should start with the Poe-Hawthorne-Melville sequence, as I've so often thought? So often reading of something, say [Sir Walter Scott's] *Peveril of the Peak*, has been a suggestive waste, because of not having the essential clues.

[212] Farrar confirms that *Revelation* came from meditation on a diagram, which he calls a Pleroma or vision of plenitude.[193] Also that it's an ogdoad, seven being the number of sequence (& therefore presumably of ˥ [Tragicomedy]), & eight being the thematic stasis of 1 *repeated*.[194] He says this & Mark are the great literary innovations [306], & that Rev. comes out of Mark 13 [17]: he even says Rev. : Mark 13 :: John : rest of Mark [25]. For the Gnostics the diagram "generated a drama" of fall & redemption [310].

[213] Anyway, the diagram of meditation (cf. the Chinese I Ching) is one of the essential forms of Logos vision. (Or Thanatos, because I still think Yeats's *Vision* is demonic). I'm back to my alphabet of forms. A fourfold ogdoad would be the full compass of 32. Farrar speaks of the Gnostic 30 as the Body of Christ form of Pleroma.[195] I have a circular vision of 8, a square Eros-Adonis one of 12, a triangular katabasis-escape one of 10 (4–3–2–1) and a Thanatos cloven fiction of 2. Incidentally, *if* the 7's & 12's of Revelation are essentially astrological, then they include the *natural religion* basis of Blake's *Europe*, & the woman crowned with stars is Enitharmon. This would account for the inability of Rev. (& all Judeo-Xn symbolism) to take in the oracular mother. But it may not be essential. Incidentally, is it conceivable that the oracular mother transformed to a bride is something that even *Blake* left out, & which I have to supplement from Jung? There's Oothoon, of course, & Enion.

[214] (Re the diagram, or rather table, on p. 96) [par. 205]. Seven is the number of sequence (stations of the cross), the *drama* of fall & redemption in history. Eight is the number of thematic stasis, for reasons given above. Most mandalas & contemplative icons involve an even-number principle of symmetry. But if 8 is the thematic stasis of 7, 13 is the thematic stasis of 12, hence Yeats's 13th cone. Well, anyway: the normal plot sequence is a parabola in seven stages, hence Jaques' speech.[196]

Every beginning is an *in medias res*: it cuts into a temporal continuity already there for the reader or audience, & the end cuts it off. So we have (1) the audience before the beginning, sometimes symbolized by an exordium or prologue, along with the poet before the beginning, symbolized by an invocation of a Muse (2) the actual beginning, the opening line as threshold symbol (3) development towards crisis, or desis[197] (4) peripety or turning point (5) development away from peripety, or lysis[198] (6) the conclusion, whether catastrophe or anastrophe (7) the audience along with the poet (*Tempest*) released into detachment, symbolized by an epilogue, applause, a Victorian last chapter of how life went on after the story, & the like. This progression is infinitely flexible, & is *not* confined to tailor-made plots.

[215] The concealed eighth is the discovery or recognition of the thematic stasis of the sequence in the reader's mind. Sometimes a central emblem (white whale, scarlet letter) symbolizes this. I must go back to my analyses of [Virginia Woolf's] *Between the Acts* & [Thomas Love Peacock's] *Gryll Grange*.[199] Note that six of these are three doubled (cf. the rovescio[200] & binary patterns in music, the Narcissus-double theme in Poe, & the chess scheme, where the queen & king are respectively peripety & recognition & the other three pieces are doubled).

[216] Farrar also remarks that the past tenses of Revelation are "epistolary aorists" defining the time & position of the reader & not the writer [313–14]. History is the idolatrous reception of the presented emblem of myth: I mean historical interpretation, taking past or future as the real meaning, is.

[217] And, of course, I'm doubling back on my criticism of McLuhan. Centrifugal meaning tends to be sequential & linear: the Logos as (a) discursive logic (b) history or sequence of events. Centripetal meaning leads to thematic stasis. Here we have the simultaneous perception that takes off from recognition: totality of metaphor mandala diagrams included.

[218] On my plane diagram, romance has a connexion with the top semicircle & the novel with the bottom one, being more "realistic" & more capable of accommodating an ironic cadence. The confession has the W to S drive into the interior of the soul, & normally stops with an implied knowledge of the future. *Heart of Darkness* & most of Conrad's

"secret sharer" themes are exteriorized confession. Lawrence too, I think. Anatomy is the S to E drive. Note the theme of rubbish heaps & bits & pieces in FW [*Finnegans Wake*], in Pound's Cantoes, & earlier forms like SR [*Sartor Resartus*]. It works toward the E cena. It follows that there must be two earlier forms of continuous fiction, not necessarily in prose, which are Eros & Adonis driven, perhaps connected with gospel & apocalypse forms. The fact that I called confession introverted & anatomy extroverted is connected with the fact that the individual descends & the group returns (my Blake's Job paper).[201] As I called them intellectual forms, it seems most likely that the Eros & Adonis forms would be prose, however: mystical affinities of Eros (pre-Socratic oracular cosmology?) and systematic ones of Adonis. Thucydides (A [Adonis]) vs. Pythagoras or Heraclitus (E [Eros]); the Jahwist vs. the prophets. Further, as there is a distinction between naive & sentimental romance, so there is a form of naive novel, inherent in W.P. Ker's distinction between romance & the greater realism of epic and saga.[202]

[219]

Eden	P.L. [Promised Land]	Canaan	Jerusalem Zion	Rebuilt Temple	Cleansed Temple	New Jerusalem & earth
(Adam)	Abraham	Moses-Joshua	David-Solomon	Zerubbabel-Ezra	Maccabees	Jesus
wilderness	Chaldea	Egypt	Philistines	Babylon	Syria	Rome
Genesis	Genesis	Exodus	Kings	Ezekiel-Zechariah	Daniel	Revelation

(The above are the seven ages of man, with the ideal kingdom, the Messiah, the demonic kingdom of bondage, and the literary source or prophet). Should add of course giants (Goliath) & monsters (leviathan) and tyrants (Pharaoh, etc.) to the demonic.

[220] Note how often the Messiah figure has a double who carries on and completes his work. Moses has Joshua; David has Solomon; there are two waves of return from Babylon with two figures in each (Ezra & Nehemiah; Zerubbabel & Joshua) & the work of Judas Maccabeus was completed by Simon. The symbol of effort in time is completed by the symbol of epiphanic vision. Similarly with the first & second coming of Christ. Even Elijah has Elisha, though that's more the continuity of

prophetic tradition, corresponding to hereditary succession among kings. Incidentally, so far as the S of S [Song of Songs] is the wedding of the king & the land, the king has the role Christ takes later of the only symbolic male (I mean people, of course, not land).

[221] Somehow or other the two creation myths, the rational one that it was made by an authoritarian sky-father, & the oracular one that it was born from an earth-mother, seem to be an antithesis suggesting that one ought to try to get past. The real creation has something to do with manifestation or appearance: I wonder if [Karl] Barth says anything helpful. Both creation myths are, within the context of literature, projected from man's creativity, & combine to form the paradox of becoming & nothing (ex nihilo).

[222] The devil's music in P.L. ii [*Paradise Lost*, bk. 2, ll. 546–51] sounds like Wagner because it *is*, prophetically, Wagner. The Angria of Charlotte & Branwell Bronte is called the infernal world, sometimes the country below the earth.[203] It's actually Africa, but of course that's a regular symbol of the underworld. Milton's life is death to Keats[204] because Keats was trying to reverse his world. The whole underground-mother world as an inverted reflection of the above ground-father world seems to be there, all right. In Blake (and occasionally in Yeats) the Romantic cosmos is the revolutionary antithesis to the authoritarian one, and the vision of what the revolution could achieve is the old pattern, reborn into freedom. (That's true of the old model, too, except that there the redeeming agent has descended from the sky in the first place).

[223] The two worlds are of course the old Apollo-Dionysus business; but that, promulgated as it has been by obsessed lunatics like Nietzsche & Lawrence, has been badly buggered. It's true that the individual descends and the group returns; but the group isn't just a mob that's exchanged a projected slave-god for an internal one. It's an *individuated* group, and the only real revolutionary force is Nous, not Thymos.[205] The Communist parody, where the leader incarnates a dialectic, can't get past the cycle formed by the n-n [Nomos–Nous] axis.

[224] I am going to scrap the title Theseus for the W > S quadrant and replace it with Hermes. But the S > E one will continue to be Prometheus, forethought, and *not* Dionysus, or Adonis redivivus. He has many Dionysiac characteristics—the feminist revolt, the release of the bumptious

or brash word or action as the naked truth, the revolt against censorship & authority, the cult of youth, are all parts of the Orc uprising. So is the idealizing of the black or African rebel whose mother is the black African bride. Nevertheless there is a Dionysiac fallacy, or taking Prometheus to be the terrible reborn Orc, and we're right in the middle of it now.

[225] Creation myths about the world as *made* usually modulate into the world as decreed, as called into existence by a word. Man made in the image of God thus means: man is essentially the answerer of the Word, which makes the Tower of Babel story the central fall myth. This word creation myth is in the Popul Vuh, where the theme of response is even clearer (man was made a lord of the animals because they couldn't speak).[206]

[226] Mother nature is partly a revolutionary force & partly Sade's old tormenting hag. The latter, the devil's dam, is left behind in Thanatos; the former turns into the redeemed bride.

[227] I think I know where the major writers, Dante, Shakespeare, Milton, Virgil, Ovid, the Bible, belong in what I have to say. It has obviously been a suppressed premise of criticism that, just as Dante is the definitive statement of the Logos complex, so Goethe's *Faust* is of the Thanatos one, the first part Hermes, the second part Prometheus & reversal into Logos. Jung calls it an alchemical poem, which belongs. But I shouldn't confuse the fact that we need a poem like *Faust* there with the judgement that *Faust* is that poem. Or is that really a confusion when I'm really looking for content?

[228] Eros moves backwards in time: Adonis moves from birth to death, but from the past, not towards the future. That's why the conceptual displacement of Adonis is the sacramental or memory-centered analogy. Hermes is future-directed, more self-conscious & therefore ironic, modern, and "realistic": reincarnation themes appear towards the end of it as *reconciling* factors. Prometheus also moves backwards in time, but from the future towards the present.

[229] In Adonis the five wounds of the passion express the five senses, as in Blake: the recognition by birthmark is a natal-wound image. The pleading with the archetype of beauty to marry & propagate goes under the p. of e. arch. [point of epiphany archetype].

[230] The development of tragedy in Greece & the giving of the Adonis passion-role to Christ in Christianity has, as its conceptual displacement, the Aristotle-Aquinas systematic-sacramental development of an *analogical* (analogy of being) Logos consolidating on Nomos. Hunting, especially of the deer, is a sexual symbol, hence all the English puns on "hart" & "deer," the horns jokes, & so on. But the Adonis hunt, which turns away from Venus, is a sublimation, so the allegro-penseroso double focus is here too.

[231] Metamorphosis is a fall symbolism in its strict sense of a human form becoming an unresponding object, but the general theme of transformation is hermetic, and links with reincarnation and similar themes.

[232] The sacramental synthesis of Adonis is founded on *memory*, which implies the mirror & Narcissus images, human knowledge as analogy of revelation.

[233] In Hermes the quester is moving towards his vision, seeing it & trying to interpret it. In Prometheus he moves forward with it behind it [him] like a horse pulling a buggy: to look back is to lose Eurydice or be turned into a pillar of salt. This points to an Apollonian fallacy, or may do: I don't know.

[234]

CENTRIPETAL	Manifest: Verbal Icon Latent: Mental Landscape	Individual ← Poem Poet →	Manifest: Representation Latent: Psychomachia	CENTRIFUGAL
	Manifest: Conventions, Genres Latent: Myths & Archetypes	Historical ← Artifact Document →	Manifest: History of Ideas Latent: Social Significance	

The theoretical aim of the verbal icon stage is the vision of the poem's unity, but explication is so preoccupied with retracing the process of reading that it often doesn't get that far. The first line is the McLuhan axis, the communication determinism balanced by the extreme formalism of identifying medium & message. (Of course he goes into the second stage a good deal too). By mental landscape I mean the sort of thing Yeats does with Shelley;[207] by psychomachia I mean Freudian criticism. By social significance I mean essentially Marxist criticism.

[235] I'm beginning to see how my Cornell-Indiana paper[208] really follows the pleroma:[209] Sidney belongs in the conscious Logos vision, where the norms are set by writing and calculation, and Shelley [in] the descent to the cave of the poetic process of oracular wit.

[236] There's no essential difference that I see between the making of the world & the decreeing of it by the word: Faust takes the conception "Word" & follows it back through "Sinn" & "Kraft" to "Tat," but it's the same creation myth.

[237] Once a myth of concern is recognized to be such, it becomes clear that you can't express its truth without lying. Because you're contradicting accepted truth with something which is going to be made true but isn't true now.

[238] Further on my remarks on reconciliation vs. interpenetration: a great thinker attracts hordes of followers who want to revise & improve him, but the greater he is, the more he resists "revisionism" (vide Marx & Freud). One either accepts his main construction lines (as I did Blake's) or not, but revisionism, like other kinds of eclecticism, just doesn't seem to work. Is this a characteristic of the myth of concern? Does it apply to Christianity?

[239] Descriptive language is objectified language, and belongs in the world of the cloven fiction; symbolic language is the language of incarnation. To do anything with Christianity we have to separate the everlasting Gospel from its institutional perversions, and that may be really a task for literary criticism.

[240] Flying over the Rockies recently I thought how human civilization cuts into the continuum of nature, which is really doing something else,

with another rhythm & dimension from another world. From the perspective of that world, nature is "fallen," down under it. There is such a thing as creation, something that neither evolution by mutation nor any revolution that starts with a *culbute* can explain. *How* did we get to warm-blooded animals? *How* did we get to consciousness? *All* the links are missing. Nothing very new here, of course, except as a feeling.

[241] Marvell's garden establishes three levels of Eros vision: the red & white level of sexual fulfilment; the physical absorption into the womb-like garden mother; the penseroso reversal of this, where the garden is "annihilated" by the mind. At this last point the soul becomes a bird on the Tree of Life, in the alchemical "peacock" stage, awaiting a "longer flight" [l. 56] or Logos vision.[210]

[242] Over the last page (middle) [par. 240], I missed the only real point I had: the conceptual displacements of our two creation myths are the maternal (gradual Fabian natural gestation traced by natural selection and the DNA molecule) and the paternal (revolutionary act of seizing power by the control of technology, symbolized by the thunderbolt. There must be a third creation myth that works through manifestation or epiphany.[211]

[243] If I go back to my hundred-sections idea, section 1 is the centripetal-centrifugal conspectus, with, perhaps, a note distinguishing the categories of literature from the mnemonic devices for grouping them. Section 2 begins with the literature-inheriting-a-mythology stuff, the two creation myths, & the two worlds of upper & lower consciousness. Somewhere along here I want to embark on a historical survey of the Logos myth: how the mathematical vision, for example, declines after Newton, & then either turns demonic (Blake's *Europe*, Nietzsche's eternal recurrence, Yeats' *Vision*) or else gets reborn by way of some kind of games theory. Hesse's Glasperlenspiel [*The Glass Bead Game*] & Mallarmé's *Igitur* & *Coup de Dés* belong here, though I don't just know how yet. I suppose chess in Bardo gets attached. One of the things I find encouraging about this project is the way I'm being compelled to face things I've ducked in the AC: Poe's *Eureka*, the epic circle, & the like. Browne's quincunx, too.[212] Because a lot of things seem to be converging on Yeats' double gyre or hourglass figure, of which the X is one form: a conscious world where the mind is at the centre or top; a lower world where the

mind is looking into itself below. "Poetic Cosmology": it sounds like Vico.

[244] I should not sell myself on the assumption that all Eros patterns are comic & all Adonis ones tragic. I must adopt more flexible criteria, of which the most promising at the moment is the view of time (Eros: present > past; Adonis: past > present; Hermes: present > future; Prometheus: future > present). As Jay [Macpherson] pointed out to me, the birth of the child is an important Adonis pattern. The father-mother-child Trinity is the Incarnation of the Trinity itself in time: Berdyaev quotes a theologian named Bulgakov, who calls Mary the hypostatic form of the Holy Spirit.[213] The transfer of the hero from mother to father is important, and so is the intermediate hermaphroditic conception of Shakespeare's beautiful youth, which is of course involved in the Narcissus complex.

[245] Browne says of chess that in its original form it figured "the whole world, the motion of the planets, with eclipses of sun & moon."[214] Invented by Thoth, according to *Phaedrus* 270. This is the GC [*Garden of Cyrus*], where the quincunx takes the X form mentioned above [par. 243],[215] an upper & lower pyramid representing perception from a centre & circumference respectively—close to Yeats' hour-glass & Blake's vortex, & one of the things I'm looking for.

[246] Re the Adonis theme of father, mother & child, note how Shakespeare's PT [*The Phoenix and the Turtle*] reverses this in its upward Eros movement. From Reason's point of view, at least, they leave no posterity.

[247] The accordion folds again, as it must: Part One, The Light World (Logos vision with Eros & Adonis cycles); Part Two, The Dark World (Thanatos vision, with Hermes & Prometheus cycles); Part Three, The Nomos-Nous axis, with narrative movements of tragedy & comedy & perhaps the contract-Utopia displacement; Part Four (which may not be a separate part), the symbols of the centre, the epiphanic creation, the myth of concern, the source of authority.

[248] Or, more simply, One, The World Above; Two, The World Below; Three, The World Between. Paradiso, Inferno, Purgatorio; Virgo, Scorpio, Libra. This has to be the modern order. Past, Future, Present; faith,

hope, love. I see the third part as a *nobile castello* or House of Alma ringed round with pericopes. The house of communion after the periplus.[216]

[249] I should like to try keeping the argument to small sections (after all, even the *Anatomy* does that, really) because a reasonably heavy amount of documentation is required, and each section can be "thickened" by additional reading.

[250] Each major character in a myth tends to become individualized, even though every literary treatment of him or her is totally different. Characters in folktales are typical shadows like the Trickster; gods & goddesses are real enough to have visions of & build temples to. Yet Venus the mother of Aeneas in Virgil seems to have little in common with Venus the muse of Lucretius.

[251] As a child I had a board with 33 hollows for marbles, the central one empty. The puzzle was by jumping over marbles & removing them from the board to leave one in the middle. There were four side areas to be cleared. This game has the solution to my projected book on an I Ching or model of augury. I record this because anyone reading these notes would assume that they were the work of a psychotic, so I may as well furnish the definitive proof of the fact.

[252] The opening & closing of the accordion means simply my permanent axiom: write every book as though it were your last. Shoot the works; tell all you know at that point. The present book is my *Burnt Norton*: it's the first of four, yet it contains all four. Further, as I now conceive it, it's a voyage into the unknown for me: I have some notion of Part One, a dimmer notion of Part Two, & only the vaguest hunches about Part Three. Yet Part Three is the real balls of the book: the rest is just mapwork, or map reading.

[253] Browne's GC [*The Garden of Cyrus*] (the remark about chess, by the way [par. 245], comes from Suidas, S.V. *tabula*, according to L.C. Martin:[217] cf. similar games in the Utopia, and, of course, the labyrinth-dance or game of Troy in Virgil)[218] is about the quincunx, but is fascinated by the crux ansata or sign of Venus, the circle with a cross below it. In me, the cross is the four forms of fiction & the circle the episodes of drama & lyric. I kept trying to inscribe the cross in the circle in AC, with indiffer-

ent success. Ultimately, I suppose, my L [Liberal] is a circle & my ˥ [Tragicomedy] a cross, but I can't think of that when I'm writing L: I have to inscribe it within again.

[254] One hurdle to get over is this: you originally thought of the Eros-Adonis semicircle as innocence & the lower one as experience, or greater realism. Now you think of the upper semicircle as daylight consciousness, which makes *it* realistic, & the lower one as an area of fantasy. I suppose part of the answer is a double gyre, broadening out to its greatest displacement at the N-N [Nomos-Nous] axis & then narrowing again. Well, assuming that any circle is a projected sphere, my cross, or what I used to call the axes of speculation & concern, is really the four forms of fiction as a fictional meridian running from romance (N.) down to parable (S.) & back up again, and a thematic equator running from confession (W.) to anatomy (E.) and around back. Now if the poles of the sphere are undisplaced, apocalyptic & demonic respectively, then the centre must be the place of greatest displacement.

[255] Part Three, then, would begin with a panorama of the displacements of the quadrants. The sun cantoes in the *Paradiso* show the Eros-Adonis displacements, Platonic mysticism & Aristotelian-Thomist teleology, as going up & down the same ladder.[219] There's a corresponding point in the black sun inside Leviathan where the existential & the revolutionary, Nietzsche & Marx, Jung & Freud, can be similarly seen. Hints of this are in Yeats' antithetical primary cycle, Joyce's Shem & Shaun struggle, and perhaps in Pound. After that comes the mapping of the centre.

[256] If, like Coleridge, I were writing a Christian book, it would be easy to show the centre as the incarnate Logos, the balancing power that has come down from the sky & up from hell. And I suppose I do have to take the Gospels as my basis, if only because that has been the answer given us by our mythological tradition. The place of the greatest displacement is the place of revelation, where myth has been superseded by the greater & non-symbolic reality of a person in eternity. Hence the realism of the parables . . . If I can bring it off, it really will be the Divine Comedy of criticism, perhaps a greater *poem* than the Pound Cantoes. Add paranoia to psychosis, & the hell with it. I think I'm on to something, something I've been revolving around for twenty dark but profitable years.

[257] The N-N [Nomos–Nous] axis moves west to power, east to wisdom. The elect group becomes an Arthur's court, & hence a tragic comitatus, as it moves west; it becomes a symposium group towards the east, moving through a last supper or Phaedo group on the way. Perhaps the pericopes are on a horizontal axis of feeding, the group becoming a man, and a vertical axis of healing, the man becoming a group. The former move from kernels of commandment through parables at the centre to kernels of aphorism; the latter move from birth & epiphany appearances to the Passion.

[258] Ever since Seattle I've seen a point near the d.e. [demonic epiphany] where oracle becomes wit, where the visitor to Trophonius recovers the power of laughter.[220] What's the corresponding point in the N? Is it where the allegro & penseroso ecstasies touch? I suppose it must be.

[259] In Eros, at least, sexual differentiation comes out of & returns to a hermaphrodite, as in the transvestite comedy roles & the Spenser-Shakespeare complex. Virgin mothers and divine fathers form a similar pole: the latter is in the Jupiter-Athene & God-Wisdom patterns. I wonder where the childlike fantasy world belongs: the Peele-Gozzi-Lewis Carroll type of thing.[221] Somewhere nearby, because MND [*A Midsummer Night's Dream*] & the Tempest are so close to it. The Alice books seem to me to be "innocent" parodies of descent themes.

[260] *A Rebours* is a penseroso Tower (I begin to see how my circle of phases is working in), and Mallarmé's poem *Prose pour des Esseintes* is the corresponding allegro vision. (I suppose I should look at those phases again to see if they correspond to what I keep thinking of as a series of stages in Eros & Adonis & the other patterns. If they do, the danger of reduplicating AC will be increased, though there'll be other advantages).

[261] The two most frequent persons in primitive myths are the supreme being & the Trickster, who become the God & devil of our framework. In the Hermes descent the psychopomp is often some variant of the Trickster: the identity of Mephistopheles puts *Faust* I firmly in this quadrant, though I doubt if Marlowe's Faustus is there. The grateful dead man (Tobit var. [variant]),[222] the clown (Sancho Panza mod. [modulation]), and others: cf. too Edmund in *Lear* vs. the benevolent but somewhat ectoplasmic Edgar. Counterpart of the old wise man & such in Eros.

[262] The sacred is the symbolic, the holy marked off temenos [sacred circle]. What's it symbolic of? Ultimately, the profane is the symbol of it: the sacred represents an eternal world where there are no symbols. As with the Temple symbolism of the Bible, what begins as a centre ends as a circumference.

[263] We experience Time as a mixture of the linear & the cyclical. But there are two cyclical movements. The cycle of nature is a guarantee of permanence, as after the flood. The human cycle is neurotic, an assimilation of man to the nature he grew out of, & which keeps trying to pull him down to its automatism.

[264] I've been looking at a book on Gurdjiev,[223] not that I find either him or Ouspensky very rewarding, but just to see if his enneagrams & such are a genuine Logos vision or just a put-on. They could be both, of course: the emphasis is on oral teaching, as with other religious leaders, and those who just try to read the book are outside in the court of Gentiles. But I wonder if the higher consciousness he talks about exists only as an experience, or can't be attained in creative work.[224] There's no evidence that Shakespeare or Bach habitually attained higher consciousness, but what they wrote certainly manifests that world. Perhaps this is the real basis for the traditional distinction between active & contemplative life.

[265] The book quotes St. Thomas, naturally without giving a reference, as saying that in order to move into a higher grade of vision, man must cease to exist.[225] In a sense this is what Sartre says about ordinary consciousness, & as the same thing on a higher plane is described in the N.T. [New Testament] as "out of the body" or "in the spirit," there may be a link I could use between the ultimate apprehension of the myth of concern & a life beyond death.

[266] My three worlds link with the Gunas: Rajas above, Tamas below, Sattva in the middle, where the projections are recovered.[226] The world corresponding to Dante's purgatory, which is both part of this world & a world of imaginative sense, has to be the final one. The general historical movement is from the ear to the eye, as in Job. Literature begins in oral tradition and religion in a creative word in the dark: religious poetry is sing-song and echoic, full of puns and jingles & assonances. Hence, e.g., even the Book of Revelation is echoic, and, though said to be a vision, is

poorly visualized. The ear is a whirlpool fierce to draw *creations* in,[227] but its product is the projected vision which tends to become in its turn hypnotic & idolatrous, making us become what we behold, until it's recovered & possessed. The driving of action by formulaic units is still going on in Maoism.

[267] I have been saying that this book was concerned with external relations, which means it's partly centrifugal. The end of the process, where literature merges into the myth of concern, has two aspects. First, the centre becomes the circumference: Jerusalem the New Jerusalem, the *temenos* magic circle the zodiac. Second, the specific "Western" *cadre* derived from Classical and Biblical myth turns out to have a strong family likeness to all other developed myths of concern.

[268] *So* much to do: I don't see how I can make even my introduction convincing until I draw up a series of *linguistic* criticisms: say structural, transformational, philosophical & anthropological.

[269] The turning inside out of the *temenos* is in Revelation, at the end of the *Paradiso*, and is perhaps in the relation of Yeats' S to B to B [*Sailing to Byzantium* to *Byzantium*]. For the final *descent* of the bride Jerusalem to the earth (the Sattva world between),[228] & remembering that the bride is closely connected with the bird or Spirit, cf. the fact that the change in the elements in the Greek rite takes place during the prayer for the descent of the Spirit. Cf. the Eros form of this in [Dylan] Thomas' Winter's Tale, where of course it's been influenced by PT [*The Phoenix and the Turtle*]. Jerusalem (Zion) the bride is symbolically at the highest point of the world, vs. Babylon the Whore & its heaven-rending Tower. Both are on seven hills (Enoch & II Esdras for J [Jerusalem]).

[270] It could be quite a book if I bring it off, but, oh gee, one hundred sections is a bloody long book, especially if the documentation is heavy. A laborious but perhaps effective procedure would be the FS one, which originally had the 100 sections structure: write a hell of a long MS, then cut it down by polishing sentences into aphorisms.

[271] The third is beginning to take some kind of shape: it introduces or recapitulates the two great historical movements of myth: (1) from the ear to the eye [cf. par. 266] (2) from the eye (projected) back to circumfer-

ential possession, where the unity of literature disappears in the myth of concern. I'm beginning to think that, in the general theme of recovery of projection which is central to Part Three, that [*sic*] *nomos* will turn out to be the recovered *logos*, and *nous* the recovered *thanatos*. This was not at all what I originally expected; but, after all, nomos only begins as something arbitrary & external: it's actually the centre of *objective* recovery, the point of incarnation. Similarly, nous is the centre of *subjective* recovery, & it's the point of resurrection, and what resurrection is recovered from is obviously death. But of course the risen body, like the dead body, has ceased to exist: that's that point just above [par. 265] that unites St. Thomas & Sartre.

[272] So I come back to the great doodle: the W. point is neither infancy (N.) nor passion (S.) but the generation of the presence, the sort of thing the baptism epiphany is, and it's clear how the other end of P.R. [*Paradise Regained*], the pinnacle elevation, is a Nous point, a prototype of resurrection. Milton in Blake's poem goes through the same two points: the vortex descent and the rejection of Satan. So that puts those two crucial poems in something like the appropriate place. But it's all very vague still: what's *Paradise Lost* in these terms? What's *Don Quixote*?

[273] I notice that Christian themes are closing in: they're difficult to sell, because even people who can see how wrong Whitman was about the Trojan war[229] are still in a frenzy of impatience to cancel out the Christian accounts. It'll take tact to show how difficult it is to break out of a mythological framework. The poets keep reminding us of this, because so many good ones are religious.

[274] The world above projects into the past: the Exodus narrative moves toward the *original* contract, thençe to a world typologically identified with Eden. This is why the theme of *nostos* or return is so bound up with it. Now, I've always known that descent themes were connected with knowledge of the future, so my existential-Angst & Promethean revolutionary-ideals themes also fit. I should also notice the Eros theme of return to the past in Shakespearean late romance, the Pygmalion theme in WT [*The Winter's Tale*] (& the RR [*Le Roman de la Rose*]), the constant reference to a past in *The Tempest*.

[275] Lévi-Strauss says that in the Dark Ages the sub-Arctic peoples

were in communication all around the world, & that the Grail cycle is closer to forest-Indian myths in North America than anything else.[230] Diffusion has the same relation to the inner designs of the myth of concern that source & direct influence have to the analogy of inspiration. I need this kind of thing for the opening sections of Part Three, (unless they're further on) about the myth of concern.

[276] Blake's hundred plates are on a quaternary division,[231] but I seem, for the time being at least, to be on a ternary scheme, despite the four quadrants & cardinal points. Well: my Logos vision is the projection into the past of the actual or recovered or incarnate Logos, & the past projection of the Son is obviously the Father. The Spirit is the voice of inspiration & prophecy, the Christian oracle, of whom the Mother is a hypostatic form: hence it's involved in all future-centered revolutionary constructs like that of Joachim of Floris.[232] I saw this when I was writing about Shelley, & referred to Heine.[233] Jews (Heine, Marx) brought up in a future-Messiah creed, have a natural affinity with Promethean symbols. Negroes connect with the African underworld: cf. Hart Crane's "Black Tambourine," where Negro : world :: poet : society. Coming out of the oracular cave, where the Earth-Mother becomes the World Spirit or Anima Mundi (cf. Browne's identification of this with the Holy Spirit),[234] you have to form an inner spirit or anima, which is what I think Valery's Jeune Parque is all about. If you sin against the Spirit, you're left in the lower world.

[277] Even my tragedy sequence fits this, because I'd always thought of the tragedy of isolation, *Lear* in particular, as a W to S descent. But what Joachim thought of as the age of the Son was really, of course, the Age of the Father, to whose wrath the Son was continually being sacrificed.[235] And the secular revolutionary-movement that began in the 18th c. was the Age of the Spirit. That age has taken us straight into the great pile of shit in the bottom of hell. Maybe the third age, the recovered Age of the Son, will start in 1996, the traditional year of the millennium. For it we need a new view of creation that gets out of the chicken-egg alternation.

[278] Curious how I've practically reversed my earlier notion that Nomos-Nous was speculative and Logos-Thanatos concerned. I'm now beginning to think of Nomos & Nous as ultimately the same thing, but that doesn't mean two circles. The wisdom of each quadrant has to expand into the other quadrants, the most difficult being the one above or below. That is,

Eros wisdom soon grasps the connexion with Adonis, but finds it very hard to understand that its roots are in Prometheus. Similarly, Prometheus is soon aware of Hermes, can easily think of itself as a reborn Adonis or Dionysus, but resists the notion that it is completed by Eros. This is the form of the fourth, the elusive final breaththrough. The river Lethe runs between Nomos & Nous. *Paradise Lost* is built around Adam in Adonis & Satan in Hermes. Satan is turned away from the Logos descent, & thinks he started with Nomos (which of course he also misinterprets). So do all atheistic existentialists since. They see the descent to Thanatos, but can't believe that the source of the descent is Logos. Similarly, evolution is an upward movement: Milton has Eros forms of it in Raphael's speech to Adam [*Paradise Lost*, bk. 5, ll. 469–505]. The grosser feeds the purer, things naturally ascend to God; digestion of food is part of a rising operation; our bodies may at last all turn to spirit. But Milton doesn't see in P.L. [*Paradise Lost*] that the roots of this process are in Prometheus, though he had been a Promethean poet. Modern evolution is Promethean, tracing things from origin, going from lower to higher, realizing that the ultimate source of the ascent is Thanatos, death, the limit of opacity. But it won't see that there's an Eros movement completing it that ends in Logos again. I think each quadrant is aware first of its opposite (Eros of Hermes, etc.), next of its cyclical complement (Eros of Adonis, etc.), & last of its dialectical complement (Eros of Prometheus, etc.).

[279] I've often wondered why I disliked abstract expressionism so much, and now I think I know: it's pictorial anarchism, the same thing student unrest begins in, the renunciation of the community. I remember some Clyfford Stills I saw in Buffalo:[236] wonderful pictures, but they wouldn't endure anything else in the same room except another Clyfford Still. (I was told later that Still was personally almost a psychotic, and of course I disapprove of putting that fact into a causal relation to the pictures, but the effect of the pictures is unmistakable). But going through the Uffizi one can see how the pictures of the most towering geniuses still belong in a pictorial community, and hang in a room with other pictures.

[280] Thinking, of course, is not something I do: it's something that happens where I am. It gets done in spite of what I do: everything I "do" is mental automatism, running along prefabricated tracks that look like a map of the London subways.[237] There's the black sado-masochist line, consisting of remorse (in the literal "agen-bite of inwit"[238] sense) over the

past & stewing about a future invented for the purpose of stewing about it. There's the blue line of all the good things I've written or said in the past and am going to write or do in the future (the future part of this is the only one I feel as voluntarily-assumed self-indulgence). This is the anecdotage line: I might call it the Narcissus line, except that Narcissus was a comparative realist: the image he fell in love with really did resemble himself, & wasn't one invented out of mainly imaginary qualities. Whenever this line stops at a station, we instantly transfer to the black line. Then there's the inner circle, or what Beckett calls the Belacqua line, of diddling & twiddling & meandering around what is in front of one.[239] I resent other people's automatisms excessively because they run over the same lines, & delay or impede mine.

[281] At the centre of my diagram is the unity, or recovery, of what I've been calling Nomos & Nous, which become respectively the natural & the reasonable aspects of recovered vision. A line running from Logos to Thanatos also intersects them. Contract & Utopia are not so much Nomos & Nous conceptions as the recovered forms of the projections into the past & the future respectively. Thus they're north & south on my diagram, if I'm right; but if I am I'm back to the old speculation-concern axis. Also I seem to have Blake's Zoa diagram lying on its side, with the "parent power" or Tharmas north instead of west. I don't know if this is serious: I can't change it at this stage, surely: but it's so like me to get it wrong the first time.

[282] Anyway: I think my Table of apocalyptic & demonic images [*GC*, 166–7] relates only to the father-centered creation myth, which is one reason why Revelation, & the Bible generally, is a guide to it. For the world below as oracular I need a wholly different model. Alchemy? The other one is astrological, or at least Ptolemaic.

[283] It is a relatively old idea that after I box the compass of my quadrants & cardinal points I come around to the recognition of Eros again. Now The Tempest seems to me to belong with *Milton* and *Paradise Regained* in the purgatorial world,[240] being in so curious a way on the other side of this one.

[284] But, of course, while *Milton* & *P.R.* [*Paradise Regained*] & *T.* [*The Tempest*] will probably bulk large in Part Three, Part Three isn't about a

specific kind of literature but the recovered way of reading literature. It's obvious that we can't read *Inferno* as a projection, believing in an objective hell; less obvious that we can't read the Gospels historically; still less obvious that contracts & Utopias are myths in the present tense, and yet not kidnapped by present historical conventions. I'm starting to gabble, which is one phase but a tedious one: what I wanted to note was the Heideggerian "thrown-ness"[241] of the Court Party in *The Tempest*.

[285] There's a bad or demonic descent to hell and a good or oracular descent to a lower world, often the point of demonic epiphany, as in T [*The Tempest*], The Aeneid, The Descent of Odin,[242] the point of the thriller I noted in Dickens (Orlick is a shadow-brother figure who "lays" the sister-mother out), etc. I have to read—series of satiric oracular descents starting with Lucian's *Kataplous* & Apuleius (ass fucking the whore is the demonic parody of the bird-woman conjunction in Yeats & in A's [Apuleius's] own Cupid & Psyche story) (cf. of course Yeats & the glint of the copulating ass in The Herne's Egg),[243] Rabelais, with great attention to the final chapters, perhaps (besides of course GT [*Gulliver's Travels*], TS [*Tom Sawyer*] & FW [*Finnegans Wake*]) Melville's *Mardi* & Gurdjieff's *All & Everything*. Don't forget the search for the *future*, Kurtz's "intended" & FW's [*Finnegans Wake*'s] "futurousn," parodied in the Rip van Winkle type of sleep through time in Celtic stories.

[286] Recently in teaching Graves' Juan poem [*To Juan at the Winter Solstice*] I thought how complete & unifying the hero cycle is, and how unnecessarily fragmented my present method of taking it apart is. But I don't know. Perhaps, ignoring the ⅂ [Tragicomedy] factors, I could take John Barleycorn[244] as the basis of an Adonis cycle that covers the mysterious birth, exposure, finding & all the rest of it of the hero (indicated by Burns when he replaces the three western men of his sources with three eastern kings). This goes on until the Adonis death which creates a solemn sympathy with nature, Orpheus' magic achieved by *death*, and a reintegration of society through the Eucharist rite. The separation from the brother is part of this. The journey below is different: the hero appears mysteriously, as in Mark & John, in the desert or over sea, then goes through the dragon fight & the rest of it. But the logical exposition would lead up in Part Three to the *total* cyclical journey of the incarnate Logos, or great doodle. In the purgatorial context (e.g. the Eliot quartets) the infernal aspect of the dark world disappears.

[287] At the nadir the Heidegger-shaped knowledge of being from nothing is attained. Being is qualitatively distinct from beings, I suppose because it's really a Thanatos vision. At the other end, God is qualitatively distinct from gods, including God when he is a god, a human-shaped myth. I'm back to the point that revelation must be something else than the mythical presentation of the Bible. Now the traditional God of the Logos vision is a person, and *therefore*—this is a point I find it hard to get around—the creator of the natural order. When does the universe begin & end? Tradition has a confident answer, though beginning & ending are human notions & have nothing to do with the universe. We have to *recover* both the God and the being that we've projected into past and future.

[288] Adonis literature isn't all tragic, as I've said: my instinct to put the confession on the west side stories was a sound one. All the big encyclopedic confessional novels like Keller's Green Henry,[245] or Proust himself, that move from the past into the present, that take one deeper into experience, that have a teleological shape and an over-all sacramental or analogy-of-being feeling, belong here. Incidentally, the Virgilian archetype of moving from pastoral to epic belongs in this quadrant, as I've doubtless said somewhere. In any case the sequence Virgil-Proust seems the organizing one: the motto of Adonis movement is always "The only paradises are those we have lost." It seems to me too that *Glasperlenspiel* [Herman Hesse's *The Glass Bead Game*] is a movement from Adonis pastoral to Adonis reality, & that at the end the Master enters death at Nomos, in a reversal of the Eros Socrates-pupil situation, leaving the labyrinth a Hermes Oedipus inheritance.

[289] Some years ago I tried to read [Herbert] Marcuse & Norman Brown. They were Freudians, & both referred to Jung in passing as a "reactionary," therefore useless. People who talk that way are nits. Marxists are therefore nits. Nobody is inherently reactionary or revolutionary: it's the use made of him that determines what he is. It doesn't matter what opinions he held: Freud had a lot of "reactionary" views too. The belief in the magical inherence of reaction or what not is a squalid humanized version of the Mark Apocalypse, which is about sheep & goats, but could never have been about people, as nobody is good enough for heaven or bad enough for hell.

[290] Note how Rimbaud's Sonnet des Voyelles runs from the ear to the eye. We go from the "bombinating" A, Alph the sacred underground river with its roar, to the Omega in the visual world, "yeux" being the last word.

[291] I need Rimbaud's Bateau Ivre, Baudelaire's Voyages, Huckleberry Finn, Moby Dick, Poe's Maelstrom & Gordon Pym, The Ancient Mariner & Kubla Khan for the particular Hermes complex of white goddess, black slave, descent down the river or sea to the lower world of leviathan, & the like.

[292] Something tells me that my Paradiso & Inferno won't really be so tough. It's the Purgatorio that at present I have so few clues to. Anyway, I'm getting bored with my present introduction, which is really not very new stuff, and would like to scrap it in favor of a section 100 which will be a genuine conclusion. This book doesn't need the driving rhetorical force of FS, or won't need it if the drive is properly taken care of in the sequence: what I'd like to make of it is what the magicians mean by objective art, where "inspiration" is something known, planned, and calculated.

[293] I shall of course have to return to my Kentucky question about how far words can inform[246] in Part Three, and I can hardly write the third part without learning something about linguistics, transformational grammar, structuralism, and philosophical linguistic problems. In my Notes I should have, as an addendum, a list of references to my own works.

[294] Prometheus symbolism is only incidentally about revolution, which is really a vulgarization of it. What it's really about is resurrection. I suppose alchemy has to do with some kind of psychosomatic discipline that could end in the resurrection of the body [see also par. 282]. Anyway, the group would include, to begin with, visions of white-goddess tyranny like Tennyson's Hesperides; it would include PU [*Prometheus Unbound*] & MHH [*The Marriage of Heaven and Hell*], of course, and Verlaine's Crimen Amoris, & Hopkins' Heraclitean fire sonnet, and perhaps [Valéry's] La Jeune Parque. And [Yeats's] Byzantium. I must pray for luminousness, the quality my work has at its best when I really know

what I'm talking about . . . I wonder if the unfinished or destroyed masterpieces of the past, resentful at being excluded from history, keep trying to come back, or yelling like the martyrs under the altar, & if they are part of the imagination of other works.

[295] Eros imagery after Rcsm. [Romanticism] tends to become a search for a *historical* period of lost innocence, the age of chivalry, the age of innocent paganism, the noble savage, or whatever was before a historically-conceived fall. The key to Don Quixote is somewhere in here. Of course the extraordinary provincialism of Xy, which regarded everything pre-Xn as subhuman, played into the hands of such anti-Xns as Swinburne.

[296] It would be lovely to be able to keep to a *Commedia* approach, and yet it may be too much like the AC again. Perhaps this is rather what will take shape: Part One, a survey of the four quadrants; Part Two, the four cardinal points, which involves studying two quadrants together, plus the two opposites, Eros-Hermes & Adonis-Prometheus. Part Three as I now think of it, that way would be a spiral initiatory development, along with very obvious tactical dangers, following the general movement from the episodic to the encyclopedic, the great doodle monomyth[247] beginning the last part [cf. par. 272].

[297] One conception I stumbled over by accident was that of the *apocryphon*, the book hidden or sealed up in a bad time to be released at the right time. It connects with the following:
1. Mysterious birth of hero > ark in desert > word in desert
2. Epiphany of hero > temple > proclaimed or found word
3. Defeat & death of hero > destroyed Temple > hidden word
4. Restoration of hero > restored Temple > received word.
But I'm beginning to think now of a separate short book on the Bible, which would help prevent too much Bible from getting into this one.

[298] The contrast between the sexual & the sublimated goals of Eros imagery derive[s] ultimately from the contrast in Ovid between *Ars Amatoria* and *Remedia Amoris*.[248]

[299] Just as AC was an anatomy & not a confession or novel or romance, though it surveyed all four impartially, so this book is, I think,

going to be an Eros book & not an Adonis or Hermes or even Prometheus one. The three parts are three turns on the winding stair. Only it goes to a centre.

[300] It's obvious that Yeats's S to B [*Sailing to Byzantium*] & Byzantium are related as projected vision to recovered process; similarly, the third part is concerned with the incarnate or indwelling Logos, & hence with its relation to Nomos & Nous, not forgetting Thanatos. Is this also the relation of Dante's Convivio, which I gather is later, to his Paradiso?

[301] I've said that the central area radiating from the crossing point of the axes is not a third area of literature but the area of recovering what's been projected above & below. But in this new scheme there would be things belonging to section 2 at least, perhaps 3 as well. These would be my "central" things, *Milton, P.R.* [*Paradise Regained*], *Tempest*, the Eliot *Quartets, Mental Traveller*.[249]

[302] Or, more likely, these go in the 3 summary: I'm reverting to 2 as a miniscule ㇕ [Tragicomedy], dealing with long fictional syntheses. Just as there's a young lover & an old wise man in Eros, with an informing dialogue between them, so there's a Urizenic full-close aspect to Adonis: even the Odyssey may be that. I've mentioned Proust as Adonis literature, and those huge 19th c. educational novels like *Der grüne Heinrich*[250] also belong.

[303] I can't quite rid myself of a feeling (and I'm by no means sure that I should) that there are two circles, the low point of the Eros-Adonis one being the centre, & the top of the other. The Mental Traveller might work out better on the top level. But I don't know: I thought at first FQ [*The Faerie Queene*] might be an upper cycle, but isn't really. I is Prometheus, II Nous, III Eros, IV Adonis, V Nomos, VI Hermes, in spite of Acidale & the rest. That leaves the Logos-Thanatos axis for the Mut. Coes. [*Mutabilitie Cantos*]. Though even there Cleopolis & Acidale may indicate the centre, which needs a name. Kairos?[251]

[304] One main theme of Part Three is: the N-S axis of concern is revolutionary, & the W-E one is liberal, not speculative, but simply broadening & enlarging. Revolutionary characteristics are: the enforced loyalty of a minority group (Jews, early Christians); belief in a *unique* historical rev-

elation; resistance to "revisionism"; establishment of a rigorous *canon* of myth; rejection of knowledge for its own sake (demand for relevance or *Zweckwissenschaft*).[252] Judaism was the only *revolutionary* monotheism produced in the ancient world, and Christianity inherited the characteristics that made Tacitus scream & Marcus Aurelius talk about their *parataxis*.[253]

[305] So Arnold has something in equating the *liberal* element of our culture with Hellenism. *Liberal* elements include: the mores of a writing culture, philosophy as the pursuit of dialectic, history & the like as research. Knowledge is in large measure for itself: this is the expansion that takes place as soon as the demands for "relevance" are quieted. There is also less suppression of the sexual, and more emphasis on confronting a *visible* objective world. So sculpture, the hypothesis of biology, and drama are Hellenic.

[306] I must work this out in more detail somewhere else. Meanwhile, if my hunch is right that Aristotle & Plato are, respectively, the guardians of Nomos & Nous, a lot of things will clear up.

[307] Hermes journey: the black attendant, either diabolic like Mephistopheles or a servant (Jim, Queequeg, the black-servant figures behind *Bateau Ivre*) or an obsession like the Nigger of the Narcissus. Sometimes, as with *Moby Dick* and *Heart of Darkness*, the ultimate terror is a white one. Note how when *The Ancient Mariner* comes to its climax in the appearance of the female Thanatos figures Death (p.d.e. [point of demonic epiphany]) and Life-in-Death (hell), there's a dice-play: the Mallarmé archetype.

[308] One more recasting: Part One is the compass-boxing of quadrants; Part Two is the extended or encyclopedic forms and the conceptual displacements; Part Three is a general comparative mythology survey.

[309] For example, I was looking at some Australian drawings of what is called (very well) the Eternal Dream Time, where huge giants in vaguely human form became animals & natural phenomena. Metamorphosis: I fell over something similar in Blake, or something I was able to attach to Blake. Metamorphosis & the myth of earth-Titans or giants can be traced from Part One, where it's mainly a SSE and, through Rabelais & Vico in

Part Two to something which is part of what all words say in Part Three. Three books, maybe, of course. If so, the Dante shape might recur for the first one.

[310] The black & blonde double heroine I noticed in AC [101] is mainly a feature of Adonis fiction. Often they're heroines of, respectively, experience & innocence, hence the blonde one is sometimes fragile & dies early ([Poe's] *Ligeia*, [Gottfried Keller's] *Green Henry*). In more domesticated fiction, of the Ivanhoe type, it's the brunette who has the Adonis role. Query: is an Adonis romance with a happy ending an Eros form? That's one of my Part Two problems that has to be settled by Part One.

[311] Divination is part of the attempt to evoke a Logos vision, or something akin to it, out of a Thanatos one: a hidden order that the divination elicits. Hence the catalogue in Rabelais. So dice, Tarot cards, most chess, & for that matter astrology, conceived as a knowledge of the future, are all p.d.e. [point of demonic epiphany] visions.

[312] Chambers' *Beowulf*, p. 27: Princes whose lives are threatened by powerful usurpers should go in pairs.[254] Hrothric & Hrothmund vs. Rolf Kraki; Malcolm & Donalbain vs. Macbeth, Edward V & Richard vs. R3 [Richard III]. Modulation of the hero-as-twin theme. I should also look at the bear's son tale: the bear, with his hibernation habits, is a natural for descending to the cave.[255] He usually rescues princesses & his companions desert him: the Beowulf story is like but not identical. Also: I say [par. 153] that father-mother-child trinities are hypostatic forms of father-son-spirit trinities above the p. of e. [point of epiphany]. Is the three-son theme, with the third successful, a further hypostasis of this below about NNW?

[313] I often have the feeling that my thought is an elaborate rationalization of my own temperament and social attitude, & that its profoundest areas are verbal formulas connecting one prejudice with another. I used to worry about this & feel I ought to become more objective and impersonal & what not. But now I think it's only what's true only for me that's really true. That is, it's all that gets into the higher area of personal truth, & thereby becomes absolutely or universally true on the flight-of-the-alone-to-the-alone principle. Impersonal truth is only a drop in the ocean of the petty omniscience of a God who hasn't yet been incarnated. The

model of personal truth is the poet's vision which only the poet can see, and I think I understand more clearly now Blake's identification of the imaginative and the divine. (Of course, everybody ought to have a Rintrah or outsider-principle inside him).

[314] One real handicap in my scholarship is the immense difficulty I find in finishing long works of fiction. I seem to get the point after about 100 pages. Right now it's [Italo] Svevo's *Confessions of Zeno*. My distinction of fictional & thematic, in its product-vs.-process form, glances at the phrase "various devices of repetition." This means that such books as Svevo's, which belong on the Hermes line, are really theme-&-variation forms. Given the anti-hero postulate, everything else—the cigarette habit, the father, the wife—are all essentially variations. They're exceedingly ingenious & searching variations, & I read each page with pleasure, but a long-run impatience bothers me. What I notice in this story is (a) the "hero" in the grip of karma whose central identity is confusion, so that he marries through the ascendancy of the wrong ego-government (b) the fighting with time & the preoccupation with death (c) the use of certain devices, like table-rapping spiritualism & the Proustian "bunch" of girls (four A's) which suggest disintegration of personality. For "Zeno" cf. Valéry: the motionless philosopher. (Xenios?).[256]

[315] Also: the falsity of fiction, established by the psychoanalyst's note at the beginning. *And*, he's off the natural integrated rhythm symbolized by music. Beethoven, the variations composer, haunts this area: Wagner ought to be (P.L. [*Paradise Lost*] ii) right at the bottom of it [cf. par. 222], but there's a formulaic quality about the leitmotif that pushes Wagner over into the Promethean quadrant. In the *Ring* & in his Promethean (not Dionysian) Parzival, Wagner was right & Nietzsche wrong. The "confession" form is very central to Hermes, because of all the lying it permits. Even reincarnation is mentioned in Svevo.

[316] And I've just read a detective story by [Friedrich] Dürrenmatt, very standard stuff: it contains the theme of two men whose lives are bound together by a wager & are hunter & hunted—stock, of course, but interesting for that reason, a modulation of the twin theme.[257]

[317] I'm confused by the way that a dramatic form that I put in the N.E. quadrant now seems to belong around the S. end. Two possible points:

(a) there may be a distinction between the S. of irony, realism, & experience & the S. of sentimental romance which establishes its typology (b) there are several lanes on the Eros highway of which the penseroso & death of the old shadow themes is one.

[318] I have always wanted to write a book that would sit there while I worked on it. My ideal for this book is a general overall scheme clear enough for me to fill in, in an unhurried fashion, whatever details my current reading suggests. Every other book I've done has been done on the kitten-in-the-ball-of-yarn principle, every new piece of reading suggesting a new idea, every new idea revolutionizing the whole structure, the whole making an obsession that had to be given every priority possible until it was off my hands. I can never read library books, partly because I work with marginalia in books I own, perhaps because every book out of sight is also out of mind. If I could only get a firm enough doodle for my controlling scheme, so that the book could gradually evolve! Not just a mechanical filling in of a design, like a hooked rug, but with something of that principle.

[319] Two things might help: one, cutting away of introductory harrumphs into separate books or articles. This has happened already with *The Critical Path*. Two, having a future volume or two in mind, definitely & not as something to be collapsed into the present task. Now that I'm within a decade or so of retirement this might become possible. The present L [Liberal]-ʎ [Rencontre] project can be done before retirement: I'm not sure about the others.

[320] The eight trigrams of the I Ching can be connected with my Great Doodle.[258] The N-S contrast of Logos & Thanatos visions is the primary yang-yin contrast of Ch'ien (☰) and K'un (☷). The W-E axis of Nomos & Nous is the water-fire contrast of K'an (☵) and Li (☲). The sinking descent of Hermes is Ken (☶) and the initial Promethean rise is Chen (☳). The Adonis penetration theme is Sun (☴) and the joyous reflecting Eros soul is Tui (☱). Sun & Tui are the human creature as the full-grown daughter of Logos, breaking away as Eve & returning as Sophia, Alice the queen. K'an & Chen are the son of the earth-mother, buried under the mountain with the Titans & returning in Viconian thunder. The middle child can hold the horizontal balance of nature & reason. Tui is Psyche also, of course.

[321] This association of the upper world with a daughter-figure clears up a point or two: the descent of innocence, Alice & the Dickensian girl-child, Marvell's drop of dew. It would be wonderful if I could see AW [*Alice in Wonderland*] consistently as an Adonis descent, or parody of one, with the red & white roses, the beheading queen, the cards, & the final trial, & ATLG [Alice *Through the Looking-Glass*] as an Eros descent, I mean ascent, with chess, red & white queens, & the white knight as the melancholy Virgil-guide who can't go all the way. Even the mirror fits, Tui being a lake.[259]

[322] I need a much clearer sense of Nomos & Nous, which seem to be shaping up in a curious way as the *end* of the book. If I could only shove the Great Doodle off its course, & think of Adonis & Hermes as going toward & away from Nomos. The arrangement on my plate has Li (Nous) at the top & K'an[260] (Nomos) at the bottom; but the others are all buggered up. Well, anyway, the theme of the descent of innocence into experience runs all through Nomos: the heroic-Christ descent of Adonis, the Quixote-Idiot descent of Hermes. But I see this as a continuous descent: I don't yet see it as a contrasting movement. The Adonis tragic movement is polarized by Nomos at the end, as a kind of *telos*, and an *aition*, a hidden mysterious cause up somewhere in the *hortus conclusus* of the mother with her invisible wind-lover. (But I should keep my plate arrangement in mind, as Wilhelm calls it the later or inner-world arrangement, the horizontal synthesis.[261] So it may be the telos of the book after all).

[323] Blake, the Chinese, & the Egyptians put the south at the top. But it's no use my trying to think of the south as anywhere except at the bottom of all maps whatever. And that's closer to the Logos-dominated Western tradition I'm following: the Ancient Mariner goes south, & the Mississippi.

[324] Anyway, the fact that the I Ching has a primal (= unfallen) arrangement & a later or inner-world one connects with my old pre-Rc. [pre-Romantic] & Rc. [Romantic] diagrams, to some extent. I doubt if one is really a simple reversal of the other. They also link with some of Boehme's diagrams, as interpreted by Law, about the generation of the Trinity.[262] I seem to be working out from my Logos-Thanatos diagram towards one organized around Nomos & Nous, is the point. The first would dominate

my symbolic-universe and narrative-displacements volumes; the second the conceptual displacements and search-for-the-centre volumes.

[325] In my anti-clockwise, or north at the top, form, the inner-world arrangement starts at K'an, the watery abyss, goes through the stillness of Ken to the arousing of Chen, thence through the gentle penetration of Sun to Li, the fire. Then down, first through K'un, the earth, then through the reflecting joy of Tui to heaven, Ch'ien, at which point the narrative seven ends & the octave begins again.[263] I think this is the Heraclitean gyre that Yeats uses for *Byzantium.*

[326] The Ch'ien-K'un axis seems to be Tharmas-Enion, the K'an-Li one Los-Enitharmon, Chen-Sun Orc-Vala, & Ken-Tui Urizen Ahania.[264]

[327] I am intensely superstitious; but there are two kinds of superstition, related as self-destructive melancholy is to penseroso melancholy. There is the superstition based on fear of the future: this is based also on my character as a coward & weakling, & is of course to be avoided. There is another kind which consists of removing all censors & inhibitions on speculation: it's almost exactly what Coleridge calls fancy. It may eventually be superseded by imagination: but if there's no fancy to start with there won't be any imagination to finish with. Let's call it creative superstition. It works with analogies[,] disregarding all differences & attending only to similarities. Here nothing is coincidence in the sense of unusable design; or, using the word more correctly, everything is potential coincidence—what Jung calls synchronistic.

[328] Thus, noting that Blake's Zoa-Emanation scheme & the I Ching trigrams are both an ogdoad or Noah's Ark family of eight,[265] I seize on every resemblance there is, invent a great many there aren't, and disregard all differences, determined to find an analogy in the teeth of the facts—not that there are any facts, of course. There are two arrangements of the trigrams, given above, & they seem to me to correspond to the schemes of FZ [*The Four Zoas*] and M-J [*Milton-Jerusalem*] respectively.[266] In my own book they're respectively a diagram to work from and a diagram to work toward. The shift over in Blake seems to be what the two versions of Z7 [*The Four Zoas, Night the Seventh*] registers [*sic*].

[329] The myth of the fall incorporates a fact which is non-mythically

true: that with sex came death and individuality. Amoebas are immortal, because they aren't sexually split; and their essence and existence are the same, diffused through the total amoeba. See a book called *African Genesis.*[267] Similarly, the Eros ascent backwards in time has a non-mythical analogue. When we look at stars many light-years away, we are looking directly into the past—sometimes a very remote past.

[330] My present doodle, an ogdoad or double cross forming a circle, is more complicated than the single-cross pattern I worked the prose-fiction forms out on. But that's still there. Its four points are the tetragrammaton: Y as the Son or Logos principle, V as the spirit, the two H's as the Father and his dark shadow (cf. Boehme).[268]

[331] Silberer gave me the principle of anagogy as an idealism parodied by the psychoanalytic sexual phenomenon.[269] Dante's purgatory is an erection pointed at a *female* heaven or multifoliate rose. Sitting opposite a girl in a mini-skirt with her legs open, on the subway, I thought of how the cunt is the focus of vision, and thence of attainment, on Yeats's soul-look-and-body-touch principle.[270] It's also, of course, the most elaborately concealed part of the body: even "nature" conceals it when the body is stark naked.

[332] I must find out more about the conceptions of *taxis* and *thesis* in the *Poetics.*[271] I could have used them in AC, but they may be the organizing conceptions of the first two parts. The first part is the *topoi* or places of imagery, the second part narrative displacements.

[333] All my critical career has been haunted by the possibility of working out a schematology, i.e., a grammar of poetic language. I don't mean here just the stuff in FS & AC & elsewhere, but the kind of diagrammatic basis of poetry that haunts the occultists & others. Whenever I finish a big job I seem to return to this. Right now, Poe's *Eureka* is turning up on my agenda again, and I'm beginning to think it's the time for reading Boehme. In other words, once again I have a hope reviving of making precise & detailed suggestions about—let's say the diagrammatic basis of schematology.

[334] Thus with these I Ching trigrams:[272] the first is a kind of "astrological" inventory of the elements of reality as they're spread out in the

Logos vision, the four Zoas & their emanations all balancing. It's not exactly the unfallen perspective: it's rather the *simultaneous* one, so to speak. The second arrangement, the one on my plate, is an "alchemical" process-arrangement. Here water moves up to fire, the Heraclitean movement, the K'un-Li being the only Zoa & emanation relation left, & corresponding to Los & Enitharmon in Blake. On the way it absorbs the three cyclical relations: the father-daughter one (Ch'ien-Sun), the son-mother one (Ken-K'un), and the bridegroom-bride one [Chen-Tui] (i.e., the brother-sister, Christian, all relationships here being incestuous).

[335] Hermes themes: I've said that divination is part of the Coup de Dés complex at the p.d.e. [point of demonic epiphany]. So is the descent to the oracle, or diving for the cipher (Poe's Pym narrative; Book 3 of *Endymion*). I suppose the Gospel equivalent is Jesus' quotation [Mark 15:34–5] of Ps. 22 on the cross, where "Eloi" is mistaken for "Elias." Rabelais, natch. Then there's the father-daughter pattern: Job & Lear have three, Oedipus two. And the "swell-foot" aspect of Oedipus: cf. the heel imagery in Lear, Achilles, of course, & Philoctetes, & the literal meaning of "Jacob."[273] For Eros, read the Old English poem on the Phoenix, noting the music, the alchemical pretty colors, & the identifying of e.p. [epiphany point] & Eden.

[336] Boehme is neither theologian nor philosopher, much less a scientist, but he does try to explain why we have a Trinity.[274] The "Father" is the hidden ground of being, the essence-existence, which we can connect with only by mystical identification, if that, Kant's noumenal world. The "Son" is the Logos-world, related to the mind as the Father is to the soul, the intelligible order which is a real presence in the world. As the Word, the Son is the subjective consciousness that withdraws from existence, and which consequently takes on the capacity to suffer. The Spirit is the *community* of consciousness, the church or body of Christ, which starts with society & eventually adds nature, thus returning through the Son to the Father. I don't say all or any of this is Boehme. Incidentally my Tetragrammaton [par. 330] is wrong: the two H's are Christ as glorified Logos and as harrower of hell, J (probably) is Nomos, the Father-Son complex, & V Nous, the Son-Spirit complex. I've been confused by thinking of language & communication in terms of the Son as Logos, forgetting Pentecost with its gift of tongues and the inspiration of the prophets. Well, anyway, a lot of Heidegger & Nietzsche seems to me to

come out of Boehme,[275] with his conceptions of the "nothing" & the "anxiety," so I better investigate. But, oh God, it's a discouraging blather: when the alleged simple & saintly cobbler begins to write with knowing winks & leers & nudges, one suspects the wrong kind of spiritual dictation.

[337] Eros imagery was the great breakthrough into the first book, and perhaps the displacement of imagery in the New Comedy form is the corresponding crack in the second one. I'm wondering whether what I used to think of as *the* Great Doodle, the cyclical quest of the hero, isn't at once the conclusion of ∟ [Liberal] and the starting point of ㄱ [Tragicomedy].

[338] I suppose what's essentially occult about the occultist tradition is the Dionysian (pseudo) conception of a "hidden divinity," or what I used to call the deification of the void. [276] Boehme's Father, associated with such words as Unground, Abyss, Nothing, dark fire, & the like, put him in this camp. I could never see that it was Blake's: Blake condemned the solitude-and-chaos conception of creation as pernicious. But it is Romantic, obviously, more particularly German Romantic, and Heidegger & Jung & possibly Nietzsche follow in the Hermes procession. Boehme's creation myth, by the way, is an emanation myth, neither sexual nor artificial: but it leans to the former.

[339] My "Logos" is hopelessly chaotic: I've never thought of it as the top point of the circle, but as an area above & beyond the circle. I've got about five things snarled up in it. One, the Shekinah, or revealed presence of God, symbolized by the sun.[277] Two, the musico-mathematical vision of intelligible order symbolized (among other things) by dance, correspondence & the music of the spheres. Three, the apocalyptic consolidation of metaphors, or the pulled-up chain of being, contained in the city. Four, the point of epiphany, which includes the earthly paradise as a female body and the penseroso dark night.

[340] Now, what's the corresponding series at Thanatos? One, the abyss or unground or nothingness or, in more than one sense, what the hell. Two, the coup de dés or chance glimpse of design through divination. Three, the demonic consolidation of metaphors. Four, the point of demonic epiphany, which includes an Isis vision or sibylline oracle.[278]

What would correspond to the dark night would, I suppose, be something like an epopteia[279] or radiance in the gloom, just before the Chen thunder.[280]

[341] What I'm getting at is, is there a corresponding series for Nomos & Nous, and, if so, is there a series of concentric spheres? Why leave out the quadrants?

[342] The word of recognition out of the past (Beatrice's "Dante")[281] belongs to the p. of e. [point of epiphany], & I suppose some prophecy or oracle of the future—Anchises' vision of Rome or Teiresias's "you will die at sea"[282] for the p.d.e. [point of demonic epiphany].

[343] Everybody assumes an affinity between Boehme & Blake, yet Blake describes Boehme's notion of creation proceeding out of an unground, abyss or nothing as the most pernicious idea that can enter the mind.[283] Boehme says that the primary reality, identified with God the Father, is a will, & that creation arises through an efflux of will.[284] Blake says that will is always evil & that if God is anything he is an influx from the understanding into the will.[285] Blake & Boehme are not reconcilable, but neither are they really opposed: on my diagram they're the same myth going the opposite ways, one hermetic & one promethean. Boehme is carrying Protestant voluntarism to its logical conclusion; Blake is not returning to Thomism, but going around the other way to Nous. Yet at one time I thought *Luther* was the originator of the Promethean quadrant, & so he still may be.

[344] I've been reading a science fiction novel called *The Mind Parasites*, by Colin Wilson. Silly book in many ways, which is a pity, because its central idea is a genuine Promethean archetype, the Gospel driving out of the devils symbolized as malignant small creatures like insects (Beelzebub as lord of flies, the Q1 [*The Faerie Queene*, bk. 1] & P.L. 1 [*Paradise Lost*, bk. 1], rats in Poe references; Lilliput, Wyndham's Triffids, Tolkien).[286] Note that the aeroplane or space ship escape theme occurs in *Erewhon*, *Rasselas*, and Medea. Wilson is interested in Blake, & links the parasites to a polypus.[287] He says they are linked somehow with the moon: this doctrine of the sinister or lunatic moon recurs in C.S. Lewis,[288] and he (Wilson) refers to Velikowski, Hörbiger, Gurdjieff, and other lunatics.[289] Below consciousness, in the mind, there's a paradisal "nurs-

ery" or child's world of moral impulses. Below that is a deep sea, Blake's heavens beneath Beulah, where the parasites are [137]. As long as they're there, we feel there's a paradise at the bottom of which they are the Covering Cherub, but once they're expelled we simply feel that our whole mind is ours—he compares this to the Israelites entering the Promised Land.[290] Note how often in science fiction (Wyndham's Midwich Cuckoos, Hoyle, etc.)[291] the theme of the ring of impregnable minds turns up: the comitatus that, as in *Beowulf*, deserts the descent but re-forms in the ascent.[292] Note that whether the "parasites" are giants or insects depends on perspective only: Blake's Og & Sihon are also germs or viruses.[293] As I say, the book is silly, but he does touch on significant themes. Descending into the mind & seeing all one's memories there, *not* examining them closely because each is a world in itself, is described in language recalling Alice's descent down the rabbit-hole. Of course this is really an Eros journey into the past; this is part of that difficult interchangeability principle.

[345] He speaks of the moon as a world of imprisoned life, like Ariel before Prospero [169–70]: the life is solidified, like Urizen fighting with the fire.[294] Everything that exists is alive, because to exist is to thrust out from non-existence. They expel the parasites by going out in a spaceship: they're terrified of going out into the deep. They're symbols of self-alienation, the mind as a "fairground crowded with strangers" [162]. He says "stillness is natural to man" [157–8] and speaks of "hovering" over his own mind-depths [157]. The alienated self is compared to an alter-ego as a reflection in a mirror [162].

[346] This book has to pull together all my ideas—my Raphael & Blake on Newton existential point of the poet as primitive Protestant as a Promethean symbol.[295] Also parody symbolism: the deasil & withershins swastikas, Oriental & Nazi: solar wheel (cf. triskelion) & its parody the sun under the moon: third eye of wisdom (Hindu caste mark, if that's what it is, & the Buddhist depression) parodied by the cyclops.[296]

[347] The effect of organized and institutional religion on society, for the most part, is evil. It isn't just reactionary or superstitious; it is evil, and stinks in the nose of God. One has to remember this when thinking of the easy conquests of secular revolution over it. They, of course, become evil in their turn.

[348] The natural man sits at the mouth of his cave, afraid he'll lose his way if he explores in either direction. I suppose the outward one, Urizen exploring his dens, is the parody-opposite of Los prowling in Albion's bosom with a lantern.[297] I think that this may be part of an extensive Nomos-Nous parody, which I've already found in the tragic-comic opposites. It's fundamentally the contrast of the risen Christ & the divine Caesar. Eros from the Nous point of view (I've been treating it so far as a Logos-aspect) is the quadrant of purifying the soul & the casting out of demons. Adonis from the Nomos point of view is the leader destroying his enemies and so restoring past glories. Urizen exploring his dens is Hermes from the Nomos perspective, the alteration of the temporal power of the ruler into the democratic technological power of science. It'll be quite a business to find my way around this hall of mirrors; but certainly Christ & Caesar polarize the historical process.

[349] So my two axes are not speculation & concern, unless I reverse those categories: they're rather the diachronic historical process (E-W) and the synchronic imaginative vision (N-S). The synchronic or layout vision is the L [Liberal]-⅄ [Rencontre] one; the diachronic, featuring centrally the teleological plot, is the ⅂ [Tragicomedy]-⊢ [Paradox] project. The third I don't know, but its theme (Λ [Anticlimax]-⊥ [Ignoramus]) is conceptual displacement, so I suppose it enters a new dimension. The fourth returns to the first perspective, I should imagine: the arts as a unit.

[350] The essay which has now taken over the title *The Critical Path* turned out to be one of the most articulate & central pieces of writing I've ever done. Also, it kept siphoning off ideas that didn't really belong, at that stage & that context, to the Great Instauration.[298] What I'd like to ponder now is an essay on comparative religion of about the same length, making a normal length book with the other.

[351] The next thing to grasp is the central diachronic pattern: I have a hunch its archetype is the second I Ching circle, as I've said.[299] The imagery is alchemic & Heraclitean, and it probably recurs in V [Mirage] (⅂ [Tragicomedy]): I don't see how Λ [Anticlimax] (⊥ [Ignoramus]) can be anything but synchronic.

[352] The pattern I see in the Bible is a synchronic one; and I'm right, because all "keys" to meaning are synchronic keys. The Koran is a

completely synchronic Scripture: Mohammed has some sense of sequence, specifically a sequence of prophets, but no sense of history. He has Jesus born under a date palm beside a stream—in other words in the p of e [point of epiphany] or h-c. [hortus conclusus], not the diachronic manger. And Mary is evidently identical with Moses' sister Miriam. I know Islamic culture produced distinguished histories (Ibn Khaldun)[300] but its typical products are mystics, mathematicians, and geometrical arts.

[353] The periods of "dryness" that accompany all quests of the spirit are the journey through the purgatorial desert to the e.p. [epiphany point]. It's probably not just coincidence that our great leaders came out of deserts: so powerful an Eros drive couldn't have *started* in a jungle. The theme of false e.p., bower of bliss, P.R. [*Paradise Regained*] banquet & the like, is a desert mirage too—explicitly so in P.R.

[354] I should realize that if I ever live long enough to get anywhere near ∧ [Anticlimax] (⊥ [Ignoramus]), it won't be a book about philosophy, or even about the metaphorical substructure of philosophy, but about the transformation of ideas and concepts and propositions in literature. That keeps literature, & more particularly the anatomy, strictly in the centre of the picture. It's ridiculous to deal with Aristotle or Kant or Heidegger in terms of "displacement," but not so ridiculous to deal, say, with Locke in Sterne (positive) or Blake (negative) in those terms.

[355] The synchronic is the total range of possible plots. The diachronic is the *given* form of participation: it's Heidegger's being *there*, thrown down in front of us. I have elsewhere [11f.81] a note on Samuel Johnson's strictures on the Leibnitzian tendency of critics to rationalize a given sequence as the best possible one. If this is true (I mean my present general approach) then I can't simply identify the mythos & dianoia as moving & frozen forms of the same thing. The *mythos* is the Scotist real individual; the dianoia identifies this, not simply *as* itself, but *with* the Thomist real universal, the knowable form of the individual, which is the object of criticism & not of precritical sensuous response. (New Criticism, of course, is a half-assed development of Hopkinsian Scotism).

[356] Because the synchronic is the simultaneous, its temporal projection is the continuous & teleological. It's the Los creative rhythm, ex-

pressed in recurrent pulsation or repetition. The diachronic is the same rhythm from the inside, a sexually-based, discontinuous, rise-&-fall, tumescent-detumescent rhythm of Orc in Beulah. One is the father-artificer, the other is the mother "sewing away" in Kenneth Patchen's phrase.[301] In the Biblical, the synchronic is the polarized apocalyptic & demonic symbols; the diachronic is the manic-depressive series of enslavements & deliverances, out of which the Messianic narrative comes.

[357] In our day the synchronic view, expressed in a sense of tradition, of the continuity of tradition, and of teleological art, is greatly weakened, and a discontinuous, sexual-centered, diachronic view has separated from it. I say separated, because it's still there, mainly in the form of a set of technologically feasible possibilities to be achieved in the (near or remote) future.

[358] The acquisitive, the cumulative, the selective (keeping the things that are *worth* keeping) are synchronic. This synchronic mentality has traditionally been interrupted, every so often, by war or revolution. War, especially, is based on a potlatch mentality, sacrificing lives, money, tools—anything to "win" the war. It comes as a tremendous relief, psychologically, to a conserving society. Today, in the economy of waste, the decline of craftsmanship, in technological obsolescence, in the sense that anything is expendable when money itself is not stable & thrift no longer a virtue, in the ephemeral art of the happening—in all this we may be finding William James' moral equivalent of war, & incorporating it into our society. Today's mood is intensely bellicose, yet it hates war; it is intensely revolutionary, yet it has no real sense of revolution, or what it has takes the form of the mean & squalid ideology of separatism.

[359] One diachronic illusion is the democratic election ritual: the pretence that the new leader will begin afresh. Actually, every leader *inherits* a situation; almost everything he can do is prescribed for him. The head of a great power, like the President of the U.S., has a considerable potential power of destruction, but relatively little chance for creativity or innovation. Again, many things are technologically feasible which will not be done without a sufficiently powerful economic or political compulsion to do them: hence the sense of science-fiction unreality in so many gazes into the future.

[360] Well, anyway: there's an important critical issue about universals and particulars that I've never quite worked out. It's time to read St. Thomas & see why he says the individual is unknowable. Scotus, as I get it, says this is only true when you identify knowing solely with conception: you know the individual in a mental act which includes perception. For Samuel Johnson & [Joshua] Reynolds, great thoughts are always general. The basis here, as Blake saw, was the epistemology of Locke, where perception is associated with passivity because it's followed by "reflection," the "shadow" of Eliot's *Hollow Men* falling between the two. Reflection is the withdrawal by the (death-principled) consciousness from engagement, hence its Olympian, "objective" (i.e., judgement in the next world) quality. Blake strongly hints that the whole idea of "another" world, a life "after" death, is of this Lockian origin. What Blake calls Lockian is medieval too (*prius* in sensu).[302] But the relation of the 18th c. general to the medieval universal is another matter. I can understand Blake's association of the former with abstractions and death-wishes, but his "states" surely have something in common with universals.

[361] Blake's minute particular and, even more, his outline of identity, are closely related to Hopkins' Scotus-inspired inscape, or perception of individual reality.[303] And just as the new critics & their followers rely on this quasi-Scotism in attacking my archetypes as "reductive" conceptions, so they could, if they knew enough Blake, quote Blake against me. But Blake has some program of short-circuiting the general and going directly from particular to universal, which I think would eventually involve my anagogic & interpenetration ideas.

[362] This sequential progress from sensation to reflection has many ramifications. Religiously, a sensational world is polytheistic & full of presences; the progress to conception brings monotheism and the judge after death. The ambivalence of death & higher consciousness projects the heaven-hell duality.

[363] I've got Logos on the top & Nous on the east because that's where they traditionally belong; but I'm going to run into trouble towards the end when the terms reverse. That is, the Logos vision is ultimately a Nous; it's not the centre of Christianity but its Greek natural-theology extension, & runs from the Great Pyramid to T. [Teilhard] de Chardin's "noosphere."[304] Similarly Nous keeps focussing on the real Logos, the

resurrection from, and of, the dead. This is, I suppose, where the synchronic ∟ [Liberal] perspective turns into the diachronic ⌉ [Tragicomedy] one, and I have to start a new book. Ultimately, Agape is not God descending from heaven; agape is God coming up from hell, treading the winepress. Eros is not the counter-movement to agape but its consequence. After Christianity destroys death, mystic, Buddhist & other ways destroy birth—for the opposite of death is birth, not life.

[364] In Keats particularly note how the descending metamorphosis movement, focussing on Narcissus & Adonis, is counter-balanced by the Cupid-Psyche Eros rise.

[365] I was given *Hamlet's Mill*[305] for Christmas, but so far there doesn't seem to be much new in it. I suppose though my synchronic pattern really is astrological, spread out, where the sky is the mirror of the world & the world the shadow of heaven. I want a Prologue in space-time, to be followed, after I box the compass once, with a second book starting with a Prologue in time-space, where the symbols are diachronic & Los-centered & alchemical, not synchronic & Orc-centered & astrological. As there's no such thing as a constellation, it follows that all star-myth is created from something else, where its centre of gravity is. There are planets, and it was a colossal imaginative effort to see the sun and moon as planets, but calling them Mars & Jupiter & the like is something else.

[366] Still, the authors have two characteristics of good mythographers: they're cranks or near-cranks, and they have no use for the hazy gradualism that insists that all men were Calibans ten thousand years ago. If we realize that human beings quite as intelligent as ourselves have been around for half a million years, we get quite a different slant on things. And they start from where I did, thrilling to the numinous account of the sources of the Hamlet legend in the Reverend Henry H. Hudson's expurgated edition.[306]

[367] My zodiac, if I haven't it already, starts at Nous (Aries) & goes around: low & high Eros are the Bull & the Twins, the Logos summer vision the backward moving Crab; high & low Adonis are the Yeatsian lion & Virgin; Nomos is of course the Balance; the scorpion & archer dominate Hermes; Thanatos is on the Tropic of Capricorn & the winter solstice; the water-bearer & the fish take us up Prometheus. Now, if

there's a precessional reverse-movement to take care of, we sank into high Prometheus with Christ & our outlook has had something fishy about it ever since: the universe recedes on all sides like the ocean. Alice goes into the mirror world & hears poems about fish: asks why & is given a riddling answer about undishcovering the fish or dishcovering the riddle.[307] Chess, by the way, is another mirror-image: one social establishment manoeuvering against another, its demonic shadow. Maybe this precessional movement will account for some of my mirror-reversals. Alice is a girl-child created queen in the mirror-world: the creation of the youngest daughter, *la jeune parque*, is SE, Lear being the tragic & failing version of that arch. [archetype]. Perdita & the winter solstice.

[368] The fundamental aim of the second book being to establish the legal contract of the past, it follows that the apocalyptic end is left vague or incomplete. Hence what might be called, borrowing Spengler's term, apocalyptic pseudomorphosis.[308] Otherwise, the buggering of the latter end. When the Jews decided that law & prophecy were both finished, imaginative writers had to call themselves Enoch or Moses or Ezra. Perhaps the whole heaven-and-hell projection is part of the pseudomorphosis.

[369] Or perhaps it's also a projection of the Adonis theme, the wrapping up of the human tragedy in a teleological system. This begins with Aristotle, the biologist, turning his back on Platonic Eros myth & mathematics, & starting to construct an *imperial* philosophy that winds up in the expanding gradualism of our day. Note the importance of becoming aware of the mythical shape of our assumptions. The Darwinian myth is all in the upper air, hence it's romantic & revolutionary.

[370] Jessie Weston's Frazerian treatment of the Percival story[309] also keeps in the upper air, or tries to: she plays down the importance of the "question" P. [Percival] should have asked. To ask the "why?" question is to descend, with Oedipus, into the Hermes world. The question to Adam, *quid fescisti*,[310] does not do this, but any questioning of the *origin* of original sin, of the hardness of Goneril's & Regan's hearts, of the suffering of Job, makes the descent. Cf. the aetiological song, curing a wound made by iron by chanting a rhyme about the origin of iron.

[371] As for the planets, I suppose Saturn is the point of epiphany,

Jupiter high Eros & Adonis, Mars low Eros & Adonis, the sun the axis of Nomos & Nous, Venus high Prometheus & Hermes (high Prometheus has a lot to do with rising out of the water & being foam born[)], Mercury, as the name suggests, low Prometheus & Hermes, & the moon the point of demonic epiphany. Logos is Ouranos, the heaven, the cynosure or pole of the ecliptic; Thanatos is the earth.

[372] Re the Hermes question: this goes with, & is a part of, the theme of abstaining from action: don't touch food in the underworld, etc., & so on to the renounced quest of Shelley & Tolkien (also Blake's forgiveness of sins: the action of *Jerusalem* takes place in Albion's guts). The quest as question is of course future-directed, & its ultimate answer, which goes beyond any origin or first-cause answer (as in Job), is resurrection in the present.

[373] My zodiac leads to a division between high & low in the four quadrants, suggesting NW-SE & NE-SW axes. *H's M* [*Hamlet's Mill*] says that astrological schemes of journeys after death provide for a change in direction either between Scorpio & Sagittarius in the south, or between Gemini & Taurus in the north.[311] As I get it, these are the points where the Galaxy crosses the ecliptic. The SE point is the one just ahead of us, where one goes into (or comes out of) the water: the NW one is where the hero comes out of the forest, or, as above, goes into it.

[374] Why is there so much accurate observation of the stars in mythology & so little of animals & plants? Because the stars suggest *design*, and observation of animals & plants suggests realism, which comes later. Myth is verbal design, & goes with such stylizing as the Altamira bison, which is presented as an object-event in space-time.

[375] *H's M* [*Hamlet's Mill*] has some interesting stuff I've met before—in G.R. Levy's *Sword From the Rock*, in some essays in [S.H.] Hooke's *Labyrinth*—about a combination of whirlpool, tree and stone images associated with the bottom of the world.[312] There's a plug that prevents the maelstrom from draining away the world into the abyss, or vice versa it prevents chaos from rising & creating a new flood. This plug may be a holy mountain or temple, or a charmed safeguard like the Gordian knot, or it may be linked to Thor's cat[313] or to the sword-in-the-stone motif.

[376] I'm reading Jewish apocalyptic, the Book of Enoch & the like, in search of the pseudomorphosis[314] & other themes. Rabbinical Judaism of course repudiated apocalyptic: Xy took in enough to assimilate the Resurrection & Apocalypse themes, but it's interesting that it turned into an establishment Rabbinical religion around 400, with Augustine & Jerome, & that it was exactly then that Enoch was dropped as a serious book. Enoch says in its opening verses that it's an apocryphon in the sense of being sealed up in its own evil day & released when its time came. Actually, it was sealed up during the Christian ascendancy & released during the Romantic movement, which was symbolically the right time. My reference to Rowley & Ossian as pseudepigrapha, taking the psychologically primitive to be chronologically primitive,[315] could be followed up, I think, either here or in the CP, or both. The theme of the fall of angels in Enoch, another theme picked up in Rcsm. [Romanticism], expands the Adonis-Adam theme into a Thanatos one.[316] Nothing in the OT [Old Testament] itself does this except the prologue to Job, which also has the enemy in heaven.

[377] Woman is the *best* work of creation, and the *jeune parque* theme is important in the Prometheus quadrant: the successful father-daughter relationship that fails with Lear. Hence the Promethean significance of Esther, Judith, & Susanna. The last is the clearest because of her release from two chortling elders associated with trees, who are thrown into an abyss & burned with fire from God. Here Daniel has the Messiah heroine-deliverer role, & she escapes through confusion of testimony, reflecting the calumniated-mother theme above.

[378] As for Esther, I wonder if the Ishtar-Marduk element in the names[317] doesn't imply the reversal, not simply of Jewish fortunes in Persia (which means, of course, the Day of Jehovah overthrowing Haman), but of the whole Babylonian-Persian religious complex. Similarly, the Song of Songs reverses the Adonis cult in an Eros setting.

[379] The upper cycle, as I've said, imposes & abandons order—Plato's *Politicus* cycle. The Resurrection transforms, but the Ascension merely repeats the Astraea myth,[318] & all Eros journeys, including Shakespeare's PT [*The Phoenix and the Turtle*], leave the world to its fate.

[380] I notice how in free association I seem to have a white dove & a

black raven or screech owl on my shoulders. One keeps trying to turn the associations into pleasant & complacent reflections, mostly about phrases & other bits of writing or speaking or story-telling I'm pleased with. The other, far noisier & more aggressive, keeps gibbering and croaking away about all the damn fool things I've done, all the embarrassing or humiliating things that have happened to me. This must be a pretty standard setup—I wonder if the old conceptions of good & bad angels or daimons, or, closer, an advocate (go'el)[319] and an accuser, arise from it.

[381] Nietzsche buggered himself with one desperately silly remark: "Dionysus versus Christ." The sane thing to say would have been: "Dionysus, or Christ as the dying god, versus Prometheus, or Christ as the rising and life-giving god."

[382] In the story of Ahikar a father showers a son with proverbs: the son proves ungrateful & treacherous, the father returns in wrath, imprisons him & showers more proverbs on him, of a more menacing kind.[320] The story is slightly confused: Ahikar has no son, but adopts one at the command of God, hence the fact that the son is a no-good makes a monkey out of God. It was immensely popular: Ahikar is said to be a relative of Tobit, & either directly or through Tobit influenced the Gospels: he's the Greek Aesop & the "Lokman" of the Koran.

[383] The archetype is a Hermes one, the anxiety of continuity. Wisdom is the beaten path, & is symbolized by a father handing wise sayings down to a son. Polonius in *Hamlet* is significant: the anxiety about legitimacy (original right, vs. Oedipus original sin) in the histories is parallel. Chesterfield in the 18th c.: cf. too the relation of Tobit & Tobias. (Sometimes it's literally a beaten path—anxiety turns to hysteria in Proverbs & Ben Sira, where it's said to give your son wise maxims & beat the shit out of him if he doesn't listen. As for the confusion in the story, I suspect a displacement of something like the Prodigal Son story where the son is a lout who wants to do his own thing, so that the story is related to the central anxiety of Judaism & Xy: the breach of covenant between God & his disobedient son Man. The covenant is a testament (*diatheke*) or will, the last "will" of God (which becomes the unconditioned human will of the people in the Prometheus quadrant): it's not a contract (*syntheke*) on equal terms. Satire in *Tale of Tub*. Originally the ordeal of A. [Ahikar]

may have been instigated by God, for A's [Ahikar's] education (Hermes: it would also be God's education in Prometheus), as in Job.

[384] I suppose Xy is related to the Maccabean rebellion[321] somewhat as Marxism is to the French Revolution (reversing the categories, of course), the Ahikar archetype adopted by Rabbinism being parallel to such things as Burke & Newman.

[385] The more I read Ahikar the more fascinating it gets. There are riddle contests, & when the bad nephew gets his thrashing (Matthew 24:48 ff.) [written above parenthesis: Luke 12:43 ff.][322] he asks forgiveness, because God forgives, & says he'll be his uncle's hired servant. Ahikar keeps on droning his damn proverbs & finally the nephew blows up & busts. Sounds as though Jesus was deliberately improving on the story for the Prodigal Son. Then again, the man commanded to kill Ahikar keeps him hidden instead, substituting a criminal in prison condemned to death. The themes suggest Shakespeare's MM [*Measure for Measure*], which also has to do with the superiority of forgiveness to this kind of morality: Shak. [Shakespeare] might even have got hold of the story, though it's not in the Aesop version very fully—it's there, though, & in Aesop the usurper is forgiven. There are resemblances between the Ahikar proverbs & the fragments of Menander that suggest a link with the whole sententious tradition in comedy. If one could only write the secret history of literary forms! In stories like this one sees their elusive ghosts disappearing around the corner.

[386] Thus Tobit combines Ahikar, the grateful dead folktale, and the Egyptian Tractate of Khons.[323] The last at least is reversed (cf. the reversal of Esther & Song of Songs, above, & add the P source reversal of Babylonian hymns of creation, also assoc. w. Marduk). Perhaps the other great Lucan parable, the good Samaritan, reverses the morality of the grateful dead story much as the Prodigal Son one does Ahikar. Ahikar influenced the N.T. [New Testament], directly or through Tobit, at least in the story of the (Saturnalia of) the unjust steward, MT. 24 48 [Matthew 24:48], in the story of the barren fig tree, Luke 13:6, in the Prodigal Son (above) in the death of Judas (the unforgiven: the Gospel writers can't consistently manage the Jesus morality) & in the quotation of proverbs in II Tim-iv 17 & II Peter 2 22. I don't see much Tobit in these links.

[387] Tobit has the Hermes theme of burial, & as his life is in danger for doing so, the Antigone theme is there.[324] The ascension & benediction of Raphael is said to have close verbal links with the Transfiguration & Ascension in the Gospels. Ahikar is referred to in terms that bring out the light & darkness archetype of the reversal of fortunes; Tobit's blindness & Tobias' delay in return are both death-rebirth links: the whole story is a descent & return. He's very well aware (the author) of the assimilation of his story to the story of Israel. Tobit is blinded & Sarah calumniated at the same time: their prayers are made & heard at the same time. Note the *jeune parque* redemption theme. I don't understand a) the bird turd b) why the fish tries to swallow Tobias' foot (cf. Dan in Gen. 49: Tobit is Naphtali).[325] But I suppose Sarah is really divided from the Great Whore that Asmodeus gets, symbolized by the fish-smell & by Egypt. The fish could be astrological, & in some readings it's all of Tobias he tries to swallow, which does make him Leviathan, & his gall & liver labyrinth-charms, reversing the danger into a help. Tobit is a kind of Jacob-figure, Ahikar a Joseph, & Tobias the descending, protected, & returning Israel. I suppose Tobit's cataracts interested Milton in the story.[326]

[388] In the Tractate of Khons,[327] an Egyptian god, with priest, exorcizes a spirit from the Pharaoh's intended bride, living in a foreign country, but the spirit bargains for a festival to be held in his honour before he'll leave. In cpt. [counterpoint?], the prince tries to hold the god with him, but he flies back to Egypt as a falcon. (Back to Tobit: I suppose Mary Magdalen, with "seven devils in her pen," as Blake says, or Mary of Egypt, absorbs Sarah).[328] (Back to Ahikar: note the generic development from maxim-collections addressed to a son to the later pastoral epistles of the NT [New Testament] (Timothy & John especially). If one only had the erudition to write the secret history of literature!

[389] My conception of "Adonis" is fundamentally sound, I think: it's the tragic human situation in which all death has the feeling of the premature about it. But one has to be cautious about following Frazer and identifying all the dying gods. Osiris, for example, is really an underworld or Prometheus figure: a prototype of the Jesus with whom & in whom we rise. Dionysus, again, is the mob, as Yeats saw with a partial penetration: the disintegrating of individuality caused by "enthusiasm" of drugs or drunkenness. Dionysus has to have an Apollo he can revolt

against, but the overtones of Adonis are different. Perhaps I have the wrong word; perhaps Adonis doesn't survive the high stage: perhaps low Adonis is really more like Adam, the boy of the Mental Traveller grown old. I've thought of calling this quadrant Apollo, but that, like Dionysus, is only half true. Or perhaps the Adonis quadrant, like the Eros one, has two climaxes, the violent one of youthful tragedy (Absalom) corresponding to allegro & the aged one, reconciling life with the cycle of natural law, being the penseroso climax in the opposite direction. Because Adonis travels from past to present, the future *narrows*. For the young hero it's cut off: from the baby it's no more innocence. The old man hasn't any future: to find one he has to dive underground.

[390] I must hang on to this idea: I mean of the Adonis quadrant being polarized by a Dionysus mob & an Apollo individual. In the first place, it confirms my hunch that long lifetime 19th c. novels of the *Green Henry*[329] type belong to it. In the second place, it takes me back to Yeats. Dionysus and Apollo are his phases 1 & 15 respectively, placed at the ideal poles of the sparagmos & the complete telos of individuality.[330] The association with youth & age may be incidental. This may mean that there is, as I've often thought, an upper circle, with its p.d.e. [point of demonic epiphany] where the centre of my total diagram is, & that Yeats' *Vision* fits inside *that* p.d.e. The one above is of course the regular double-gated Beulah or G. of A. [Gardens of Adonis]. And *that's* maybe where Ahikar goes—trying to preserve the continuum in time. Certainly, whether it's incidental or not, there *is* a David-and-Absalom side to that double focus.

[391] In the Trinity, the Father is the decree, the unspoken Word, symbolized here by the act, or rather by the process of which the act is a secondary symbol. The Son is the articulation, the spoken Word, of which the symbol here below is the visible object (the identity, the bounding outline, the haeccitas).[331] The Spirit is the written word, of which the symbol is the class or community, as the Son is the individual. Well, the primary symbol is the *intelligible* objective world. As I've thought for so long, as soon as God speaks, the objective world is created (hence "light"); but as soon as God speaks, he condemns himself to death, for he then retires from existence into the contemplating theoria world.[332] Death entered the world, then, not with the fall of Adam or Satan, but with the creation of the *objective* world by thc birth of consciousness.

[392] The written word *democratizes* a community by providing an accessible source: I'll have to get this into the CP, I think. It provides a centre: the oral tradition is linear.

[393] I start with a Prologue outlining the upper & lower worlds. Then Part One, the Logos vision and the Eros-Adonis (complete) cycle, now reconciled, I think, with the Orc-Urizen one in Blake. Part Two, the Thanatos vision. Out of these *two* cycles there emerges one gigantic cycle, and out of that, one gigantic dialectic of resurrection, where the total cycle turns on its side and we get the alchemical great work. I hope the Chinese tradition that it takes superhuman intelligence to grasp the second I Ching arrangement is wrong, or that Xy *has* the answer to it.[333]

[394] The natural way to think of the upper cycle is to think of a soul entering a body & then leaving it. The Resurrection is of the spiritual body, the reverse movement of the Hermes descent to *physical* death. The Eros ascent is rather the soul evaporating—the Greek heresy of the immortality of the soul which is in Plato & is adopted perforce by Dante. Pound's remark, a far more incisive one than Nietzsche's, about the difference between those who thought fucking was good for the crops & those who thought it was bad for them,[334] defines the contrast between the shy virginal Adonis, the women lamenting his virginity like Jephtha's virginal daughter, Attis with his castrating priests, Jesus with his "touch me not" & his homosexual refinement—chaste, anyway—& his elusive ascension, are all in the upper sphere of the purified soul. The syntax went off the rails: the contrast is with the improvement of sensual enjoyment.

[395] There's a book of essays on Joyce I have, one by Father Noon who says that epiphany is Neoplatonic as well as Christian, & is in the Mackenna Plotinus. A footnote refers to the interest of Thoreau & Emerson in this form of it, & to an article on the subject.[335] Ellmann says the original term in Joyce was epiclete rather than epiphanies,[336] & this, of course links with the bird-woman symbolism in Yeats & the "bird descended" climax of Dylan Thomas's *Winter's Tale*. Both are Adonis themes, of course, one Son & the other Spirit: the Orc-tragic & Urizen-fulfilment double focus corresponding to the Eros allegro-penseroso one. Wonder why the West plumped for the Son theme (*et homo factus est; filioque* [and was made man; and from the Son])[337] & the Eastern Church for the

father-as-spirit one. Of course in Dylan Thomas the bird is female, a bride, & the dying old man a kind of Simeon figure.

[396] I'm told that an early book of Norman Brown, called "Hermes the Thief," has just been reprinted, & makes a connexion between Hermes & Prometheus.[338]

[397] Clive Hart's book on FW [*Finnegans Wake*] says it uses an Arabian Night's tale of a caliph whose head was pushed underwater by a magician: in a split second he dreamed of spending years transformed to an ass & condemned to marry some monstrous female.[339] Sounds like the folktale underlying the main story of Apuleius. He also says Shaun is the sun & travels E-W & Shem goes N-S.[340] I wonder about FW [*Finnegans Wake*].

[398] I wonder too about Robinson Crusoe, Vico's contemporary, who has a black attendant (acquired on Friday), steps out of society into isolation, & journeys to a new land. The line from this to *Heart of Darkness* might be curiously straight. The opening pages, whatever the irony, tell of a fey or fated wanderer who deliberately walks out of a middle-class environment: the prodigal son & Jonah are explicitly referred to, & there seem even to be echoes of *The Tempest*. The arguments with his father sound very like the unborn chapter in *Erewhon*,[341] except that the bourgeois starting point is so obviously Nomos & not the p. of e. [point of epiphany]. He's with the Adam of P.L. [*Paradise Lost*], Gulliver, & Theobald-Cibber of the *Dunciad*, and points forward to Ishmael, the Ancient Mariner, & Kurtz, who echoes his name. He's the third son: the first was killed in battle & the second disappeared, & he bears the name of Cross (Kreutz). It would be tempting to start with the Hermes descent, but surely it would introduce the Prometheus theme too quickly, & I'd have to work back to the simpler & more traditional pattern. I have so far so little help with the Prometheus quadrant: Dante leaves it out entirely. In fact it's the mysterious return theme that's omitted from all the epics.

[399] Jonathan Edwards speaks of wanting to act as he will wish he had done if after all he were damned.[342] We think what hideous superstitious nonsense. And yet: we can only understand life after death through what we know of it, which is reputation in posterity, and surely there are infinite numbers of good, upright, honest, pious men who are damned in

the sense that their actions were based on what we can see to have been wrong, insufficient, mistaken premises.

[400] I may be going off on another critical path here, but even that might be useful. Superstition is, etymologically, what persists out of habit. Faith then would be the resurrection of superstition, in the way that, in Shelley, imagination is the resurrection of knowledge. Take the Biblical superstition about Lilith & Azazel, the demons of desolate places.[343] In the age of Hitler & Stalin we aren't more rational: it's just that with a crowded civilization the demonic forces have become visible in human form. Similarly, of course, with God in Christ, but that's different.

[401] Man is awake at night, & sees that the moon & stars are orderly as well as the sun. He also sees the sun vanish into the dark world & reappear. The Logos & Thanatos visions, then, may begin as bordering haloes of one world; but each *is* the world, & they interpenetrate. The morning has come, and also the night [Isaiah 21:11–12].

[402] This is of course a more difficult conception than the four quadrants, but it emerges as soon as the Narcissus principle of imitation begins to operate. Thus I think now of my three favorites, *Tempest*, *P.R.* [*Paradise Regained*], & [Blake's] *Milton*,[344] as all beginning essentially with Hermetic meander-&-descent patterns. Similarly, Shakespearean romance differs from comedy in containing tragedy, that is, in making the dip below the axis of Nomos & Nous & coming up again. But this isn't separable from their Eros patterns.

[403] Is there a consistent and encyclopedic center—Bible? I know Blake thought the Bible contained its own counter-Bible, hence his technique of superposition: the romance of Palestine on the reality of England. (You can think of the top half as reality & the lower half as dark illusion, or of the top half as spectral ghost or shadow & the lower half as substance). The point is that I'm thinking of beginning with an abridgement of my lecture course on the Bible, as an introduction to the Logos vision. Now, is there a Thanatos vision that finds the oracle in the dark, & doesn't get obsessed by ironic stereotypes so that, like FW [*Finnegans Wake*], it dissolves in general tee-hee? Suppose my Avatamsaka hunch turned out to be something like that?[345] Suppose the Jewish-Christian & the Hindu-Buddhist sequences were the only two possibilities open to us?

[404] Of course I know about the Christian-*Classical* opposition, but who doesn't know about that? Xy's comic & the Classics have the tragic Dionysus: Xy sublimates & the Classics have Eros; Xy has compassion & the Classics have the Iliad gutcut. Likewise Rabelais & the high priests of the p.d.e. [point of demonic epiphany], Heidegger & Proust & the like. But I wonder . . . I wonder, first, if such people aren't examples of an *anima naturaliter buddhistica*.[346] It would be awkward & probably useless if any counter-Bible turned out to be something written in Sanskrit, but my hunch still remains. Against the drama of the God who becomes man in daylight, saying that we are born but never die, there *can only be* the night vision of the triumph over Maya of the Enlightened One who says that we die but have never been born. And that, of course, had to come first in time.

[405] There is, then, if I'm right, a lesser & a greater antithesis. The lesser is the Christian-Classical one, Yeats' primary & antithetical—as usual, Yeats gets it wrong, & Nietzsche may have confused the two in his idiotic Christ-Dionysus formula. In Eros, Xy sublimates & Eros fucks; in Adonis, the contrast is the Oedipus-Christ one that Yeats got: there must be similar antitheses in the two lower ones. Perhaps in Hermes there's one of oracular & hidden knowledge descent vs. the experience of death or hell. Prometheus then would perhaps have the rebirth-resurrection antithesis.

[406] But all this is superficial, a mere difference of emphasis, compared to the Xn-Buddhist one. Except that reincarnation belongs to one & not to the other, & the obvious fact that one is personal, theistic, & voluntary & the other depersonalized, atheistic, & enlightened, I haven't a clue how to proceed. It would be strange if I turned out to be a Great Reconciler after all. In any case, if this tremendous antithesis is really there, & if two or three volumes are really involved, a very different direction of development is certainly indicated.

[407] Of course the foreground antithesis, a very minor one, is the contrast represented by McLuhan & myself. I hold to the continuous, encyclopedic, linear-narrative Christian structure, and, of course, "discontinuous" is very much an in-word at present. There is no such thing as a discontinuous poem, though there are poems, like Pound's Cantoes, that try to force the reader to establish the continuity of what he's reading, instead of providing it for him ready-made.

[408] I imagine the construction of this book will have to proceed differently from my usual habits. First writing a thin outline, then gradually thickening it with illustrations drawn from reading. Thus I begin with the father & mother myths of creation, & then my reading will suggest other examples: e.g., the separation of Izanagi & Izanami in Shinto myth, the Sumerian descent of Ishtar, etc.[347]

[409] The introduction outlines the two creation myths, & their contrasts. Everything that includes the female *is* female. If God made the world out of anything, that material cause must be co-eternal with God. Blake's female will notion is unshakable here. Further, the artificial creation defines time & space: if Augustine cautiously associates our experience of time with the fall, still the world must have been made at a point of time—"so late," as Milton says—as the week symbolism indicates.[348] In all sexual myths there's ultimately nothing but an unending cycle, for even if the world began, the process of beginning worlds didn't. So Judaism & Xy annihilated the female creator & denied or ignored reincarnation.

[410] Identity, immortality, & the *dialectic* of symbolism is bound with the artefact creation myth. Unending cycle belongs with the mother, so rebirth is the opposite of resurrection. This is part of the general principle that becoming is the (cyclical) analogy of being, combined with Blake's principle (which I've finally decided really is Blake's principle) that all analogy is demonic parody.

[411] I suppose after the introduction, when I discuss the Logos vision & talk about *Orchestra*[349] & the Mutabilitie Cantoes, I'll doubtless need the *Timaeus* & the way it gets up the pattern of the cycle revolving below the world of being, the cycle being the analogy of the metaphorical unity of being. But all I need to say just then is that the artefact myth was believed in up to the 18th c., outline its four levels, & start in. Later on, however, I'll have much tougher problems to think about.

[412] I've got some repetition from the AC, but I think no more than I have to have for the sequel to it. The chain of being is first of all not a chain: as being it's pulled up inside Zeus,[350] & is my apocalyptic table. Its demonic opposite is involved in its whole conception, however, so I'll need the Biblical pattern. The revolutionary Jewish outlook, which starts with the parody-possession, can account for evil, as the Platonic-

Neoplatonic-Gnostic-Cabbalistic approaches can't. That only tries to account for descent, and descent gives us the two patterns of linearity (the chain *as* chain) and cycle. The latter, in the *Timaeus*, is becoming's imitation of being. (The word *ouroboros*, I understand, occurs somewhere in the *Timaeus*).[351] So we have the bright sky-father (being), the dark earth-mother (non-being, or perhaps necessity in Plato) and the revolving child, the annual eniautos dying-god.[352]

[413] The next step is to set up the four levels; heaven, the earthly paradise (Eden-P.L. [*Promised Land*] in the Bible, Atlantis in Plato), the world of experience & the demonic world. The point of epiphany is two-gated (Beulah) and *must* become either the lower part of heaven or (G.A. [Gardens of Adonis]) the top of the cycle. The final step is to see the cycle itself as demonic, part of the unending female will. At this stage Moses isn't excluded: he's torn in two by Michael & Satan. That's why the demonic vision also appears in the *Purgatorio*. Not so much new here. *Lower* Eden gets washed away in Milton.

[414] Yes, the demonic comes first in Hebrew myth: they really did learn good by evil, & their God became true because the others were false. Hence not only all the repudiated gods & cults, but the more urbane taking over of heathen structures (Esther, Song of Songs, tehom from Tiamat & the dragon-killing myth, etc.).[353]

[415] I wonder if the great Jewish revolution wasn't the shift of the king-as-Son from the son of the earth-mother to the Son of the sky-father and if the Christian revolution wasn't the identification of the latter with the Adonis ritual. This made Christ descend from Logos vision & identified Adonis & Agape, giving to Xy that dramatic pattern which is so central to it but centering it on resurrection instead of rebirth. I think I'm on to something pretty big here. If I could only figure out what's important & valid *now* about the Logos vision I'd have this program clear.

[416] So here I am again, right bang up against that. Genesis *is* an alternative theory to Darwin, even though Reagan & Co. are the most miserable kinds of fool for saying so. The astronauts reading Genesis were right, & the God-is-dead people are wrong: God didn't annihilate himself as Creator of the order of Nature at the Incarnation: he just went underground.

[417] The Owl & the Nightingale (13th c.) is an early form of the allegro-penseroso contrast. In its deeper aspects (e.g., the crucifixion of the owl) it expands into a Yeatsian Logos-Thanatos debate.

[418] Of course Shaw & the others of his time were right in connecting what was left of the artefact myth with *leaps* in the evolutionary process (e.g. the warm-blooded animal). There must be a great deal in Butler that is not just cranky & futile anti-Darwinism, even though his attempt to internalize the evolutionary process doesn't help my present problem.

[419] Maybe what's true of the Gospels is also true of Genesis. If you'd been there, you'd have seen nothing miraculous in the career of Christ. If you'd been there, in all those millions of sunny days when Nature wasn't doing a damn thing but laying down chalk, you'd have seen nothing but the laying down of chalk. The meaningless sunny day, the commonplace life of zero-century Palestine, were *what happened*, just like that. Is the cyclical Thanatos vision also the *perceptual* vision, what you see without the Logos, Rabelais' empty bottle?

[420] Xy stands for the triumph over death; Buddhism for the triumph over birth. The latter is a Thanatos vision because death is the only visible symbol of Nirvana, just as life after death, or rebirth, is the only visible symbol of heaven. Yet rebirth is the opposite of resurrection, & death the opposite of Nirvana. But the ultimate identity of Nirvana & Samsara indicates the identity of the perceptual vision with Thanatos.

[421] I haven't as yet got much out of the *Bateau Ivre*, but notice how Rimbaud uses the image of the starry *floor*, the stars on the other side of the world, below the bottom of the Hermes descent, as alchemical symbols of the great fire-work.

[422] Footnote to across [par. 420]: in Xy the triumph over death is a new birth; in Buddhism the triumph over birth is the new death of Nirvana.

[423] General note, separate or prefatory: fitting literary works into their archetypal contexts does away with a lot of source-hunting. If a writer specifically refers to, quotes from, or paraphrases the wording of another work, that other work is a source. A work assumed to be a source because it is archetypally analogous may not be a source at all. Joyce

hadn't read Alice before somebody called his attention to the analogy: he hadn't read Rabelais either, he says, and adds "though I suppose nobody will believe this." That is, on a rigidly historical or *Wissenschaft* framework, if he says he hasn't read his most direct generic ancestor he *must* be lying. Chambers tried to show that the Beowulf poet might have read the Odyssey, but if he had he'd have preferred Prudentius.[354] And Dante got more out of Lucan than he would have got out of Homer—I mean that once a job has been definitively done, an equally great successor may tend to avoid it, as Milton avoided Dante.

[424] Under the mythical framework of being x nothing = becoming, we get the following associations for the cyclical element in experience: a) analogical continuation, or sacramental analogy b) the demonic unending cycle when in the same time-unit as the apocalypse (that is, identification of the cyclical with the linear aspect of time) c) identification with nothingness d) the demonic consolidation of metaphors, or the hell conception of unending life in death e) Kierkegaard's "repetition" image, a restatement of the sacramental-analogy one which is founded on (I mean K's is) the habit-memory of practice rather than the straight anamnesis memory.

[425] The thing is, can you find a framework different from this becoming-as-being-X-nothing for the Rc. [Romantic] period?

[426] I've said[355] that the *bateau ivre* MHH [*The Marriage of Heaven and Hell*] Orc-Urizen construct is the fundamental one of the modern world: it fits Schopenhauer, Marx, Freud, Darwin, & Rousseau, & that nobody can make a major contribution to modern mythology outside it. What about Einstein—that is, the mythical analogy of Einstein, relativity as a myth? Does the Newtonian universe occupy the upper portion of that? Certainly the quantum theory floats the universe on a chaos of chance like the older cosmology used in P.L. [*Paradise Lost*].

[427] I suppose in our day physical myths belong to the upstairs Logos vision, and biological ones to the Thanatos one. Some analogy here with the intellectual Christian myths versus the old popular pagan ones.

[428] Some modern mythologists of evolution (e.g., Alexander's *Space, Time, and Deity*) seem to be trying to reconstruct the chain of being from

the bottom up.[356] "Evolution" thus occupies the place of the old creature-returning-to-its-maker Eros conception, and God becomes the supreme donkey's carrot, whatever the telos of human evolution is. (Of course it's Eros plus Prometheus, as somehow or other life has to evolve from death).

[429] I suspect that my alternative mythical framework is something like: being apprehended as time becomes being in time or space (the world, that which is, Dasein). I'd hoped Alexander[357] would say this, or at least give me a lead to what can be said, but it doesn't look as though he's going to. In this myth that which is apprehended becomes pure thereness, Blake's Satan or Limit of Opacity, hence consciousness is ultimately consciousness of death. And Alexander *does* say that time is the mind of space.[358] My first glimpse into this was through Beddoes.[359]

[430] The individual, when he falls asleep and dreams, joins the general dream of man, which is why dreams are archetypal.

[431] In Joyce, Finnegan can't wake up because he's overlaid by the individual dream of HCE, who gives a cyclical shape to the Finnegan dream: HCE is the continuing analogy of Finnegan, or Albion as Luvah. He takes over ALP from F [Finnegan]: it's very important that ALP is the "wife" of both of them. Of the children, Shem is the time-spirit closer to F [Finnegan], Shaun the receptive (postman) space spirit (the cycle of the sun, or the E-W Nomos-Nous axis, is his) is closer to HCE. So it's Shaun who goes through the "inquest" of memory & ends in death, & Shem who's ALP's favorite.

[432] This is doubtless CP material, but it's diffused through this scheme as well: the more I think about McLuhan's *obiter dicta*, the more the exact opposite of what he says seems to me to be true. As I say earlier in this notebook, the oral tradition is linear: we're pulled along by it in time, & at the end there's nothing. Writing provides a spatial focus: the *process* of reading a book is linear, but at the end you have the "simultaneous" possession of the whole thing. Also in a newspaper. That's why writing is democratic, potentially: the oral tradition is much closer to the mob, with its easy access to "lend me your ears" rhetoric. Its revival today goes with anarchism, and also with unscripted improvised dramas, music, and socio-political "happenings."

[433] I said [par. 429] I got my lead into the being x time = world formula through Beddoes, & I did, but probably Whitehead is more articulate than Alexander, and Whitehead was fascinated, from all accounts, by *Wordsworth*.[360]

[434] In the development of the city, the aggregating of dwellings is inevitable: the real imaginative revolution connected with the city is the street, the *way through* the city. Why didn't houses just grow up higgledy-piggledy? I suppose they often did, and that there are quarters in old cities, at least from Morocco to Japan, which are pure labyrinths, where everyone who doesn't live there gets lost & where postmen go insane. But the street represents the Logos domination of city-dwellers, & I notice its prominence in the Bible (also Isaiah's "highway in the desert," the desert being *all* highway, in contrast to the forest).

[435] I've said earlier [par. 414] that God, in Judaism, Xy or Islam, is a conception qualitatively different from anything expressed by "a god." It's also equally different from a monotheistic unity. Any Greek or Roman intellectual would have said that all gods were manifestations of one supreme spirit. The early Christians believe that gods, so far as they resembled their own God, were demonic parodies, but of course demonic parody is only one aspect of analogy. So we're back to the quagmire of analogy again.

[436] Being, similarly, is qualitatively different from beings. Everything that exists, like every god, is a manifestation of one "being"; but this "being" is not Being, it is *world*, the analogy of Being. Now, how is Being related to God? Theologians say Being is an analogy of God, philosophers say that God is an analogy of Being. Some, like [Paul] Tillich, simply identify the two. In my diagram we have a Father God & a Mother Being, the former Hebrew & the latter Hellenic. Buddhism, the definitive night vision, seems to me to ask a different question.

[437] The Roman intellectuals of the later Empire said that gods were imaginative creations of man. Hence there was no limit to their creation: every phenomenon that repeated itself could be deified. Hence the catalogue satire in St. Augustine.[361] One could raise the question of psychological archetypes: what gods "exist" in the sense of being projected mental states? This is Blake's preoccupation. There's an interesting anal-

ogy with saints in Catholicism. When the Pope says that St. George & St. Christopher never existed, that's a question, or could be one, of historical fact. But when he goes on to say that it's all right to venerate them even if they never existed, that raises some very complex epistemological problems. Surely once the distinction between divine revelation and human imagination, and of the corresponding contrast in what they create, is given up, traditional Christianity pretty well goes down the drain, and you can no longer ignore the challenge of Blake's identification of the two.

[438] Ultimately, I suppose, one can't have the two things, God & Being. There isn't room for them both in hypothesis. Heidegger says the fundamental philosophical question is: why are there things rather than nothing?[362] This is the ghost of the Christian question: why did God create? The totality of things is world or universe, and there's nothing to relate that to except its origin.

[439] According to the old dispensation, man as creator could only either imitate God, by producing a second-hand copy of his work, or act against him by creating ("worshipping") other gods. For Blake, of course, as soon as you worship even the true God, you're denying his creativity by objectifying him. And you imitate him properly only by creating. Nothing new here.

[440] In the gospels note the pericope of dilemma. Jesus is asked a two-way question; either way gets him into a difficulty, & trying to avoid the dilemma would get him into an unseemly (for a prophet) wriggle. What he does is to break through the dilemma formulation.

[441] I must look up Tolkien's Beowulf article: he says something about the Scandinavian gods: they fight the forces of chaos & lose, but this doesn't invalidate their cause.[363] Clue here to something profound in the North & the furor Teutonicus: the renounced quest in Tolkien himself & Wagner: the Nazi cult of loss (cf. the *Gothen linie* business);[364] the medieval adoption of the Troy legend, etc.

[442] One thing about the four forms of prose fiction: the article I wrote & incorporated into AC is all right.[365] But when I come to trace the development of four prose forms out of the kernels of concerned prose

there's something wrong with the *novel*: it doesn't fit. Partly because it's a displaced form and its development is a historical accident. The four kernels I think are commandment, oracle, aphorism, and pericope.[366] Now there's no doubt about the S, demonic, sparagmos associations of the anatomy: there's the last chapter of Rabelais, the first chapter of Walter Map, the chopped-up encyclopedic mess of Aulus Gellius & Macrobius (both referred to in FW [*Finnegans Wake*]), the kataplous theme in Lucian, etc., etc.[367] But the cena or symposium may be W (Last Supper & commandment), S (encyclopedic sparagmos cf. the mod. [modification] of this in the Tale of a Tub) or E (supper at Emmaus & Plato).

[443] If I put the kernels of concerned prose thus: commandment W at Nomos, oracle S at Thanatos (riddling, ambiguous, cipher or shored fragment), aphorism E at Nous (the *journey* of the aphorism is the Eros journey of dialectic) and pericope N at Logos (revelation in sunlight) I might have something.

[444] I still have to do a great deal of hard thinking before I can start writing: it's not just what to put in but the whole conception of what kind of book it's to be that isn't clear. An ultra-schematic framework, *very* full of lattice-work, is being invaded by a more integrated scheme incorporating the philosophical displacements. Naturally I'd prefer this: I hate the thought of producing just one more big doodle, unless it's a really definitive one. But I think I'll hold on to my hundred sections for a while.

[445] It's been a long interval between this & the previous note. I'm not sure that I've done any hard thinking, but I've done some brooding. The book is now becoming something more on the analogy of Pound's Cantoes or Finnegans Wake, only I certainly will want to do the reading & documentation of a scholarly work. Like the original Cantoes, I think of three main divisions. The first is my cycle of topoi, what I used to call the Druid analogy.[368] It starts at NNW with the birth of the hero & follows the Great Doodle around to Eros at the end, 27–32, with 33 the Logos vision. It's Druidical & mother-centered because it's a cycle, a spatial & temporal cycle of then & there. So it's really a kind of Inferno, for all its ending in heaven, an Inferno close to FW [*Finnegans Wake*] & the Yeats vision. It's the cave of the dromena,[369] the bound vision of shadows. It's full of literature, yet literature in it is circumferential & Tharmas domi-

nated. Its ogdoad is: N, Tharmas, Ch'ien; NW, Vala, Sun; W, Los, K'an; SW, Urizen, Ken; S, Enion, K'un; SE, Chen, Orc; E, Li, Enitharmon; NE Tui, Ahania.[370]

[446] It has, as I say, 33 sections. I start with the up & down, sky & cave, father & mother, landscape, & a general conspectus of the ogdoad. That's, let us say, 1; 2 would be the Great Doodle, which never got into the AC. Adonis symbolism takes us down to the Absalom cluster (8?) and the Nomos world of the Oresteia (9?). Thence we go undersea into the Hermes world of clocks & mirrors & doubles & descents & labyrinths. Somewhere around 16 we hit Thanatos & the eternal cycle (17?). Then the throw of dice, the birth of the youngest fate, the struggle with giants, & so on up to the Resurrection & Nous (I think I hit Easter morning around 25). Eros symbolism, & the final vision of Logos, takes up the rest. So I shan't mind the one-level aspect of it so much if I realize, & warn the reader, that this *is* an Inferno, & part one only, though the only part 20th c. literature has achieved. It has lyrical topoi & loci strung along as episodes on the Great Doodle which is the underlying form of all epics, or quest-epics at least, so it keeps the ∟ [Liberal]-ㅅ [Rencontre] formation.

[447] The second part is the Paradiso, the heavenly projection, & what it does is test the *mythos* hypothesis: that everything in words has a narrative shape. If so, a study of literary plots & of metaphysical & theological arguments can proceed *pari passu* as *mythos* & *dianoia* of one thing. Of what thing? Perhaps my version of the "perennial philosophy."[371] It starts at 34 with a modulation from Dante to St. Thomas, & probably involves the cycle again. The *Mikado* or Adonis complex, imperial sovereignty with a continuously martyred son, takes place in Aristotle's teleology in the NW. Thence we go down into Heidegger & the existentialists, re-emerge with the revolutionaries & then go up Eros with Plato & the Hermetic people, ending at Logos again in the Avatamsaka or universally decentralized vision.[372] Still spatial & temporal, but when & where rather than then & there.

[448] The third part, the recovered Purgatorio, I don't know much about as yet. It doesn't deal with the circle as such, but works alchemically from Nomos & Nous, W to E, the Adonis-Hermes & the Prometheus-Eros quadrants being taken together as unities. It's of course Biblical,

historical, & deals with literature as an informing power: the existing world (Nomos) & the world that completes existence (Nous) are finally related.

[449] Anyway, back to Part One, hereafter ∠ [Part I]:[373] in the diagram of Section One, the same sun rising contrasts with the different life emerging from nature, so that resurrection, the pattern of the same rising again, is the opposite of rebirth. And *the* resurrection, for Xy, is the conquest of the lower world of rebirth. The Eros journey is the soul's response to this, and is of two degrees: the Eros journey proper, leading to a lower Paradise which can also be a place of rebirth, and the logos journey or full resurrection. The e.p. [epiphany point] journey is discarnate, as in Yeats' Byzantium.

[450] Rabelais is probably as definitive for Promethean imagery as Dante is for Eros. Milton's SA [*Samson Agonistes*] is also of that quadrant. Defeat of giants (Harapha): prototype of resurrection, agent of a (necessarily temporary) revolution. Keeping the secret (of the oracle) is central to the cave cluster: Samson is bound for being a "blab." Swarms of insects in his opening speech.

[451] Eros journeys are also to wisdom, to a Utopia conceived as a structure of arts & sciences. Hence morality structures like that of Hawes belong to it.[374] Also dialogue & dialectic. The latter is the *journey* of the idea, attained in the penseroso tower. But I don't know yet where the Utopia belongs. The traditional Utopia is revolutionary & aristocratic, & so suggests Eros. But there's an equally traditional City of *God*, as well as the city-state of Plato informed by the symposium and balanced by the Laws (Nomos). I suppose the answer is that there's a city for each point in the ogdoad.[375] The SW one is labyrinthine; the NE one emphasizes the street or way through.

[452] In the progression of Joyce's books I notice a retreat from the eye into the ear, from the meticulous realism of D [*Dubliners*] to the dream of FW [*Finnegans Wake*]. I wonder if I could get away with a similar retreat from the spread-out panorama of ∠ [Part I][376] to a discontinuous form that would be written in the aphoristic form of my notebooks, and so come closer to what I listen to, as the theme also moves from projection to recovery?

[453] The Jewish-Christian tradition moves in a historical sequence: creation, burning bush, incarnation, descent of the Spirit on the Church. Romantic imagery converges on reincarnation and cycle & repetition. Faust, weary of the *journey* of knowledge, wants only to be reborn.

[454] In myths of ascent, descent or quest, we *go* only in dream, with the soul leaving the body. The goal of the quest is to integrate what we're getting with what we've got, and the only way to reach the goal is to wake up & find ourselves in the same place. Jacob's ladder.[377]

[455] In Eliot's Burnt Norton there are seven points of time, corresponding to the seven directions of space. Thus:

rose-garden	north	(backwards)
subway	south	(forwards)
past	west	(one side)
future	east	(other side)
correspondence	up	(up)
yew-tree	down	(down)
still point (present)	centre	(around)

[456] The point of epiphany is of course the end of the line for Eros because the same ego-power that pulls you up also pulls you down: that's why Buddhism (a) accepts reincarnation (b) denies the substantiality of the ego. In Xy you're at the point represented by the climax of Milton's PR [*Paradise Regained*] & SA [*Samson Agonistes*], where the will is taken over.

[457] Re the eight cities on the last page [par. 451]: the Nomos city of the W. is the Utopia of adjustment, the conventional Utopia. Its E. counterpart is the genuine Platonic Republic in the wise man's mind. As soon as we look closely at the Utopia of adjustment, it becomes the nightmare city of Dis.

[458] All Utopian projects, including the Marxist empires, envisage an alternation of physical & mental effort (More, Brook Farm, etc.). It doesn't

work (& in Communist countries is explicitly intended not to work) because physical exercise addles the brain. However, the real alternation is work & play; physical work needs physical play & mental work mental play. In words, descriptive and informing language is working with words; literature is playing with words. Ruskin's distinction of ornament & imitation applies here.[378]

[459] Comedy attains, romance contains; comedy drives toward an erotic or dialectical telos, romance revolves around it in the circular quest shape. Comedy is primarily dramatic, romance narrative. The Purgatorio is archetypal comedy, Paradiso archetypal romance.

[460] The imaginative world is not a world to see but a world to see by.[379]

[461] One possible method would be to tie the quadrants up with an initial survey of some epic which really covers it. I'm sure the reason I understand Eros so much better than the other three is that I've gone through the Purgatorio recently. I assume Rabelais will take me through Prometheus. I don't know why I think Proust is a guide to Adonis, but I do. I suppose Dostoievsky has a lot to say about Hermes, along with Conrad & perhaps Nietzsche.

[462] Jung talks about embracing the demonic principle or shadow. In my scheme, to embrace the demonic is to embrace (incorporate or include) the *cycle*. That's why all the "square" (cubic) numbers have to turn into rolling ones (7, 11, 13, 17). At the last supper there is the normal establishment number of twelve: thirteen includes the demonic figure, and eleven is the centrifugal movement of gospel into world. In PT [*The Phoenix and the Turtle*] & its parliament of fowls there are seven birds, one banished. (By the end of the poem there are 5).

[463] One of the Hermes themes is: what is property? i.e., how much can be taken away from a man and still leave his identity? This is of course a central theme of the Book of Job; it's equally central to King Lear, searching for the state of nature and tearing off his clothes (also to Timon, who unlike Lear falls into the Stoic rat-trap). It goes back to the stripping of Ishtar in the Sumerian underworld;[380] it enters *Everyman*, and it's an element in the desertion or betrayal of the hero by his comrades.

[464] I have a note on Joyce's i-c-cl [integritas, consonantia, claritas] progression as the beginning, middle & end of every action, the "middle" being also the fourth point, outside.[381] The mythoi have these too. The claritas of irony is bondage in Egypt, and the comic, which starts with the irrational law, sees this claritas as absurd. The Promethean cannibal giant is absurdity of this kind.

[465] The pictures of the Crucifixion show a human being assimilated to an abstract pattern. The mutilation of the abstract, especially the moral law, is presented in *Euthyphro*: this is the law that the Promethean Christ shatters.

[466] It's possible that my underlying scheme—at least the conspectus part of it—is an incredibly simplistic one. 32 points, minus four for the cardinals, gives four quadrants of seven steps (I don't have to have a sequence, of course) each. Maybe the seven steps of Eros have exact counterparts in Prometheus, and reversed ones in the other two. My beads-and-string metaphor seems to be going into reverse: get the 28 in proper alignment and the string will take care of itself. I hope there's enough variety in the string, i.e. the great doodle, to overlay or even disguise the fundamental simplicity of the conspectus. Otherwise, every fool in the country will shake his bells—not that that bothers me much, & they're not all fools.

[467] In playing through an edition of Dussek's sonatas,[382] I had a curious sense of the ambiguity of the word "invention." The greatest composers, we think, are those who make up the best music out of their own heads. This is part of the subjectifying of creation that we've come to take for granted. It's the ghost of the old idea that God is the only objective creator. Gurdjiev has a remark about "objective" art that impressed me, although in his context it was probably all balls.[383] But I wonder about "invention"—I get a strong feeling that Mozart and Beethoven *found* things that were really there, in the ground Dussek surveyed. (Of course Dussek found things too, especially in the fine F minor sonata). Maybe the "greatest" artists are also the greatest realists: they discover, like the scientists, patterns & constructs actually latent in nature. This would explain the sense in, e.g., Eliot, that the poet is a fisher king trying to hook and land one thing, his poem, which is his only because he happened to catch it.

[468] The role of convention, then, is to define an area of search. I keep feeling that the book I'm about to write doesn't depend only on subjective or mnemonic constructs but describes something there. Also that Yeats, who I think may be inferior to me as a theorist of literature, surveyed the ground in *A Vision* where I've found something. I suppose I can't really articulate this point about "invention," but if I could, at least in ⩘ [Part III],[384] it would certainly shut my critics up. Not that that's a very noble aim: what I'd like to shut up is a voice inside me, not of honest doubt, but of genuine malice.

[469] There's an odd "homunculus" image in Sterne & Diderot, & perhaps elsewhere (I mean apart from *Faust*, of course) that's somewhere underground: it may be part of the *jeune parque* complex. Just as there's a child, lover, & old man in Eros, so there may be a daughter (j.p. [*jeune parque*]), bride and mother (Isis in Apuleius) below.

[470] It's early days to speculate about ∠ [Part I],[385] but I imagine it will expose contract & Utopia as the essential social roots of, respectively, tragic & comic metaphysical structures. Here the individual is related to visible & invisible society W & E, and to different kinds of concern N & S (educational contract N, related to Sophia, & the mob at S, where the individual as such is a pharmakos). The thing is that contract & Utopia are the master keys of that book. As for ⩘ [Part III],[386] it will probably be polarized between Ruskin & Morris, along with the sentimental romance sequence from Poe to Henry James, on the W, & something more "light-colored" & discontinuous E, symbolistes (Mallarmé & Hopkins), bits of Samuel Butler, etc. Blake's theory that art *is* resurrection, clothing spectres or animating the separated bones in the dry valley, seems the logical informing principle of ⩘ [Part III]. Incidentally, one of the key authors of ˥ [Part II] would be Montaigne.

[471] The debate on the point of epiphany has, on one side, Dante, who insists on going on, and the later Yeats, who goes back. In Prometheus there's a much more formidable rivalry, between Rabelais, who crashes through, and Don Quixote, who remains shut up in his illusion, though with of course also a vision of the real thing. The realism of Don Quixote's surroundings makes him a Prometheus rather than an Eros figure, just as the fantasy of Rabelais puts him there. Funny. Only it isn't pure fantasy: the shit is real.

[472] Analogy is the *opposite* of identity, hence demonic parody is, as in Blake, the only real analogy. The sacramental analogy at Nomos is illusion, and so is the rebirth-revolution analogy at Nous. This is one of the things discovered in the cycle, which helps overlay the compass.

[473] Of course there's a debate in Quixote's mind on the 24 points of Nous epiphany: what he believes is apocalyptic; what he thinks he believes is a childish regression, hence cyclical. This develops out of the whole Promethean struggle between the existential (a *liberating* force here, in contrast to Hermes) and the systematic (the Aristophanic comic form, reproduced in the teleological New Comedy in a different way, Eros being on the other side of Plato). (That is, dialectic has, or may have, a redeeming power in Eros, in contrast to Prometheus: perhaps Eros turns its back on Prometheus as Prometheus does on Hermes). Anyway, this conflict begins somewhere around 18 with the Solomon-and-Saturn dialogue,[387] the Rameau's nephew type of thing.

[474] In tragedy the hero is sprung from the gods because the gods exist to ratify the order of nature and the hero is not so much individual as generic man, a product of nature, like Butler's Townley. That's the kernel of truth in Yeats' notion that the top of his cycle is towards nature.

[475] Incidentally, the theme of tragedy turns on the illusion of achievement, the kind of thing I spoke of in my sermon on humility.[388] They've done things; they expect to be remembered for, and identified with, what they've done, & the reality of death for them is burial, getting planted *there*. The surviving shade in Hades hasn't nearly the reality of the tomb demanding sacrifices.

[476] The gate of death is the dung-gate of nausea: death is the last crap, the last defecated stool. Dante, as I've said, emerges from hell as Satan's turd. Our whole notion of the "dirty" is excremental. The gate of birth is the entrance gate, connected with curiosity & discovery. And why do I make the return on the point of epiphany depend solely on Yeats? The great book of return is Ovid's Metamorphoses: it's Ovid, not Virgil, who returns from there.

[477] Every ordered structure, in art or scholarship, represents an ethical victory over the anxieties of the ego, which express themselves by di-

gressions. In Prometheus digressions are exuberance, part of the victory over established order: in Hermes they're part of the labyrinth, the genuine bewilderment of the soul.

[478] A father sky-god myth makes the soul female & submissive: maybe the jeune parque complex (that's only a guess: I don't know if it exists or not) is part of a revolt against this, along with Milton's shifting of the Church from mother to virgin.[389] Certainly it's part of the revolt against the mother.

[479] Marvell's Garden: the saving remnant of introversion, of communion with something that isn't society. Pastorals generally, and all the stuff about the quiet mind. It has a lot to do both with the recovery of childhood & with attaining freedom of will, but is different from both.

[480] Re the excretory symbolism of the S: I imagine that it will be a long time before we have public toilets without distinction of sexes. That seems to be the last stronghold of the primitive passion for separate houses & initiation rites for the sexes: I'm noting a strong desire for co-educational residences & the like, & am wondering if excretion rather than sex is the real basis for sexual segregation. E.g. puberty rites & seclusion at menstruation.

[481] Marx was a Promethean writer, not merely in his Promethean imagery & the fact that he read Aeschylus, but in his truculence, his excremental imagery, and his inability to finish books. The Prometheus element on the other hand is the one Dante left out: he turned his back on hell and didn't harrow it. This is the element I used to call schalk, I forget why.[390]

[482] I have half a dozen Prometheus themes now, or hunches: 18 (say) anal imagery; 19 (not necessarily a sequence) the fight with or escape from cannibal giants; 20, the throw of dice or the reading of the cipher; 21, the struggle of the systematic & the existential (Solomon & Saturn dialogue);[391] 22, the emergence of the jeune parque; 23, the oracular message (not the same as 20); 24, the debate at the mouth of the cave. Note how the *Frogs* theme fits 24: Aeschylus is taken and Euripides left behind. The Alpha & Omega business goes in 20: the rivers of the underworld are here too.

[483] For Hermes, I think 10 is the maze in the wood, where you either find a guide or go through the cycle of violence: Comus & Inferno openings; the Golden Bough. Perhaps this is also both the "bloody wood" of Eliot's Agamemnon[392] & also the world of Oedipus, the Nemi father-conqueror[393] who plunges downward. The Biblical equivalent of Oedipus is Cain, Abel being a displaced Adam.

[484] I have a notion that something as simple and obvious as the four quadrants themselves has still to fall into place. It may have something to do with the fact that every one of the 32 points on the circumference *is also* a centre, the centre of the whole thing. The place of the Odyssey circle is something I'm wondering about now: it's most simply the p. of e. [point of epiphany], of course. The rejection of both Circe (lower) & Calypso (upper) for Penelope (purgatorial or existent world) may make it the basis of ⩘ [Part III].[394]

[485] But I wonder (Rev. 21:13)[395] if each cardinal point may not have *three* gates, one to enter, one to leave, & one opening into the world it's a gate to. Thus at W, or Nomos, there's a "debate" at the entrance between the Absalom-Adonis-Abel martyr & the avenger who enters Nomos at the end of the Oresteia. There's also an exit gate: Adam & Oedipus leave by it after killing or insulting their fathers. And there's the Western Gate into the world of Nomos itself. This is probably the world of praxis or event. Theoretically, the eastern gate would be closed, as the Western Gate of Nous (Resurrection) is in Blake—it may be the same gate.

[486] In the Adonis quadrant there are two climaxes corresponding to the allegro & penseroso climaxes in Eros. The Adonis death itself corresponds to sexual fulfilment in the Earthly Paradise. That is, the premature death illustrates the fundamental disharmony between organic time and duration time. The Urizenic climax is entropy time, energy subsiding into the predictable. But Nomos itself, as the Bowlahoola founded by Tharmas, is the world of predictable law, which gradually turns inside out into creative or teleological law, communication conquering entropy.[396] The evolution of *nature* has a good deal of the Hermes pattern in it, the scansion-and-action pattern of the computer, which is the Darwinian mutation-and-direction one, being symbolized by the meander-and-descent Hermes one.

[487] Before I can do any serious work on this book I have to free myself from the domination of the overall flat pattern. The typical Eros pattern is a climb, but it can also be a descent, as it is in the Alice books, and there can be, as in the Eliot Quartets, a down and an up pattern at the same time. Similarly Hermes may be an ascent: onward & upward into the future, as in progressive theories. Maybe Proust (cf. "Bergotte")[397] takes this view and turns it around in the last volume. Anyway, each quadrant, like each cardinal, is a universe in itself.

[488] In reading Rabelais (for Prometheus) I've rediscovered the principle of the *ludens* shift,[398] the change in perspective from experience to innocence. The bird's song is sexually aggressive, but we interpret "tweet, tweet" as the voice of innocence. The sound of children playing is a cliché of innocence, though the more closely we attend to it the more aggressiveness & hysteria we find in it. Similarly the appalling practical jokes of Panurge, like the gigantic mowing down of enemies by the giants, are childish aggressive fantasies transmuted into "horseplay."

[489] Along with the ludens shift goes the Lilliput-Brobdingnag shift, of titans to swarms of insects. The mischievous imp (Huckleberry Finn, at the end; Lord of the Flies (title significant); the Katzenjammer kids, who are twins) is a standard modulation of the devil, cf. of course the end of *Paradise Lost* I.[399] In Rabelais the sexual aggressiveness seems rather laid on: it's the excretory aggressiveness, piss-floods and the like, that seem really spontaneous: it corresponds to the polymorphous pre-sexual fantasies near the top of Eros. Cf. also the core of innocence in female vanity, as in Milton's Eve, even though it's attachable to pride. The Rabelaisian aggressiveness recurs in Jarry's *Ubu Roi*.[400]

[490] I've spoken of the three A's of irony, Anxiety, Alienation & Absurdity: to these one should add a fourth, Aggression.[401]

[491] Irony observes, or operates, a sado-masochistic cycle, not just a masochistic complex. The ludens shift[402] works in reverse in television programs, where we're expected to transmute the aggressive desire to sell us something as pure entertainment. The principle that the medium is the message, for any form of *interested* communication, lasts only so long as we remain relatively unconscious of the form: as soon as we become conscious of it the content separates from it.

[492] Rabelais has all the symbols I associate with Prometheus: the emphasis on games and dice, a tremendous emphasis on divination, cannibal giants, shifts of perspective from giants to swarms of insects, oracles and caves, female sibyls (if that isn't a tautology), and the ridicule of all intellectual structures and systems, including those of the professions. Also determinism as a feature of this quadrant. He's quite explicit about trying to remove the curse from the descent to the belly and anus of Man, but he's enough affected by it to give us only a teasing conclusion. Goethe's Erdgeist and Shelley's Demogorgon are much more direct attempts to explain what the genuine Thanatos vision is: in them we see that the Hermes structure is essentially Kantian: reality *behind* a veil.

[493] What's missing from Rabelais, according to my hunches, are the *jeune parque* and homunculus themes. He does have a somewhat abortive rejuvenation theme in the fifth book, and his female "Lanterns" seem to have some wise-virgins connexions.[403] There appears to be a double-peaked Nous of Dionysus *and* Christ (or whatever); Carnival *and* Lent, Lent being the great enemy of the quest in Rabelais.

[494] I suppose the Hermes quest turns its back on the Word, the Logos vision, and that's why the insufficiency of words as compared to life and action seems so insistent. In Goethe, Wagner is satisfied with words. How to distinguish Logos from Nomos visions in such things as the Prolog is an unsolved problem.

[495] Ups and downs: I'd better transcribe my old note[404] here: "high katabasis: incarnation or descent of superior spirit; drop of dew in Marvell; lady, or rather attendant spirit, in *Comus*: microcosm imagery. Middle katabasis: death; identification with bleeding flower; metamorphosis; wheel of fortune turning down. Low katabasis: descent into hell; no exit; sparagmos. Low anabasis: escape from hell or prison; Cyclops; Mutability; Satan in Eden; rebellious release of chaos like the Gunpowder Plot imagery in Milton; Harrowing of Hell; Jonah and fishing. Middle anabasis: birth of individual or society in comedy; marriage; revival; return from absence; piled logs; tower and mountain climbing. High anabasis: redemption; sacred marriage; king & beggar maiden; black bride; green lion.[405] High assimilated to dialectic; middle cyclical; low *are* the cycle."

[496] What about Pentecost & the descending Spirit: is it part of the

Adonis-Agape descent or a reverse Eros movement? What about the metamorphic descents of a fucking Jupiter who forsakes his queen in heaven? What about the distinction between fixed and temporary (Proteus) metamorphosis?

[497] Also the fatal foreshortening process has begun. I'd thought of the *second* book as concerned with conceptual displacements [par. 447]. Thus: the Logos vision in Thomism; the journey of the Logos itself through the seven realms; descent down the Aristotelian teleological path, further descent down the Kant-to-Heidegger existential road, ascent through the Hegel-Marx dialectical pattern; further ascent through the Platonic mystics, ending the journey with the Avatamsaka interpenetration[406] which annuls all distinctions and brings in the Kingdom of the Holy Spirit. But it's going to be tough keeping that out of One.

[498] Still, that does give me a terrific formula if I can bring it off: the conception of a sky-father creating a dialectic against the other half of creation, which is associated with evil, with death, with strange oracles of "heresy," with sex and excrement and revolution. Then the quest of the Logos, who brings up what is redeemable from this world (sexual & excretory imagery, revolution, & heretical oracle) and leaves behind what isn't (death and unending misery or pain). The crisis of the narrative is at E with the Resurrection, but we have to have the rest of this as the *conquest of order*, the consummation of love. *That's* what leads to the interpenetrating Spirit. But here are all three of my themes, God help me. And I mean that.

[499] So far as CP was about religion, I put its theme to myself as: ["]mythology being a human language, it is not revelation." This turned into: "this book raises no specifically religious issues, only issues concerned with the human understanding of religion." These two formulations were based on [Karl] Barth's principle that God is never identical with what we call God. Now it's turned into something like this: "The use of revelation to bind societies together in a myth of concern is perhaps ultimately illegitimate. If so, a myth of concern is a perversion of revelation." I suppose the moral is that all religions are one and that revelation can only come through an individual. For Blake the sin against the Spirit was natural religion, but a society with a *closed* myth of concern perhaps defines it more accurately: "Synagogue of Satan."[407]

[500] Proust speaks of the prosiness of habitual surroundings which become poetry to those who visit them but don't live with them. I'm very familiar with this feeling: it seems to imply that the creative impulse begins in some kind of deliberately set up type of confrontation.

[501] The women in Rabelais range from Grandgosier's wife, splitting her guts eating guts, to the sybil—I mean sibyl, dammit—figure of Baqbuq. In between are a number of fucking machines. Rabelais is one of the boys. I've said one should preserve the adolescent in oneself as well as the child, but a lot of adolescence goes in Prometheus, and I wonder if this adolescent turning off of women isn't a Promethean characteristic. Even Blake speaks of women, like a damn Nazi, as "born for the sport and amusement of man."[408] Mephistopheles in Goethe takes a similarly contemptuous view. (I don't mean that it's contemptuous in Blake, but it looks like a blind spot in his vision). And of course women complain bitterly about Freud.

[502] I must of course get over the notion that every major work of literature has to follow *my* sequence, as though every melody in music had to follow the notes of the scale. My 32 points have to be more discontinuous than that.

[503] The conception of interpenetration is that of natural inclusion. We are in God; God is in us. Therefore there are two worlds, as at the end of *Paradiso,* one the other turned inside out. My consciousness of things puts those things inside me, but whatever is conscious has me inside them. I fell over this years ago in dealing with art & nature: in art nature is turned inside out. But I didn't see it as interpenetration, or an aspect of it. Perhaps this mutuality of awareness *is* identity. My memory holds my past selves in me; my growth, or body of fate,[409] or what the hell, holds my future selves. And there's that point at the end of the Morality of Scholarship essay,[410] plus my treatment of Keats' democracy of forest trees.[411] This democracy is my "fraternity," or redeemed aristocracy, and perhaps the myth of concern is a necessary stage in its development which becomes in the end a perversion of it.

[504] And of course there's always the possibility that the seven steps of each quadrant are six, and that I'm just rewriting my theory of phases. But I don't really think so: the phases are generic in a way that these

quadrants aren't. Still, there does seem to be some connexion. My 24 phases are actually 12 double phases, and if the quadrants are six phases each the cardinal points are each double.

[505] Thus Logos as the end of Eros is city & music of spheres; Logos as beginning of Adonis is consolidation of metaphors. Nomos-Adonis is Oresteia; Nomos-Hermes Oedipus. Nous-Prometheus is the Rabelais-Plato symposium; Nous-Eros the Quixote alien. Thanatos-Hermes is oracle; Thanatos-Prometheus wit (Trophonius).[412] Each cardinal is a Beulah double-gate (or triple, as above).

[506] I suppose it's around Eros 2 (26 or 27) where we get the exhaustive psychological analysis of a sexual relation (*Adolphe*, the Odette & Albertine sections of Proust, the Regina books of Kierkegaard). In Swann's Way the Combray section is Adonis 2 & the Swann in Love section Eros 2, directly opposite, suggesting another schematism in the Yeats *Vision*.[413]

[507] I've said that the original writer continues convention at a deeper level: this is an application of the general principle of shallow & deep consistency. Shallow consistency is continuity, habit, doing what one has always done. At certain points a deeper consistency emerges which is discontinuous with the shallow repetitions of habit. Proust remarks that the actions which most deeply reveal people's character are often overlooked by others as though they were hallucinations.[414]

[508] Thirty-two stations of the Logos; thirty-two voices of revelation.

[509] Eros, being Platonic, is hierarchical: it talks about the "lower" and "higher" aspects, the "lower" being sense and the "higher" approaching the disembodied soul. The "lower" aspect of man is always the "animal" aspect, never the social or *idées reçues* aspect. It's a thin and impoverished outlook until it discovers its Promethean ancestry and understands how crucial the resurrection of the body is. I suppose the risen *social* body is the disciples going into all the world from the upper room, in contrast to the Platonic symposium of the *Laws*.

[510] In the Poimandres God, or his equivalent, falls into this world like Narcissus, drawn into it by gazing at his reflection.[415] In Xy the Father gazes at his reflection in the Son (cf. *Paradiso*, I think X)[416] and the *Son*

then descends to the lower world & performs the cycle of death & resurrection. This means that the cycle itself, even when closed, is not just an ironic parody of apocalypse, but brings to the apocalypse the thing it needs. I'm increasingly inclined to think that this is the point FW [*Finnegans Wake*] is making about the cycle.

[511] The boundary of Prometheus & Nous (24) is the Harrowing of Hell, where the hero crashes through and the tanist[417] has to return to the cycle. Rabelais gets through; Quixote remains imprisoned, though something in him is redeemed.

[512] FW [*Finnegans Wake*] may go back, though, as above, I have doubts. But I note how my scheme is collapsing again: the alchemical theme in Rabelais is absolutely central, and I can't deal with him without dealing with it. The Holy Bottle contains the elixir, and Rabelais calls himself something like the master of Quintessence.[418]

[513] Perhaps my first volume treats the circle as the unconscious unity underlying literature, and the second volume follows the deliberate and progressive movement of a Logos which always knows where it's going and why it has to go there. Maybe I should have called my E. point Soma rather than Nous: on the other hand, what the bodily resurrection makes possible is the ultimate power of life, the individual. Note that in my present view the Logos traverses the cycle *and returns to itself*, bringing the cycle as the image of itself. That way, perhaps I can incorporate the turning-on-its-side movement without making the Eros movement an anticlimax.[419]

[514] If the real Eros is not simply the creature returning to its creator, but the complete individual, united to the risen body of God, on its way to the community of the Spirit which is interpenetration, then one can see how the future-Utopian city is an illusion. (It's an illusion of Hermes, and *those* illusions reappear in another context in Eros).

[515] I've been reading Proust again, with many misgivings about the wisdom of committing myself to so gigantic a work at this stage. What I'd hoped (and still hope) is that he would illuminate for me the whole west side of the cycle. In RR [*Romanticism Reconsidered*] I referred to him (in SER [*A Study of English Romanticism*], actually) as an Adonis writer,[420]

and began him with that quadrant in mind. But he may deal with the entire half of experience that depends on memory and habit, as distinct from the imagination that reverses their current.

[516] I'd thought (see above) of the enormous analysis of an erotic situation as an Eros genre, but I may be wrong. *A l'Ombre des Jeunes Filles en Fleurs* is a title that suggests the forest retreat stage of the Adonis hero. Gilberte is explicitly called an Undine or Melusine figure, but she's overshadowed by her parents, especially Odette, whose tremendous epiphany at the end of the first part of that book is typically Adonis, Cleopatra on her barge. My hunch is that we enter late Adonis with the Guermantes volume, reach Nomos with the death of his grandmother, cross into the Hermes underworld with *Sodome et Gomorrhe*, & stay there through the Albertine books.[421]

[517] I've previously warned myself against assuming that all literary melody just goes up & down the notes of the scale. But perhaps my "guide books," if they are that, do this more than other books would have to do. Anyway, I've thought of this (i.e. the sequential structure of a *mythos*) as a later problem.

[518] So, if I'm right, the "Prisonniere" ["Prisonnière"] theme is typical of a Hermes labyrinth, and the theme of abandonment, *Albertine Disparue*,[422] corresponds to what I still hope is the *jeune parque* theme on the Prometheus side. One thing Proust is very strong on is the recovery of projection: we're not inspired by the woman we love, but by our own love for her. In *Le Temps Retrouvé*[423] he finally reaches the cave of Thanatos and the oracular vision of giants.

[519] The fact that the "hero" is so unheroic, a querulous invalid and hypochondriac clinging to his mother or grandmother[,] has several advantages. It anchors archetypes in common experience, like Wordsworth & the low mimetic generally, and weakness in him, as in Emily Dickinson in a different way, clarifies those archetypes through its increased sensibility: e.g. the sense of hostility in a strange room that one is trying to sleep in.

[520] I don't know even yet whether I can impose the MT [*Mental Traveller*] grid on my diagram. But as far as the cyclic aspect of it goes I

think it's probably there. The Boy is born NNW, is overshadowed by a mother down to Nomos; as he gets older & deeper into Hermes the father-daughter relation becomes more prominent. He dies at Thanatos; the *jeune parque* appears somewhere in the SE, then becomes an Isis-figure that draws him on, becoming steadily more maternal while he becomes more infantile, moving backwards in time up Eros, until we reach the garden again. That's got it, I think: very simple too, once you really look at it.

[521] This suggests that the lover-to-infant, mistress-to-mother Eros pattern is the cyclical aspect of Eros: that consequently Eros, & the other quadrants, also has [have] other aspects. Let's say a dialectical-separation aspect (old man in the tower) and an apocalyptic-consummation aspect (the sacred marriage). Perhaps even another deasil-shaped cycle (e.g. the Marcel of Proust's book is going down Adonis but Marcel Proust himself is going up Eros). Isolating the withershins pattern is clearly what I have to do first.[424]

[522] Meanwhile, if I'm right about the controlling theme, there are *three* major organizations in literature, not two, the dialectical, the cyclical and the *genuinely* apocalyptic or interpenetrating. These develop from, respectively, the Father, the Son & the Spirit. It's the conception of the sky-Father that splits the world in two between a Heavenly Creator and a demonic Mother Nature. Out of this my apocalyptic-demonic *tables* come [*GC*, 166–7], & the entire cycle of nature here is demonic, the guts of Leviathan.

[523] Now: the Logos-Son descends to the world and activates the cycle, redeeming it as he does so. That's why Xy picks up a lot of dying-god imagery that Judaism dropped. The Trinity enters time in the hypostatic form of Father, Mother, & Child, & leaves it as Father (old man in tower), Hero (returned son) and Bride (descended from Mother).[425] As long as the sky-Father is there the demonic world has to be there too: once the Logos emerges from the cycle, what Boehme calls the Father's empty shell of wrath & pain is abandoned.[426]

[524] There must be something to this hunch, because so many things hook on to it. I wonder, first, if I can get the outline for the Birks lectures;[427] second, if I can get ∟ [Liberal] & ˥ [Tragicomedy] in the right

order. It's beginning to look as though the cycle were the *second* part, ethos as L is mythos. Or maybe my still very vague hunch about turning it over on its side[428] was the real ⌉ gimmick. 1–33, dialectic & cycle (L & ⋏ [Rencontre]); 34–66, the regeneration of the cycle; 67–100, the "anticlimax" or decentralizing of the cycle, which would take in the conceptual displacements. I think I've got either an idea or a brain tumor, or possibly both. But, if the former, how long a book have I got?

[525] This makes it look for the moment as though Part One were on comparative mythology and cosmology as a literary form; Part Two on the cycle of literary themes I'm working on now; Part Three, as above, on conceptual displacements. The thing is that I can't go traipsing around that compass three fucking times: if this is it, I have to have separate organizations for two of the parts at least. Also, the present scheme reverts to the Dante order, with the Paradiso last. Yet maybe one is places and two plots or movements around, hence the purgatorial regeneration theme, which is what I had: as the Great Work, however, it would have the spiral alchemical shape. There ought to be one major part where all my Zohar-Pseudepigrapha-Pistis Sophia interests would go.[429]

[526] So: at the moment, Part One is this book; Part Two the religious book I want to write (comparative mythology, the Biblical Tradition, etc.), Part Three is on the metaphors of philosophy. One sets up the dialectical structure of mythology from its *telos* in literature, and goes round the quadrants & cardinals, as now planned, 1–33. It contains the whole religious theme, or the Trinitarian theme, but only by implication.

[527] Two is the religious book I've always wanted to write: its theme is the regeneration of the cycle by the Logos, but it is actually another approach to literary symbolism. Alchemical & turned on side.[430] Begins with comparative religion & follows the Biblical-tradition reading I've been doing. The theme is of course thrown forward, towards the spiritual climax. Three, based on this & on conceptual displacements, takes over from here, but I don't know what direction it goes.

[528] What will bring off One if it comes off will be the coherence of its vision of a symbolic universe, the way it accounts for literary cosmologies like Yeats' *Vision*, the MT [*Mental Traveller*], the "discarded image,"[431]

perhaps *Eureka* & perhaps Ruskin, & works out a single theory to account for them, besides giving a contextual reading of many very difficult works.

[529] The present scheme accounts very well for my instinct in buying books, which I think, apart from a few aberrations here & there, is pretty sound. The advantages of this scheme are enormous; the chief disadvantage I see is that I'll have to finish One before anything except the vaguest notion of Two will come clear.

[530] I used to think that this kind of fumbling was just masturbation, which perhaps it is, though that's really just a deviant form of the polymorphous instinct, which is very in now, & has connexions with the state of innocence. I suppose I'm in a female role here: I let these book-forms paw me over before I get fucked by them.

[531] Two would bring off a general theory of what the schematic constructs of occultism are all about: it would do the "heroic quest" job, even though the hero is only one of many Logos symbols. It would be a completely new recasting of the symbolic universe from the compass one, I think, even though it retained the ogdoad elements. So I shouldn't actually have to continue the 100–section scheme, though I'd like to, & the Trinity organization would I suppose carry through. So will the ogdoad: it'll be in Three too. I must look up my three awarenesses and my soul-mind-body notes, of course;[432] but Two is the book where I Say Something Original About Religion.

[532] The physical roots of Eros are in Prometheus; but I don't think Prometheus has a definite sexual climax at the boundary of Nous. A lot of fucking goes on in the SE; but the later female figures are guides or Isis figures. Maybe that's why Eros *begins* alienated. Shift from excretion to the homunculus figure: Pantagruel creating men with his farts.

[533] Female figures in early Adonis calumniated or otherwise stained. I pulled a pornographic novel off the shelves in a bookshop & found the heroine forced to take a bath in the early pages: this erotic fantasy of cleaning up the dirty girl occurs in a displaced form in Macdonald's [George MacDonald's] *Lilith*; in a story of Baron Corvo's (heroine blown on to a ship's deck, I think, by an explosion, stark naked & covered with

dirt), & the kind of sentimental romance that's really soft-core pornography, such as Gene Stratton-Porter's *Michael O'Halloran*.[433]

[534] The general feel of the first two books is all right. One is astrological & a conspectus, based on the wheel or compass, the first I Ching arrangement (Ch'ien-K'un)[434] and a collection of topoi or places. Hence it's based mainly on lyrics, on themes or image-clusters in fiction, and on, so to speak, general centres of gravity in longer works. But the real containing form is the Great Doodle, the circular journey of the Logos from the Father to the Spirit. Two is alchemical and a process, based on the vortex or spiral, the second I Ching arrangement (K'an-Li),[435] and a collection less of image-clusters than of image-sequences. So, if I bring it off, it's a study of the permutations of plots leading from repetition to resurrection. Each book, especially One, has to be complete in itself, as though I had nothing further to say.

[535] I've occasionally wondered if there were horizontal bars, connecting not only Nomos & Nous but the last Adonis phase & the first Eros phase. Or if there are diagonal opposites as well as the quadrants. The May morning love vision is Eros, but it often opens in a thick wood like Hermes. It's things like this that make me realize that something utterly obvious has still to be said about One.

[536] Perhaps the obvious thing is that image and place on wheel have no necessary connexion at all. They may be related as note to key. Any note on the piano could appear in any one of at least seven keys, but it would have different functions: G# would be tonic in G# minor, leading note in A major, & so on. I may well be trying to work out a gigantic development of folktale study; first a study of image-clusters (themes), then of image-sequences (motifs). Maybe I should start by trying to analyze & reduce to a central scheme the catalogues in Aarne-Thompson & Bolte-whatsit.[436] More likely that comes much further along, towards the end of One.

[537] So maybe the Great Doodle is like reading the *staff*, where you see the notes from A to G in sequence but not yet involved in the circle of fifths. I think the homunculus is typically a mid-Prometheus theme, but it might occur elsewhere. It's not impossible that I could name the topoi, though that at the moment sounds gimmicky.

[538] Of the elements, fire represents the world above & earth the world below. The cycle is the world of air & water. Regenerate man, according to Jesus, is born of water & the spirit: air is the symbol for the Holy Spirit in the world & water the symbol of the casting off of the earth or death-element, & so being able to break through the cycle into the world of fire.

[539] But there are variants of this: the conception of "firmament" in Genesis distinguishes upper from lower water, & in the latter there's a lurking traditional idea of waters *below* the earth, connected with the sea & chaos clusters. Meanwhile, air is associated particularly with the upper world of *human* nature & consciousness; water with the lower world of physical nature and its liquid "humours," the essence of the body before it starts producing "spirits" on a higher level.

[540] And of course there are two levels of fire as well as water: cf. the fire-spirits in *Comus*. Spenser has a Pyrochles as well as a Cymochles [(malis)?].[437] There's also in Milton & elsewhere an upper & lower air, though both are above ordinary air, the cold air which is Satan's headquarters & the paradisal air of Eden (Eden being also an upper *earth*).

[541] I still should do some thinking about the I Ching: 64 is the number of squares in chess, 32 of pieces. The hexagrams would have to be in sequence, & no doubt I should study the sequence. Of course they have a primary connexion with divination, oracle, knowledge of the future, & hence Thanatos. But my six phases, each three overlapping with another three, indicates [indicate] some connexion in my own mind.[438]

[542] I have two levels in reading: the level where I'm looking for what to look for before I start writing, and the level where I do know what to look for because I've already started writing about it. Which level I'm at now when I'm reading Rabelais I don't quite know.

[543] In Xy, the true form of the Adonis descent is the Agape incarnation of the Son. The true Eros ascent (the Ascension itself is just there to complete the pattern, I suppose) is the return of the Holy Spirit to itself. Of course the Spirit descends just as the Logos ascends: the duality of descent is important: I have my note on Dylan Thomas' Winter's Tale. The sequence of events in Acts is interesting: after the Son ascends the Spirit descends, meeting the Lord in the air, and in between comes Peter's ac-

count of the death of Judas, the self-destructive Thanatos traitor of mankind who's shucked off as soon as Jesus completes his victory over death. Query: if the Son describes a withershins cycle, does the Spirit describe a deasil or clockwise one, moving against the current of humanity, i.e. bringing life & inspiration to a rhythm headed toward death & expiration? Is that a clue to, not only the persistent association of the Holy Spirit with inspiration, but to the double gyre in Yeats, the power of dream & creativity moving against life & death? Is it possible that the difference between the creature returning to its creator & the creator returning to its own Byzantium or Golgonooza is not a real difference at all, but only a shifting of emphasis within the identity of man?

[544] That is, I think I don't believe in the two natures of Christ: I think what he represents is the identity of God and Man, in which the part of man that isn't God, symbolized by Judas, goes to his own place. This is straight Blake, & so isn't new, but the context may be, & anyway the obvious always comes last in my muddled head. But of course Jesus, the second Adam, follows the withershins rhythm of human life. In Blake the Holy Spirit represents the identity of God & Man that man starts with, the imagination or Poetic Genius in him, & which works against the Selfhood or death-principle. Marcel *in* Proust goes down the W, but Marcel Proust recreating that life goes up the W (not that that works out in the sequence of events, which is still the life of Marcel *in* Proust).

[545] So maybe the Son regenerates the cycle & achieves, or rather completes, the life-death dialectic created by the Father. Then the Spirit regenerates the dialectic, & after him there's the second death [Revelation 20:14 and 21:8], the state of sin which is unforgivable because it doesn't exist: that is, it's the death which is non-existence or the abyss of nothing.

[546] I think my paper on Old & New Comedy had something,[439] & I'm sure there's a corresponding tragic contrast, the Adonis tragedy of rupture & the Hermes tragedy of isolation. The Oresteia & the tragedy of order sit on the Nomos boundary, just as the symposium sits on the Nous boundary. Also, I might be able to find a Prometheus pattern of symbolism in Milton on which I might base my Samson paper.[440]

[547] Check Lydgate's *Reason & Sensuality*, founded on *Les Échecs*

Amoureux for erotic chess, not that I expect much.[441] Also check Catullus on the marriage of Peleus & Thetis for Spenser & Yeats references.[442] I wonder if Eros 1 is the Barbara Allen theme of ritual death by a cruel mistress (echoing the Adonis theme across)[443] & if Eros 2 is the vision of the community of love (lists of great lovers, the temple of Venus, etc.). I shall have to wait until I get my own copy of *Hypnerotomachia*,[444] but note: a) the symbol of Pegasus as indicating that creation is also associated with *rising*: the art of sinking, or bathos, is a failure to create, b) the Ionic column as a spiral symbol associated with the neck of a viol where the strings are tuned into a concord. Note the frequency of emblematic designs on the walls of buildings in Eros: it recurs in the Purgatorio.

[548] Somewhere, possibly Eros 3, is the great dream of "paganism": rapprochement between man and nature as though man were physically natural. In *Hyp* [*Hypnerotomachia*] the hero meets five nymphs who take him along to their bath, & he gets a terrific erection while they laugh at him. The point is that these five nymphs are his own senses. Then of course there's the moral or Bower of Bliss approach to it. Query: does every topos have both a paradisal and a demonic side?

[549] The logical order I suppose would be (a) the myth of the quadrant, e.g. the ascent motif in Eros (b) the genres which find their centre of gravity in that quadrant, e.g. New Comedy in Eros (c) the archetypes or typical images of the quadrant, which don't have to be a sequence of phases, though it might be useful to have some sequential arrangement.

[550] The Frobenius maypole stuff that so fascinated me is I think part of the Absalom complex around Nomos.[445] In each section I could perhaps start with the myth or folktale (e.g. the Two Brothers[446] theme in Hermes), then proceed to the literary developments on the assumption that literature is always the telos of myth. This principle need not enter the text, but could be one of the axioms listed at the beginning (perhaps 33 of these). The value of the book will be in this deductive expounding of the myth, not in spotting the archetypes around the compass.

[551] I suppose my original atomic notion of 32 points was influenced by my desire to have for once a piece of writing where I could isolate units, instead of going into my usual tizzy. Probably I can't, even though

the Anatomy itself broke up into bits—large bits, it's true. I suppose I should introduce the archetypes on their "tonics": the chess game seems to be in upper Eros with the earthly paradise and the associations with music & dance (Hyp, T [*Hypnerotomachia, The Tempest*]) though there are demonic forms in Eliot & Poe. Similarly with the Alpha-Omega business associated with usually underground rivers (Coleridge, Kenneth Patchen, etc.)[447] & the feast of languages stealing the scraps, where the tonic is lower Hermes. There are games in all the quadrants, but the game of athletic contest (the epic game) has its tonic in Adonis, the game of fate (cards) in Hermes, the game of chance (dice, divination) in Prometheus, & the game of strategy (chess & board games) in Eros. Note however the Adonis chess games in medieval romance (if so).

[552] If I superimpose the narrative of the Bible on my diagram, the Age of the Father extends from Logos to Nomos. That is, the original God included Christ: all efforts to conceive of God apart from Christ end in Nomos, the vision of natural law. That's the Old Testament. The Age of the Son, covering the four Gospels, extends from Nomos to Nous, through Thanatos. It takes thirty years, or "three" days, or one split second, or the whole of time. The Age of the Spirit stretches in the Bible from the beginning of Acts (Pentecost) to Revelation or the Everlasting Gospel. In the diagram it's the (ultimate form of the) Eros quadrant. And just as the Father without the Son ends as the sky-god of causation, so the Spirit without the Son has no roots or human beginnings, but is a mere "soul" without a body, increasingly associated with a life "after" death.[448]

[553] God is rarely called "Father" in the Old Testament: he isn't really revealed as Father until the Incarnation. The word "father" sometimes means artificer or inventor (Gen. iv, 21;[449] cf. the metaphor in "patron" saint). I may be wandering off here into another book or article, as I so often do at the end of a notebook, but I can't help it.

[554] Forget all thoughts of a second or third book. Shoot the works on this one, including conceptual whatsits & all the rest of it. The Spirit will tell you what to read, and, if you leave it to him, when to read it.

[555] Two stitches dropped above: The chess game in *Hyp* [*Hypnerotomachia*], with its overtones of music & dance, suggests the dancing spirits on the palace floor in Yeats' *Byzantium*; the "pagan" episode the

Pan stage in Ash Wednesday. Also the detailed vision of buildings & "mathematic form" in *Hyp.*: cf. Yeats' *Statues.*

[556] To create is to identify the creature, & to identify is to extrude, to cut it away from its surroundings. Hence the creature is "fallen" or separated in the act of creation. Creation means a struggle with the unidentified surroundings, hence the idea of creation suggests wrath, the separation of light & darkness, in which the creature, separated equally from both light & darkness, is partly under the wrath. In the instant of incarnation, a kenosis [emptying] took place in which the Nomos-God vanished and the Father-Son relationship appeared. (This is my version of the "God is dead" notion). In the instant in which Christ was preserved from death the Thanatos world disappeared & the Son-Spirit relation took its place. The Holy Spirit *in time,* therefore, is the reborn elder brother, the Lucifer brought up from the depths.

[557] Query: do I have to take each quadrant through *all* the displacements, from myth to irony? If I start with myth & go on to literature via folk tale, it certainly looks that way. Thus the Adonis myth would start with the birth-of-hero stories, go on through romance to rupture-tragedy (Romeo & Juliet) & from there to *Green Henry* & other time-novels to Proust. The conceptual displacements can hardly be kept out of anything like this.

[558] Medieval literature, with its ruler-God imported from Aristotle, its life after death, & its minimizing of underworld symbolism, has the idealized, romantic quality of the upper half of the diagram. Could I dare to think that the sense of revolutionary Incarnation really entered the world with Luther, and, in literature, with Rabelais?

[559] Lapidaries, herbals & such catalogues belong in Eros because that's the world of named animals, where everything regains its original function and identity. I suppose Raphael's speech in Milton [*Paradise Lost*, bk. 5, ll. 469–505], prophesying the turning of bodies to spirit in an upward movement, is an Eros vision. *Hyp* [*Hypnerotomachia*] also has the Beatrice-Pearl theme of the woman loved on earth who reappears at the top of Eros. In fact *Hyp* is so remarkable an Eros vision that I wonder if Rabelais wasn't revisiting it in the key of Prometheus: certainly it's a connecting link between Dante & Rabelais. One of the gifts of the Spirit that I

definitely don't possess is the gift of tongues: if I had it I'd look up Merlin Cocci's *Baldus*.[450]

[560] I have an immense sense of release in finishing *The Critical Path*. The present book is one that I've wanted to write ever since finishing FS: it's older than the AC, which I thought was going to be it. But everything I've written since 1945 has been hacking away at underbrush, and I have a feeling that the last big clump of underbrush is now cleared away. Of course there are still unsolved problems: I still have to work out the right verbal formulas for the similarity-identity business. All religions are one, not alike; "that they may be one," not that they should all think alike: community means people thinking along similar lines & motivated by similar drives; communion means that all men are the same man. The Hegelian-Marxist "synthesis" is this identity projected as the end of a process, but that's illusory. These are of course only hunches, but the right formulas are there if I can find them. And identity is important because it's the key to the interpenetration climax.

[561] The central image of the Logos vision is the dance; of the Nous vision the symposium (including the New Testament upper room); of the Nomos vision the assembly (of gods, judges, Arthur's court) with a plaintiff (more rarely dependent) before it (Oresteia end; Job beginning); of the Thanatos vision the sibyl in the cave. Of course the court (or temple) of Venus is a common Eros setting; but love is a law too in the early stages. In the martyrdoms of Socrates & Jesus the Areopagus & the Sanhedrin of Nomos are in the background; they & their disciples are the Nous foreground. Of course these images can go anywhere: it's where their centre of gravity or "tonic" is that matters.

[562] The Narcissus complex I have: it appears in reverse sometimes (Davies' *Nosce Teipsum*)[451] as a kind of censor or self-blocking power, rather as original sin is conceived in Auden's *For the Time Being*. As such it's the archetype of the absurd.

[563] This is first of a series of books that I have wanted to start writing for at least thirty years, but I have had to spend most of my professional career cleaning away the underbrush to reach them. The underbrush is stacked and tied in bundles at the beginning, in the form of (no.) [numbered?] "postulates," that is, critical axioms or assumptions derived

from my earlier writings, which I had to try to establish before the present work could be intelligible . . . How many sequels to this book I shall be able to write I do not know, but it is obvious that the present volume is introductory only. It has the two qualities which most dismay my [written above previous word: some] readers: it is ahistorical, and it outlines a self-contained poetic universe. Literature does have an ahistorical & a self-contained aspect, though in this panic-stricken age there are many who do not wish to be told about them. Hence the present book is not necessarily wrong in its approach, but it is incomplete, which is hardly surprising.

[564] I should remember that my ogdoad consists of the home and seven steps of the Logos. Therefore the Logos takes the complete Logos vision with him to every stage, adapting it accordingly. That's where the "analogical" or mimetic displacements of apocalyptic and demonic imagery come in.

[565] I have to start, then, by thinking about creation myths. There are two kinds, as I've said, the natural & the artificial: the first descends from an earth-mother, the second from a sky-father. I've associated the latter with a tool-using, urbanized, patriarchal society: but there's more. A creation myth, as such, often takes the form of a cross-section cut into a continuum: there's already a society of gods, & for their amusement they created us—i.e., men & nature. But the idea of *a* creator, the absolute beginning, is projected from the *telos*, the latest development of man, the *individual* consciousness.

[566] As soon as the individual feels consciousness, objective nature springs into being. Creation and fall, in the sense of separation or alienation from the community, are thus the same thing. Adam naming the animals is the true form of creation. But nature, the thing lying there to be created, inspires guilt, and the nostalgia for a lost paradise, the community in origin, becomes correspondingly intense. The scriptural myth of absolute beginning survives in Genesis & Ovid; the cutting into a continuum survives in the *in medias res* beginning of epic.

[567] Concern pulls man back to his community, with which he associates God or his gods: the freedom that is to emerge from his contact with nature confronts him as something demonic. One must violate one's

mother (nature) & kill one's father (community) to be free; the only end of such freedom is death. This consolidates in the Nomos vision of a martyred son, a weeping mother, and an inscrutable & wrathful father.

[568] The Logos comes first: the Father is the (Nomos) product of the Logos vision. If this is the Sabellian heresy, the Sabellian heresy makes a lot of sense.[452] The individual as such is a Son: Father is a relative term, not discovered until the consciousness is conscious of itself. (The Son *as* Son, of course, is part of the Father idea, & so is co-eternal with the Father). The discovery of the self polarizes the world into a light community and a dark eternal individuality, Milton's Satan. To be aware of oneself, to be conscious, is to know death. I've already said [par. 391] that God condemns himself to death as soon as he becomes a Word and recognizes the light. Similarly in Shakespeare's MM [*Measure for Measure*] & the Alonso business in T [*The Tempest*]: the confronting of nothingness is the discovery of identity.

[569] So the stations of the Logos have to include the descent into Satan's kingdom of eternal individuality, which is also the kingdom of total alienation and isolation. It's here that the community is rediscovered: it's abandoned at Nomos and all through the Hermes descent, where Jesus is deserted by his disciples & Beowulf by his companions.[453] Thanatos is also the world of dream, where the skull is the circumference of reality. So, just as creation and fall are the same thing, so resurrection and the harrowing of hell are the same thing. We go through what Proust calls the mystery of annihilation and resurrection every night: to wake up is to recognize one's true naming from the context, to discover one's original identity, starting with the community.

[570] The discovery that all men are the same man is the point of Nous, the symposium disappearing into the wise man's mind and seeing there the pattern of the just state. Incidentally, Dante's Inferno is a reverse movement: Dante descends into a community and returns (except for Virgil) alone.

[571] In Joyce's *Ulysses* we have a Jewish father-figure, a Christian (so to speak) son-figure, a mother-wife-whore figure, and a spiritual visitant whose name suggests fire and water (Blazes Boylan). I think I see why HCE is Protestant: the descent into alienation is the real point of Protes-

tantism. Also, many great cultures have arisen from an invasion which split society into an ascendant & a subjected class, the latter producing most of the women, & their indigenous beliefs forming the dark half of the culture. Thus Egypt; thus India; thus the North, where Grimm's & Margaret Murray's reconstructions of the submerged cult merge.[454] So I see why HCE is associated with the English & Scandinavian invaders of Ireland: what I don't see is why Finnegan, the original husband of ALP, is Scandanavian too. Anyway, it's Finnegan who is deserted by his companions. I need the Two Brothers & the Bear's Son folktales for Hermes.[455]

[572] One of the freshest & most attractive poems in English of the Logos vision is Davies' *Orchestra*,[456] which is sung to Penelope by the chief of her suitors, Antinous. Why? Primarily because he wants to make the point that the weaving & unweaving of Penelope's web is one of the images of the dance of nature. But I wonder if there isn't also some feeling about the Odyssey as an unconscious prophecy of the stations of the Logos. The opposite end would be Ulysses on the island of Calypso, which is referred to in *Hyp* [*Hypnerotomachia*]. The vision of the cosmic dance is part of the Saturnalia of the absent master, whose coming stops the weaving.

[573] I arrive at the last page of this notebook on August 30, 1970. My mother & father[,] who were exactly the same age to a day[,] were born on August 30, 1870. My mother died in November of 1940, when Western culture entered the point of demonic epiphany.

[574] I think there is a historical projection of my diagram as far as Christianity is concerned. Medieval culture kept to the upper half, with a Nomos-God of Nature and an Eros "soul" leaving the body after death. Dante backs into hell the wrong way round & the underworld, being almost wholly demonized, was not seriously explored, unless there's more going on in the Percival legend than I've yet grasped. The miserable whimpering of *Everyman* is more typical. The final great plunge into the lower world occurred at the Reformation, with the great Prometheans Luther & Rabelais. (It would be interesting to compare the Protestant Boehme, who I think is a Hermes figure, with St. John of the Cross, who's restating, if reversing the customary direction, of Eros).

[575] Hermes doesn't really begin to open up, however, until the Ro-

mantics: Byron, Goethe's *Faust*, Shelley's Alastor figures, and the later French *symbolistes*. My present hunch is that Proust sums this up. Meanwhile the Promethean segment, which Blake had explored, developed into *Finnegans Wake*.

[576] Freud & Marx, in different ways, had mined other areas of Prometheus, the social & physical roots of the resurrection. The two met in 1940 as the West began to walk along the abyss of non-being, preserved from Nazi domination, Communist domination, oligarchical domination, & the total destruction of atomic war.

[577] I would hope to be able to contribute a vade mecum to the present journey through the valley of the shadow. *The Critical Path* (the significance of the title is greater than I realized) may be such a vade mecum, a small unpretentious book of some sanity and sequence. The present book, if I bring it off, may be much larger in scope than that—it will certainly be larger—and it may even become prophetic, a sacred book like the ones it studies.

[578] I say this, not to start swelling my head prematurely, but to indicate my willingness to try to do what may be expected of me, however grandiose & even paranoid it may sound at this stage, before I've written a line of it. If I think of it as something I shall write, I shall be too paralyzed with stage fright even to produce that first line. If I think of it as something that may get itself written where I am, I can at least stand and wait. All revelations have the problem of the stupid medium: my job is to try to be as transparent as possible while it struggles past me.

Notebook 24

Notebook 24 most likely dates from 1970–72. In some of the earlier entries, Frye struggles to decide how to focus the Birks Lectures, which he gave in October 1971 at the McGill Divinity School in Montreal. At some point, while continuing to use Notebook 24 as a place to develop the Third Book project, he spun off Notebook 21 as a place for ideas about the Birks Lectures and perhaps ultimately a whole book on religion; this is one of the earliest intimations of GC. By paragraph 230, the Birks Lectures are spoken of as in the past, and the final entries, contemplating a four-volume opus called The Critical Comedy, *closely parallel the description of that project in the "Work in Progress" Notes, so the notebook closes somewhere in 1972. Notebook 24 is in the NFF, 1991, box 25.*

[1] I suppose a good deal of this is material to be put in the "postulates" at the beginning, but still it may help here. Meaning is derived from context; for a work of literature there are two contexts, intentional discourse and literature as a whole. This duality is related to, & if not suggested by perhaps itself suggested, the distinction of content and form. For a myth there are similarly two contexts, the cultural or anthropological one, and the context within a mythology, which is structural or formal. Then comes the argument that literature descends from mythology.

[2] For anything with a history that history is part of the context which determines meaning. Hence the descent of a literary work from a mythical structure is part of its critical interpretation. For anything with a *telos* or direction of development that *telos* is similarly part of the context and the meaning. Many people have written on comparative mythology, fascinated by the resemblances in patterns, & most of the results are

pretty unconvincing, because their *telos* was either part of their own myth of concern (i.e. they "believed the Bible," or were certain that Xy as they understood it was the *telos* of myth) or the particular ideas or doctrines or moral lessons they most admired. The real *telos* of mythology is literature.

[3] Original myths are social and collective in reference, and so far as they are that, their *telos* is not literature but ritual. Ritual in turn expands into ritual habit, the *nomos* vision of predictable order which modulates from the [Bishop] Butler "analogy" of an unseen world to a totalitarian state. But the literary direction moves from the collective & anonymous to the individual, and that direction goes through the individually broken-off part of myth, the dream.

[4] We've heard a lot about the Promethean aspect of dream, its revolt against "reality" (i.e. ritual habit) in the name of wish-fulfilment. But primitive dreams are full of a sense of the perils of the soul, which may never get back to the body. The sense of guilt in breaking off from the group is always there, hence de Quincey's remark (which Joyce got, according to Budgen) that every dream recapitulates the fall of man.[1]

[5] Mythology begins with creation myths, and the primary creation myth, I should think, is the sexual or earth-mother one: the cycle of nature once started turning as it continues to do. The secondary or derived myth (of course it may not be that) is the sky-father artificial myth. This is in two stages. The first is the coming into consciousness of the individual. This is a withdrawal from existence: man ceases to be a function of his society and becomes a "subject." As a subject, he discovers nature or the objective world as something set over against him. The vision of nature is an *alienating* vision, a vision of what is *not* human. Conceptions of guilt, wrath & the certainty of death are bound up in it.

[6] In the Bible, the phrase "let there be light" shows how the artificial creation myth is projected from the sense of individual consciousness. In the older Babylonian story the *tehom* was Tiamat, a demonic monster to be killed, and with Xy this myth recurs.[2] The creation of light and the fall of Satan in the dark, the eternal or undying individuality or total alienation, are the same event, and, as I say elsewhere,[3] as soon as God speaks he condemns himself to death.

[7] There follows the act of creation itself. Creation becomes increasingly thought of as something the individual does. Concerned or social creation is done by the king or projected social individual (e.g. the Pyramids, "built by Pharaoh," a form of speech still recurring in modern dictatorships). I suppose the king represents individuality without guilt: he can do as he likes, but the ordinary citizen is relieved from the guilt of individuality by the king's existence. The other side of this, which makes the king a sacrificial victim, is Frazer's theme. The princes dig the well in the Book of Numbers.[4]

[8] To create is to transform consciousness, or identity as, into identity with. Creation is thus a raid into the world of the dark, part of a conquest, and its goal is total identity. Milton was right: creation is de Deo,[5] & the ex nihilo business is a pseudo-issue. Because the idea of divine creation is projected from human creation, that tohu-wa-bohu[6] co-eternal principle just won't go away. Anyway, to create is to identify with the creature: God is Man, Blake says, because he is the creator of Man, not because he is so perceived by man. Hence creation is the (voluntary) fall of God into death.

[9] The Creation hymn in Genesis is a cycle, not a sequence: as a sequence it makes no sense to create the trees before the sun. There are six days, but eight acts.[7] First, N, light appears, and the whole light-darkness dialectic of consciousness, half a loving Father and half a power of wrath and mystery, is established. Then, NW, the firmament or lower heaven appears, the Narcissus mirror through which the Logos descends. At W the land & sea, the elements of hearing, are separated; at SW the vegetable world, Blake's Hyle,[8] appears. I refer to Blake because you have to think of his "forests of space," "stems of vegetation," & "vegetable glass" to see why plant life appears here. Directly opposite the initial act of awareness, S, the lower lights of the cycle of nature are formed. At SE, the region of birds & frogs & the giants, the creatures of water & air, are formed, & at E the land animals. Still using Blake's terms, these are the gates barring Paradise, the Covering Cherub, Leviathan & Behemoth respectively. At NE there is man, the Narcissus image of God, & the Logos completes his work by reversing the Narcissus movement & bursting through to his original home. Then a return to the light, and rest.

[10] At this point the *Spirit* descends with a contrary movement, & man

turns round the other way. With consciousness comes the sense of man as lord of animals, a dominion given him by virtue of the power of naming them. As civilization advances, he extends into water & air: he even makes a successful raid on the moon. But he still has to harness his unconscious or vegetable powers.

[11] Every so often I get an itch to get a grip on what I think of as the Egyptian tradition in thought, the one that runs through Plato's *Timaeus*, Plutarch, the Alexandrian neo-Platonists, the Hermetic literature, & so on. The Egyptians kept the descent to the mother open. The hieroglyphic is one of the cipher-images in deep Hermes.

[12] Another is the macaronic language. Rabelais, whose Panurge is so polyglottal, is close to the macaronic tradition, though his sources, Colonna's *Hyp* [*Hypnerotomachia*][9] & Folengo's (Merlin Coccai) *Baldus*[10] are closer to it, as is in fact his translator Urquhart. The remark in LLL [*Love's Labour's Lost*] about stealing the scraps from a feast of languages [5.1.40] is made mainly about Holofernes, whose name is the one link between Shakespeare & Rabelais (I'm not counting "Gargantua's mouth" in AYL [*As You Like It*, 3.2.38–9]). Also in *The Waste Land* & *FW* [*Finnegans Wake*], where it's closer to verbal sparagmos (Hieronimo's play in Kyd's Sp. Tr. [*The Spanish Tragedy*] is another link with the former).[11] Too bad that in the late 15th c. English poetry had things like Stephen Hawes,[12] who's macaronic in reverse, English conceptualized with Latin for solemn moral purposes, instead of, as in *Baldus*, Latin undercut with Italian for satiric purposes.

[13] Aristotle's comparison of discursive & poetic writing with syllogism & enthymeme[13] is precisely the distinction Valéry makes between walking & dancing, instrumental & disinterested writing. Or rather, the first *is* writing, progressive & sequential movement; the second is the metaphorical leap. That's how I can speak of philosophy as a conceptual displacement of poetry. Cowley says of Pindar's odes that they consist more in digressions than in the main subject:[14] as in *Lycidas*, these digressions are the mythical archetypes of the subject,[15] which tend to disappear in purely sequential writing. In philosophy & science, dominated as it is by the chain of being, there is an abhorrence of the missing link: everything must proceed by gradations.

[14] After I get some grip on this "Egyptian" cosmology I shall go back to reading about contracts & Utopias. One easy inference from CP is that these myths occur in the personal life. One's contract is one's social context, which includes the beliefs, or myth of concern, in which one has been brought up. This occupies the Nomos vision, the community of the alike, founded on the conception of analogy (I need Hooker, Butler, Burke & Newman for this as well as Hobbes or Locke).

[15] Opposite is the Nous point of identity or communion of the same. Hence the axis of Nomos & Nous is the quest for identity, moving from likeness to sameness. As I say, the Utopia which hovers around Nous is an allegory of the identified individual. It's symbolized by the Platonic symposium & the Christian communion supper (or perhaps the Agape love-feast), baptism & the eucharist being defined by Blake as the formation of the appropriate society. But the real focus is the identity of risen man: the real form of Nomos is the identity of the Christian "Adam." The core of tragedy is this form of identity, the individual defined only by his social function.

[16] The conventional or traditional hope of immortality is that of the indefinite survival of the *individual* within the risen body of Man. All our individualized virtues, at least, are the result of a private myth of identity. We are only honest, e.g., if we are *consistently* honest, if it forms part of an identity we build up in life. The hope for immortality is a *projection* of this identity. The private myth or visionary model necessarily has both social & individual aspects.

[17] At present Xy wanders between two worlds, a resurrection in the past and another in the future. The everlasting Gospel of the Spirit would anchor it in the present. Our private myth of identity, which makes an honest man honest, a martyr stubborn, an artist creative, & so on, is the gift of the Spirit[,] the use of which is the faith that justifies us, & the non-use of which is the essential sin of self-denial, in a literal sense, which forgiveness cannot reach. The myth of identity is really the integrating of individual consciousness, the first stage toward freedom and away from mere acceptance of contract & environment.

[18] Proust says of Elstir that he painted the original act of vision, before

it became habitual through repetition and so assimilated by memory into our "regular" perceptions (i.e. regulated).[16] This is exactly the function of poetry as defined by Shelley. Proust even uses the figure of Ovidian metamorphosis to illustrate this subsiding of a "god" into an object. The original perception may not be pleasant: for Marcel a new room to sleep in is generally hostile.

[19] The implications of this are immense: the feeling of a paradisal spontaneous first act or perception buried underneath the habits & compulsions that instantly take it over runs all through experience. I used to connect it with the Tibetan Book of the Dead, & its doctrine of the flash of recognition of eternity that comes at the instant of death, & which everybody misses.[17] Of course it's also the still point of Eliot & so on. Joyce's FW [*Finnegans Wake*] suggests that dream also has something to do with reversing the current of habit & bringing us back each morning to the place where we might find that instant again.

[20] One application of this principle is in the history of science. The speculative cosmology in Browne, Kepler, Berkeley, even Newton, is partly "obsolete" science & partly too a large complex response which science cuts down in its progress & assimilates to its own "habit" or memory. But these other elements still remain, & it's part of my job to show their "relevance."

[21] Another application, which is what I'm reading Proust for, is to the theme of Adonis descent from a state of innocence, where our primal or paradisal ideas are corrupted by sense. The Eros climb, on its intellectual side, tries to reverse this & get back to the primary innocent light.

[22] My principle that linear participation is followed by a simultaneous apprehension should be extended to thought. Writing helps to bring in the sense of insensible gradations, the chain of being, space as a plenum, a step by step movement through argument corresponding to a similar advance in nature. One could trace back this sense of significant sequence to the processional hieroglyphics on Egyptian monuments. The Eros ladder or staircase (Osiris is the god at the top of the staircase)[18] is a modification of this: here the sequence is "upwards," and backwards in time to the original moment. This latter is the preternatural paradisal experience of which simultaneous comprehension is the analogy.

[23] Now: just as the first response, or participation, is a sequential progress toward a goal (note the lockstep of the *terza rima* in Dante), so the second response is integration, or seeing all the steps as parts of a whole. For the Eros sequence, the second response is encyclopedic, an intuition of unity or oneness. This is why there's such a drive toward encyclopedic synthesis in the concern-myths of writing ages. This is just my old notion that the dianoia *is* the mythos conceived as a unity. The second response is circumferential, the circuit of the Logos having returned to the original point: there's a third response involving a centre & a conception of interpenetration which I haven't yet got.

[24] Eros symbolism is normally hierarchical, and goes from body & sense up to mind. There's a rough political analogy, as in Plato, among: God-king-brain; Forms-aristocracy-intelligence (I mean mind rather than brain above). It's a tradition with many teasing analogies to Blake; but Blake is Prometheus, not Eros: the resurrection of the body & the Eros ascent as the last act of a human Logos, is his point. This means that the form of the Eros quest which ends in sexual consummation is hard to distinguish from Prometheus. Thus we might think of Jean de Meun as adding the Promethean ground bass to William de Lorris;[19] similarly perhaps Yeats as compared with Eliot. I suppose the ultimate quest possesses the Virgin Mother & disposes of the Father.

[25] Myth seems to me to occupy a position similar to that of the law in Christian theology. One aspect of it is emancipated by being fulfilled in the gospel of literature, where belief is similarly emancipated into imagination. Another aspect is that of belief which becomes so fixed that it controls a strategic area of action. This is ritual, or action expressing an unchangeable belief. Ritual is an analogy of art which gradually becomes a demonic analogy in proportion as it takes over the rest of life. It's part of the analogical Nomos vision, the assimilation of life into the predictable which can only be kept going by the donkey's carrot of a "future" life, whether Christian or Marxist in reference.

[26] Consequently, in studying any major convention or genre of literature, it is always useful to look at the ritual analogy: the Adonis lament in the elegy, the Olympian games in the Pindaric ode, *komos* in comedy, & so on. The twisting of this into a pseudo-historical conception of source & derivation I have already attacked in AC. The mass is not a "work of

art": the use of the contact senses of smell & taste shows that it's ritual, an analogy of art, capable of repetition but not of recreation. As repetition, it's memorial, and as memorial it's a starting-point of recreation.

[27] The "ideal" state of affairs (i.e., the upper semicircle with the axis of Nomos and Nous at its base) is founded on the Nomos vision of social conformity: everybody thinks alike, because belief is manifested by action, & everybody is united in the same ritual acts. From this the individual breaks off by means of epopteia,[20] vision revealed to the individual within the context of mystery. Hence initiation is the culmination of ritual, & mysticism its end product. The great Western mystics, at least, have arisen in periods of intense & repressive social conformity (e.g. St. John of the Cross).

[28] Such an attitude is hierarchical, founded on the Nomos sacramental analogy. The mover is superior to the moved, which *imitates* the mover, the conception of mimesis being fundamental to Nomos. The cause is superior to the effects: knowledge of effects, gained through sense experience, is not real knowledge, which latter is knowledge of things by their causes. Hence the brain is superior to the "merely physical" aspects of the body.

[29] Idealism is connected by Marx with the ascendancy of a ruling class: it should also be connected psychologically with a resistance to the sexual and the excretory. Middle-class women who go in for soulful religions and uplifting thoughts are idealistic in this sense. The idea of dirt is inseparable from (a) shit (b) whatever is thought of as "lower," in whatever context. Anyway, I'm working toward my next hunch, which is that there are two ways of getting from Nomos to Nous. The real way is around by Thanatos; there's the more direct but incomplete way just mentioned.

[30] In the Nomos vision death, being inevitable, is the most legal of all laws: the direct passage from Nomos to Nous involves two forms of death. One is a *mimesis thanatos*, or ritual death. This is the dying to the world of ascetics, the *via negativa* of the mystics, St. John's dark night, Eliot's way of vacancy. The other is actual death conceived as a prelude to an "after" life, which is perhaps ultimately a vision of rebirth rather than resurrection, & is in any case nearly always thought of as a separa-

tion of soul from body. In both cases, this point of death occupies the *centre* of my diagram, the "heart" of the world.

[31] But it isn't what I mean by the real Thanatos vision, which follows the Logos to the world explored by Rimbaud, Goethe, Rabelais, Joyce, Swift: the world of irony and satire, of the sources of human "pollution," shit & corruption, sex in all its sado-masochistic disguises & deviations, & isolation, not the isolation of solitude but the isolation *from* an alien society & nature. This is the world of Job & King Lear & Oedipus: in the Gospel narrative the descent into it takes place *after* the Crucifixion, but of course the Crucifixion is what it was the culmination of[,] what Blake calls the Deist or Druid vision.

[32] Hence it's utter nonsense for Eliot to say that the dark night is *lower* than the world of the subway. The Quartets have only a purgatorial world, & the world of *The Waste Land* & *The Hollow Men* is far lower than anything they reach. Blake is closer when he says that the *loins* are the place of the Last Judgment, & Yeats when he speaks of the foul rag & bone shop of the heart. *Measure for Measure* is, if I'm right about it, Shakespeare's "heart" play, with the Duke-as-Friar its Hermes psychopomp. I have a notion too that when Thanatos is really explored it turns out not to be there, & that Lear & Oedipus & Job are reunited with their daughters or young-fates.

[33] Anyway, institutional Xy seems to me to have given a revy. [revolutionary] form to the "Egyptian" tradition, reversing the everlasting Gospel into a peculiar one. It seems to me that in that context it's mystery religion gone berserk, just as institutional Marxism, founded like capitalism on the conception of productivity, is capitalism gone berserk. The dreadful subversiveness of the real descent to hell it just can't take.

[34] Previously I've felt that there was no centre because every point on the circumference is the centre. But perhaps there is a *provisional* centre, Eliot's still point, a moment of consciousness where we project our own sense of timelessness *and* time into a "heaven" above and a "hell" below. This is the moment of definitive experience we don't really get but keep revolving around. Perhaps what I'm doing in the above is incorporating my apocalyptic & demonic worlds into the cycle: I've always thought of them as outside the cycle, because of the undisplaced imagery. Inciden-

tally, the association of Thoth-Hermes with *writing* [in Plato's *Phaedrus*] is parallel to my hunch that it takes literature to explore Thanatos. Luther, Marx, & Freud explored it, but as lawgivers they couldn't take it either, though as visionaries they released greater forces.

[35] I understand the new critics' insistence on texture as against structure because they're haunted by the evaluation spectre. Dussek & Beethoven both wrote in the sonata form, & their structures are much alike: Beethoven's superiority is in his texture, which a critic by explicating can "demonstrate."[21]

[36] In Kierkegaard's *Either-Or* there's a brilliant analysis of a Scribe comedy. Obviously the play is just a meccano-set contraption, though with considerable practical theatrical experience behind it. K. [Kierkegaard] makes it sound like late Henry James. Well, maybe he "reads more into it than is there." This is illiterate nonsense: if he quotes the play as saying something it doesn't say, that's another matter, but who the hell can say "what" "is" "there"? The opposite inference is that Scribe is a challenge to the critic, whereas HJ [Henry James] forces them to comment on the obvious. A comparison of the amount of criticism on HJ & on Scribe will lead either to a very melancholy inference about critics or to a suspicion that something is wrong with that suggestion. Or, more likely, to both.

[37] What is really exciting is the possibility that the convention itself says something. This after all, is precisely what Shakespeare demonstrated about *Pandosto* or *Promos & Cassandra* or Lodge's *Rosalind*: not his superiority but the solidity of his foundation. And a complete criticism of Shakespeare would demonstrate that along with the texture. We're still blinkered by private property & competition metaphors about such things. That's why it's wrong to regard the source as irrelevant to the criticism of Shakespeare.

[38] I should try out, perhaps in the Birks lectures, my notion that Xy was the definitive revy. [revolutionary] form of the Hellenistic religion. The Incarnation was its solution of the Eros problem of how man can get in touch with God. Without the Incarnation, the only possible answer is "through wisdom" (which includes initiation). This was the "counter-revy." [counter-revolutionary] answer, which meant among

other things that the whole Sophia-myth got squeezed out of Xy. The Xn myth however can't stop with the Resurrection, or God from the rock myth: it has to have the Ascension to keep from becoming a mere humanism. But nevertheless the Incarnation was also a kenosis: it emptied the sky, even though it took, as Blake shows in *Europe*, 18 centuries to realize it.

[39] The first revy. [revolutionary] element in Xy was anchoring the descent of the God in history; the second was its "realistic" view of man, who was a mudball animated by God, not a Titanic being falling through seven planetary spheres. The third was its social realism in associating the death of its god with criminals & outcasts—a proletariat. These features establish the axis of Nomos & Nous: man is born earthbound, & his contract starts there: yet the contract has to be scrapped as the man it rejected rises again.

[40] These three revy. [revolutionary] characteristics, in a way I'm not clear about, express themselves in practical social organization. Xy is not anti-intellectual, nor did it prefer unintelligent leaders: but it did renounce individual speculative wisdom as a goal: it put speculative limits to the intelligence which forced it outwards into a reduplication of temporal authority. The apostles developed into bishops, not into gurus or teachers of illumination.

[41] Maybe my provisional centre is simply the cycle of revolution and ascendancy. Its basis is justification by faith, or adhering to a myth of concern. The individual may escape from it by some kind of gnosis, where the nomos analogy, of higher law obeyed by imitation, has become ideal, a conviction of the superiority of the invisible to the visible.

[42] Or perhaps my turning-on-side hunch[22] means that there is a series of stations on the road from Nomos to Nous, proceeding from the community of similarity to the communion of identity. Various contract myths & sacramental analogies & conservative rationalizations hover around the "west"; revolutionary & Utopian attitudes are "east": the Miltonic view of the free individual as containing the law is further "east," until finally, *at* the "east," we join up with a power that's gone around by the "south" & come up again. This power has to be conceived as an imagination that's explored the whole Thanatos semicircle.

[43] Dante doesn't really go all the way, because the dark world isn't wholly demonic. Just as Satan shits Dante, so Dante shits Satan, arriving at the foot of Purgatory without bringing anything from below, & one with the Eros "souls" who haven't any bodies. Treatments of the point of Nous epiphany include the terrible parody of Beckett's *Malone Dies* and D.H. Lawrence's *Man Who Died*.[23]

[44] It is possible that I ought to write two short books articulating the skeletons of what may be Books I & II[24] when combined with documentation from literary imagery. The first book, which could conceivably be the Birks Lectures, would be on the three awarenesses of religion,[25] that of the light-dark dialectic of the Father, of the journey of the Logos through the seven creative stages, and of the decentralized interpenetration of the Spirit. Caution: don't say "solving the problem of," which is projection: say "finding the verbal formulas for."

[45] The second one would then be the progress of human freedom through contracts & Utopias: from the community of the alike at Nomos to the communion in the same at Nous. If there were a third one, I'd have the plan of my Commedia, which may be 36-28-36 in its dimensions.[26] Perhaps the circle of topoi is really just a Father-book, the Logos coming into its own in the Nomos-Nous axis. Note that we need not only the progress up from Thanatos but the original descent from Logos for the second stage.

[46] As for the third volume, that would have to be a monadology of some kind. It would establish one work, or group of works, as a centre of experience, the search for the centre being its main theme. My encyclopedic commentary on *The Phoenix & the Turtle* would be one possible type of it, or a series on my favorite "centre" poems, *Milton*, *P.R.* [*Paradise Regained*], *T* [*The Tempest*].[27] In older Xy the conception of "person" was the decentralizing conception: Leibnitz' is a demonic or Nomos monadology,[28] based on substance, harmony, and man as simply rational creature.

[47] I've just read Glanvill's *Vanity of Dogmatizing*,[29] which in itself is a wise and sane book. Unfortunately he takes his main thesis in a "holiday" direction: if our knowledge is uncertain, a lot of things may be possible that a closed system denies. So he goes off on considering

sympathetic magic, telepathic action & communication, & so on: I call it unfortunate because its later product was a desperate defence of witch-craft.* He thinks the *anima mundi* is possibly the best "explanation" for sympathetic magic.

[48] The first volume[30] establishes the vertical line of a cross, the dialectic of light & darkness. The second establishes the horizontal line. A circle, which however does not *enclose* the cross, also appears. The third book, which radiates from a centre & demonstrates that every work of literature is a circle whose centre is anywhere & circumference nowhere, may possibly have an X-shaped cross at its basis: in other words it may deal with the four cardinals as conceptual displacements rather than with the quadrants. It is not impossible that the form of the fourth would then appear, forming a 28-22-28-22 tetralogy,[31] and returning to the quadrants.

[49] In the Hermetic tradition the starting point is the Virgin Birth of the Logos in the human "heart," which of course is also Milton's Word of God in the heart. The Gospel myth may be a projection of this: I don't want to remain content with a psychological or subjective reality, but, just as Xy seems to me the revy. [revolutionary] form of the whole "Full Moon in March" religious impulse,[32] so the imgn. [imagination] seems to me the revy. [revolutionary] form of the nature-reason truth, which is always a Nomos vision, hierarchical, analogical, & *purely* concerned.

[50] So I have, after all, reversed my original idea. The N-S axis, founded on the light-dark, life-death dialectic, is the axis of speculation:[33] it is in fact the great chain of being. As that, it's the ultimate source of *all* hierarchies: those of society, of philosophy (cause above effect, reason above sense, form above matter, etc.), of psychology. Whenever man is defined as reasoning or conscious, we get this hierarchy. Its root is the dialectic of duality, the analogical or sacramental conception of life.

[51] I'm not sure whether the N-S axis belongs in L or not: perhaps the three books are simply circle, cross & spiral. In any case, the axis of

---

* I mean of the belief in it, of course. Here, as in Yeats, the analogy between magic and poetry is considered in its aspect of occult vs. imgve. [imaginative] *communication*.

concern runs W-E,[34] & the book dealing with [it] is the ladder of human freedom. By is I meant was. Judaism was the revy. [revolutionary] form of ancient religion, Xy of the Mediterranean second religiousness; in our day the elements of a third religion are scattered through democracy, Marxism, the sexual revolution, & the replacing of reason by imagination which is the essential cultural revolution. I daresay in the course of this the three groupings of son-mother, brother-sister, father-daughter, will disclose themselves as elements. The climax has to be Resurrection, which so far as I can see now means having to go through Xy, but of course the everlasting gospel that it brings to light is less exclusive.

[52] That's ℸ [tragicomedy], I think: perhaps Λ [Anticlimax] might be a double gyre based on a commentary on two works, widely removed in language, culture, time & space. Commentary on A expands outward to the circumference of the verbal universe, at the heart of which we discover work B; then commentary on that expands to another vision of the v.u. [verbal universe], at the centre of which is work A.

[53] I suppose though that the real Nomos radical is not simply the analogical vision, but the supremacy of the one over the many which produces kingship in society, monotheism in religion, monism in philosophy, the idea of the "uni-verse" in science, & the dialectic of the same & the other, identity & alienation. Only the everlasting gospel of interpenetration can resolve this tension.

[54] If one believes that the soul is *by nature* immortal, with Plato, a doctrine of hell seems logical, because after death an immortal soul would go into the state it had itself created, or helped to create. But if man is mortal by nature, & is made immortal only by the power of the Word of God, then hell implies a supreme maliciousness in Jesus, who raises people from the dead simply to stick them in hell. The dumbest person can see that he should of left them lay.[35]

[55] I have always held that when will is informed by a vision the antithesis between free will & compulsion of the will disappears. I suppose the idea of unconditioned will comes from ascribing such a will to God, who is thought of as not having a will subjected to a vision. (The vision is always ascribed to something that comes later in order, such as the Son or Spirit). So the idea of unconditioned will is a kind of projection

in reverse. It makes an infinite ego out of God, the eternal childishness that says "I want," & don't dare ask why.

[56] The contrast of one & reason as hierarchical against many and imagination as equal is pure Blake on generalizing & minute particulars, and there's nothing new as such in it. But the evolution from the regressive Nomos, the individual projected from the alike, to the progressive Nous, the individual incarnating the same, needs some essential links—I still don't know why individuality also means *total* identity.

[57] I can't get rid of the chapter unit, & shouldn't try. Twelve chapters, in three sections each. Part One: The Symbolic Universe. Chapter One: The Myth of Creation. Chapter Two: The Myth of the Quest. Part Two: The Circle of Images. Chapters Three to Ten, going around the Ogdoad & starting (as I now think) with Logos (traditional). Part Three: The Renewal of Vision. Chapter Eleven: The Myth of Apocalypse. Chapter Twelve: The Myth of Interpenetration (if it is a myth: there ought to be at least one thing in a new book I know balls-all about). One sets & Eleven completes the dialectic of light & darkness.

[58] The first chapter will have to be one of my "brilliant" efforts, a survey of creation myths which gradually separates into an up & a down, light & darkness, a sky-father & an earth-mother, an artificial & a sexual myth of origin. The varieties of this ranging from deifying the cosmos (Cicero & the Stoics) to diabolizing it (the Gnostics). The return of Gnosticism in the Romantic period.

[59] The important sub-myth of the buried fire comes into this. There are usually sparks buried in the darkness, or a diffused fire or heat which is the *anima mundi* or life principle of the dark world. This is why Promethean fire is always stolen, I think, & why the final consummation is a burning. The tradition runs from Heraclitus through the Stoics & Hermetics (including the alchemists) and is still going strong in Berkeley's *Siris*. Alchemy is included because gold is often a symbol of buried fire.

[60] Chapter Two is on the Great Doodle, summarizing the Joseph Campbell theme of the life, death & resurrection of the hero.[36] It should discriminate among the dying-god myths, the centre of gravity being different for Osiris, Adonis & Dionysus. Things like Blake's MT [*The*

Mental Traveller] come in to[o], as well as a restatement of my cyclical-epic points. Mysterious return as the suppression of Prometheus.

[61] Three is on the Logos vision, both in its traditional form (St. Thomas, the Paradiso; later poems like *Orchestra*[37] & the Mut. Coes. [*Mutabilitie Cantos*]). Literary cosmology: Poe's *Eureka* for the modern version. Sylvester's Du Bartas,[38] Palingenius' Zodiac,[39] & medieval poems like the Cursor Mundi,[40] either here or one [chapter 1]. Reincarnation as a poetic theme: the contrast of cycle & separation, the theme of Eleven, perhaps anticipated.

[62] Four, on Adonis, I have least grasp of at the moment, though I know about the fall-from-innocence Vaughan-Traherne-Dylan Thomas themes, John Barleycorn,[41] *Paradise Lost* as the Adonis epic, Tennyson, etc. Virgil, I should think: certainly the elegy & the Adonis lament. Adonis ends in the Nomos vision, which has two sides: the young man crushed by it & the old man settling into it.

[63] Five, on Nomos, outlines the sacramental analogy & studies the Oresteia. Incidentally, I'm thinking of alternating chapter titles: "The Imagery of Adonis," & "The Nomos Vision" being the pattern for the quadrants & cardinals respectively. That means I can put my "conceptual displacements" into the cardinal chapters.

[64] For Six, on Hermes, I have the labyrinth & the descent to the bowels of the monster; the clock & the mirror; the double, twin, tanist,[42] demonic & angelic companions; the stripping away of everything not part of one's identity; the journey into the future; the ouroboros[43] circle of returning to the knowledge of the sin of birth. Oedipus, Lear, Job, & very probably Kafka & Dostoievsky's idiot; Conrad's *Heart of Darkness*, *The Waste Land*, Aeneid VI.

[65] I haven't much for Thanatos, Seven, as yet distinct from the two quadrants. There's the double focus again of the utter peace of death & the nightmare of hell: the paradox of total alienation and of the *formillante cité*:[44] the parody of the Logos light in the vision of anguish of the pure detached consciousness: the Tithonus-Struldbrug motif[45] & its logical complement: the soul which is immortal by nature can't die.

[66] Prometheus symbolism for Eight comes mostly out of Rabelais. It begins in the oracular message, the deciphered code, the "symbol-essences" of *Endymion*[46] concealed in the scraps of languages. This in turn is connected with divination, the coup de Dés,[47] the game of chess in the lower world.[48] Cannibal giants, the paradox of stupid power & articulate intelligence, anal imagery, Dante shat out of Satan, the piss-floods in Rabelais, all belong—Birds & Frogs. Ariel & Caliban. The soul & the sleeping body vs. the rising body.

[67] FW [*Finnegans Wake*] belongs here, along with most of Blake—or at least the MHH [*The Marriage of Heaven & Hell*] & *Europe* Blake. Some Lawrence. Harrowing of Hell, & the contrast of Rabelais breakthrough to Nous & Quixote's return to illusion (though of course qualified). I don't yet know why I think Valéry's *Jeune Parque* belongs here & represents a major Promethean theme: the homunculus theme, in Goethe & by implication in Rabelais, is clearer.

[68] The *jeune parque* hunch has to be examined later: meanwhile, other things are getting clearer. Goethe's *Faust* is, as I thought, a Hermes descent in the Gnostic tradition (cf. Simon Magus's Helena & his name of Faustus).[49] So is *The Scarlet Letter* (cf. the name Pearl). The theme of buried sparks is a favorite one of Hopkins, & helps place him in Prometheus (kingfishers, the windhover, the Heraclitean fire: cf. the birds & frogs archetype).

[69] Nous is the one category that I don't think I've named properly. Its radical is resurrection, the identical body of the sun that has set turning up again. The space in which it turns up is Blake's Enitharmon, & a lot of city & garden images surround it. The risen *body* is important—I've mentioned Lawrence's *Man Who Died* [par. 43]. The symposium group around Christ *and* Socrates, and so on: I have to get it unsnarled from the climax of my next book.

[70] The word "reality" should not mean statically a certain form of what is perceived, but dynamically a quantum, a certain charge or energy of perception—in practice, I suppose, the minimum consistent with consciousness. Any change of perception over that contains an element which is unreal in some contexts and a greater reality in others. As

unreal, it's generally called subjective, or perhaps emotional, or sometimes imaginary; as more real, it's imaginative or creative.

[71] This is pure Blake—I'll never get out of that framework, I suppose—also Shelley's doctrine of poetry as the overcoming of the inertia of habit.[50] (Whether Wiener's formula that communication overcomes entropy[51] is anything more than a vulgarization of this I don't know). Anyway. I got to this, as usual, through the back door: remembering that very unpleasant book, the *Story of O*,[52] it seemed to me that no actual woman's body could bear that charge of fetishism: it's only in fantasy that all that flogging & branding & chaining could exist as an experience with its own kind of reality.

[72] Creatively, of course, the surcharge of reality takes the hallucinatory form of Van Gogh's sunflowers. *That* kind of excess is acceptable as *potentially* real; but the question remains unsolved: to what extent, & in what sense, is it actually there? Probably if I knew that I'd know too much to want to write books. However, the objective world is only "material": it's there, but it could be there in a great many different forms and aspects. I suppose even here there [are] still possibilities: it can't be just anything. But perhaps extracting a finite schema from the variety of mythologies, literatures, & religions might contribute something to the understanding of what some of these possibilities could be. The individual can't create his own world, except in art or fantasy: society can only create a myth of concern. What fun if one could get just a peep at what some of the other worlds are that a new humanity could create—no, live in.

[73] If I could arrive at a suggestion about that the *commedia* would have four parts after all: an Ulro of images on a cave wall, a Generation of the attainment of freedom, a Beulah scherzo of fourteen sections taking me to 78, the Tarot number & a favorite of the Rabelais,[53] & then a Last Twilight of 22, in which the different languages of the arts (V [Mirage]) might suggest a way of climbing up Babel again. The scherzo might not only deal with but be the chess in Bardo problem: the opposed forces each with its own centre. I talk as though I were about seventeen years old: actually I feel more like a bull in a ring, learning fast but therefore soon to die.

[74] I have already defined coincidence as unusable design. Inconsistency seems to me to be verbal discontinuity: I mean of course logical or

verbal inconsistency. Critic A, working on thinker J, says idea X is inconsistent with idea Y. Critic B says it may not be after all: this means that J hasn't provided the connecting verbal formulas PQR that make X & Y consistent, but that he can. Verbally, everything is potentially consistent with everything else: in written language, & thought derived from it, there are no missing links anywhere. Inconsistency of action, being a coward one day & a hero the next, can never be patched up, though again on a verbal plane it may be "accounted for."

[75] The shape of the second book may be like a plot: first the Nomos vision as one of uniformity which *must* have a scapegoat to squeeze out. Ultimately there is only one possible scapegoat, of which all actual ones are symbols, & that one is the rejected stone that becomes the head of the Nous corner. Further, when he's squeezed out, there's only one place for him to go, & that's round by the S. He reappears in the revolutionary chaos near Nous, trampling the winepress . . . There really isn't much to distinguish my writing from an obsessional neurosis like that of Norma or Henry Rowland,[54] & I should stop fussing about the resemblances. I just happen to have something, that's all.

[76] Proust's remark about Elstir's painting of the first vision or perception before habit takes over: of course it isn't necessarily the first vision, any more than the Edenic state of innocence is necessarily the condition of the baby.[55] It's a potential perception which gets liberated by the arts, & it may not be there at all, though with normally sensitive people there's usually more of it in first impressions, where there's still some strangeness in them. The trouble is that habit takes over the arts too, & they can become only conventional guides to experience—not that that's their fault.

[77] I want to start with my horizon opening, but I should also consider the possibility of (1) Typology of the Bible, which could be published separately (2) Typology of Classical myth (3) The four-level world & the cycle (4) The Romantic world. Easier to do, but more repetitive.

[78] The world of time provides analogies. Rev. xi: 8:[56] historically there are cities, Egypt, Sodom, Jerusalem, with certain likenesses. "Spiritually" (pneumatikos), which certainly includes the idea of symbolically, they are seen metaphorically, as identities of the demonic city. Similarly,

Proust sees his people as young & in the last book as aged: he has difficulty in seeing the likeness to their younger selves. But he sees them metaphorically as giants in time.

[79] Descent patterns: the thunderclap, or sound that focuses attention, is in FW [*Finnegans Wake*] (from Vico), at the end of *The Waste Land*, and in a vestigial form in certain sounds in *Le Temps Retrouvé*. The effect of thunder is to focus attention on the sky, & so to separate the overworld & underworld (giants crawl into caves). The oracular response of the lower world is always in the context of repetition or cycle—the same anew. In Proust it's the world recreated by repetition out of the "lost time" which is its analogy in experience. In Proust the stupid giants are the habit-lives of his characters: they recur, in a non-gigantic form, in Beckett's clowns.

[80] Naturally the Jack-the-giant-killer theme is a Prometheus archetype: David & Goliath & its ramifications in guerrilla warfare today. I wonder what connexion the skyscraper has with the stupid giant. It would make an effective conclusion if I could wind up the book with a kind of organized LSD trip: a walk through the contemporary world like the one the film on me indicated.[57] A supermarket, for instance, is a shoddy symbol of an embryonic paradise: one wanders at will gathering food off the shelves, then departs by the turnstile of birth.

[81] One of the symbols of the point of demonic epiphany is the facing of death with a reprieve. MM [*Measure for Measure*] of course: it's also a normal crisis in a thriller. But Dostoievsky actually did experience it in his life,[58] which is what helps to give *The Idiot* such terrific power. Lazarus & Jesus actually go through death. Browning makes a very creditable effort to examine Lazarus' state of mind, but of course hasn't the intensity of Dostoievsky. Besides, his mind is on other things: whether the all-great is the all-loving too, & similar horseshit—he should have kept his mind on his subject.

[82] I hoped to find Adonis symbolism in Proust, & perhaps there is some, but he's more romance than anything else, with a most ingenious modulation of the romance endless form. He brings it around into a circle, the end of the life being the beginning of the writing, so that a commentator on him is bound to start with the end of the book. At the same time this end-beginning is also a cognitio, almost of an upper Eros,

or pulling oneself out of the mirror, type. Or maybe it's upper Promethean, emancipation *by means of* the cycle, as in FW [*Finnegans Wake*]. Speaking of Adonis symbols, Milton's haemony means the bloody flower (αἱμα [αἵμα]).[59]

[83] Check Plato's *Timaeus* for the distinction of the cycle of the same (east to west) & the cycle of the other (west to east).[60] Also Blake's developments of this in J [*Jerusalem*].[61] The idea of the open-ended beginning with the Bible attracts me, first, because I could start writing on it at any time; second, because it would be relatively easy to rearrange the material if a more effective order presented itself; third, it might suggest ways of shaking off the tyranny of that one circle.

[84] I've read Velikovsky's book,[62] which is much more convincing than I thought it was going to be, even granting that he proves far too much. Naturally he's deterministic: myth is an effect, for him, following a natural event as its cause. He perhaps underrates the absorptive power of mythical language. It's another aspect of my point that there's no such thing as a constellation.

[85] What he suggests is the importance of a demonic Logos vision: synod unbenign, running from Plato's *Statesman* through Chaucer to Blake's *Europe*. Creation, according to Blake & Shelley, overcomes the inertia of habit. Habit is founded on the security of predictability, the promise *after* the flood. But what if the last three lines of the Introduction to the SE [*Songs of Experience*] are wrong? What if part of the broken-off infinite human is destructive?

[86] Well: a demonic Logos vision is merely the divine-spiritual end of the chain of being having a demonic as well as an apocalyptic side. Nothing new there. But I do have to begin with my Descartes-Crusoe reduction & see emerging from it the primitive root of the *Timaeus* conception of *two* cycles:[63] the light-cycle of the same and the darkness-cycle of the different. Plato says they revolve in opposite directions, a point partly concealed by my uniform diagram. The question is one of tactics & sequence: can I really work it out with two cycles, one descending & the other ascending to identity? I doubt it.

[87] Eliade says in primitive societies everything is a later imitation of an

archetype existing *in illo tempore*.[64] That's west: the Eliot waste land sense of the slipping away of time, knowledge as recollection. The essential S oracle must be the transformation of this into repetition. This connects with one of my biggest themes: the articulation of the mirror, which is the cyclical analogy of the apocalyptic vision. It's through here that the ironies of Proust & FW [*Finnegans Wake*] break through to myth. Maybe I could work this out as the ultimate form of the Romantic reversal of the four levels: actually of course it's the theme of *Jerusalem*. The cycle of the other becomes the reflection of the cycle of the same, which is its repetition. Molloy's bicycle.[65]

[88] The key to the whole business, of course, is time, as I started to say above. In the waste-land/hollow-men world of time time is always time *after*: its clock-tick is an ostinato bass against an inaudible mighty melody (the *real* music of the spheres) of moments that we hear only as "might have been." The whole business (damn that stupid phrase) of recovering time begins in the recollection in tranquillity: the use of the moment *after* to start rolling back the Red Sea of habit & inertia.[66] The stupid giants, Polyphemus & Goliath & the rest, are the giants of habit, Blake's Og & Sihon,[67] & they are both Blake's giants who formed this world & Proust's giants immersed in time. Myshkin's supreme moment [in Dostoyevsky's *The Idiot*] occurred the second before his epileptic fit.

[89] One thing that's been nagging me: in modern design, music & painting a good deal is left to chance. Chance in poetry means the "untranslatable" elements: the accidents of a specific language that aren't calculated but just appear as an undercurrent of assonance & alliteration. Of course the calculated effects are partly accidental too, or at least coincidental: whatever associations are of sound rather than sense, of rhyme rather than reason.

[90] I said in *Fools of Time* [4–5] that death was what defined life: perhaps it's also what permits of the variety of life which is the other aspect of its unity. If there were no death, life would be uniform, as in the monotonous visions of heaven. This connects with one of my favorite superstitions: that *the way to* [written above previous phrase: in order] rationalize the utterly pointless & hideous tortures men have inflicted on each other, one has to think, not of reincarnation, but of one man getting the total variety of all possible experiences, of hell as well as of heaven. In the Last

Judgment everything that has done this becomes part of the body of death & disappears: everything that has suffered it is part of the redeemed body of Albion or Adam Kadmon.[68] One comes to a focus in Barabbas & the other in Jesus: the former is the "scapegoat" sent out to Azazel, the Gadarene swine driven over a cliff (the word Azazel means cliff)[69] out into the deep of annihilation. The scapegoats or Gadarene swine are the temporary kings, i.e., Blake's "Elect," the rulers of the time-establishment. Not as people, but as phenomena: the sinister goat-world that's abolished.

[91] I've often said that a man's religion is defined by what he wants to identify himself with. I was speaking in social terms, but what I most *want* to identify myself with is my own second self, the kind of person I wish I could be, desiring this man's art & that man's scope. There are two levels of this. One is the straight reincarnation one—what would I do differently if I could do it over again, the same situation but with the present perspective? This is the bull-in-the-ring-for-the-second-time situation, where the bull could kill any toreador. (Note that this isn't exactly reincarnation, because the shadow of the dial would move back to 1912 again).[70]

[92] Well, I'd have a much happier & fuller life & would be able to avoid some mistakes, but it wouldn't be ideal. For an ideal, I'd want to get a much better deal from nature physically, without losing the mental intensity I've developed partly out of compensation. Yet again the shadow of the dial would have to go back: the social context of such an ideal would still be early 20th c. Canadian white middle class. One's risen body is still rooted in history & a specific culture. I'd want to be an excellent pianist & composer, but in terms of 20th c. music.

[93] This speculative fantasy is of a type that's run through culture from the tenth book of the *Republic* to the Eliot Quartets. I note that my ideal or perfected self would *not* be a saint: that I've never been able to grasp as a personal ideal. And I'm not sure that the real key to the fantasy is the rose-garden: the Eliot return to childhood with the might-have-been glimpse of Eden informing it. I do notice a large antithetical or compensatory element: I'd want first-rate physical coordination & a strong practical sense, the opposite of what I have, without losing what I have. This is the Yeats mask, & indicates both a strong positivistic & will-to-power streak in my writing.

[94] Dostoievsky speaks of Myshkin [in *The Idiot*] as having a tremendous overmastering desire, "almost a temptation." We so seldom think of temptation as a mortal struggle, Christian fighting Apollyon: we feel that the military metaphor is simply a way of making the decision power more interesting. Even Milton in *Comus* (partly because it isn't a Christian poem) portrays the Lady as essentially un-tempted. Nothing gets inside her. Christ in P.R. [*Paradise Regained*], though exhausted like Guyon in Spenser, is also "immoved." But if we think of temptation as being what it is we get a very different view of the soul. The result of yielding to temptation is demonic possession, the state in which Christ found so many people. The students I call the little buggers are in this state: they cannot be tempted because they are already possessed. They are allowed to retain a set of moral standards (racism & the like) for their self-respect, but whatever the demonic in them decides they "want" to do [they do], and rationalize doing it accordingly. They would regard resisting temptation as an unhealthy hang-up.

[95] To fight a temptation one needs a crystal-clear vision of society which the temptation itself violates. This vision is the justifying faith of Luther, but its ramifications are much broader. Every martyr dies for the same cause: any social vision to which one will commit his life is genuine. And of course a revolutionary's social vision may be quite intense enough for that: the sense of demonic possession is partly superstitious. But it's partly too the serpent body of Orc. One *is* a citizen ultimately of an invisible kingdom: the Christian kingdom of heaven in one context, the Platonic Republic in another, the kingdom of ends in the context of the Kantian ethic.

[96] Some things are clearing in, of all places, Blake. Thus:

Plato: the soul sees the form
the body sees the thing.
Blake: the imagination sees the spirits of things (AROI [*All Religions Are One I*?])
the body sees things.

Simple, & nothing I didn't know, but is a formula for such things as: "the stars threw down their spears." Then there's my old diagram:

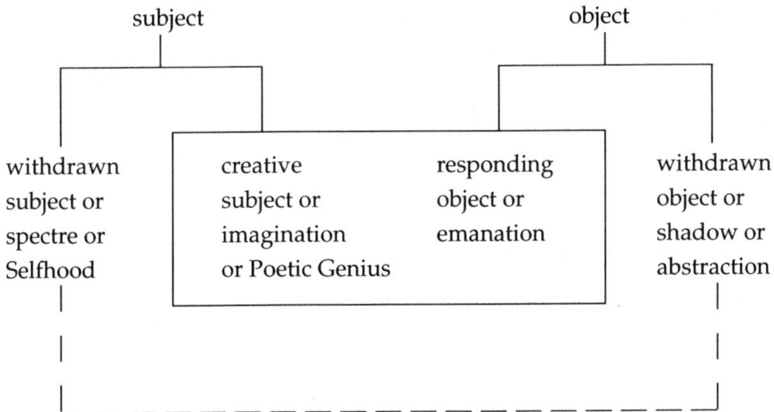

Nothing new, again, but note that the emanation, when manifest or created, surrounds the imagination: when uncreated or embryonic, it's within. Neither state is strictly speaking androgynous or hermaphroditic. These are the demonic parodies, Tirzah the mother with the male inside her (Gwendolyn & Hyle) & Rahab or Religion hidden in war.[71]

[97] I'm beginning to distrust my old creator-creature, lover-beloved hierarchy. I'm trying to work out what seems to me a central preoccupation of philosophy (Hegel) and poetry (Wallace Stevens) alike: the formulation of the identity which starts with the subject confronting the object. Stevens seems to think in four stages:

1. Stage of estrangement: the imagination looking at the bleak world, the arrogant X, the final slate, Crispin's sea, the world of the snow man.
2. Stage of subordination of imagination to reality. The sun vision, thunderstorms in Yucatan.
3. Stage of subordination of reality to imagination. The moon vision of "evasions." Cf. the So-&-So Reclining poem.
4. Stage of absolute identity, where "things as they are" become also things as they could or should be because imagined. The first section of the "Blue Guitar," & "Description Without Place."[72]

[98] Love, like criticism, may assume value-judgments, but is not directed towards them. "Thou shalt love thy neighbour as thyself" is nonsense unless one loves oneself. Nygren, in Eros & Agape,[73] denies

this because he can't separate self-love from self-admiration, thinking that one is not so bad considering. But love is, as I've said elsewhere, clairvoyant vision backed by infinite concern. The soul one is trying to save is as precious as any other. Normally, one likes the person one loves, or else is sexually attracted toward her. But those are not essentially forms of agape.

[99] There's still, I feel, something essential to this book I haven't yet got the right clue to. Suppose I started with the Bible, & the penumbra of Biblical writing. That would give me the *hierarchical* diagram which is half of the book. This could then be expanded through Classical mythology and the medieval-Renaissance four-level *centre*. But something *else* is involved in the Bible of hell that begins with Blake. So far I've thought of it as a straight Heraclitean reversal: the undifferentiated alienating Absolute at the top, under it the two estrangements of ascendant object & ascendant subject, & under that the identity.

[100] The book that started me on all this was Colin Still's book on *The Tempest* [*Shakespeare's Mystery Play*], which I found by "accident" in the Public Library (Toronto) in 1930. Its influence is earlier than Blake's. Eventually I picked up both it & its successor, *The Timeless Theme*[,] & put them on my shelves, where they sat for years uncracked. Now I'm reading the second book for the first time & it's a bit disconcerting to see how much of it is already part of my makeup. *And* my diagram.

[101] He says the "timeless theme" is the fall and return of the soul, & that the mystery plays were all about the reversal of movement from fallen to unfallen state [90]. My four levels he equates with the four elements: heaven as aether or fire, Paradise as air, experience as water, the demonic (oracular) as earth. There are three transitional points: mire, mist, & rainbow or ring of fire. Water he says is the separating & air the unifying consciousness—psyche & pneuma.[74]

[102] I think he's undoubtedly right that a four-level element symbolism is involved in both the pagan mysteries and the New Testament. Paul does speak of four bodies, physical, psychical, pneumatic or spiritual & heavenly, & Jesus speaks of birth by water and air (spirit). The contrast of air or spirit as uniting Logos & water as separating or individualizing perception seems to be there too. And on my diagram the Nomos-Nous

axis is his "mist," the purgatorial progression of Milton's P.R. [*Paradise Regained*] & the Court Party in *The Tempest*.

[103] *This* book at the moment is clearer than the first one,[75] except that the first one may be it, once I work out the contrast of world left & world returned to. But one has to improve on Still. He's got the mirror right: the Narcissus fall through water, but coming the other way there are two stages, the *jeune parque* or Psyche-water stage (SE) & the Eros-air stage (NE). There's an implicit fire-idea, air-word, water-image, earth-thing equation. But "earth" life is unconscious, and it seems to me that water & air between them are really the separating object & the unifying subject. There's a higher water, the Genesis waters above the firmament, a lower water or chaos, & a middle water which is where we are. The thing to do is change one's water. Similarly, ether or quintessence could be thought of as higher air, & chaos as the abyss or lower air.

[104] The sun & moon are the two eyes of heaven, but the moon, reflecting the sun's light, is the mirror-principle, the symbol of everything below that "reflects" the above. So is the lake. Hence moon & water are symbolically very close, the closeness being illustrated by the boat or ark symbol.

[105] Things are solids, symbolic earth; liquids, s. [symbolic] water; gases, s. [symbolic] air[;] or living things or organisms, s. [symbolic] fire (i.e. things that preserve their form but not their content or volume).

[106] No, the four post-Newton levels appear to be:[76] (1) The death-level of the first phase of Hegel's absolute, where all cows are black.[77] This is the old heaven recreated as abyss or empty space where everything is alien. (2) The ordinary world of experience, where conscious awareness is dominated by the sense of the objective. It's the paradisal Beulah world recreated as abstraction. (3) The world of suppressed wish or desire, where consciousness is revolutionary and manipulative, the Generation world of substance recreated as subject. (4) The world of deep identity, where creation is *below* the conscious will & where, as Yeats says, chance & choice are one.[78]

[107] That's fine: I can see that in Hegel, less clearly in Kant, & in a good deal of Blake, Shelley, Yeats & Wallace Stevens. But what is its relation to

the other diagram? Is it a separate cycle of the other that revolves in the opposite direction, with the south at the zenith? If so, what pre-Blake literature belongs to it?

[108] Anyway, I have to pound this notion into my stupid noddle. The world of creative identity is, to use a musical metaphor, parallel (standing in the same place) to the old demonic world, relative (representing the same thing) to the old heaven. The objective world watched by the observing subject is parallel to the world of experience, relative to the old (lost) paradise, an abstract world that keeps eluding us as we try to grasp it, going mostly into the sky. The substance-as-subject[79] world is the (regained) paradisal world (relative key) but parallel to the vanished Eden, now underground. The night-of-black-cows Absolute is the death-vision, parallel to the old sky, now seen as "outer space," relative to the demonic world. That's something, however little I make of it.

[109] The only thing to do is to keep hammering at these categories. Suppose I call the conventional set Heaven, Paradise, Earth, Hell. The second set can go for the time being by their Blakean names. Well: The Urizen world is parallel to lost innocence (cf. My Spectre Around Me) because it's a receding or vanishing world. It's the Alastor world of Shelley, and is a world in which the Romantic "organic" keeps getting assimilated to the "mechanical." It's investigated by mathematics—a faint recall of the old music of the spheres—and it's the world of experience "understood," i.e., stood under.

[110] The Orc world is the Romantic world of unspoiled nature, where man makes contact with a process bigger than himself but "vital." The "city" is always getting wizzled up by geometry: that's our contemporary geometrical world that pollutes nature. Note that the conservative Romantic takes a view of the Urizen & Orc world which brings them close to the old set-up. That's the queasy view of the drunken boat. Nothing new here, but I've been confused about the precise location of these levels.

[111] Anyway, my three levels of awareness hunch comes in here.[80] The first awareness is expressed in philosophical reconciliation; the second in revolutionary action; the third in imaginative interpenetration. Which leads me to the utterly crazy hunch: there are two mythical frameworks.

The traditional four-level one achieved its first awareness in St. Thomas, whose Two Summae reconcile everything reconcilable within the real universal. The second awareness was achieved through a revolutionary authoritarian tradition of which Luther is the centre, with Machiavelli & Calvin connected in different ways. The third awareness is Shakespeare, at least as culmination.

[112] The second framework gets its great reconciler in Hegel, with his conception of the Absolute as spirit. The second awareness is in the breakup of Hegel that has Marx at its centre, flanked by Kierkegaard & perhaps Nietzsche. The third awareness starts in Blake & informs the whole 1920–50 mythopoeic period. Goethe has a relation to Hegel rather like that of Dante to St. Thomas.

[113] My central problem however isn't much helped by this. Is the second framework something that can be applied to pre-Newtonian poetry, or to some of it, or can the first one be applied to all or some post-Newtonian poetry? Are there some poems that *essentially* belong to one or the other? If so, why? Is it the poets' beliefs or assumptions? What about Eliot or Hopkins, or all the poems I put on the first circle? And in conclusion: do I need a second diagram, with eight new names, that I can only read standing on my head?

[114] I may scrap all this: it's not yet a breakthrough, but I'm tunnelling. I think there is a second diagram. At its top, corresponding to the bottom half of the older diagram, is the point of total identity, Yeats' Phase 15, the sunken Atlantis, Los & Jerusalem, the birth-marriage-death of Dylan Thomas' *Winter's Tale*. At the other end is the Covering Cherub,[81] Yeats' Phase One, God as mob. There are debates at both points. At the top are *Le Temps Retrouvé* & *Finnegans Wake*. Note that here the *cycle* can represent the total identity, which is a *repetition* of it, & not as in the older p. of e. [point of epiphany], the stasis of anamnesis, the Sabaoth's sight of Spenser.[82] At the bottom are the Yeats debates, though there's the same ambiguity that there is at the other bottom (oracular & tormenting). I don't know, though; the Dialogue of S & S [*A Dialogue of Self and Soul*] & Vacillation are different.

[115] Anyway, the top half is Orc, historical, revolutionary, and Yeats's antithetical; the bottom half is Urizen, natural, "established," & primary.

The conception of the "sublime" has moved from the C.C. [Covering Cherub] down through Urizen's mountains to Orc's deserts, after which "unspotted nature" settles in the genitals. The quadrants are different too.

[116] It will be easier to study the second diagram under the same form as the first, anti-clockwise with the north at the top. In relation to its predecessor, it really goes clockwise with the south at the top, but it doesn't really matter whether north & south are up or down.

[117] Well, then, the new Eros quadrant is best represented by D.H. Lawrence: it's the Freudian drive from the sexual to the polymorphous perverse. The quadrant begins E (really W, on the other diagram) with the epiphany of the risen hero, the kind of thing Nazism sold itself on, hence *The Plumed Serpent*. Note the drive *away* from the Urizenic intellectual, hence all the warnings about sex in the head. Note too the earthly paradise Rome-Rananim[83] or whatever it is—the *pastoral* ideal. Henry Miller & the jerkoff squad are there too—Christ, I hope I don't have to read too much of it. This quadrant corresponds to the older Hermes one, & there's a good deal of Hermes "show-through" (an important principle I must get used to) in it.

[118] The Prometheus quadrant, the new one, corresponding to the old Adonis one, is perhaps best described as a "Dionysus" quadrant. It's the quadrant particularly of Nietzsche & of Rimbaud, the theme of finding identity in individual isolation. The E point, the old Nomos, has a lot to do with the "Romantic agony," the beauty of pain. I don't know whether Dostoevsky's Idiot is here or not.

[119] I may resolve my muddle about experience & realism in the older diagram by the fact that there is a straight progression of modes: the first diagram is mythical, romantic, high mimetic, but keeps *remembering* myth; the second is low mimetic & ironic and *breaks through* to myth. I think I can keep my Bildungsroman hunch about the *new* Adonis: the theme here is loss of vitality or integrity through age or compromise. So far, I think the past & future set-ups are much the same, except for the difference in the role of the cycle.

[120] I haven't a name for the new Adonis & perhaps don't need one—in

view of the Blakean & I Ching parallels[84] perhaps I should have some female names. But I used to think of the Hermes quadrant as the Oedipus one, & perhaps that is the central theme of the new Hermes—the growing isolation at the centre, the increased objectifying of everything, the clock-double-mirror world. My old Poe-Hawthorne-Melville hunches may work out after all for this section—also some of my naive romance ones.

[121] In the older diagram W isn't exactly the point of crucifixion, which I think is more SW, but it's implied in the Adonis-Absalom death. In the new one W is the achieving of identity through isolation, or perhaps it's really "enthusiasm" in the sense of possession by an ambivalent Orc power, which could be why Nietzsche contrasted Dionysus & Christ. No: that won't work. W is the new Nomos, the power of self-objectification, & so particularly the double-clock-mirror point. E, the new Nous, is the point of internalization: Lawrence's Man Who Died. The N-point is, like the S-point on the other, ambivalent. It doesn't have to be pure alienation; it can also be pure objectivity, hence Yeats' Dialogue SS [of Self and Soul] & Vacillation & AMS [*Among School Children*] debates really do belong there, because it's the phase of Yeats's Phase One & of his primary annunciation of dove & virgin.

[122] E tunneling toward S is Lawrence, Dionysiac enthusiasm. The wild old wicked man as the post-Romantic counterpart of Simeon.[85] At the point of identity, S., Yeats' Phase 15 & Blake's Jerusalem, we reach the corresponding point of the Logos vision, which is the *Atlantis* vision, the completion of the internalizing vision that begins in the E. Here is the FW [*Finnegans Wake*] & Proustian confrontations, where (as in the old S.) the cycle may represent redemption.

[123] One thing has certainly emerged from all this brainstorm, & that is the parallel between a "catholic" reconciling and a "protestant" existential awareness in both periods. I'm reasonably sure of Shakespeare as the third awareness of the first period too.

[124] Further on Colin Still's element symbolism,[86] air is the unifying subject & water the separating object, so that normal life is a mist—Maya, hebel. Earth is the unifying object, Stevens' final slate,[87] and fire is (here I'm picking up a traditional occult view, found in Berkeley's *Siris* &

elsewhere) the separating subject or principle of vitality. Earth = solid, water = liquid, air = gas, and fire = organism or form of the fourth. So the air is where the *Logos* is, the common unifying principle.

[125] I need to get a much clearer impression of the *confrontation* at the points of epiphany. My new diagram has one at Atlantis, between real identity & the total chaos in which all culture is assimilated to news, which links with an emerging thesis about education as an encounter with reality, communication as an encounter with appearance or phantasmagoria. At the CC [Covering Cherub][88] there's the encounter between total alienation or objectivity and the redemptive cycle (this suggests that FW [*Finnegans Wake*] & Proust are at the *same* point as the Yeats debates & not the opposite as I've thought). At the Atlantis I suppose the real contrast is between two approaches to the present moment.

[126] In the older diagram the confrontation patterns are familiar—oracular knowledge, sometimes crippling like Jacob's angel or Odin, touch of redemptive cycle in Aeneid 6 & Rabelais against the life-in-death of hell. But I haven't thought much about the confrontation of Jove & Mutability. The latter has the plagues of Egypt & all the apocalyptic whoop-de-doo; all the storm & tempest & epiphany of Antichrist imagery. Remember that the Beast & Whore are placed there in Dante, & that the whole apoc.-dem. [apocalyptic–demonic] table belongs there.[89] The demonic consolidation in hell is, as in Dante, only the shadow of this. Also the p. m. [Primum Mobile] in [Chaucer's] the Man of Law's Tale moving against the rest of the universe[90] needs thinking about.

[127] I've crammed a lot of stuff into my circle, post as well as pre-Romantic. Theoretically, I suppose, it could go all on one diagram: it's just more convenient to have a second. If so, then Mallarmé's Igitur & dice-playing,[91] Valery's jeune parque, Dostoevsky's Idiot, *Heart of Darkness*, the breaking of language in FW [*Finnegans Wake*], *Byzantium*, the Eliot Quartets, all ought to have more convenient locations. Also the Alice books. It's a lot better for the new Adonis, which I might call the Narcissus quadrant: this is a Kantian area, & it's where the Bildungsroman goes, the blonde & dark heroines, & the rest of it. It ends in the new Nomos, which is the point of objectification, where the double theme begins. In this Adonis, as in the other, the double theme goes with a knowledge of good & evil.

[128] Then we go into the new Hermes, which may be Oedipus (as I originally called Hermes). Here double & shadow & mirror themes deepen & alienation increases. Socially, this is the theme of dystopia. The ego of Beckett & Dostoevsky's *Notes From Underground* belongs here as demonic imagery belongs in the old S: that is, I may have to introduce it as part of a confrontation at the other end. Anyway, there's a big complex involving Eliot's Wasteland, the "deeper" purgatorial descent (the reversal from the old diagram is significant) of his dark night, Mallarmé's *Igitur* & the dice-throw, the Ancient Mariner's dice, & a lot of other things ending in the defining of consciousness as non-being before the Covering Cherub. This is Yeats's Phase One: my new diagram makes a lot more sense of Yeats.

[129] Nympholepsy, the alastor & spectre around me themes[92] belong in the new Hermes too, as do most of the Romantic Wanderers. Over on the Prometheus side is the *jeune parque* recovery, a progress toward internalization, individual and social, that reaches a new integration at the new Nous point, where we go through the Narcissus mirror from the Narcissus side. Then we get into a new Eros: D.H. Lawrence is central here. Note that in the spatial metaphors we're descending, not going up, so Lawrence's dark gods & such are all right, also Yeats' Byzantium that you reach through the sea. Probably a lot of second *Faust* belongs here. I suppose my new Prometheus could be called Pan or Dionysus, because I think this is Nietzsche's hangout, & the vehicular-form enthusiasm in Romanticism belongs to it. What the new Eros is I don't know—maybe *it's* Dionysus. It's sexier than the other Eros, of course, but its *telos* is polymorphous & pre-sexual.

[130] I don't know if a new table of apocalyptic & demonic images is needed: certainly gold seems to be involved. One end is the Covering Cherub full of gold & gems; the other is the alchemical work accomplished. At the Atlantis end there's more emphasis on man as creator & as participating in the divine nature than in the old heaven, but it's not committed to that: Hopkins & Claudel must belong here too, even though, like Eliot, there'd be a lot of "show-through" from the older model. Incidentally, *if* Blake is the 3rd awareness of II, & *if* he has both models, does Shakespeare, the 3rd awareness of I, have the second model also?[93]

[131] Commentator on the first awareness: Dante. On the second, Milton.

On the third, Shakespeare. In the second construct the first commentator I think is Goethe. The second I'm not sure of: it could be Dostoevsky. The third, represented by Blake, hasn't been born yet.

[132] Do I need new names for the second construct? I'd thought of Dionysus for the new Prometheus, Oedipus for the new Eros (difficulties here, as it's a tragic theme in its literary aspects), perhaps Perseus for the new Hermes, and (doubtfully) Apollo for the new Adonis. Actually Prometheus for the S to E movement hardly fits the older framework at all: it's mostly new in its overtones. Names or no names, I think I'm getting somewhere.

[133] In both frameworks the first & central myth is the myth of alienation, which in our culture is the myth of fall. The myth of creation is not really first: it's been displaced to the first position, like law & gospel in the Bible. In the first framework it's the compensating myth, founded in the sense of objectivity; in the second it grows out of alienation.

[134] Now if, for the whatsit [Birks] Lectures at McGill, I could do: One, the two frameworks; two, the three awarenesses of the first framework; three, the th. aw. [three awarenesses] of the second fr. [framework], (it's probably far too neat & chopped off), I'd be very close to the position of the man who said his new play was finished and he had only to write it. Except that I also have to do a lot of the reading for it.

[135] In gematria,[94] the numerical value of the Tetragrammaton (or four-letter word) is 26, so that a Trinity would be 78. The word for salt also has that number. Don't know what Rabelais[95] knew or cared about this: I should look at Revelation. The old southern hemisphere is curtailed but still there: Boehme is still in Hermes & Luther & Rabelais in Prometheus. But most of the mirrors & clocks go into the second framework: that will throw a heavier weight on metamorphosis, the older form of W. objectification.

[136] In the red book I've got the MT [*The Mental Traveller*] stuck into the older framework, as I remember with fair plausibility.[96] In the new one I think it's the *female* who follows the cycle. That is, the Boy is born at the Phase One or C.C. [Covering Cherub] end, and the female babe is what comes at the other end instead of identity. The Tirzah[97] stage is in (new)

Prometheus, the garden stage in Eros, the shadow and maiden stage in Adonis (Persephone & Pluto), & the renewed boy & mother in Hermes. The apocalyptic overtones of the new birth are part of the C.C. [Covering Cherub] ambivalence: the cycle is regenerative at that point.

[137] The connection of MT [*The Mental Traveller*] & Yeats *Vision* cycles, which Yeats himself insists on so much, is getting clearer in my mind. But my version of his cycle goes round the other way. I wonder if this is because he classifies his phases by will instead of creative mind, which in Blake's terms means classifying by the female instead of the male principle.

[138] The first diagram, as I've said, includes a macrocosmic human body, with the head at Logos & the arse at Thanatos. In its day very little was known about the lower part of the body: if one knew one's bodily processes completely one would also know the moment of one's death, which is why Thanatos is the place of knowledge of the future and of the sinister or forbidden.

[139] This is the tentative outline for the book:

Part One: The Traditional Framework.

Chapter One, Sections 1–4. The Poet in His Universe: The Upper Cycle of the same & the Lower Cycle of the different:[98] analogy of the body; creation myths (as projections).

Chapter Two, Sections 5–8. The Four Traditional Levels. The axis of Nomos & Nous; the quadrants & their chief archetypes.

Chapter Three, Sections 9–12. The Symbolic & Typological Structure of the Bible. Plato's Bible. The Logos vision.

Chapter Four, Sections 13–16. Adonis imagery and the Nomos vision.

Chapter Five, Sections 17–20. Hermes imagery and the Thanatos vision, with its ambiguities.

Chapter Six, Sections 21–24. Prometheus imagery and the Nous vision.

Chapter Seven: Eros imagery and the regained Logos vision.

Chapter Eight: The Three Awarenesses,[99] or stages of mythical self-consciousness. The first awareness, "catholic," conceptual, and working by inclusion & reconciliation, in St. Thomas Aquinas: spokesman, Dante. The second awareness, "protestant," existential & revolutionary, in Luther: spokesman, Milton (but keep Rabelais in mind). The third awareness, imaginative, based on interpenetration: spokesman, Shakespeare. Seven has sections 25–28 & Eight 29–32. Eight may have to come before the quadrants.

Part Two: The Post-Romantic Framework.

Chapter Nine, Sections 33–36. Newton Demands Another Muse.[100]
Ten, Sections 37–40. The Four Levels of the Romantic Framework. Eleven, Sections 41–44. The Bible of Hell.
Twelve, Sections 45–48, The Three Awarenesses (I really think these do have to precede the quadrants: if they do, each part splits exactly in two, a deductive & theoretical part being followed by a practical & applied part. Anyway, the three awarenesses here are: first, Hegel (spokesman Goethe), second, the "protestant" or existential reactions to Hegel, notably Kierkegaard & Marx: spokesman undefined, perhaps Dostoevsky. Third, the whole mythopoeic development from Blake to Stevens, pending the birth of a second Shakespeare).
Thirteen, Sections 49–52: The new Adonis (title unassigned: I don't like Apollo). The movement from the old Logos & new Covering Cherub or point of alienation or surrender (Phase One) down to the new W. Nomos or objectification. Bildungsroman, black & fair heroine stories, etc.
Fourteen, Sections 53–56: The new Hermes or Perseus. Doubles, clocks, mirrors, nympholepsy & alastor figures:[101] growing mechanistic & conspiratorial worlds (Poe, Kafka, Borges); the dystopia; breakup of language as we approach Phase One. (I was asleep above: we start from the new Logos which is Atlantis or the point of identity, Phase 15). As we pass Phase 1 we go through Mallarmé's *Igitur* & dice-throw complex,[102] the regenerative aspect of the Proust & FW [*Finnegans Wake*] cycles, the dark night aspect of the Eliot Quartets, etc.
Fifteen, Sections 57–60: The new Prometheus or Dionysus. Rimbaud's hell, Nietzsche, & the "vehicular form" energy as we approach the new Nous, or internalization.
Sixteen, Sections 61–64. The new Eros, or Oedipus. D.H. Lawrence & the dark gods; the Freudian drive to the polymorphous; Yeats' wild old wicked man,[103] & so back to the point of identity with the Yeats debates & the Byzantium alchemical progress.

It could be four volumes, └ [Liberal], ┐ [Tragicomedy], ∧ [Anticlimax] and ⅄ [Rencontre]. Straight, not mixed. And 25 sections each, making 150 in all.

As amended, then, └ is: (1) The Poet and His World (2) The Four-Level Universe (3) The Symbolic Structure of the Bible (4) The Three Awarenesses of the Myth. So ┐ is the quadrants of the pre-Romantic wheel, followed perhaps by brief essays on Dante, Milton, & Shakespeare. Fifty sections.

[140] In Plato's *Timaeus* [26c–d] somebody exclaims about the resemblance, or identity, of the hypothetical state of the *Republic* and the actual one of the ancient Athens contemporary with Atlantis. We see here a scripture in process of formation:[104] the Bible of Plato would naturally begin with a creation myth (the *Timaeus*): this would be followed by a proto-historical Israel-Egypt legend (the *Critias*) and that in turn by an account of the ideal social contract (the unwritten Hermogenes which eventually turned into the *Laws*).[105] Here as in the Bible the *Torah* vision is founded on the prophetic one, sc. [social contract?] of Socrates, whose *Republic* has much the same kind of relation to the *Laws* that the arse-end of Ezekiel has to the Holiness or Deuteronomic codes. The martyrdom of Socrates recurs in the Hebrew prophetic tradition: there's still something in this I haven't got.

[141] If we ask how Plato thought he could write a Bible singlehanded, the answer is that he didn't have the stage fright that anyone who knew about the eventual importance of the Hebrew Bible would have. In any case his task was simplified by his belief in aesthetic arguments. Did the Demiurge look to the upper or the lower model? The upper one, of course: it would be blasphemous to choose the lower. The right or true doctrine is the one that ought to be there, the one that fits, so it's much less difficult to discover. This belief in truth as the pleasantest or most elegant argument is connected with what I call the ritual purification of words, which I noticed in the *Summa contra gentiles* & had earlier found in the *Republic* itself.

[142] In Dante's Purgatorio we have the Beast & Whore in the earthly Paradise.[106] In Apuleius we have the Beast and Whore in that brutal story about the ass (Lucius) fucking the whore in public, depriving her of every vestige of human dignity. The contrasting figure, corresponding to Beatrice, is Isis. In the second construct the Atlantis-identity point, Phase 15, is also where the reborn female babe (Rahab)[107] passes across in transit.

[143] I have started finally on the first chapter, The Poet and his World. Only this chapter should be a complete outline of the symbolic universe,

or what I used to call the Druid analogy.[108] The Bible chapter, which should follow it, should condense my whole R.K. [Religious Knowledge] course & be publishable separately.[109] After that, I should think, would come the four-levels, part one, the two upper levels, then part two, the lower levels, then the three awarenesses (which really can't be done until I've examined the quadrants). Five chapters, then. Dante is the hero of Three: maybe Rabelais can take Four, I don't know. The subject of Five, incidentally, is the Axis of Nomos & Nous, & this is where *this* book turns over on its side.[110] Not that I haven't a contract-and-utopia shot left; but my motto is, shoot the works every time.

[144] The thing is, should I draft the first four chapters on the same model? Take Eros symbolism, which is central to Three. In One perhaps I should establish the kernel of this: the hillock image in Egypt, stylized as the pyramid;[111] the corresponding ziggurat image in Mesopotamia; the Hittite god in the mountain discussed by Miss Levy;[112] the link with ascending fire imagery. In Two this becomes the image of Jerusalem as the highest point in the world: the anabasis ritual in the Psalms; the sublimation of this in the Song of Songs; the Ascension & Transfiguration imagery in the Gospels.

[145] This book I suppose will get duller as I start writing & strategy succeeds to tactics. But although I have never had serious doubts that I could bring this book off, writing an oratorio in a hundred and fifty contrapuntal parts has its difficulties.

[146] I have four directions, and of course there are six. But there is a strong tendency to identify the north-south and the up-down ones, so frequent that I wonder if I do have to allow for six. What seems more important, at the moment, is the establishing of the Logos-Thanatos axis. Creation myths of the artificial type come to a climax in the real Logos vision, creation by the Word, the consciousness which withdraws from existence, & the *direct* projection of the myth-maker. Once again, as soon as God speaks he condemns himself to death.[113] At this point the mystery of *ex nihilo*, the touching of creation and death, is established. In the *Faust* passage, either Goethe is making some profound point about a Faust-Mephisto axis being made at the word (die) "Tat,"[114] or Goethe himself is being an ass, and braying through Faust. I have a horrid suspicion that Goethe was an ass.

[147] Anyway, this creation by the withdrawal from creation is the archetypal tragic movement, containing both Adonis & Hermes descents. The corresponding rising movement I suppose must have something to do with winter-solstice birth, life at the point of death. Only I think what gets born is a female babe, a Perdita figure, perhaps a Psyche or jeune parque, and that the whole comic movement, Prometheus & Eros both, is an anabasis of Kore. Kore was the *daughter* of the earth-mother, just as the Logos is the *son* of the sky-father.

[148] Still, that won't altogether do: there *is* an anabasis of Kore, of course, but the threatened male infant ("if it die")[115] that achieves resurrection (*not* rebirth) is the main character. Query: where does the Female Babe in the MT [*The Mental Traveller*] go after she finds her man? I suspect she then becomes a Psyche or *jeune parque*, & goes all the way up. She's a Rahab figure only to the male babe of rebirth, who, being that, comes from the alienation end.

[149] Is there, then, a descending figure which is female? Cf. Ishtar[116] & a humiliated heroine of comedy who stoops to conquer (and often pretends to be male). What's the female consort of the Word? Perhaps idea or thought: that which is conception rather than emergence. Sophia.[117] An ogdoad is taking shape: the rising god & his Kore in E; Logos & Sophia N; the devil & his dam, the shadowy mother & dark son S, & some kind of dying god & staring virgin W.[118] The I Ching pattern suggests Sophia NE,[119] the dark son SE, the dark father SW, & the staring virgin NW.

[150] I must remember that this is a book about literature by a literary critic, using incidental & illustrative material from comparative mythology. What I've said about mythology I can keep, but I shouldn't make Frazer's mistake all over again, especially when it was I who pointed out that it was a mistake.[120] I'm not out to make a single construct out of mythology, but out of literature.

[151] The first thing man does is *project*: reality for him is at first the shadows on the wall of his cave. Mythology makes sense to the degree that he recovers his projections. Thus the recovered projection of the artificial creating God is the Word, which dies. The core of Nomos is *trial* & judgement. The core of Thanatos (and the hell with Dante, in more

than one sense) is new birth, the ultimate whisper in the dark from the oracle which is both knowledge of the future and of oneself, & what the Preludium to [Blake's] Europe is all about.[121] The core of Nous is symposium or communion in one body, eating, as the Nomos trial is, I suppose, ultimately a form of excretion. In his trial man is what his society takes him to be, hence the worst of all enemies is the *diabolos* or slanderer, the Blatant Beast, the false tongue. At the centre, I suppose, is the self-trial of the apocalyptic parable of the sheep & goats, the parable of the building of the community out of shoats & geep.

[152] So I should get as quickly as I can, I think, to the four levels. The *second* level appears when our poet realizes that his light & dark dialectic is a projection of his own cycle, & that he's habitually on the third.

[153] If there's a sky below, there's a concentric mythical universe. There's an earthly paradise on the other side, a fairy world inside the mountain, Alice's underground & mirror worlds, Dante's purgatory or otherworld trial on the "other side." There's an antipodal world of experience, the source of mirror satire. I don't know whether the Thanatos world splits in this way: the oracular-infernal split is the apocalyptic-demonic ambivalence that's also in Logos.

[154] One of the commonest medieval topoi is the fortiter et justus king.[122] In the Nomos trial, the great vision is of justice, balance or equity (Libra) crystallizing out of power. In the Nous symposium, the great vision is of the power of the rising god crystallizing out of the dialectic form of the just state. The divine king (basileus de jure)[123] is not necessarily the ruler (tyrannos de facto). Elizabeth II reigns but does not rule; the ruler is the prime *minister*, the *servant* of the prince. In the Renaissance the wise courtier was the servant of the *ruling* prince.

[155] In Egypt the sun, Ra, is male & the sky, Nut, female. This image of making the sky female to the sun (cf. the later Queen of Heaven in a blue cloak) is part of the practice of making the focal centre male & the periphery or surround, the home or environment of the focus, female. Similarly with the king-and-land imagery in the S of S [Song of Songs]. However, don't rush things: Ra is not one of the Ennead, strictly, & Nut is not his wife: she's the daughter of a male earth. No, she isn't: I'm more or less right.[124]

[156] Creation seems to be the opposite of Milton's de Deo:[125] it begins in a withdrawal from chaos and (in the Egyptian myth)[126] ends by resting & contemplating, or withdrawing from creation. As Blake saw, this is the point of death, a retreat into non-being. There's more about the name as the principle of creation I haven't got: gods existing in their names, the secret or real name as the principle of existence, etc. The name seems to be or represent a Sein that isn't Dasein.[127]

[157] Where do I put (I hate this kind of question, but sometimes I have to ask it) the simplest of all archetypes, the story of the man who journeys or wanders & eventually arrives back home? The home of the soul is theoretically in the Logos vision, but that doesn't apply to the Sinuhe[128] & Odyssey archetype, or even the prodigal son. The centre may be a place after all. Of course when I talk to my students about the four levels of time and space, I say that the *second* level is home, the third being the world of accustomed experience and yet not home. Going home is a lower Eros motif: it has the present-to-past element in it. It's the underside of the point of epiphany, in a way. The desire to be buried honorably polarizes this in the lower world: sometimes it's the same spot. The body that keeps journeying, in death as in life, is the theme of *Gerontion.*

[158] Note that the rising body in Nous is regularly a figure in a doorway.[129] Ra rises between two "turquoise" trees in Egypt[130]—I don't know if that's literally jewelled trees or just a color word. Jesus & the tomb. Samson's pillars & the three crosses in the west; Jachin & Boaz[131] in Kabbalism is Nous: the risen body coming out between the framing posts of arms & legs.

[159] In the contest of Horus & Seth, the archetype is the struggle of brothers. Seth is the Esau figure, stupid, powerful, Lord of Upper Egypt but also the god of the foreign (wandering) peoples. There's some red & white symbolism too. Incidentally, my diagram makes it easy to understand the dropping of the prick into the water where it's eaten by fish (Osiris myth, also in the Two Brothers).[132] It's the beginning of the talisman of recognition & rebirth that comes out of the water (ring in *Sakuntala;*[133] cf. *Rudens*).[134] J. p. [*Jeune parque*] themes in Perdita & Marina. In the Two Brothers note assoc. of wandering & female will: My Spectre Around Me arch. [archetype].

[160] In Egyptian myth, where the south is the zenith, the place of the rising of the Nile is the e. p. [epiphany point]: the hillock of creation (ANET, p. 31).[135] The Nile rises through two caverns. Source of the later Ethiopia-Alph[136] business. Note that both Alice books end on the N-N [Nomos-Nous] axis: W [*Alice in Wonderland*] with a trial about tarts, LG [*Through the Looking Glass*] with a catechism & a dinner.[137] I have a feeling that if I thoroughly understood the Alice books I'd have the key to the whole of mythology.

[161] A certain formal symmetry, based on the three awarenesses,[138] is shaping up. Let's call them A, B, and C. The first two chapters, if that's what they are, deal with A & B mythology respectively: the first reconciling by identification, & so arriving at monotheism, as world-state unifying; the second, the Bible, dealing with the revolutionary-existential aspect of this, is a future-directed & Saturnalia-culbute version of monotheism. Next follows the great wheel in two parts, A the Logos vision, uniting-reconciling & ruling, & B, the Thanatos vision, revolutionary & dividing. And yet *this* A and B, taken together, constitutes C. So the fifth chapter, dealing with Thomas as A & Luther as B, can logically end with a C (I think at the moment of a *tour de force* Shakespeare coda).

[162] The organization of Part Two will have to be different, though the same general pattern recurs with Hegel seeking identity through the reconciling of alienation (where Leibnitz & Kant perhaps have roles corresponding to Plato & Aristotle in I). The anti-Hegelian revolutionary-existential Kierkegaard-Marx movement is B. In I, Dante & Milton are A & B poets respectively: I've spotted Goethe as A in II, but the B I dunno: I may have to settle for Dostoevsky, but I strongly suspect it's Beethoven. The second C doesn't exist, but I can reconstruct him through Blake, and perhaps partly through Ruskin in a different way: note the V [Mirage] theme.

[163] Anyway, the difference between the great-power mythology that reaches monotheism and the Word by adding, including & reconciling, and the revolutionary kind that proceeds by dialectic and opposition has always been pretty clear in my mind, and now, with this analogy with Thomism & Lutheranism, Dante & Milton, it's getting almost incandescent. The Logos Christ of order & the revolutionary Promethean treader of the winepress has always been there too. That the core of the

revolutionary vision is *Thanatos* is probably the most important point I have.

[164] I suppose the fundamental difference between Parts One & Two is the fact that One turns on the principle of the *projection of creation*. In both Testaments Law & Gospel are projected out of their historical order, Law to get a creation myth, Gospel to get the authentic revolutionary starting point in history. (That's oversimplified, of course). Anyway, the sense of residual mystery in objective nature, which the Egyptians & others symbolized by "animal forms of wisdom," projected the creation myth. The Hebrew discovery of "idolatry" removed some of this, but left the creation myth, in their own version, intact. The Newtonian revolution shifted the focus of reality from Logos to Thanatos, & set up an unprojected myth polarized between alienation and identity. As for interpenetration, that of course has always been theoretically there: it's in the great circle definition of God that appears, most appropriately, at the end of Rabelais.[139]

[165] Projection means fundamentally the finding of something in the order of nature to correspond to the existing social order. In another words a scientific proof of faith. Projection means alienation, and identity now begins at the point of *chance* birth in & out of death. I say chance because of the *igitur*[140] business—it's really the identity of chance and choice.[141] Yet there's a difference between projection and idolatry, between the Egyptian divine king and Hebrew iconoclasm. The latter is equally projected: similarly with Protestant iconoclasm and Catholic ecclesiolatry, Marxist iconoclasm and Hegelian ideolatry. When the activity that projects is recognized to be itself the essential creative power, belief assumes its proper role as axiom of conduct in the light of a social vision. And when that happens an immense decentralizing movement in society takes place, the social counterpart of interpenetration. Has it ever taken place in the past? I think so, but it's always called "breakdown." The intense reality of place-names in Israel & Greece is part of it.

[166] Try again. The first awareness[142] concentrates on visible symbols: its focus is the sun, the source of visibility. It identifies the sun, or what the sun symbolizes, with the centre of social order, and its mental tendency is toward the conceptual. When writing develops, especially. Myth consolidates by reconciliation & cannibalism: local myths are ab-

sorbed into the general cult; monotheism develops as a rationalization of a world-state. There's no fixed belief, only a prescription of ritual habit.

[167] The second awareness is represented by the Judaeo-Christian tradition as compared with that of the rest of the ancient world from Sumeria & Egypt to Rome. It's dialectical: first of all it seizes on the *new* conception of "false god": the true god is theirs, & he has a specific name and social context—he's at least potentially incarnate. It's revolutionary, leading to a future *culbute*, & existential because of the partisan incarnation of its god. The first awareness of the first stage is represented by Homer & Greek drama; the second awareness by the Bible & by tendencies in the late Plato. Above all, the second awareness is iconoclastic: it *internalizes* imagery, & shifts from visible to audible symbols, from the sun to the thunder, & eventually the Word. (Desert nomads, if that is what the Hebrews originally were, have no great affection for the sun anyway). All these characteristics throw a heavy emphasis on literal belief, with little toleration of variety & a strong sense of heresy unknown to the first awareness.

[168] Passing over the third awareness for the moment, the second awareness was consolidated in Christendom, where, on this second-stage basis, the pattern of first & second awareness repeated itself. Medieval Catholicism had no tolerance of belief, but it did have some for local cults & absorbing pre-Xn rituals, even some quasi-beliefs, into its own pattern. Its imagery was again visible, (or tangible, as in the Corpus Christi complex of ritual & dogma) focussed on the visible church, & its conceptual web spread all over the universe, swallowing Plato *and* Aristotle. Against this came the Reformation, Luther with his revolutionary conception of Xy as revolt against a devil-controlled world, an existential recall from sacramental ritual to faith, and an iconoclastic internalizing of the imagery & renewed emphasis on the hearing of the Word. Dante & Milton are the protagonists here, of course.

[169] The great Hebrew discovery of "idolatry," a charge repeated later by Protestants against Catholics (with what justice doesn't concern me now) didn't stop projection: it was the halfway-house of internalization, & through [threw] a much heavier weight on tradition & received belief, both of which are projections. Note that the first awareness has a consistently spatial focus, the second a temporal one. One leans to the Logos

vision & demonizes the lower one; the other begins in a revolutionary Thanatos movement and finds something alienating about the great imperial "systems."

[170] The third awareness is the imaginative recovery of projection, in which the dogmatic tolerance of the first one is recaptured—this is why Shelley so venerated the Greeks, along with some Germans—being German, of course, the notion drove most of them mad. Here man sees himself to be the only source of creation, and consequently of communication. This latter is an intricate problem I haven't worked out, but it's connected with the fact that *interpenetration* & complete decentralizing, *of time as well as space*, is the key to the third awareness.

[171] In the first stage there was no real awareness of the third type, though it was possible for a later age to get something of it out of Ovid, which is why Ovid is the world's greatest poet for Shakespeare. In the second stage only Shakespeare reached it—though, mind you, it's always potentially there in the creative process itself. With Newton & the decline in the symbolic force of the Logos sky vision, the third awareness entered with Romanticism. Then the three awarenesses repeated once again, this time on a third-stage basis. First was Hegel, who established a conceptual imperialism stretching from alienation to identity, where the light of the sun is replaced by the light of the mind. Then came the revolutionary-existential reactions against Hegel, including both Marx and Kierkegaard, where again the idea is internalized into social or individual action. The third awareness of the third phase is Frye, of course, but I'll have to locate it in the mythopoeic poets from Blake on. Goethe is the great poet of the first or Hegelian awareness, & perhaps Blake is of the second: the third is unborn, except for his John the Baptist. I know I've been saying Beethoven is the second & Blake at least the model of the third. I suppose I'm trying to resist or be suspicious of the way this scheme ties up everything I've ever thought. But I'm not really suspicious of it. It's the book, all right. God knows I've waited long enough for it.

[172] How does the third awareness decentralize time? Essentially, of course, by the process suggested by Blake in the SE [*Songs of Experience*] Introduction, line 2, & by Yeats in the last line of SB [*Sailing to Byzantium*].[143] In time the cycle combines with the irreversible. Hence the

historical cycle is of the alike. Decentralizing this means first of all to assimilate it to the cycle of the same.[144] Thus the Babylon cycle in the Bible is not just a later analogue to the Egypt cycle: it *is* the Egypt cycle. In the second awareness there has to be a historical beginning: the burning bush, the birth of Christ. This is also the absorption of the upper cycle, which begins, into the Thanatos world. The historical fact is "given in its poetic vigor as it always happens,"[145] just as the concept is given in the way that it oft (always) was thought.

[173] The second awareness is the Exodus awareness: it begins in the kidnapping of the upper cycle, so to speak. Genesis begins with God creating the unchanging firmament: Exodus begins with a new (historical) life starting with the burning bush at the Thanatos point in Egypt. The S to E Promethean progression to Nous is the *stolen* fire of the upper world breaking through to its own place. I know all this, but I have to keep repeating it.

[174] I wonder why I've always thought sentimental romance so central a hinge of the argument? S.r. [sentimental romance] begins with Scott & more particularly with the Germans (Hoffmann, Novalis). In America it runs through Poe, Hawthorne & Melville; in Britain through George Macdonald & William Morris to the Godly Church: Charles Williams, C.S. Lewis, & Tolkien. I suppose Scholes' *Fabulators* (?) is about them.[146] It's often considered a branch of science fiction, but it isn't: it's predominantly anti-scientific. The popularity of Tolkien has caused two other "trilogies" to be reprinted, Eddison's [Zimiamvian trilogy] & Mervyn Peake's [Gormenghast trilogy].[147] I'm reading [E.R. Eddison's] *The Worm Ouroboros*, which I may not finish. S. r. [sentimental romance] is rooted in Gothic revival, in a continuation of naive romance in a different key. It's endless, Boys' Own Paper in formula (sexless adventures; no women; the fantasy world of elves, dragons, magic, hypostatized). But this is all in AC. Incidentally, the Mormon Bible, said to be derived from an obscure romance of the same genre, belongs here, as does Gurdjieff's *All & Everything*.[148] And of course there's James Branch Cabell & M.P. Shiel,[149] two authors I've always had difficulty reading. I'm not as fond of this stuff as I used to think I was. The W.O. [*The Worm Ouroboros*][150] is written in a silly yea-verily-and-forsooth gobbledygook that the bemused hack who wrote the introduction compares to Sir Thomas Browne.

[175] Well, I did read *The Worm Ouroboros*, & am very glad I did. It knocks the pins out from under Tolkien as far as originality goes. Its date is 1926: Tolkien has taken his war-of-light-and-darkness theme, his return-of-the-king theme, his elves-orcs etc. characterization theme (though he improves it a good deal), his mock-chronological apparatus, all straight from the earlier book. Tolkien is more intelligent, I think: there's a silly streak in Eddison, but there's a genuine imaginative focus that I kept missing in Tolkien.

[176] The structure reminds one a little of Ariosto & it raises a question similar to his. In Ariosto there's a war, in fact a crusade, going on, and Paris is besieged. Meanwhile the heroes bugger off on quests, & the great champion Orlando is off somewhere mad. Similarly with the role of Achilles in the Iliad. The war represents social duty, the quest the nihilistic aggressiveness of the individual hero. In fact the whole code of Courtly Love tends really, neither to weaken nor to rationalize warfare, but to atomize it into a number of feats. The Odyssey set-up is different, but in the house of Penelope & Telemachus there is still the sense of the *absent* champion, and what the hell does he think he's doing? The convention is always that the absent hero is a military Messiah, whose return will finish the war. In fact the same theme is central to the Messianic Biblical theme, & to all religious themes of the agon or temptation type. Samson Agonistes point, I suppose.

[177] The later books[151] suggest something obvious I haven't really studied. Some actions go on in the world of experience, while at the same time and in the same space the same action is taking the form of romance. Joyce does this by parody, which is the easiest way of understanding it; in Spenser "Faerie" is the second *form* that English history is taking. Similarly with the melodrama point I fell over in Dickens. Characters are in experience to others but in romance to themselves, & both sides have their own validity. I've said I'd know all about literature if I understood the Alice books, but maybe I'd need to understand [Lewis Carroll's] *Sylvie & Bruno* also, which is about this.

[178] Doesn't look so impressive now I've got it down, but it may grow. Eddison's "demons" & "witches" mean nothing, but Tolkien's Orcs & hobbits & the like do mean something. What they mean is something connected with elemental spirits I haven't yet all got. Religion often

begins with numinous animals, plants, etc., which survive as nymphs & fauns & satyrs. The next stage is elemental spirits,[152] as in *Comus*. Fairies & elves & such seem to turn up mainly in higher Eros, as part of a nature assimilating to the human. Elemental spirits are the internalized images of a visible numinous nature: they are controlled by a magician's aural formulas. How this applies to Hades and the world of the dead-as-shadows I don't know.

[179] Another point in the W.O. [*The Worm Ouroboros*]: the ouroboros[153] is the emblem of the bad guys, who have a series of kings who are all the same king. When they're conquered by the heroes, the heroes go all sulky and withdrawn because there's nobody to fight anymore. So the heroine "prays," & the answer to the maiden's prayer is that the action begins all over again, the last line being the first one. So the ouroboros wins, & the heroes, as in Yeats, choose the "self's" circle of recurrence.

[180] What is the *real* connexion between heroism and recurrence? I get so impatient with this idiotic maudlin hero-cult in Yeats & Nietzsche, which is also, as Graves shows, a female-will cult, that I can hardly discuss it with any patience or objectivity. Yet I've written a book myself [*The Critical Path*] which says that man is not capable of continuous freedom, only of cycles of concern from which freedom is a (gradually increasing) secondary derivative. What is true about Nietzsche's "Dionysus versus Christ" is that Christ stands for resurrection and Dionysus for continuous death and rebirth. The astigmatism that sees this as Dionysus = Life and Christ = Death should, of course, be examined more carefully than I've yet done.

[181] In every notebook I've kept, plans for a big book funnel into what is soon perceived to be a separable article or shorter book. It's happened again. The Birks Lectures are to be the basis of a short book on five stages of religious consciousness, as follows:

1. The first awareness[154] is natural religion as practised in Egypt, Mesopotamia, Greece & Rome; the second is what's characteristic of Hebrew & Biblical religion.
2. These two awarenesses form a cycle in which the second never completely breaks away from the first. (My hermeneutics lecture goes into this one).[155]
3. The structures of reason & experimental [experiment?], embodied

in science & philosophy, represent the liberation of the first awareness. Scholarship or *scientia*.

4. The structures of the creative imagination, embodied in the arts, represent the liberation of the second awareness.

5. Revelation itself is the reversal of the current of all four types of awareness.

Now, that's that, & I got it out of here.

[182] People get so fucked up with clichés. As I've said so often, we tend to assume that the genres of poetry & fiction are "creative" in themselves, because of our habit of calling people who write poems & stories "creative." Similarly, graduate students writing a thesis are apt to get self-distrustful if they feel creative about writing it.

[183] The main problem in a book of this kind is the overlooking of the most obvious patterns. In Eros there's the sex-fire association, the other side of which is the snow-chastity one. The thawing out of the snow maiden or Pygmalion's statue & the constant cold-purity associations ("butter wouldn't melt in his mouth") is the other side of this.

[184] With the Fall man lost good & got the knowledge of good & evil, a cyclical & interpenetrating knowledge in which evil is primary & good a secondary derivation from it. So much I've always got clear. Man also lost life, life which is the *opposite* of death, life where death is an alien & non-existent possibility like unicorns, and got the interpenetrating cycle of life & death, where death is not only natural & inevitable, but implied in the very conception of life itself.

[185] I'm intellectually a prisoner of my own profession: for me, to know anything is to find a verbal formula for it. Hence the above represents something I've always known but never really knew. I suppose the good-evil & life-death cycles are only aspects of a total pattern of double-gyre or antithesis which can "exist" only in that form, as CP says. Youth & age, male & female, master & slave, & so on. So the cycle is the demonic analogy of interpenetration.

[186] Pike's *The Other Side*.[156] It's impossible that Pike is a liar or that he's in any obvious or crude way a dupe. There remains what he calls the "fundamentalist" objection that the experiences are genuine but de-

monic, & I feel there may be something in this. We never hear about *evil* spirits in these séances, yet Christ in the Gospels never has dealings with any other kind.

[187] The body is a mechanism, & the mind (psyche) is equally mechanical, obeying mechanical laws of association & the like. The body is "material," but matter is really energy, & the mind could well be a series of vibrations. At death it's quite conceivable that a discarnate mind could go on quacking for years, perhaps centuries, holding its memories & mental reflexes intact. But we never seem to *learn* anything from that world that we couldn't learn better in this one. The dead seem more detached from time & space, but, like the [purgers?] in Dante, rather more ignorant & childish that we are.

[188] It's possible that they are in a purgatory & are learning something—Jim [James Pike, Jr.] seems to think so, though he hasn't learned much by the end of the book. And I don't see why they have to go back into bodies, as the Hindus & Buddhists say. But neither do I think that, if there is a redemptive process, that [*sic*] these discarnate souls are what get saved, or can save themselves, any more than our physical bodies are.

[189] I think there's a higher principle connected with whatever is creative in man that gets saved, or develops, or whatever. We might get the spirit of Beethoven saying Donnerwetter & tausend Teufels but it's peaceful on this side. What we never get is anything like a 10th Symphony. Yet surely "heaven" has more to do with music, just as Pike's "heaven" would be a world where he could finally get to work on Christian origins.[157] Query: did Pike's immediate & violent death have anything to do with his exposure to this world? Query: we're told that two or three people had a hell of a bad time while Jim was suiciding. Why should the suicide of a very self-centered young man make such a whoop-de-do when thousands of people may die of hunger or cholera or in genocidal wars & never disturb our sleep?

[190] Jim [James Pike, Jr.] seemed to have got one thing clear: that the whole point of this other-side world was the production of the Bodhisattva. Blake & Yeats say definitely that there are teaching spirits, and I've had many intimations of them. But I wonder if every dead

person involuntarily enters such a world? Don't you get to some degree what you expect? Including nothing?

[191] I'm thinking of a poem by Thomas Hardy where a number of people speak of death as a total release from the anxieties of life.[158] That seems to me to have dignity; revenants of all kinds seem to me to be psychic neurotics. I suppose the doctrine of reincarnation is the only one that gives people enough claustrophobia to attempt "liberation."

[192] Elie Wiesel, *Legends for our Time*. The last chapter, "A Plea for the Dead," describes how nobody made any real fuss when six million Jews were murdered in Germany. Nobody to blame, except everybody. This is the kind of thing that makes it impossible for me to be a Buddhist, to accept ignorance and enlightenment as *ultimate* categories. The terrible burden of guilt simply has to be accepted: we can't cast it off even on Christ.

[193] What we can *do* about it involves organization—*moral* organization. Communism cannot produce this: it's only the other side of capitalism, and accepts all its economic-man stereotypes. Teaching people one by one to be more sympathetic is futile. Western organization is the key, though no Western society at present has it. Our fumblings for "participatory democracy" really have as their goal a society in which one almighty yell can go up, almost automatically, when East Pakistan or black Rhodesia or whatever gets out of line of our moral sense. We don't really lack the moral feelings; what we lack is a social structure in which to embody them.

[194] Gurdjieff talks about objective art:[159] as usual with him, I get the feeling that he doesn't know what he's talking about but has talked to somebody who does. I feel that this is the central mystery of art. Everything that, say, Beethoven writes is in his style, it sounds like him, it couldn't have been written by anyone else, etc. All this is subjective. But coming through it, somehow, is the tremendous authority of objective music, a music beyond any one composer's music, however great. A very obvious convention gives us a slight hint of an objective quality. I've said this before in the "voice of music itself" part of the AC [344], but there I had a different issue in my mind.

[195] Mircea Eliade's book on alchemy[160] says that alchemical symbol-

ism is an application to the mineral world of the dying-god vegetative symbolism. Wonder if this could be extended to the whole chain of being, thus:
1. Divine world. Mandala symbolism (e.g. the Trinity diagram in Dante's *Paradiso*).[161] The human universe seen as a geometrical pattern.
2. Spiritual world. Astrological symbolism, mostly in sevens & twelves (planets & zodiac), along with some 13's & 28's.
3. Human world. Leave this for a bit.
4. Animal world. Pastoral symbolism: flocks & herds; an easy & relaxed nomadic wandering. Passover symbols & such: animal gods & beast-headed carnival figures.
5. Vegetable world. Dying god & other agricultural symbolism: bread & wine (and oil).
6. Mineral world. Alchemical symbolism.
7. Chaotic world (water). The symbolism of chance: oracles, divinations, coincidences, found objects.

[196] A belief is a course of action inspired by a shaping vision. This shaping vision is the opposite of idolatry. In both cases you become what you behold. One is the total "I am" building up inside you; the other is the tabula rasa approach to the objective. The Hebrews, in attacking idolatry, first of all demonized the *oracular* objective, as in the Witch of Endor (note *where* Bishop Pike died).[162] The scapegoat ritual & casting out devils develop from this, I don't know just how. The thing that's wrong is divinizing this world. I've been reading about Edgar Cayce,[163] who's evidence that we may be getting near the point where we can plug into the big phone exchange of *spiritus mundi* without getting silly ideas about *gods*. The Hebrew tradition was not scientific, but by demythologizing nature it helped the growth of science. But of course this too can develop idolatry if it becomes founded on dogma. The doctors who *a priori* attacked Cayce were working on the same principle that W.H. Auden ascribes to Herod.[164]

[197] Of course the oracular fallacy operates here too: if Cayce is "right" (tuned in to the spiritus mundi exchange) in one area, say medical diagnosis, I don't see that he must necessarily be right about, say, Atlantis. (Why does Atlantis have to be in the *past*? If it's a myth, of course, it's present, an example or warning). In Plato Atlantis is only the projected ghost of the *Republic*.

[198] All religions are, Blake says, different forms of the Poetic Genius, so that there's objective religion as well as objective art. My job in this world appears to be that of a mantra-gleaner, a picker up (inventor) of possibly useful verbal formulas. One set has to do with the role of art as a potential liberator of whatever gets liberated. Again, I suspect (and I hope, rather than at present believe) that Xy has at least as much to be said for it as any other religion, & I'd like to keep this comparative aspect of my Bible book open. If I could suggest this I'd be very grateful.

[199] I'm not ready to buy the reincarnation bit at the moment, and certainly not the transmigration bit, which so far I think is horseshit. Yet it seems clear that there's a cyclical as well as a dialectical rhythm in religion, as in art, & the evidence from objective religion seems to be in favor of a life-death-rebirth cycle. It's the there's-that-man-again side of it I can't buy. Art is the model of dialectical liberation: what an artist gives through his art is a pattern for understanding what's redeemable in him, & in man generally.

[200] I don't see why I couldn't present the Biblical tradition in an "objective" context. When I read Blofeld or Evans-Wentz[165] on Tantrism I read almost uncritically, because I want to be as responsive as possible. Yet what do these immensely long & laborious efforts aim at? At the Bodhisattva. And what does the B. [Bodhisattva] do? Perform charitable acts. And how does this differ from what the Christian, accepting Christ as the definitive Bodhisattva, does or is enjoined to do? Perhaps the Chinese conquest of Tibet will diffuse the Tantric light over the world, as the Turkish conquests of the Roman Empire spread Greek over Europe. But the knowledge of Greek was essentially new light on Europe's own past, & we might get an "objective" Xy in the same way.

[201] Christ isn't a "reincarnation" of anybody: he's a "repetition" of the Law, and the apocalypse "repeats" him, in Kierkegaard's sense. Yeats says [in *A Vision*] the discarnate soul moves from death towards birth: this could be a cyclical process or a dialectical one: Dante's Purgatorio moves from death to dialectical rebirth in Paradise (= Eden). Cyclical rebirth isn't possible except in the obvious sense that we're our reborn ancestors (reincarnation seems to ignore the one aspect of itself that nobody can deny). The vision of this is in Aeneid VI.

[202] The "real" world is one of infinitely possible ones—not necessarily the best one, as Leibnitz urges,[166] but the one we're stuck with for whatever reason. Blake says it's not the best but nearly the worst of all possible worlds; Buddhists say it's the best of the six "existing" ones but pretty awful. Blake revolves around the conception of art as a form of liberation, & this is something I should come to grips with. Long before the drug-cult craze I realized that Rimbaud had something to do with the yogic nature of art. So do the Eliot Quartets. Obviously art can only operate this way if it's a stimulus to the reader's creativity.

[203] The soul's return to birth starts in this life, as one's past, & eventually one's childhood, becomes more vivid. I suppose the Catholic saint is the institutional equivalent of the teaching Spirit, but I doubt if things are set up quite as the R.C. Church teaches in the other world.

[204] *Liberal* is the Bible book as I'm now planning it: *Tragicomedy* is a book on Shakespeare, probably not to be thought of until after retirement. *Anticlimax* is a long book on education, for God's sake. It takes in my Utopia & *Critical Path* stuff; it leads to a kind of Mahayana Christianity, I think; and it's probably identical with the book on its side.[167] My CRTC [Canadian Radio-Television Commission] work[168] will probably correspond to Section VI of CP, and it will go in the direction indicated by two recent koans of mine: that nothing happens in the world except the education of the people in it, and that knowledge is of the actual and leads to wisdom which is of the potential. If the book has to be "on" something, I suppose it's really "on" Plato. *Rencontre* is *Fearful Symmetry*, or a rewritten version of it.

[205] In the second series, *Mirage* is the present *Anatomy*, and *Paradox* what I've been calling the Third Book. Those don't have to stick, of course, and I haven't thought further at present.

[206] Although separated by ⅂ [Tragicomedy], Λ [Anticlimax] is really the sequel to L [Liberal], & a lot of what I've been trying to stick on to L, which would make it impossibly long, goes in Λ. L is Urthona, ⅂ Orc, Λ Urizen, and ʎ [Rencontre] Tharmas. So Γ [Twilight] is Enion, & perhaps V [Mirage], ⊢ [Paradox] & ⊥ [Ignoramus] are Enitharmon, Vala & Ahania respectively.

[207] It isn't much to do for the Liberation, but there's always the hope that my industrious search for koans & verbal formulas may be useful. In some contexts they could outlast the thoughts of Chairman Mao. Anyway, that's the sort of thing I should keep in front of me.

[208] ∟ [Liberal], then, deals with the Logos dialectic of heaven & hell, and, I suppose, stops there. ¬ [Tragicomedy] is the cycle of the Spirit, and the Third Book is its emanation. It's partly a book about Ovid, the Classical counterpoint to the Christian myth, because, as is obvious, the plays of Shakespeare were really written by Ovid. Honest Ovid among the Goths,[169] that is. Things like the use of folktale & ballad (e.g. the bed trick) instead of myth are parts of the counterpart to Scripture that Shakespeare produced. I can use it for expounding things like the discontinuous moment (from MM [*Measure for Measure*]).

[209] Recently I had to read *Lord Jim, The Caine Mutiny* & *The Ship of Fools*, to advise an audiovisual company.[170] As always, my approach was through *anagnorisis*. With the Wouk & Porter this meant simply recognition, seeing certain things done. With the Conrad, which of course I had often read before, it also meant discovery. In other words I do have a value-system, whatever my critics say. The Wouk & Porter are second-rate, which means they're damn good but not quite first-rate. Second-rate literature is whatever I can't *learn* from. At the same time I have a curious compulsion to read detective stories. I don't know why: it may have something to do with organizing my dreams.

[210] Well, anyway, ∧ [Anticlimax] is perhaps the polarization-in-unity of the Father, the deus absconditus & the mother-naked Abyss. Of course if I identified ⅄ [Rencontre] and the Third Book, I'd have a complete encyclopedia. ⅄ would then be the comminution[171] book it's always been, & there'd be a lot of Blake in it—*Europe* & *Milton* at least.

[211] I must do more thinking about Tharmas. He's Cronos, Hyperion, Atlantis; the Parent Power who first fell. So he's the original state (circumference) of the Los-Orc-Urizen process. It'd be more plausible to see ∟ [Liberal] as the Tharmas book, & ⅄ [Rencontre] as the fourth immortal starry one. Anyway, the Frye encyclopedia seems to be taking shape. Either 100 sections (28-22-28-22) or 96.

[212] ʎ [Rencontre] is a book of riddles, as my course is,[172] & the riddle is a verbal trap. As soon as you *name* "what it's about" (in some cases pronounced the name of the riddler) you've sprung the trap & escaped from it. Riddle is also the cognate object of read. I read riddles; I don't "solve" or destroy them. But what's riddling about them, in this sense, is their egocentricity, their isolation from the rest of literary experience. So the motto of the book is interpenetration, the identity of the one and the many. You don't reduce the many to one, nor do you keep them many, as you do when you solve or "explicate" them.

[213] No: at present it looks as though ʎ [Rencontre] were the Tharmas book. Remember that the Chinese ☰, Ch'ien, is Tharmas.[173] ∟ [Liberal] and ∧ [Anticlimax] are the Urthona-Urizen axis, from imagination to articulate intelligence. ¬ [Tragicomedy] & ʎ [Rencontre] are on the Ovidian axis, & are episodic as the other two are continuous. Perhaps, then, I'd better block out ∧ as well as ∟, so as to determine where one stops & the other starts.

[214] ∧ [Anticlimax] is ostensibly a book on education founded on Plato: it's the old Second Essay,[174] of course, dealing with contracts & Utopias.[175] The traditions of both, the theory of education, the 4k thinkers,[176] whatever CRTC [Canadian Radio-Television Commission] stuff[177] I pick up, & so on. Plato (and his Neoplatonic developments) raise the question why Atlantis & reincarnation myths turn up so often: he also defines faith as realization of knowledge in experience (nous as distinct from mere pistis). ∟ [Liberal] is spear & grail, wand & cup (or rod & staff as in Ps. 23); ∧ is sword & dish. ʎ [Rencontre] may be the greater trump sequence after all & ¬ [Tragicomedy] the mandala of peaceful & wrathful deities. Oh, hell: maybe this stuff is just a lot of masturbation.

[215] Anyway, with luck I should finish the Encyclopaedia by the time I retire, & can spend the years of retirement drafting the emanation-encyclopaedia. A *Mirage* full of music, a *Paradox* full of Poe, Hawthorne, Melville, Scott, Henry James & William Morris: an *Ignoramus* full of God knows what, a *Twilight* full of me—what could be sweeter?

[216] And I certainly mustn't forget that it *is* an encyclopaedia, & that it couldn't matter less what order the books are written in or published.

Also that, even if ideas for an emanation cycle do take shape, like the Scott-Morris-American one for *Mirage* or *Paradox* above, I must utterly shoot the works on this one: it's to be the ideal systematizing critique of me that I've often wished somebody else could write.

[217] I'm often attacked for deliberate pattern-making, but that's how I've learned a lot of things. If A & B have opposites R & S, & A & B are followed by C & D, then these probably are T & U. In the present scheme L [Liberal] & ʎ [Rencontre] have been reasonably clear, but far too long & schematic & elaborate, & if I think of an opposite book it should help a great deal. With L it's the sequel; with ʎ it's the preliminary understructure. The whole father-mother creation myth, and perhaps the pre-Rc & post-Rc [pre-Romantic & post-Romantic] structures, can now go in ⅂ [Tragicomedy] where they'll prop up commentaries on (perhaps) *The Tempest*, *Comus* & the like, so that the long & elaborate ogdoad which is the basis of ʎ can emerge more clearly.

[218] L [Liberal] is perhaps after all the Book of Urizen, & Λ [Anticlimax] the Book of Tharmas, thinking of Tharmas as Atlantis concealed by the sea. This new conception of a very old hunch hinges on Philo, & raises the question: what would Xy be like if its tradition had gone through Plato, the *Greek* Fathers, Clement & Origen, some of the Gnostics, the school of Chartres, & on to the Klibansky people?[178] That is, the Western Church, being Roman, legal, authoritarian, & rationalizing sterility as a sense of reality, found a deep kinship with Aristotle: St. Thomas set up realism, the nominalists knocked it down, & so created a schizophrenic split between experience & knowledge, which buggered the conception of "faith," by taking it out of the area of realized vision.

[219] As the last note shows, I must keep well out of the history-of-ideas quagmire I've been skirting for at least thirty years. Starting with Plato doesn't mean plodding through every Platonist, century by century, down to Whitehead. It means pulling together my Utopian, educational & communication interests—the Second Essay, in short[179]—along with the mythical importance of the Atlantis & reincarnation themes. The Platonic tradition is or can be actually misleading, as Blake warns—Plotinus, for instance, tends toward cosmos-worship & away from the recovery of creation.

[220] By Mahayanic Xy I mean the repudiation of the legal substitute, the "outward ceremony" or sacramental system that replaces realization. Patanjali begins: "Yoga is the suppression of the metamorphoses projected by the mind. This suppression is freedom. Without it, you become what you behold."[180] Blake uses art as a yogic discipline, a counter-idolatry of vision.

[221] ∟ [Liberal] & Λ [Anticlimax] are "male" books, progressive in style, alchemical in schematism, though naturally they contain their emanations as well. ˥ [Tragicomedy] & ⋌ [Rencontre] are "female," astrological, circumferential, Ovidian. Male is the postlapsarian I Ching sequence,[181] the book on its side; female the prelapsarian & simpler one. It (female) also contains the Druid analogy.[182]

[222] Let's say, just to get it said, that V [Mirage] is devoted mainly to the post-Rc [post-Romantic] conception of yogic & objective art, that ⊢ [Paradox] deals with the romance trdn. [tradition] in 19th c. fiction, & that ⊥ [Ignoramus] is largely concerned with Kantian & Hegelian developments in thought & the reactions against them. Γ [Twilight] will still be me.

[223] First I sought for an authentic prophet, & wrote FS. That enabled me to write AC, my Deuteronomy.[183] Now I must write the vision of the fourfold Law & Gospel. I have an odd feeling too that I'm past the stage of Ulysses beating off the ghost of his mother.[184] After 30 years it's about time.

[224] I'm no nearer understanding Atlantis or reincarnation symbolism, but I do understand more clearly that it polarizes the Bible in some way. Similarly, I don't understand the *ahimsa*,[185] or "leave everything alone," side of yoga. In yoga you go up the Eros quadrant, splitting in two into an old man & a *kouros* [male youth]. The old man gets reborn; the youth goes into the Logos vision, then voluntarily forces himself down the Adonis chute as a Bodhisattva, like Christ. Sure, but *then* what does he do? Charitable acts. But these are dialectic, garden-weeding, acts. They're mosquito-swatting acts. The Word cuts like a sword. It's still possible that without Christ there's no *vision* of what to do except achieve self-liberation.

[225] A Buddhist book I was reading says: "first of all, one has to acquire

an abhorrence of death & rebirth," or words to that effect. A completely happy kanzzanic existence,[186] with an eiron-reserve so you wouldn't fall out of it, where you'd die only to get some variety out of a sequence of lives ("change delectable, not need"),[187] where the community was so well organized that your happiness wasn't at anybody's expense—that would knock the bottom out of the Buddhist system, and it is, I think, in Xy.

[226] I've often said that if I understood the two Alice books I'd have very little left to understand about literature. Actually I think the Alice books, while they carry over, begin rather than sum up—a new twist to fiction that has to do with intellectual paradox & the disintegrating of the ego. Borges especially, along with some Kafka, FW [*Finnegans Wake*], some conspiracy novels like [Thomas Pynchon's] *The Crying of Lot 49*, some *elements in* detective stories & science fiction, come down from this. In science fiction it's the world within that's really existing, & the world without is only a projection of it. At least, when the within isn't interesting the without isn't either. My one fiction idea (24 Preludes)[188] also relates to this. My remark in the Beddoes essay [*SR*, 62–3], that fantasy is a "distinctively modern" quality, also relates to it.

[227] I'm beginning to feel that while ⌉ [Tragicomedy] is a book about Shakespeare, & while drama is its centre of gravity, it also incorporates a theory of fiction, the lead into which, at various times, I've looked for to (a) comparative folktale (b) sentimental romance (i) Scott-Macdonald-Morris (ii) Poe-Hawthorne-Melville. I think Lewis Carroll is of some help here, and I also wonder if Sylvie & Bruno, despite all its silliness & dismal cuteness, doesn't have something in its double-focus alternation of two worlds. Eddison's books seem to me to have some relation to S & B [*Sylvie and Bruno*] (unconscious, I think) & the whole conception latent in S & B, of an action in "real life" as an action within the l. m. [low mimetic] mode, & going on simultaneously in a romantic mode, is worked out by Eddison.[189]

[228] ⌉ [Tragicomedy] is probably the Tharmas, not the Orc book, & ⋏ [Rencontre] is Orc. ⋏ is about Ovid, I think, in the sense that ∧ [Anticlimax] is about Plato. And Ovid, of course, wrote not only Shakespeare's plays[190] but the Phoenix & the Turtle as well, along with its encyclopaedic context. It's always been a thematic & episodic book, & ⌉ gives the

interconnecting principles of narrative that are the necessary prolegomena to it. So far I've kept dodging this theory of narrative: it was the "epic" chapter that got squeezed out of AC. I doubt if I can dredge up much that's new to say about drama, in the context of *scene* or dianoia.

[229] My "recluse" existence is not wholly laziness & inertia. My work depends on a good memory, & the way to keep a good memory is not to make too many waves of experience in between. The hours I spent in Mob Quad reading about Old English literature[191] are as vivid to me still as the hours I spent last week at a CRTC [Canadian Radio-Television Commission] hearing,[192] & of course I remember the content of those hours far better.

[230] The thing that crystallized from the Birks Lecture was the consequence of the eye & ear business.[193] Eye religion makes, eventually, the physical order of nature the symbol of God—remember the horror of Plotinus at the Gnostic suggestion that the order of nature might be evil. Thus there's a *meta*physical world which is the invisible world behind the visible order which is its symbol. The tendency of this is to drop the anthropomorphic mask of a personal Deity, to move from an essential Him Who Is to a That Which Is, the ground of being.

[231] Ear religion leads not to a metaphysical but a spiritual world. The word spirit contains the metaphor of breath, air, wind. We can't see air: if we could we could see nothing else. Similarly with light: we don't see light; we see *by* light: what we see is a source of light [*GC*, 124]. Creation begins with light: the *source* of light comes on the fourth day. Here's a conception in which the invisible is the *medium* of the visible, the power by which the visible is brought into being. This is a revolutionary, existential & phenomenological conception. What's invisible is the inner Word of God, which is not projected on the outer world.

[232] The spiritual world is a *bodily* world, not a metaphysical one. It's most easily seen in the arts, which em*body* the spiritual vision of a people. And here, by way of Yeats' *Byzantium* is a link between imagination & life that would, if I could grasp it, clear up the whole "after-life" business.

[233] The "yoga" intuition is founded on the notion of transforming the

body, & I don't know if there's any Christian alternative answer to it. Our present body is almost wholly unknown to the consciousness which inhabits it. Yoga creates an imaginative body in its place, & goes to work on that. Christian imagery concentrates on the social body, the city & garden which are also the body of the one man who achieved resurrection. The next step connects with the contrast between the crumbling monument & immortal because dying & rebirthing papyrus, & somewhere in here is the mystery of why the Bible tells a story.

[234] I've been wondering, partly as a result of a dream I had, whether our memories & impressions of other people don't become to some degree autonomous after those people die. Maybe the spirits that turn up at séances are autonomous projections of this sort, i.e., Bishop [James] Pike wasn't talking to the spirit of his son but to his own memory of his son that had become autonomous.[194] It would be interesting to know if a spirit came to a séance who was the spirit of someone who, unknown to the enquirer, was still alive. If this has never happened, the hypothesis is still possible, but indicates some essential but hidden link with the living person.

[235] This would account for the popular belief that if you see your *own* fetch you're going to die. For such autonomous creatures of memory could be projected visually as ghosts as well as aurally as voices. This I suppose is why Blake speaks of the memory as a desert where spectres of the dead wander,[195] & why the notion of repose, and, symbolically, burial, is so important. It's for us, not them. In Blake the use of the imagination, specifically in art, is *a resurrection* of the dead. Art, the spiritual vision of a culture, harrows the hell of human misery.

[236] Such memories, resting in peace with the inscriptions of our own impressions written above them, form the continuous illusion which is the sense of identity in this world. (Cinema, I suppose, is what Susanne Langer would call "virtual memory").[196] The plowing & harrowing (Blake's terms) of these memories is the imaginative resurrection, which is the permanent reality of Man, brought to life by the practice or habit-memory of constructive skill. If the memories don't rest but wander restlessly about, they become neuroses or blocking points.

[237] ⋏ [Rencontre] is to be a book of riddles, riddle being the cognate

object of read. Hence it's to focus on difficult poems or other relatively brief things: Rimbaud's *Illuminations*, Valéry's *Jeune Parque*, Blake's *Europe*—that sort of thing, only it becomes a magical total riddle or mandala. The Alice books. And it'll probably be the second of the four to be written; ⅂ [Tragicomedy] probably the last. I alternate between wanting to close the Bible book off & wanting to start planning the whole encyclopedia; but I should keep the whole thing in mind, without forcing the pace. I've waited a long time. What I'm waiting for at the moment, mainly, is some huge, central & utterly simple organizing idea for ⅂. That will probably come out of the last two chapters of L [Liberal]. My graduate course keeps ⅄ percolating, or would if I recorded my teaching of it more fully & carefully. I think I shall open a new notebook for Λ [Anticlimax].

[238] The *transition* from L [Liberal] to ⅂ [Tragicomedy] will come out of the intuitions that have been swirling around me for twenty years (at least) connecting the Christian *commedia* with the Tempest, which is the telos of ⅂, with Sakuntala,[197] Menander, *The Birds*, & the *dianoia* of romantic comedy generally. The transition from ⅂ to ⅄ [Anticlimax] starts with the St. Clair enlightenment,[198] also nearly twenty years old. Note the Blake rhythm, and the recapitulation of my four undergraduate years.[199] The transition from Λ to ⅄ [Rencontre] probably revolves around the oracle-wit business at Seattle.[200] Then Λ presents literature as a cycle of discontinuous epiphanies.

[239] I think I'd like to go back to my original experiences with comedy & anatomy: in the excitement of identifying new genres I missed a great deal of their actual content.

[240] There has been a very long interval between this note & the last one. I get periodically bored with notebooks, because so much of what I put into them is just a form of masturbation: an empty fantasy life making the scene with beckoning fair charmers who don't exist. However.

[241] At present I'm thinking of four books under the running title of *The Critical Comedy*,[201] with the same secret names & symbols as before, & the same general characteristics. L [Liberal] is a book on the Bible and literature. ⅂ [Tragicomedy] is my conspectus of mythoi and themes, the great doodle,[202] and evolves out of my graduate course. Λ [Anticlimax] is about

philosophy as a conceptual displacement of myth, contracts & Utopias, literature as a form of communication, & prose forms. I think it may follow the communication-community-communion line of my Keats article.[203] ⋌ [Rencontre] is a summarized history of English literature, following the outline of my HBJ introduction.[204] Of these, only ∧ is really in the masturbation stage now. This means that the book of riddles is now absorbed into ┐, & ⋌ seems discontinuous only because the history idea, which I'd always resisted, is a snapper-up of otherwise unconsidered trifles.

[242] ┐ [Tragicomedy], then, like ∟ [Liberal], will have 12 chapters, 3 parts of 4 each. The three parts may follow the Joyce progression: Part One is the Great Doodle *and* the book of riddles, such poems as [Mallarmé's] Igitur, Jeune Parque, Phoenix & Turtle turning up in place. Part Two is on epic & fiction, a rationale of fictional structures (sentimental romance figures here: it's the informing principle of Balzac, not that I'm going to read all of *him*). Part Three is on drama & probably ends once more with *The Tempest*.

[243] ∧ [Anticlimax] then starts with my old drama-to-prose gyre,[205] and while it's in three parts again, there's more of a narrative drive to it. It's also what I used to call the book on its side,[206] & it incorporates the old three-awarenesses scheme.[207] Note that the four books expand the structure-imagery-narrative-language scheme in ∟ [Liberal].

[244] Coryat's Crudities, ii, 328: typology of Q [Queen of] Sheba : Solomon :: Magi : infant Jesus.[208]

[245] I notice that every major change of the last few years has been in the direction of *naturalizing* my themes, fitting them to the obvious things I know, or can most easily discover at my time of life. Anchoring ⋌ [Rencontre] in the old history of English literature scheme does away with having to learn linguistics & such; similarly, if the ┐ [Tragicomedy]–∧ [Anticlimax] drama-to-prose gyre (St. Clair)[209] goes through sentimental romance I wouldn't have to try to mug up any communication theory. One could start with the four forms of fiction & work through a turned-on-side version[210] of the descent theme of ┐.

[246] That is, the Promethean turn is radically rebirth, the coming around of the cycle. Then it becomes revolution, or a move to a new plateau, but

eventually revolution, as in Blake's view of the Exodus, collapses into rebirth. Then comes resurrection, the full dialectical opposition to rebirth. On the way at least two other elements are involved. One is the passage through oracle to wit, recovering the power of laughter;[211] the other is a kind of incarnation from below, Blake's wandering spectres of the dead taking on bodies.

[247] This is chapter 7 of L [Liberal] and the last part of ⅂ [Tragicomedy]. In ∧ [Anticlimax] it becomes the nostos theme of romance, the polarization of beginning & end points as contract & Utopia, & the neo-romance, Utopia-transcending apocalyptic vision. (Or perhaps I leave that out & go on to some conceptual displacements as the "anticlimax" ending).

[248] Bloom's Anxiety of Influence:[212] an embarrassing book to me, because it's about him & not its subject, & I'm one of the influences he's anxious about. I think the fear of death, which the existentialists say is *the* anxiety, is really just the centre of a much larger anxiety of metamorphosis. The question *ubi sunt* may turn up in snow or flowers long before it's realized to be death. The anxiety of continuity is salvaged from this, just as the knowledge of good is salvaged from the knowledge of evil. Continuity actualizes itself in the O.T. [Old Testament] forms of wisdom (hokmah) & law, & thence develops towards a neo-metamorphosis ("we shall all be changed," says Paul). The Jews, & the Pharisaic survivals in Xy, knock themselves out keeping their identity continuous (e.g. apostolic succession).

[249] Progress & evolution & the Burke-Newman notion of *contained* metamorphosis belong to the revolutionary halfway stage. The *acceptance* of the anxiety of metamorphosis leads to reincarnation & the whole *maya*[213] doctrine. What this ignores is the reality of the past, the polarized opposite of resurrection, perverted by Xy into its appalling notion of hell. A book called, even if secretly, Liberal must lead to a vision of total liberation. Recognition of the eternal reality of the *has been* is the beginning of this. On the other hand, Rencontre stays in the region of intermediate dialectic which is also the region of *history.*

[250] That is, a revolution, whether Christian or Marxist, looks out of & beyond history. But once it's actualized in history, & has to establish continuity with what *was* there, the trans-historical ideal becomes a

donkey's carrot, & history keeps right on going, a rebirth or revolution in the sense of a turning cycle.

[251] Just as death is the focus of the anxiety of metamorphosis, so life after death is the focus of the anxiety of continuity. Hence the Egyptian obsession with burial. The whole of Biblical symbolism, the O.T. [Old Testament] Exodus & the N.T. [New Testament] resurrection, is founded on the *symbolic* Egypt as the land of the dead.

[252] The Tutankhamen grave was discovered in 1922, too late to be a source for *The Waste Land*. But *The Waste Land* is one of the definitive poems, because Eliot fished all his life for what was down there, & *The Waste Land* IS what's down there. Even Pound's job on the MS was an archaeological clean-up, the real stuff separated from the debris.

[253] Egyptian-Eliot links:[214] the board game. Hunting scenes. The ship of death (Cleopatra on her barge: Elizabeth on the Thames playing with the idea of making Leicester king by marriage). The fear of premature resurrection, i.e., the grave-robber: cf. the scratching dog. Lil & Lilith (it's a very white-goddessy poem too). Egypt as synecdochal for Africa, Carthage, etc. Still larger pattern, much of it cut by Pound, takes in the South Pole, with Ancient-Mariner & Gordon Pym[215] links. Contest in former of death & life in death (subterranean & submarine, reversed, in Eliot). Tutankhamen was a boy, an Adonis figure. To get back to Bloom's book,[216] the anxiety of influence combines continuity & metamorphosis.

[254] Also Egyptian is the boxes-of-Silenus mummy cases, of one inside another: Rabelais.[217] Anointing the body for burial: Mark 14:8,[218] so it survives. Evidently it was *dice* games that were found in T's [Tutankhamen's] tomb. Cards are Adonis & Hermes; dice is Thanatos; chess & the like Prometheus & Eros.

[255] Two forms of incarnation: one is the katabasis from Logos to Nomos. This is the actualization of consciousness. When this enters the world of experience, the latter turns objective, a place of obstacles to be contemplated in order to discover in it the predictable element of law. On this science is founded. The other is the anabasis from Thanatos to Nous. This is the creative unconscious rising from a spectral world to the embodiment of art, hitched to dream.

[256] The argument of Λ [Anticlimax] gets a little clearer. I start with naive romance as a displacement of myth. The Two Brothers, the Hymn of the Soul, the Clementine Recognition[219] stream, & so on to the Grail romances, Spenser & Ariosto. Then my study of 19th c. sentimental romance, shading off to the main "realistic" tradition by way of Melville, Conrad, Henry James, etc. The essential point is that romance *contains* realism, its structure being what holds realism together.

[257] That's Part One: Part Two is devoted first to confessions & anatomies, then to contracts & Utopias. William Morris bulks large here, but the St. Clair illumination[220] does too. Three, revolving around Plato, deals with the informing patterns of thought. Note that Λ [Anticlimax] occupies the *theoria* territory & ⅄ [Rencontre] the *praxis* one. Hence ⅄ has to be historical in its outlook.

[258] So what's vaguest, now, in the whole series is the *third* part of L [Liberal]. It should be, of course, on the historical & conceptual projections of the Bible.

Work in Progress

The set of typed notes that Frye titled "Work in Progress" is located in box 36 of the 1991 accession of the NFF, and is indexed as file 11h. Buried for some time among masses of disorganized typescripts, it is one of the extraordinary finds among the unpublished papers, for it explains, as if to an uninitiated audience, the history and structure of the ogdoad scheme (see Introduction). The notes are accurately datable to 1972 because Frye says in paragraph 8 that he reviewed Charles Williams's Shadows of Ecstasy *twenty-two years ago, which he did in 1950. The outline of a four-volume project to be called* The Critical Comedy *is more or less identical to the late entries of Notebook 24, providing a cut-off date for that notebook. The history of English literature listed here as* Rencontre *is identical, except for the sequence of its numbered parts, to the introduction Frye wrote for a Harcourt Brace anthology. The project collapsed, but a surviving 184–page unfinished typescript of NF's introduction survives, with a letter attached to it dated 1972.*

[1] When I was about fourteen, I developed the ambition to write eight great novels. The ambition was founded on something still earlier, connected with music, and is probably based ultimately on some ogdoadic diagram in my unconscious which enabled me to respond to Blake, among other things. I can still remember having this ambition as late as my freshman year at college. In a fourteen-year-old's typically pretentious way, I had given them all impressive titles, one word each: Liberal, Tragicomedy, Anticlimax, Rencontre, Mirage, Paradox, Twilight. Why those names have stuck with me all these years I don't know, but they have. They also had certain characteristics, and in fact have kept them to some degree ever since, through all their modulations.

[2] Then I discovered at university what my real vocation was, and plunged into the Blake book. When I finished it, the old scheme came back again, only this time they were to be works of criticism and scholarship and thought. I pondered these books while walking down to the College from Bathurst Street—1944, it would have been.[1] My lucubrations eventually produced the Anatomy of Criticism ten years later: by that time I had realized that the Blake didn't belong in the series, but would have to be, as I put it, numbered zero. After the Anatomy was published, it seemed to me that that too would have to be numbered zero.

[3] At that point I decided that the Eight Books were not to be books I would write, but books to be read: astral volumes surrounding me in a circle, so to speak. But during my first sabbatical after the Guggenheim year of 1950, in 1964, I again tried drafting a sequence of four books. By the [that] time I advanced enough in years to realize that four would be absolute maximum that the time and intelligence left me could manage. Meanwhile, I was doing various series of public lectures and writing short books, all numbered zero.

[4] In 1964 the four books were worked out in Four Zoas diagram, and the sequence has been, pretty consistently, Urthona, Orc, Urizen, Tharmas.[2] The next four are "emanation" books, contained by implication in the first four, but most unlikely ever to be written out.

[5] For a year or two it's been becoming clear that the Liberal of the series, the first book, is a book on the Bible and its relation to literature, more particularly as the source of the mythical framework of the Western imagination.[3] Tragicomedy, then, becomes a book on the conspectus of literary imagery derived from my present graduate course. It begins, probably, as a book of "riddles," showing how various difficult poems become more intelligible when placed on what I call the Great Doodle. Then it goes on to the interconnecting mythoi.

[6] Anticlimax is at present vaguer than the others, but will be concerned with: prose forms; contracts and Utopias; the relation of these to the theory of education; communication, community and communion as progressive stages in identity;[4] conceptual displacements of myths. Rencontre, I've just realized, is to be a history of English literature,

following the general outline of the sketch I'm doing for the Harcourt Brace Anthology.[5]

[7] The four books will have, I think, the running title of The Critical Comedy,[6] and the Dante and Balzac echoes will be frequent. Each book, as I see it now, will have twelve chapters, making the whole scheme my "Forty-Eight."[7] If each chapter were divided in two, or thought of as double in construction like a prelude and fugue, that would make, with four introductions to the single books, one hundred sections. (I've always felt that Dante's trinitarian obsessions made him fail to see the real fourfold form of his poem, Purgatorio 27 to Paradiso 9 being the missing fourth world and scherzo movement).[8]

[8] Sentimental romance, then. Starting with Morris, there's the fact that he's an indefatigable collector of epics and traditional stories, and in the Earthly Paradise fits a number of them together in what is evidently a significant way. I've just bought his translation of the Volsunga Saga in paperback, forgetting that I'd bought it before without realizing it. The introduction to this book links Morris with Wagner, who is also deeply involved in the sentimental romance business, apart from the fact that the Volsung story is close to the centre of what I'm interested in. And now comes Levi-Strauss saying that Wagner was the first person to make a structural analysis of folk tale,[9] in the Ring anyway, only he made it in music, as I wish I could do myself. Twenty-two years ago I reviewed a series of novels for the Hudson review, one of them being Charles Williams' Shadows of Ecstasy, which I said was "by Zanoni out of She."[10] Now I have Zanoni and She, and they're also close to the centre of something.

[9] I had always thought of Tragicomedy, perhaps because of its name, as based on drama in general and Shakespeare, especially the late romances, in particular. Also as going back to Classical mythology, which means primarily Hesiod and Ovid (with Apollodorus), as a complement to the Bible book. And, partly because of Shakespeare's consistent use of folktale for his comedies and his avoidance of Christian myth, it would also deal with the morphology of folk tale.

[10] Two types of plot: the repetitive (forward to recognition, and repetitive in the Kierkegaardian sense),[11] and the anamnetic (backward to

recognition). The former includes the Odyssey, the primary example of a story of the regathering of a separated family, where the central figure is at first in disguise, then assumes his proper shape. Measure for Measure is Shakespeare's example, though the main point of that play is different. In Shakespeare it goes on to include the curious plot that starts with the Clementine Recognitions[12] and goes through Chaucer's Man of Law's Tale and Gower's Apollonius story to Pericles and the Comedy of Errors. Here one theme is the recognition of one's unfallen identity, as in Eliot's Marina and the end of the Purgatorio. The Apollonius story starts with incest, the demonic form of the united family.

[11] The other story develops from the Hymn of the Soul in the Acts of Thomas,[13] where the soul is nobly born and is sent to discover a pearl in the depths of the sea, and then forgets what the hell it was supposed to do. In other developments of this, like Sakuntala,[14] the talisman of recognition gets swallowed by a fish, which brings that archetype in; the one that's sprawled all over the New Testament and that I've been chasing through Rudens and Moby Dick and God knows what else. Wonder if God does know.

[12] Anyway, this type is close to Cymbeline and the Winter's Tale—I had a strong feeling when doing the Bampton Lectures that the four romances corresponded to four primary types of mythos. The Tempest starts beckoning in the direction of that chess-in-Bardo[15] will-o-wisp I've been chasing for thirty years. Also Lear's search for the natural man.

[13] I can't forget that the conspectus of plots, if I can do it, arises out of the Great Wheel of Archetypes,[16] which I already have. The Eros quest as a displaced lover's activity, typically going up a mountain to the earthly Paradise. The Adonis quest, on the other side going down, has the birth-of-the-hero stuff, the Adonis elegy, and the symbolism of hunting I originally got out of Surtees.[17]

[14] For the descent to the lower world I must reread Rabelais and try to recollect the various hunches I was getting then; also that Merlin Coccaius epic.[18] The Inferno is compulsory but not attractive: I wish the bloody Christians could think of something better than just shit and corruption. Here's where sentimental romance really could help: Rider Haggard, for example, writes what in explicit meaning are adventure stories, but in

implicit meaning they're searches for the buried mother, or what he calls the heart of the world. Incidentally, I have to make the point again, though it's clear in the Anatomy, that what our value-judgements subordinate as popular and sub-standard is actually better literature than a lot of stuff we give higher ratings to. I'd like to begin, for example, with a comparison of Katherine Anne Porter's Ship of Fools with Paul Gallico's Poseidon Adventure.[19] The former has nothing except a certain amount of allegory, as wooden as her Sebastian Brant original. The latter is busting with archetypes—Christmas tree, Exodus climb, with very explicit references indicating that the author knows exactly what he's doing, a clergyman who's a Moses figure and goes mad near the top (the theme is climbing up a ship that's turned upside-down), references to the lake of hell, and so on. The highbrows prefer the Ship of Fools for the same reason that highbrows in Anglo-Saxon times preferred saints' lives to Beowulf.

[15] The Prometheus quadrant is really sparse: I haven't much except my birds-and-frogs hunches about Aristophanes, and revolution as a vulgarization (not a demonic form) of resurrection. On the other hand my fishing stuff almost certainly goes here.[20]

[16] Then there's the difficulty about the post-Romantic wheel,[21] trying to see whether it's really different or whether my nagging feeling is right that the earlier carries on out of habit for much if not most of the period. Anyway, I have the poles of identity and alienation, and the relation of the wheel to Yeats's Vision and Blake's Mental Traveller. The Bildungsroman as the most usual way of describing the new Adonis quest away from identity toward alienation. I have various hunches about the congregates at the other pole, much of it carrying on from the old Hermes descent: the grateful dead companion, the doppelganger, the symbolism of clocks and mirrors (one's own identity as an object), the breakup of language, the muttering ego in Dostoievsky and Beckett, the reduction to chance and the throw of dice in Mallarmé, which is also connected with (new) creation in Igitur.[22]

[17] The new[23] Prometheus seems to deal mainly with Rimbaud but to include a few things like Valery's Jeune Parque: the movement toward a new identity. Where the Huckleberry-Finn and Confidence-Man journeys down to the great river belong I'm not sure. The new Eros is mainly

D.H. Lawrence, so far as I can see now. Is the work I did on [Virginia Woolf's] Between the Acts, on Morris romance, on Peacock and Meredith, of any relevance here?

[18] I must consolidate on this point: I have a Bible book in my mind, fairly complete except for the last two chapters, and I have another book which sticks together a conspectus of narrative structures and my graduate course material—I can't imagine how they can ever be unstuck. So that's two books: I can't pretend I've got only one in mind, and I haven't as yet the ghost of an idea for the last two, and should forget them, for the time being anyway. Two books, one revolving around the Bible and the other a conspectus of narratives. Both of these, I notice, are subjects that keep turning up in the avant-garde critics, of the kind that read Barthes and Derrida. As usual, they'll probably get more credit for saying it ought to be done than I'll get for doing it, like twenty years ago when people like Francis Fergusson were saying somebody ought to do something about the four levels of meaning.[24]

[19] I can do the second book, as well as the first one, I think, if I can get over one of my silliest vices, which is reading a book and then being too lazy to take notes on it. For thirty years I've been reading at the sentimental romance area, and now, after Jay and Anne[25] have gone into it, for God's sake, it looms up as a new idea. Well, I have to read the same goddamn books I've been reading or thinking of reading for thirty years and take notes on them.[26] [Edward Bulwer-Lytton's] Zanoni and [H. Rider Haggard's] She. Not much other Bulwer-Lytton except A Strange Story—The Coming Race didn't have much. Some more Rider Haggard, enough to get his context. George MacDonald. Maybe some Wilkie Collins. Dickens wasn't as rewarding as I'd hoped,[27] but perhaps Barnaby Rudge. And the Americans—Poe, Hawthorne, Melville, Lewis Carroll, very much including Sylvie and Bruno. And some Scott—I read Peveril of the Peak and was too lazy to analyze it afterwards. William Morris again. Sheridan LeFanu—again I never analyzed Uncle Silas. Mary Shelley. That Gogol story I did take notes on, not that it did me any good. Some of the Germans, of course—Novalis and Hoffman, though I never could see much in Jean Paul. I have a hunch Scott ties a lot of it together.[28]

[20] One's literary values, as I have already mentioned, take a bit of adjusting. I've been reading She and [Wyndham] Lewis' Apes of God,

and find I spend all my time on the latter. The ostensible reason is clear enough: that's a book that's been staring me in the face for forty years as A Book I Ought to Read, although I know quite well that the only reason for reading it is to have documentary evidence that it isn't worth reading. However, I felt an overmastering urge to transform it from the most boring book I never read into the most boring book I ever read, so that, at the age of sixty, I could be in a position to reflect that never, never, never, would I have to read that fucking book again. A book that one has this attitude to one naturally reads fairly fast. (No doubt it's my obsession with the time philosophy that makes me feel that a book six hundred and fifty pages long ought to say something and get somewhere). But, I realized, the compulsion to read it was simpler. I was reading it for relaxation. Pretentious as it is, it's not a serious book: one simply stares at it page by page and reacts with some such reflection as "the Sitwells, I presume." Whereas She is a very serious book: it has to be read with great concentration, noting all the archetypes, the images, the aphorisms, the plot devices, in their different contexts.

[21] Not that I'm likely to make the elementary blunder of assuming that the more archetypes there are in a book the more serious it is: I've expressed myself on that point a good many times. As I've said, the book with the greatest number of demonic images in it I ever read (the Inferno of course doesn't count) was [Charles Maturin's] Melmoth the Wanderer.[29] And I've certainly read better books than that. But still the images have to be noted, and noting them will eventually lead to some enlightenment about the shape of plot-structures.

[22] I have a feeling that I need to get as clear an idea of the shape of Tragicomedy as I now have of Liberal before I can really write Liberal with much conviction. Because there is a good deal of over-lapping: Chapter Nine of Liberal, as I now have it, is the infra-structure of Tragicomedy.

Rencontre

[23] Just as Anticlimax is a study of the conceptual and theoretical displacements of myth, so this book is a study of the historical displacements of it. Its focus therefore comes in the imagery of time. A specific historical field must be chosen, i.e., English.

Part One: English Poetry[30]

[24] The cycle of conservative and radical movements; expansion of this to show how each cycle comes nearer to the circumference of a range of possibilities. Recurrence of such devices as imitative harmony; how the characteristics of the language imprint themselves on the poetry.

Part Two: English Prose

[25] A similar but later cycle; problems of spoken and written word surviving in English; discontinuous, rhetorical and discursive prose; the realistic tradition of fiction, its rhetorical structures; the development of sentimental romance and its eventual absorption of the realistic tradition.

Part Three: The Imagery of Space

[26] The discarded model and its reflexion in English literature; the inversion of its model from the eighteenth century on.

Part Four: Displaced and Conceptual Imagery

[27] As in the summary of Part Five at present; the philosophical traditions and their characteristics from nominalism to the anti-existential tradition of our day. A good deal of 4d,[31] and an extended treatment of Ruskin as the transitional figure from humanism to myth criticism.

Part Five: The Imagery of Time

[28] I'm putting this last because it seems to me that it's the differentiating feature of this book; but it may belong earlier, as I have it now.[32] The cycle and the telos: the myths of history that exert a counter-historical force and yet inform history too.

Anticlimax

Three main parts, as follows:

Part One: The Fictional Displacements of Myth

[29] One: Naïve Romance (Grail stories, folk tales, notably the Two Brothers and the Hymn to the Soul in the Acts of Thomas; the comic tale embodied (or embedded) in the Clementine Recognitions and developing through Gower and Chaucer to Shakespeare). Probably climaxing in Spenser and Ariosto. Also, e.g., Surtees on fox-hunting.

[30] Two: Sentimental Romance (Scott, Wilkie Collins, Poe, Hawthorne, George MacDonald, LeFanu, William Morris, Tolkien, etc.). The formulas of popular fiction (detective story and science fiction formulas coming out of Poe and Collins, e.g.).

[31] Three: Realistic Romance (Melville, Conrad, Virginia Woolf, etc.). The absorption of romance into the fictional tradition (I don't naturally always mean realism; Virginia Woolf represents a kind of psychological absorption, as do the Brontes).

[32] Four: The Main (quasi-realistic) Fictional Stream. Henry James, perhaps; Meredith's Egoist and the like.

Part Two: Conceptual Displacements of Fiction

[33] One: Confession and Anatomy forms; absorption of the rite de passage into the former and the conceptualizing of ritual (i.e., the symposium) in the latter. The dialogue, including the dialogue of the dead; the kataplous[33] and reversal of normal life in the lower world, etc.

[34] Two: Contracts and Utopias.[34] The development of these quasi-political myths from myth itself and its fictional displacements. Study of William Morris.

Part Three: Conceptual Displacements of Myth

[35] One: Plato and the conceptualizing of dialogue and symposium forms; also the quasi-Biblical contract-Utopia polarizing in the later work, from the Republic on. Eros quest in Hegel; Promethean quest in Marx, etc. Summary of the philosophical forms of the Great Doodle.

[36] Two: Back to Myth: the embryonic containing forms of concepts.

[37] This makes Anticlimax more of a maroon-colored book, and less gray than it's traditionally been, but all my colors are getting pretty hazy. Also, it seems to me that this book lends itself to division better than Liberal or Tragicomedy. By division I mean three short books, of four chapters each, interconnected to anybody who reads them all, but possible to read separately. The first four chapters, for instance, could be a series in its own right.

Notes

Preface

1 In *Rereading Frye: The Published and Unpublished Works*, ed. David Boyd and Imre Salusinszky (Toronto: University of Toronto Press, 1999), 3–18. See also Dolores Signori, *Guide to the Northrop Frye Papers* (Toronto: Victoria University Library, 1993), 191–4.

Introduction

1 See Bertrand Russell, *A History of Western Philosophy* (New York: Simon and Shuster, 1945), 203; and Alfred North Whitehead, *Science and the Modern world* New York: Free Press, 1953), 7. NF quotes both passages in *LN*, 530–1. See also *MM*, 168–9 and *WP*, 150. NF's further comment on the passages is cited from "Literature as a Critique of Pure Reason" (1983), *MM*, 169.

2 For example, *LN*, 150: "It's a good thing this notebook is not for publication, because everyone else would be bored by my recurring to Helen."

3 As NF writes in *LN*, 45: "One does not understand the logos by hearing it, only by speaking it and listening to what one says. Writing, to me, is essentially this action of speaking and self-listening."

4 Sometimes not even to that. No reference appears more often in the Third Book notebooks than the one to the *jeune parque* or "young fate" in Valéry's poem *La Jeune Parque*; for NF, she represented the appearance, at the bottom of the descent towards the demonic epiphany of "Nothing" in Thanatos, of a young girl, often a daughter-figure, in relation to the aging male quester. Examples include the "Female Babe" of the second half of Blake's *The Mental Traveller* and Cordelia in *King Lear*. But she seems to have disappeared beyond the event horizon of the Thanatos black hole, for she is never mentioned in *WP* or any of NF's other published writings.

5 "Long Sequacious Notes" (1953), *NFCL*, 172.

6 As reprinted in *CyberReader*, 2nd ed., ed. Victor J. Vitanza (Boston: Allyn and Bacon, 1999), 277. The source is Jay David Bolter, *Writing Space* (Hillsdale, N.J.: Lawrence Erlbaum, 1991).
7 Bolter, *Writing Space*, 279–80.
8 "Long Sequacious Notes," 176.
9 See Jorge Luis Borges, "The Library of Babel" and "The Garden of Forking Paths" in *Ficciones* (New York: Grove Press, 1962), 79–88 and 89–101 respectively. NF uses the image of the garden of forking paths in *WP*, 142–3, to describe the "chaos of echoes and resemblances that we find in comparative mythology."
10 See Wallace Stevens, *Oak Leaves Are Hands*, in *The Collected Poems of Wallace Stevens* (New York: Knopf, 1954), 272.
11 See Sigmund Freud, "The Antithetical Meaning of Primal Words," in *The Standard Edition of the Complete Psychological Works of Sigmund Freud*, gen. ed. James Strachey, 24 vols. (London: Hogarth Press, 1953–74), 11:155–61.
12 See Joseph Campbell, "The Symbol without Meaning," in *The Flight of the Wild Gander: Explorations in the Mythological Dimensions of Fairy Tales, Legends, and Symbols* (New York: Viking, 1969). See especially sec. 6, "Mythologies of Engagement and Disengagement" and sec. 7, "The Flight between Two Thoughts" (168–92).
13 *StS*, 109–34. A related discussion occurs in chap. 7 of *CP*, 158–71.
14 It is possible that NF took the terms "Nomos" and "Nous" from Francis Cornford, *From Religion to Philosophy: A Study in the Origins of Western Speculation* (1912; New York: Harper and Brothers, 1957), an annotated copy of which is in the NFL. Chap. 1, "Destiny and Law," contains a lengthy discussion of Nomos, while Nous is mentioned on p. 154 as deriving from Anaxagoras, though it was later used by Plato.
15 "The Problem of Spiritual Authority in the Nineteenth Century" (1964), *StS*, 241–56.
16 The essays on Butler, "Some Reflections on Life and Habit" (1988), and William Morris, "The Meeting of Past and Present in William Morris" (1982), are both in *MM*, 141–54 and 322–39 respectively.
17 "Speculation and Concern" (1966), *StS*, 38–55.
18 "Design as a Creative Principle in the Arts" (1966), *StS*, 56–65.
19 The third listing is that of 12.442. A rare public discussion appears in a single paragraph of *CP*, 41–2. Here, the listing is commandment, aphorism (adapted to different social contexts as proverb and oracle), parable (along with fable and riddle), and pericope, the "brief anecdote in the life of a teacher," as in the Gospels.
20 It has been little noticed that NF had already developed a consistent intellectual system in his student papers, one that preceded both *FS* and the ogdoad project of the 1940s. In it, art appears (as it will later in *AC*) as an intermediate unity integrating the poles of action and thought,

morality and logic, will and reason, etc. But in the student papers it is more obvious that this involves an integration of time phenomena and space phenomena—and this is clearly a derivation from Spengler. The point here is that Tragicomedy and Anticlimax are the temporal and spatial unfoldings of what appears as a totality in Liberal and as fragmented in Rencontre. See *SE*.

21 "Structure then can be *methodically* threatened in order to be comprehended more clearly and to reveal not only its supports but also that secret place in which it is neither construction nor ruin but lability. This operation is called (from the Latin) *soliciting*. In other words, *shaking* in a way related to the whole (from *sollus*, in archaic Latin "the whole," and from *citare*, "to put into motion." From "Force and Signification," in *Writing and Difference*, trans. Alan Bass (Chicago: University of Chicago Press, 1978), 6. In the same paragraph, Derrida says (5–6), "Thus it is in no way paradoxical that the structuralist consciousness is a catastrophic consciousness, simultaneously destroyed and destructive, *destructuring*, as is all consciousness," a formulation related to the existentialist notion that so fascinated NF during the Third Book period, that being arises out of its opposite, out of nothingness, a nothingness identical with consciousness itself. Where Derrida says "catastrophe," which literally means "overturning," NF might say *katabasis*, a descent into the underworld. Derrida himself elsewhere uses the phrase *mise en abime*, "put into the abyss."

22 See Pauline Kogan, *Northrop Frye: The High Priest of Clerical Obscurantism*, Literature and Ideology Monographs 1 (Montreal: Progressive Books and Periodicals, 1969).

23 "New Directions from Old" (1960), *FI*, 52–66.

24 "The Drunken Boat: The Revolutionary Element in Romanticism" (1963), *StS*, 200–17.

25 See Gertrude Rachel Levy, *The Gate of Horn: A Study of the Religious Connotations of the Stone Age, and Their Influence upon European Thought* (London: Faber and Faber, 1948), annotated copy in the NFL.

26 "The Revelation to Eve" (1969), *StS*, 135–59.

27 See 12.503.

28 *StS*, 130. NF's note to this passage cites *De Genio Socratis*, 21, but adds that "The statement in the text comes partly from Pausanias, 9.39."

29 To qualify this, however, NF is able to accumulate a fair number of examples in the history of symbolism that turn, so to speak, upon a contrast of two wheels or circles: the *I Ching* trigrams, Plato's Circles of the Same and the Other in the *Timaeus*, the double cycle in Blake's *The Mental Traveller* and its developments in Yeats's *A Vision*, and so on.

30 See 50.799: "Now I'm wondering if I could explore the Great Doodle. Erikson says little boys make tower structures & little girls enclosure ones. Islamic countries have the minaret & the mosque; Christian ones the bell-

tower & the basilica; Toronto the C.N. Tower & the retractable Skydome. I've written about the axis mundi & only hinted at the G.D. [Great Doodle]. I am not a historian: I'm an architect of the spirtual world. I should start with the female or group aspect of God, the Schekinah."

31 See Richard A. Lanham, "The 'Q' Question," chap. 7 in *The Electronic Word: Democracy, Technology, and the Arts* (Chicago: University of Chicago Press), 154–94.

32 See 19.92, 107, 245; 12.243; 24.73. It also occurs outside the Third Book notebooks, as in 50.313, where it is the creative act that establishes a meaningful pattern: "A chess move is a decisive choice that may not abolish chance, but sets up a train of consequences that forces it to retreat into the shadows."

33 See 19.3. But NF retained this notion throughout his career, up to the close of his life: *LN*, 238, 318.

Notebook 19

1 Identification is uncertain in both cases: the ideas cited do not appear in any surviving notebooks of the appropriate colours. It is possible, however, that the "red book" is NB 20, which dates from the late 1950s, immediately post-*AC*, and contains a lengthy sequence of notes about the possibility of setting a novel in "Another world, occupying the same space as this, which we enter at the moment of death" (20.2). The likelihood that this is the notebook being referred to is perhaps increased by the fact that in par. 11, below, the work of fiction with death as *cognitio* is linked with two other plot ideas which also occur in NB 20: the discovery of a fifth Gospel and a time machine that reconstructs the past. These are recorded in 20.26 and 20.27 respectively. As for "centuries of meditation," whatever the "green book" was, the idea of a book of aphorisms, sometimes called "centuries of meditation" after the work of that title by Thomas Traherne, was the form NF most commonly envisioned for the last member of the ogdoad, Twilight.

2 See *A Vision* (New York: Macmillan, 1966), especially bk. 3, *The Soul in Judgment*, 219–40.

3 From the final paragraph of Joyce's *Finnegans Wake*.

4 This is the first of three states in the sequence given in *The Tibetan Book of the Dead*. Called Chikhai Bardo, it is the moment when the soul has a chance to escape from the cycle of rebirth; if it fails, it goes on to the other two phases and to eventual reincarnation. NF refers to the Chikhai Bardo state frequently throughout his notebooks.

5 T.S. Eliot, *The Dry Salvages*, pt. 3: "'on whatever sphere of being / The mind of a man may be intent / At the time of death,'—that is the one action / (And the time of death is every moment) / Which shall fructify in the lives of others . . ."

6 The fictional idea of a machine to see into the past also occurs in 20.25. The idea of the discovery of a fifth Gospel occurs in 20.23, 34.12, and 3.165. The idea for a work of fiction with death as the *cognitio* or recognition scene occurs in 20.26, as well as in par. 3, above.

7 The paragraphs beginning here contain a number of ideas NF developed in "Varieties of Literary Utopias" (1965), *StS*, 109–34.

8 See Georges Dumézil, *Archaic Roman Religion*, trans. P. Knapp, 2 vols. (Chicago: University of Chicago Press, 1970). A copy of Dumézil's *Gods of the Ancient Northmen* (Berkeley: University of California Press, 1977) is in the NFL. However, since Dumézil's studies were not available in English when NB 19 was composed, NF may have read about them in the works of Mircea Eliade or some other specialist in the history of religions or comparative mythology.

9 The virtues of wisdom, power, and love in Tommaso Campanella's sketch of an ideal state in *Civitas Solis* [*City of the Sun*] (1623).

10 The society of *1984* is divided into three classes: party bosses, party workers, and the masses or "proles."

11 *Fay ce que vouldras*: "Do what you will," the motto of the Abbey of Thélème in Rabelais's *Gargantua*.

12 See Andrew Marvell, *The Garden*, ll. 63–4: "Two paradises 'twere in one / To live in paradise alone."

13 In *A Modern Utopia* (1905), H.G. Wells classes the samurai in the first of his four social groups: the Poietic (creative), the Kinetic (executive), the Dull, and the Base.

14 Plato, *The Republic*, 592b: "'But in heaven,' I said, 'perhaps, a pattern [*paradeigma*] is laid up for the man who wants to see and found a city within himself on the basis of what he sees. It doesn't make any difference whether it is or will be somewhere. For he would mind the things of this city alone, and of no other.'" Trans. Allan Bloom (New York: Basic Books, 1968).

15 Par. 33, below, somewhat clarifies what NF is thinking about here. Despite having written in the *Republic* about a utopia ruled by philosopher-kings, Plato in the Seventh Epistle, 334c–d, urges the friends of Dion of Syracuse, "Let not Sicily nor any city anywhere be subject to human masters—such is my doctrine—but to laws. Subjection is bad both for masters and for subjects, for themselves, for their children's children, and for all their posterity" (trans. L.A. Post). In other words, there is no such thing as an enlightened dictatorship, which is really only the projection of the discipline of a wise man's mind.

16 In Sinclair Lewis's *Main Street* (1920), Carol Kennicott, a librarian, marries a doctor and moves to Gopher City, Minnesota. In chap. 4, secs. 1 and 2 catalogue in Joycean detail the buildings, stores, and people as Carol takes her first walk through the town; but, by coincidence, Carol's Swedish maid Bea Sorenson is taking the same walk at exactly the same time. When the

same buildings and people are described all over again in sec. 3, from Bea's point of view, everything that had been ugly and unpleasant to Carol seems exciting and full of promise to Bea.

17 I.e., "The Vocation of Eloquence," the sixth of NF's Massey lectures, published as *EI*.

18 Cf. William James, *Principles of Psychology* (1890), 1:488: "The baby, assailed by eyes, ears, nose, skin, and entrails at once, feels it all as one great blooming, buzzing confusion."

19 The later paintings of Erastus Salisbury Field (1805–1900) were on historical and Biblical themes. *Historical Monument to the American Public* (Springfield, Massachusetts Museum of Fine Arts), originally conceived as part of the celebration of the American centennial in 1876, is said to stand alone in American folk art in size and scope. Eight towers (two more were added in 1888) are linked by railway bridges with trains at their tops; scenes from the history of the United States cover the surfaces of the towers in low relief. Edward Hicks (1780–1849) painted a series of *Peaceable Kingdom* paintings, their iconography based on Isaiah 11:6–9, in which "The wolf also shall dwell with the lamb . . . and a little child shall lead them." NF contrasts the two paintings in "Conclusion to *A Literary History of Canada*" (1965), *StS*, 309–10.

20 David Riesman, *The Lonely Crowd* (1950); Theodore Caplow, *The Academic Marketplace* (1958); Vance Packard, *The Hidden Persuaders* (1957); John Keats, *The Insolent Chariots* (1957); Vance Packard, *The Status Seekers* (1959); William H. Whyte, *The Organization Man* (1956). When this note was developed into a passage in *MC*, 112, John Kenneth Galbraith, *The Affluent Society* (1958), and Eric Berne, *Games People Play* (1967), were added to the catalogue.

21 Refers to the theory in David Hume, *A Treatise of Human Nature* (1739–40) and *An Enquiry concerning Human Understanding* (1748), that ideas are discrete units connected by three possible types of association: resemblance, contiguity, and cause-and-effect.

22 See Thomas Carlyle, *Heroes and Hero Worship* (1841).

23 See n. 15, above.

24 See *FT*, 93.

25 See Paul Tillich, "Existential Philosophy: Its Historical Meaning," *Theology of Culture* (New York: Oxford University Press, 1959), 76–111. Also "Existentialism against Essentialism" and "The Transition from Essence to Existence and the Symbol of 'the Fall,'" *Systematic Theology*, (Chicago: University of Chicago Press, 1957), 2:24–6, 2:29–44.

26 Alludes to the "principle of the best" in the philosophy of G.W. Leibniz, for example in his *Theodicy* (1713), that God chooses to create the best of all possible worlds; satirized by Voltaire in *Candide*.

27 See Thorstein Veblen, *The Theory of the Leisure Class: An Economic Study of Institutions* (1899).

28 See "The Drunken Boat: The Revolutionary Element in Romanticism" (1963), *StS*, 208: "The original form of human society is also hidden 'within.' Keats refers to this hidden society when he says in a letter to Reynolds: 'Man should not dispute or assert but whisper results to his neighbour . . . and Humanity . . . would become a grand democracy of Forest Trees.' Coleridge refers to it in the *Biographia* when he says: 'The medium, by which spirits understand each other, is not the surrounding air; but the *freedom* which they possess in common.'"

29 The distinction between ornament and imitation is more or less defined in par. 47, below, and the terms recur in 12.458. The source in Ruskin seems to be diffuse rather than localized, however, although it probably derives from the first two volumes of *Modern Painters*, in which Ruskin first established the theoretical framework of his criticism of art. There, Ruskin's opinion of imitation may be inferred from some of the section titles in pt. 1, sec. 1, chap. 4, "Of Ideas of Imitation": e.g., sec. 4, "The pleasure resulting from imitation the most contemptible that can be derived from art"; sec. 5, "Imitation is only of contemptible subjects"; and sec. 6, "Imitation is contemptible because it is easy." Art's central task is to convey ideas of *truth*, and truth refers to form rather than to content or subject. When Ruskin goes on to treat of ornament in chap. 11 of *The Stones of Venice*, "The Material of Ornament," he says that ornament must follow God's laws, which are the essential *forms* of nature, beginning with abstract lines.

30 "And we indeed justly; for we receive the due reward of our deeds: but this man hath done nothing amiss."

31 Diatonic scales, including the major, minor, and certain modal scales, divide the octave into five whole-steps and two half-steps, whereas the chromatic scale divides the octave into twelve half-tones. *The Depiction of Chaos* at the beginning of Haydn's famous oratorio *The Creation* employs a degree of chromaticism unusual for the period; it is followed by the chorus singing "And there was light" on a C-major chord.

32 Bach's secular cantata *Der zufriedengestellte Aeolus* (BWV 205). Henry Purcell's opera *The Tempest, or the Enchanted Island*, adapted from Shakespeare by Shadwell (1695?).

33 Bach's secular cantata *Der Streit zwischen Phoebus und Pan* (BWV 201).

34 "Che faró senza Euridice?" from Gluck's *Orfeo* (1762).

35 See also 12.454.

36 See par. 37 and n. 29, above.

37 "Allusion" derives from late Latin *allūsiō*, a playing with, from Latin *allūdere* (past participle of *allūsus*), to play with.

38 Juan Eduardo Cirlot, *Dictionary of Symbols*, trans. Jack Sage (New York: Philosophical Library, 1962).

39 J.L. Austin (1911–60), English "linguistic" philosopher, only published a few papers during his life, transmitting his ideas chiefly through discussion and lecture. Ludwig Wittgenstein (1889–1951), Austrian-born British philosopher, wrote mostly in the form of short, individual notes, frequently numbered.

40 See Marshall McLuhan, *Understanding Media: The Extensions of Man* (1964). NF and Marshall McLuhan (1911–80) were the most famous Canadian intellectuals of their time, rival theorists on the same campus. McLuhan began as a literary critic and developed into a philosopher of communications, studying the changes in human consciousness produced by the electronic media. At one time, his distinction between "hot" (print, radio) and "cool" (telephone, television) media, his phrase "the global village," and the aphorism in his title *The Medium Is the Message* (1967) were internationally famous. Because the Third Book began as a study of criticism and society, NB 19 in particular is itself preoccupied with the theme of communication, and NF is conscious throughout that he is writing in competition with McLuhan. He eventually became impatient with some of McLuhan's more simple-minded disciples and their claim that books were not only obsolete but imprisoned the mind in a linear consciousness inferior to the dynamic and simultaneous consciousness of a medium like television.

41 *Paravritti*: The turning of the mind away from illusion towards freedom and ultimate reality; translated "revolution" or "revulsion" in NF's probable source, D.T. Suzuki, *The Lankavatara Sutra: A Mahayana Text* (1932).

42 In Helmut W. Ziefle, *Dictionary of Modern Theological German* (1982), *die Wiederkehr* is defined as "return, reappearance, recurrence, repetition."

43 The references are to McLuhan's *Understanding Media: The Extensions of Man* and Butler's *Erewhon*.

44 See *A Vision of the Last Judgment* (Erdman, 566).

45 For the Utopia paper, see n. 7, above. The Bampton Lectures were published as *NP*. The Random House book is *SR*.

46 The works referred to here are Richard Jefferies, *After London* (1886); Yevgeniy Ivanovich Zamyatin, *We* (1920), a description of a totalitarian state; George Orwell, *1984* (1949); *The Land of Cockayne*, an anonymous fourteenth-century poem; Tommaso Campanella, *City of the Sun* (1623); Edward Bellamy, *Looking Backward* (1888).

47 Descent to the underworld. The term, which literally means "sailing into port," derives from the *Kataplous* of Lucian of Samosata (2nd century A.D.), a satire in dialogue form that takes place before and during the ferryboat journey to the underworld.

48 A communal experiment by a group of Transcendentalists at Brook Farm,

in West Roxbury, Mass., which lasted from 1841 to 1847. Nathaniel Hawthorne's experiences at Brook Farm gave him material for *The Blithedale Romance* (1852).

49 See nn. 14 and 15, above.

50 "The Garden Within," the fourth of the Huron Lectures, published as the fourth chapter of *RE*. See *RE*, 114.

51 See n. 13, above.

52 John MacNie (pseud. Ismar Thiusen), *Diothas, or, A Far Look Ahead* (1883). Ignatius Donnelly, *Caesar's Column* (1892).

53 See "The Instruments of Mental Production," StS, 7–8: "Plato divides knowledge into two levels: an upper level of theoretical knowledge (theoretical in the sense of *theoria*, vision), which unites itself to permanent ideas or forms, and a lower level of practical knowledge, whose function is to embody these forms or ideas on the level of physical life. What I have referred to in my title as the instruments of mental production consist of the arts, and we may see the major arts in Plato's terms as forming a group of six. Three of these are the arts of *mousike*: music, mathematics, and poetry, and they make up the main body of what Plato means by philosophy, the idenifying of the soul of man with the forms or ideas of the world. The other three are the imitative or embodying arts, the arts of *techne*, painting, sculpture, and architecture, which, along with all their satellites and derivatives, unite the body of man with the physical world." The distinction between arts of *mousike* and *techne* seems to be NF's own, and does not occur in Plato. On a blank page at the beginning of NB 9 (dating from the early 1960s), NF has drawn a pie-shaped diagram. One semicircle, marked *mousike*, consists of three wedges, Mathematics, Music, and Literature; the other semicircle, marked *techne*, consists of three wedges, Architecture, Sculpture, and Painting. The *mousike* semicircle is labeled "Platonic"; the *techne* semicircle is labeled "Aristotelian." See also the references to this binary division in pars. 75 and 86, below, and also in 12.16.

54 See William Morris, "The Decorative Arts, Their Relation to Modern Life and Progress," An Address Delivered Before the Trades' Guild of Learning, 4 December 1877 (London: Ellis and White, n.d.), par. 4 of 11 pars.: "For, and this is at the root of the whole matter, everything made by man's hands has a form, which must be either beautiful or ugly; beautiful if it is in accord with Nature, and helps her; ugly if it is discordant with Nature, and thwarts her; it cannot be indifferent; we, for our parts are busy or sluggish, eager or unhappy, and our eyes are apt to get dulled to this eventfulness of form in those things which we are always looking at."

55 The *Avatamsaka* or *Flower Ornament Sutra* of Mahayana Buddhism and Alfred North Whitehead's *Science and the Modern World* (Cambridge: Cambridge University Press, 1938), annotated copy in the NFL, are sources for

NF's key concept of "interpenetration," indirectly referred to here. An annotated copy of *The Flower Ornament Scripture: A Translation of the Avatamsaka Sutra*, Volume 1, trans.Thomas Cleary (1984) is in the NFL, but during the period of NB 19, NF probably relied on the discussion of the Sutra in D.T. Suzuki, *Essays in Zen Buddhism*, 3rd ser. (London: Rider and Co., 1958), annotated copy in the NFL.

56 An old observation repeated. In 31.76 (from the late 1940s), NF writes of Morris, "He has one personal symbol that's obviously important: hair."

57 See n. 53, above.

58 Barry Goldwater, right-wing Republican candidate for the U.S. Presidency in 1964.

59 The Oneida Community, established in 1848 in Oneida, New York, believed that sin could be eliminated through social reform.

60 For the "Locke programme" of reading, see Introduction, p. xxxiv. The romanticism book is probably *SR*, but many years earlier, in NB 32, NF had contemplated a book on Romanticism that he linked with the Locke programme.

61 "The Problem of Spiritual Authority in the Nineteenth Century" (1964), *StS*, 241–56.

62 Probably "Design for Learning: Introduction," *OE*, 46–61; or *WE*, 127–42. Outlines the idea of a "spiral curriculum" moving through primary, secondary, and tertiary phases of education.

63 "Design as a Creative Principle in the Arts" (1966), *StS*, 56–65. It is not clear why NF regarded it as a "flop."

64 See n. 53, above.

65 An explanation of this enigmatic reference occurs almost twenty years previously, in NB 3, par. 75: "A much more recent dream concerns a maroon-colored book which mentions St. Augustine & explains everything; an archetype that started with Spengler in Edmonton & grew through the spring of 1940 when I was holding Lovejoy's Chain of Being in my hand and trying to find out about Neoplatonism. In my dream I don't write the book myself; when I wake up I know I have to." See also par. 106, below.

66 *Le Jardin d'Épicure* (1894) is a discontinuous collection of essays, dialogues, epigrams, and other short prose fragments stitched together by Anatole France out of material he had at hand.

67 In "Varieties of Literary Utopias," NF had contrasted B.F. Skinner's *Walden Two* and Robert Graves's *Watch the North Wind Rise* (both 1949) as Utopias by a social scientist and humanist respectively. See *StS*, 116.

68 Samuel Alexander, *Space, Time, and Deity: The Gifford Lectures at Glasgow, 1916–1918* (London: Macmillan, 1966), annotated copy in the NFL; J.McT.E. McTaggart, *The Nature of Existence* (Cambridge: Cambridge University Press,

1921–27), annotated copy in the NFL; for Whitehead, see n. 55, above.

69 For NF's desire to write a novel about "chess in Bardo," see Introduction, p. liv.

70 J.A. Cramb, *Germany and England* (1914).

71 NF's articles for *The Canadian Forum*, of which he was editor 1948–54.

72 "Trends in Modern Culture" (1952), *RW*, 300–15; "Religion and Modern Poetry" (1959), *RW*, 228–41. Both originally published in collections of essays by Ryerson Press, Toronto.

73 "The Analogy of Democracy" (1952), *RW*, 219–28. Orig. pub. in *Bias*.

74 See n. 61, above.

75 Sheridan LeFanu's *Uncle Silas* (1864); George Meredith's *The Egoist* (1879). These novels are discussed in the same paragraph of *SeS*, 81, as both linking their heroine to "the Iphigenia situation."

76 NF's graduate course "Principles of Literary Symbolism" was based upon analyses of lyric poems that belonged to the *topoi* of the Great Doodle diagram, the clusters of imagery that form its four quadrants in the Third Book project. NF did not mention the diagram or the project to his students, though he did deal with such issues as the contrast between pre- and post-Romantic mythologies. NF taught the course up through the late 1980s.

77 See n. 60, above.

78 Ibid.

79 See n. 7, above.

80 The title character in Samuel Beckett's *Murphy* feels an affinity with Belacqua in canto 4 of Dante's *Purgatorio*, also mentioned in Beckett's *Molloy*; see NF's explanation in "The Nightmare Life in Death," his review of *Molloy* and two other Beckett works, *NFCL*, 221. In the *Purgatorio*, Belacqua remains outside the gates of Purgatory with the Indolent, who are one variety of the Late Repentant; nevertheless, he excuses his failure to begin the climb by claiming that he will not be allowed beyond the gates until he has spent as much time in the Antepurgatory as he spent delaying his repentance during his lifetime (ll. 127–32). See also 12.280.

81 Norma Arnett was an early student of NF's at Victoria College, 4T9. After she graduated, she began writing NF on the average of a letter a day for nearly ten years, full of what NF described in a letter to William Fennell dated 14 May 1980 as "psychotic blither." Finally, as the letters bore no return address, NF instructed his secretary to begin discarding them.

82 See par. 86 and n. 65, above.

83 See Introduction, p. liv.

84 Jay Macpherson, originally NF's student, joined him as a colleague at Victoria College from 1957 onward. With the publication of *The Boatman* (dedicated to NF), which won the Governor General's Award for 1952, she instantly became one of the most important Canadian poets of her genera-

tion. It and her other book of poetry, *Welcoming Disaster* (1971), were republished together by Oxford University Press in 1981. She is also the author of *The Spirit of Solitude* (1982), a study of the imagery of romance. For Norma Arnett, see n. 81, above.

85 NF seems to have intended to write "objective" here rather than "subjective."

86 In NBs 21 and 24, NF develops an elaborate theory of the evolution of religious consciousness through "three awarenesses." This and the following two paragraphs predate those notebooks but anticipate the later theory. *Sein* and *Dasein* are terms from Heidegger's philosophy, usually translated "Being" and "individual human being." For Whitehead and the *Avatamsaka Sutra*, see n. 55, above. All three are here being associated with the concept of "interpenetration," in which "simple location is destroyed."

87 *Forza* and *froda* are "force" and "fraud," the two Sins of Deliberate Malice punished in the lower part of Dante's hell. In *SeS*, 65–6, NF links *forza* and *froda* with tragedy and comedy respectively, and with the heroes of the *Iliad* and the *Odyssey*, Achilles and Odysseus.

88 See n. 7, above.

89 Pierre Charles L'Enfant (1754–1825), American engineer, architect, and soldier, born in France.

90 William Billings (1746–1800), composer and singing teacher who spent almost all of his career in Boston. In *MC*, 64, NF says that "When the eighteenth-century American composer Billings developed contrapuntal hymn-settings which he called 'fuguing-tunes,' he remarked that they would be 'more than twenty times as powerful as the old slow tunes.' The quantitative comparison, the engineering metaphor, the emphasis on speed and power, indicate a new kind of sensibility already present in pre-Revolutionary and pre-industrial America."

91 Carfax is a place where four roads meet; hence, the proper name of a place formed by the intersection of two principal streets in certain towns such as Oxford and Cambridge. The *OED* does not indicate any connection with vampires, despite the folklore commonplace that they were often killed by being staked out at crossroads, which are sinister places where boundaries become ambiguous and opposites meet. But in Bram Stoker's *Dracula*, Carfax is the name of the estate in London that Dracula buys through the negotiations of Jonathan Harker's firm. It becomes his base of operations after he emigrates from Transylvania to England.

92 "Late civilizations turn extended" is a theme out of Spengler, as his parenthetical appearance in this sentence indicates. See *The Decline of the West*, trans. Charles Francis Atkinson (New York: Knopf, 1928), vol. 2. Sec. A, "The Soul of the City," of chap. 4, "Cities and Peoples," contains such remarks as the following: "Even now the world-cities of the Western

Civilization are far from having reached the peak of their development. I see, long after A.D. 2000, cities laid out for ten to twenty million inhabitants, spread over enormous areas of country-side, with buildings that will dwarf the biggest of to-day's and notions of traffic and communication that we should regard as fantastic to the point of madness" (101).

93 The connection of nomadism with cultural creativity is an old one in NF; there is some evidence in NB 42, pars. 5–17, from the mid-1940s, suggesting it might have originally derived from his reading of Toynbee's *A Study of History*. Whatever may be true historically, the imaginative pattern includes the founding of Rome and England by wandering refugees from the fall of Troy, the founding of all human civilization by wanderers from the garden of Eden after the fall, and the settling of the Promised Land by wanderering refugees from Egypt.

94 The "great wheel," copied from NB 8, appears in par. 191, below.

95 A *summa* is a comprehensive work definitively synthesizing or summarizing either a particular subject or all human knowledge.

96 See William Blake, *The Marriage of Heaven and Hell*, pl. 6.

97 This has not been identified.

98 A traditional saying about the effort and discipline required in Zen: achieving enlightenment is like a mosquito trying to bite through an iron bar.

99 See n. 55, above.

100 *Paradise Lost*, bk. 3, ll. 194–5: "And I will place within them as a guide / My Umpire Conscience."

101 Thomas Rymer, seventeenth-century Neoclassical critic whose *A Short View of Tragedy* (1693) ridiculed *Othello* and other plays he judged according to what he thought were the strict rules of the ancients; F.R. Leavis, famous twentieth-century critic, leader of the *Scrutiny* group, a school of moral criticism. In other words, two fiercely evaluative critics.

102 R.S. Crane, *The Languages of Criticism and the Structure of Poetry* (Toronto: University of Toronto Press, 1953). NF especially has in mind Crane's account of the formal cause in chap. 5.

103 NF repeats this idea throughout the Third Book notebooks, even though Norbert Wiener, early communications philosopher and inventor of cybernetics, does not draw out the social implications in the word "overcomes" quite as explicitly as NF does. In *The Human Use of Human Beings* (Cambridge: Riverside, 1950), Wiener writes: "In the case of the pessimists, the scientific idea which has seemed most in accordance with their interpretation of the universe is that of *entropy* . . . This notion is associated with that of *pattern*, and represents the amount of disorder in a class of patterns. It is also closely associated with the notion of *information*, and of its measure, which is essentially a measure of order. Amount of information is a measure of the degree of order which is peculiarly associated with those pat-

terns which are distributed as messages in time" (20–1). Later, he says: "In the first chapter, we have seen that communication is based on a notion allied to entropy, known as the amount of information. This amount of information is a quantity which differs from entropy merely by its algebraic sign and a possible numerical factor. Just as entropy tends to increase spontaneously in a closed system, so information tends to decrease; just as entropy is a measure of disorder, so information is a measure of order" (128–9). See also 6.1; 12.29; 24.71.

104 The three aspects of an epiphany of beauty in Stephen Dedalus's theory of art: "Aquinas says: *ad pulcritudinem tria requiruntur, integritas, consonantia, claritas.* I translate it so: *Three things are needed for beauty, wholeness, harmony and radiance.*" See James Joyce, *Portrait of the Artist as a Young Man*, ed. Chester G. Anderson (New York: Viking, 1968), 212.

105 The conflict between the aesthetic and the ethical in Kierkegaard's *Either/Or*.

106 In Blake's mythological system, reality is ultimately created by the imagination and not merely external or given; the state in which this is true is called Eden. Beulah, Blake's secondary redeemed state, is the state of passive reception rather than active creation; hence it has a tendency to fall back upon the "mattress" of some underlying given or noncreated reality, whether objective ("substance") or subjective ("mind"). NF uses his own slang phrase "Beulah mattress" elsewhere in the notebooks.

107 The School of Practical Science at the University of Toronto, i.e., the faculty of engineering.

108 See n. 29, above.

109 See Sir James Jeans, *The Mysterious Universe* (Cambridge: Cambridge University Press, 1948: orig. pub. 1930), whose final chapter, "Into the Deep Waters," was cited in *AC*, 352, for its central idea, which is, in Jeans's words, that "we have already considered with disfavour the possibility of the universe having been planned by a biologist or an engineer; from the intrinsic evidence of his creation, the Great Architect of the Universe now begins to appear as a pure mathematician" (122). The private-language theme NF speaks of is evidently Jeans's notion that "The universe cannot admit of material representation, and the reason, I think, is that it has become a mere mental concept" (123). That is, the commonsense language of everyday empiricism can no longer adequately represent reality, but only the arcane, and yet universal, symbolic language of mathematics.

110 See n. 4, above.

111 *Ding an sich*, "thing-in-itself," the term Kant uses in his *Critique of Pure Reason* for the unknowable reality beneath the phenomenal world.

112 "The Drunken Boat: The Revolutionary Element in Romanticism." See par. 36 and n. 28.

113 Cleopolis is the city of earthly glory in Spenser's *Faerie Queene*, bk. 1, canto 10, ll. 58 ff., representing an ideal vision of London as well as the highest state fallen humanity can achieve.

114 The lectures for *MC* were presented at McMaster University in 1967, the centennial of Canadian confederation.

115 Gentile da Fabriano (ca. 1360–1428) is the greatest painter of the Byzantinizing school of the Marches. NF has in mind his only surviving painting (as opposed to fresco), the *Adoration of the Magi* in the Uffizi. Benozzo Gozzoli (ca. 1424–97), a Florentine influenced by Gentile, was also the favourite pupil and collaborator of Fra Angelico.

116 For *integritas* and *consonantia*, see n. 104, above.

117 Marshall McLuhan, *Understanding Media: The Extensions of Man*. See n. 40, above. McLuhan states his "the medium is the message" thesis in the first chapter.

118 See William James, *A Pluralistic Universe* (New York: Longmans, 1920), 309: "We may be in the universe as dogs and cats are in our libraries, seeing the books and hearing the conversation, but having no inkling of the meaning of it all."

119 "Aunt Lily" is Helen Frye's Aunt Lilly Maidment. For Jay Macpherson, see n. 84, above.

120 "Design as a Creative Principle in the Arts," presented at a festival of the arts at the University of Rochester. See n. 63, above.

121 NF explains in "Letter to the English Institute: 1965" in *Northrop Frye in Modern Criticism*, ed. Murray Krieger (New York: Columbia University Press, 1966), 28–9: "One of the most accurately drawn characters in drama is Reuben the Reconciler, who is listed in the *dramatis personae* of Ben Jonson's *Sad Shepherd*, and whose role was apparently to set everybody right at the end. Jonson never finished the play, so he never appeared. I wish we could throw away the notion of 'reconciling,' and use instead some such conception as 'interpenetration.' Literature itself is not a field of conflicting arguments but of interpenetrating visions. I suspect that this is true even of philosophy, where the place of argument seems more functional. The irrefutable philosopher is not the one who cannot be refuted, but the one who is still there after he has been refuted."

122 "Fancy . . . has no other counters to play with, but fixities and definites." Samuel Taylor Coleridge, *Biographia Literaria* (1817), chap. 13.

123 *Othello*, 5.2.144–6: "If heaven would make me such another world / Of one entire and perfect chrysolite, / I'ld not have sold her for it."

124 In 32.59–65. The progression in these notes, dating from the late 1940s, is from body to mind to soul or spirit, roughly paralleling the progression through the three awarenesses in par. 111, above, as well as their further development in pars. 175–81, below. These in turn lead to the related yet

rather different, and much more elaborate, theory of three awarenesses in NB 24 in the present volume, and in NB 21. Below, 12.531 links mind–soul–body and three awarenesses as part of a single complex of thought.

125 Sir Thomas Browne, *Religio Medici* (1642), pt. 1, sec. 9: "I can answer all the objections of Satan and my rebellious reason with that odd resolution I learned of Tertullian, *Certum est, quia impossibile est* [It is certain, because impossible]." Tertullian's often-quoted phrase occurs in his *De carne Christi.*

126 Friend of Ernest Pontifex in Samuel Butler's *The Way of All Flesh*, for whom he exemplifies Butler's own theory in *Life and Habit* that behaviour has to be learned so deeply as to become habitual and unconscious. NF discusses him in "The Problem of Spiritual Authority in the Nineteenth Century," *StS*, 247–8.

127 "New Directions from Old" (1960), *FI*, 52–66. Pt. 2, dealing with ascent and descent journeys, deals with the *Purgatorio*, Eliot, and Yeats, among other things.

128 On Leontes and Prospero as *idiotes* figures, see *NP*, 114, 156.

129 A reference to what NF called the Seattle epiphany; see Introduction, p. li.

130 The "drama notebook" is NB 8, dating from the 1950s and containing notes on drama in general and Shakespeare in particular. Intended as a reservoir of material for Tragicomedy, it was probably kept concurrently with NB 7, which began as material on epic for Liberal or Anticlimax. The "great wheel" here is copied directly from par. 248 of NB 8. The cardinal points and their titles are verbatim, while the descriptive details vary considerably. The importing of the "great wheel" at this point marks the beginning of a move away from consideration of the horizontal and vertical axes towards a focus on the circle and its quadrants that will be the main preoccupation of NBs 6, 12, and 24.

131 "Secundum scripturas" means "according to the Scriptures"; the original version of this passage in NB 8 discloses that its source is the Nicene Creed: "and rose again on the third day according to the Scriptures."

132 See Proverbs 20:27: "The spirit of man is the candle of the Lord, searching all the inward parts of the belly."

133 A blank verse tragedy (1682) by Thomas Otway.

134 See n. 46, above.

135 Perhaps NF has in mind *Erewhon* (New York: Penguin, 1970), chap. 26, "The Views of an Erewhonian Prophet Concerning the Rights of Animals," 228–9, in which the prophet says: "Now it cannot be denied that sheep, cattle, deer, birds, and fishes are our fellow-creatures. They differ from us in some respects, but those in which they differ are few and secondary, while those that they have in common with us are many and essential. My

friends, if it was wrong of you to kill and eat your fellow-men, it is wrong also to kill and eat fish, flesh, and fowl."

136 NF's "motto" is quoted from William Blake, *The Marriage of Heaven and Hell* (Erdman, 37). NF's review, broadcast on CBC radio on 25 January 1965, was revised and published as the "Foreword" to a Canadian Educational Edition of *1984* (Don Mills, Ontario: Bellhaven House, 1967), vi–xii. In the passage NF is referring to, he says: "Orwell thinks of truth less as a virtue than as a sign of a healthily functioning mind. Lying weakens the will power, and it leaves one without the strength to resist the will of someone else, a mechanical instrument" (x).

137 William Blake, *Jerusalem*, pl. 91, ll. 36–7: "Los reads the Stars of Albion! the Spectre reads the Voids / Between the Stars" (Erdman, 251).

138 A juxtaposition of Luke 22:19 with John 13:27: "this do in remembrance of me" and "That thou doest, do quickly." The latter is said to Judas after Jesus gives him the sop dipped in wine, an ironic parody of the Eucharist in the verse from Luke.

139 For the "St. Clair revelation," see the Introduction, p. xli.

140 See *AC*, 61 and note.

141 See n. 46, above.

142 See par. 203 and n. 136, above. NF has apparently forgotten and is repeating that paragraph in this and the next sentence.

143 See *Gulliver's Travels*, bk. 4, chap. 4.

144 See n. 104, above.

145 Ishtar is the later Babylonian name for the Sumerian Inanna, who descends to the underworld to redeem her consort Dumuzi (Babylonian Tammuz). In order to complete the descent, she has to be ritually stripped, and arrives in the underworld naked and dead. See also Introduction, p. l.

146 There are four Solomon and Saturn dialogues dating from the Middle Ages, two in a combination of verse and prose and two in prose. They are a combination of catechism and Christian apologetics, as Saturn, the pagan god of wisdom and contemplation, challenges Solomon, his Christian counterpart, with various difficult theological conundrums. See also 12. 473.

147 Loki, the trickster god of Norse mythology.

148 *AC*, 151–5.

149 "The Anatomy in Prose Fiction," *Manitoba Arts Review*, 3 (Spring 1942): 35–47. It appeared in a substantially revised form as "The Four Forms of Prose Fiction," *Hudson Review*, 2 (Winter 1950): 582–95, which, after further revisions, became a part of the Fourth Essay of *AC*.

150 See n. 47, above.

151 Lucian's dialogue *Timon, or the Misanthrope*, one of the sources for Shakespeare's *Timon of Athens*.

152 See n. 7, above.
153 See Introduction, p. li.
154 In *SR*, NF wrote on Beddoes, Shelley, and Keats. In par. 322, below, he identifies these as South, East, and North on his Great Doodle diagram (see Introduction), and toys with the idea of adding a chapter on Wordsworth to represent West, along with a final commentary on Blake's *Milton*. See also *SR*, 169, note to p. 102.
155 See n. 7, above. "Varieties of Literary Utopias" was originally published in *Daedalus*, 94 (Spring 1965): 323–47.
156 NF never delivered any of these lecture series.
157 The Page-Barbour Lectures, delivered in March 1961 at the University of Virginia, became *WTC*.
158 See n. 7, above.
159 See n. 45, above.
160 See n. 87, above.
161 See *FS*, 382 ff.
162 The five Megilloth or Scrolls, traditionally read during the Synagogue services during the course of the year, are Song of Songs, or Song of Solomon, Ruth, Lamentations, Ecclesiastes, and Esther.
163 The identification is far from certain, but in the opening scene of Aristophanes' *The Birds*, two Athenians are carrying birds they have been promised will point them towards Tereus the Hoopoe. Pisthetairos's crow keeps cawing backwards, but Euelpides' magpie points straight ahead—right at a cliff, which happens to be the domain of the Hoopoe after all.
164 I.e., the ogdoad, the eight interconnected works NF contemplated writing for most of his life. See Introduction, pp. xx, xl–xli.
165 The lecture referred to here was presented at the University of Kentucky in October 1965 and published as "Speculation and Concern" in *The Humanities and the Understanding of Reality*, ed. Thomas B. Stroup (Lexington: University of Kentucky Press, 1966), 32–54; rpt. in *StS*, 38–55.
166 See Introduction, p. xxi.
167 Daydreaming hero of James Thurber's satiric story "The Secret Life of Walter Mitty" (1942).
168 A misquotation from "Of Reformation." See *Complete Prose Works of John Milton* (New Haven, Conn.: Yale University Press, 1953), 1:525: "Then was the sacred BIBLE sought out of the dusty corners where the prophane Falshood and Neglect had throwne it, the *Schooles* opened, *Divine* and *Humane Learning* rak't out of the embers of *forgotten tongues* . . ."
169 See Introduction, p. liv.
170 "Dragon" derives from a Greek epithet meaning "the sharp-sighted one."
171 See n. 53, above.

172 The former line, "Prescribe us not our duty," is Regan's in *King Lear*, 1.1.279. The latter is Goneril's, 1.3.58.
173 Irving Layton (b. 1912), perhaps the most famous Canadian poet of his generation and author of almost fifty books, including *In the Midst of My Fever* (1954), *A Laughter in the Mind* (1958), and *A Red Carpet for the Sun* (1959, winner of the Governor General's Award). The relationship between Layton and NF was complex, in many ways a tension of opposites. NF reviewed several of Layton's most important books for the *University of Toronto Quarterly* during the 1950s, praising his talent and insisting upon his importance, yet critical of what he regarded as the tendency of the poet's ego to intrude upon his poems. Layton in turn made intermittent satiric comments about NF as an academic who, unable to comprehend Layton's own brand of romantic vitalism, fostered instead a school of self-consciously academic myth-poets.
174 The "blue book" is NB 18, in which NF refers to par. 44: "Ordinary social relationships are a mixture of sincerity & hypocrisy: sometimes we mean what we say, sometimes we speak ironically or hypothetically; but in any case *personal* sincerity switches on & off like an electric light. (One may be sincere in irony, as when a panegyrical obituary is felt to be 'right,' though nobody regards it as more than an aesthetic conventionalizing of the truth). Similarly in poetry or discursive writing: the relation of any given passage to personal sincerity is unpredictable. Clergymen, especially Protestant preachers, find it hard to adapt to this: they feel they're hypocritical if they don't believe all they say. But nobody but a paranoid does send his personal consent through every statement, just as nobody but a hopeless pedant or cynic believes nothing he says. You can't go on being a hypocrite: that's just an illusory vice for the most part, & a prolific breeder of pharmakoi."
175 Cf. par. 63, above.
176 See Isaac Newton, *Opticks* (New York: Dover, 1979), 370.
177 "Baudelaire," in *Selected Essays* (New York: Harcourt, 1950), 371–81.
178 Dagwood Bumstead is a character in the comic strip *Blondie*, created by Chic Young.
179 The "blue book" is NB 18, whose "drafts" are not drafts in the ordinary sense but the usual NF-style prospectus for the volumes of the ogdoad, including a volume, probably Liberal, on epic.
180 See Introduction, p. xxxi.
181 "Comminution" is a fragmentation, or division into small parts. For the "deepest passages" referred to, see *WTC*, 104–8.
182 Samuel Alexander, *Space, Time and Deity*, vol. 1 (London: Macmillan, 1920), passim.
183 R.G. Collingwood (1889–1943), English philosopher and historian, associ-

ated with historicism, the theory that all knowledge is situated, and therefore limited by the horizon of its particular place and time. Thus there can be no universally valid laws or patterns of history, a challenge to the kind of total vision represented by something like Spengler's *Decline of the West*.

184 See Introduction, p. xxxiv.

185 NB 41 consists of two pages of notes on Robert Smith Surtees's novels *Jorrock's Jaunts and Jollities* (1838) and *Handley Cross* (1843); see also *SeS*, 146–7. For Meredith, see *SeS*, 81.

186 The Browning and Yeats references are to *The Bishop Orders His Tomb at St. Praxed's Church* and *Among School Children* respectively. As for "Blake's Pyramid," *FS*, 104, says that "The purely mathematical symbol of Egyptian pyramid is the product of a fantastically inert tyranny: its builder, in Blake's drawing, has a face combining stupidity and ferocity in a hideously self-satisfied leer." Another reference on 130 also identifies it as an exemple of "mathematic" rather than organic or "living form," and on 364 it is linked to Egypt as the "furnace of iron."

187 For R.G. Collingwood, see n. 183, above. Isaiah Berlin (1909–97), English philosopher-historian, espoused a variety of non-relativistic pluralism.

188 See n. 174, above.

189 See Introduction, p. liv.

190 NF was one of twelve consultants from across Canada who met with a Joint Committee each year for three days, beginning in 1965, to produce the *Hymn Book of the Anglican Church of Canada and the United Church of Canada*, published in 1971. Attempts to be politically and theologically correct produced various controversial additions, alterations, and deletions; NF was distressed when Blake's *And did those feet in ancient time* was excluded as too bellicose.

191 See Introduction, p. xxxiv.

192 John Henry Newman, *An Essay in Aid of a Grammar of Assent*, ed. C.F. Harrold (New York: Longmans, 1947). See especially 33–64.

193 See Hans Vaihinger, *The Philosophy of "As If": A System of the Theoretical, Practical and Religious Fictions of Mankind*, trans. C.K. Ogden (London: Routledge, 1965).

194 See John Bunyan, *Grace Abounding to the Chief of Sinners* in *"Grace Abounding" and "The Pilgrim's Progress,"* ed. Roger Sharock (London: Oxford University Press, 1966), 103: "Wherefore, thought I, the point being thus, I am for going on, and venturing my eternal state with Christ, whether I have comfort here or no . . . for I am resolved, (God give me strength) never to denie my profession, though I have nothing at all for my pains . . ."

195 The course designated 4d was a 3-hour-a-week English course offered as a pass option in a limited number of honour courses. The course description

from the 1963–64 University of Toronto calendar says it was "the same as courses 4m and 4n," which were the honour courses in modern drama and poetry and the modern novel respectively. NF seems to be implying that, in addition to drama, poetry, and fiction, there was a fourth component of rhetorical works.

196 Georges Sorel, *Reflections on Violence* (New York: Macmillan, 1972).

197 In *The Witch-Cult in Western Europe* (1921), Margaret Murray argued that what the Christian authorities called witchcraft was actually the survival, throughout the Middle Ages and up to the Reformation, of a pre-Christian fertility cult. A copy of Murray's *The God of the Witches* (Garden City: Doubleday, 1960) is in the NFL. See also 12.571.

198 Thomas Aquinas held that we cannot know God directly, because his infinite and perfect nature transcends any names we could apply to it. But we can have limited, indirect knowledge of his being through analogy with our own being.

199 See the "General Note: Blake's Mysticism," *FS*, 431–2, where NF contrasts Blake's *analogia visionis* with "the more orthodox analogies of faith and being."

200 See n. 198, above.

201 See n. 203, below, for representative books by the women named.

202 See n. 198, above.

203 Representative books by the women named: Maud Bodkin, *Archetypal Patterns in Poetry* (1934); Jessie Weston, *From Ritual to Romance* (1920), annotated copy in the NFL; Gertrude Rachel Levy, *The Gate of Horn: A Study of the Religious Conceptions of the Stone Age, and Their Influence upon European Thought* (1948), annotated copy in the NFL; *The Sword from the Rock: An Investigation into the Origins of Epic Literature and the Development of the Hero* (1953), annotated copy in the NFL; *The Phoenix' Nest: A Study in Religious Transformations* (1961), annotated copy in the NFL; Helen Flanders Dunbar, *Symbolism in Medieval Thought* (1929); Helena Petrovna Blavatsky, *The Secret Doctrine: The Synthesis of Science, Religion and Philosophy* (1908), annotated copies of both the full and abridged versions in the NFL; Frances Yates, *Giordano Bruno and the Hermetic Tradition* (1964), annotated copy in the NFL; *The Art of Memory* (1966), annotated copy in the NFL; Enid Welsford, *The Fool: His Social and Literary History* (1935), annotated copy in the NFL; Jane Ellen Harrison, *Themis: A Study of the Origins of Greek Religion* (1912), annotated copy in the NFL; *Ancient Art and Ritual* (1913), annotated copy in the NFL; Bertha Phillpotts, *The Elder Edda and Ancient Scandinavian Drama* (1920); *Edda and Saga* (1931); Ruth Benedict, *Patterns of Culture* (1934).

204 NF knew many of Jung's works, but the greatest influence on his own earlier thinking was *Psychology of the Unconscious: A Study of the Transfor-*

mations and Symbolisms of the Libido. A Contribution to the History of the Evolution of Thought, trans. Beatrice M. Hinkle (1916); annotated copies of it and its later revision, *Symbols of Transformation* (1956) are in the NFL. In 1954, NF reviewed Jung's *Two Essays on Analytical Psychology* (1953) and *Psychology and Alchemy* (1944; 2nd ed., rev., 1952) in *The Hudson Review*; the review, "Forming Fours," is included in *NFCL*, 117–29. The work of Leo Frobenius that seems to have influenced NF was *The Childhood of Man*, trans. A.H. Keane (1909). There is a discussion of it and Jung's *Psychology of the Unconscious* in NB 7 from the late 1940s–early 1950s. Sir James Frazer produced an edition of Apollodorus's *The Library* in 1921; there are annotated copies of both the abridged and unabridged editions of *The Golden Bough* in the NFL, along with an annotated copy of *Folklore in the Old Testament* (1918); NF's talk on Frazer, "Symbolism of the Unconscious," is included in *NFCL*, 84–94. The Cambridge school consisted of Gilbert Murray, Jane Ellen Harrison (see above), Arthur Cook, and Frances Cornford, whose *The Origins of Attic Comedy* (1912), annotated copy in the NFL, was an important early influence on NF.

205 I.e., *Patterns in Comparative Religion*, trans. Rosemary Sheed (1958), and *The Forge and the Crucible*, trans. Stephen Corrin (1971). Annotated copies of both are in the NFL. NF's review of five books by Eliade for *The Hudson Review* in 1959 appears as "World Enough without Time" in *NFCL*, 95–106.

206 This imagery is discussed throughout Levy's book, but for the term "conditional entry," see pp. 133, 157, 159.

207 *The Gate of Horn*, pt. 3, "Ziggurat and Pyramid," 167–210.

208 Gonzalo to Alonso in *The Tempest*: "By'r Lakin, I can go no further, sir: / My old bones ache: here's a maze trod indeed / Through forthrights and meanders" (3.3.1–3).

209 Harold Bayley, *The Lost Language of Symbolism: An Inquiry into the Origin of Certain Letters, Words, Names, Fairy-Tales, Folklore, and Mythologies* (1912).

210 For the image of the plow in Blake's *Milton*, see *FS*, 335; in Levy's *The Gates of Horn*, see p. 145. See her index under "spiral" and "red ochre."

211 A.M. Hocart, *Kingship* (1927), cited in *The Gate of Horn*, 171, 176.

212 *The Gate of Horn*, 47, 51.

213 See n. 154, above, for NF's reason for wanting to add the chapter on Wordsworth (which he never did) to *SR*.

214 Apparently a reference to "Dickens and the Comedy of Humours" (1968), *StS*, 218–40. The reference to Strindberg appears on p. 219.

215 See n. 203, above.

216 For the importance of this triad of works in NF's thought, see Introduction, p. xlii.

217 The "blue book," 18.132, plays with the notion with something less than

ridicule: "For a long time I've been obsessed by the notion of writing a definitive history of English literature. I'll never do that, of course, but why should the idea fascinate the author of the *Anatomy of Criticism*? Could it be that there's a possibility of writing a history, based on but not confined to English, that would have the form of an incredibly complicated fugal structure?" The rest of the paragraph goes on to speculate about that "fugal" pattern.

218 NF has apparently already agreed to write the General Introduction to a historical anthology of English literature to be published by Harcourt, Brace and World (Harcourt Brace Jovanovich as of 1970), for which he was to have been the general editor. In 1972 NF completed the first three parts of the Introduction, a portion of pt. 4, and a 3-page outline of pt. 5. The project never materialized, but an unfinished 184-page manuscript survives (see *Northrop Frye on Literature and Society, 1936–1989: Unpublished Papers*, ed. Robert D. Denham, CW, 10 [Toronto: University of Toronto Press, 2002], 3–130), with an attached letter dated 12 December 1972 addressed to the project's other editors. See "Work in Progress", pars. 23–8 and n. 30.

219 NF never taught a course in the theory of drama.

220 Reference to the Ontario theme song that was part of the Canadian Centennial celebration of 1967: "Give me a place to stand and I will include the world."

221 Apparently sarcastic for "Truth."

222 See the final paragraph of "*Endymion*: The Romantic Epiphanic," *SR*, 164–5.

223 Vera is NF's sister; the book he is referring to is probably *The Sleeping King*, by Aubrey Hopwood and Seymour Hicks (1900), a children's fairy tale.

224 Matthew Arnold, *Literature and Dogma*, in *The Complete Prose Works*, ed. R.H. Super (Ann Arbor: University of Michigan Press, 1963), 6:173.

225 See the penultimate paragraph of "*Endymion*: The Romantic Epiphanic," *SR*, 163–4.

226 Diotima is the wise woman who instructs Socrates about the nature of love in Plato's *Symposium*. Egeria is nymph of a spring in the grove sacred to Diana at Lake Nemi near Aricia. In Roman legendary history she was the wife and invaluable advisor of Numa, second king of Rome, assisting at his task of civilizing a savage people, and appears as such in both Virgil and Ovid. See also 6.8.

227 Nicholas Berdyaev, *The Destiny of Man* (1948).

228 See par. 6 and n. 2, above.

229 Ernst Robert Curtius, *European Literature in the Latin Middle Ages*, trans. Willard Trask (1953), annotated copy in the NFL; for the books by Yates and Levy, see n. 203, above.

230 See *The New Science of Giambattista Vico* (1744), trans. Thomas Goddard

Bergin and Max Harold Fisch, rev. and abridged (Ithaca: Cornell University Press, 1968), xliii, 117. Annotated copies of this and the 1961 edition are in the NFL.

231 I.e., "Prometheus: The Romantic Revolutionary," *SR*, 87–124.

232 Alessandro Della Ciaja, a minor seventeenth-century Sienese nobleman, composer, singer, and performer.

233 Carlo Gesualdo, Prince of Venosa (ca. 1560–1613), composer of madrigals characterized by an expressionistic chromaticism that looks forward to Wagner.

234 *Fuente Ovejuna* (1619).

235 Norman O. Brown, *Life against Death: The Psychoanalytical Meaning of History* (1959), annotated copy in the NFL.

236 See Edmund Wilson, *To the Finland Station: A Study in the Writing and Acting of History* (New York: Harcourt, Brace, 1940), 316. See also 12.481.

237 Michelet says this in the first sentence of his *Introduction to Universal History* (1830), quoted by Wilson in *To the Finland Station*, 8.

238 Expo '67, the World's Fair at Montreal, highlight of the Canadian Centennial celebration of 1967. The exposition cost Canada, Quebec, and Montreal $283 million, despite the fact that most of the 120 participating countries built their own pavilions. The theme of the Fair was "Man and His World," and was subdivided into five groups: "Man the Creator," "Man the Explorer," Man the Producer," "Man the Provider," and "Man and the Community." It is no accident that reference to NF's visit to Expo '67 occurs in NB 19, in which he is interested in Utopian thinking—though NF was clearly dubious about the kind of Canadian nationalist fervour that inspired the undertaking, as par. 384, below, makes clear.

239 See chap. 7 of Albert Bates Lord, *The Singer of Tales* (Cambridge, Mass.: Harvard University Press, 1960), annotated copy in the NFL.

240 The story is told by Giorgio Vasari that Giotto drew a perfect circle in a single stroke and without the aid of a compass for an emissary of Pope Benedict XI, who was so impressed that he called him to work in Rome.

241 In Blake's *Milton*, pl. 2, l. 17 (Erdman, 96).

242 Milton's description in *Paradise Lost*, bk. 4, ll. 239–40, of how the four rivers of the garden of Eden, flowing from their single source, "With mazie error under pendant shades / Ran Nectar."

243 In *Paradise Lost*, bk. 2, ll. 650–9, Sin is described as being beautiful above but horrible and serpentine from the waist down; hellhounds creep in and out of her womb.

244 Urizen explores his dens in Blake's *The Book of Urizen*, chap. 8 (Erdman, 81–2), and in the opening of *Night the Sixth* of *The Four Zoas* (Erdman, 344 ff.). Los explores Albion's bosom with a lantern in *Jerusalem*, pl. 45 [31] (Erdman, 194). NF elaborates on this contrast in 12.348.

245 Yeats's symbol of the double gyres, two interpenetrating spiral movements in opposite directions, appears in both his poetry and prose, but is most fully explicated in *A Vision*. For the "dream cycle," see par. 6 and n. 2, above.

246 *Nel mezzo del cammin di nostra vita,* "In the middle of the journey of our life," the first line of Dante's *Inferno*.

247 See n. 198, above.

248 Bks. 11 and 12: "Imagination, How Impaired and Restored," and "Same Subject (continued)." Bk. 11 sets forth Wordsworth's theme of the "spots of time," the vivid examples of which may correspond to a structure of education and a vision of plenitude. As a consequence of the healing power derived from such experiences, Wordsworth is reintegrated into the human world, the subject of bk. 12, and decides that his vocation is the poetry of common experience. The first book is more experiential, the second more reflective; NF may have in mind a parallel with bks. 11 and 12 of *Paradise Lost*. In bk. 11, Adam is shown visions of the first cycle of fallen history; in the second, he is told rather than shown, but the central redemptive message, while less vivid, is more profoundly heartening to Adam.

249 This idea goes back at least to 1957, as it is mentioned in 7.256 in such a way as to indicate that it was not new then. In 24.226 it is referred to as "my one fiction idea," so it is apparently a scheme resembling the encyclopedic collection of twenty-four tales in William Morris's *The Earthly Paradise*. The ancient editors divided the Homeric epics into twenty-four books in part because that was the number of letters in the Greek alphabet, so the suggestion of an alphabet of forms is implicit. See *FS*, 417, where the idea of an alphabet of forms is also extended to Blake's twenty-two plates illustrating the Book of Job, which have been associated with the twenty-two cards of the Tarot pack. There is no doubt also a link with the four *mythoi* of the Third Essay of *AC*, each of which has six phases, forming a complete "circle of keys."

250 See Introduction, p. xxxi.

251 See n. 76, above.

252 I.e., the ogdoad, minus the final work, Twilight, which was to be a sort of epilogue (see par. 377). See Introduction, pp. xl–xli.

253 The word "religion" comes from *religio*, conscientiousness or piety, which in turn derives from *re* + *lig* ("bind" or "tie"); as NF explains in par. 382, religion as *religio* is therefore a sacred affliliation or bond. "Butterslide" is NF's occasional term for any theory of history that is really a displaced or conceptualized version of the myth of a fall from original perfection.

254 See n. 196, above.

255 See *FS*, 92–3.

256 See n. 238, above.

257 The Field of the Cloth of Gold was a site near Calais where a meeting took place between Henry VIII and Francis I in 1520; Francis was hoping to gain English support against the Holy Roman Emperor Charles V. He failed, but the event became renowned for its lavish clothes and tented pavilions.

258 Prospero's speech after the vanishing of the masque of Ceres, 4.1.146–58, which includes the famous lines: "Our revels now are ended. These our actors / (As I foretold you) were all spirits, and / Are melted into air, into thin air . . ."

259 The terms are taken from Sartre's *Being and Nothingness*. Being, as such, is the in-itself: it simply *is*. Consciousness, however, is the for-itself, being conscious *of* something, namely, of itself; thus, it is self-conscious, and therefore other than being. It in fact arises by negating being. Presumably, mythology for itself would be from the perspective of the ordinary ego in the process of transformation; mythology in itself would be the apocalyptic perspective as described by NF in *GC*, 165, "the way reality looks after the ego has disappeared."

260 In Cantos 10–13 of the *Paradiso*, Dante, in the sphere of the sun, finds himself surrounded by two circles of contemplatives in harmonious interrelation, one led by the Dominican St. Thomas Aquinas, the other by the Franciscan St. Bonaventure. In the present context, as confirmed by the reference in par. 419, below, NF seems to be using this as an image of an open myth of concern, with the Aristotelian Thomistic tradition united in equality with a mystical Neoplatonic tradition whose members, historically, were frequently suspected of heresy by the Church hierarchy.

261 See Introduction, p. xlii.

262 See Introduction, p. xli.

263 See n. 181, above.

264 See n. 219, above.

265 See n. 218, above.

266 See n. 196, above.

267 Chief of state in Communist China from 1959 to 1968.

268 The last line of Browning's *Cleon*: "Their doctrine could be held by no sane man."

269 "The Revelation to Eve" (1969), *StS*, 135–59.

270 In the mid-nineteenth century, J.J. Bachofen argued the existence of a pre-patriarchal period of mythology dominated by the figure of a goddess. See *Myth, Religion, and Mother Right: Selected Writings of J.J. Bachofen* (1967). See also 12.155. In "The Revelation to Eve," 138, NF writes, "Eurynome means wide-ruling: Milton's gloss, the 'wide-Encroaching Eve perhaps,' is somewhat puzzling, but it seems to say that the memory of the fallen Eve is the

source, for the heathen, of the myth of a great mother-goddess from whom all deified principles in nature have ultimately descended, even though their fathers are the fallen angels."

271 René Wellek (1905–97), well-known critic and literary historian; one of the original reviewers of *FS*, he thereafter wrote briefly about NF at intervals in several of his books—none of which puts his argument exactly as NF frames it here. Yet Wellek's most persistent disagreement with NF was on the functionality of value judgment in literary criticism. Even in the review of *FS* he faults NF for evading the value judgment of Blake's poetry as poetry; NF's belated response was in his review of Wellek's *A History of Modern Criticism*, vols. 1 and 2, in which he claims that the unintended moral of Wellek's historical narrative is the expendability of critical value judgments. See "An Indispensable Book," *Virginia Quarterly Review*, 32 (Spring 1956): 310–15.

272 For Maud Bodkin, the Jungian literary critic, see n. 203, above. A slightly modified version of the quip about Sarah Bernhardt appears in *CP*, 16.

273 See n. 253, above.

274 In 1881, William Robertson Smith was dismissed from his post by the Free Church of Scotland for his theories about the development of the Old Testament out of the totemistic religion of the early Semites. He went on to write a famous book, *The Religion of the Semites* (1889), and to help steer his friend Sir James Frazer towards the researches that later resulted in *The Golden Bough*.

275 As a missionary in Africa, Bishop J.W. Colenso had such difficulty defending to his congregation the credibility of some Old Testament narratives that he went on to write *Pentateuch and the Book of Joshua, Critically Examined*, a five-volume work that argued that some of the Old Testament could not be literally true. He was excommunicated for his trouble.

276 The higher criticism of the nineteenth century consisted of source-analysis of Biblical texts, inspired by the attempt of contemporary German historians such as Mommsen and Ranke to write history in a critical spirit, based upon evidence rather than tradition. While the lower criticism limited itself to evaluating the status of the various Biblical manuscripts, the higher criticism was concerned with interpretation, in particular with discovering what "really happened." It replaced the tradition that Moses was author of the Pentateuch with the theory that there were at least four different authors or narrative strands, and in New Testament studies engendered a "search for the historical Jesus." Consequently, it not only became controversial in itself but led to various attempts on the part of the church hierarchy to make its clergy swear allegiance to a literal interpretation of Scripture.

277 A reference to chap. 15, "The Musical Banks," of Samuel Butler's *Erewhon*

(New York: Penguin, 1970). The chapter is a satire on institutional religion: the Banks' currency is not the true currency of everyday life, and maintaining the institution is of considerable inconvenience to the society, yet adherence to it is an article of faith, despite the fact that "So far as I could see, fully ninety per cent. of the population of the metropolis looked upon these banks with something not far removed from contempt" (146).

278 One of the most influential theologians of the twentieth century, Rudolf Bultmann believed that the essential proclamation or *kerygma* of Christianity had to be "demythologized," i.e., refined from the mythological language that was inevitable in the time when the New Testament was composed, but whose supernaturalism forms an obstacle for contemporary readers. When demythologized, Christ's message is existential; it speaks the possibility of a spiritual transformation in the present moment. See *Jesus Christ and Mythology* (1958) and (with other authors) *Kerygma and Myth: A Theological Debate* (1953), annotated copies in the NFL.

279 See n. 260, above.

280 Wilhelm Dilthey (1833–1911) believed that the human sciences cannot be organized on the same principles as the natural sciences because the perspective of the observer cannot be eliminated and must itself therefore become an object of study. Every person has a *Weltanschauung* or world view, and the first task of the *Geisteswissenschaften*, the human sciences (literally, sciences of the spirit), is to formulate a typology of possible world views. Dilthey's major book, in which he lays this project out, is the *Introduction to the Human Sciences* (1883).

281 See Susan Sontag, *Against Interpretation* (1966).

282 An annotated copy of *Phantastes and Lilith* (Grand Rapids: Eerdmans, 1964) is in the NFL.

283 From the 1951 Diary, par. 1: "The second half of the century opened with me drinking some rather oversweet Cointreau with Helen after seeing Vera [Frye, NF's sister] off on the plane. We went to bed soon after midnight. New Years is a dull holiday if one makes one's festive effort at Christmas, and the news from Korea was bad enough to spoil whatever of that spirit remained. But, if the first half of the century saw the passing of Fascism, the second half may see the passing of Communism. I don't look for catastrophic war, but for restricted bleeding wars, threats, interdicts, and an attempt on the part of each side to wait for the enemy to blow up through internal contradictions" (*D*, 452).

284 The phrase derives from Jack Kerouac's novel *The Dharma Bums* (1958).

285 *MC*, 97.

286 Echoes the last line of "The Revelation to Eve," *StS*, 159.

287 I.e., replacing Beddoes, Shelley, and Keats respectively: the chapter titles of *SR* designate these as the Romantic Macabre, Romantic Revolutionary, and

Romantic Epiphanic. On the Great Doodle diagram, as set out in par. 222, they would be South, East, and North.

288 *Tannenbaum, mit grünen Fingern,* in *The Harz Journey: Poems of Heinrich Heine,* rev. ed., trans. Louis Untermeyer (New York: Harcourt, 1923), 160–2.

289 See *GC,* 85; also 12.272. The typological proclamation of three world Ages by Joachim de Floris (or Fiore) has shown a continuing power to inspire other writers, including Dante, from the time that the Calabrian monk first expounded it around 1200. In slightly popularized and oversimplified form, the Age of the Father is that of the Old Testament, the Age of the Son the period of the New, which has been dominated by the institutional Church; but history is on the verge of a Third Age of the Holy Spirit, in which the Church and clergy will be superseded by direct inspiration from God. The scheme is developed in his *Book of Figures, Exposition on the Apocalypse,* and *Book of Concordance.* See the Introduction to pt. 3, "Joachim of Fiore," in *Apocalyptic Spirituality,* trans. Bernard McGinn (New York: Paulist Press, 1979), 97–112.

290 *AC,* 190. Specifically, W.K. Wimsatt, in his essay on NF, "Criticism as Myth," in *Northrop Frye in Modern Criticism,* 95, had complained of NF's describing Tom Sawyer and Becky Thatcher's adventures in the cave as a displaced version of the dragon-slaying myth.

291 William Cowper (1731–1800), English poet, author of *The Castaway.*

Notebook 6

1 See 19.141 and n. 103.

2 *Nativity Ode,* ll. 38–9: "She woo's the gentle Air / To hide her guilty front with innocent Snow."

3 In canto 19 of the *Purgatorio,* Dante dreams of a deformed woman who turns into a captivating Siren, until Virgil rips open her garment and reveals her "belly," whose stench wakes Dante from sleep. At the end of canto 31, Beatrice is entreated to unveil her mouth for Dante.

4 See Norman O. Brown, *Life against Death: The Psychoanalytical Meaning of History,* 2nd ed. (Middletown, Conn.: Wesleyan University Press, 1985), 29.

5 See 19.339 and n. 226.

6 The phrase comes from the famous last lines of Goethe's *Faust,* pt. 2: "Woman Eternal / Draws us on high" (ll. 12,110–11), trans. Walter Arndt.

7 From Ibsen's *Peer Gynt.* See *AC,* 195. The contrast is between female figures who attract and draw forth, and who therefore have erotic connotations in a larger sense, and nurturing or caretaking figures: Isis was the wife of the Egyptian Osiris, but her most famous task was to gather together again all the fragments of his body that had been scattered by his enemy Set.

8 The version of this idea in "Approaching the Lyric," *EAC*, 131, reads: "Here the blocking point makes the lyrical poem part of what biologists call a displaced activity, as when a chimpanzee crossed in love starts digging holes in the ground instead." In the source, however, Konrad Lorenz, *On Aggression* (New York: MJF Books, 1963), annotated copy in the NFL, Lorenz actually speaks of "the process we call, with Tinbergen, a *redirected activity*. It is characterized by the fact that an activity is released by *one* object but discharged at *another*, because the first one, while presenting stimuli specifically eliciting the response, simultaneously emits others which inhibit its discharge" (169). Initially, Lorenz speaks only of redirected aggression, as when someone slams drawers or throws crockery instead of striking someone; later, he does widen the concept to include the redirection or sublimation of the sexual as well as the aggressive drive (279). The chimpanzee example, though, appears to be NF's. See also 12.3.

9 *I and Thou*, trans. Ronald Gregor Smith (New York: Scribner's, 1958), 24–8. Buber describes how our experience and understanding of the "primary word" I–Thou is mediated by the original connection to the mother, while the other primary word, I–It, is mediated by maternal separation.

10 For J.J. Bachofen, see 19.411 and n. 270. For Robert Graves, see *The White Goddess: A Historical Grammar of Poetic Myth*, 2nd ed. (London: Faber and Faber, 1948), annotated copy in the NFL.

11 "Prometheus" means "forethought"; the name of his brother Epimetheus means "hindsight"; "Pandora" means "all gifts" or, some suggest, "all giving." In the myth as told by Hesiod in *Works and Days*, it was a jar (*pithos*) which Pandora opened, but NF is implying an obscene pun.

12 See "The Revelation to Eve" (1969), *StS*, 135–59.

13 See *The Complete Works of W.H. Auden: Plays*, ed. Edward Mendelson (Princeton: Princeton University Press, 1988), 353. In *The Ascent of F6*, 2.5, the figure at the summit of F6 at first appears in a monk's habit but is later revealed as a "young mother," who is Mrs. Ransom, Ransom's mother.

14 In *The Diary of Søren Kierkegaard*, trans. Gerda M. Andersen, ed. Peter P. Rohde (New York: Wisdom Library, 1960), 23, no. 26, annotated copy in the NFL: "Since my earliest childhood a barb of sorrow has lodged in my heart. As long as it stays I am ironic—if it is pulled out I shall die."

15 See n. 3, above.

16 Rahab the prostitute hid Joshua's spies and enabled them to escape from Jericho, thus enabling the Israelites to gain the Promised Land. In canto 9 of the *Paradiso*, Dante works from the tradition that, as a reward, after the Crucifixion she rose from Limbo directly into heaven. Beatrice in the garden of Eden and Rahab, the last figure seen in the sphere of Venus at the end of the moon's shadow in the *Paradiso*, mark for NF a hidden fourth section of the poem structurally, a division whose associations are with Eros.

17 See n. 6, above.

18 Paul Valéry's *La Jeune Parque, or The Young Fate* (1917), is the monologue of a female figure struggling with dawning self-consciousness and knowledge of mortality. She finally decides to accept her own tears, which are thereby transformed into seaspray in the sunlight. NF associates her with a father–daughter complex close to the dead South on the Great Doodle, at the point of demonic epiphany that divides Hermes from Prometheus, with a link to the Female Babe and Old Man of Blake's *Mental Traveller*. References occur almost obsessively in NB 12 (pars. 276, 294, 367, 377, 387, 469, 478, 482, 493, 518) and in NB 24 (pars. 67, 103, 127, 129, 147, 148, 159, 237, 242); also in "Work in Progress," par. 17. Yet the *jeune parque* never makes it into the final *WP* scheme, or into any of the late essays affiliated with it.

19 NF did go on to consider some of these questions in "Old and New Comedy," *Shakespeare Survey*, 22 (1969): 1–5, incorporated into pt. 1 of "Romance as Masque," *SM*, 148–56.

20 In other words, not so much the Hermes of Greek mythology as Hermes Trismegistus ("Thrice Great") in the *Corpus Hermeticum* of approximately the 2nd c. A.D., which became the source of Renaissance Hermeticism after its translation by Marsilio Ficino in 1463.

21 Milton, *Arcades*, ll. 68–70: "Such sweet compulsion doth in musick ly, / To lull the daughters of Necessity, / And keep unsteddy Nature to her law."

22 The phrase comes from William Blake's annotations to Berkeley's *Siris*, 219: "Man is All Imagination God is Man & exists in us & we in him" (Erdman, 664).

23 Refers to the diagrammatic schemes of Yeats's *A Vision* (1937) and Poe's *Eureka* (1848).

24 In *I and Thou*, Martin Buber maintains that the true relationship to God is personal and intimate: neither a distanced, objective I–It relationship on the one hand nor, on the other, the dissolving of all relationship in total mystical union. Such a relationship could only be constituted through dialogue, not through abstract contemplation or ritual observance. See also n. 9, above.

25 Anders Nygren, *Agape and Eros* (Philadelphia: Westminster Press, 1953). See pt. 2, "The History of the Christian Idea of Love."

26 *Shah mat*: Arabic, "the king is dead," origin of the word "checkmate."

27 The reference has not been found.

28 From the last stanza of Poem 1260, *Because that you are going*.

29 Goethe, *Faust*, pt. 1, ll. 1,236–7.

30 William Blake, *Milton*, pl. 35 [39], l. 42 (Erdman, 136): "There is a Moment in each Day that Satan cannot find."

31 *The Four Zoas, Night the Eighth*, p. 101 (first portion), l. 1 (Erdman, 373).

32 From Luke 2:29–32, the so-called canticle of Simeon, which begins in the Vulgate, *Nunc dimittis servum tuum* ("Now lettest thou thy servant depart").

33 The twin of the hero-consort of Robert Graves's *The White Goddess*; the tanist can be the hero's deputy, but often there is an alternating co-kingship. Graves names Hercules and Iphiclus, Castor and Pollux, Idas and Lynceus, Romulus and Remus, Cain and Abel, among other examples. See n. 10, above. See also 12.35, 36, 164, 511; 24.64.

34 Eros and Anteros (i.e., Anti-eros) are children of Aphrodite and Ares in Cicero's *De Natura Deorum*, 3. See also 12.56.

35 For Anders Nygren, *Agape and Eros*, see n. 25, above. In his Conclusion, Nygren states that, "In attacking the Catholic doctrine of love, Luther has no thought of putting an end to love. What he seeks to destroy is that interpretation of Christian love which finds expression in the idea of Caritas, which fundamentally contains more Hellenistic Eros-love than primitive Christian Agape-love. Here, as elsewhere, Catholicism is a *complexio oppositorum*, a synthesis of opposed fundamental motifs. In Luther, on the other hand, a clear distinction is made. His view of love is throughout determined by the Christian Agape motif. We look in vain here for any single feature of Eros" (739).

36 In his disquisition on temperance in *Paradise Lost*, bk. 11, ll. 518–19, Michael speaks of "ungovern'd appetite" as "a brutish vice, / Inductive mainly to the sin of Eve." For Kierkegaard, see n. 14, above.

37 *Paradiso*, canto 10, ll. 1–6 (trans. Mark Musa):

> Looking upon His Son with all that love
> which each of them breathes forth eternally,
> that uncreated, ineffable first One,
>
> has fashioned all that moves in mind and space
> in such sublime proportion that no one
> can see it and not feel His Presence there.

38 In Shakespeare's *Venus and Adonis*, ll. 1,055–6, after Adonis has been fatally wounded by the boar, "No flower was nigh, no grass, herb, leaf, or weed, / But stole his blood and seemed with him to bleed." The next line says, "This solemn sympathy poor Venus noteth."

39 In *Hyperion*, ll. 70–2, quoted in *SR*, 139: "that second war / Not long delay'd, that scar'd the younger Gods / To hide themselves in forms of beast and bird."

40 *The Waste Land*, l. 383.

41 In fact, the *Tempest-Aeneid-Exodus*-Dante parallel reiterates in a new context the argument of one of NF's earliest influences, Colin Still, *Shakespeare's Mystery Play: A Study of "The Tempest,"* (London: Cecil Palmer, 1921), annotated copy in the NFL.

42 See Joseph Conrad, *The Nigger of the Narcissus* (1898).

43 Psalm 45:3 urges: "Gird thy sword upon thy thigh, O most mighty, with thy

glory and thy majesty." Verse 5 continues: "Thine arrows are sharp in the heart of the king's enemies; whereby the people fall under thee."

44 See n. 31, above.

45 "Thingness," the flat, objective description in the earlier work of Alain Robbe-Grillet. See *WP*, 87–8.

46 Protagonist of Carlyle's *Sartor Resartus;* the name does mean what NF says it does.

47 *Odyssey*, bk. 13, ll. 109–12. The cave of the Naiades or Nymphs has two entrances, a northern one for mortals and a southern one for immortals. This mysterious detail was allegorized by later tradition, especially the Neoplatonic, the most elaborate example of the latter being Porphyry's *De antro numpharum.*

48 Evidently a reference to Jean Genet's *The Balcony (Le Balcon)*, trans. Bernard Frenchtman (New York: Grove Press, 1962), annotated copy in the NFL. In the play, customers in a brothel enact various role-playing fantasies, dressing up as those figures of conventional society whose roles have an archetypal glamour: bishop, judge, general, etc. Such play-acting is supposed to be a "perversion," yet when a revolution deposes the old order and forces the play-actors to take on their roles for real, everything goes on exactly as before, so that the roles are now the perversion of a perversion, the mirror-image of a mirror-image. The implication is that the distinction between "reality" and "fantasy," "normal" and "perverted" in social life is untenable. Everything is a matter of role-playing and imagery, and the only distinction is that of context. A discussion of the play is in *MC*, 84–5. References to the "perversion of a perversion" occur in 12.24, 30, 45.

49 Indifference, apathy. From the sceptical Pococurante in Voltaire's *Candide.*

50 *John Barleycorn* is a traditional folk ballad existing in many versions, from the sixteenth century to modern folk-rock; in his graduate course on "Literary Symbolism," NF taught the version by Robert Burns. The story reads like a variant of the dying-god figure studied by Frazer's *Golden Bough.* A personification of the grain, John Barleycorn is put to death and buried by three men out of the East (in Burns's version; West in other sources); when he grows up again out of the ground, he is ritually killed all over again by the three men, and turned into the very drink they toast him with. See also 12.9, 286; 24.62.

51 *To Juan at the Winter Solstice*, a poem about the White Goddess by Robert Graves, also taught by NF in his graduate course "Principles of Literary Symbolism."

52 See n. 49, above.

53 The sermon by Rev. Gideon Hawke in chap. 49.

54 "The Nature of Satire," *University of Toronto Quarterly*, 14 (October 1944): 75–89. Incorporated, with major revisions, into *AC*, 223–39.

55 In Sartre's *Being and Nothingness*, the anguish of consciousness is that it must constitute itself by the negation of being, and is itself, then, a kind of nothing. Lear and Timon learn their identity only after they strip themselves of everything they possess; what they learn, however, is that, as pure consciousness, they are nothing.

56 Identification is uncertain here: the two essays which more or less fit the description are "New Directions from Old" (*FI*, 52–66) and "The Drunken Boat: The Revolutionary Element in Romanticism" (*StS*, 200–17), the only problem being that neither has any apparent connection with Harvard or Yale; "my Romantic book" is *SR*.

57 In *The Man of Law's Tale*, Chaucer tells the story of a long-suffering, patiently enduring wife named Constance. Antigonus is pursued and killed by a bear in Shakespeare's *The Winter's Tale*, 3.3.

58 "The *critical* path alone is still open." Emmanuel Kant, *Critique of Pure Reason*, trans. Norman Kemp Smith (London: Macmillan, 1933), 669.

59 See Introduction, p. xli.

60 See *FT*, 29, 89–90. "Thrown-ness" is an allusion to Martin Heidegger's term *Geworfenheit*. See *Being and Time*, trans. John Macquarrie and Edward Robinson (New York: Harper and Row, 1962), sec. 38, "Falling and Thrownness," 219–24.

61 *Milton*, pl. 33 [36] (Erdman, 133). The Mundane Egg's relation to the "Four Universes" of the four Zoas is treated in the text on pl. 19 [21], ll. 15–24 (Erdman, 112–13).

Notebook 12

1 For the Kant reference, see 6.n. 58. "Expo" is Expo '67, the 1967 World's Fair in Montreal.

2 See 19.n. 269.

3 See 6.8 and n. 8.

4 See 6.57 and n. 50.

5 The reference is to NF's theory that Dante's *Divine Comedy* can be seen as fourfold rather than threefold by considering the narrative from the garden of Eden through the sphere of Venus as a lower level of paradise—Eros rather than Logos, to use the language of the Third Book, though the inspiration is also Blake's lower paradise of Beulah, with its feminine associations. Matilda or Matelda appears in the garden of Eden in *Purgatorio* 28, while Rahab is the last figure Dante meets in the sphere of Venus in *Paradiso* 9. See par. 32, below; also "Work in Progress," par. 7.

6 *GC*, 166–7. NF had not yet written *GC*, but he had been using the table for many years in his undergraduate course on the Bible.

7 For "comminution," see 19.n. 181.

8 See 19.73 and n. 53.

9 For Norman O. Brown, see 19.348 and n. 235, and 6.6 and n. 4. The phrase "infantile polymorphous" alludes to Freud's theory that infantile sexuality, as yet lacking a genital focus, is characterized by a "polymorphous perversity" that can make an erotic object out of almost anything.

10 The "plot" of Blake's *Milton* is that Milton in eternity, dissatisfied at having left tasks unfinished, descends like a Boddhisattva back into time in order to (1) confront and cast out his shadow and (2) redeem his emanation or female counterpart Ololon, depicted as a young virgin.

11 As Matelda explains to Dante in *Purgatorio*, canto 28, ll. 127–33, these two rivers have their source in a common spring. The waters of the Lethe (from Classical mythology, now relocated in the garden of Eden) wash away the memory of sin, while the waters of the Eunoe restore the memory of good deeds. Matelda draws Dante into the waters of the Lethe in canto 31, ll. 91–102; he drinks the waters of the Eunoe in the final lines of the *Purgatorio*, canto 33, ll. 127–45.

12 That is, Dante's mirror and sphere symbolism. An explanation of this phrase is found in NB 45, a set of notes on the cantos of the *Purgatorio* and the first ten cantos of the *Paradiso*—i.e., to the limit where NF considered that Eros gave way to Logos in the *Divine Comedy*. Internal references date NB 45 concurrent with NB 12 and 24. One of the most recurrent images it records is that of what par. 81 calls "The extraordinary mirror imagery." To this, par. 46 adds that in the opening of canto 17 of the *Purgatorio*, "Light in mist continues, the word 'spera' [sphere] being used of the sun (5)." It is significant that this canto is sometimes called Dante's apostrophe to the imagination, which can be moved by sense perception, but can also be stimulated by the sphere of spiritual light. NF says in par. 87, "I don't quite know why, but I'll have to collect all these specchio & spero references."

13 T.S. Eliot, *The Waste Land*, l. 383. NF quotes this line in 6.50, to describe "Dante's escape from hell through the centre of the earth."

14 The last three symbols in this paragraph do not correspond to NF's normal usage. Judging from the total number of symbols listed, they are most likely irregular forms of Paradox, Ignoramus, and Twilight.

15 For Blake's "bounding outline," see *A Descriptive Catalogue* (Erdman, 550): "The great and golden rule of art, as well as of life, is this: that the more distinct, sharp, and wirey the bounding line, the more perfect the work of art." For Hopkins's "inscape," see n. 303, below.

16 See 6.56 and n. 48.

17 Joseph Campbell traces the career of the hero as a cyclical quest in *The Hero with a Thousand Faces* (New York: Pantheon, 1949), annotated copy in the NFL. NF's own "wheel" is the "great wheel" from NB 8, adapted into the

Third Book project in NB 19 to become ultimately part of the Great Doodle. See 19.122 and n. 94, and 19.191.

18 See 6.45 and n. 37.

19 In late passages of NB 18 and the earlier section of its successor, NB 19.

20 See Geoffrey Hartman, "Ghostlier Demarcations," in *Northrop Frye in Modern Criticism*, 109–31; rpt. in Geoffrey Hartman, *Beyond Formalism: Literary Essays, 1958–70* (New Haven, Conn.: Yale University Press, 1970), 27–41. The remark occurs on p. 31 of the latter: "Archetypal analysis can degenerate into an abstract thematics where the living pressure of mediations is lost and all connections are skeletonized. These faults appear clearly in the little book on T.S. Eliot and the essay on Milton's 'Lycidas,' inexpensive world tours of myth." The "little book on T.S. Eliot" referred to is *TSE*; the "essay on Milton's 'Lycidas'" is "Literature as Context: Milton's *Lycidas*" (1959), *FI*, 119–29.

21 1 Corinthians 9:1: "Am I not an apostle? am I not free? have I not seen Jesus Christ our Lord?" and 1 Corinthians 15:8: "And last of all he was seen of me also, as of one born out of due time." Since Paul lived after Jesus and never met him, he must be speaking of another kind of experience, one he identifies with both his conversion and the recognition of his vocation as apostle.

22 See the ending of "The Top of the Tower: A Study of the Imagery of Yeats" (1969), *StS*, 255–77.

23 See 19.141 and n. 103. The same idea is repeated by NF in the first paragraph of NB 6.

24 In the very last speech of *Back to Methuselah*, Lilith says of humanity: "Best of all, they are still not satisfied: the impulse I gave them in that day when I sundered myself in twain and launched Man and Woman on the earth still urges them: after passing a million goals they press on to the goal of redemption from the flesh, to the vortex freed from matter, to the whirlpool in pure intelligence that, when the world began, was a whirlpool in pure force."

25 See 6.56 and n. 48.

26 See n. 5, above.

27 "The Story of Two Brothers," an Egyptian folk tale with strong resemblances to the story of Joseph falsely accused by Potiphar's wife, also mentioned in 24.159. NF refers to it a number of times in the Third Book notebooks. See *Ancient Near Eastern Texts Relating to the Old Testament*, ed. James B. Pritchard (Princeton: Princeton University Press, 1955), 23–5. Perhaps fittingly for a story about doubling, however, there is a folk tale in the Grimm collection, also called "The Two Brothers," which is a kind of doublet of the Egyptian tale and is mentioned by NF in *SeS*, 111. See pars. 35, 550, 571, below.

28 See n. 48, below.

29 *Purgatorio*, canto 9, ll. 94–102.
30 For the "folk tale of the Two Brothers," see n. 27, above. For the "tanist theme," see 6.40 and n. 33. In *SeS*, 111, NF speaks of "the medieval story of Amis and Amiloun" as a development of the "Two Brothers" folk tale pattern: "In this type of story one brother goes out on a quest or in search of adventure, the other remaining home, though able to tell from some sign how his brother is faring, and going into action when help is needed."
31 Azazel is the demon to whom the scapegoat was sent out on the Day of Atonement in Leviticus 16. Lilith was not originally a single figure but a type of female demon, mentioned once in the Bible (Isaiah 34:14). In Talmudic literature, she preys lustfully upon men or strangles babies and women in childbirth. Midrashic sources sometimes made her the first wife of Adam, before the creation of Eve. In certain Kabbalistic texts she achieves an apotheosis as a kind of anti-Shekhinah, mother of the race of demons as the Shekhinah or Divine Presence was the mother of the House of Israel. NF discusses her in *GC*, 140–1 and *WP*, 273–83.
32 *Prometheus Unbound*, 1.1.191–4. Zoroaster meets himself walking in a garden.
33 A variation of the Shaun–Shem brother conflict in *Finnegans Wake*, based on Joyce's own relation to his brother Stanislaus. Primas is Shaun, the firstborn; Caddy (the cadet, and also the "cad") is the younger brother Shem. Both are Oedipal parricides; but Shaun, in his guise as Buckley, shoots his father HCE (the Russian general) with a gun, while Caddy kills him with words: as Hosty, he composes the satiric "Ballad of Persse O'Reilly." Spirit of slander, the cad is a form of Satan, the Accuser. Yet both brothers are also of one substance with the father.
34 NF's Alexander Lectures at the University of Toronto in 1966 became *FT*. See the first essay, "My Father as He Slept: The Tragedy of Order."
35 The epithet *pius*, repeatedly applied to Aeneas, can by translated "pious" or "dutybound," according to whether the emphasis is on his sense of religious or social duty; both, however, are included in the *Aeneid*'s central theme of "piety." Here, it is used by Aeneas himself in one of its early appearances in the poem, bk. 1, l. 378, when Aeneas, landed upon the shores of Carthage, addresses his mother, the disguised Venus.
36 Spenser, *Epithalamion*, sec. 18, ll. 330–1.
37 Goddess of the "bitter" or salt waters in the Babylonian Creation myth, from whose body both heaven and earth are fashioned; in *GC*, 146, NF notes how certain features of the myth are reflected in the Biblical Creation story.
38 The Welsh board game was *gwyddbwyll*, according to a footnote on p. 68 of *The Mabinogion*, trans. Gwyn Jones and Thomas Jones (London: Everyman, 1949); the editors say it is not a battle game (or a love game) but a hunt game: from the centre of the board, the king tries to make his way to the

outer edge while a hunting party attempts to capture him. For the Egyptian Book of the Dead, see E.A. Wallis Budge, *Chapters of Coming Forth by Day or the Theban Recension of the Book of the Dead* (1910) and *Hieroglyphic Vocabulary to the Theban Recension of the Book of the Dead* (1911).

39 I.e., Lil in *The Waste Land*, sec. 2, "A Game of Chess," ll. 142 ff. Line 157: "And her only thirty-one."

40 In *Berenice*, the story of a man so obsessed with a woman's beautiful teeth that he collects them after her death.

41 For the table of metaphors, see n. 6, above. For the "great wheel," see 19.122 and 191, and par. 24 and n. 17, above.

42 NF is preoccupied with this story idea in the early pages of NB 19, e.g., pars. 3 and 11.

43 For the importance of Rahab and *Paradiso*, canto 9, to NF, see n. 5, above.

44 Wyndham Lewis, *Paleface: The Philosophy of the "Melting Pot"* (1929), is a plea to the white race of America to stop feeling inferior to the black. For fairly obvious reasons it was never published in the United States during Lewis's lifetime.

45 Robert Briffault's *Europa: The Days of Ignorance* (1935), is an autobiographical *Bildungsroman* of the man who wrote *The Mothers* (1927), an enormous, once-eminent three-volume study arguing for the existence of an early matriarchal stage of society.

46 See 6.56 and n. 48.

47 See *SR*, 135: "Keats, speaking of the blind Homer, also thinks of the poet as encompassing the entire world of the *diva triformis* from the moon-drawn sea to the moon: *There is a triple sight in blindness keen; / Such seeing hadst thou, as it once befel / To Dian, Queen of Earth, and Heaven, and Hell*" [italics in original]. The Keats poem is "To Homer."

48 For his distinction between the paraphrasable overthought and metaphorical underthought, see Gerard Manley Hopkins, letter to Alexander Baillie, 14 January 1883, in *A Hopkins Reader*, ed. John Pick (New York: Oxford University Press, 1953), 113. See also *WP*, 57.

49 See *The Use of Poetry and the Use of Criticism* (London: Faber and Faber, 1964; orig. pub. 1933), 151. The poet provides "meaning" for the reader "as the imaginary burglar is always provided with a bit of meat for the house-dog."

50 In *Gertha's Lovers, The Early Romances of William Morris in Prose and Verse* (London: Dent, 1907), 174, annoted copy in the NFL: "and they had a mighty faith withal that they should one day ring the world, going westward ever till they reached their old home in the east, left now so far behind."

51 I.e., the early 1940s. NF was living on Bathurst St. when he composed NB 42, the "Pentateuch" notebook, in 1944; the Fryes bought their home on Clifton Rd. in 1946.

52 This observation is repeated in the "Work in Progress" typescript, par. 21.
53 In Poe's story "The Oval Portrait," an obsessed and narcissistic painter insists, despite her reluctance, on painting his young wife's portrait. Although he is too absorbed in his work to notice, her health progressively declines as the portrait takes shape. In the end, the artist adds the final brushstrokes, looks in triumph at his wife—and realizes she has just died. Since the wife had been of uncertain health, a naturalistic explanation is possible, but the suggestion is that the portrait has, like a vampire, sucked the life out of its subject.
54 Possibly referring to an organizational scheme lying behind NB 12, a version of NF's recurrent desire to write a book in one hundred sections. In par. 506, below, for example, he refers to "Eros 2 (26 or 27)." When thinking in terms of such mythical schema, NF often regards 28 and 29 as lunar numbers.
55 See Wallace Stevens, *Description without Place*, pt. 2, ll. 8–9: "An age is green or red. An age believes / Or it denies."
56 The stories of Enoch and Noah are the last to be recounted to Adam by Michael in bk. 11 of *Paradise Lost*. Both represent the saving remnant who contrast with the wickedness and corruption that mostly precede them. Thus, they mark the end of the first cycle of human history, which is why Milton broke the text here for the second edition of *Paradise Lost*, creating the present bks. 11 and 12.
57 See 6.42 and n. 34.
58 Inaccurate reference to Anders Nygren, *Agape and Eros*. See 6.28 and n. 25.
59 William Blake, *Jerusalem*, pl. 91: "Los reads the Stars of Albion! the Spectre reads the Voids / Between the Stars," ll. 36–7 (Erdman, 251).
60 See 19.58 and n. 40.
61 See 19.108 and n. 84.
62 Probably a general reference to Nietzsche's ambivalent fascinaiton with systematic thinkers, as exemplified by Hegel.
63 NF's lecture at Cornell in the spring of 1968, entitled "The Social Context of Literary Criticism" (see *Northrop Frye on Literature and Society, 1936–1989: Unpublished Papers*, 347–65), was an early version of material that later ended up in *CP*.
64 The occasion has not been identified. A reference in NB 36, one of the *AC* notebooks from the early 1950s, speaks of planning to follow the "history chapter," i.e., the First Essay, with "a pep talk about Spengler and the containing forms of cultural history" (par. 9), which may or may not be a clue as to the content of the talk. A more substantial clue perhaps lies in the following passage from "New Directions from Old" (*FI*, 53–4): "We notice that when a historian's scheme gets to a certain point of comprehensiveness it becomes mythical in shape, and so approaches the poetic in its structure.

There are romantic historical myths based on a quest or pilgrimage to a City of God or a classless society; there are comic historical myths of progress through evolution or revolution; there are tragic myths of decline and fall, like the works of Gibbon and Spengler; there are ironic myths of recurrence of casual catastrophe. . . . A Canadian historian, F.H. Underhill, writing on Toynbee, has employed the term 'metahistory' for such works." See also par. 115, below.

65 See Introduction, p. xli.

66 "The Top of the Tower: A Study of the Imagery of Yeats" (1969), *StS*, 257–77.

67 William Butler Yeats, *A Vision*, A Reissue with the Author's Final Revisions (New York: Collier, 1966; orig. pub. 1937), 27.

68 According to a story not told by Homer, Eris (Discord), out of spite for not being invited to the wedding of Peleus and Thetis, threw down amidst the company a golden apple inscribed "To the most beautiful," resulting in the Judgment of Paris and thus the Trojan War.

69 See the Introduction to *The Mabinogion*, xii: "There has been no lack of attempts to explain the term *mabinogi*, but by common consent of Welsh scholars today it is derived from the word *mab* (youth), and is equated in meaning with the Latin *infantia* and the French *enfance*. It means first 'youth,' then a 'tale of youth,' then a 'tale of a hero,' and finally little more than 'tale' or 'story.'"

70 Jessie Weston's 1894 translation of the *Parzival*. NB 14 is closely linked to this paragraph. It begins, "This notebook is for the collecting of observations on what I now think of as the red or Adonis vision," and goes on to a lengthy book-by-book analysis of Wolfram von Eschenbach's *Parzival*, with page numbers keyed to the translation by Helen M. Mustard and Charles E. Passage (New York: Vintage, 1961), annotated copy in the NFL.

71 NF is possibly thinking of the following remark in "Ezra Pound: His Metric and Poetry": "Very few people know the Arthurian legends well, or even Malory (if they did they might realize that the *Idylls of the King* are hardly more important than a parody, or a 'Chaucer retold for Children'); but no one accuses Tennyson of needing footnotes, or of superciliousness toward the uninstructed." In *To Criticize the Critic and Other Writings* (New York: Farrar, Straus and Giroux, 1965), 166.

72 Jessie Weston, *From Ritual to Romance* (Garden City: Doubleday, 1957; orig. pub. 1920), annotated copy in the NFL. Famous for its influence on T.S. Eliot's *The Waste Land*, Weston's study not only found vestiges in the Grail romances of dying-god fertility-cult imagery of the kind studied by Sir James Frazer in *The Golden Bough*, but went on to postulate controversially that the Grail romances contain vestiges of the secret ritual of a fertility cult that had actually survived into the Middle Ages from pagan times.

73 Poem by Robert Chester, originally published in the same volume as Shakespeare's *The Phoenix and the Turtle.* A lengthy analysis of the poem is in NB 14.

74 NF is quoting from *Paradise Lost*, bk. 4, ll. 277–80: "where old Cham, / Whom Gentiles Ammon call and Lybian Jove, / Hid Amalthea and her Florid Son / Young Bacchus from his Stepdame Rhea's eye." Milton's allusion is to a legend out of Diodorus Siculus in which Jupiter Ammon (the Biblical Ham or Cham) protects Bacchus, child of Amalthea, from Rhea. Elsewhere, however, Amalthea was owner of the goat (or else the goat itself) that suckled and protected the infant Zeus while Rhea and Gaia were hiding him on Mt. Dicte in Crete from the Titans.

75 Echo of Blake's *The Mental Traveller*, ll. 101–2, with connotations therefore of the cyclical birth of Orc: "And none can touch that frowning form / Except it be a Woman Old."

76 NF is referring to the symbolism of Tarot cards, whose normal suits were cup, baton, sword, and coin. However, one strand of tradition associated those suits with what were called the four Grail Hallows, four sacred objects out of the Grail legend: cup, lance, sword, and dish. Though explanations differed, one version lists these as the Grail itself, the lance used to pierce Christ's side in the Crucifixion, the sword that killed John the Baptist, and the platter on which his severed head was placed. This has affinities with the kind of view represented by Jessie Weston's *From Ritual to Romance*, in which the Grail legend grew up as a spiritualization of an original sexual and fertility symbolism. In this version, the two pairs of objects are linked with the defining points of the natural cycle, the two solstices. The two associated with Christ, Grail and lance, are thereby linked with the winter solstice of Christ's Nativity; for symmetry's sake, the Church designated the summer solstice as the feast of John the Baptist, St. John's Eve, based on John's remark in the Gospels on beholding Christ: "He must increase, but I must decrease." NF explains some of this in *NFS*, 41–2. See also n. 92, below.

77 Reference to Blake's *The Mental Traveller*, ll. 43–4: "Till from the fire on the hearth / A little Female Babe does spring." In the poem, male and female move in opposite cycles, the one growing younger as the other grows older, and there is always an opposition between them, as between the white and black players in chess.

78 Possibly Helen Creighton, a copy of whose *Songs and Ballads from Nova Scotia* (Toronto: Dent, 1932) is in the NFL. Other books by her include *A Life in Folklore* (Toronto: Ryerson, 1965) and *Bluenose Magic: Popular Beliefs and Superstitions in Nova Scotia* (Toronto: McGraw-Hill, 1968).

79 See n. 39, above.

80 It was a folk custom in the British isles for children to go wren-hunting on St. Stephen's day, the day after Christmas, as described in a folk lyric, "The

Wren Song," sung by the children door to door as they collected money for the wren's "funeral." The wren, who was placed in a decorated holly tree, is clearly a kind of Frazerian dying-god figure, and was called "the king of all birds." However, Beryl Rowland says in *Birds with Human Souls: A Guide to Bird Symbolism* (Knoxville: University of Tennessee Press, 1978), 186, "As is often the case with birds and animals, the wren had ambivalent values, and by its sacrifice, the powers of darkness were defeated, and light and life triumphed"; hence NF's reference to Leviathan.

81 In the first stanza of Shakespeare's *The Phoenix and the Turtle*, the "bird of loudest lay" is called to be the herald, summoning the birds to the funeral rites of the phoenix and the turtle.

82 See n. 73, above.

83 Wolfram von Eschenbach, *Parzival*. See n. 70, above.

84 Probably because some of the symbolism of von Eschenbach's *Parzival* shows the influence of alchemy, this paragraph is a fantasia on alchemical imagery: lead, gold, Saturn, the black sun or hidden fire within nature, etc.

85 See *RE*, 14: "In the *Aeneid* there is what from Milton's point of view is a most important advance in this conception of a total cyclical action. Here the total action begins and ends, not at precisely the same point, but at the same point renewed and transformed by the heroic action itself. . . . The end is the beginning as recreated by the heroism of Aeneas."

86 See n. 81, above.

87 For "Beatrice's unveiled mouth," see 6.5 and n. 3.

88 See n. 63, above.

89 See Martin Heidegger, "The Origin of the Work of Art," in *Poetry, Language, Thought*, trans. and intro. Albert Hofstadter (New York: Harper and Row, 1971), 17: "In themselves and in their interrelations artist and work *are* each of them by virtue of a third thing which is prior to them both, namely that which also gives artist and work of art their names—art."

90 Tennyson, *Flower in the Crannied Wall*, ll. 4–6: "*if* I could understand / What you are, root and all, and all in all, / I should know what God and man is."

91 In *Margaret Fuller: From Transcendentalism to Revolution*, Radcliffe Biography Series (Delta: Seymour Laurence, 1978), 86–7, Paula Blanchard writes, "It was in this sense of embracing one's experience as a whole that she later made the famous statement, 'I accept the Universe'—at which Carlyle reportedly remarked, 'By Gad, she'd better!'"

92 May Day, the Celtic Beltane and German "Walpurgis night," is one of four hinges of the year as explained in *NFS*, 42, the others being the summer and winter solstices and Halloween or 1 November. See also n. 76, above.

93 See also par. 280, below.

94 See *The Romance of Tristan and Iseult, as Retold by Joseph Bédier*, trans. Hilaire Belloc and completed by Paul Rosenfeld (New York: Pantheon, 1945).

95 See D.H. Lawrence, "The Spirit of Place," *Studies in Classic American Literature* (New York: Penguin, 1964; orig. pub. 1923), 8: "Never trust the artist. Trust the tale. The proper function of a critic is to save the tale from the artist who created it."

96 *King Lear*, 4.6.206–7: "Who redeems nature from the general curse / Which twain have brought her to."

97 From the first paragraph of chap. 4: "They must without pause justify their life to the eternal pity that commands toil to be hard and unceasing, from sunrise to sunset, from sunset to sunrise; till the weary succession of nights and days tainted by the obstinate clamour of sages, demanding bliss and an empty heaven, is redeemed at last by the vast silence of pain and labour, by the dumb fear and the dumb courage of men obscure, forgetful, and enduring."

98 Andrew Marvell, *On a Drop of Dew*. See *WP*, 264.

99 In 18.76, NF writes, "here's an ancient note I've just rescued from five years back: "high katabasis: incarnation or descent of spirit: drop of dew (Marvell), lady in *Comus*, microcosm imagery. Middle katabasis: death; identification with bleeding flower; metamorphosis, wheel of fortune turning. Low katabasis: descent into hell; no exit; sparagmos. Low anabasis: escape from hell or prison; Cyclops; Mutability; Satan in Eden; rebellion & loosening of chaos (Gunpowder Plot explosion in Milton); Harrowing of Hell; Jonah & fishing. Middle anabasis: birth of individual or society; marriage; revival or return from absence; piled logs; tower & mountain climbing. High anabasis: redemption; sacred marriage; king & beggar maiden; black bride; question. High assimilated to dialectic; middle cyclical; low *are* the cycle." It is possible that the "ancient note" of five years previous was 32.84–5, which also tries to sort out various types of anabasis and katabasis. See also pars. 107 and 495, below.

100 See P.D. Ouspensky, *In Search of the Miraculous: Fragments of an Unknown Teaching* (1949), which has many geometrical diagrams; annotated copy in the NFL along with annotated copies of two other books by Ouspensky. See also Aldous Huxley, *The Doors of Perception and Heaven and Hell* (1959), annotated copy in the NFL.

101 On pl. 1, ll. 20–1, Bromion says to Oothoon, "Thy soft American plains are mine, and mine thy north & south: / Stampt with my signet are the swarthy children of the sun." On pl. 2, l. 8, Theotormon hears another reference to the American slave trade: "The voices of slaves beneath the sun, and children bought with money." Oothoon, then, identified with America, is presumably sun-darkened with labour like her children.

102 For the Utopia paper, see 19.n. 7.

103 See n. 64, above.

104 The result of this desire was "Old and New Comedy," *Shakespeare Survey*,

22 (1969): 1–5. Incorporated into pt. 1 of "Romance as Masque," *SM*, 148–56. The remarks about Old and New Comedy in the next several paragraphs look toward those articles. See also par. 142, below.

105 The other context is in 19.111–13. Those paragraphs and the present reference predate and somewhat differ from the elaborate theory developed later in NBs 21 and 24 of the evolution of religious consciousness through "three awarenesses." See also 19.174 and n. 124.

106 The Beddoes essay is "Yorick: The Romantic Macabre," in *SR*, 51–85. The early comedy paper is "The Argument of Comedy," *English Institute Essays, 1948*, ed. D.A. Robertson, Jr. (New York: Columbia University Press, 1949), 58–73. Incorporated into *AC*, Third Essay.

107 Disceopolis, or Dikaiopolis = Just-City. Lysistrata = Ending-Army.

108 See n. 106, above.

109 See chap. 28, "Aristophanes in London." The play is a satire on technological progressivism.

110 For the Utopia paper, see 19.n. 7. The Chicago paper is "The Instruments of Mental Production"(1966), *StS*, 3–21. Originally presented as an address at the University of Chicago, 1 February 1966, as part of the university's seventy-fifth anniversary liberal arts conference.

111 The spiritual authority paper is "The Problem of Spiritual Authority in the Nineteenth Century" (1964), *StS*, 241–56. The Kentucky paper is "Speculation and Concern" (1966), *StS*, 38–55. Versions of a paper later incorporated into *CP* were originally delivered at Cornell University in 1968 and at Indiana University. For the Cornell paper, see n. 63, above. For the Indiana paper, see n. 154, below.

112 Wolfram von Eschenbach, *Parzival*, 249. In the extensive notes about *Parzival* in NB 14, keyed to the Mustard and Passage translation, par. 44 quotes from the same passage.

113 From the 1950 Diary, par. 423: "In the letter to the clergymen he [Jonathan Swift] says it's his duty to preach & practise the contempt of human things, which not only establishes the link between preaching & satire, but associates both with the whole *Paradise Regained* withdrawn vision of wrath, the rejection of all act, within which the universe of myth is reborn" (*D*, 382–3).

114 See *AC*, 243.

115 See pars. 113 and 115, above.

116 As in 19.3 and 11; also 20.23.

117 At the very end of the *Symposium*, 623d, when only Socrates, Agathon, and Aristophanes are still awake, Socrates maintains that the same man might potentially be capable of writing both tragedy and comedy. NF's remark about Euripides presumably derives from the fact that Euripides not only wrote in both genres but also invented the tragicomedy. Aristotle reports

(*Poetics*, 1451b) that Agathon invented some of his plots and characters rather than receiving them from tradition, which perhaps suggests some of Euripides' kind of freedom.

118 See 6.45 and n. 37. Also n. 12, above.

119 Or "year-daimon," name given by Jane Ellen Harrison to the dying and reviving god figure, as studied by Sir James Frazer in *The Golden Bough*, in his capacity as totemic focus of the social group. See her *Themis: A Study of the Social Origins of Greek Religion* (London: Merline, 1977; orig. pub. 1912), annotated copy in the NFL.

120 See n. 119, above.

121 Kairos is defined by Paul Tillich in *Systematic Theology* (Chicago: University of Chicago Press, 1963), 3:369, as "the moment at which history, in terms of a concrete situation, had matured to the point of being able to receive the breakthrough of the central manifestation of the Kingdom of God. The New Testament has called this moment the 'fulfilment of time,' in Greek, *kairos*." It is contrasted with *chronos*, or clock time.

122 A reference to the Seattle revelation. See Introduction, p. li.

123 For the Seattle revelation, see Introduction, p. li. For the mind–soul–body and "three awarenesses" notes, see 19.174 and n. 124. The "mystical" notebook in 1946 is NB 3.

124 For the St. Clair revelation, see Introduction, p. xli.

125 See Introduction, p. xxxi.

126 In *Paradise Lost*, bk 7, ll. 169–72, just before he sends the Son out to create, the Father makes a speech that has been variously interpreted:

> Boundless the Deep, because I am who fill
> Infinitude, nor vacuous the space.
> Though I uncircumscrib'd my self retire,
> And put not forth my goodness, which is free
> To act or not, Necessitie and Chance
> Approach not mee, and what I will is Fate.

NF accepts the view that Milton's God is creating out of himself (*de Deo*), by filling infinitude; where he has retired, there is nothing. In other words, Milton denies the theory that God created *ex nihilo*, out of nothing, a theory in conflict with Genesis 1 but adopted by theologians to avoid postulating a substance co-eternal with God. However, creation *de Deo* also avoids that difficulty. See also 24.8.

127 "Edgar Poe on the Theme of the Clock," John-Paul Weber, trans. Claude Richard and Robert Regan for *Poe: A Collection of Critical Essays*, ed. Robert Regan (Englewood Cliffs, N.J.: Prentice-Hall, 1967), 301–11.

128 The first two books mentioned are: Stanley Stewart, *The Enclosed Garden: The Tradition and the Image in Seventeenth-Century Poetry* (1966); Maren-

Sofie Rostvig, *The Happy Man: Studies in the Metamorphoses of a Classical Ideal, 1600–1700* (1954). "Hils's translation of Casimire" is a reference doubtless derived by NF from discussions in Stewart and Rostvig. Casimire Sarbiewski was a Jesuit whose poetic paraphrase, in Latin, of the Song of Songs was translated by G. Hils as *Odes out of Salomons Sacred Marriage Song* and published in 1646 in *The Odes of Casimire*. It is alleged to have influenced Marvell's *The Garden*.

129 See n. 67, above.

130 To prevent a battle between Satan and Gabriel in bk. 4 of *Paradise Lost*, God hangs "forth in Heav'n his golden Scales, yet seen / Betwixt Astraea and the Scorpion signe" (ll. 997–8).

131 There are variant spellings, including "woodhouse," but a woodwose was a wild man of the woods or savage.

132 See sequence beginning with par. 116, above.

133 The *mystes* was the initiate in the Eleusinian mysteries.

134 See William Butler Yeats, *If I Were Four-and-Twenty*, in *Explorations* (New York: Macmillan, 1962), 279.

135 Jorge Luis Borges, "The Immortals," in *The Aleph and Other Stories, 1933–69* (New York: Dutton, 1970), 161–8.

136 See "Pierre Menard, Author of Don Quixote," in *Ficciones* (New York: Grove, 1962), 45–56. NF mentions the story in *SeS*, 162.

137 See *The Presocratics*, ed. and trans. Philip Wheelwright (New York: Macmillan, 1966), 69–79. NF is synthesizing several of Heraclitus's aphorisms. For the "double gyre," see Fragment 28: "There is exchange of all things for fire and of fire for all things, as there is of wares for gold and of gold for wares." Souls should aspire upward, towards the condition of fire, though they are tempted downward towards the heavy elements of water and earth; hence Fragment 46: "The best and wisest soul is a dry beam of light," whereas in Fragment 49 "It is death to souls to become water, and it is death to water to become earth." Fire is the image of the universal Logos; Fragment 1 says that "all things come to pass in accordance with this Logos."

138 The symbolic colours of *Spelt from Sibyl's Leaves* are white and black, Logos and Thanatos.

139 Although born in Sherbrooke, Quebec, NF spent his early years in Moncton, N.B.

140 See 19.62 and n. 47.

141 Bacbuc, the priestess of the holy bottle in bk. 5.

142 Jacob Jordaens (1593–1678), the third great Flemish painter in the Baroque period after Rubens and van Dyck.

143 In *RE*, 69–73, NF defines lust and greed as the primary categories of sin in Milton, comparable to Dante's *forza* and *froda*, respectively: sins of outward

aggression and of inward withdrawal. In the council of devils in bk. 2 of *Paradise Lost*, Moloch represents the "aggressive swimming in blood" of lust, not on superficial appearance, but because war is perverted sexual energy. His opposite, Belial, represents the passively-withdrawing principle of greed. The vision of the lazar-house in bk. 11 is cited (71) as an image of greed; although there are no miserly suicides in shit, the lazar-house shows the consequences of intemperance.

144 See 19.411 and n. 270.

145 See Søren Kierkegaard, *Repetition: An Essay in Experimental Psychology*, trans. Walter Lowrie (Princeton: Princeton University Press, 1946), annotated copy in the NFL.

146 Keats, *Endymion*, bk. 2, l. 198. The story is recounted in Apollodorus and other ancient mythographers that Orion was blinded by Dionysus's son Oenopion for raping Oenopion's daughter Merope. An oracle told Orion he would regain his sight by travelling to the easternmost point of the world, where his eye-sockets could catch the first rays of dawn. Led by Cedalion or Kedalion, a diminutive apprentice from Hephaestus's workshop, Orion travels to the rim of the Ocean-Sea, where Eos, the dawn, falls in love with him and her brother Helios restores his sight. Poussin has a painting called "Blind Orion Searching for the Rising Sun," and the myth is alluded to in *Hamlet's Mill*.

147 Plural of *nostos*, meaning "a return home."

148 See *Iliad*, bk. 24, ll. 527–33. In these famous lines, the very heart of the vision of the *Iliad*, Achilles, grieving for Patroclus, tells Priam, grieving for the son whom Achilles has killed, that excessive grief gains nothing; we must submit, for there are two great jars that stand in Zeus's halls: in one lie blessings and in the other all our miseries. Zeus scatters handfuls from them both arbitrarily, and that is how life is.

149 In the *Odyssey*, bk. 11, ll. 465–540, Odysseus speaks to the underworld shades of both Achilles and Heracles, though he is aware that the latter is only a phantom, the gods having granted Heracles a unique double fate: while his shade is in Hades, his real self feasts on Olympus with Hebe as his consort. At the very end of bk. 11, ll. 627–35, Odysseus says he had to flee before he could meet Theseus and Pirithous, who ventured into the underworld to kidnap Persephone and were trapped themselves instead. Odysseus does not mention the story that Theseus, but not Pirithous, was rescued by Hercules, Pirithous thus becoming what Robert Graves in *The White Goddess* called a "tanist," the hero's twin and, often, his scapegoat.

150 See 6.55 and n. 47.

151 Dardanus was the original ancestor of the Trojans.

152 A fusion of lines from two of Yeats's poems: "The lion and the honeycomb:

O what does Scripture say?" from *Vacillation* and "The foul rag and bone shop of the heart" from *The Circus Animals' Desertion*.

153 Neither Prometheus nor Esau are mentioned by name in Blake's *The Marriage of Heaven and Hell*, but Prometheus is one of "The Giants who formed this world into its sensual existence and now seem to live in it in chains" (pl. 14). Esau was reputedly the ancestor of the neighbouring kingdom of Edom, for which a day of vengeance is prophesied in Isaiah 34, cited by Blake on pl. 3. However, since Blake is inaugurating his revolutionary "Bible of hell," which turns conventional Biblical ideology upside-down, the same plate also proclaims that "Now is the dominion of Edom, & the return of Adam into Paradise." Both Edom and Esau come from a root meaning "ruddy," and the dominion of Edom and return of Esau signify an uprising of revolutionary energy coming from an oppressed and rejected quarter, the kind of revolutionary explosion associated with the fiery-haired Orc. *GC*, 195, notes that Job's Uz is sometimes said to be in Edom: "Job lives in enemy territory, in the embrace of heathen and Satanic power," and his restoration is thus metaphorically identical to the emancipation of Edom.

154 "Mythos and Logos," *The School of Letters, Indiana University: Twentieth Anniversary, 1968*, 27–40. Originally delivered as a lecture at the summer session of the Indiana School of Letters, Bloomington, June 1968. The discussion of Sidney and Shelley was later incorporated in *CP*.

155 Edwin Honig, poet, critic, translator, author of *Dark Conceit: The Making of Allegory* (1959).

156 See n. 5, above.

157 One of NF's many references in the notebooks to Mallarmé's poem *Un Coup de Dés* (1895). He uses the famous opening phrase, "A throw of the dice will never abolish chance," in *SeS*, 176; in "The Symbol as a Medium of Exchange," *MM*, 39; and in *WP*, 292, each time in a discussion of Mallarmé, but each time without explaining that he is quoting from the poem.

158 See 6.72 and n. 60.

159 See Stephane Mallarmé, *L'Après Midi d'un Faune* (1865).

160 Thomas Lovell Beddoes, *Death's Jest Book*, 5.3.316–29.

161 See pars. 116 ff. and par. 142.

162 Stephane Mallarmé, *Toast Funèbre à Théophile Gautier* (1873).

163 See n. 157, above.

164 See "Crisis in Poetry," in *Mallarmé: Selected Prose Poems, Essays & Letters*, trans. Bradford Cook (Baltimore: Johns Hopkins University Press, 1956), 34: "Pursuing his mysterious task, Hugo reduced all prose—philosophy, oratory, history—to poetry; and since he was himself poetry personified, he nearly abolished the philosopher's, speaker's, or historian's right to self-

expression. In that wasteland, with silence all around, he was a monument."

165 See p. 225 of "The Nightmare Life in Death," NF's review of *Molloy* and two other works by Samuel Beckett, in *NFCL*, 219–29.

166 See 19.391 and n. 260.

167 See n. 157, above.

168 See Introduction, p. xxxi.

169 See 19.191 and n. 131.

170 See Richard Broxton Onians, *The Origins of European Thought about the Body, the Mind, the Soul, the World, Time, and Fate* (Cambridge: Cambridge University Press, 1951), 108–10. Onians argues that the head and the "cerebrospinal substance" (109) were considered "holy with potency" (108). But "Elsewhere and, as we shall see, in earliest Greece it was those parts of the body [the testicles], that were the seats and sources of life in this sense, that were revered, counted holy, so that men made appeal or oath by them." Thus it seemed natural "to see in the seed, which carries the new life and which must have seemed the very stuff of life, a portion of the cerebrospinal substance which was the life of the parent."

171 See Introduction, p. li.

172 Ibid.

173 See 19.n. 181.

174 Written in 1968 about the Seattle revelation of 1950.

175 See *FS*, 278–81.

176 See 19.96 and n. 76.

177 See Introduction, p. xli.

178 The reference to alchemical imagery in Andrew Marvell's *The Garden* is explained in par. 241, below.

179 See Gertrude Rachel Levy, *The Gate of Horn: A Study of the Religious Conceptions of the Stone Age, and Their Influence upon European Thought* (London: Faber and Faber, 1948), 248–9, annotated copy in the NFL. Levy in turn is drawing upon W.F. Jackson Knight's *Cumaean Gates* (1936).

180 *L'Après-Midi d'un Faune* (1876) and *Prose (Pour des Esseintes)* (1885).

181 For Agape, see stanza 20, ll. 134–6: "Out of the bosome of eternall blisse, / In which he reigned with his glorious syre, / He downe descended." As Adonis, see stanza 23, ll. 155–7: "O huge and most unspeakeable impression / Of loves deepe wound, that pierst the piteous hart / Of that dear Lord with so entyre affection." The usual Elizabethan pun on "heart" and "hart," cited in par. 30, below, is probably implicit throughout this poem.

182 A fusion of two references, cited one right after the other in *WP*, 268: "In one of Poe's stories, 'A Predicament,' we read of a woman caught in a clock tower where one of the hands cuts her head off, both head and trunk being convinced that they are the real psyche (the woman calls herself

Psyche). In Yeats's play 'The King of the Great Clock Tower' there are again a clock tower and a severed head."

183 See Jay Macpherson, *The Spirit of Solitude: Conventions and Continuities in Late Romance* (New Haven: Yale University Press, 1982).

184 See *WP*, 274: "Another starting point is the mysterious passage in Genesis 6:1–4 which tells how the 'sons of God' were attracted by the 'daughters of men,' descended to the earth and begat on them a race of giants."

185 The discussion of Ecclesiastes in this and the next paragraph resembles that of *GC*, 123–5. See also par. 490, below, for the "three A's," a joke NF also used regularly in the lecture on Ecclesiastes in his undergraduate Bible class, and in several published works.

186 See Herbert Marcuse, *One-Dimensional Man: Studies in the Ideology of Advanced Industrial Society* (1968).

187 See William Butler Yeats, *Blood and the Moon*, l. 49: "For wisdom is the property of the dead."

188 The word rendered as "Ecclesiastes," i.e., assemblyman, by the Greek translators of the Bible. Hence the author of the Book of Ecclesiastes is sometimes referred to as the Preacher or Speaker, and sometimes is even taken to be named Koheleth, as here.

189 NF has apparently been working on "Dickens and the Comedy of Humours" (1968), *StS*, 218–40. In *SeS*, 5, he says that "One of the roots from which these chapters grew was an abandoned essay on the Waverley novels of Scott."

190 The Davidson paper is "The Church: Its Relation to Society" (1949), *RW*, 203–19, *NFR*, 253–67, so called because the collection it originally appeared in was a memorial volume for Richard Davidson, principal of Emmanuel College. The essay in the Woodhouse Festschrift was "The Problem of Spiritual Authority in the Nineteenth Century" (1964), *StS*, 241–56.

191 For the Locke programme, see Introduction, p. xxxiv.

192 For NF's notes on Surtees, see 19.n. 185.

193 The next several entries have been inspired by NF's reading of Austin Farrer, *A Rebirth of Images: The Making of St. John's Apocalypse* (Westminster: Dacre Press, 1949), annotated copy in the NFL, a book that influenced him in many ways. When it was republished by the State University of New York Press in 1986, NF supplied the following cover blurb: " Everyone concerned with the influence of the Bible in Western literature and thought needs a good clear study of Biblical typology, and Farrer's *A Rebirth of Images* is not only the best book available in English, but almost the only one." The discussion of the diagram and the Pleroma or "Fullness" is on pp. 306–11.

194 *A Rebirth of Images*, 71. Farrer's thesis is that the Book of Revelation is

structured in the form of six sevenfold sequences, the latter being antitypes of the seven days of Creation. NF's list of the works of each day in the P account in *WP*, 157, is taken from Farrer, 41.

195 See *A Rebirth of Images*, 309. For the Valentinian school of Gnosticism, thirty "was *pleroma* or fulness for the physical body of Christ; and St Luke tells us that it was at thirty years that Christ judged himself to have sufficiently 'advanced in wisdom and age' and so began his ministry. So as the body of Christ built itself up in thirty years, the Pleroma must eternally articulate itself in thirty aeons."

196 Jaques's famous speech on the seven ages of man in Shakespeare's *As You Like It*, 2.7.139–66.

197 Aristotle, *Poetics*, 1455b, 26–8 (sec.18); often translated "complication."

198 Aristotle, *Poetics*, 1455b, 28–31 (sec. 18); often translated "resolution."

199 See 19.185.

200 A musical passage that can be performed backwards, either retrograde or inversion. In 18.42, NF says, "The binary form in music (A tonic to dominant; B dominant to tonic) is really based on the mirror principle, as the stunt known as 'rovescio' makes clear (in e.g. a Haydn minuet)."

201 "Blake's Reading of the Book of Job" (1969), *SM*, 228–44.

202 In *Epic and Romance: Essays on Medieval Literature* (New York: Dover, 1957; orig. pub. 1896); see especially chap. 1, sec. 2, "Epic and Romance," and chap. 1, sec. 3, "Romantic Mythology." NF first noted the same distinction in Ker in 32.82—about twenty years previously.

203 Angria is the imaginary country in the juvenilia of Charlotte and Branwell Brontë. See Fannie Elizabeth Ratchford, *The Brontës' Web of Childhood* (New York: Columbia, 1941), 159: "Charlotte and Branwell both referred to their dream world as 'the infernal world' or 'the world below.'"

204 Letter to George and Georgiana Keats, 17–27 September 1819, in *Letters of John Keats: A New Selection*, ed. Robert Gittings (London: Oxford University Press, 1970), 325–6: "Chatterton's language is entirely northern—I prefer the native music of it to Milton's cut by feet[.] I have but lately stood on my guard against Milton. Life to him would be death to me. Miltonic verse cannot be written but it [in] the vein of art—I wish to devote myself to another sensation—."

205 In the utterly physical and non-abstract vocabulary of Homer as analysed by Onians in *The Origins of European Thought* (see n. 170, above), *thymos* is the "breath-soul" (44–5) which gives a man fierceness, energy, and courage (50). *Nous* is not mere intellect (as it is sometimes translated) but the dynamic and purposive ordering factor that moves through *thymos* as a current moves through water (83).

206 See *Popul Vuh: The Mayan Book of the Dawn of Life*, trans. Dennis Tedlock (New York: Simon and Schuster, 1985), 78–9. An annotated copy of the

translation by Delia Goetz and Sylvanus G. Morley (Norman: University of Oklahoma Press, 1950) is in the NFL.

207 See "The Philosophy of Shelley's Poetry," in *Essays and Introductions* (New York: Macmillan, 1961), 65–95.

208 See par. 120 and n. 111.

209 The world of plenitude and divine perfection in some Gnostic cosmologies.

210 See also par. 196, above. The *cauda pavonis*, the rainbow-coloured peacock's tail, was in alchemy a culminating stage signifying successful production of the Stone.

211 See also par. 221, above.

212 The quincunx, an arrangement of five objects in a square or rectangle with one object in each corner and one in the centre, is a ubiquitous natural symbol in Sir Thomas Browne's *The Garden of Cyrus*. See par. 245, below.

213 See Nicholas Berdyaev, *Truth and Revelation*, trans. R.M. French (London: Geoffrey Bles, 1953), 144–5: "The iconographic theology of Sergius Bulgakov which would see in the Mother of God a human hypostatic image of the Holy Spirit is a matter of dispute as is all his sophiology, but it does not actually conflict with the spiritual interpretation of revelation. It is entirely untrue and superficial to set up an opposition between spirit and the cosmos, between spiritual revelation and cosmic." Bulgakov was the lifelong friend, mentor, and collaborator of Berdyaev.

214 See n. 217, below.

215 See Sir Thomas Browne, *The Garden of Cyrus*, in *Religio Medici and Other Works*, ed. L.C. Martin (Oxford: Oxford University Press, 1964), chap. 2, 139, which speaks of the cycles of the Same and the Other from Plato's *Timaeus*: "Of this Figure *Plato* made choice to illustrate the motion of the soul, both of the world and man; while he delivereth that God divided the whole conjunction length-wise, according to the figure of a Greek X, and then turning it about reflected it into a circle; By the circle implying the uniform motion of the first Orb, and by the right lines, the planetical and various motions within it. And this also with application unto the soul of man, which hath a double aspect, one right, whereby it beholdeth the body, and objects without; another circular and reciprocal, whereby it beholdeth itself."

216 Or *periplum*. From Ezra Pound's *Cantos*, which use the word as a leitmotif; it has been taken from Victor Bérard's *Les Navigations d'Ulysse*, where it means "not as land looks on a map / but as sea bord seen by men sailing" (*Canto* 54).

217 See *The Garden of Cyrus*, chap. 2, 139: "In Chesse-boards and Tables we yet finde Pyramids and Squares, I wish we had their true and ancient description, farre different from ours, or the *Chet mat* of the *Persians*, which might continue some elegant remarkables, as being an invention as high as

Hermes the Secretary of *Osyris*, figuring the whole world, the motion of the Planets, with Eclipses of Sunne and Moon." The note to this passage cites "Suidas (SC), iii, (1705, p. 423): . . . Tabula."

218 See n. 179, above. Levy cites *Aeneid*, bk. 2, ll. 238–40.

219 See 19.391 and n. 260.

220 See Introduction, p. li.

221 NF mentions Robert Peele's *Old Wives' Tale* in *SeS*, 55, among "highly romantic forms of drama." Carlo Gozzi (1720–1806) is also mentioned there (38) as the "eighteenth-century Italian dramatist who is useful to a study of romance because he writes undisplaced fairy tales full of magic and metamorphosis. We are not surprised to find that it was Gozzi who maintained that the entire range of dramatic possibilities could be reduced to thirty-six basic situations."

222 See *WP*, 233.

223 See Kenneth Walker, *A Study of Gurdjieff's Teaching* (London: Jonathan Cape, 1967), annotated copy in the NFL; the reference is given in *GC*, 244, note to page 216.

224 This idea, in relation to Gurdjieff, also occurs in "Expanding Eyes" (1975), *SM*, 99–122, on p. 120. It also shows up in *GC*, 216.

225 See Walker, *A Study of Gurdjieff's Teaching*, 48: "The condition which, above all others, is demanded of those who enter this realm of the spirit to discover unity with it is that they should shed for the moment the selfhood of space and time, that tyrannous selfhood which Jalal'-uddin has called 'the dark despot.' All who have had experience of this other state are agreed upon this point. 'No creature,' wrote St. Thomas Aquinas, 'can attain a higher grade of nature without ceasing to exist,' and it is the existence of the everyday self which has to be sacrificed."

226 In the system of Samkhya-Yoga, the primordial substance, *parkṛti*, manifests itself in three modalities or *gunas*: *sattva* (pure luminous intellect), *rajas* (physical and emotional activity), and *tamas* (inertia, confusion, animality); these are both objective qualities of nature and subjective modes of consciousness.

227 Blake, *The Book of Thel*, pl. 6, l. 17 (Erdman, 6).

228 See n. 226, above.

229 Walt Whitman, *Song of the Exposition*, sec. 2:

> Come Muse migrate from Greece and Ionia,
> Cross out please those immensely overpaid accounts,
> That matter of Troy and Achilles' wrath, and Aeneas', Odysseus' wanderings,
> Placard "Removed" and "To Let" on the rocks of your snowy Parnassus . . .

NF cites Whitman's "anti-archetypal view of literature" in *AC*, 101–2, as a "low mimetic prejudice."

230 See Claude Lévi-Strauss, *Tristes Tropiques*, trans. John and Doreen Weightman (New York: Atheneum, 1974), chap. 24, "The Lost World," 255–6. An annotated copy of the earlier (and somewhat abridged) translation by John Russell (New York: Atheneum, 1968) is in the NFL, in which "The Lost World" is chap. 21: "The people of Alaska were using iron tools about the beginning of the Christian era, and yet they knew nothing of metallurgy; the same pottery is found from the area around the Great Lakes of America to central Siberia, and also the same legends, rites and myths. While Western Europe remained shut in upon itself, all the northern communities, from Scandinavia to Labrador by way of Siberia and Canada, seem to have maintained the closest possible contact with each other. If the Celts borrowed certain myths from this sub-Arctic civilization, of which we know practically nothing, it is easy to understand how the Holy Grail cycle happens to be more closely akin to the myths of the forest-dwelling Indians of North America than to any other mythological system."

231 Blake's *Jerusalem* consists of one hundred engraved plates; the poem is divided into four parts.

232 See 19.438 and n. 289.

233 *SR*, 169, note to page 102.

234 In the passage quoted in n. 217, above, Browne goes on to say that Plato's World Soul or Spirit, with its cycles of the Same and the Other, is actually a trinity, consisting of "the indivisible or divine, the divisible or corporeal, and that third, which was the *Syntasis* or harmony of those two, in the mystical decussation" (168).

235 See 19.438 and n. 289.

236 In the permanent collection of the Albright-Knox Art Gallery in Buffalo, New York.

237 See also par. 99, above.

238 Archaic for "remorse of conscience," in James Joyce, *Ulysses*, the Corrected Text, ed. Hans Walter Gabler, Wolfhard Steppe, and Claus Melchior (New York: Random House, 1986), 14, l. 481, and elsewhere.

239 See 19.106 and n. 80.

240 See Introduction, p. xlii.

241 See 6.n. 60.

242 Odin descends to the underworld, Hel's kingdom, on his eight-legged horse Sleipnir in *Balder's Dream*, a poem from the *Elder Edda*. There, he questions a dead seeress about the interpretation of an ominous dream of Balder. Another demonic point of epiphany involving Odin is in *Hávamál*, another poem from the *Elder Edda*, in which he hangs on the World Tree

Yggdrasill, pierced with a spear, for nine days and nights, in order to gain secret knowledge.

243 I.e., the conjunction of bird and woman in Yeats's play *The Herne's Egg* echoes the copulation of the whore and the ass in Apuleius's *The Golden Ass.*

244 See 6.n. 50.

245 Gottfried Keller, *Green Henry*, trans. A.M. Holt (London: John Calder, 1960; orig. pub. 1854–55; rev. 1880), annotated copy in the NFL. See also pars. 302 and 310.

246 Refers to the lecture presented at the University of Kentucky in October 1965 and published as "Speculation and Concern." See 19.n. 165.

247 NF took the term "monomyth" from Joseph Campbell's *The Hero with a Thousand Faces* (2nd ed. [Princeton: Princeton University Press, 1968], 30), which in turn took it from James Joyce's *Finnegans Wake* ([New York: Viking, 1939], 581).

248 As their titles indicate, Ovid's two works are about the art of love (which in his case means the art of seduction) and the remedies for love.

249 See Introduction, p. xlii.

250 For *Der grüne Heinrich* (*Green Henry*), see n. 245, above.

251 For Cleopolis, see 19.n. 113. Acidale was originally a fountain in Greece, haunt of the Graces, but Spenser expands it into a whole *locus amoenus.* In the *Faerie Queene*, bk. 6, canto10, Mount Acidale is the site of Colin Clout's epiphany of his mistress amidst 104 Graces. For *kairos*, see n. 121, above.

252 See *CP*, 155.

253 *GC*, 95: "Marcus Aurelius spoke of the *parataxis*, the military discipline, of the Christians as their strongest asset." NF first recorded the remark in 42.20, in the late 1940s. See also, *CP*, 49.

254 R.W. Chambers, *Beowulf: An Introduction to the Study of the Poem with a Discussion of the Stories of Offa and Finn*, 3rd ed. (Cambridge: Cambridge University Press, 1967; orig. pub. 1921). The first two sets of characters come from Saxo Grammaticus.

255 The "Bear's Son Tale" is an enormously widespread folk tale, with over two hundred European and non-European variants. The similarities to the story of Beowulf, long pointed out by scholars, become even more suggestive in light of the possibility that the name "Beowulf" may mean "bee-wolf," i.e., the bear, enemy to bees. A synopsis of the tale is given by Klaeber in the Introduction to his edition of *Beowulf* (1922).

256 The Valéry reference is to the following stanza of *The Graveyard by the Sea*, which plays upon the philosopher Zeno's paradoxes, seeming to prove that motion and change are impossible. See *Paul Valéry: An Anthology*, ed. James R. Lawler (London: Routledge, 1956), 277:

> Zeno, Zeno, the cruel, Elean Zeno!

You've truly fixed me with that feathered arrow
Which quivers as it flies and never moves!
The sound begets me and the arrow kills!
Ah, sun! . . . What a tortoise shadow for the soul,
Achilles motionless in his giant strike.

However, the single, cryptic word "Xenios" added to the Valéry reference indicates that NF is thinking in terms of his own complex paradox about time. *Xenios* is an epithet often attached to Zeus as guardian of the laws of hospitality. NF has been talking about Italo Svevo's *The Confessions of Zeno*, a novel famous for having been an influence on Joyce's *Ulysses*, whose plot is structured by a continuous series of parallels with the *Odyssey*. Odysseus is a wanderer, continually striving to get home. That is, he is continually in motion; and yet, he is motionless in a sense after all, because he is repeatedly trapped or delayed. Moreover, he is a stranger (*xenos*) in strange lands, reduced to begging for hospitality on the grounds that, in the old saying frequently quoted, "Guests and strangers come from Zeus"; in fact, they may even be Zeus Xenios himself in disguise.

257 *A Dangerous Game* (1960).

258 NF had a lifelong interest in the *I Ching, or Book of Changes*, but the translation by Richard Wilhelm and Cary F. Baynes (Princeton: Princeton University Press, 1950) was of particular interest because of the appearance of two diagrams with a haunting resemblance to the Great Doodle diagram of the Third Book project. The trigrams represent the primal forces whose constellations and interactions produce the changes both in nature and in human life. The primary opposition is the yin–yang opposition of male and female, Creative and Receptive; a significant footnote on p. 286 of the Wilhelm-Baynes edition says that these approximate the Greek principles of *logos* and *eros* respectively. The trigrams form an "ogdoad" of four pairs of linked opposites, and the first pair, Ch'ien and K'un, are the primal parents, father and mother respectively. Each trigram is composed of a combination of three vertically stacked horizontal lines, so Ch'ien, the archetypal father, is represented by three unbroken or male-creative lines, K'un by three broken or female-receptive lines. There are also three brothers and three sisters, whose trigrams are varying combinations of broken and unbroken lines; the whole family is likened by NF in par. 328 both to Blake's four Zoas and their emanations and to Noah's family of wife, three sons, and their three wives. But what most interests NF in the following sequence of paragraphs is the arrangement of the eight trigrams in two different constellations of circle and axes. The one he describes in par. 320 is the Sequence of Earlier Heaven (in roman), or Primal Arrangement (Wilhelm and Baynes, 266), to which he adds the associations of the Great Doodle (in italics), thus:

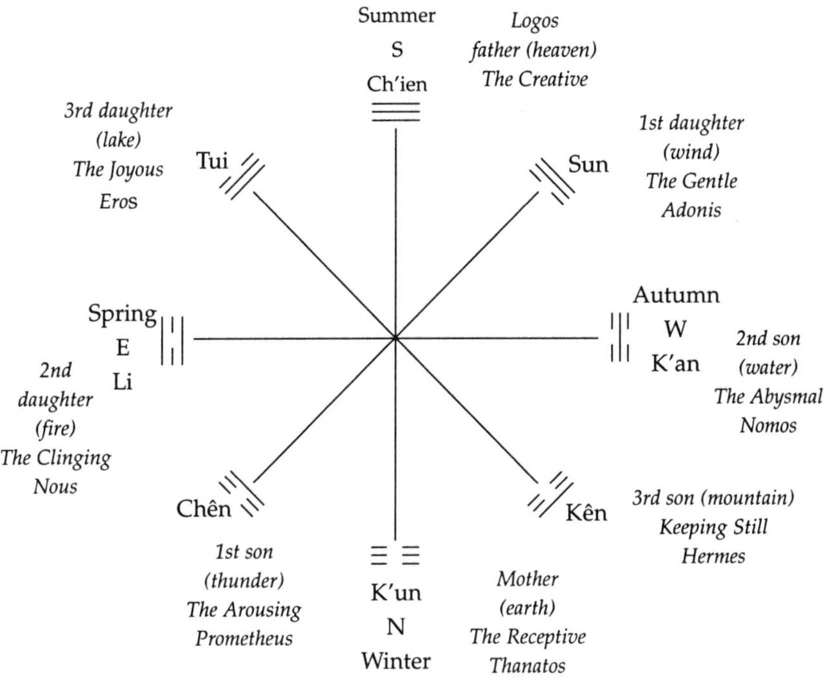

Sequence of Earlier Heaven, or Primal Arrangement

259 See n. 258, above.

260 Ibid.

261 NF is referring here to the second diagram (269) in the Wilhelm and Baynes edition of the *I Ching*, the Sequence of Later Heaven, or Inner-World Arrangement. Also a mandala or circle-with-axes diagram, it differs from the Primal Arrangement given in the note to par. 320 in that "The trigrams are taken out of their grouping in pairs of opposites and shown in the temporal progression in which they manifest themselves in the phenomenal world in the cycle of the year" (Wilhelm and Baynes, 268), (again, NF's associations are in italics). See diagram top of next page.

262 See *The Works of Jakob Behmen, the Teutonic Philosopher. With Figures, illustrating his principles, left by the Rev. William Law, M.A.*, 4 vols. (London: 1764–81).

263 See n. 261, above.

264 NF has gone back to the Primal Arrangement in this paragraph. See n. 258, above. His point is that this is the arrangement that pairs Blake's Zoas with their emanations.

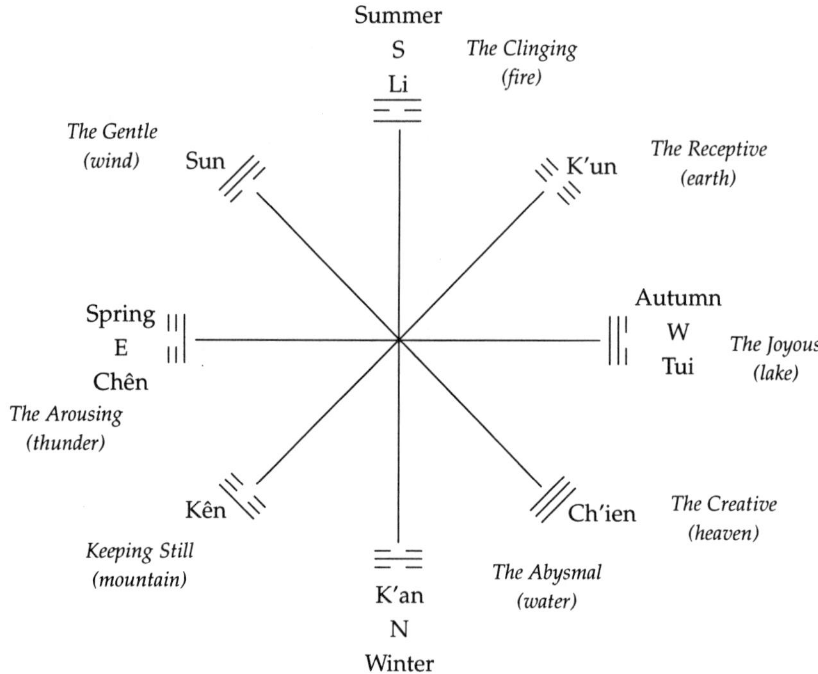

Sequence of Later Heaven, or Inner-World Arrangement

265 Ibid.

266 See nn. 258 and 261, above.

267 Robert Ardrey, *African Genesis: A Personal Investigation into the Animal Origins and Nature of Man* (New York: Dell, 1961), 218–19.

268 Of the four annotated books by Jacob Boehme in the NFL, the most readily accessible is *Six Theosophic Points and Other Writings* (Ann Arbor: University of Michigan Press, 1958). Boehme's central ideas recur throughout his labyrinthine works, but see pp. 16–20 for one treatment of the theme of the light and dark faces of the Father.

269 See Herbert Silberer, *Problems of Mysticism and Its Symbolism*, trans. Smith Ely Jelliffe (New York: Moffat, Yard, 1917), annotated copy in the NFL. Later republished as *Hidden Symbolism of Alchemy and the Occult Arts* (1971).

270 The reference is to *The Lady's Second Song*, ll. 19–20: "If soul may look and body touch / Which is the more blest?"

271 The conceptions are not discussed in the *Poetics*. Possibly a slip for the *Rhetoric*, where *taxis*, or arrangement, typically of the parts of a speech, is discussed in bk. 3, chaps. 13–19.

272 See nn. 258 and 261, above.

273 The name "Oedipus" means "swollen foot," and the name "Jacob" means "heel-grabber" (Genesis 25:26). Achilles and Philoctetes were both wounded in the heel or foot. Heel imagery in *King Lear* seems somewhat oblique: Kent deliberately trips Oswald (1.4.86), and is punished by having his feet put in the stocks (2.2); Gloucester, whose eyes are put out like Oedipus's, has to have someone guide him, but claims not to mind, saying, "I stumbled when I saw" (4.1.18–19).

274 For Jacob Boehme, see n. 268, above. For a representative passage in Boehme concerning the generation of the Trinity, see *Six Theosophical Points*, 8–10.

275 Nicholas Berdyaev's introductory essay, "Unground and Freedom," in *Six Theosophical Points*, claims that Schelling, Fichte, Hegel, Schopenhauer, and Eduard von Hartmann all derive from Boehme.

276 See, for example, 32.32, from the mid-1940s, where one kind of "false occultism" is designated "the deification of the void which places divinity in the non-human so that it can only descend into the human world in terms of force. Force is the source of all external compulsion, hence of all mystery & causality." During the same period, 31.33 speaks of "Carlyle's and Blavatsky's common deification of the void." Other occurrences are 10.112 and 11f.137.

277 The "Presence" of God, here used in its original sense as God's glory or theophany. Gershom Scholem, in *Major Trends in Jewish Mysticism* (New York: Schocken, 1961), 116, annotated copy in the NFL, speaks of "'the Shekhinah of our Creator, the spirit of the living God,' i.e., His 'holiness,' which in spite of everything is almost defined as the *Logos*." However, in some places in Kabbalism, for instance the Zohar, the Shekhinah became the female aspect or emanation of God.

278 In *The Golden Ass* of Apuleius, the vision of Isis is only attained after a long ordeal of suffering, including metaphorphosis into an ass. The sibylline oracles were collected in the Sibylline Books, which were brought to Rome from Cumae and contained, in the words of Plutarch, "many mirthless things" (Joseph Campbell, *The Masks of God: Occidental Mythology*, 322). Their most famous prophecy commanded Rome to introduce the cult of Cybele, with its castrated priests and orgiastic rites.

279 The epiphany experienced by the initiate in the Eleusinian mysteries.

280 See n. 258, above.

281 In the *Purgatorio*, canto 30, ll. 55, when Beatrice calls out to him it is the first time Dante has heard his name in the *Divine Comedy*.

282 Prophecies in the underworld in bk. 6 of Virgil's *Aeneid* and bk. 11 of the *Odyssey* respectively.

283 See *A Vision of the Last Judgment*, p. 91 (Erdman, 563): "Many suppose that

before [*Adam*] <the Creation> All was Solitude and Chaos. This is the most pernicious Idea that can enter the Mind . . ."

284 See *Six Theosophic Points*, 8: "For the eternal will . . . is Father."

285 See annotations to Swedenborg's *Divine Love and Wisdom*, Flyleaf (Erdman, 602): "There can be no Good Will. Will is always Evil. It is pernicious to others or selfish. If God is anything he is Understanding. He is the Influx from that into the Will Thus Good to others or benevolent . . ."

286 In Spenser's *Faerie Queene*, bk. 1, canto 1, ll. 22–3, Error while fighting the Redcrosse Knight excretes "serpents small," who annoy the Knight as gnats in a field annoy a shepherd. In *Paradise Lost*, bk. 1, ll. 777–92, the devils shrink to fit into Pandemonium. In Poe's "The Pit and the Pendulum," the narrator escapes the descending pendulum blade by allowing rats to crawl over him, gnawing away his bonds. *Day of the Triffids* (1951) is a science fiction novel by John Wyndham.

287 The "present natural order of spawning and preying, the aggregate of which Blake calls the 'Polypus,' a huge wriggling mass of life," *FS*, 130.

288 In *That Hideous Strength: A Modern Fairy-Tale for Grown-Ups* (New York: Macmillan, 1965; orig. pub. 1946), 273–4 (chap. 13), annotated copy in the NFL.

289 Colin Wilson, *The Mind Parasites* (New York: Bantam, 1967), 153–4.

290 The reference has not been found. However, on p. 162, the narrator does describe this experience of descent to a source which is beyond both existence and nonexistence by saying, "I understand what Jacob Boehme meant when he talked of a 'sabbath of the spirit,'" thus indicating a link between NF's thinking about Boehme in the previous paragraph and his interest in the Wilson novel.

291 John Wyndham, *The Midwich Cuckoos* (1951); Fred Hoyle, *The Black Cloud* (1957).

292 Beowulf's companions desert him during his final fight with the dragon, but come slinking back once the dragon is dead.

293 *FS*, 366–7. Once the Israelites have crossed the Jordan into the Promised Land, Og and Sihon "roll away from them into a vast dead heaven over their heads," turning from gigantic obstacles into distant, dead abstractions; the process is an example of a Blakean vortex that turns perception inside out.

294 In Blake's *The Book of Urizen*, chap. 2, stanza 5 (Erdman, 72).

295 Discussing Raphael's advice to Adam, in bk. 8 of *Paradise Lost*, not to be overly concerned with astronomical questions, a conversation in which Galileo is alluded to, NF writes in *RE*, 59: "The Galileo vision in Milton sees man as a spectator of a theatrical nature, and such a vision is opposed to the vision of human liberty. It is not idolatrous in itself, but the demonic basis of it is. The vision of liberty pulls away from the world and attaches

itself to the total human body within, the Word that reveals the Eden in the redeemable human soul, and so releases the power that leads to a new heaven and a new earth."

296 "Deasil" means towards the right, clockwise, or following the course of the sun from east to west, a direction considered auspicious in Celtic tradition. "Withershins" or "widdershins" means counterclockwise, or west to east, a sinister direction. The triskelion (three-legged cross) and swastika were both originally solar symbols, and could rotate in either direction. See Philip Wheelwright, *The Burning Fountain: A Study in the Language of Symbolism* (Bloomington: Indiana University Press, 1954), 123–30.

297 See 19.357 and n. 244.

298 A joking reference to the Third Book in terms of Sir Frances Bacon's Great Instauration, "a total reconstruction of the sciences, arts, and all human knowledge raised upon the proper foundation" (Bacon's own words in the *Prooemium* to *Instauratio Magna*). See *Francis Bacon: A Selection of His Works*, ed. Sidney Warhaft (Toronto: Macmillan, 1965), 299. NB 21, roughly concurrent with NBs 12 and 24, contains several references to the "GI."

299 See n. 261, above.

300 Ibn Khaldun is a famous Islamic historian, author of *The Muqaddimah* (final revision, 1402).

301 See n. 447, below.

302 The full Latin aphorism is *Nihil est in intellectu quod non prius fuerit in sensu*: "Nothing is in the understanding that had not previously been in the senses." A tenet of Lockian empiricism, it had, as NF says, also been maintained in the Middle Ages by such thinkers as Aquinas.

303 Letter to Robert Bridges, 15 February 1879, in *A Hopkins Reader*, rev. and enlarged ed., ed. John Pick (New York: Image, 1966), 149–50: "But as air, melody, is what strikes me most of all in music and design in painting, so design, pattern or what I am in the habit of calling 'inscape' is what I above all aim at in poetry." But inscape was not confined to art: in a journal entry for 24 February 1873, Hopkins wrote: "All the world is full of inscape and chance left free to act falls into an order as well as purpose: looking out of my window I caught it in the random clods and broken heaps of snow made by the cast of a broom" (*Hopkins Reader*, 111).

304 See Pierre Teilhard de Chardin, *The Phenomenon of Man* (London: Collins, 1959), 180–4, annotated copy in the NFL.

305 Giorgio de Santillana and Hertha von Dechend, *Hamlet's Mill: An Essay on Myth and the Frame of Time* (Boston: Gambit, 1969), annotated copy in the NFL. NF may be disappointed that there is not much new in it, but what may be striking to other readers is the number of images and preoccupations it happens to share with the Third Book project: not only such recurrent images as the celestial ladder, the maelstrom and other spiral descent

imagery, the tree, the stone, etc., but also board games (161), the cycles of the same and the other in Plato's *Timaeus* (306), even Robert Burns's *John Barleycorn* (91). The basic theme of the book is the precession of the equinoxes through the Great Year of 26,000 years as an image of a cosmic fall (see NF's discussion in par. 367, below). The precession is caused by the wobbling of the earth upon its axis, the mythological image for which is a wheel or grinding mill that has gone out of control. Such a mill appears in the common folk tale about "why the sea is salt," where it sits submerged like Atlantis beneath the sea, perpetually grinding out salt, and is called "Amlodhi's Mill" in Snorri Sturluson's Icelandic work on poetic diction (87). Amlodhi is related to the Icelandic Amleth, whence Saxo Grammaticus derived his version of the source of the Hamlet story.

306 Eminent nineteenth-century scholar whose edition of Shakespeare appeared 1851–56.

307 See the White Queen's song at the end of chap. 9, "Queen Alice," in *Through the Looking Glass*: "Which is easiest to do, / Un-dish-cover the fish, or dishcover the riddle?"

308 Pseudomorphosis is Spengler's term in *The Decline of the West* for the deformation that occurs when a new culture grows up within the sphere of influence of an older one.

309 In *From Ritual to Romance*. See n. 70, above.

310 That is, the question Percival should have asked, "the 'why' question," would have raised the question of the Fisher King's wound, and thus the question of human suffering. God's accusing question to Adam after the fall, "What have you done?" closes down all questioning, reducing the mystery of evil to a simplistic violation of moral law.

311 According to *Hamlet's Mill*, Sagittarius and Gemini are the constellations rising at the solstices, and therefore located at the Tropics of Capricorn and Cancer respectively, where the Zodiac and the Milky Way intersect, called "Gates" by Macrobius (242), where souls ascend (by way of Capricorn) or descend (through the Gate of Cancer) to be reborn. The Mangaians of Polynesia agreed that "they could go to heaven only on the two solstitial days. Because, in order to 'change trains' comfortably, the constellations that serve as 'gates' to the Milky Way must 'stand' upon the 'earth,' meaning that they must rise heliacally either at the equinoxes or the solstices" (244).

312 NF seems to be remembering principally Eric Burrows, "Some Cosmological Patterns in Babylonian Religion," in *The Labyrinth: Further Studies in the Relation between Myth and Ritual in the Ancient World*, ed. S.H. Hooke (London: Society for Promoting Christian Knowledge, 1935), 54–7, which speaks of "The legend that God cast a stone into the *tehom* [the deep] and made it the keystone of the earth and foundation of the temple" (55),

comparable to images in Babylonian and other mythologies. Gertrude Rachel Levy's *The Sword from the Rock* deals with creation myths that divide the upper and lower waters with barriers, but does not mention the image of the stone as "plug." The tree and stone images are from her earlier book, *The Gate of Horn*, and are not particularly connected with this complex, except in being related to *axis mundi* and labyrinth imagery.

313 See *Gylfaginning* ("The Tricking of Gylfi"), in Snorri Sturluson, *Edda*, trans. Anthony Faulkes (London: Dent, 1987), 45. Thor is set various challenges by the giant Utgarda-Loki, one of which is to lift a cat off the ground. Straining with all his might, he manages to lift one paw off the ground. Later, Utgarda-Loki explains that the cat was really the Midgard Serpent which encircles the universe.

314 See n. 308, above.

315 In "Towards Defining an Age of Sensibility" (1956), *FI*, 136.

316 There is a foreshadowing here of chap. 8 of *WP*.

317 Because the names "Esther" and "Mordecai" resemble or are related to "Ishtar" and "Marduk," names of Babylonian deities, some scholars theorize that the story originally goes back to Persian or even Babylonian New Year celebrations.

318 In Greek mythology, Astraea was identified with both the constellation Virgo and with Justice, or Dike; she lived on earth during the Golden Age but fled into the skies when humanity became wicked. In Shakespeare's time, Astraea was identified by writers with Elizabeth, the virgin queen, for propagandistic purposes; see Frances A. Yates, *Astraea: The Imperial Theme in the Sixteenth Century* (1975).

319 See *GC*, 195.

320 The next several paragraphs became the basis for *GC*, 122–3.

321 Revolt beginning in 167 B.C. against the attempts of Antiochus IV Epiphanes to foster Hellenism by repressing Judaism. In the Apocrypha, 1 and 2 Maccabees chronicle the story of the rebellion led by the Maccabee family, which got its name from the nickname "Maccabbeus" ("the hammer") given to one of its members, Judas.

322 Matthew 24:48 ff. and Luke 12:43 ff. are synoptic versions of Jesus' story of the unjust steward. If an evil servant, put in charge over his master's household in his absence, abuses his power, the lord shall return one day when he is not expecting it and "cut him asunder."

323 The Tractate of Khons was inscribed on a stele dated ca. 500 B.C., belonging to the cult of the Egyptian god Khons at Thebes. See par. 388 for a plot summary. Its purpose was evidently to encourage apostasy among Jewish exiles in Egypt; the Book of Tobit is a rival tractate, remodeling the Tractate of Khons in order to show the superior power of Yahweh in the business of expelling demons. NF's probable source for this is the introduction to the

Book of Tobit, sec. 8, "Sources," in *The Apocrypha and Pseudepigrapha of the Old Testament in English*, ed. R.H. Charles (Oxford: Oxford University Press, 1913), 1:187–8.

324 A brief discussion of Tobit appeared many years later in *WP*, 233.

325 In Genesis 49:17, "Dan shall be a serpent by the way, an adder in the path, that biteth the horse's heels, so that his rider shall fall backward"; in Genesis 49:21, "Naphtali is a hind let loose: he giveth goodly words."

326 In *Paradise Lost*, bk. 4, ll. 166–71, Satan likes the smells of Eden better than Asmodeus liked the "fishie fume"; in bk. 5, ll. 221–3, Raphael is contrastingly introduced as "the sociable Spirit" who travelled with Tobias.

327 See n. 323, above.

328 From a section of Blake's *The Everlasting Gospel* now exiled into the Textual Notes of the Erdman edition (877):

> Was Jesus Born of a Virgin Pure
> With Narrow Soul & looks demure
> If he intended to take on Sin
> The Mother should an Harlot been
> Just such a one as Magdalen
> With seven devils in her pen . . .

329 See n. 245, above.

330 A reference to the typology of human personality types according to the phases of the moon in Yeats's *A Vision*. Phase 1, that of the new moon, represents "primary" or collective consciousness; phase 15, that of the full moon, represents "antithetical" or individualized consciousness.

331 Duns Scotus's *haecceitas* is the individuality or particularity of a thing. Scotus rejected the Thomist notion that the intellect cannot know individual things directly, since the intellect knows through universals; he accepted universals, but believed that we have an intuition of particularity as well. The idea of knowledge through the particular appealed to Gerard Manley Hopkins.

332 A version of this passage appears in *GC*, 111. See also par. 568, below, and 21.7.

333 See n. 261, above.

334 See Ezra Pound, *Make It New* (New Haven: Yale University Press, 1935), 17: "The opposing systems of European morality go back to the opposed temperaments of those who thought copulation was good for the crops, and the opposed faction who thought it was bad for the crops (the scarcity economists of pre-history)."

335 See William T. Noon, S.J., "*A Portrait of the Artist as a Young Man*: After Fifty Years," in *James Joyce Today: Essays on the Major Works*, ed. Thomas F. Staley (Bloomington: Indiana University Press, 1966), 65–6. The footnote is

on p. 172: "Emerson and Thoreau were both much interested in the idea of epiphany as they found it set forth by Plotinus: see, for example, Joel Porte's recent book, passim, *Emerson and Thoreau: Transcendentalism in Conflict* (Middletown: Wesleyan University Press, 1966)." The "Mackenna Plotinus" is Plotinus, *The Enneads*, trans. Stephen MacKenna (1957), annotated copy in the NFL.

336 See Richard Ellmann, *James Joyce*, 2nd ed. (New York: Oxford University Press, 1982), 163. *Epiclesis* (Latin), *epicleseis* (Greek): the invocation still used in the Eastern Churches, though dropped from the Western, in which the Holy Spirit is prayed to descend and transform the host.

337 The *filioque* controversy led to a rupture between the Western and Eastern Churches in 1054. The subject of debate was whether the Holy Spirit descends from both the Father and the Son (*ex Patre Filioque*), as was held in the West, or, as the East maintained, from the Father only.

338 Norman O. Brown, *Hermes the Thief: The Evolution of a Myth* (New York: Vintage, 1969), 21–4, annotated copy in the NFL.

339 See Clive Hart, *Structure and Motif in Finnegans Wake* (London: Faber and Faber, 1962), 107–8, annotated copy in the NFL.

340 See "Shaun's Cycle," 114–16; "Shem's Cycle," 116–28. Moreover, the very next section, "Chapter Five: Spatial Cycles: II—The Cross," 129–34, asserts that Shem and Shaun embody Plato's cycles of the Same and the Other, a recurrent preoccupation of NF in NBs 12 and 24.

341 Samuel Butler, *Erewhon*, chap. 19, "The World of the Unborn."

342 See *Resolutions*, in *Jonathan Edwards: Letters and Personal Writings*, ed. George S. Claghorn (New Haven: Yale University Press, 1998), 754: "Resolved, that I will live so as I shall wish I had done when I come to die."

343 See n. 31, above.

344 See Introduction, p. xlii.

345 See 19.74 and n. 55.

346 A play upon *anima naturaliter Christiana*, "the soul is naturally Christian," a phrase from Tertullian (3rd c. A.D.), meaning that even pagans can have natural knowledge of the existence of one God and of a moral law.

347 In the Shinto myth, Izanagi and Izanami together produce the eight islands of Japan and other natural phenomena, but Izanami dies in giving birth to fire. Izanagi goes to the underworld, but, like Orpheus, fails to rescue his beloved, who becomes ruler of the dark realm as he is ruler of the light. For Ishtar, see 19.n. 145.

348 *Paradise Lost*, bk. 7, ll. 90–3: "what cause / Mov'd the Creator in his holy Rest / Through all Eternitie so late to build / in Chaos . . ."

349 Sixteenth-century poem by Sir John Davies in which Antinoos, the suitor of Penelope, sings to her of the ordered pattern of the universe, an order reflected in the pattern of her weaving.

350 NF was criticized by at least one reviewer of *GC* for saying that Zeus threatens to pull all the gods and goddesses up into himself at the end of a golden chain (10). In fact, Zeus only says that he would win a tug-of-war with them and leave them dangling from Olympus (*Iliad*, bk. 8, ll. 18–27); the chain-of-being interpretation was a later allegorization.

351 Erich Neumann says that the *Timaeus* contains, not the word "ouroboros," the ancient symbol of the serpent with its tail in its mouth, but a passage about "the universe as a sphere revolving in a circle, one and solitary, yet by reason of its excellence able to bear itself company, and needing no other friendship or acquaintance." See *The Origins and History of Consciousness*, trans. R.F.C. Hull (Princeton: Princeton University Press, 1954), 10.

352 See n. 119, above.

353 See *GC*, 146. *Tehom*, "the deep," is etymologically cognate with Tiamat. See n. 37, above.

354 R.W. Chambers, *Beowulf: An Introduction to the Study of the Poem* (see n. 254, above), says that "Perhaps, however, some remote and indirect connection even between *Beowulf* and the *Odyssey* is not altogether unthinkable, about the year 700" (329). It does not mention Prudentius.

355 In many places, but see "The Drunken Boat: The Revolutionary Element in Romanticism" (1963), *StS*, 200–17.

356 Samuel Alexander, *Space, Time, and Deity: The Gifford Lectures at Glasgow, 1916–18*, 2 vols. (London: Macmillan, 1966), annotated copy in the NFL.

357 Ibid.

358 Ibid., 2:38–9.

359 See *SR*, 78.

360 In the Preface to *Science and the Modern World*, Whitehead says: "I am especially indebted to Alexander's great work" (i.e., *Space, Time and Deity*). The formula "being x time = world" is a roughly accurate summary of Whitehead's philosophy of process, which begins with a rejection of the idea, inflicted upon us by seventeenth-century mechanistic physics, of "simple location": the idea that reality consists of discrete entities in space. Such a notion leaves out the element of time, so Whitehead replaces discrete entities with "events." Each object, and each subject as well, is an event or process which cannot be considered apart from all the other subject- and object-events in the universe, which "interpenetrate" in an indivisible organic whole, Blake's world in a grain of sand, Wordsworth's notion of something "deeply interfused." Each being in time *is* the whole world.

361 See Augustine, *The City of God*, trans. Henry Bettenson (London: Penguin, 1972). Augustine spends a good portion of bks. 4 and 6 satirizing what he calls the "functions assigned to the gods, portioned out in minute penny

packets, with instructions that each of those divinities should be supplicated for his special responsibility" (bk. 6, chap. 9, 243–4). "Catalogue satire" is a very apt name for these passages, some of which sound more like Rabelais than like a Church father. See, for example, bk. 4, chap. 8, sec. 8, and bk. 6, chap. 9, sec. 9.

362 See the first sentence of chap. 1, "The Fundamental Question of Metaphysics," in *An Introduction to Metaphysics*, trans. Ralph Mannheim (New Haven: Yale University Press, 1961).

363 See "Beowulf: The Monsters and the Critics," in *An Anthology of Beowulf Criticism*, ed. Lewis E. Nicholson (Notre Dame: University of Notre Dame Press, 1963), 70. Tolkien is actually quoting W.P. Ker.

364 The German words are hard to read, but are an apparent reference to the Gothic Line, one of several defensive positions set up by the retreating German army to resist the advance of Allied forces northward through Italy. Some of the most brutal and costly fighting of the Italian campaign took place along this line, in part due to the "Nazi cult of loss," presumably a reference to the ideology of heroic nihilism as urged by Hitler in some of his late speeches, in which he urged his soldiers to "fight to the last man."

365 "The Anatomy in Prose Fiction," *Manitoba Arts Review*, 3 (Spring 1942): 35–47; incorporated into *AC*, 303–14.

366 See Introduction, p. xxxvii.

367 Of this catalogue, Macrobius's *Saturnalia* survived into the discussion of the anatomy form in *AC*, 311. The rest appear in the original *Manitoba Arts Review* article: Walter Map's *De Nugis Curialium* on p. 44, Aulus Gellius's *Attic Nights* on pp. 43–4, Lucian's *Kataplous* on p. 41.

368 See Introduction, p. xxxi.

369 See *GC*, 48: "Myth is thus inseparable from *dromena*, things to be done or specified actions. The ritual actions that accompany the rehearsing of myth point in the direction of the original context of the myth." The passage goes on to make the point that the original context of the myth is the social context of law, "the prescribing of certain forms of action." This makes it a "bound vision," stressing obedience and repetition, turning the cycles of time.

370 See n. 258, above. This is the first, Earlier Heaven or Primal Arrangement, moving clockwise, but with the traditional directions reversed: Ch'ien is normally S and K'un normally N.

371 See Aldous Huxley, *The Perennial Philosophy* (London: Fontana Collins, 1958), annotated copy in the NFL. An early discussion of the book (late 1940s) appears in NB 3.

372 See 19.74 and n. 55.

373 For a number of pages hereafter, NF uses this symbol, which may be a

fusion of L [Liberal] and ʎ [Rencontre] (see the end of par. 446) to designate pt. 1 of his new multi-volume version of the Third Book project, the "Inferno" volume. A second symbol, ˥, appears beginning in par. 470 and evidently designates the second volume, which (departing from Dante's order) is the "Paradiso." A third symbol, △, begins to appear in par. 468, and seems to designate a third, or "Purgatorio" volume (cf. "purgatorial" in par. 484). These identifications are far from certain, however, and it is possible that the second and third symbols should be in reverse order.

374 Stephen Hawes turned his medieval Courtly Love poems into encyclopedic allegories on love, death, education, and the liberal arts, modelling himself upon such philosophical writers as Martianus Capella and Jean de Meun.

375 See also par. 457, below.

376 See par. 449 and n. 373, above.

377 The phrase "we *go* only in dream" appears also in 19.46. The Jacob's ladder image makes this paragraph one of the earliest harbingers of the *axis mundi* diagram that will organize the second half of *WP*.

378 For Brook Farm, see 19.n. 48. For Ruskin's "ornament" and "imitation," see 19.n. 29.

379 See "Expanding Eyes," *SM*, 117.

380 See 19.n. 145.

381 See 19.211: "In each mythos there seems to be a sequence of the integritas-consonantia-claritas kind, which I suppose is simply the beginning, middle & end of any action at all." See also 19.143 and n. 104.

382 Jan Ladislav Dussek (1760–1812), Bohemian-born composer whose piano sonatas may have been an influence on Beethoven.

383 See n. 223, above.

384 See n. 373, above.

385 Ibid.

386 Ibid.

387 See 19.213 and n. 146.

388 Probably the "Baccalaureate Sermon" preached to the graduating classes of Victoria and Emmanuel Colleges in the Victoria College Chapel, 19 March 1967 (*NFR*, 280–6).

389 See *GC*, 85–6: "Milton, who, being a poet, understood that changes in metaphor were far more important than changes in doctrine, remarked that this involved thinking about the Church not as a 'mother' but as a young bride about to be instructed in her duties." NF's note to this passage gives the source as Milton, *Complete Prose Works* (New Haven, Conn.: Yale University Press, 1953), 1:755. The passage occurs in *The Reason of Church Government*, chap. 1 (746–61).

390 For Marx's reading of Aeschylus, see 19.351 and n. 236. *Schalk*: knave,

rogue, joker. For example, see 7.2 (from the late 1940s), in which Goethe and Joyce are characterized as "both representing the *schalk* disruption pattern which was the one thing Dante couldn't include, the form of the fourth . . ."

391 See 19.213 and n. 146.

392 Final stanza of *Sweeney among the Nightingales*: "And sang within the bloody wood / When Agamemnon cried aloud . . ."

393 I.e., the King of the Wood at Nemi in the opening of Frazer's *Golden Bough*.

394 See n. 373, above.

395 "On the east three gates; on the north three gates; on the south three gates; and on the west three gates."

396 A phrase NF took from his reading of Norbert Wiener; see par. 29, above; also, 19.141 and n. 103.

397 Bergotte is an art-for-art's sake novelist with a highly artificial style and a witty yet melancholic manner, supposed to be modelled in part upon Anatole France. He does not survive until Proust's last volume. On the day of his death, he goes to see Vermeer's *The Lace Maker*, which is on exhibition; the consummate artistry represented by its "little patch of yellow" means to Bergotte that he has wasted his life. Marcel undergoes a similar disillusionment with his previous life in the last volume, but with the opposite result: he decides that the only possible redemption of his failed life will be through art.

398 See Johan Huizinga, *Homo Ludens: A Study of the Play-Element in Culture* (1955), annotated copy in the NFL.

399 See par. 344 and n. 286, above.

400 Savagely ironic absurdist drama (1896) by Alfred Jarry.

401 See par. 208 and n. 185, above.

402 See n. 398, above.

403 See Rabelais, bk. 5, chap. 33, "How We Landed at the Port of the Lychnobii, and Came to Lantern-Land."

404 See par. 105 and n. 99, above.

405 The green lion is an image in alchemy for the prima materia, the substance from which the Philosopher's Stone is to be made. See 34.97.

406 See 19.74 and n. 55.

407 From Revelation 2:9 and 3:9. Blake uses it to mean false religion, the structure of conventional morality founded upon nature and reason, as embodied in the worldly church; it worships Satan, mistaking him for God, and judges the Lamb of God to death.

408 *The Four Zoas, Night the First*, p. 10, ll. 277–8 (Erdman, 306): "And wilt thou slay with death him who devotes himself to thee / Once born for the sport & amusement of Man now born to drink up all his Powers."

409 "Body of Fate" is a term from Yeats's *A Vision*.

410 See "The Knowledge of Good and Evil" (1967), *StS*, 37: "We belong to something before we are anything, nor does growing in being diminish the link of belonging. Granted a reasonably well-disposed and unenvious community, perhaps our reputation and influence, what others are willing to think that we are, comes nearer to being our real selves than anything stowed away inside us."

411 Quoted in *SR*, 159: "Man should not dispute or assert but whisper results to his neighbour and thus by every germ of spirit sucking the sap from mould ethereal every human might become great, and Humanity; instead of being a wide heath of Furze and Briars with here and there a remote Oak or Pine, would become a grand democracy of Forest Trees!"

412 Refers to the Seattle revelation. See Introduction, p. li.

413 *Adolphe* (1816) is the autobiographical novel by Benjamin Constant. The Regina books are the three works of Kierkegaard in which NF had the greatest interest: *Either/Or, Stages on Life's Way*, and *Repetition*. All were composed during a tremendously prolific period in 1843–44; they employ the same set of characters and narrators, many if not most of them masks for various aspects of Kierkegaard himself; and they attempt, through a meditation on Kierkegaard's categories of the aesthetic, the ethical, and the religious, to work their way through the crisis provoked by Kierkegaard's broken engagement to Regina Olsen and her subsequent marriage to another man. *Fear and Trembling*, also written during this period, could be considered a Regina book as well, but does not employ the same characters and stands a little apart. *Swann's Way* is the first of the seven volumes of Proust's *Remembrance of Things Past; Combray* and *Swann in Love* are (after the *Overture*) its first two sections, the latter being identical to the Odette section. The Albertine sections are vols. 5 and 6, *The Captive* and *The Fugitive*.

414 If NF had a specific passage in mind, it was not found. However, the general idea is something of a Proustian commonplace. See Raymond T. Riva, *Marcel Proust: A Guide to the Main Recurrent Themes* (New York: Exposition Press, 1965), especially chap. 3, "Multiplicity of the Ego (The Technique of Varying Perspective)," 59–73, and chap. 8, "Reality," 160–72.

415 The *Poimandres* is the first and most influential work in the *Corpus Hermeticum*, a collection of Greek texts written in late antiquity. Translated by Marsilio Ficino in 1463, they were the basis of Renaissance Hermeticism, and have exerted a continuing fascination beyond that. See *Hermetica: The Greek "Corpus Hermeticum" and the Latin "Asclepius"*, in a new English translation, with notes and introduction by Brian Copenhhaver (Cambridge: Cambridge University Press, 1992).

416 See 6.45 and n. 37.

417 See 6.40 and n. 33.

418 A specific reference was not found. However, in bk. 5, chap. 19, the questers arrive at the kingdom whose Queen is named Quintessence, or Entelechy.

419 See Introduction, p. xxx.

420 See *SR*, 43: "Perhaps we have to wait for Proust before we find the full tragic counterpart to the great Romantic epics: Proust's account of a growing consciousness which, like Wordsworth's, has intermittent flashes of paradisal vision, but finally realizes that there are no paradises except lost ones, that this realization confers on the narrator the tragic dimension of defeated heroism, the ability to see mankind as giants immensed in time, and that maturity means among other things the irreparable and final loss of the mother."

421 *A l'Ombre des Jeunes Filles en Fleurs* is vol. 2 of Proust's *Remembrance of Things Past*, published in English as *Within a Budding Grove*. The Guermantes volume is vol. 3, *The Guermantes Way*. Vol. 4, *Sodome et Gomorrhe*, was published in English as *Cities of the Plain*. The Albertine vols. are 5 and 6, *The Captive* and *The Fugitive*.

422 I.e., vol. 6, *The Fugitive*.

423 I.e., vol. 7, translated both as *The Past Recaptured* and *Time Regained*.

424 For "deasil" and "withershins," see 12.n. 296.

425 See par. 153 and n. 142, above.

426 See par. 330 and n. 268, above. The reference there to *Six Theosophic Points*, 16–20, also helps gloss the reference in the present paragraph.

427 NF delivered the Birks Lectures at the Divinity School of McGill University in Montreal in October 1971. Substantial portions of NBs 21 and 24 are taken up with explorations of possible subjects for the three lectures. For the eventual titles of the lectures, see 24.n. 193.

428 See Introduction, p. xxx.

429 I.e., NF's interests in the esoteric visionary religious tradition, including the Jewish Kabbalah (the *Zohar*) and Gnosticism (the *Pistis Sophia*).

430 See Introduction, p. xxx.

431 Reference to C.S. Lewis, *The Discarded Image: An Introduction to Medieval and Renaissance Literature* (1964).

432 See 19.174 and n. 124.

433 The Baron Corvo story is Frederick Rolfe, *Don Tarquinio: A Kataleptic Phantasmatic Romance* (London: Chatto and Windus, 1929), annotated copy in the NFL. Gene Stratton-Porter's *Michael O'Halloran* dates from 1915.

434 See n. 258, above. The identification here is by the north and south poles of the Inner Arrangement diagram, Ch'ien and K'un.

435 See n. 261, above.

436 Antti Aarne and Stith Thompson, *The Types of the Folk-Tale* (1928) and

Johannes Bolte, with Georg Polivka, *Commentaries to the Nursery and Household Tales* (1932). The former indexes common patterns in folk tales; the latter updates Grimm from modern archives.

437 The brothers Pyrochles and Cymochles, foes of Sir Guyon, the knight of Temperance in Spenser's *Faerie Queene*, bk. 2, cantos 5–8, are false fire and false water. Pyrochles is a kind of Hotspur, choleric and rashly aggressive; Cymochles, associated with water and sleep, is passive and dissolute.

438 Presumably the four *mythoi* with six phases, each three overlapping with another three, in the Third Essay of *AC*, though that gives a total of 24 rather than 32 or 64.

439 For "Old and New Comedy," see 6.n. 19.

440 "Agon and Logos: Revolution and Revelation" (1973), *SM*, 201–27.

441 Lydgate's poem is unfinished, though it has expanded the 4,873 lines of its original into 7,042. After looking into the well of Narcissus, the auctour-lover describes a chess game with his beloved. Actually, he spends so much time allegorizing the various chess pieces (her queen = grace, whereas his first pawn = idleness) that he never gets to the actual game. In the French romance, the lover is checkmated by the beloved.

442 Poem 64 of Catullus is an epyllion or miniature epic, a kind of fantasia of themes and narratives from the Golden Age of Greek mythology, including the marriage of Peleus and Thetis. In "The Structure of Imagery in *The Faerie Queene*," *FI*, 85, NF notes the symbolic importance of the wedding of Peleus and Thetis in the *Mutabilitie Cantos*. For Yeats, see *News for the Delphic Oracle*, stanza 3.

443 "Bonny Barbara Allan" is no. 84 in Francis James Child, *The English and Scottish Popular Ballads* (1882–98). The "Adonis theme across" likely means in the Adonis quadrant of NF's diagram, across from the Eros quadrant.

444 The *Hypnerotomachia Poliphili* (1499) attributed to Francesco Colonna, literally "Poliphilo's Strife of Love in a Dream," is a symbolic dream-quest full of alchemical symbolism. NF obtained a reprint of the 1592 English translation (Amsterdam: Theatrum Orbis Terrarum, 1969), annotated copy in the NFL. See also pars. 548, 559, 572, below.

445 In 7.18–22, dating from the late 1940s, NF has recorded this early fascination with Leo Frobenius's discussion of solar symbolism in *The Childhood of Man: A Popular Account of the Lives, Customs, and Thoughts of the Primitive Races*, trans. A.H. Keane (New York: Meridian, 1960), annotated copy in the NFL. In par. 20, he records the "maypole stuff": "A grisly African rite linked with the sun, spiders, death & resurrection (wonder why cutting hands off recurs too?) is a dance round a pole with strings attached, indicating that the maypole was the *rayed* sun & the webbed spider—also, as Frobenius doesn't see, the spreading tree, which links the solar and vegetable cycles" (Frobenius, 341–3). But the larger reason for NF's excitement becomes clearer in the same paragraph: "I'm a fool about the ladder of

arrows: it's the whole symbol of a heaven-earth connection we get in the Rapunzel, Jack & Beanstalk & Jacob's ladder stories (Dante too) & in the great chain of being & ladder of love ideas which go back to Homer & Plato." In other words, somewhere around 1948, NF has discovered the symbol of the *axis mundi* that he will return to, after the cyclic pattern of the Great Doodle in the Third Book period, as the organizing pattern for *WP*. "Absalom complex" is because Absalom's hair, tangled in the tree of his death, is said to indicate solar associations.

446 See n. 27, above.

447 For Coleridge and underground rivers, see 24.160 and n. 136. The references to Kenneth Patchen here and in par. 356, above, are something of a puzzle. The only book by Patchen in the NFL is an extensively annotated copy of *The Journal of Albion Moonlight* (New York: New Directions, 1941), a highly poetic, visionary work clearly influenced by Blake, as its title indicates. Albion Moonlight is conducting a motley crew of outcasts across a landscape that seems basically American but is really a kind of dreamlike underworld (hence "Moonlight"). The problem is that there is no specifically underground river mentioned in the text. On the second page, however, the narrator says that "My idea was to travel along rivers whenever it was feasible to do so," and nearly every scene does take place near some kind of river or water. The reference to a mother "sewing away," referred to in par. 356, above, was not found, although there are intermittent references to Albion's dead mother.

448 For Joachim of Fiore's three ages of the Father, Son, and Holy Spirit, see 19.n. 289.

449 "And his brother's name was Jubal: he was the father of all such as handle the harp and organ."

450 Teofilo Folengo (1491–1544), also known as Merlino Coccajo, was one of the chief Italian macaronic poets. His first work, *Merlini Coccai Macaronicon*, was about the adventures of Baldus. See also 24.12; "Work in Progress," par. 14.

451 In the first section, "Human Knowledge," of Sir John Davies's *Nosce Teipsum*, the mind is said to avoid looking at its own reflection because it shrinks from the image of its own ugly and terrifying fallenness; because of this, few people know themselves. See *Silver Poets of the Sixteenth Century*, ed. Gerald Bullett (Dent: Everyman, 1947), 349.

452 The early-Christian Sabellians believed that Father, Son, and Holy Spirit were not three beings of one substance but one being in three aspects, the body, soul, and spirit of one God.

453 See also par. 344, above.

454 See 19.302 and n. 197.

455 See par. 33 and n. 27, also par. 312 and n. 255.

456 See also par. 411 and n. 349.

Notebook 24

1 See Thomas De Quincey, *Confessions of an English Opium-Eater and Other Essays* (Oxford: Oxford University Press, 1985), 212. NF quotes the passage in "The Survival of Eros in Poetry" (1983), *MM*, 57. For the Joyce remark, see Frank Budgen, *James Joyce and the Making of "Ulysses" and Other Writings* (London: Oxford University Press, 1972), 294.

2 Genesis 1:2, "the deep." See *GC*, 146.

3 See 12.391 and 568.

4 Numbers 21:18, sometimes called "The Song of the Well," is an enigmatic and unexplained miraculous provision of water: "The princes digged the well, the nobles of the people digged it, by the direction of the lawgiver, with their staves."

5 See 12.136 and n. 126.

6 Genesis 1:2: "without form, and void." See *GC*, 146, where *tobu* is a misprint for *tohu*.

7 This account of the P Creation myth differs from that in *WP*, 157, which follows closely the version in Austin Farrer's *A Rebirth of Images*.

8 One of the Sons of Albion, whose name is Greek for "matter."

9 See 12.547 and n. 444; also 12.548, 559, 572.

10 See 12.559 and n. 450.

11 Eliot uses the subtitle of Kyd's *Spanish Tragedy*—"Hieronymo's Mad Againe"—at the end of *The Waste Land* (l. 432), in significant conjunction with the line "These fragments I have shored against my ruins" (l. 431), embedded amidst quotations from English, Italian, French, and Sanskrit.

12 A poet of the school of Chaucer and Lydgate who wrote long, Latinate moral allegories. See also 12.n. 374.

13 *Rhetoric*, 1356b. An enthymeme is a syllogism with one premise suppressed. Aristotle says that as the example is the rhetorical equivalent of induction, the enthymeme is the rhetorical equivalent of the syllogism.

14 In Cowley's Introduction to his version of the Second Olympic Ode of Pindar. See *The Complete Works in Verse and Prose of Abraham Cowley*, ed. Alexander B. Grosart (New York: AMS, 1967), 2:5.

15 A point NF makes in his essay on the poem,"Literature as Context: Milton's *Lycidas*" (1959), *FI*, 121.

16 See Marcel Proust, *Swann's Way*, trans. C.K. Scott Moncrieff and Terence Kilmartin (New York: Vintage, 1982), 893 (sec. 3). Marcel visits the studio of the painter Elstir: "Naturally enough, what he had in his studio were almost all seascapes done here at Balbec. But I was able to discern from these that the charm of each of them lay in a sort of metamorphosis of the objects represented, analogous to what in poetry we call metaphor, and that, if God the Father had created things by naming them, it was by taking away their

names or giving them other names that Elstir created them anew." What does not seem to appear in this passage, however, is the Ovidian metamorphosis of a god subsiding into an object. Perhaps NF has in mind a passage much later, in *The Captive*, in which Marcel is listening to a piece by the composer Vinteuil and thinks: "I was truly like an angel who, fallen from the inebriating bliss of paradise, subsides into the most humdrum reality. And, just as certain creatures are the last surviving testimony to a form of life which nature has discarded, I wondered whether music might not be the unique example of what might have been—if the invention of language, the formation of words, the analysis of ideas had not intervened—the means of communication between souls" (260).

17 Chikhai Bardo, the first of three stages in the *Tibetan Book of the Dead*. See 19.n. 4.

18 See E.A. Wallis Budge, *The Gods of the Egyptians* (New York, Dover, 1969; orig. pub. 1904), 2:116–17.

19 Jean de Meun added another 18,000 lines to Guillaume de Lorris's original 4,000 of the *Roman de la Rose*, but he also added a new, Promethean tone of encyclopedic satire to the Eros vision of the original poem.

20 For *epopteia*, see 12.n. 279.

21 This observation is repeated from 12.467.

22 See Introduction, p. xxx.

23 See NF's review of the trilogy of which *Malone Dies* is the middle work, "The Nightmare Life in Death" (1960), *NFCL*, 219–29. For Lawrence's *The Man Who Died*, see *SeS*, 151 and *GC*, 96.

24 Apparently a continuation of NF's thinking about a three-volume project in 12.445 ff.

25 The theory of the historical evolution of religious consciousness through "three awarenesses" is continued both in the present notebook and in NB 21, which NF spun off from NB 24 precisely to have a repository for ideas relevant to a book on religion and perhaps to the Birks lectures. These were preceded, however, by references to "three awarenesses" in 19.111–13 and 12.116. These earlier references differ from and yet seem to anticipate the later theory.

26 In other words, a total of 100 sections, like the 100 cantos of the *Divine Comedy*, though perhaps with an implicit joke about vital statistics. NF spoke all through his career about his yearning to write a book in 100 sections. See Introduction, p. xxv.

27 See Introduction, p. xlii.

28 The reference is to Gottfried Wilhelm Leibnitz's *Monadology* (1714), with its thesis that every substance is a "windowless monad."

29 A member of the Cambridge Platonists who claimed in *The Vanity of Dogmatizing* (1661), his most important work, that fallen human nature could at

best achieve only a partial and probabilistic knowledge of nature through empirical invesigation.

30 See n. 24, above.

31 See n. 26, above.

32 See "The Rising of the Moon: A Study of *A Vision*" (1965), *SM*, 262. Explaining Yeats's version of the "Great Year," 26,000 years long and formed by the precession of the equinoxes, NF says: "One of these Great Years ended and began with Christ, who rose from the dead at the 'full moon in March' which marks that point. Caesar was assassinated at another full moon in March a few decades earlier."

33 This reverses the identifications of earlier notebooks, where the N–S axis is the axis of concern and the W–E the axis of speculation.

34 Ibid.

35 The grammar is NF's.

36 See Joseph Campbell, *The Hero with a Thousand Faces* (New York: Pantheon, 1949), annotated copy in the NFL.

37 See 12.n. 349.

38 *La Semaine* (1578) was an attempt at a Protestant epic by Guillaume de Salluste, Seigneur DuBartas. It was translated into English by Joshua Sylvester in 1592 as *Divine Weeks and Works*, and influenced Milton, among others, especially because it is based upon the six days of Creation.

39 The *Zodiake of Life*, a translation by Barnabe Googe in 1565 of the original by Stellatus Palingenius in 1537, was a twelve-part meditative-didactic poem that influenced Spenser's *Shepheardes Calendar*.

40 A thirteenth-century poem of some 24,000 lines, harmonizing Classical, Biblical, and apocryphal traditions into a unified history of the world as it revolves around the axis of the Incarnation.

41 See 6.57 and n. 50.

42 See 6.40 and n. 33.

43 Or *uroboros*, the serpent with its tail in its mouth. In its ideal form an emblem of eternity but in demonic form an image of natural life cycling in time like Blake's Luvah, it appears in many contexts from alchemy to E.R. Eddison's romance *The Worm Ouroboros* (1926), a book that interested NF and upon which he comments in the notebooks.

44 Opening phrase of Baudelaire's poem *Les Septs Vieillards*. Literally, "Swarming city," but T.S. Eliot attaches a note quoting the first two lines of Baudelaire's poem to his phrase "Unreal City" (l. 60) in *The Waste Land*.

45 Both the title character of Tennyson's *Tithonus* and Swift's Struldbrugs in *Gulliver's Travels* achieve immortality but not eternal youth; cf. also the Cumaean Sibyl cited by Eliot at the beginning of *The Waste Land*.

46 As NF says in his essay on *Endymion* in *SR*, 143–4, Endymion and Glaucus find a scroll that "informs them that they have to learn magic, like Prospero,

and this magic is an art of releasing the 'symbol-essences' of nature, delivering the spirits in the prisons of subject and object alike," a reference to bk. 3, ll. 699–701 in the poem: "*If he explores all forms and substances / Straight homeward to their symbol-essences; / He shall not die*" [italics in original].

47 See 12.176 and n. 157.

48 See Introduction, p. liv.

49 Simon Magus, i.e., Simon the Magician, sometimes held to be an early Gnostic, appears in Acts 8 as a convert from magic to Christianity who nevertheless becomes corrupted and invents the sin of simony. In a later series of legends called the Clementine Recognitions, discussed by NF in *SeS*, 140–2, Simon Magus implants his face on a man named Faustus and is accompanied by a prostitute named Helena. He becomes the great opponent of St. Peter, his opposite: Simon Magus versus Simon Peter.

50 Shelley, *A Defense of Poetry*, in *Critical Theory Since Plato*, ed. Hazard Adams (New York: Harcourt Brace, 1971), 53: "Poetry lifts the veil from the hidden beauty of the world, and makes familiar objects be as if they were not familiar . . ."

51 See 19.141 and n. 103; also 6.1, 12.29, and 24.71.

52 The famous pornographic novel of sado-masochism by Pauline Réage (1954).

53 NF speaks again of the symbolism of the number 78 in Rabelais and the Tarot in a late series of typed notes, Notes 52.177, 180 (*LN*, 458–9). The latter paragraph notes the recurrence of the number in Rabelais, particularly in the fifth book.

54 For Norma Arnett, see 19.106 and n. 81. Henry (Hank) Rowland was a member of the Vic class of 1933 with NF, and apparently became obsessed, according to 42.34, 34.17, and 7.20, with the symbolic colours and images on national flags.

55 See par. 18 and n. 16, above.

56 "And their bodies shall lie in the street of the great city, which spiritually is called Sodom and Egypt, where also our Lord was crucified." See *GC*, 56.

57 *Fearful Symmetry: Northrop Frye Looks at the World*, produced and directed by Jon Slan, Toronto, 1969; 27 minutes, colour, 16 mm. A documentary that links interviews with NF to scenes from contemporary life in order to show how literature is related to experience.

58 Dostoevsky, imprisoned for political reasons, was sentenced to die but given a reprieve at the last minute.

59 The magical root given to the brothers in Milton's *Comus*, ll. 629–40, by the Attendant Spirit to protect them against Comus's enchantment, evoking the *moly* that Hermes gave Odysseus to protect him against Circe's magic in the *Odyssey*, bk. 10. The plant has been identified as St. John's wort, also called androsaemon, Greek for the colour of blood.

60 In the *Timaeus*, 36c, the Demiurge divides the World Soul into two parts,

and bends these into two interlocking circles moving in opposite directions, the motion of the same and the motion of the other. See also par. 86, below. In *Plato and Platonism: An Introduction* (New York: New York Times Books, 1978), 189–90, J.N. Findlay gives an explanation that helps suggest why NF was interested in the notion at a time when his Great Doodle diagram had split into two opposing circles: "One circle is called the Circle of the Same, and is responsible for the absolutely uniform motion of all the stars from East to West every twenty-four hours. The other is called the Circle of the Other, and is cut into seven subcircles, each responsible for the motion of a nonfixed star—that is, the Moon, Sun, Venus, Mercury, Mars, Jupiter, and Saturn. Each of these circles, while all are dragged round by the Circle of the Same's daily rotation, has complex movements of its own at an angle to the Circle of the Same and in an opposite direction. . . . We must note, however, that Plato thinks that the same inbuilt structures which control movement also control opinion and thought: the daily revolution of the Circle of the Same enables the World-Soul to run through the whole gamut of the eternal Ideas, while the vastly complex movements of the Circles of the Other enable it to keep in contact with contingent facts and probabilities in the instantial world. And both circles are paralleled in the human head, which lends itself therefore to both ideal and instantial cerebration, and has a shape which resembles that of the spherical cosmos."

61 See *FS*, 380–2.

62 See Immanuel Velikovsky, *Worlds in Collision* (New York: Dell, 1967), annotated copy in the NFL.

63 See n. 60, above.

64 "In that time," the sacred time of the Origin. Eliade uses the phrase in several of his books, but see *The Myth of the Eternal Return, or, Cosmos and History*, trans. Willard R. Trask (Princeton: Princeton University Press, 1954), 4: "they are repeated because they were consecrated in the beginning ('in those days,' *in illo tempore, ab origine*), by gods, ancestors, or heroes."

65 Another of NF's frequent references in the Third Book notebooks to Samuel Beckett's trilogy of *Molloy*, *Malone Dies*, and *The Unnameable*; see also n. 23, above. Molloy's bicycle is an image of the unending cycle of fallen time, the wheel that goes nowhere but around in a circle.

66 Cf. 3.184, dating from the late 1940s: "I wonder what it would really be like to get one's mind completely clear of the swirl of mental currents. It would be like walking across the Red Sea to the Promised Land, with walls of water standing up on each side."

67 The Giants who objectively constitute Blake's Mundane Shell, the globe of the heavens that entomb us in the fallen world; subjectively, they are the walls of habit, inertia, and inhibition that keep us from eternity, and there-

fore their social projections are such stifling institutions as factories, prisons, and workhouses.

68 The "primordial man" in the system of the Lurianic Kabbalah. See *FS*, 125: "This myth of a primeval giant whose fall was the creation of the present physical universe is not in the Bible itself, but has been preserved by the Cabbala in its conception of Adam Kadmon, the universal man who contained within his limbs all heaven and earth, to whom Blake refers." See also p. 287.

69 It is not clear why NF thought this. Traditionally, "Azazel" had been said to mean "goat that escapes," i.e., "scapegoat." Modern scholarship, according to the *Harper's Bible Dictionary*, translates it as something like "angry god."

70 NF was born 14 July 1912.

71 Blake's mythological vocabulary at its most condensed. Rahab is natural religion, Mystery, the Whore of Babylon, associated with seven because she sits upon the seven hills of Rome (see *FS*, 139–40, 301, for Blake's phrase "Religion hid in War"). Tirzah, her daughter, is maternal nature itself, keeping the male imagination embryonic inside her, and also the five senses (*FS*, 301). Thus, in pl. 5 of *Jerusalem*, ll. 40–5, Rahab is said to unite into seven of the twelve Daughters of Albion and Tirzah into the other five, including Gwendolyn, the emanation of Hyle. Gwendolyn is female sexual repression intoxicated with war; at the end of *Jerusalem*, her kind of love reduces Hyle to a worm on her bosom, hoping that he will be reborn as a kind of dragon or "rough beast" that will be the totality of the fallen world (*FS*, 402).

72 Allusions to specific Stevens poems, as they occur in *The Collected Poems of Wallace Stevens* (New York: Knopf, 1954), run as follows: "arrogant X": *The Motive for Metaphor* ("The vital, arrogant, fatal, dominant X") (288); "final slate": *The Man Whose Pharynx Was Bad* ("Perhaps, if winter once could penetrate / Through all its purples to the final slate . . .") (96); "Crispin's sea": general reference to *The Comedian as the Letter C* (27–46); "the world of the snow man": general reference to *The Snow Man* (9–10); the sun vision: general reference, but possibly including such poems as *Credences of Summer* ("Trace the gold sun about the whitened sky / Without evasion by a single metaphor") (372–8); "thunderstorms in Yucatan": "Concerning the Thunderstorms of Yucatan," pt. 2 of *The Comedian as the Letter C* (30–3); "the moon vision of evasions": *The Comedian as the Letter C* ("Moonlight was an evasion") (35), but see also *An Ordinary Evening in New Haven* ("in the intricate evasions of as") (486); "The So-&-So Reclining poem": *So-And-So Reclining on Her Couch* (295–302); "Blue Guitar": *The Man with the Blue Guitar* (165–84); "Description Without Place": *Description Without Place* (339–46).

73 NF's usual inaccurate title for Anders Nygren's *Agape and Eros* (1954). See 6.n. 25.

74 *The Timeless Theme*, 19–56. See especially the charts on pp. 21 and 23.
75 Another apparent reference to the three-volume project first announced in 12.445 ff.
76 See *WP*, 248, for a later version of this four-level post-Romantic cosmos.
77 A joke directed against (probably) Schelling in Hegel's Preface to the *Phenomenology of Spirit*, 1.3: "to pass off one's absolute as the night in which, as one says, all cows are black—that is naivete of the emptiness of knowledge." See *Hegel: Texts and Commentary*, trans. Walter Kaufmann (Garden City: Doubleday, 1965), 26.
78 "*Solomon and the Witch*, l. 14: "Chance being at one with Choice at last."
79 For "substance-as-subject," see G.W.F. Hegel, *Phenomenology of Spirit*, trans. and commentary A.V. Miller and J.N. Findlay (Oxford: Oxford University Press, 1977), 10 (sec. 18). See also *DV*, 36; or *NFR*, 194.
80 See par. 44 and n. 25, above.
81 Blake took the term Covering Cherub from Ezekiel 28:16, a denunciation in mythological terms of the King of Tyre. It suggested to him an identification of the angel with the flaming sword who keeps humanity out of Eden with the fiery serpent himself, and thus with Satan in his dragon or leviathan form. The Covering Cherub is one form of the Selfhood, the anticreative death-principle in us by which we keep ourselves blocked from paradise. See *FS*, 137–43.
82 See the last line of Spenser's *Mutabilitie Cantos*: "O that great Sabbaoth God, graunt me that Sabaoths sight."
83 For Lawrence's "sex in the head," see *Fantasia of the Unconscious* (London: Martin Secker, 1923), 76. Rananim was the name Lawrence used in his circle of friends and disciples of an ideal community he planned to establish as a refuge from what he saw as the impending collapse of European civilization. He hesitated for years over its location, although the American Southwest was the choice he considered most seriously.
84 See 12.320 and n. 258, and 12.322 and n. 261.
85 Yeats's *The Wild Old Wicked Man* and Eliot's *A Song for Simeon*.
86 See par. 100 ff.
87 *Maya* is the Sanskrit term for "illusion," both in the sense of a false appearance and the power that creates that appearance. *Hebel*, the word translated "vanity" in the Book of Ecclesiastes, has a metaphorical meaning of fog or mist; see *GC*, 123. For Stevens, see n. 72, above.
88 See n. 81, above.
89 Another instance where NF seems to be thinking in very general terms. Canto 6, stanza 4, ll. 1–4, say of Mutability, "So likewise did this *Titanesse* aspire, / Rule and dominion to her selfe to gaine; / That as a Goddesse, men might her admire, / And heauenly honours yield, as to them twain," which fits the definition of Antichrist. The rest is a bit conjectural. In canto 6,

stanzas 14–15, earth is plunged into what might be characterized as a plague of darkness when Mutability delays the passage of Cynthia, the Moon, and men begin to fear that Chaos has come again, while Jove worries lest Typhon break loose, though there is no actual tempest. But surely the real "confrontation of Jove & Mutability" is on Arlo Hill; it is this scene which is comparable to the Beast and Whore in canto 32 of the *Purgatorio*, where the seven-headed Beast and the Whore of Babylon appear in the garden of Eden in the seventh of seven tableaus of the persecution of the Church. The table of apocalyptic and demonic images that would explain all this imagery came from NF's course on the Bible; later, he would incorporate it into *GC*, 166–7.

90 See ll. 295–8:

> O firste moevyng! crueel firmament,
> With thy diurnal sweigh that crowdest ay
> And hurlest al from est til occident
> That naturelly wolde holde another way . . .

The basic idea is, roughly, that in the Ptolemaic cosmos, the ninth sphere, the Primum Mobile, runs from east to west and thus creates the appearance of the sun's movement in a direction opposite to its natural motion through the zodiac.

91 Another of NF's frequent references to Mallarmé's prose piece *Igitur*, in which a young man throws dice, then lies down and dies in the ashes of his ancestors; with an implicit reference to Mallarmé's *Un Coup de Dés*, with its famous line, "A throw of the dice will never abolish chance." See 12.n. 157; *WP*, 291–2; *MM*, 39.

92 Allusions to Browning's *Nympholepsy*, Shelley's *Alastor*, and Blake's *My Spectre around me night & day* respectively.

93 I and II refer to the two frameworks of the pre-Romantic and post-Romantic cosmoses, each with their cycle of three awarenesses, as set out in pars. 111–12, above.

94 In Kabbalism, finding a hidden meaning in a word or phrase by giving numerical values to each of the letters and then performing various operations upon the values.

95 For the symbolic significance of the number 78, see par. 73 and n. 53, above.

96 See 6.14.

97 See n. 71, above.

98 NF's adaptation of the cycle of the same and the cycle of the other in Plato's *Timaeus*, 36b, identifying them with his two versions of the Great Doodle in this part of NB 24, the Upper and Lower Cycles of the pre- and post-Romantic cosmoses. See n. 60, above.

99 See n. 25, above.
100 Playful allusion to Marjorie Hope Nicolson's *Newton Demands the Muse* (1946).
101 See n. 92, above.
102 See n. 91, above.
103 See n. 85, above.
104 This idea of "Plato's Bible" recurs many times in the later notebooks, and ends up in *GC*, 80.
105 The *Timaeus* was supposed to be the first work in a trilogy, its creation myth comparable to Genesis. The *Critias*, of which we have only a few pages, was to have told the story of the war between tiny Athens and powerful, imperialistic Atlantis, the latter being drowned under the sea after losing the war much as the Egyptians were drowned in the Red Sea. As NF says, the *Hermogenes*, the third work, gave way to Plato's equivalent of Leviticus-Numbers-Deuteronomy: the *Laws*.
106 See n. 89, above.
107 See n. 71, above.
108 See Introduction, p. xxxi.
109 NF's undergraduate course on the Bible. Almost the entire course was subsumed later into *GC*.
110 See Introduction, p. xxx.
111 See par. 160 and n. 135, below.
112 See *The Sword from the Rock*, 19–35. The link with NF's Eros symbolism is the motif of the Sacred Marriage in a large hall.
113 See *GC*, 111. Also, 12.391.
114 In Goethe's *Faust*, pt.1, ll. 1,224–37, Faust, struggling to find a translation of "In the beginning was the Word" that satisfies him, toys with translating "Word" as "Sense" and "Force," finally settling on "Deed." NF mentions this many times in the notebooks.
115 Seemingly a reference to John 12:24: "Verily, verily, I say unto you, Except a corn of wheat fall into the ground and die, it abideth alone: but if it die, it bringeth forth much fruit." This would make the "threatened male infant" a seed planted in earth, an image consonant with the imagery of chap. 7 of *WP*, whose presiding deity is Adonis and whose central image is the seed buried in the earth or cave.
116 See 19.212 and n. 145.
117 The "Wisdom" (*hokmah*) of God in post-Biblical Jewish thought; in some cases, Wisdom rather than the Word is said to be God's instrument by which he created the world.
118 The "staring virgin" is from the first line of Yeats's *Two Songs from a Play*, the woman who rips out Dionysus's heart in the dying-god ritual. The two songs were originally from Yeats's play *The Resurrection*.

119 In many passages in NB 12, NF explores the relation of his Great Doodle diagram to the two circular arrangements of the trigrams of the *I Ching*, as illustrated in the Wilhelm and Baynes edition. See 12.320 and n. 258, and 12.322 and n. 261. His general tendency is to associate the first or Primal Arrangement with what he is calling the "first framework" in NB 24 (see pars. 111–12, above), i.e., the pre-Romantic cosmos, and the second or Inner-World Arrangement with the "second framework" or post-Romantic cosmos. That seems to be the case here, only with the N-S directions reversed: that is, in the Inner-World Arrangement, K'un, the mother figure, is SW instead of NE; Ch'ien, the father, is NW, etc.

120 NF says of Frazer in "Expanding Eyes" that "he thought he was a scientist, and collected a great deal of illustrative material from anthropology, but that did not make him primarily an anthropologist," *SM*, 111. The larger point of the discussion is that to do what Frazer, Spengler, and Jung all did, making a single construct out of data removed from its original context, is the task of the cultural or literary critic, not the anthropologist, historian, or psychologist.

121 In the *Preludium* to Blake's *Europe*, the "nameless shadowy female" has mated with Orc and laments that she is giving birth to devouring flames, yet looks forward to the advent of some redeeming power. She is nature (in *FS*, 228, NF identifies her as Tirzah) looking for the descent of spirit, which is why the actual "Prophecy" part of *Europe* begins by echoing Milton's *Nativity Ode*.

122 NF may be speaking in general terms. At any rate, the famous study of medieval *topoi*, Ernest Robert Curtius, *European Literature and the Latin Middle Ages*, trans. Willard R. Trask (Princeton: Princeton University Press, 1953), 178, gives *sapientia et fortitudo* as the standard binary term.

123 The Greek *basileus* was the king by the regular process of succession, as opposed to the *tyrannos* who achieves kingship through talent and action.

124 NF is trying to get straight in his mind the various and competing Egyptian cosmogonies. It was the solar theology of Heliopolis in which Ra (or Re), the sun god, created Shu and Tefnut, who became parents of Geb, the earth, and Nut, the sky. So Nut is the sister and not the daughter of a male earth, and NF is right that she is not the wife of Ra either because she is the wife and consort as well as the sister of Geb. It was the so-called "Memphite Theology" that postulated an Ennead of nine gods, an ogdoad plus the later god Ptah, who clearly interested NF (see next paragraph) because he created by the power of his "word."

125 See 12.136 and n. 126.

126 See *Ancient Near Eastern Texts Relating to the Old Testament*, ed. James B. Pritchard (Princeton: Princeton University Press, 1955), 5: The "Memphite Theology" says, "And so Ptah was satisfied, after he had made everything,

as well as all the divine order." As he makes explicit in par. 160, NF is making repeated use of this anthology in this area of NB 24.

127 Central terms in Heidegger's philosophy, often left untranslated, though *Sein* can be translated as "Being." *Dasein* means "being" in the sense of "human individual" or "the mode of being human."

128 See *Ancient Near Eastern Texts*, 18–22. "The Story of Sinuhe," from the Egyptian Middle Kingdom, the climax of the title character's life is his return from voluntary exile in Asia to his beloved native land.

129 In fact, NF had noted it as early as 1948, in 7.37: "The figure in the doorway is the analogy of the risen God in the midst of two witnesses (opposite of the two false witnesses of the Passion), the tree of life or Branch of Zechariah (tree of Jesse symbolism in Isaiah), flanked by the two olive trees, identified as Moses & Elijah in Rev. xi."

130 Alludes to a Mortuary Text found in *Ancient Near Eastern Texts*, 33: "I know those two sycamores of turquoise (-green) between which Re comes forth, the two which came from the sowing of Shu at every eastern door at which Re rises." The headnote says, "The eastern horizon of heaven [at sunrise] was thus an analogue for entry into paradise."

131 Jachin and Boaz were the pillars at either side of the entrance to the Temple in Jerusalem. Cf. 7.35: "However, the tree of knowledge is a split tree .... This split tree suggests Jachin and Boaz, Samson's pillars & Jesus' flanking crosses. It suggests in short the figure in the doorway, the image of the hanged sun-god in the eastern gate of the oriented Druid temple, the ram horned with gold appearing at the spring equinox."

132 See 12.33 and n. 27.

133 Indian drama by Kalidasa, 5th century. See *AC*, 191 and *SeS*, 147.

134 Plautus's comedy *The Rope*; linked with *Sakuntala* in *AC*, 191.

135 ANET = *Ancient Near Eastern Texts*. The page number refers to the following passage in "The Tradition of Seven Lean Years in Egypt": "There is a city in the midst of the waters [*from which*] the Nile *rises*, named Elephantine. It is the Beginning of the Beginning, the Beginning Nome, (*facing*) *toward* Wawat. It is the *joining* of the land, the primeval hillock, *of earth, the throne* of Re, when he *reckons to cast* life beside everybody. 'Pleasant of Life' is the name of its dwelling. 'The Two Caverns' is the name of the water; they are the two breasts which pour forth all good things. It is the couch of the Nile, in which he becomes young (again). ..."

136 In *Archetypal Patterns in Poetry: Psychological Studies of Imagination* (Oxford: Oxford University Press, 1963; orig. pub. 1934), 93, Maud Bodkin explores Coleridge's sources in *Kubla Khan*: "he had found the Nile and the Alpheus—whose confluent names no doubt explain 'Alph, the sacred river'—associated by Pausanias as rivers flowing underground and reappearing." The source of the Nile is in Abyssinia, i.e., Ethiopia, which some

early writers believed was the location of the garden of Eden. See *FS*, 212–13.

137 Cf. par. 154, above, in which trial and symposium mark the Nomos and Nous points respectively.

138 See n. 25, above.

139 In the final chapter of bk. 5, Bacbuc "filled three small leather vessels with fantastic water, and giving them into our hands, said, "Now, my friends, you may depart, and may that intellectual sphere, whose centre is everywhere, and circumference nowhere, whom we call GOD, keep you in his Almighty protection" (trans. Urquhart, chap. 48). The definition is originally from the twelfth-century Hermetic *Book of the Twenty-four Philosophers*.

140 See n. 91, above.

141 See n. 78, above.

142 See par. 44 and n. 25, above.

143 The lines referred to are "Who Present, Past, & Future sees" and "Of what is past, or passing, or to come."

144 See n. 60, above.

145 Blake, "A Descriptive Catalogue," p. 43: "In this Picture, believing with Milton, the ancient British History, Mr. B. has done, as all the ancients did, and as all the moderns, who are worthy of fame, give the historical fact in its poetical vigour; so as it always happens, and not in that dull way that some Historians pretend, who being weakly organized themselves, cannot see either miracle or prodigy; all is to them a dull round of probabilities and possibilities; but the history of all times and places, is nothing else but the improbabilities and impossibilities; what we should say, was impossible if we did not see it always before our eyes" (Erdman, 543).

146 Robert Scholes's *Structural Fabulation: An Essay in Fiction of the Future* (1975) is about Lawrence Durrell, Kurt Vonnegut, Terry Southern, John Hawkes, Iris Murdoch, and John Barth.

147 E.R. Eddison's Zimiamvian trilogy, *Mistress of Mistresses, A Fish Dinner in Memison*, and *The Mezentian Gate*, is tangentially related to his earlier romance *The Worm Ouroboros* (1926), discussed by NF below. Annotated copies of all three are in the NFL. Mervyn Peake's Gormenghast Trilogy consists of *Titus Groan, Titus Alone*, and *Gormenghast*. An annotated copy of *Titus Groan* (1969) is in the NFL.

148 Georges Ivanovitch Gurdjieff, *All and Everything*, Ten books in three series, of which this is the first series (London: Routledge and Kegan Paul, 1967), annotated copy in the NFL.

149 James Branch Cabell (1879–1958), fantasist who wrote eighteen volumes of a satiric and witty romance sequence called *The Biography of the Life of Manuel the Redeemer*; its most famous volume was *Jurgen* (1917), subject of

a widely publicized obscenity trial, a copy of which is in the NFL. M.P. Shiel is best known as the author of the early science fiction novel *The Purple Cloud* (1930), annotated copy in the NFL.

150 E.R. Eddison, *The Worm Ouroboros* (New York: Ballantine, 1967), annotated copy in the NFL.

151 I.e., E.R. Eddison's Zimiamvian trilogy. See n. 147, above.

152 Many years later, NF was still interested in this subject. In 44.400 (1986–91) (*LN*, 189–90), he says, "But as I started thinking about that [ghost stories and the nineteenth-century occult] I got increasingly attracted to an article on 'Fairies and Elementals.' . . . What I'm interested in is mainly: 1. The Paracelsian tradition of the spirits of the elements in Shakespearian comedy & romance . . . and in early Milton, especially *Comus*. I have always had the feeling that there was something to be pinned down there that I never did pin down. . . . 2. Romantic developments of this in the Germans (Novalis especially) and in George MacDonald. Morris' romances of course, early & late. . . . 3. Lewis Carroll's Sylvie & Bruno . . . 4. John Crowley's *Little, Big*, a book the author handed to me at Smith. . . ." But the article never got written, although the typescript notes 55.3 (in the NFF, 1991, box 50) consists of notes towards it.

153 See n. 43, above.

154 See n. 25, above.

155 No record of this lecture has been discovered, although it is referred to four times in the concurrent NB 21, pars. 31, 42, 74, 252, in the third of these being referred to as "my fall lecture." But certain passages in NB 21 at least suggest that NF has picked up the term "hermeneutics" because of the way his first and second awarenesses are trapped in a cycle resembling the traditional "hermeneutic circle." Par. 75 describes "The first two awarenesses as an antithesis (Orc–Urizen)" and "as a cycle, i.e., the hermeneutic dilemma of the second forces it back into the first." What is obviously the same trap is described in par. 85 as "The hermeneutic dilemma and the return to legalism. The recurrence of the iconic-iconoclastic cycle in Xy: medieval & Protestant tendencies." Likewise, in par. 80, "The second awareness is conceived as a revolutionary social movement. Such a movement cannot break out of the circle of the law." Once iconoclasm has rid itself of images, it is left with mere abstraction and literalism.

156 James A. Pike, *The Other Side: An Account of My Experience with Psychic Phenomena* (Garden City: Doubleday, 1968). Pike, a bishop, radical theologian, and prolific author, claimed to have communicated through a medium with his son Jim after the latter's suicide. The claim was highly publicized even before the publication of the book, since Pike was a controversial figure, and was in fact embroiled in proceedings against him for heresy when the story broke, but NF might have had his attention drawn

to the case for an additional reason, since Pike first spoke of his experiences on a Toronto television program in September 1967 (*The Other Side*, 196). Pike's newly acquired interest in Edgar Cayce (160–2) may explain NF's own interest later in NB 24 (see par. 196, below).

157 See *The Other Side*, 186. Pike's publishers were pressuring him to write a book about his psychic experiences, but his own desire was to pursue research on early Christian origins that had already been delayed by the heresy charges and the death of his son.

158 NF may be referring to Hardy's *Friends Beyond*, a poem about the spirits in a Mellstock graveyard who see death as an achievement that "turns the bane to antidote, / Unsuccesses to success, / Many thought-worn eves and morrows to a morrow free of thought."

159 A version of this paragraph shows up in *GC*, 216. The theme of "objective art," and also "objective religion," preoccupies NF off and on over the next several dozen paragraphs.

160 See Mircea Eliade, *The Forge and the Crucible: The Origins and Structures of Alchemy*, 2nd ed., trans. Stephen Corrin (Chicago: University of Chicago Press, 1978), 30–1, annotated copy in the NFL.

161 *Paradiso*, canto 33, ll. 127–38.

162 In August 1969 Pike became lost on a trip in the Israeli wilderness and was found dead in a cave.

163 Given the proximity of this note to the passages about James Pike, it seems likely that NF was inspired to read about Cayce because of Pike's references to him in *The Other Side*, 160–2. In Pike's words, "I later learned that Cayce was a medium who was able to prescribe treatment for illnesses and give 'life-readings' for people while in a deep trance. The life-readings seemed to tell the history of a living person's previous incarnations, the very suggestion of which had been disturbing to Edgar Cayce himself in a waking state because of his strong orthodox Christian upbringing." NF does not say what he has been reading about Cayce, but Pike mentions Thomas Sugrue, *There Is a River: The Story of Edgar Cayce* (1967), and lists Jess Stearn, *Edgar Cayce: The Sleeping Prophet* (1967) in his bibliography.

164 See W.H. Auden, *For the Time Being*, in *Collected Poems*, ed. Edward Mendelson (New York: Random House, 1976), 301–4.

165 John Blofeld was the author of numerous works on Buddhism, including *The Tantric Mysticism of Tibet: A Practical Guide* (1970). W.Y. Evans-Wenz was the editor of *The Tibetan Book of the Dead* (1949); *The Tibetan Book of the Great Liberation* (1954); *Tibetan Yoga and Secret Doctrines* (1958); and *Tibet's Great Yogi Milarepa: A Biography from the Tibetan* (1951), annotated copies of all four books in the NFL.

166 See 19.34 and n. 26.

167 See Introduction, p. xxx.

168 NF served as a part-time commissioner for the new Canadian Radio-Television Commission from 1968 to 1976 (when it was renamed the Canadian Radio-television and Telecommunications Commission), partly through the endorsement of Prime Minister Lester Pearson. For a few years, he even reviewed Canadian television, writing reports on shows ranging from *Sesame Street* to *The Carol Burnett Show* to the Miss Canada beauty pageant (Ayre, 329–30). The reviews are included in *Northrop Frye on Literature and Society, 1936–1989: Unpublished Papers*, 273–301.

169 Touchstone in *As You Like It*, 3.3.7–9: "I am here with thee and thy goats as the most capricious poet, honest Ovid, was among the Goths."

170 NF compares Katherine Anne Porter's *Ship of Fools* to quite a different sea story, Paul Gallico's *The Poseidon Adventure*, in "The Search for Acceptable Words" (1973), *SM*, 19–20. In the one case, the Porter novel is being compared to another example of "serious" literature; in the other, it is compared with popular literature that uses archetypes rather than allegory.

171 Fragmentation; Rencontre has always been about the fragmentation of modern culture since the Romantic period.

172 See 19.96 and n. 76.

173 When the trigrams of the *I Ching* are considered as members of a family, Ch'ien is the father; hence NF identifies him with Blake's Tharmas, the "parent power" among the Four Zoas.

174 The term "Second Essay" evokes *AC*, but during the period when *AC* was an evolving project rather than a finished book, the terms "First Essay" and "Second Essay" tend to shift their subject matter, as they do in NBs 30m and 37. In *AC*'s final form, it is the First Essay which is historical and horizontal; the Second Essay is conceptual and vertical—yet it actually retains more of a link with the themes of contracts, Utopias, and education.

175 NF never wrote a book on education, contracts, and Utopias, but he entertained the notion frequently from the Third Book period right up to the end of his life, where some of his last notebook entries contemplate beginning such a work after the completion of *WP*. This theme was pursued in several articles, however, including "Varieties of Literary Utopias" and "The Problem of Spiritual Authority in the Nineteenth Century." The final chapter of *CP*, 158–71, deals with contracts, Utopias, and education, and may contain in microcosm the book NF envisions in this paragraph.

176 The prose writers NF taught in the honour course on "Nineteenth-Century Thought," including Burke, Newman, James and John Stuart Mill, Carlyle, Ruskin, Huxley, Arnold, Morris, and Butler.

177 See n. 168, above.

178 Raymond Klibansky was associated with the Warburg Institute, so his colleagues would have included such scholars as Erwin Panofsky and Fritz Saxl, with whom he in fact collaborated on *Saturn and Melancholy*, as well as Paul Oskar Kristeller and Edgar Wind.

179 See n. 174, above.

180 The *Yoga-Sutra*, attributed to Patanjali, ca. 3rd century A.D. An annotated copy of *The Yoga-Sutras of Patanjali*, 4th ed., ed. Manilal Nabhubhai Dvivedi and Pandit S. Subrahmanya Sastri (Adyar, Madras, India: Theosophical Publishing House, 1947), is in the NFL.

181 Of the two circular diagrammatic arrangements of the trigrams of the *I Ching* in the Wilhelm and Baynes edition used by NF (see 12.nn. 258 and 261), the first or Primal Arrangement would be prelapsarian because it is structural, built symmetrically out of pairs of opposites. The second would be postlapsarian because it follows the cycles of time, and is thus an image of process rather than structure. This contrast of the same pattern considered synchronically and diachronically, structurally and dynamically, parallels NFs long-standing plans to write one volume of the Third Book founded on the static diagram of the Great Doodle, but to follow it with a volume, the "book on its side," that considered the same pattern dynamically and dialectically.

182 See Introduction, p. xxxi.

183 Not only in the sense of the discovery of the law, but perhaps also in connection with the five-volume scheme of NB 42, the "Pentateuch notebook" of 1944, where the fifth and last book, Deuteronomy, was to deal with general aesthetic problems and theory of language.

184 After thirty years (his mother died in 1940), NF is past the stage of beating off the ghost of his mother's Methodist fundamentalism, as Odysseus had to beat off the shades in the underworld descent of the *Odyssey*, bk. 11; his mother is among the shades, although he also tries futilely to embrace her later.

185 Literally, "non-harming," abstaining from injury to any living creature by thought, word, or deed; one of the five virtues on the first step of Raja-Yoga, as stipulated in the *Yoga-Sutra* of Patanjali. See n. 180, above.

186 "Kanzan" is the Japanese form of "Han-shan," the Chinese Zen Buddhist layman of the T'ang period, who lived as a mountain hermit. His poems, which he is said to have written on walls, trees, and the faces of cliffs, were later collected into an anthology called *Poems from Cold Mountain*.

187 See *Paradise Lost*, bk. 5, ll. 628–9: "(For wee have also our eevning and our Morn, / Wee ours for change delectable, not need)."

188 See 19.372 and n. 249.

189 See par. 174 and n. 147, above.

190 See par. 208 and n. 169, above.

191 The reference is to NF's studies at Oxford in 1936. The Mob Quad is the quadrangle at the southwest corner of Merton College.

192 See n. 168, above.

193 NF's Birks lectures at McGill in October 1971 were titled "The City of the

Sun," "The Burning Bush," and "The Postponed Vision." Later in October he lectured at the University of Minnesota on "The Ear and the Eye in Literature" and "The Spoken and Written Word" (Ayre, 336). Typescripts for the lectures have not survived. The ideas in the following paragraphs are clearly related to NF's scheme of the "three awarenesses": see par. 44 and n. 25, above.

194 See n. 156, above.

195 Evidently a generalizing reference, since "the Spectres of the Dead," who do show up repeatedly in Blake's later poetry, are never spoken of in exactly this way. Perhaps the closest approximation is a passage in a letter to Thomas Butts, 11 September 1801, in which Blake says that "my Abstract folly hurries me often away while I am at work, carrying me over Mountains & Valleys which are not Real in a Land of Abstraction where Spectres of the Dead wander" (Erdman, 716).

196 See p. 112 of "Art in a New Modulation" (1953), *NFCL*, 111–16, NF's review of Suzanne Langer's *Feeling and Form*.

197 See n. 133, above.

198 See Introduction, p. xli.

199 The explanation for this cryptic reference is buried in a set of typed notes towards *GC* from the early 1970s (Notes 54.3, par. 9): "I have long had a sense that the four books had some kind of connexion with the four years of my undergraduate career here, though of course nobody can understand how except me. My first year was bits and pieces academically, and in retrospect the New Testament Greek course was pretty central to it: anyway the Bible book is connected in my mind with that year. The second year brought Pelham [Edgar] teaching Shakespeare, the stock company at the Empire Theatre, and my discovery of Colin Still on the Tempest. That's the bedrock of Tragicomedy. The third year was the discovery of Blake, and I'm just beginning to realize that Anticlimax is in many respects a book revolving around Blake: my treatment of Blake was, after all, very largely a conceptual and Urizenic treatment. The fourth year was the year of the Romanticism essay, and that has always seemed to have some relation to Rencontre." A slightly different version can be found in a set of "Autobiographical Notes" (NFF, 1991, box 50, file 1), in which see par. 2.

200 See Introduction, p. li.

201 Both the title *The Critical Comedy* and the prospectus of the four volumes match that in the "Work in Progress" memo, included in the present volume, and are evidently contemporary with it.

202 See Introduction, pp. xxviii–xxix.

203 See "Endymion: The Romantic Epiphanic," *SR*, 150, where NF writes: "In

Christianity this act of worship [of a god or numinous presence] is expressed in a symbolic act of communion, in the response of faith to a revelation symbolized by a divine Word, and in the forming of a church, or community of response. The Romantic counterparts of these would be, respectively, communion, or the identity of the poet and his theme which the poem itself articulates; communication, or the reader's understanding of the poem; and community, or the forming of a society of readers, or a literary tradition."

204 A five-part introduction, written in 1972, to a projected Harcourt Brace Jovanovich textbook anthology of English literature, for which NF was general editor. See 19.n. 218.

205 See Introduction, p. xli.

206 See Introduction, p. xxx.

207 See par. 44 and n. 25, above.

208 This got into GC, 178, minus the reference to Coryat: "The visit of the wise men to Christ is the antitype of the Queen of Sheba's visit to Solomon, the connecting link being Isaiah 60:6." The latter reads: "The multitude of camels shall cover thee, the dromedaries of Midian and Ephah; all they from Sheba shall come: they shall bring gold and incense; and they shall shew forth the praises of the Lord." See Thomas Coryat, *Coryat's Crudities*, 2 vols. (Glasgow: James MacLehose and Sons, Publishers to the University, 1905; orig. pub. 1611); the passage is Coryat's translation of some engraved tablets he saw in the Cologne Cathedral.

209 See Introduction, p. xli.

210 See Introduction, p. xxx.

211 See Introduction, p. li.

212 Harold Bloom, *The Anxiety of Influence: A Theory of Poetry* (New York: Oxford University Press, 1973).

213 See n. 87, above.

214 The following are all references to characters and images in *The Waste Land*.

215 "The Narrative of A. Gordon Pym," a story by Edgar Allan Poe which ends at the South Pole.

216 I.e., *The Anxiety of Influence*; see par. 248, above.

217 According to the first page of the "Author's Prologue" to bk. 1 of Rabelais, Alcibiades in the *Symposium* compares Socrates to the Sileni or boxes of Silenus, painted with humorously grotesque pictures on the outside but preserving fine drugs and precious stones within—an emblem for Rabelais's own book.

218 "She hath done what she could: she is come aforehand to anoint my body to the burying," Jesus's words about the woman from Bethany who poured a precious ointment on his head.

219 For "The Two Brothers," see 12.33 and n. 27; for the "Clementine Recognitions," see n. 49, above. The "Hymn of the Soul" in the Acts of Thomas is discussed by NF in *SeS*, 156–7.
220 See Introduction, p. xli.

Work in Progress

1 NF recorded this scheme in NB 42, the so-called Pentateuch notebook, because it assimilates the ogdoad scheme to a five-volume project.
2 I.e., Liberal, Tragicomedy, Anticlimax, Rencontre.
3 The plan for *The Critical Comedy* (see par. 7, below) as NF works it out from this point is exactly paralleled in the series of entries beginning with 24.240, which says, "There has been a very long interval between this note & the last one." Pars. 240–58 (i.e., to the end) of NB 24 were thus clearly written during the same period as "Work in Progress."
4 See 24.241 and n. 203.
5 See 19.n. 218.
6 See 24.241.
7 In Joshua 21, the Levites, because of their priestly character, are not given a land of their own but are granted forty-eight cities scattered through the lands of the other tribes. In Blake (*Milton*, pl. 38 [43] [Erdman, 138]) these are identified with the forty-eight constellations of the Mundane Shell.
8 See 12.11 and n. 5.
9 See Claude Lévi-Strauss, *The Raw and the Cooked* (Chicago: University of Chicago Press, 1969), 15.
10 On p. 214 of "Novels on Several Occasions" (1950), *NFCL*, 207–18.
11 That is, in the sense described in Kierkegaard's *Repetition: An Essay in Experimental Psychology*, trans. Walter Lowrie (Princeton: Princeton University Press, 1946), annotated copy in the NFL.
12 See *SeS*, 140–2, and *GC*, 205. Also, 24.256.
13 See 24.256, where the "Hymn of the Soul" is mentioned in conjunction with the *Clementine Recognitions*, mentioned in par. 10, above. See also *SeS*, 156–7.
14 See 24.159, 238. Also, *AC*, 191, where *Sakuntala*, the play by the fifth-century Indian dramatist Kalidasa, is linked, as here and in 24.159, to Plautus's *Rudens* (*The Rope*), and *SeS*, 147.
15 See Introduction, p. liv.
16 See 19.122 and 191.
17 See 19.n. 185.
18 See 12.559 and n. 450; also 24.12.
19 See "The Search for Acceptable Words" (1973), *SM*, 19–20. In 24.209, NF compares the Porter book with *Lord Jim* and *The Caine Mutiny*.

20 The reference is uncertain, although 12.495, lists "Jonah and fishing" amongst images of "low anabasis" such as the Harrowing of Hell.

21 Another link with NB 24, in whose latter half the Great Doodle fissions into two circle diagrams, one for pre- and one for post-Romantic myth and literature.

22 NF refers to Mallarmé's throw of the dice in *Un Coup de Dés* and *Igitur* countless times in the Third Book and *WP* notebooks. See 12.n. 157 and 24.n. 91.

23 The repeated "new" in this paragraph refers to the fact that NF has recently split the Great Doodle into two separate wheels, and is now dealing with a new, second diagram for modern myth and literature.

24 The phrase "twenty years ago" means that NF almost has to be referring to Francis Fergusson, *Dante's Drama of the Mind: A Modern Reading of the "Purgatorio"* (Princeton: Princeton University Press, 1953). Fergusson does not really say that "somebody ought to do something." He recites the medieval rhyme about the four levels of meaning, a passage (179) whence NF derived his frequent tags *quid credas* (what is to be believed, the allegorical level) and *quid agas* (what is to be done, the moral level). In the following paragraph, he says, "There is fairly general agreement among students of Dante that the *Divine Comedy* is somehow composed in imitation of Scripture, and with all three spiritual meanings, or dimensions. But there is little agreement about just how this works in detail" (180).

25 "Jay" is Jay Macpherson, Canadian poet and NF's colleague at the University of Toronto. See 19.108 and n. 84. "Anne" is probably Anne McWhir, whose M.A. thesis was on Shelley and whose doctoral dissertation, supervised by Milton Wilson, was on the imagery of rivers and caves in the Shelleys. Later, she published an edition of Mary Shelley's *The Last Man*.

26 NF in fact did this in a concerted way: almost two hundred pages of typed notes synopsizing and analysing various romances survive, and formed the groundwork of *SeS*, which contains references to most of the works catalogued in this paragraph.

27 Alludes to the research that resulted in "Dickens and the Comedy of Humours" (1968), *StS*, 218–40.

28 In *SeS*, 5, NF writes that one of the roots of the book was an abandoned essay on the Waverley novels of Scott.

29 See 12.50.

30 The five parts of the Rencontre project as described below in pars. 23–8 correspond closely, though in a different order, to the five parts of the 184-page surviving typescript of the introduction to the Harcourt Brace Jovanovich anthology (see 19.n. 218), which are titled as follows: Part One: The Language and Its Poetry; Part Two: The Language and Its Prose; Part Three The Imagery of Time; Part Four: The Imagery of Space; Part Five Retrospect. Much of the content is also repeated.

31 See 19.n. 195.
32 The phrase "as I have it now" may refer to the HBJ introduction, outlined in the note to par. 23, in which "The Imagery of Time" is pt. 3 rather than pt. 5.
33 See 19.62 and n. 47.
34 The Third Book notebooks return full circle here, as NB 19 began with speculations about contracts and Utopias. See also *CP*, 158.

Index